MUSIC *for the* MELODRAMATIC THEATRE *in Nineteenth-Century* LONDON & NEW YORK

STUDIES IN THEATRE HISTORY AND CULTURE

EDITED BY

Heather Nathans

MICHAEL V. PISANI

MUSIC *for the* MELODRAMATIC THEATRE *in Nineteenth-Century* LONDON & NEW YORK

UNIVERSITY OF IOWA PRESS, IOWA CITY

University of Iowa Press, Iowa City 52242

Printed in the United States of America

Design by Richard Hendel

www.uiowapress.org

The University of Iowa Press is a member of Green Press Initiative and is committed to preserving natural resources.

Printed on acid-free paper

Library of Congress Cataloging-in-Publication Data
ISBN: 978-1-60938-230-8 (pbk)
ISBN: 978-1-60938-265-0 (ebk)
LCCN: 2013953635

Once the theatre was cleared of audience, Elliston, fancying himself the equivalent of Alexander the Great, Henry V, or Napoleon Bonaparte, came striding onto the stage and then stopped, rapping his "wand of authority" on the floor and calling out to all.

"Carpenters, fall in and take close order. Leader of the band, marshal your men in the van—yes, have them all in the orchestra, and prepare to sound the alarm. Prompter, take up your position on the left-wing with your call-boy, property-man, and assistants. Acting-manager, be prepared at the right-wing. Scene-shifters, you will form in double file, two deep. Flymen, you will occupy the heights. Wingmen, you will skirt the rear. Trapmen and cellarmen, be prepared to act as sappers and miners . . . Dismiss, you others, and to your work. Call on the opening chorus, prompter. Play the first melos, leader. Band, strike up in the orchestra, for Judah's lion is o'erthrown for ever. Yes, now I'm satisfied—I've triumphed!—greatly triumphed! . . .—so quick, quick!—off with the flats, and on with the rehearsal!"

Robert W. Elliston, rehearsing a melodrama
at the Surrey Theatre, London, 1809
(W. T. Moncrieff, "Ellistoniana, No. XII: Elliston's Valour,"
New Monthly Magazine 69 [1843])

CONTENTS

ACKNOWLEDGMENTS

This book is the result of nearly twenty years of research. It would not have been possible without the pioneering work and continuing encouragement of David Mayer, theatre historian and professor emeritus of drama at the University of Manchester. He is the first and lasting inspiration for this study. I am also grateful to my editor at the University of Iowa Press, Thomas Postlewait, especially for his keen eye, sharp pen, and sage advice. I am unable personally to thank Anne Dhu McLucas, one of the first musicologists to undertake serious research in music and English-language melodrama, but I know that before her untimely death she was looking forward to the completion of this study and would have been pleased to find in its pages much evidence of her foundational work.

Other historians of theatre and music as well as research librarians deserve special thanks for their generous responses to requests for information and advice. Chief among them are Stephen Banfield, Philip Carli, Stephen Cockett, Annette Davison, Richard Divall, Joseph Donohue, Victor Emeljanow, Annette Fern, Christina Fuhrmann, Aubrey Garlington, John Graziano, Sarah Hibberd, David Hulme, Bridget Keown, Marian Wilson Kimber, John Koegel, Bob Kosovsky, Alan Lewis, Katherine K. Preston, Margaret Sherry Rich, Deane L. Root, Emilio Sala, Laurence Senelick, Denise Walen, and Don Wilmeth. Also special thanks to my supportive colleagues and friends throughout this project: Ralph P. Locke, T. J. Hochstrasser, Karen Robertson, Mark and Qin Stubis, and Christopher Huebner.

What really fueled my passion for this topic was a deep and abiding love for drama, already in evidence at age twelve when I tried to inveigle neighborhood kids to participate in a backyard production of Gilbert and Sullivan's *H.M.S. Pinafore*. I owe my practical experience with the theatre to years spent as an assistant conductor for several major opera companies, including the Houston Grand Opera, the Seattle Opera, Milwaukee's Skylight Opera, and the Opera Company of Boston. In this capacity, I worked with remarkable singer-actors such as Karan Armstrong, Mirella Freni, Marilyn Horne, Diane Kesling, Jon Vickers, and Thomas Stewart and directors such as Colin Graham, Jean-Pierre Ponnelle, Götz Friedrich, Sarah Caldwell, Stephen Wadsworth, Francesca Zambello, and Frank Corsaro. I witnessed effective collaboration between such visionary artists and equally visionary orchestra conductors, especially Leonard Bernstein, John Mauceri, Steuart Bedford, and John DeMain. Any identification that I was able to establish with the larger-than-life but long dead nineteenth-century actors, managers, and orchestra leaders was possible largely through my associations with these remarkable twentieth-century figures.

INTRODUCTION
Genres, Concepts, and Terms

However it may be defined today, "melodramatic theatre" for the first hundred years of its existence simply meant stage action or dialogue accompanied by music. Audiences may recognize "mood" music, but they typically take this aspect of a production for granted. Why is such music necessary and who is responsible for it? What do we know about this technique of persuasion and how it changed over time? My focus here is on the transatlantic enterprise of Anglo-American theatre, where for at least two hundred years—and to some extent still today—authors, managers, and actors relied on music's unique power to draw audiences into the story world of the drama.

The history of this technique undoubtedly stretches far back in time. Documents from the late eighteenth century reveal that theatrical managers were beginning to rely more frequently on orchestras to provide an interpretive role in play production. Typically, the more elaborate the theatre, the more abundant the music. Yet aside from a few later examples by famous European composers such as Felix Mendelssohn and Edvard Grieg, known largely through concert suites, what real evidence do we have of the music written for stage productions? The successor to this practice, music in narrative film, has been a subject of intense interest since the 1970s. Like film directors and composers, nineteenth-century theatre managers and their orchestra leaders employed a variety of musical styles and techniques. Also like film, these styles varied depending on the dramatic genre. It was practically impossible to see plays such as *Frankenstein*, *Oliver Twist*, *Uncle Tom's Cabin*, *Lady Audley's Secret*, *The Corsican Brothers*, and *The Three Musketeers*, if not also historical romances by William Shakespeare and Friedrich Schiller, without hearing some type of background music. Yet the musical dimensions of these productions are almost entirely lost to us. The irony is that good dramatic music—like good film music—was most effective when it was unobtrusive; hence few spectators seemed able to recall it. Yet people in those days heard more music in the theatre than anywhere else. The theatre was to audiences then what radio, film, television, YouTube, and similar platforms are to us today.

In the nineteenth-century theatre music and storytelling formed an inseparable melodramatic bond. We are going in search of this lost art, particularly the music of the "popular drama," a once ubiquitous theatrical genre that has now been absorbed into other media. This book is a chronological history, beginning when the popular drama first emerged and ending as a fully integrated art form when it was taken over by the cinema and eventually by radio and television.

These nineteenth-century dramas were "popular" because they were performed everywhere, from the most elegant theatres in Paris and London to the tiniest outposts in rural English and American towns. The stock characters, complicated plots, heightened emotional situations, and spectacular action sequences have been the subject of many close analyses (not to mention parodies). The form, it is commonly explained, originated with the melodramas of René-Charles Guilbert de Pixerécourt and spread quickly to other theatres and countries. But many of the structural characteristics of melodrama emerged well before the late eighteenth century and extend back at least to Roman farce, with its archetypal characters. Its plot devices contributed to the scenarios of the commedia dell'arte and merged with influences from Italian commercial opera, English Restoration tragedy, and French pantomime to form a new and hybrid genre in which instrumental music was deemed absolutely essential for success. The traditional assumption that music eventually became a much weaker (and even expendable) third sister to dialogue and spectacle, however, is based not on facts but on music's historical "invisibility." Today melodramas are more likely to be read than seen and heard. It is all too easy to ignore the widespread mandate for mood and action music in most nineteenth-century theatrical venues.

Popular music, like other commercial products, can easily become outdated. Modern re-creations of a play like *The Lights o' London* could hardly be expected to use the music of Wilson Barrett's original 1881 production (if available). Dramatic music then as now was calculated to appeal to the emotions of its audiences. As audiences change, so do musical fashions. And yet we have much to learn about *how* music was used in this melodrama, which includes when and where music appeared, length, style, instrumentation, order and frequency, and the pacing and dramatic shape that it brought to the production. This information may be of interest to stage directors, actors, and theatre composers who want to know more about historical performance practices, given the many misconceptions and stereotypes that abound. For other readers, this investigation of a once prevalent genre takes us through unique musical retellings of stories that have moved audiences again and again.

The musico-dramatic techniques with which this book is principally concerned most likely originated in the Parisian fairs of the early eighteenth century. These same traditions were still alive in 1843 when Charles Dickens visited the Greenwich country fair. There he saw the itinerant acting company of John Richardson. At this immense and colorful booth with a front stage brilliantly illuminated by glass oil lamps, Dickens witnessed a dozen or more actors and acrobats and some ten musicians presenting "a melodrama (with three murders and a ghost), a pantomime, a comic song, an overture, and some incidental music, all done in five-and-twenty minutes."[1] This mélange typifies a kind of popular entertainment that was then called burletta, a genre that included not only songs (which in some theatrical venues were a legal requirement) but also acting techniques borrowed from the Italian and French popular stage, such as pantomime and *mélodrame*. By this time, the genre could be seen in fully blown form in one of London's best-known playhouses. At the Adelphi Theatre, then under the management of Thomas Gladstane and Edward Stirling, the same mélange took four and a half hours. The Adelphi playbill of 23 October 1843 lists a "dramatic burletta," a "locomotive farce," a "farce burletta," and a "grand operatic ballet spectacle," all in one evening! Each piece except the "locomotive farce" was loaded with songs, choruses, dances, and other instrumental pieces played by the Adelphi's band of some twenty musicians. The "dramatic burletta" was actually a play, John Baldwin Buckstone's *The Wreck Ashore, or A Bridegroom from the Sea*. This was a gothic melodrama, complete with a crazed villain who terrorizes two young women as he attempts to break into their cottage.

The same type of programming could be found in America as well. The first major financial crash in 1837 had produced a disastrous effect on New York's theatres. But, like the Hollywood studios a hundred years later, William Mitchell at the Olympic proved that theatre could lift people's spirits in times of need. Mitchell produced burlettas (popular dramas) and musical travesties "to which the despondent came, and at which the despondent laughed, and continued to come and to laugh," as Laurence Hutton wrote.[2] By 1843 New York's Olympic had become one of the finest stock theatres in America.

The playbills of nineteenth-century theatres announced such a dizzying variety of genres that it is difficult to imagine the exact nature of these plays in performance. But audiences then expected a variety of entertainment for the price of admission, whether it was a resident stock company or a traveling troupe. The Richardson's and Adelphi examples cited above occurred at a turning point in English dramatic history. That year the British Parliament relaxed some of the statutes in its theatre laws. Many of these had been in effect since 1752, when theatrical licensing enforced a two-tiered system for British theatres. In the late eighteenth century the royal or patent theatres (in London: Covent Garden, Drury Lane, and the King's Theatre in the Haymarket) were the places to go for Shakespeare, classical drama and comedy, and opera, while the popular or "minor" theatres like the Adelphi catered to broader tastes for sensation and farce. Hence the repertoire at the minors generally came under tight scrutiny, with restrictions applied to style of performance, genre, subject matter, language, and even the use of music. No less than sixty-six dramatic categories appeared on manuscripts sent to the Lord Chamberlain for his approval between 1790 and 1843, in the playbills that announced the performances, and on the title pages of published plays.[3] Plays were circulated and produced under these labels throughout the United Kingdom and in English-language theatres around the world. Besides burletta, other genres that required music were ballet-pantomime, burlesque, comic drama, comic pantomime, dramatic farce, divertissement, extravaganza, melodrama, musical romance, spectacle, and vaudeville.[4] Furthermore, labeling was not always consistent. Musical romances, for example, which tended to privilege songs and dances, were often indistinguishable from so-called English opera, with its alternation of dialogue and sung numbers. Furthermore, labels could be misleading as to how plays were actually produced, as managers of English popular theatres often exceeded the boundaries of their licenses.

Though playbills only occasionally noted the composer of the melodramatic music, songs featured in plays or between the acts were routinely advertised. Music publishers recognized that sheet music showcasing the names (and sometimes portraits) of actors and actresses who performed them on the stage had commercial value. The project of identifying the songs and dances, not to mention analyzing their relationship to the plays and the theatres where they were produced, is beyond the scope of this book. But the presence of a song meant that there was an orchestra or band of some kind to accompany it. Hence I try to answer some important questions raised by the existence of these musical ensembles. For example, if music was mandated in Britain, at least until 1843, why did many theatres maintain orchestras even after music was no longer legally required? A band of musicians, even a small one, could be a significant expense for a theatre manager, many of whom struggled financially from season to season. Surely the orchestra's role was not just to accompany songs and dances but also to add color and excitement to the plays. Who provided the music and what did this music sound like? Was there a common practice shared among managers and theatres? Were there exceptional cases that stood out from the rest?

Genres, Concepts, and Terms

The theatre band, especially before the formation of orchestra unions in the 1860s, was a much more fluid concept than is found today in, say, a traditional musical. The musicians were often visible from the waist up, at least until the advent of the sunken orchestra in the 1870s. They typically faced the stage and could view the action in progress. Some infrequently used musicians might occasionally even slip away to double as extras onstage. Their essential role, when not playing overtures or entr'actes before the curtain or between plays, was to assist the actors by establishing mood, communicating aspects of characterization, and invigorating the action. Their leader was frequently a violinist, who also played along.

"Background music" (affective or situational music used *during* the play) has been defined historically in different ways. The most common labels used in nineteenth-century sources were "appropriate," "characteristic," "melodramatic," and "incidental." The first of these began to show up around the time of Samuel Arnold's "appropriate music in *Obi, or Three-Fingered Jack*" (Haymarket, 1800). "Appropriate" indicates that the music was more or less consistent with the emotional contours of a scene or speech and with the way audiences were expected to react. For instance, in 1821 in New York, Mrs. Barnes was the latest in a long line of elocutionists to recite William Collins's famous *Ode to the Passions* "with appropriate music."[5] The term "characteristic" applied to instrumental pieces was already in use in the 1790s. In Johann (Jan) Ladislaus Dussek's *Naval Battle*, a "characteristic sonata," music not only depicts events but evokes specific images. In this sense the term continued to be used for any music of a quasi-descriptive nature, as in Felix Mendelssohn's *The Temperaments, or Seven Characteristic Pieces* (London, 1845). Dussek's *Characteristic Airs of Different Nations* from about 1794 suggests that the term was also applied to a collective national or ethnic identity. The term "characteristic" often relates to music that attempted a literal embodiment of an actor's physical demeanor (stately or groveling, for example) or ethos (heroic, demure, or sneaky).[6]

(By the 1890s the "characteristic" had developed into a separate light music genre, where it still retained allusions to personality or ethnicity.)

Though the term "melo-drame" was already in use in the late eighteenth century, the phrase "melodramatic music" first appears in publication in 1808, with Joseph Mazzinghi's *Marches and Melo-Dramatic Music in "The Exile, or The Deserts of Siberia,"* an operatic play by Frederick Reynolds performed at Covent Garden with songs composed by Henry Bishop. As it was commonly used throughout the early nineteenth century, the phrase referred to music required to accompany any necessary action in the play. Commentators often complained of "humdrum melodramatic music." But affective music pervaded theatrical productions of all types and was often of greater diversity and originality than such terms of abuse tend to imply. Such music also engaged with the spoken text in ways that required special skills from both orchestra leaders and actors.

The label "incidental music" begins to show up in print around 1816, including "the incidental music by [Tom Simpson] Cooke" for Edmund Kean's *Timon of Athens* (Drury Lane) and "incidental music by Mr. West" for John Fawcett's adaptation of *Oedipus* (Tottenham Court Theatre). In its earliest usage "incidental" appears to refer to music *added* to an existing play, such as songs and dances that supplemented or retarded the dramatic progress. The insinuation is that "incidental music" is superfluous to the drama and more or less interchangeable from production to production. In practice, however, such music was required to depict important "incidents" occurring onstage or to set up an act or make smooth transitions between scene changes. This is how we normally think of Mendelssohn's "incidental music" to *A Midsummer Night's Dream* (written to accompany a production in Berlin in 1843). In this purer sense "incidental music" seems useful as a generic label.[7]

These four terms, while overlapping in meaning, refer to somewhat different musical components of stage music. Mendelssohn's *Dream* music, for example, contains *both* incidental and melodramatic music, which is only reproduced in concert if there are actors to deliver the lines. Charles Martel, preparing the Library of Congress classification system in 1913, assigned different numerical categories for publications about "incidental music" and "melodramatic music" (by then associated more with concert melodramas).[8] And yet the interchangeability of these terms hints at the flexible nature of nineteenth-century theatre music and its capacity for multifunctionality. When not filling the intervals between acts or accompanying a song or dance, music breathed life and soul into the architectural space, lent buoyancy or gravity to the actors, and even alerted audiences to the dramatic shape of the play.

Of course, countless instances of the addition of music are found throughout the history of Western drama. Ancient Greek theatre used music, though we lack specific details. Roman pantomimes had musical accompaniment. The commedia dell'arte of the sixteenth and seventeenth centuries was known to incorporate songs and use music for effect (even if played only by a single instrument).[9] Furthermore, Shakespeare and other seventeenth-century playwrights requested music in published editions of their plays, usually songs or stage music such as parleys and tuckets. For the dance of "several strange shapes" in *The Tempest* Shakespeare calls for "solemn and strange music" (Folio 1, 3.3). During a funeral sequence in Thomas Middleton's *A Chast Mayd in Cheape-Side*, the text specifies the playing of "a sad Song in the Musicke-Roome" (Quarto 1630, 5.4). Court masques had music and dance, and the first revivals of Shakespeare in Restoration England used small orchestras for "curtain tunes" and to accompany onstage songs and processionals.[10]

Opera had employed small orchestras since the first commercial opera houses in Italy in the 1630s. But spoken dialogue remained separate from musical insertions, even in the uniquely English ballad operas, with their alternating speech and songs. Music first began to play an almost continuous role in nonoperatic works on the fairground stages of early eighteenth-century Paris and to accompany French and English pantomime from the 1720s on. In fact the requirements for theatrical music seemed to increase from this point onward, even in the legitimate drama. When eighteenth-century British tragedies such as George Lillo's *George Barnwell*, Edward Moore's *The Gamester*, and John Home's *Douglas* were first published, the texts included no musical indications of any kind. By the 1820s at least one edition of all three plays observed that each final curtain "descends to slow music."[11]

Over the course of the late eighteenth century several plays would be performed in one evening, with a central main fare followed by an afterpiece, usually farcical or burlesque in nature. Major theatres in cities like London and Philadelphia maintained small orchestras, so music was employed strategically throughout the evening's entertainment. It was necessary to welcome the audience into the house (an English tradition stemming from the old "first," "second," and "third" music that persisted well into the nineteenth century). An overture might precede the main fare, and light musical numbers might clear the air after a drama and set the tone for the afterpiece. Furthermore, some plays required a character to sing or dance. Even if the author had not specified any music, an actor might interpolate such a piece to show off vocal or terpsichorean skills.

Gradually, however, the orchestra became more and more involved in the play itself, sometimes rendering melodrama as much a musical genre as a dramatic one. An important recognition of this distinctive form comes from the German music historian Adolph Bernhard Marx. Writing in 1839, by which time the popular drama was long established in most theatres, Marx identified four separate genres of theatrical music. Ballet and opera were two of these. But he drew an equally clear distinction between the other two, which he called the play with music and the melodrama. In the "play with music," Marx wrote, "we find much employment for music in the poetical objects of the drama. In these compositions, the poet requires music conformable to the circumstances of his plot—for example, marches, convivial music, songs (pastoral or warlike), solemn church music, and so forth, *just as the like might occur in real life* [my emphasis]."[12] Thus the long-popular *Guy Mannering*, first performed at Covent Garden in 1816 with text by Daniel Terry after Walter Scott and music principally by Henry Bishop, included a typical English combination of airs, ballads, duets, quintets, glees, marches, and dances. With the exception of the overture, the characters participate in making music, usually by singing. This conformed to traditional eighteenth-century operatic conventions, where situations set up in recitative or dialogue tended to culminate in a musical number. Even an instrumental piece in *Guy Mannering* must be justified. The mysterious flute music over which Julia speaks near the beginning of act 2, for example, turns out to be Harry Bertram serenading beneath her window.

In contrast to the play with music, the "melodrama," as Marx explains,

> shows us instrumental music as an accompaniment to, or as phrases intervening with, discourse, whereby the latter becomes deeper in its meaning, and more powerful in its impressiveness: the action is illustrated and rendered intelligible in its preconcerted situations, and the melodramatic intentions, in general, are accomplished. Here, the music has only to give gentle, passing indications, and is heard, occasionally only, with marked expression. It is to be considered, throughout, as secondary and subordinate to the speech and action.
>
> *Melodramatic music, therefore, is employed during the action, principally in easily interspersed passages, harmonic successions, occasionally returning phrases (or otherwise) and introduced now and*

then only as a march or a dance when the action of the drama requires it [my emphasis].[13]

Here Marx describes music that is completely inseparable from the design and production of a play. Though rarely published in conjunction with the script, by the middle of the nineteenth century a whole industry existed for its dissemination. The *Era* newspaper noted in 1853, for example, that a theatrical and musical agency in Covent Garden called Fairbrother and Harroway's furnished "pantomime and melodramatic music at the shortest notice and on the most reasonable terms."[14] Most of this music, at least until the 1870s, circulated only in manuscript.

Marx made a clear distinction between music that occurs in the course of the play as it might have occurred in real life (to accompany an onstage procession, for example) and music that is "unheard" by the characters but is intended largely for the audience, which he identifies as "melodramatic music." The published scores of *Guy Mannering* and surviving orchestra parts from early in the century do not employ such "melodramatic music." But in a set of parts rented by the Arthur Tams theatrical agency in New York for performances in the 1880s, someone has penciled in instructions for the death speech of Meg Merrilies: "play slowly 'Rest the babe, rest the babe.'" The reprise of the gypsy woman's ballad from the first act added an emotional layer of dialogue underscore. The technique *melodramatized* the play in a way not specified by its original authors, even though Henry Bishop himself wrote quite a bit of original melodramatic music for other plays when the situation warranted.

Three Categories of Theatre Music

Given the range of music in the popular British and American theatres of the nineteenth century it would be difficult to generalize about a common stylistic practice to accompany the popular drama: music was often tied to the genre of entertainment, legal restrictions, or class of house and audience. For a stage performance that is neither opera nor ballet, we can usually identify all music used in the course of an evening by three categories or types. The first category applies to music that fills up the intervals between plays and acts: overtures and entr'actes. With the curtain usually closed, attention is generally on the orchestra. Managers and leaders sometimes but not always attempted to link this type of music to the nature of the dramas being performed.

The second category applies to music with a precise visual or aural reference within the play, such as bringing up the curtain, assisting a scenic or lighting effect, or accompanying a song or dance performed onstage. Some music of this type may be highly integral to the conception of the play and thereafter closely associated with it, such as the glee that opens act 1 of Alfred Bunn's historical drama *Kenilworth* (1832) or what J. L. Toole referred to as "the well-known march" in *Timour the Tartar* (1811).[15] A selection from this category of theatre music might even be published, especially if it had commercial value (Charles Grobe's "*Camille* Polka," for example) or if publication might lead to concert performances, such as the famous orchestral suites by Franz Schubert, Georges Bizet, and Edward German. Such music may also be interpolated according to an actor's whim or director's concept. John Kerr's *Rip van Winkle* (1826) requires a dance for Rip and the grotesque dwarves that he meets in Sleepy Hollow, but it is unlikely that the same music was used for this sequence in every theatre.

The third category encompasses the great invisible mechanical apparatus of melodramatic music. The adjective "melodramatic" is applied here in a functional sense and without any value judgment, as nineteenth-century practitioners viewed it. "As a writer of melodramatic music," an obituary describes the Boston-based Charles Koppitz, "he was particularly skilled and justly esteemed."[16] Melodramatic music occupies a more subordinate position than theatrical music in the second category. The most interesting and original "hurry" or "plaintive" fails in its purpose if it distracts rather than heightens the progress of the drama. But melodramatic music could move the spectator as much as could actors, lighting, or stagecraft. One sharp-eared playgoer at a performance of Dion Boucicault's *The Colleen Bawn* in 1860 was impressed by "the strain accompanying the entrance of Corregan into the death-chamber of the murderer, [Danny] Mann, which comes as unexpectedly and falls as deliciously upon the scenes as a genuine Van Dyck in a second-hand printshop."[17]

The principal subject of this book is the various uses of "category three" theatrical music in the development of the popular drama. For many of the dedicated orchestra leaders who provided such music for the nineteenth-century stage, this practice was embodied in the concept of *melos*, once deemed an inseparable component of melodrama. A prominent composer such as German-born Carl Maria von Weber, who came from a large family of theatre musicians, was clearly familiar with the term: in 1810 he began to use "Melos" as a nom de plume when signing his published music criticism.

Melos is today known largely from German musicological writings, where it has been particularly associated with the music dramas of Richard Wagner. Wagner, one critic in the 1890s wrote, "uses his 'Melos' in one continuous stream." Wagner himself employed the word in his instructions to the opera conductor, who needed to comprehend the dramatic *melos* of a passage fully in order to find its correct tempo.[18] To the critic, *melos* presumably meant the threads or leitmotifs that were seamlessly interwoven in an orchestral fabric. In some situations the word is used in this way, referring to bits of music that needed to be strung together. But for Wagner, *melos* seemed to be an inherent quality embodied in musical language, relating to its *affect* or mood, and did not refer solely to isolated themes or musical numbers.

The term *melos*, of course, is from the Greek, where it is indeed sometimes defined as "limb," a part of the whole.[19] *Melos* was mentioned often in Hellenic theories about music and in this context was revived by aristocratic Italians in the early seventeenth century as one justification for the singing of drama. For a long time the word appears to have been used only in reference to the Hellenic period. It begins to show up in a vernacular sense in eighteenth-century music dictionaries (*melos* = melody), but it is clear that theatrical musicians from this time through Wagner considered it more broadly. "The ancient dramatic writers," observed the noted eighteenth-century composer and music historian Charles Burney in *A Brief History of Music*, "had different kinds of *melos*, for the declamation of the actors and for the songs of the chorus." Modern scholars of ancient Greek music are a bit less certain what was meant by the word over two thousand years ago. The first phrase of the systematic study of music *Elementa Harmonica* by Aristoxenus was written as *Τῆς περὶ μέλους ἐπιστημῆς* and is usually translated as "the science concerned with melody." But it is clear, as Andrew Barker and other scholars of Hellenic music theory note, that Aristoxenus generally meant *melos* in a wider sense. Elsewhere, for example, he uses the term when he refers to different colors of modes. Plato's use of the term was also well known in the eighteenth century and was quoted by such eminent Greek scholars as Francis Stiles. "Our music," Stiles translates Plato, "was then divided according to certain species and figures thereof . . . hymns, threni, paeones, dithyrambus, citharoedic nomi . . . It was not allowable to use one species of *melos* for another."[20]

Informed by this research, eighteenth-century playwrights, directors, and musicians began to revive the concept as they sought to find the appropriate *melos* for a given dramatic situation. Though the term itself does not show up in printed theatrical sources until the early nineteenth century, it should be obvious from the following examples that the principle was in use before that time.

Theatre Music and Audiences

Theatre historians in recent decades have uncovered much new social and economic information about eighteenth- and nineteenth-century audiences. But melodramatic music was not a measurable commodity. Audiences who recounted their theatregoing experiences hardly ever seemed to mention it. Hence the recollections of an avid playgoer like John M. Morton, the son of playwright Thomas Morton and author of many nineteenth-century farces such as *Box and Cox*, whet the appetite to know much more about what audiences actually heard. Writing in 1882, Morton looked back on his youth in London, in the 1830s and 1840s. "Did you ever see Celeste in *The French Spy*, in *Janet Pride*, or in *The Green Bushes*?" he asked (referring to the French-born mimist and actress Céline Celeste).

> In the first play she sets the part of a dumb [i.e., mute] young lady, who for military and romantic purposes assumes a male costume and becomes a spy for the French army before Algiers. Of course, in this part, Celeste acted entirely by pantomime and was followed by the orchestra with the utmost devotion. When she appeared as the lively French officer, the orchestra seemed to lose their heads and assume a devil-may-care style quite in harmony with the situation. Then when Celeste appeared as the Arab boy in that wonderful costume . . . and fought double-handed with two gigantic Algerian warriors, the orchestra fairly thrilled with excitement. When Celeste fell on her knees and fought all over the stage in that attitude, the orchestra was equal to that trying occasion and found appropriate music, which conveyed not only the critical nature of the situation but their entire sympathy with the over-matched but not overpowered little Spy.[21]

By the time Celeste toured in England and the United States, nearly every theatre in the larger cities maintained an orchestra. The amount of music used and the degree of coordination between stage and band depended upon several factors, including the genre of play, the licensing of the theatre, the actor-manager in charge, and the class makeup of the audience. For example, a *London Times* review of a melodrama entitled *Darnley, the Knight of Burgundy, or The Field of the Cloth of Gold* (Coburg Theatre, 1830) observed with obvious pleasure that "a fight, in which the combatants strike in accordance with the notes of the orchestra, elicited unbounded applause."[22] The Coburg—situated south of the Thames in one of the danker areas of town known at the time for prostitutes and pickpockets—had a loud gallery of representatives from the neighborhood. Its audience earned the theatre a reputation for this kind of tight visceral coordination between music and action.[23] In contrast, when the Coburg that same year produced *The Mutiny at the Nore,* Douglas Jerrold's serious attempt at a national drama, an impressed reviewer admitted that he feared the author "might be tempted to vulgarise his style in order to propitiate the [Coburg] audience." The reviewer was surprised, however, that Jerrold "succeeded in raising their tastes to the capacity of understanding" where they were disposed to interpret "his best passages most deeply."[24] While no reviewer of *Mutiny* commented on the music—and no music sources have yet been found—the Coburg's orchestra and leader under Jerrold's watchful eye surely bore some responsibility for this elevation in taste. Had the opposite been the case, we likely would have heard about it, because this was usually when critics bothered to acknowledge the music. Meanwhile, in the same season at the Drury Lane Theatre, Charles Macready had opened Lord Byron's five-act drama *Werner.* Macready would have been horrified to have an orchestra shadow his movements as it did the Coburg players, given his insistence on the artistic separation between highbrow and lowbrow entertainment and his contractual agreement that he not be required to perform any parts that might be viewed as "partaking of a melodramatic character."[25]

Of course melodrama did not begin at the Coburg; nor did dramas with "a melodramatic character" end in the 1890s with the advent of the new social dramas of Oscar Wilde, Henrik Ibsen, and George Bernard Shaw. In fact the popular drama continued to evolve, taking on new subjects or retelling old stories in new ways. Some of these, like *The Prisoner of Zenda,* were mostly escapist fantasies, looking back with nostalgia on more chivalrous ages. This book traces this development until the beginning of the twentieth century, through its transformation by major actor-managers and producers in London and New York. This genre certainly continued well beyond that date and in one sense is still very much alive today in the modern cinema. The one link in all of this is music, unacknowledged or forgotten as it fulfilled its indispensable role.

Overview of This Book

The three-part structure of this book reflects the development of the popular drama, which occurred in roughly three overlapping stages. The first of these, the pantomime-burletta period, lasted from 1752 to the 1820s. Chapter 1 explores the roots of *melos* in the legitimate productions of David Garrick and Richard Brinsley Sheridan, the "action ballets" of Jean-Georges Noverre, the classical *mélodrames* of Jean-Jacques Rousseau and Georg Benda, and the comic and serious pantomime. Chapters 2 and 3 focus on the development of the early melodrama: first in Paris, where it originated, then in London. England imported this new musico-dramatic form as an afterpiece in the patent houses, but it quickly spread to the minor theatres, where as an "illegitimate" form of drama it began to reflect the tastes of its managers and the character of its local audiences. America too began to contribute original works, though the bulk of its repertoire during the burletta period was borrowed from Great Britain. In chapter 3 we visit three theatres in London: the Coburg, the Adelphi, and the Surrey.

A clear second stage began in the 1820s with the emergence of the Anglo-American popular drama, an adaptation of the earlier genre to reflect contemporary economic and social concerns. Part two explores the spread of this repertoire through the proliferation of the nineteenth-century stock theatre, which included a leading actor-manager, a company of actors (with occasional visiting stars), and a music director. Chapter 4 surveys the musical sources and discusses the various ways in which theatre managers procured and disseminated music. Though aspects of this practice still remain shrouded in mystery, evidence from legal documents sheds some new light on the value of theatre music and how it exchanged hands. Chapter 5 introduces the main artistic and economic factors that determined the makeup and sound of the Victorian-era theatre orchestra. Chapter 6 takes us behind the scenes to see how music was devised and applied in rehearsals. By drawing on evidence from eyewitness accounts, we learn how playwrights, managers, prompters, and actors worked with music directors to achieve their dramatic goals. The apex of the second stage was the "sensation drama" of the 1860s—the subject of chapter 7. A study of Boucicault's *The Colleen Bawn* at Laura Keene's Theatre in 1860 forms the centerpiece of this chapter and of the book. *The Colleen Bawn* was also among the first long-running sensation dramas in New York and London. Ironically, the competition for long runs posed a major threat to the stability of the stock system.

Authors as much as managers of stock theatres thought of their dramas in terms of music. But tastes began to change, and the mandate for *melos* experienced a crisis in the 1870s. Chapter 8 considers a range of decisions made by influential managers and playwrights, from those who sometimes used music to subvert melodramatic conventions, such as T. W. Robertson and David Belasco, to those who nearly dispensed with music altogether. This chapter examines how the managers and orchestra leaders of three theatres in the 1870s—the Grecian and the Lyceum in London, and Booth's in New York—used music to transform the popular drama. Until the first decade of the twentieth century managers who sought to legitimize the Anglo-American popular drama struggled to compete with variety, music hall, operetta, and other rival forms of theatrical entertainment. As the stock system began to deflate—hastened by a major financial panic in 1873—a star system rose to take its place, aided by combinations of productions that toured the provinces.

On the heels of this crisis the popular drama clearly entered its third phase around 1880. The increased value of the music was partly stimulated by continental European composers who brought greater prestige to dramatic music by composing for the spoken play. Shrewd managers like Henry Irving in London and Charles Frohman in New York also incorporated a rich tapestry of music into their increasingly sumptuous and glamorous productions. Chapters 9 and 10 thus explore music's role as the popular drama moved to new levels of technical professionalism.

As clear as this evolution of the popular drama seems now, I did not begin my investigations with any such outline. The conclusions in this book are the result of an extended engagement with a vast array of surviving documents. These include playtexts and (especially) specific promptbooks used in production, orchestra parts actually played by the musicians in various theatres (and sometimes corroborating copies), documents of production such as music and lighting plots, actors', managers', and other accounts in published books and articles, and comments by drama critics in newspapers and journals. I am immeasurably grateful to the expanding digitization of nineteenth-century resources by the Internet Archive, Google books, Gale, and others over the last ten years, which made some of these discoveries possible. But the search for promptbooks and especially surviving music was a long and fairly traditional process, aided by countless helpful librarians in theatre collections on both sides of the Atlantic. The venues examined here are mostly in London and New York, for which most sources were available. When possible, I cite information from other theatres, particularly when such examples help to provide perspective.

Contrary to popular notions, a great deal of nineteenth-century theatre music does indeed survive, as David Mayer, Anne Dhu McLucas, Emilio Sala, and others have demonstrated. Most of it resides quietly in theatre archives, often uncatalogued. This music, however, remains something of an enigma. I have had to negotiate the reality of the existing documents with narratives of modern theatre historiography. Hence I could not always privilege a well-known or influential play if its music could not be found. At times I may seem to give greater prominence to some long-forgotten play whose music and other performing materials survive to offer a vivid practical example. I hope that the large amount of theatre music that I was able to consult—which I plan to list in an online database—will serve to minimize the dangers of a skewed argument. These manuscript orchestra parts offer a wealth of evidence about the performance of nineteenth-century popular dramas, including timings, changes made in rehearsals, and even when and where the parts were used. Perhaps most surprisingly, they demonstrate that popular dramas were rarely performed as they are handed down in published versions. David Belasco's promptbook for *The Darling of the Gods*, for example, was long thought to have disappeared. But I was thrilled to discover a copy signed by him among the orchestra parts sent to London for performance at His Majesty's Theatre. This guide to production—including minute attention to details of stage business—differs considerably from the version published later, which is how *The Darling of the Gods* has been known. Interpreting this play and many other popular dramas through the musical scores that once accompanied them opens a whole new level of emotional and psychological understanding of the nineteenth-century popular drama.

ONE

Forging a New Musico-Dramatic Genre

1

The Eighteenth-Century Roots of *Melos*

Throughout the eighteenth century it was essential that public theatres engage a band of musicians to play for dramatic genres that were expressly musical in nature, such as masques, operas, *opéras-comiques*, ballets, and pantomimes. The services of musicians were only nominally required, however, in performances of tragedies, histories, and comedies. In these so-called legitimate forms of the thespian arts, a small instrumental ensemble was only necessary to provide music before and between plays and on occasion perhaps to offer "curtain tunes" to open an act.

The traditionally limited participation of an orchestra in the legitimate drama did not stop directors like David Garrick, famous eighteenth-century British Shakespearean, from pressing it into service from time to time. John Burgoyne, the military general turned playwright, wrote in 1781 of his astonishment when Garrick, then manager of Drury Lane, introduced "soft music" into the awakening scene of *King Lear* when Cordelia returns to her father. Though Lear's physician in the 1608 quarto edition of this scene calls for music, Shakespeare's tragedy had been performed since the Restoration in Nahum Tate's version (and George Colman's revision), which eliminated the character of the doctor. But at Drury Lane Garrick introduced sentiment. Over some tender melody playing in the background, Lear slowly came to recognize his devoted daughter, moving the audience to tears. Burgoyne found himself startled by the "encrease of sensibility" on the part of the spectators that this use of music provoked.[1]

In the same writing the retired general observed another unexpected instance of Garrick's affective use of music, in a revival of Edward Moore's *The Gamester*. "At the close of the tragedy," Burgoyne wrote, when the distress is raised to such a pitch that language fails under it, how forcibly is the impression left upon the audience by music, accompanying the slow descent of the curtain over the mournful picture! How preferable such a conclusion to the usual one of an actor straddling over dead bodies to deliver a tame moral in tame rhime to the pit, in the same breath, and often in the same tone, in which he is to give out the play.

The orchestra's usual custom for a legitimate drama was to retire backstage during the acts. The Drury Lane musicians were on hand to accompany this peroration: since at least 1774 Garrick had insisted that they remain in place throughout the play.[2] Considering that musicians were seated at the same level as the pit audience and their movements were visible throughout, it would have been impossible for them to play unobtrusively. Any reason to engage their instruments during the progress of the drama needed to conform to certain conventions. In Shakespeare's time, music would normally have been onstage or situated in a small gallery above, the musician in *Lear* (perhaps a single lutenist) having been brought in to soothe the anguish of the dying king. But Burgoyne recognized in Garrick's experiment a relatively *new* technique: using music in ways that worked on his spectators indirectly, while their attention was riveted on the actors. In *The Gamester* music was a logical expressive recourse when language could no longer serve a meaningful purpose and helped to sustain a mood during the final tableau. In reaction to instances such as these, Burgoyne surmised: "I am convinced that under judicious management music is capable of giving [our dramas for the stage] effect beyond what our best authors can attain without it."[3] Garrick's promptbooks for these two plays do not specify the music, so we must rely on this eyewitness account.[4]

Burgoyne acknowledges how unusual it was for Garrick to add affective music to the play. The device of having music speak on behalf of the actors (or some unseen narrator) was of course already used in pantomime. Garrick had close associations with many important mimists, both French and English. Some kind of narrative or affective music was also a prominent—even *dominant*—feature of the *mélo-drames* of Jean-Jacques Rousseau and Georg Benda in the 1770s. But it is not clear from Burgoyne's references whether his cited examples came before or after these *mélo-drames*, because Garrick produced those two plays a number of times over the course of his career. Yet the technique of using bits of music (very often a borrowed tune) to introduce certain characters must have infiltrated the English stage by the 1770s, because in his play *The Critic, or A Tragedy Rehearsed* of 1779 (Drury Lane), Richard Brinsley Sheridan was able to invoke the practice with a bit of tongue-in-cheek.

In act 2, scene 2, the characters are rehearsing a historical tragedy called *The Spanish Armada*. They have been working out the mechanics of cannon fire. Mr. Puff, who is author and director of the play, expresses exasperation after two volleys go off in succession. "This is always the way at the theatre," he complains. "Give these fellows a good thing, and they never know when to have done with it." After getting an assurance from the prompter that the crew has discharged all its explosions, Puff continues:

Puff. Now then, for soft music.
Sneer. Pray what's that for?
Puff. It shews that Tilburina is coming. Nothing introduces you to a heroine like soft music. Here she comes.
Dang. And her confidant, I suppose?
Puff. To be sure: here they are—inconsolable to the minuet in Ariadne! *(Soft music.)*

The "minuet" referred to is the most famous overture tune in George Frideric Handel's *Arianna in Creta* (1733). Perhaps Sheridan's locus of satire is Garrick and his recent recourse to such devices at Drury Lane, as the playwright-director here is apparently trying to introduce what seems like a new idea to his prompter. "Soft music" had been used as curtain tunes since the days of John Dryden and William Congreve, when women actors were introduced to the English stage. In Congreve's *The Mourning Bride* (1697) the curtain "rises slowly to soft music" in Almeria's chambers. But Almeria immediately reacts to the music that she hears, thereby justifying its existence, whereas Sheridan provides no source for the soft music that ushers in Tilburina—indeed she carries on, oblivious to it. It is perfectly within the rights of a modern playwright, Puff seems to be saying, to engage the orchestra without any textual or visual justification for the presence of music and to do so anywhere that the emotional arc of the play warrants. Furthermore, the author-manager is free to draw from a storehouse of well-known tunes to enhance characterization, much as an opera composer would shape a specific type of orchestral ritornello or characteristic melody to introduce a singing actor to the operatic stage.

How did this operatic technique work? Let us take a look at a few eighteenth-century examples that both Garrick and Sheridan would have known well. The first is an aria from one of the most successful comic operas of the eighteenth century, Niccolò Piccinni's *La buona figliuola*. Carlo Goldoni's libretto, drawn from Samuel Richardson's famous novel *Pamela, or Virtue Rewarded* (1740), italianizes the names and adds several stock character types. In the version performed at the King's Theatre, Haymarket, in 1766, the first entrance of the maid Sandrina is preceded by thirteen measures of *Larghetto* in G minor. Unlike Cecchina, the savvy Pamela-heroine who dispatches her gardening and other duties with Columbine-like alacrity, this disaffected and envious *servetta* grumbles her way through her tasks. The mournful strings and forceful changes in dynamics suggest her exaggerated burdens well before she begins to sing about them. Such an introduction (including all its musical qualities, tempo, mode, and articulation) heralds a dramatic *melos*, which here serves to establish a mood and to alert spectators to the arrival of a new character. Like a shadow projected from the wings, it precedes a character onto the stage in somewhat exaggerated proportions.

A second example is from an *opera seria*, Christoph Willibald Gluck's *Orfeo ed Euridice* (1762). As Orpheus enters leading Euridice from the gloom of Hades in act 3, the strings play a heavy, gasping figure, suggesting that the characters have come a long way and are already physically exhausted. Hence they are more susceptible to a weakening of resolve, which is what eventually happens. This four-bar characteristic music precedes and ushers the singer-actors onto the stage, establishing both the emotional and the psychological framework for their conversation, which of course is sung in accompanied recitative (this being an opera).

Though these two examples go well beyond Sheridan's "soft music" in terms of detail and affect, they were certainly representative of the kinds of aria-like introductions that a playwright in 1779 was likely to know and would have imagined appropriate to borrow for his characters, particularly for those that enter in similar states of mind. Once Puff's Tilburina is on, of course, music no longer serves any purpose: neither playwright nor audience has any expectation that she will sing her lines.

Throughout the eighteenth century a series of elaborate international debates took place about genres, both dramatic and musical. As we will see, English playwrights and adapters borrowed heavily from the French, and with this came certain musical conventions. Among these was the addition of a specific tune, such as the *Arianna* music, to provide supplemental denotative information. The device was not always welcome, however, especially during more incendiary political times. Such information could be subversive, as in this example from a French play by François-Marie Mayeur de Saint-Paul. In *Le Baron de Trenck,* a "pièce historique" written in verse for the Théâtre de l'Ambigu-Comique in 1788, Mayeur put the specifications for music directly into his playtext. In act 1, scene 3, the uniformed Trenck emerges to address his officers:

Trenck. Ce bienfait de mon Roi me devient plus flatteur	*Trenck.* This kindness from my king is more gratifying
Depuis que l'amitié partage mon bonheur.	Now that I have friends to share my happiness.
AIR: *Déjà la trompette guerrière* (8 mesures)	AIR: *Déjà la trompette guerrière* (8 measures)
Qu'il est doux pour un guerrier	How sweet it is for a warrior,
Brûlant de l'amour de la gloire	Burning from love and glory,
De cueillir un beau laurier	To choose a beautiful laurel
Dans les champs de la victoire.	In the fields of victory.
(7 mesures)	(7 measures)
(etc.)	(etc.)

Trenck does not sing but continues speaking, with intermittent musical interruptions. After each couplet or quatrain, the orchestra plays a phrase or two of music, ranging from four to fifteen measures. The tune is a heroic aria from *Renaud,* Antonio Sacchini's *tragédie-lyrique* (L'Opéra, 1783). Even for spectators at the Ambigu-Comique, a secondary theatre that specialized in pantomimes (and eventually melodrama), it may have had just enough currency that many in the audience would have made a literal connection. The French had a name for such borrowed melodies: *airs parlants* (talking tunes). As Marian Smith has shown, this was an effective device for communicating information to audiences in pantomime, where speech was not legally permitted, or in ballet, where dancers were neither trained nor expected to deliver lines.[5] In any case, the *melos* of a military call-to-arms would have served to stimulate emotion not just among the spectators but among the actors playing the baron's troops, who might even be inspired to rally around their leader physically.[6]

Playwrights such as Sheridan and Mayeur are not known to have used the term *melos* for this process, but they and their educated contemporaries certainly understood the concept: some affect or sentiment was communicated through the relationship of melody, key, harmony, and tempo and even an allusion to a known text. Some of the composers in the later eighteenth century who would go on to write music for pantomimes and melodramas, such as Samuel Arnold (1740–1802), came from a background in opera. Arnold and John O'Keeffe's comic pastiche-opera *The Castle of Andalusia* (Covent Garden, 1782), for example, is entirely sung. But each air is introduced with an appropriate *melos*. Victoria's "By woes thus surrounded" begins with an eight-bar introduction labeled simply "plaintive." A similar plaintive introduces Phillip's air "Severe the pangs of slighted love." Arnold did not live long enough into the nineteenth century to have composed for melodramas, but he composed many pantomimes and was obviously very familiar with the concept of *melos*. The plaintive, used as a curtain tune since the days of Dryden, would serve as a clearly defined *melos* for the entrance of a wronged or suffering heroine.

Certainly by the late 1770s some authors or managers besides Garrick were already asking their small band of musicians to find an apt tune to assist in the service of the drama, particularly to introduce certain characters or moods on which the actor could then build. For a time this practice largely seemed to involve appropriating well-known airs and folksongs. As we will see with *Black-Eyed Susan*, this procedure continued well into the nineteenth century, creating melodramatic underscoring that consisted almost entirely of familiar melodies. But the idea of employing original music also began to accrue some cachet. This complicated the issue considerably: why would a manager go to the trouble and expense of commissioning an original score when borrowed tunes—especially in the days before copyright lawyers—would do just as well, if not better? Herein lies a paradox of this study. The most effective music in melodramatic genres functions best "invisibly," subordinate to the action onstage. So the more prominent or inventive the musical score, the more likely it is to draw attention to itself and possibly diminish an actor's efforts. Those tensions between new and borrowed music, between an original score and apposite or formulaic music, make even the most effective theatrical music resistant to traditional forms of analysis.

The Passions and the Art of Mimic

In the eighteenth century the value that music added to drama was perceived as an extension of the various passions, categories of feeling and emotion discussed at great length in the literature of the time. "When Music . . . was young," wrote the eighteenth-century poet William Collins of the ancient Greek muse, "the Passions . . . thronged around her."

Exulting, trembling, raging, fainting,
Possess'd beyond the Muse's painting.
By turns they felt the glowing mind
Distub'd, delighted, rais'd, refin'd.

Every personified passion—fear, anger, despair, hope, revenge, pity, jealousy, love, hate, melancholy, cheerfulness, and joy—drew from the Muse its own expressive power and unique characteristics. But without the nourishment of music, the poet warns, the passions eventually run dry.

'Tis said, and I believe the tale,
Thy humblest reed could more prevail,
Had more of strength, diviner rage,
Than all which charms this laggard age;
E'en all at once together found,
Cecilia's mingled world of sound—
O bid our vain endeavours cease;
Revive the just designs of Greece:
Return in all thy simple state!
Confirm the tales her sons relate!

Written in 1746, Collins's great testimony of the power and indeed the necessity of music served well into the nineteenth century as an inspiration for elocutionists and actors, who used accompanying music to confirm the truthfulness of the tale.[7]

As appropriate music formed the essential background to any actor's performance of Collins's ode, a series of normative poses and physical expressions associated with each passion also arose. These were the subject of many treatises on speech and acting, especially those by Aaron Hill (1746), Thomas Wilkes (1759), James Burgh (1761), and Johann Jakob Engel (1785) and in the early nineteenth century by Gilbert Austin (1806) and Henry Siddons (1807). These treatises were concerned more with the art of gesture ("mimic") and its relationship to the various passions (states of being) than specifically with music. Burgh analyzes Collins's ode in detail, but all wrote in the light of the poet's stern warning that the passions, no matter how well an actor might embody them, would seem hollow without music.

Eighteenth-century actors clearly thought in these terms, if we consider the "ten basic passions" as described by Aaron Hill in 1746, a topology referenced by Siddons and others in early nineteenth-century acting manuals.[8] Hill believed in six "primary" passions—joy, sorrow, fear, scorn, anger, and amazement—and four "secondary" ones—jealousy, revenge, love, and pity. All others were variants of these ten, aided by specific gestures that qualified the passion. As Denis Diderot further explained in 1773, the passions begin as ideas in the mind of the actor and are then translated by means of artifice into voice and gesture, the refinement of which forms an essential part of an actor's training.[9] Today we are more likely to speak of emotions than of passions. Even in the field of cognitive science a body of literature recognizes six basic emotions detectable in the human face, which closely correspond to Hill's primary ones: happiness (= joy), surprise (= amazement), anger, sadness (= sorrow), fear, and disgust or contempt (= scorn).[10]

But to realize any tragic role an actor clearly needs more than six basic passions and the ability to manage more than just facial expressions. "Every part of the human frame," Burgh observed, "contributes to express the passions and emotions of the mind."[11] Engaging the full body as an expressive instrument, Burgh itemized no less than seventy-five distinct passions. Pride, for example, "borders on the aspect and attitude of anger; the eyes open, but with the eyebrows confidently drawn down; the mouth pouting out, mostly shut, the lips pinched closed." An actor can only be said to convey such passions faithfully, qualified Engel, "when an audience perceives these passions as natural, not imitative."[12] While allowing for some national and regional variation, Engel—borrowing from Wilkes and others—identified several universally recognized gestures as the body's natural way of reflecting emotions. For Engel, pride is physically communicated by a combination of a hand placed high on the breast, the shoulders and head tilted slightly back, and space between outward-turning feet (Fig. 1). In his English adaptation of Engel, Siddons illustrates sixty-five such attitude clusters, each manifesting the psychological-emotional categories of apprehension, devotion, enthusiasm, conceit, menace, terror, dejection, jealous rage, and many more. By using a systematic combination of facial expressions and universally recognized body movements, an actor could be certain that spectators would correctly interpret the passion.

Burgh, Engel, and Siddons, however, do not discuss music's relationship to physical gesture, though Siddons often refers to music as a sister art to drama. But in his treatise on rhetorical delivery Gilbert Austin claimed that music, while less specific than speech or gesture, was nevertheless useful to delineate six distinct passions: love and pity, sorrow and joy, terror and valor. In these instances musical expression could lend an actor additional force.[13] Moreover, music could be an effective way to incite an appropriate emotion in the observer, thereby paving the way for a sense of identification

FIGURE 1.
Images from Henry Siddons, Practical Illustrations of Rhetorical Gesture and Action, Adapted to the English Drama from a Work on the Subject by M. Engel, *2nd ed. (London: Sherwood, Neely, and Jones, 1822):* left to right: *Pride, Terror, Menace,* left: *Enthusiasm*

with the actor's passions. "Music," wrote the Scottish philosopher James Beattie in 1762, "is pleasing not because it is imitative, but because certain melodies and harmonies have an aptitude to raise certain passions, affections, and sentiments in the soul."[14] Beattie identified eight passions specifically roused by music: love, hatred, ambition, fear, hope, remorse, jealousy, and revenge. Austin must surely have known of Beattie's categories when he reduced their number to six, combining some and jettisoning others.

These elocutionists speak of passions in music as a science of affect (or, in eighteenth-century phraseology, as an expression of "the affections"). Music theory treatises from the seventeenth and eighteenth centuries that describe various types of musical affect and their relationship to human passions are legion.[15] Some composer-theorists, such as Marc-Antoine Charpentier (1692), thought in terms of the emotional colors of various modes, similar to the way Aristoxenus had used the term *melos*: E-flat minor was "horrible, frightful," E major was "quarrelsome and clamorous," F major was "furious and quick-tempered," F minor was "gloomy and plaintive," G major was "sweetly joyful," and so on.[16] Others, such as Johann Mattheson (1739), catalogued the affections according to rhetorical figures. Very fast notes "running" up a scale, for example, could suggest anticipation or surging hope, whereas the same notes running down would suggest resignation or defeat. "Even in instrumental music," Mattheson wrote, "each melodic line always focuses its attention on the presentation of the reigning affection, so that through their notes the instruments deliver a presentation as if they were speaking and understandable."[17]

Mattheson's formulation embodies a mode of thinking that would divide into two camps by the nineteenth century: those who felt that musical expression is always abstract or limited to general emotions (and therefore could be made more specific by the helpful addition of words) and those inclined to believe that music was capable of greater specificity than words or, rather, offered an entirely *different* kind of expression (and was therefore limited or cheapened by any text associated with it). From an actor's perspective, an attitude- or gesture-cluster associated with a particular passion, when united with the appropriate affect of music, could unmistakably intensify the affective significance of any dramatic incident. As Garrick and his successors no doubt realized, this was a sure way to win over the hearts and minds of an audience.

Original Music and the Classical Mélo-drame

The Swiss philosopher and composer Jean-Jacques Rousseau (1712–1778) wrote his *Pygmalion* in the midst of these debates about the dramatic passions. Begun in 1762, this "lyric scene" for two characters was perhaps the first major experiment to apply music to the passions. Even by this time, as we have seen, music had been used in tragedy to introduce a scene or a new character, thereby making the spectators receptive to the following dialogue. For Rousseau, the French language (specifically related to the theory of its rationality) needed no musical mirroring, whereas the dramatic passions (with accompanying gestures) could be made more explicit through music. Rousseau had been caught up in the Parisian controversy over French versus Italian opera and was decidedly in favor of Italian as the preferred language for singing. He may have planned his lyric scene as a parody of the French *opéra-ballet*.[18] But in the end Rousseau's solution was to have an actor deliver the lines in neoclassical declamatory style and allow for short musical insertions to accompany the various pantomimic actions and chart the emotional development of the protagonist. Rousseau's precise musical instructions ("a few measures of tender and melancholy music") were indicated in the margins of his text with a dark cross, as seen in the edition prepared by Jacqueline Waeber.[19] After composing one or two of these pieces, however, Rousseau seemed to have lost interest.

In 1770, while in Lyon, Rousseau was approached by Horace Coignet (1735–1821), a gifted amateur musician, to whom he entrusted his *Pygmalion*. Although several more prominent composers eventually wrote music for this short dramatic work, it was Coignet who crafted most of the original *melos* numbers for the first performance in Lyon in 1770; his music is most closely associated with the piece. Rousseau perhaps understood that to engage a composer of known stature would also have invited a distinct musical voice that could very well have overwhelmed his text. Coignet's music is serviceable rather than distinguished. Its short atmospheric pieces (some as brief as two measures long) unequivocally capture the drama's shifting moods without turning it into a predominantly musical piece. *Pygmalion* is classical in theme, with characters drawn from Greek mythology and intended for a private audience rather than for the public stage. But in his decision to engage a little-known musician with an efficacious rather than conspicuously original style, Rousseau established a precedent that would persist in the history of the popular drama for a hundred years.

Rousseau called *Pygmalion* a *mélo-drame*. The term was not exactly a new one. Since around 1600 Italian scholars had used *melodramma* to mean the re-creation of classical Greek tragedy, which they believed to be a union of *melos* and *dramma*. *Melodramma* has remained the term most closely associated with opera in Italy: *melos* as sung play. Rousseau's insertion of a hyphen between the two roots symbolized a departure from the operatic genre, in which *melos*, as "instrumental" as opposed to "vocal" music, was quite independent of the speaking actor. For Rousseau, *melos* and text (*déclaration*) engaged complementary modes of expression, united not in the performing space but in the sympathetic imagination of the spectator. This unique form of eighteenth-century melodrama, with the insertion of music between recitations, has been examined in great detail elsewhere. The focus here is on those ingredients that exerted a lasting influence on the popular drama.[20]

Pygmalion is principally a monodrama set in an artist's studio in which a sculptor miraculously animates his stone cast of Galatea, rather like Leontes with Hermione's statue in Shakespeare's *The Winter's Tale*, which may very well have been the source of Rousseau's inspiration. When David Garrick staged this culminating scene of *Winter's Tale* at Drury Lane in 1756, he asked William Boyce to compose some music to accompany it. Boyce's *melos*, for two winds and strings, consisted of forty-two bars. "Awake her. Strike," Pauline instructs Leontes. Boyce's music began with long dramatic notes and gradually became more animated. Garrick broke off the music in midstream to have Pauline speak the line "descend; be stone no more." The music then resumed, perhaps even continuing under Pauline's succeeding lines, to culminate in an exciting finish as the enlivened Hermione stepped down from her pedestal.[21] (The instructions for music in this scene appear in the Tonson edition of 1765, edited by Samuel Johnson.)

Instead of using music sparingly, as Garrick did to heighten the effect at the climax of *The Winter's Tale*, Rousseau expanded it over the entire length of his minidrama. To musical accompaniment, the actor playing the artist goes about his preparatory duties, chiseling away at various blocks of marble. He periodically stops and speaks in meditative soliloquies, offering insights into the agonies and ecstasies of the creative process. Though not an opera, Rousseau's *Pygmalion* is often cited in operatic annals as one of the first works to deal with aesthetic and epistemological questions raised by Romantic notions of the creative artist. It was the first treatment of the subject by a major author to involve music as well as speech. In retrospect it was perhaps as much a philosophical experiment as a dramatic one.

Unlike the classical French dramas by Jean Racine and his predecessors, *Pygmalion* is not a tragedy. The music's overall emotional trajectory is from the dark and gloom of the artist's blocked state of mind to the sunlit flow of energy channeled into the completed artwork. For the opening of the play, as Pygmalion is found slumped in a dreamlike state "in the attitude of a man anxious and sad," Rousseau asked for "two minutes" of music that conveys unrest, sorrow, and despondency ("l'inquiétude, le chagrin et le découragement"). This would at first glance seem to be mood-setting music, a technique that composers such as Jean-Philippe Rameau had already used in their operas by this time. But Rousseau's expectations for music were new: to transmit not a general mood but a character's specific emotions to the audience. Coignet wrote a piece largely in F minor, a key often associated in the eighteenth century with "mournfulness" and "anguish" (Charpentier's "gloomy" and "plaintive"). Before Pygmalion even moved or spoke, the audience members were drawn into the character's emotional state. They were then piqued for a clarification of these feelings through words.

In other places Rousseau specified that musical illustration should supersede the text. Near the climax of the piece, for example, following Pygmalion's observation of irony in a nobly smiling statue incapable of feeling anything itself, Rousseau added a cross and the words "flûtes calme." Coignet wrote fifteen bars of *amoroso*, with the oboe and violins (he had no flute) sweetly singing a surging melody in C major, during which the sculptor "gradually returns to himself with a gesture of assurance and joy." Insecurities threaten to prevent him from resuming his work, however; to reassure himself, he shouts: "Hey look, unhappy one, be fearless, dare to complete a statue" (*Eh! Regarde, malheureux: deviens intrépide, ose fixer une statüe*). Another cross appears in the margin of Rousseau's text. In response to this critical turning point in the plot Coignet composed a three-bar *andante* in A minor for ascending strings to culminate on a B dominant seventh chord, during which the sculptor "sees the statue come alive and turns away with terror" (*Il la voit s'animer, et se détourne saisi d'effroi et le coeur serre de douleur*). In these cases music reacts to stimuli in the drama rather than preparing the spectator for them. None of the musical pieces overlap with the actor's voice, so Coignet did not need to concern himself with problems of dialogue and music, the kinds of issues that composers for the popular drama would later need to tackle.

Altogether, in addition to an overture, *Pygmalion* contained twenty-six numbered *morceaux* (bits or short pieces).[22] Despite the wide range of keys, from C major and E major to such remote and spooky keys as E-flat minor, not a single one of Coignet's *morceaux* ends with tonal closure. Each *melos* hesitates on an inconclusive chord, like a sentence punctuated with an ellipsis. In other words each piece ends musically "open," awaiting direction from the drama. This is true even of the very last cue, which occurs before Galathea's awakening. Coignet specified no music for the ending, although the orchestra may have played some familiar piece to close.[23] The instrumental ensemble at the Lyon performances was small: two oboes, two horns, and strings. Coignet's music was used again in 1775 for the performances at the Comédie-Française and other locations. (The Viennese performances in 1772 had music by another composer.)[24] As *Pygmalion* spread to Madrid, London, and other European capitals the Rousseauan experiment defined *mélo-drame* in the literary, dramatic, and musical circles of the 1770s and 1780s.[25]

In Spain, for example, the playwright and musician Tomás de Iriarte (Yriarte) wrote what he termed a *melológico* entitled *Guzmán el Bueno*, first performed for a private audience in Cadiz in 1790 and then in Madrid in 1791. Iriarte subtitled this a "soliloquio ú escena trágica unipersonal, con música en sus intervalos," in other words, a unidrama or tragic scene interspersed with music. The story takes place in the interior of a castle and is narrated by a single actor, without sets or costumes. Guzmán's soliloquies were separated by ten brief musical pieces, composed by Iriarte himself. The performance at Madrid had an orchestra larger than Coignet's, about twenty-three musicians (two flutes, two oboes, two clarinets, two bassoons, two trumpets, and strings).[26] This Spanish version of the *mélo-drame* is a significant benchmark on the path to the popular drama. Instead of using a classical subject Iriarte chose an actual Castilian nobleman as protagonist, and the musical interludes served to interpret well-known events in this historical life.

The most significant transformation of the early *mélo-drame*, however, took place in Germany, with a different approach from the Rousseau-Iriarte technique of inserting set musical pieces between soliloquies. In the 1770s German acting troupes were beginning to diversify their repertory, realizing that they could better fill the public theatres if they alternated the great tragedies of Shakespeare and G. E. Lessing as well as translated French comedies by Pierre Beaumarchais and others with the increasingly popular French *opéra-comique* and its German variant, the *Singspiel*. These were plays with interpolated songs and other musical numbers. Hence even a traveling troupe of actors such as Abel Seyler's company engaged a ballet corps and a small body of musicians. Johann Brandes, one of Seyler's actors, had written *Ariadne auf Naxos*, a tragic duodrama for his wife, Charlotte Brandes, to act on the stage to the accompaniment of some music.[27] Georg Benda (1722–1795) was a Bohemian musician working in Gotha when the Seyler troupe moved to that city after the Weimar theatre burned. When Benda read Brandes's *Ariadne* he eagerly offered to compose music for it himself.

In this forty-two-minute piece, Theseus, in order to seek his political destiny, abandons the sleeping Ariadne, who wakes, agonizes over her situation, and eventually commits suicide. Benda integrated Brandes's powerful voice and his relatively large orchestra, which consisted of two flutes, two oboes, two bassoons, horns, timpani, four offstage trombones, and strings. The drama was staged in costume. In an effort at historical accuracy, Brandes wore Greek robes, rather than the usual contemporary dress. This was the early melodrama's first move toward realism, a feature that would prove integral to the popular drama. For the style of the music, Benda took his cue from French and German *opera seria*, in which the portions of the text that were not musically expanded into arias were executed in real time, at the speed and inflection of naturalistic dialogue. In an operatic sung recitative, there was a seamless flow between voice and orchestra, which punctuated and illustrated the text with brief snippets of music. These were more transitory than tuneful; they shifted rapidly between emotions, either leading into a line of text or out of it. Since accompanied (or *obbligato*) recitatives generally led directly into arias or duets, their role was to establish the dramatic conflict that would be resolved in the aria—hence the frequent *Sturm und Drang* quality of much of the music accompanying these kinds of recitatives. Large sections of *Ariadne* are composed in this style, except that the actress speaks her lines instead of singing them. The orchestra responds, however, as if she *were* singing.

The dramatic pacing of Benda's *Ariadne* as well as his *Medea*, written for Madame Seyler a few years later, is therefore maintained by the orchestra rather than the actor, which lends a more operatic or symphonic dimension to the whole. Gone are the inserted "numbers." Benda's *mélodrame* is now one continuous composition, even integrated musically with a few recurring themes. As David Joseph Buch wrote, Benda "employed vivid musical imagery to portray psychological turmoil." Choice of keys reflects some of the prevailing attitudes toward color and emotional affect. The work includes a storm scene in the grand and melancholy key of D minor, oracle scenes in the heroic and devotional key of E-flat major and the pathetic key C minor, and Ariadne's suicide scene in D minor, which exacts a return to the tragic.[28] For Rousseau, music served largely as interludes of sensation. But Benda's musical commentary was "through-composed," written around the text and in support of evolving action.[29]

Ariadne's final monologue, for example, is shot through with stage directions and even sound effects. She searches the island amid an approaching storm, ascends to the top of the cliff, and appeals to heaven. Benda's technique was to write continuous music, but in such a way as to leave space for the actress's lines to break through. The orchestra here provides mostly effects of rolling thunder (repeated notes) and unleashed torrents of rain (the ascending scales), which also serve rhetorically to suggest Ariadne's mounting fear and distress. The music is in G minor, a key that Francesco Galeazzi described as suited to frenzy, despair, and agitation (Fig. 2).[30]

The dramatic power of Benda's technique impressed many composers, including Johann André, Johann Adam Hiller, Paul Wranitzky, and even Wolfgang Amadeus Mozart, who were all eager to incorporate the melodramatic experiment into their operas. The author of the text was not so sure, however. In a published preface to *Ariadne*, Brandes wondered if Benda's music was *too* effective and perhaps threatened to overwhelm the actor.[31]

Though Benda's subjects were classical, the technique that he developed served as a powerful tool to shape dramatic intensity, not just overall in terms of pacing and drive toward the crisis but also locally by modulating the intensity within a specific monologue. *Ariadne* was first given on 27 January 1775 with a large orchestra in a fully staged production in Gotha, but Benda made a reduced version for string quartet "arranged for use in the society [public] theatres."[32] This version of the melodrama was performed throughout Europe, including at the Théâtre-Italiens in Paris in 1781. Though it generated significant controversy, it was later proven to be a decisive influence on the *opéra-comique*, particularly in the use of the orchestra to accompany passages of dialogue and pantomime between sung musical numbers.[33] Among those to feature the new technique were Jean-Baptiste Rochefort in *Echo et Narcisse*, produced at the Théâtre de l'Ambigu-Comique in 1786, and Jean-François Lesueur in *Paul et Virginie, ou La triomphe de la virtu*, produced at the Théâtre Feydeau in 1794.[34]

Original Music and the Comic Pantomime

The tender music that Garrick added to the scene of Lear's awakening was a single-affect type, as in Coignet's pieces for Rousseau, rather than Benda's through-composed music. While this *melos* type was obviously effective in

FIGURE 2. *Georg Benda,* Ariadne auf Naxos, *ed. Thomas Bauman (New York: Garland, 1985): excerpt of keyboard reduction and English translation by the author from the full score*

sustaining mood, Garrick also exploited its possibilities for making connections between the visible and invisible, between the *mise-en-scène* (the stage picture) and the *mise-en-musique* (the sound picture), to borrow a term from Emilio Sala. Using music to prolong an affect granted his actors time and space to expand upon a crucial emotional moment, which otherwise would have had to be filled with action or dialogue. This relationship of affect, gesture, and music was perhaps nowhere more developed than in the pantomime. In France and England censorship and the long-standing influence of Italian comedy performers (who did not speak the language and therefore were compelled literally to speak with their bodies) sometimes required music to do the "speaking" for them. Like the single-affect and through-composed *mélo-drames*, two distinct types of pantomimes existed in the eighteenth century, both of which involved original music. The earliest—and most enduring—was the acrobatic "dumb show" or *harlequinade*, a direct descendant of the commedia dell'arte acted by strolling players or comedians in minor theatres (eventually adopted during the Christmas season by the major theatres as well). The second type was the "serious pantomime," as Thomas Dibdin and others called it. The prototype of this kind of mime was actually invented—so observed Jean-Baptiste Dubos in 1748—by Pylades in Augustan Rome, but it was revived in the eighteenth century by dance stylists such as John Weaver in London, Gasparo Angiolini in Vienna, and Jean-Georges Noverre in France.

The harlequinades were the first to use descriptive musical pieces for each *melos*; by the 1740s they were referred to as "comic tunes" (and from the 1760s were often numbered, like Rousseau's *morceaux*, for purposes of coordination). Tunes were useful in conveying emotion in the harlequinades, because the actor's expressions were hidden behind masks. In 1751 Charles Burney wrote the tunes for *Queen Mab*, a pantomime produced by Henry Woodward, dancer and chief Harlequin of Drury Lane.[35] One of these underscores Columbine's pleas with her father's refusals ("Pantaloon's Rage"), a standard commedia scenario. Quite a few comic tunes from the eighteenth century were published, at least those written for pantomimes at the patent theatres. Most of these were single-affect and eight to sixteen bars long. Often a solo musician at the keyboard would have accompanied the mime, as Roger Fiske and Anne Dhu McLucas have shown; perhaps at most he might have had the assistance of two violins or a flute and violin.[36]

We can see how comic tunes worked in a sequence from *Harlequin Dr. Faustus*, a 1724 pantomime that Woodward revived at Covent Garden in 1766.[37] Samuel Arnold wrote the music. In the following synopsis the titles of the tunes, taken from the published score, have been interpolated into the sequence of the plot as told by an eyewitness for the *London Magazine*.[38] Scene 5 takes place in Harlequin's study, with two screens visible onstage (Music: "Doctor's Study," *vivace*, G-major, 3/8). Harlequin, in the guise of a country doctor, has charmed the miller's wife, whom he brings home with the intention of seducing her. The lady is flirtatious but coy. When the valet alarms them with notice of somebody's approach, Harlequin hides her behind one of the screens. The miller enters (Music: "The

Miller Going to the Doctor," *pomposo*, B-flat major, 4/4) and greets the disguised Harlequin. In a song ("You'll Wonder, Sage Doctor," *moderato*) the miller complains of the inconstancy of women and offers the "doctor" some money for a medicinal cure. Harlequin looks in the miller's hand and then strikes the screen, which opens to reveal the miller's wife (Music: "The Screen," no tempo specified). The irate husband runs to grab her. But Harlequin strikes the other screen, and a gruesome-looking woman in a bridal gown emerges and frightens the miller, who runs off. The action continued in this manner, accompanied by little bits of music with an occasional song. Sometimes the tunes mimicked the stage action in precise note-to-note correspondence, as in the sobbing figures for "The Miller Crying" (no. 8) or the steady *pizzicato* in "The Clock" (no. 18). Arnold's numbered comic tunes, interspersed between songs, established an important precedent for the numbering of instrumental cues in the popular drama.

Moreover, the tunes can be categorized into genera or species, with each performing a distinct dramatic function. Tune no. 12, for example, is titled "Hurry" (G minor, *allegro moderato*). As Robert Hoskins notes, the "hurry" had been in use in the comic pantomime since at least 1740.[39] This pantomime seems to contain several hurries, though called by other names such as "pursuit." As Arnold uses the term, however, a "hurry" is not just any fast-paced action but one used specifically for the unraveling of some imbroglio. Moving along these lines we can identify at least three specific musical functions in the harlequin scenario above. The first piece, "The Doctor's Study," was an establishing cue, certainly to set the lively tone for the scene and possibly also to sustain this mood during the flirtations onstage. The music for the "alarm," if there was any, does not appear in the published score (perhaps it was just a few improvised diminished-seventh chords). "The Miller Going to the Doctor" is a character or signature tune. It serves to shift attention from Harlequin as seducer to the troubled husband. It no doubt accompanied the miller's entrance to the study, soured the mood, and perhaps also conveyed some idiosyncrasics of this about-to-be-cuckolded character. Finally, "The Screen" is obviously a comic hurry, action music for a scramble and chase. Such types of functional dramatic music are the first of the many characteristic pieces that would form a staple part of the musical language of the emerging popular drama, especially in its comical or more farcical elements.

In the 1770s a spectacular new element was introduced to the *mise-en-scène* of pantomime at Drury Lane: the grand scenic paintings and lighting transformations of Philippe Jacques de Loutherbourg, soon to be inventor of the Eidophusikon (a predecessor of the panorama and moving pictures). Reviews of Garrick's *A Christmas Tale* in 1774 commented on how the production, with its enchanted castles and battles between good and evil, was a feast for the eyes (one stage direction on the objects in Camilla's magnificent garden specifies to "vary their colours"). *A Christmas Tale* seemed like a new genre, a spectacle of sound and vision aimed at popular audiences. The effects of machinery, painting, and Charles Dibdin's music (mostly songs) "seem[ed] to vie with each other for applause," wrote one reviewer. Garrick scholars generally look down on this play, and indeed many criticisms at the time were scathing. The piece is clearly a "play with music," in the genre of *Singspiel* or ballad opera, though Horace Walpole called it "a dire mixture of opera, tragedy, comedy, and pantomime." This suggests that to audiences of the time the newness of the spectacle seemed more like a confusion of genres rather than a new one.[40] Clearly, though, the essential visual and musical components for a popular drama were present, if not entirely fused, in this mélange.[41]

Pantomime took a giant step forward both musically and dramatically at Drury Lane in 1781 with Sheridan's adaptation of Daniel Defoe's *Robinson Crusoe*, devised as an afterpiece to follow *The Winter's Tale*. As Robert Hoskins has explained in his edition of this work, *Crusoe* was actually in two parts, the first being a dramatic pantomime to a scenario by Sheridan that visually depicted key events in Defoe's novel. The second part was a comic harlequinade on the same subject. The serious pantomime was a vehicle for two comic actors: as Crusoe, Carlo Delpini (who also handled most of the staging), and as Friday, Giuseppe Grimaldi, father of the famous clown. Sheridan's scenario is divided into twelve scenes. The music for the pantomime was by Thomas Linley (1733–1795). Unlike most extended pantomimes of this period, the music was published complete in piano score, affording the opportunity to examine the relationship between music and action in some detail. Linley's music included an overture (in Italian *sinfonia* style), one song, and twenty-nine comic tunes. Each comic tune was titled—as in the harlequinades—to be coordinated with dramatic changes in the pantomime and transformations in de Loutherbourg's scenic paintings.

The tune titles portray miniature episodes, such as "Robinson Crusoe Works on a Tree" and "Robinson Crusoe Shoots Birds." Unlike the earlier comic tunes of uniform length, Linley's *melos* numbers range from eight to twenty-five measures, some with repeats and pauses, and each lasts from forty-five seconds to perhaps a minute and a half (with the overture the whole pantomime would probably have taken about forty minutes). Many of the tunes, like those in the comic pantomimes, are single-tempo, single-affect pieces. But a few are composed in a more fluid manner, with fluctuating characteristics and tempos to match the arc of the dramatic event. Linley was clearly responding to the detailed plot that Sheridan had provided him. For example, in an early sequence the hero has been building a boat and just felled a tree. The tune "Robinson Crusoe Sees the Mark of a Foot" begins *largo* with staccato eighth notes, as Crusoe is dragging the tree toward his project. Suddenly there are some lightning-fast violin scales, a rhetorical suggestion of Crusoe's surprise (he's "thunder-struck" in Defoe), and then a fast descending *allegro* as the castaway starts in anticipation of a possible encounter (Defoe's "innumerable fluttering thoughts"). Seven successive tunes are matched to their corresponding descriptions in the scenario, which is derived mostly from the description in the *London Chronicle*. Hence we can get a fuller sense of how Linley's continuous music supports the evolving story.

> *Scene 3*
>
> Scene changes to a view of the sea, canoes appear full of savages, coming to sacrifice some prisoners. (no. 8: "Scene of a Sea")
>
> They paddle across, then land. (no. 9: "Savages Landing")
>
> A dance is introduced. (no. 10: "Dance of Savages")
>
> They bring Harlequin Friday on shore and are preparing to kill him. He breaks from them and escapes. They follow. (no. 11: "Prisoners Brought Forward")
>
> Scene changes to the woody part of the island. Robinson Crusoe enters on one side and Friday on the other pursued by savages. He fires at them, and they retire in the utmost consternation. (no. 12: "Scene Changes")
>
> *Scene 4*
>
> Robinson Crusoe then calls to Friday, who kneels down, kisses Crusoe's feet . . . (no. 13: "Robinson Crusoe Encourages Friday")
>
> Crusoe arms Friday in case of another attack, and they go off together. Scene changes. (no. 14: "Friday Happy")

The pantomime continued in this manner. Furthermore, music was only one of its aural components: Sheridan's notes contained plenty of instructions for sound effects from the stage. At the climax came a battle, with

Crusoe and Friday helping to overthrow a band of mutineers. The pantomime ended happily with the restored captain inviting the castaways on board and the ship sailing away.

Crusoe made a significant advance in the relationship between stage action and the use of instrumental music, engendering certain conventions already in use in opera and ballet in a popular theatrical form. We can also see here two somewhat different applications of *melos*: one where the *melos* pervades an entire episode (expressing a single passion) and another where *melos* (as in Benda's *Ariadne*) fluctuates to conform to the rising action and crisis typical of a longer dramatic scene. This second type of *melos* was further developed not in the harlequinade but in the more extended dramatic mime sequences in ballets, specifically the "action ballets" (*ballets d'action*), narrative dramas executed completely in dance and mime to continuous music.

Serious Pantomime and the Popular Drama

Jean-Georges Noverre (1727–1810), who rejected the static symmetry of French court ballets and the formal dance pieces they mirrored, was one of the developers of the action ballet. Noverre, preoccupied with the representation of character through dance, was profoundly impressed when he first saw David Garrick in Shakespeare. "Even those who understand not a word of English," Noverre wrote of the actor's skills in communicative physical gesture, "comprehend without difficulty the scene enacted before them."[42] (Some French accounts in 1751 even go so far as to describe Garrick's Macbeth as a kind of "tragic pantomime.")[43] In 1755 the two began a long friendship that ended only in 1779 when Noverre came to London to march in procession behind Garrick's coffin. In collaboration with now-forgotten composers such as François Granier in Lyon and Joseph Starzer in Vienna Noverre developed the action ballet, in which every gesture, every facial expression (for Noverre did away with traditional masks), and every design aspect of the tableau was carefully coordinated to move along a specific detailed plot, much of which was conveyed through a physicalization of the passions. "An essential part of ballet," Noverre wrote in 1760, "is that the variety of incidents and the resulting pictures must follow one another quickly. If the action does not work precisely, if scenes languish, if the plot does not heat up as the story unfolds, then the plan is poorly conceived, it sins against the rules of theatre."[44] Noverre *dramatized* dance and insisted on a type of evolving action music that would move the drama forward. His many pantomime ballets performed at the King's Theatre in the 1770s and 1780s exerted a significant impact on the development of serious pantomime in England.

Noverre's ballet subjects—like the *mélo-drames* of Rousseau and Benda—were almost entirely classical and were designed for the opera houses and patent theatres of Paris and London.[45] But in the 1770s serious pantomime began to turn toward historical subjects, which seemed to appeal to the growing audiences for such entertainment. In France, as in England, historical pantomime emerged at first in the major theatres. But beginning in the 1780s (and continuing well into the next century) the most original challenge came from the Théâtre de l'Ambigu-Comique under the ceaselessly imaginative Nicolas-Médard Audinot. The Ambigu-Comique was built in 1769 on the Boulevard du Temple, at that time still a site of one of Paris's fairgrounds. As with all secondary theatres, plays performed there needed the approval of the censor, who could strike out specific dialogue (or whole scenes). By incorporating acrobatics, pantomime, marionettes, and—in the early years—child actors, Audinot managed to skirt some of these restrictions. (*Ambigu* literally means a jumble of genres.) In 1775 Audinot invited Jean François Mussot, calling himself Arnould, to join his troupe as associate manager. Arnould wrote pantomimes that were powerful wordless dramas in which he imagined music fulfilling a significant communicative role. His first major collaboration with Audinot, who is believed also to have composed the music, was *Le siège de Montauban, ou Les quatre Fils Aymon* (1779), a "pantomime historique" based on the legend of Charlemagne. But Audinot and Arnould soon encountered a major stumbling block. The plots of their pantomimes were complicated, and the censors forbade the use of any dialogue that would clarify dramatic situations. Spectators could not follow the story without a printed libretto.

Given that many Ambigu audience members at this time were illiterate, Audinot and Arnould came up with a solution with *Dorothée* in 1782, the same year as the premiere of Friedrich Schiller's play *Die Raüber* (The Robbers), which also featured a damsel in distress and a rescue. In this extraordinarily popular *pantomime à spectacle*, Dorothée is publicly accused of a trumped-up crime and thrown into prison, principally as a result of her refusing the advances of the lascivious mayor. Her husband, a general, is away at war with England. After suffering degradations in prison, she is brought to a public place and tied to a stake bearing an inscription saying that she will be burned if no valiant knight will come forward to defend her. The general has sent such a deputy back to town to investigate, and the knight offers to fight the chief of the mayor's guard in Dorothée's defense. He wins the battle, but the infuriated mayor has already ordered the pyre set ablaze. The general arrives in the nick of time to rescue the unconscious Dorothée from the flames. Upon hearing the circumstances of her arrest, the general orders the immediate incarceration of the mayor. The plot of *Dorothée* was easy to follow because of the clearly defined archetypal characters. The authors added sentimental situations designed to appeal more to the emotions than to the intellect. When brief explanations were needed, the actors displayed simply worded signs, plaques, and banners—clever devices to circumvent censorship. Unlike the five-act classical tragedy, the pantomime was in three acts, a tradition of the *opéra-comique*. Finally, the story was imbued with a lofty moral tone, making a happy resolution on the side of good essential. Along with Schiller's *Robbers, Dorothée* launched the popular drama in 1782. With rare exceptions such as Arnould and Audinot's 1788 pantomime *La mort du Capitaine Cook à son voyage au Nouveau Monde*, audiences at the Ambigu-Comique and other boulevard theatres came to expect vice punished and virtue rewarded.[46]

While *Dorothée* engaged most of the elements of the popular drama, a "serious historical pantomime ballet" based on the legend of Captain James Cook had overtones of tragedy, including the immediacy of its connection to the recent murder of the explorer in Hawaii in 1779. It was impossible under the circumstances to invent a happy ending. For the 1785 pantomime *Omai, or A Trip round the World*, based on this tragedy and staged at Covent Garden by John O'Keeffe with set designs by de Loutherbourg, Cook was celebrated as a new kind of British hero.[47] *Omai*, like *A Christmas Tale*, was largely a "play with music." But in 1789 Covent Garden produced the original action ballet of *Captain Cook* with all of the Ambigu music by Jean-Baptiste Rochefort (1746–1819). The published text tells us that Rochefort's music (like Linley's for *Robinson Crusoe*) accompanied "Captain Cook's reception by the Natives," "the Captain's preparation for Battle," and "the Manner in which Captain Cook fell a sacrifice."[48] Rochefort's music for the *ballet d'action* unfolded in fifty-eight separate numbers: some of these were set dance pieces, others narrative pantomimes and action sequences such as battles and storms. Furthermore, a reviewer for the London performances wrote: "we scarcely ever witnessed the influence of sympathy operate so powerfully upon an audience. The passions of love, jealousy, and grief are finely blended and disposed of in the various scenes with great art."[49]

Historical pantomimes like *Dorothée* and *Captain Cook* invariably involved onstage fighting, which—in keeping with the tenets of Noverre's action ballets—propelled the drama forward toward its climax, intensified the falling action, or hastened the dénouement. These battle scenes required a special type of *agitato* music. In some pantomimes and plays, this may have been taken from operas, in which battles, for example, were depicted onstage to the accompaniment of rather formal instrumental music (as in the third act of Handel's *Rinaldo*, 1711). But from the middle of the century composers began to write commemorative descriptive pieces that vividly re-created the episodes of certain battles. Heinrich Graun's *The Battle of Rosbach* (1757), for example, was written in celebration of the king of Prussia's victory in the early stages of the Seven Years' War against France and Austria. Michel Corrette, who came from a background of writing *opéra-comique* for the Parisian fairs, depicted an ambush off the coast of Boston during the American Revolution in *Victoire d'un combat naval* (1779). The simulation of cannon fire and the hectic fury of warfare in these two keyboard works—Corrette pounded out low heavy clusters for the twenty-four-pound volleys—represented the beginnings of a new musical realism that proved irresistible to many theatrical managers.

Surely one of the most remarkable of these re-creations was the *Bataille à deux orchestres* by Johann Friedrich Klöffler, first presented in Berlin in 1782. It was composed for two full (classical-sized) orchestras and consisted of twenty-one numbers and a symphonic finale. The stages of a battle unfolded in graphic detail, from the slow entry of each army (no. 2) to the depiction of several events in the conflict, the victory, and even fireworks at the end. No. 5, for example, *allegro molto*, was in five subsections and depicted "*A*—the movement of both armies, marching from each side; *B*—the fire of the infantry platoon from each army; C—the storm and destruction of the enemy army; *D*—the last attack with musketry on the first enemy line; and *E*—the capture of the redoubt." And this was only one of the early episodes. The full cavalry on horseback is called into engagement in nos. 8 to 14, and the Hussars arrive in no. 15. The complete *Battaille* was performed in concert at the Assembly Room in St. James's (London) on 2 June 1783. An English eyewitness observed with amazement how "the different instruments should cause the ear to believe a reality of the action, whilst the eye was convinced of the inimitable deception." As our observer heard it, the warring orchestras conveyed the sound of random cannon and musket shots, the effects of bursting powder and the noise of the whistling ball. A musical storm, with simulation of thunder and lightning, brought the battle to a temporary halt, after which each side was called into a council of war (no. 7, *adagio con recitatif*). Then the full onslaught of the cavalry, the "imitation of the galloping and trotting of the horses," and the agitated "clashing of the swords" brought the battle to a climax. Two numbers for the aftermath—the groans of the wounded and lamentations of the expiring soldiers—"had a most powerful effect on the auditors," but this was joyfully superseded by a series of victory marches. The reviewer called it "one of the most extraordinary attempts to prove the power of music that ever yet has been made in this kingdom."[50]

Such "musical realism" exerted a decided influence on composers of dramatic music. Dramatized conflicts were incorporated into action ballets and the emerging popular drama by way of the *opéra-comique*, for which onstage battle sequences were acted out to the accompaniment of extended musical numbers. One of the best examples of these is Michel-Jean Sedaine's *Richard Coeur-de-Lion* (Théâtre Favart, 1784), a *comédie mis en musique*, composed by André Grétry. This play with music was adapted for Drury Lane in 1786 by Burgoyne (with a few of the characters' names changed). The music for the climactic combat in this drama is quite graphic and reflects the episodic influence of recent battle pieces. Grétry's music seems to be both illustrative as it moves through various tense stages and metaphorical in alternating emotions of conflict and victory.

Act 3, scene 2, opens with the view of Sir Owen's castle being assaulted by the troops of Countess Marguerite (Matilda, in the Drury Lane version). Until the chorus of victory, the battle is enacted entirely in pantomime. In Burgoyne's version, the troubadour Blondel, in knightly garb, leads the attack and puts himself at the head of the pioneers as the assault continues. Richard appears defenseless on the fortress, endeavoring to free himself from three armed soldiers. Blondel mounts the breach, hurries toward the king, and fatally wounds one of the soldiers, while the king grasps the sword from the dying man's hand. The two put the rest of the soldiers to flight. Blondel then throws himself at the feet of Richard, who embraces him. At this moment is heard the grand chorus of "Long live the King!" The besiegers display Matilda's flag. She goes to Richard and sinks in his arms. The governor (Florestan) is then conducted to the king by the seneschal and Sir Owen. In a valiant gesture, Richard returns to him his sword.

Grétry's music for the siege begins in D major, with heroic fanfares and a repetitive figure of mounting excitement as the troops lead the assault. As Blondel—on horseback—ascends to the head of the troops, Grétry uses rushing figures for five bars over a "gallop" rhythm: ♪. 𝅘𝅥𝅯 ♪. 𝅘𝅥𝅯

The next twenty-two bars move through several varieties of *agitato* or "conflict music"—swirling arpeggios and lightning-fast scales over minor and diminished-seventh chords—as Richard struggles with the soldiers and Blondel breaches the wall and tackles the enemy. Gallop music resumes for ten more bars, presumably as the enemy soldiers are put to flight. The opening excitement music returns as Blondel prostrates himself before his victorious king. Grétry's battle scene is action music par excellence, composed for maximum stage effect. Despite the composer's technical naïveté, as Grétry's biographer David Charlton remarked, the battle scene consists of music that truly "begins to form part of the scenery."[51]

Along with musical battles, stage warfare was also growing more sophisticated and realistic during this time. The art of sword fighting had been developed to a fine art on the eighteenth-century stage. Until the King's Theatre at the Haymarket burned down in 1789 it maintained a fencing school, partly in order to service the London stage with amply trained fighters. The school was run by the stage machinist–turned combat expert Domenico Angelo, who, with his son Henry, taught generations of actors the art of personal combat, beginning with Sheridan. (Years later Henry would fence with Edmund Kean to get him warmed up.) Domenico's standard textbook on the art, *The School of Fencing* (London, 1787), does not mention music, but it was clear that actors who trained as swordsmen often timed their set pieces and combinations to music.[52] On the evening of 16 March 1789 *The Death of Captain Cook* was nearing its climax at Covent Garden. The music was taken note-for-note from the music that Rochefort composed for the Ambigu-Comique the year before. Near the end of the second act during a long fight sequence onstage the orchestra churned away at the *grand charge*.[53] The prompter apparently had mistaken a real sword for a prop, and an actor was tragically run through. Due to the sequence in the fighting and music, it took a while for the other actors to realize what had happened. Even the audience applauded the unlucky victim's realistic collapse. In a few moments, however, the battle came to a sudden stop as the actors carried their colleague into the wings, where he later died.[54]

On another occasion sometime in the early 1790s, Philip Astley was staging a broadsword combat at his popular Amphitheatre in London and requested his leader to arrange a few bars of music. Astley, who had served as sergeant-major for a dragoons regiment and whose musical experiences were limited to fife and drum, described his needs in a typically awkward, unmusical way: "a rang, tang, bang, one, two, three, and a cut sort of thing, you know." At the subsequent rehearsal of the fight Astley wanted more sounds of combat and had an idea about how to enhance the metallic clanging of the broadswords. He shouted out to his stage manager: "Stop! Stop! This will never do. It's not half noisy enough. We must get shields!" The oversensitive orchestra leader thought that Astley was referring to the well-known theatre composer William Shield, who had used conch shells and other unusual percussion in his music for *Omai* at Covent Garden. The leader jumped out of the orchestra, tore up his music, and angrily replied, "Well *get* Shields, then, and as soon as you please for I am sick and tired of you!"[55]

Music and the Proto-Melodrama in Paris

Although the Parisian licensing restrictions lasted officially until 1791, Audinot and Arnould began to test the waters by adding dialogue to their pantomimes, which led to the creation of a new legal designation called *pantomime dialoguée* (pantomime interspersed with dialogue). Many of these were remarkable creations, made all the more spectacular because they were produced during the period from the storming of the Bastille to the fall of Robespierre (1789 to 1795) and reflect the subject matter and intense emotional fervor of the Revolution.

Thanks to the work of Emilio Sala, who has reconstructed the music of some of the Ambigu-Comique pantomimes from manuscript sources, we can see this union at work in a historical pantomime from 1790, *L'homme au masque de fer* (The Man in the Iron Mask). Audinot's *pantomimes dialoguées*—for all intents and purposes full-fledged popular dramas—require very precise coordination between the *mise-en-scène* and *mise-en-musique*. Here music can clearly be seen to shadow characters as they move about the stage, which was a common device in the early nineteenth-century melodrama. Conversely, the characters must time their actions to precise changes in the music. Both statements are true, so closely were these components fused. "The pantomimes developed by Mussot at the Ambigu-Comique," added Sala, "seem to have pushed to the limit the union of music and action theorized earlier by Noverre."[56]

Jean-Baptiste Rochefort was again the composer. Arnould wrote the text, and his response to the famous mystery was that the imprisoned man was Louis, the Count de Vermandois, a natural son of Louis XIV. True to the form of the popular drama—and unlike history (or the later novel by Alexandre Dumas)—the pantomime ends with the prisoner's escape and a general reconciliation.[57] Some aspects of Rochefort's score implement the tradition of the *air parlant*.[58] At the opening of act 1, the Marquise de la Vallière, King Louis's former lover and "one of the most beautiful women of the court," is discovered in a frozen stage picture (*tableau-stase*). She sits pensively, obviously lost in thought. We soon learn that she is the young count's mother and is awaiting his arrival. Rochefort had the orchestra play *Quand le bien aimé reviendra*, an aria from *Nina, or the Follies of Love*, a recent opera by Nicolas Dalayrac, making clear to the Ambigu spectators that the "returning beloved" alluded to in the aria reflects nostalgically on the marquise's former situation. The *melos* of the tune would have suffused the opening scene with a certain mood in any case. But for those who knew the aria, its use here managed to convey a more precise message. Even without words the music still managed to speak.

In one of the sequences that Sala transcribed from Rochefort's score, the count has escaped arrest and is fleeing Paris with the marquise's help. In the first scene of act 4 they arrive at the modest home of two villagers late at night in the hopes of finding asylum. The scene opens on a rustic cabin, with a view of two rooms. In one of these, Thomi is seated at a table, reading out loud from a book by the light of a lamp. His wife, Pauline, is knitting by the fire. Rochefort's musical numbering corresponds to Arnould's scene numbers and restarts at the beginning of each act. No. 1, a through-composed *melos* with multiple dramatic devices and tempo changes, plays throughout this opening. A gentle folk tune—possibly even a known melody—accompanies Thomi's reading, but the tempo and character of the music change as he realizes that his wife has fallen asleep. He quietly puts on his nightcap, extinguishes the light, and slips into bed. Cue no. 1 ends with an expectant musical silence (held by a fermata). This is broken by the first gentle knocks at the door, awakening Pauline, still in her chair. Cue no. 2 begins. She looks around: seeing that Thomi has gone to bed without her, she throws down her knitting and goes to join him in bed. The orchestra is silent again as she is climbing in, followed by a second, much louder knock. This one wakens Thomi, who gets up and goes to see who it might be. After the third knock, he finally opens the door.

No. 3 begins when Thomi totters into the second room, still half asleep. The tempo is *adagio* and the dynamic *pianissimo*. But the triplet figure in the violins suggests agitation and some hesitancy. As Thomi approaches the door cautiously and the knocks resume, the character of the music changes. It is more forceful, with quick downward notes underpinned by ominous diminished-seventh chords. Clearly alarmed, Thomi reaches for the door; a pause in the score again asks for a musical silence as he opens it. No. 4 follows immediately. A man and woman wrapped in cloaks stand in the doorway. Beginning with the same *adagio* music, the count and marquise enter from the shadows, inquiring about a safe place to rest, with Thomi trying to discern the purpose of their inquiry. Suddenly the tempo changes to *allegro*, and the orchestra bursts forth *fortissimo* in C major. Thomi has recognized the noble pair and falls at their feet. Not only was the scene flooded with triumphant music, but the Ambigu spectators saw the character of Thomi humbled by sonic radiance as well as the physical radiance of royalty.

For this brief episode, with its rising tension and dramatic release, Rochefort responded with a *melos* of the second type: it is fluid in construction and follows the dramatic arc. In general most of the *melos* numbers are relatively short pieces, though they vary in length (no. 3 is eight measures; no. 4 is thirty). The music sounds continuous in performance, but it is broken up into separate numbers (*morceaux de musique*). Unlike those in *Crusoe*, however, nearly every *melos* modulates in mood and character according to dramatic needs. We must thank Sala for taking the trouble to discover who wrote the *L'Homme* pantomime music, for Rochefort received no billing at the time. This set yet another precedent in the popular drama that would last a century or more: the anonymity (or invisibility) of the composer.

Music and the Proto-Melodrama in London

Even before the political dangers posed by the uprisings in France, London actors and playwrights had their problems with censorship issues. The managers of Sadler's Wells, Astley's Amphitheatre, and many other theatres that catered to working-class audiences soon challenged the existing genre limitations placed on the minor theatres. In the 1790s these theatres were still operating under the restrictions imposed by Parliament in 1752. Enterprising managers of minor theatres, to be sure, found creative ways to challenge the "burletta laws" requiring that all performance be either mimed or sung but not spoken. Among these, Jane Moody noted, were Henry Fielding's burlesques and Samuel Foote's use of puppets (both in the summer seasons at the Haymarket Theatre), John Palmer's staging of Shakespeare at the Royalty Theatre (at Goodman's Fields), and Charles Dibdin's entertainments at the Royal Circus in St. George's Fields (later the Surrey Theatre), which included "speaking pantomime, opera, medleys, drolls, and interludes."[59] Speech itself seemed to be the main threat that lurked behind the restrictions for late eighteenth-century British theatres, especially in the years during and after the French Revolution. "The stage has now no business with politics," wrote George Colman in his preface to *The Iron Chest* (1796), reminding readers that it was the Lord Chamberlain's responsibility to check any such overt connections.[60] Music, for some unstated reason, seemed less threatening to the authorities. For any secondary theatre to obtain a license, therefore, performances must either be sung or danced. So pantomime—especially the historical pantomimes with their folk heroes and proto-melodramatic elements—thrived in the minor theatres in remarkably creative ways.

Thomas Dibdin writes about the serious pantomimes that he produced at Sadler's Wells in the 1790s (*The Death of David Rizzio, The Ruins of Palluzzi, or The Black Penitent, Alonzo and Imogine*) and two or more "serious ballets of action" (*John of Calais* and *Chevy Chase*). Dibdin brought at least two of his musical directors and composers—Alexander Moorhead and John Davy—to London from the provincial theatres.[61]

Philip Astley's circus, built in 1770 on the site of a riding school south of the Thames (outside the cities of Westminster and London), specialized in "equestrian dramas"—no surprise given Astley's military career and his dazzling stunts with white horses. In January 1793 he produced *The Death of Captain Cook* as a "grand equestrian dramatic spectacle" with the dancer and mimist Louis Bologna. When this circus burned to the ground, Astley built a new theatre in 1795, where he was first known to maintain a steady orchestra. Like Audinot at the Ambigu-Comique, Astley circumvented the censors by filling up the stage with verbal clues. In the "grand spectacle romance" *The Black Castle, or The Spirit of Ravia* (1799), characterization and plot development were partly conveyed in the vocal numbers by William Upton. But during the pantomime sections—with music by an anonymous composer—performers relied upon banners and scrolls of explanatory texts, which they alternately fetched from different sides of the stage. *The Black Castle* also exhibits many aspects of the "gothic" that pervaded English culture in the last decade of the century. A reviewer in the *Monthly Mirror* noted the ghost who emerged amid a haunting blue flame.[62] Though Philip Astley was never credited with much of an ear for music (as we saw in the earlier example with his bandleader) he found ways to spotlight his orchestra. He built a special enclosure for the musicians in the new amphitheatre and commissioned a "descriptive composition" that depicted the recent burning of the old theatre. With an orchestra present, Astley discovered that it was possible to evoke visual catastrophe in the popular theatre as well as emotions associated with tragic events.[63]

Many if not all of the melodramatic elements finally came together at the Royal Circus (Surrey) in 1801 in John Cartwright Cross's production of *Rinaldo Rinaldini, or The Secret Avengers*. This was a "grand ballet of action" derived from a five-act German drama called *Rinaldo Rinaldini, the Robber Captain* by Christian Vulpius (1797), itself indebted to Schiller's *Der Räuber*. In order to comply with the burletta restrictions, Cross created a version of the play that used no spoken words whatsoever. Any crucial text was sung to operatic recitative or held up on scrolls or placards. This of course increased the need for descriptive music. The instructions for the long mimed sections were detailed and elaborate. Cross had already produced a similar "serious ballet" in 1797 at Covent Garden called *The Round Tower* with music by William Reeve (1757–1815), Cross's musical director from the Haymarket. When Cross took over management of the Surrey in 1798, he brought Reeve with him and worked with two of London's expert theatre technicians (Thomas Greenwood Jr. as scene painter and J. Branscomb as machinist), to produce these sensational generic mixtures. The story of Rinaldini was based on a real war hero, who led a rebellion between 1770 and 1773 against French control of Corsica and southern Italy.

The published text of *Rinaldo Rinaldini* begins with an elaborate description of a moody romantic scene (*The Apenines—Mountains, the tops of which are covered with snow—in various places bearing all the appearance of luxuriant vegetation . . . thunder, lightning, etc., the clouds dark and the moon obscured*).[64] Rinaldo (played by Robert Palmer) was discovered seated in a musing attitude over a fire, drawing on his tablets. His dog (incarnated by Louis Bologna) lay faithfully at his side. Altaverde, Rinaldo's chief companion and watchman, could be seen at a distance, observing him. The narrative of the act officially began with Altaverde singing an original air ("Can love thus pierce the rugged robber's heart"). This was immediately followed by pantomimed action ("Rinaldo, throwing his cloak round him, still keeps his eyes fixed on the tablet . . . an Old Man hurries on, trembling with cold and alarm"). In mime Rinaldo "demands" the trespasser's name and errand. The Old Man (a hermit figure) replies in a few sung lines of recitative ("My lamp extinguished by the boisterous wind"). Rinaldo helps him to relight the lantern and again in mime advises the Old Man to be on his way. In sung recitative, the Old Man informs Rinaldo that he lives nearby and that the young man can take shelter there if he pleases. Rinaldo offers a gesture of thanks and then gazes with rapture at what he himself has drawn. A long and elaborate mime sequence follows. Florella (the amazon of the troop) appears. As the clouds part and the moon shines bright, Altaverde is seen greeting other robbers who descend from the mountains carrying their plunder. One of them has a portrait that he gives Rinaldo, who is struck by the resemblance to the image that he has been drawing. It is obviously a likeness of his beloved, and Florella observes his recognition with marked jealousy. A robber enters holding a large sign with the words "Rewards Offered for Rinaldo's Head." Treating this warning with contempt, Rinaldo munificently showers his troops with money. The robbers joyfully engage in a Rifle Dance, in which they demonstrate their "Platoon Exercise." The scenario continues in this way for two acts.

Minus the dialogue, *Rinaldo* exhibits all the characteristics of early nineteenth-century melodrama. (Indeed spoken versions appeared in various London and New York theatres over the next ten years.) Not counting the music, it met six of the basic criteria of the popular drama. It was based on a "true story" ("founded on Historical Facts," the announcements read). It contained a moral message. The principal character was a folk hero, an outlaw, whose story was well known through ballad and song (Rinaldo was to Sicily and Calabria what William Tell was to Switzerland). Rinaldo's rival was a clearly defined villain (Baron Rovezzo, chief judge of the Secret Avengers), who would stop at nothing to ensnare the ingénue Aurelia. The pantomime offered special effects galore, including explosions and a "stupendous waterfall" sequence. Finally, it had a happy ending: instead of committing suicide rather than surrender to the agents of the French government, as did the historical figure, Rinaldo is pardoned by the grand duke of Tuscany and united in marriage with Aurelia.

Two major musical advantages of pantomimes performed in the major theatres (Drury Lane, Covent Garden, and the summer season at the Haymarket) were that the scores were generally provided by established British composers and that these scores were often published. (This was also true of pantomimes produced in Edinburgh and Dublin, both royal theatres.) But much of the theatrical music performed in the minor theatres of this time is unknown and lacks clear authorship. It circulated only in manuscript, with the exception of a song that may have been featured by a well-known actor or actress. T. Barker of London, for example, published Reeve's songs and choruses in *Rinaldo Rinaldini*, but none of the extensive pantomimic music of this Surrey production has been found.[65] In contrast, the publishing firm of Wigley and Bishop in London brought out every note of

Samuel Arnold's score to *The Corsair, or The Italian Nuptials* (Haymarket, 1801). Hence this chapter closes with a short study of this representative "popular drama without words."

The Corsair *at the Haymarket*

The Corsair, or The Italian Nuptials, produced by Charles Farley at the Little Theatre in the Haymarket in 1801, reveals the full integration of gesture and music, pantomime, and characteristic music (created in the style of the harlequinade "comic tunes"). Farley, singer, dancer, and choreographer, grew up in the theatre, having been a child actor and a call-boy at Covent Garden. His first big choreographic success was in 1797 with *Raymond and Agnes*, a pantomime based on Matthew Gregory Lewis's famous gothic novel *The Monk*. Composer Samuel Arnold was engaged to provide the music for this full-fledged "grand pantomimical drama," thirty-five years after writing musical bits for the *Dr. Faustus* harlequinade. The published score identifies Arnold's "appropriate music," and most of the forty-nine musical numbers have characteristic titles: "The Sea. Vessels Sailing. Moonlight."

The Corsair's elaborate plot is conveyed almost entirely through mime and dance. Aside from one chorus for the wedding guests the only other vocal numbers consisted of two songs sung by a pair of fishermen, minor characters in the story. Farley and Arnold also built in a number of set dance pieces. But the bulk of the plot advanced through action and a continuously evolving *melos*. Another feature was the role of stage sound and its centrality to the plot. Though the play had no dialogue, it offered plenty of crucial plot-related sound effects—battle scenes, an exploding volcano, the demolition of the castle—that Arnold's music had to negotiate.

The story centers on the wedding of Fiorita and Gagliardo in a small village near Naples (Mount Vesuvius is visible in the background). Fiorita's wealthy father owns a successful winery. Tomar, a pirate who plans to assume the old man's wealth by marrying the daughter, returns from abroad to find her marriage to Gagliardo already in progress. With the assistance of his crew he kidnaps Fiorita and carries her off to his vessel along with her betrothed, but not before killing her father in a face-off. The scene shifts to the dungeons beneath the pirate's castle, where Tomar has enslaved the couple. Tomar's black slave takes pity and helps them escape but the angry pirate pursues them. Against a rugged "romantic landscape" he kills the slave and recaptures Fiorita. Gagliardo, who breaks free, returns to the castle with the help of the fishermen and their boat and brings about Tomar's end. (Gagliardo also has the assistance of the father's ghost, who causes the pirate's castle to be spectacularly destroyed.)

The plot, as a reviewer noted, "depends for its success on the excellence of the music, the agility of the actors, the ingenuity of the mechanist, and the splendor of the scenery and decorations."[66] Grumbling that such "vehicles for music" and "dumb show" were no substitute for the legitimate drama, the reviewer observed that the story resembled many other similar dramatizations, which suggests that even by 1801 the melodramatic formulas underpinning Farley's pantomime were already well established in the popular theatre.

The abduction scene, which encapsulates many of the stylistic features of the work, begins with Tomar. The wedding guests have all gone into the vintner's mansion, so the pirate is alone. Observing the festivities through a window, he decides to steal into the house. The scene changes to a gallery somewhere inside, and Tomar sneaks from room to room in the hopes of discovering Fiorita alone. The Gallery scene in Arnold's score consists of only two numbered musical cues. But the first one, no. 18, is a long and extended piece of music in the "uneasy" and "suitable for frenzy" key of G minor that manages to accommodate different nuances with each incident. The left column in Figure 3 includes the basic details of the plot, while the right column contains the opening bars of music from each corresponding section of the score.

No. 18 begins calmly (*tenuto*) and even a bit mysteriously. It becomes more agitated once Tomar confronts Fiorita (in 18b), thereby injecting force into the drama. Fast-moving sixteenth notes suggest the flurry of physical entanglement, and the gallop effect (in the style of Grétry's battle music) sets a forward-driving pace for much of the fighting. In the final sequence shown in the figure, the beginning of no. 19, Rugoso's sons scramble in and engage heroically with the pirates, who nevertheless are successful in repelling them long enough for their master to get away. Arnold probably switched to the bright major key to align the audience's sympathy with the valorous sons, for B-flat major, in a faster tempo, was typically associated with qualities of boldness and dignity.

The elements of melodrama (minus the spoken lines) were clearly evident in dramatic hybrids such as *Dorothée*, *The Death of Captain Cook*, and *The Corsair*. When the actual melodrama with its essential dialogue component emerged around 1800, it finally solidified the musico-dramatic form out of which all nineteenth-century variations of the popular drama grew.

3.1
A gallery in Rugoso's cottage.
At opening, the gallery is empty.
Tomar, the pirate, makes a stealthy entrance. He is searching for Fiorita.

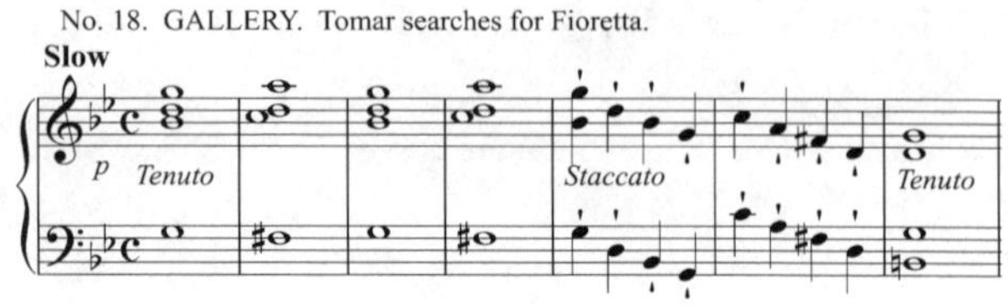

3.2
Fiorita enters the gallery and goes to her devotions. She does not realize that Tomar, in hiding, is in the room.

3.3
Emerging abruptly from his hiding place, Tomar surprises Fiorita. She struggles to pass him and escape.

3.4
Hearing the commotion, Gagliardo enters. He dashes to engage Tomar.

3.5
Drawing their swords, the two fight.

3.6
Tomar reaches for his boatswain's whistle and blows it, shrilly.

FIGURE 3. *Samuel Arnold,* The Overture, Songs, Duett, Choruses & Appropriate Music in . . . The Corsair, or The Italian Nuptials *(London: Wigley and Bishop, 1801): excerpts*

3·7
As the two men continue to fight, the door is broken open. It is the pirates, who are responding to Tomar's whistle. [The family is presumably gathering in distress and alarm at this point.]

3·8
Tomar grabs Fiorita and tries to carry her off. Gagliardo hurries after them.

3·9
The pirates prevent him from following.

3·10
Gagliardo manages to tear himself loose and jumps out the window.

3·11
The pirates fight with Rugoso and his sons to keep them from following Tomar.

2

The Rise of Melodrama in the Age of Revolution

Melodrama, the kernel of the popular drama that began to grow its many shoots in the 1780s and 1790s, overwhelmed the theatres of Europe and America by the first decades of the new century. The oppressive castles, robbers and pirates, and avenging ghosts all were in some sense manifestations of a changing society with a new emerging class that found its anxieties and fears played out in some of the most uninhibited theatre in the history of the stage. But this was no smooth path. Given the many popular uprisings that pervaded Europe in its Age of Revolution—the 1770s to 1848—the theatres of Germany, France, Spain, and England were often tightly controlled by their governments for many of these years. Speech or music that could be considered provocative or incendiary came under close scrutiny. Playwright Thomas Morton remembered that F.-J. Talma, the famous French actor, had told him that the French Revolution made slow progress until the theatres became the arena of its triumphs, after which it spread rapidly.[1] If music could enflame the passions, speech could provoke the restless to action. Religious groups also were suspicious of the theatre and legislated against the supposed immorality of specific plays or genres. Hence the development of the popular drama occurred during a period of complex licensing laws in which theatrical proprietors enthralled their audiences while toeing a fine line when it came to placating the censors and the clergy. Melodrama as popular drama—as opposed to the classically purer genres of comedy and tragedy—was shaped by these political and social circumstances. Without the mediating charms of music, this new form of expression would have been unthinkable.

Melodrama as a Genre

In modern times scholars have largely interpreted melodrama through its language, because most people engage with this genre by reading printed plays. But in the nineteenth century language formed only one part of a larger set of integrated components. These included an elaborate system of physical gestures and attitudes descended from eighteenth-century tragedy and pantomime traditions, new historical elaborations in costume and scenic design, incredible acrobatic stunts, machinery that accomplished surprising transformations, visual and sound effects, and a wide range of music, some familiar, some new. To interpret a melodrama from a copy of the play alone is like trying to visualize a building from an architect's blueprint. Acting-editions of nineteenth-century plays are like a floor plan, wherein dialogue and staging are literally represented but gestures, movement, and spectacle can at most be described and other aspects, such as the actors' vocal inflections and instrumental *melos* that equally served to buttress the drama, are very often not even mentioned at all.

The word *mélo-drame*, as noted, is a compound of two French words, each derived from the Greek. The first, *mélo*, has been interpreted variously as a musical line, coloring, or affect. *Drame* refers to the Aristotelian concept of plot, which is related by means of dialogue and action in a series of well-structured incidents. Plot is usually structured around an exposition of the protagonist and related characters, an inciting force and the emergence of a clear antagonist, a rising action, developing conflict and crisis, a tragic force (causing a reversal of fate for the protagonist), and falling action, culminating in catharsis or catastrophe (also called the unraveling or dénouement).[2] One of the key innovations in melodrama—what Peter Brooks described in terms of a Manichean duality—was the avoidance of catastrophe by some good fortune or miraculous twist of fate that allowed virtue to triumph over evil, which is obviously not the case in genuine tragedies such as *The Trojan Women* and *Othello*.[3] This aspect of melodrama was incipient in early commercial Venetian opera, and librettos by the likes of Giacinto Cicognini combined tragedy and comedy and resorted to contrived plot twists in order to rescue the mythological hero or heroine from disaster. But genuine melodrama as a vernacular "people's theatre" began to emerge only in prerevolutionary France.

The migration of the form to England was sometimes met with harsh criticism. One reviewer in 1807 called melodrama "an *olla podrida* [Spanish stew] of tragedy, comedy, opera, farce, and pantomime, partaking more or less of any of the qualities of these as the whim and judgment of the writer pleases." A writer for the *Analectic Magazine* in 1814 called it "the degenerate branch" of the dramatic arts, "not quite a pantomime, nor quite a play."[4] Professional critics penned such definitions, which reflect degrees of discomfort with melodrama's chameleonic nature.

We find an early *musical* definition of melodrama, however, by Thomas Busby (1755–1830), who composed the music for the first British melodrama, *A Tale of Mystery*. In the 1806 edition of Busby's *Dictionary of Music* he described it as "a modern species of drama in which the powers of instrumental music are employed to *elucidate the action* and heighten the *passion* of the piece." Though this definition does not account for the songs and dances sprinkled throughout most early melodramas, it is as concise an explanation of music's unique role as one could find. As the century moved forward, discussions of melodrama began to leave out this essential component. By the 1880s the term was often being applied "to plays of the coarsest emotional type," one English composer observed, "without regard to their being musically embellished or not."[5] Although melodrama had burst onto the stage as a new theatrical form in which music played an indispensable role, by century's end "melodrama" had become less a form than a coloring added to any play, as Victor Emeljanow put it.[6]

The new genre had its detractors from the start. Friedrich Schlegel described melodrama as a play in which "personages appear to be thrown into situations of forced distress and necessity, merely that they may be assisted and saved by a combination of other circumstances equally forced and unnatural and palpably contrived for the occasion."[7] This sounds like a remarkably apt definition of farce. But if this is the way audiences actually perceived melodrama, we might ask why they were not laughing instead of crying out in fear or weeping for joy, as many did. Laughter requires some detachment, while melodrama demands from its audience empathy and even identification. Melodrama produces in the audience an intense *illusion* of reality, wrote Alan Reynolds Thompson in his essay "Melodrama and Tragedy." The figures in the gallery of a public theatre recognize themselves in a melodrama, says Thompson. This illusion allows "day-dreaming" to be "conducted much more efficiently than in the case of the novel": hence the wider demographic appeal of melodrama and the successful dramatizations of many nineteenth-century works of literature.[8] The best melodramas, wrote a reviewer of Thomas Morton's *The Slave* at Covent Garden in 1817, have shown that "a composition of this nature may excite in the strongest degree emotions of laughter and sadness."[9] In other words, such plays pushed audiences to extremes—laughter at one moment and tears the next.

Melodrama has been associated with emotional excess since the very beginning and still embodies this notion today. Though almost always described by theatre historians as a genre associated with the stage, melodrama is defined somewhat more broadly by the *Oxford English Dictionary* as "a dramatic piece characterized by sensational incident and violent appeals to the emotions, but with a happy ending." Our understanding of melodrama may be filtered through two hundred years of vilification, but Eric Bentley's shrewd assessment cuts through some of this prejudice: "That we are all ham actors in our dreams means that melodramatic acting, with its large gestures and grimaces and its declamatory style of speech, is not an exaggeration of our dreams but a duplication of them. In that respect, melodrama is the Naturalism of the dream life."[10] Is it any wonder, then, that music—often operating at an unconscious level—was essential in lulling the spectator into the dreamlike state in which these grotesque conflicts were enacted?

The most revealing insight into the mechanism of melodrama comes from Richard LeGallienne (father of actress and producer Eva LeGallienne). As author and stage manager for Wilson Barrett, one of the leading producers of sensational melodramas at the end of the century, LeGallienne was clearly aware of melodrama's illusory realm when he described it as a distinct kind of hybrid form: "a play which combines the intensity of tragedy with the construction of farce and the dénouement of a fairy-tale."[11] Though music is not specified, this definition is ideal in many respects. Melodrama's recourse to a fairy-tale solution evolved partly from audiences' identification with the folklike heroes of many popular dramas. In revolutionary times the common hero must triumph over the patrician villain. Once we realize the role that farce played in the construction of melodrama, however, we understand why some were uncomfortable with situations that seemed too contrived and forced for drama. If we agree with LeGallienne's thesis of hybridity, as I obviously do, then we need to look back on the bulk of nineteenth-century popular drama as a manifestation of these intersecting (if sometimes conflicting) dramatic genres to understand exactly why music was essential. Pantomime farce relied extensively on music, whereas legitimate eighteenth- and early nineteenth-century spoken farces generally employed no music whatsoever. Tragedy occasionally leaned on music, but sparingly and judiciously, while the construction of a fantasy world in staged fairy tales and extravaganzas required huge splashes of music.

In melodrama, as in tragedy, the plotting of an antagonizing force, a crisis, and a reversal of fate still served as the structural model, except that the antagonizing force was usually embodied in a single individual (perhaps with an accomplice). The catastrophe that would normally follow the falling action in Aristotelian tragedy, however, needed to be averted somehow. The unraveling would instead follow the trajectory of a fairy tale: audiences must be assured that the protagonists and their loved ones will achieve satisfaction. (Even traditional fairy tales, however, exhibit many variations on this dénouement, as Vladimir Propp has shown.)[12]

Critics of melodrama tend to overlook or dismiss its farcical construction, which it inherited directly from the comic pantomime. In doing so, they ignore one of melodrama's most satisfying devices, what French dramatic theory has termed the *quiproquo*. Of the many obstacles that the protagonist in a farce must overcome, mistaken identity is very nearly his undoing. Writing about this device, Jessica Milner Davis has pointed out that most farces contain a symmetrical pattern created by the reversal of comic roles: the joke (*burla*) intended for the innocent recipient ends up, boomerang-like, returning to the perpetrator.[13] In a farce these situations are funny, but only if the characters are completely sincere and unaware of the absurdity of their predicament. When this farcical construction is mapped onto melodrama, the hero encounters a series of obstacles placed directly in his or her path by the villain, whose ultimate failure is foreshadowed through miscalculations (or errors). The *quiproquo* is that it is the villain who is ultimately entrapped, not the victim. In farce, as Davis puts it, "the weapon of attack is turned back upon the attacker," thereby inciting pleasure in the audience while restoring conventional authority.[14]

We can see how this works, starting with James Kenney's farce *Raising the Wind* (Covent Garden, 1803). Jeremy Diddle, a young man who has squandered all his money and now mooches off strangers, has heard of a new family in town, a wealthy man with a pretty daughter. Failing to learn their names (error one), he spies the woman that he thinks is the lady in the window (error two). Though she seems much older and homelier than he was led to believe, he gets a servant to bring her a note showing his affection (error three). As it turns out, she is actually Miss Durable, the wealthy man's aged cousin. The man's real daughter is the very girl that Diddle had courted in a different town some months before and abandoned on the day of their elopement. Miss Durable swoons at Diddle's letter and invites him into the house, but he is in fact walking into a *quiproquo*. The audience, aware of the dramatic irony, laughs at the ensuing consequences as all of the protagonist's miscalculations backfire on him. It is useful to compare this farce with John Howard Payne's *Thérèse, The Orphan of Geneva* (Drury Lane, 1821), an Anglo-American melodrama adapted from a French original. The heroine acts in ways consistent with Restoration tragedy. But the symmetrical construction that was formerly the result of the protagonist's errors in the farce is now mapped onto the antagonist. Following the death of a wealthy woman, the family accuses her adopted daughter Thérèse of forgery to gain the inheritance. The forgery was actually the work of an unscrupulous and nefarious attorney, who secretly confiscated Thérèse's adoption papers and attempted to obscure the evidence (error one). Thérèse escapes imprisonment and obtains asylum from a countess. The attorney pursues her, using every wile to win her affections (error two). When she threatens to reveal his past indiscretions, he decides to murder her and make her death look accidental (error three). This last trick leads to the *quiproquo*, for he unknowingly murders the countess instead. The shock of learning that Thérèse is still alive precipitates a speedy downfall for the attorney and catharsis for the audience.

The stages of the farce (Diddle's repeated errors) do not need music to achieve an intended humorous effect. But all of the attorney's errors—his burning of the papers, his wooing of Thérèse, his decision to do away with her—*require* music to do the major emotional work of convincing the audience that what appear to be foolish miscalculations actually have tragic consequences.[15] We should keep these intersecting structures in mind. For it is exactly this kind of dramatic construction—LeGallienne's hybrid of three dramatic genres—that is most in need of music as an emotional thread to hold together what might otherwise seem like illogical components, especially given melodrama's complex layers of subplot.

In truth, not all popular dramas employed strict melodramatic construction; nor did all end in triumph for the protagonist. But most of the nineteenth-century dramatic subgenres that were offshoots of melodrama reflect this hybrid quality, including gothic, blood-and-thunder, military, nautical, brigand, eastern, docudrama, domestic, sensation, cup-and-saucer, drawing room, detective and secret service, and even "toga" or "sacred drama." Moreover, historical tragedies by Shakespeare, Schiller, Victor Hugo, and Eugène Scribe were most often staged and musically accompanied like melodramas in the nineteenth century. The Irish diarist Lady Sydney Morgan jotted down in 1818: "Shakspeare is supreme in melodrame . . . and the melodrame of *Macbeth* is finer than any modern exhibition which has followed it."[16] Given that the Scottish Play was still performed in the nineteenth with songs and choruses more than a century old attributed to Matthew Locke, this comment is not exactly outré.[17] (The *Macbeth* music is now thought to be mostly by Richard Leveridge.) In a modern theatre, of course, we would probably find it perplexing if the witches sang instead of spoke their lines. But we would not be surprised to hear some kind of creepy music accompanying the appearance of Banquo's ghost (which it apparently did not in eighteenth-century productions that used "Locke's music").

Following the premiere of Thomas Holcroft's *A Tale of Mystery* (Covent Garden, 1802), a reviewer called it "a drama in which the language, situations, and passions are accompanied and heightened by music . . . The composer tells the story as well as the author."[18] This is the form of popular drama of which Pixerécourt is said to have been the prime architect and was imported into England and the United States via Holcroft's adaptation. In his substantial study of Pixerécourt and the early Romantic French theatre, Willie Hartog observed the various components in place in the 1790s that resulted in the emergence of theatrical melodrama. In addition to Rousseau—whom he credits with the neologism—Hartog identifies the decline of the tragedy, the rising influence of the novel, the German theatre (particularly plays such as Schiller's *Die Räuber* [The Robbers, 1781]), and perhaps mostly importantly pantomime, in which "every gesture, every feeling was reflected in a musical phrase."[19] We have already investigated some of the roles that music played in French and English pantomime. Histories of melodrama credit Pixerécourt with establishing the new genre around 1800, but several ingenious stage managers in the 1790s, notably John Philip Kemble in London, had already worked with their music directors to graft operatic techniques onto the spoken play.

French Theatres and New Mixed Genres

Mélo-drame began to take shape in the French theatres licensed for *opéra-comique*, a genre stemming from the 1710s when it arose as operatic parody. Between 1791—when a law was passed that made it possible for anyone to open a theatre—and 1806—when Napoleon Bonaparte imposed a system of authorization—popular theater in Paris evolved toward melodrama. Audinot's *L'homme au masque de fer* (The Man in the Iron Mask) and other pantomimes at the boulevard theatres in the 1790s already contained most of the defining features, as did chiefly musical stage pieces such as Sedaine and Grétry's *Guillaume Tell*, one of the most widely imitated "rescue dramas" to appear in the midst of the French Revolution (Théâtre Favart, 1791). But the genre emerged decisively—and rather accidentally, it would appear—in 1797. The playwright at the center of it all, René-Charles Guilbert de Pixerécourt, tells how it happened.[20] Showing unique entrepreneurial spirit, Pixerécourt decided to capitalize on a recent popular novel, *Victor, ou L'Enfant de la forêt*, by fashioning it into an *opéra-comique*. The novelist, François Ducray-Duminil, was emerging from his "gothic period" and had become increasingly preoccupied with French society's need for moral stability, especially in the years of deep anxiety and uncertainty following the terrors of the French Revolution. In the new postrevolutionary novel—directed toward an increasingly literate middle class—virtue and innocence would be allowed to prevail as expected, but only after a series of mistaken identities and other wildly ingenious twists in the plot. As a theatre man, Pixerécourt sensed the commercial appeal of Ducray-Duminil's plot devices. He fashioned a libretto, calling it a *drame lyrique*, and hoped it would be taken up by the Théâtre Favart, licensed since 1771 as a house for this kind of sung genre. For the music, Pixerécourt invited Jean-Pierre Solié, a musician that he knew principally as a singer. Pixerécourt handpicked his singer-actors, including Solié, and most of the music was apparently completed. But to Pixerécourt's shock he discovered that the theatre already had a *Victor* in the works, with a text by Claude de Saint-Just and music by the celebrated composer François-Adrien Boieldieu. Not to be beaten, Pixerécourt ran to Audinot at the Ambigu-Comique, a theatre originally licensed for pantomime but opened up to spoken drama since the revolution. Audinot was enthusiastic, so Pixerécourt "did away with the songs" (in his words, "je supprimai les morceaux de musique").[21] The *drame* opened in November 1797. Solié, needless to say, could not have been very happy with the arrangement, but there is no evidence for what happened to his music afterward. In this form *Victor* ran an unprecedented 392 performances and was such a success with the French public—who were delighted to see this new example of a popular novel turned into a stage play—that the administration of the Favart abandoned its project of the *Victor* opera.

In the two years after *Victor*, Audinot purchased licenses to produce what he called "grand spectacles," starting with several works by Pixerécourt and several lesser-known writers.[22] But Audinot and the Ambigu-Comique scored their next hit with Pixerécourt's *Coelina, ou L'Enfant du mystère* in 1800. Billed as a "drama extravaganza" *Coelina* (again based on a Ducray-Duminil novel) is considered the first truly original melodrama, containing dialogue as well as all the now-recognizable elements: three acts instead of the five-act structure of French tragedy, characters that included the hero and heroine, villain, comic foil, a moral message, scenic spectacle, intricate plot developments with mistaken identities and narrow escapes, mime, dance, a few songs, musical accompaniments for action sequences, and a tone of utmost sincerity. Perhaps the most original aspect of *Coelina* was not any of its individual components—which had all appeared elsewhere—but combining them all in the same play. One of the unusual combinations was the use of speaking and miming actors in the same scene, surely a direct descendant of such "dialogue pantomimes" as *L'homme au masque de fer*. As Norma Perry, a Pixerécourt scholar, noted:

> the role of Francisque, the mute beggar, is very important and requires an expert mimist [*un mime de génie*]. This character must indeed express feelings so complicated that one wonders how a mime could pull it off. Consider for example in act one, scene five, where the mute testifies that he is incapable of lying [*témoigne qu'il est incapable de mentir*] and in the last act where he expresses to Coelina his fears of one day seeing with regret the great wealth that he has lost [*ses craintes de la voir un jour regretter les grands biens qu'il lui a fait perdre*].[23]

In addition to mime, dance also played an important role in *Coelina*. Strangely, the published text for the play renders the music almost entirely invisible, mentioning only a "ronde" at the very end to be sung to the air "Un rigodon, zig, zag, don, don." In his autobiography, however, Pixerécourt reveals that an extensive amount of music was used in this play. It was composed by Adrien Quaisain, who had risen to orchestra leader at the Ambigu-Comique in 1799. The *Coelina* music seems to have vanished. But Quaisain's orchestra parts remain for a pantomime called *La forêt noire, ou le Fils naturel*, also produced at the Ambigu-Comique in 1800. The orchestration consisted of full strings, flute, two clarinets, two bassoons, two horns, and timpani. Given that the viola parts are divided, there must have been at least two viola players and therefore perhaps fifteen or so strings altogether. Among the winds, an oboe is missing. The dominant wind sonority of two clarinets, two bassoons, and two horns clearly had turn-of-the-century military associations, being a holdover from the eighteenth-century aristocratic wind bands (*Harmoniemusik*). This instrumentation for *La forêt* allows us to imagine what the orchestra for *Coelina* might have sounded like.[24]

Coelina was another in a long line of stage works—which no doubt began with *Dorothée* in 1782—that confirmed the commercial success of a popular dramatic formula. Pixerécourt followed *Coelina* with sixty-one more spectacular *mélo-drames* (which included affective and illustrative music by composers such as Quaisain, Louis Alexandre Piccinni, son of the composer of *La buona figliuola*, and Henry Darondeau).[25] With the proliferation of theatres devoted to popular dramas the Boulevard du Temple became the dominant center of Parisian theatrical life. "All sectors of the [French] bourgeoisie," wrote Peter Brooks, "began turning to the boulevard for their entertainment, realizing that here was a theatre offering much more appeal than the bloodless official houses, and even the critics began to concur."[26] Boulevard melodrama became understood as a drama of action, thrilling in its fast pace and tight coordination among the various technical aspects.

Pixerécourt's many plays catapulted him into the role of France's most imitated playwright. Many of his melodramas were adapted almost immediately and produced in Germany, the Netherlands, England, the United States, and elsewhere. Pixerécourt himself attributed the huge success of his melodramas less to the writing than "to the detailed and exacting care with which I have constantly presided over rehearsals."[27] This may be so. But clearly their sensational appeal sped them across the channel and then across the Atlantic. Theatres in Philadelphia, New York, and Charleston began producing translations of Pixerécourt melodramas as early as 1803.

One criticism leveled at early French *mélo-drame* was aimed at its growing popularity among the lower classes. It was the liberal theatrical laws, complained the attorney Amaury Duval in 1797, that led to the corruption of taste and the decline of the dramatic art.[28] In revising French theatrical law in 1806 Napoleon and his minister of the interior imposed strict guidelines. The Opéra, Opéra-Comique, and Comédie-Française were declared royal theatres. The rest therefore were referred to as "secondary theatres" (analogous to London's "minors"). Besides the Ambigu-Comique, these included the Gaîté, still licensed only for pantomimes and farces, the Vaudeville for light comedy or parody, and the Variétés, devoted to acrobats and comic skits with songs.[29] Frederick Hemmings suggests that the laws were largely enacted to contain the spread of melodrama, which he observed was becoming a rage in Paris during the first decade of the nineteenth century.[30] Any theatre that ignored licensing laws was shut down by decree, as was the Porte Saint-Martin in 1807 when it refused to stop producing its lucrative melodramas (the theatre was fully operational again by 1814, however, and went on to become one of Paris's most famous melodramatic playhouses).

Few at the time seemed to write much about the music of the early

French *mélo-drame*, although it eventually became customary to decry its use of emotionally manipulative music. "When the tyrant entered, the trumpet cried out pitifully," observed one French critic decades later, and "when the young distressed girl left the stage, the flute sighed a few notes."[31] In one of the major studies of theatrical melodrama, Paul Ginisty, former director of the Théâtre de l'Odéon, Paris, made this more far-reaching assessment of music's important role in the early nineteenth-century boulevard melodramas: "[It] highlights the dramatic situations, accompanies the entrances and exits of characters, increases the effect of emotions produced, and opens the heart and prepares for the kind of feelings that will develop before it."[32] A phrase like "increases the effect" echoes Burgoyne's 1781 comments on Garrick's use of music. But Ginisty's final phrase ("ouvre l'âme et la prépare au genre de sentiments qu'on va développer devant elle") grants to theatrical music a depth and psychological power far beyond its stereotypical imitative functions. This was a more profound understanding of the concept of *melos*. Ginisty, writing at the beginning of the twentieth century, could look back on a hundred years of melodramatic history and put into words what spectators at its inception could only intimate. Knowing the history, he also knew the full range of melodramatic music, from its most trite instances to its most stirring application. Ginisty understood that music in the drama had a far more subtle purpose that is often not even perceived let alone acknowledged by audiences and critics. That purpose had more to do with memory and cognition than with histrionics, with the evocation of an unconscious dream world latent in every aspect of melodrama's appeal to real-life characters and situations.

One major hurdle in any reconstruction of early French melodrama is the layout of the music; it is never found in orchestra or piano scores, only in individual orchestra parts. Those parts that have survived are not always complete or are in deteriorating condition and often difficult to read. Furthermore, parts that survive have been used for so many different productions that they are marked up with cuts, additions, and other changes, making it difficult to determine exactly what was played where. As scholars of opera and musical theatre have shown, reconstruction involves a consideration of these sources in conjunction with other performing materials, such as a promptbook from a specific production, which often contained precise cues for music to start and stop.

In his study of the early French mélodrame, Emilio Sala has examined surviving original sources for productions at many boulevard theatres. He found the orchestration for *Le jugement de Salomone* at the Ambigu-

Comique in 1802 to be astonishingly complete: strings, full woodwinds (including piccolo and contrabassoon) and horns, trumpets, trombones, and percussion (including timpani, triangle, and cymbals). The abundance of *melos* numbers is also rather amazing. Sala counts fifty in Pixerécourt's *La femme à deux maris* (also 1802) and eighty-four in *Salomone* (twenty-three in the first act, thirty-five in the second, and twenty-six in the third). Furthermore, he found that these numbers were of various types, some tonally "closed" (ending on the tonic chord) and some "open" (like *Pygmalion*, ending on a dominant or a diminished seventh chord). Some even consisted of just a single chord. Other numbers were "independent" (functioning as isolated action or dialogue cues). Some were "chained" (*en suite*): a series of numbered musical pieces briefly separated by dialogue or action but clearly meant to be heard as part of a continuous musical discourse. (This was not entirely a new procedure. Many *ballets d'actions* and pantomimes, like *The Corsair*, were composed as a series of linked musical pieces.)

The attribution of this music presents another difficulty. Sala relies of course on Pixerécourt's later accounts as to who provided music for his plays. But actual authorship may prove to be more complicated. First, some of the pieces employ common musical devices and could have been borrowed or adapted from any number of operatic sources. Second, when an obvious melody is introduced, how can we say today for certain whether it was original or was an *air parlant*, perhaps known to audiences at the time but now forgotten? Without a complete grasp of the cultural milieu and the collective knowledge of an audience of this time, it would be difficult to analyze the musical codes of these early French melodramas and to assess questions of originality versus referentiality. Still, many technical aspects of typical nineteenth-century *melos* practice were codified during this time. For example, each *melos* is numbered and titled only with a text or visual cue. Also, a single individual playing from the *violon-conducteur* part, which sometimes contained cues for other instruments, became the standard method for leading a theatre orchestra.

We can get a sense for the French popular drama by looking closely at one scene from *The Judgment of Solomon*. The text was by Louis Charles Caigniez and the music by Quaisain.[33] The famous biblical verdict occurs in act 3, scene 4. The published text of 1802, which credits Quaisain on the title page, mentions only one music cue in the scene: "The orchestra plays a muffled tremor during the following lines." Emilio Sala has shown that Quaisain actually composed nine separate music cues for the judgment scene, of which the "tremor" is only one. Caigniez's plot involves Tamira, the

FIGURE 4. Le jugement de Salomone, *no. 17, transcribed by Emilio Sala,* L'Opera senza canto *(Venice: Marsilio, 1995), 84 Thüringisches Staatsarchiv, Rudolstadt*

widow of Banaïas, suing for custody of his three-year-old-child with Leila, a villager. Tamira approaches Solomon with her grievances, requesting to see her son. Solomon asks a guard to bring the child. Cue no. 17 begins with the guard's exit. Leila turns to her confidante and—over music—laments "Ah, Debora! What is my destiny!" The guard returns with the child as the music changes character (from a nervous *agitato* in B-flat minor to a sweet Italianate *melos* in B-flat major.

Leila speaks to her child, perhaps even over this *andante* ("kiss me once more, in case we're separated"), and they embrace and weep. The music ends. The king now reviews the facts of the dispute, without any music, asking if one of the women would refuse her rights to the child in exchange for significant compensation. No treasure, says Leila, would make up for the loss of her child. Solomon turns to Tamira, who declares that she would rather see the child die than give him up. The king seems shocked at this. He pauses for a moment's reflection. Music cue no. 18 begins (a C-major *allegro*) as a new thought occurs to him. He calls to his minister, who hands him a tablet and stylus. As he begins to write, the ponderous music of cue no. 19 begins.

Sala observes that Quaisain enhanced the string tremolo with the dark hues of a trombone and contrabassoon playing the descending figure. This is a moment of minimal if not frozen action, and the rhythmic motive helps to sustain a few moments of great tension, with the two women in obvious consternation over the curious maneuver. Solomon hands the tablet back to his minister and calls on Éliphal, his younger brother, to read it. As Éliphal

FIGURE 5. Le jugement de Salomone, *no. 19*

takes the tablet, cue no. 20 begins. He reads and nods approvingly, handing the tablet back to the king, who gives it to the guard. As the music cue comes to rest on three C-minor chords, Solomon commands the guard to "execute the order." The mysterious "muffled tremors" of cue no. 21 follow. The cue is a series of full-measure string tremolo chords, each struck *fortissimo* and sustained while a character speaks a short aside.[34] This static *melos* is only eight bars, moving through a series of chords from G-sharp diminished to A dominant seventh. Each character reveals an emotion: Leila her fear, Éliphal his hopes, Tamira her curiosity, and Debora her despair. Here we find an operatic moment sustaining the climax of a spoken play.

Drawing on the techniques of opera and pantomime, Quaisain is helping to carve out a new musico-dramatic genre in which music functions reciprocally with dialogue and action. Scanning the music cues, we see an *agitato* that reflects the guard's hasty steps and Leila's fears. The *melos* brightens when the child comes on. An *allegro* in major with syncopations and rising series of chords graphically depicts Solomon's breakthrough moment ("the idea"). A *largo tremolo* functions as a *misterioso* for Solomon's writing, followed by an inverted and more aggressive version of the same music as the tablet passes back. The string tremolos—a central resonance in the melodramatic imagination—serve as the ultimate reminder of the potential terrors that lurk in the shadows of the unknown and unforeseen.

Melos in the popular drama is also flexible in that it can appear at any moment and in any form. The segment of the judgment scene above has five different music cues. Cue no. 17, initially a mood cue, changes *melos* at the entrance of a character (the child). The other cues maintain the same tone throughout, even if the dramatic pace intensifies, as in the *melos* accompanying Solomon's idea. Moreover, some music cues are tonally closed (no. 17), while some are tonally open (no. 19). The tonally open cues tend to usher in dialogue or action that sustains or develops the situation and yet also alerts the listener to the possibility that another *melos* is soon to follow. Tonally closed cues bring dramatic as well as musical closure and suggest that the following incident will move away from the current crisis.

Quaisain composed for many more melodramas and remained at the Ambigu-Comique until the 1810s, where he was joined by Amadée Adrien and a few others. Fewer overt indications for music are found in some of the boulevard playtexts of the 1810s. But it is clear from Ginisty's full breakdown of the Ambigu orchestra in 1817 that it remained about the same size as in 1800.[35] In 1805 the Porte Saint-Martin acquired the services of Mr. Gérardin-Lacour and Louis Alexandre Piccinni, who afterward became more associated with the melodramas of Pixerécourt than any other musician. M. J. Lanusse provided music for melodramas at the Gaîté, as did Henry Darondeau for the Théâtre des Jeunes-Artistes. While some of their music survives in manuscript, only a few songs sung in the plays were ever published.

The Path to Melodrama in London

The early years of English melodrama seemed preoccupied with the past. Perhaps this was partly due to the looming presence of the licenser of plays, who found it more acceptable to transplant the shocks and fears of the present to some safe historical distance. Issues of censorship played a crucial role: unlike the situation in Paris, where popular drama proliferated in the boulevard theatres, melodrama in London first established itself in the patent houses, Drury Lane, Covent Garden, and the Haymarket. The British Parliament maintained a much tighter control over its minor theatres than did the French. British authorities, as George Taylor has argued, were very wary of the revolution being played out on the popular French stage, in both the literal and figurative sense.[36] Therefore, when Pixerécourt's *Coelina* eventually made it to a London theatre, it was performed at Covent Garden, rather than at a working-class house. The proto-melodramas in the 1790s—with their folk heroes and dramatic rescue scenes—were to be found in English opera, such as John Philip Kemble and Stephen Storace's *Lodoïska* (Drury Lane, 1794) or in pantomime, such as *The Black Castle* or *Rinaldo Rinaldini*. The distinctively British form of melodrama also owed a great deal of its unique atmosphere to the late eighteenth-century surge in gothic literature and gothic drama. Horace Walpole, Ann Radcliffe, and Matthew Gregory Lewis catered to readers of all classes "who never tired of lengthy and absurd fictions about monks, nuns, robbers, ghosts, and haunted castles," wrote James Frederick Mason.[37] As the old century drew to a close, the gothic image of the bourgeois oppressor moved center stage. As Jeffrey Cox explains, audiences were "drawn to the villain, his mysterious milieu, and the power granted him by his position and his heroic hauteur."[38]

Matthew Gregory Lewis's "gothic mystery" *The Castle Spectre* is often cited as a key work in the development of British melodrama. It was a spoken drama presented by John Philip Kemble at Drury Lane in 1797, the same year as Pixerécourt's *Victor* at the Ambigu-Comique. Discussions of this play do not usually mention its reliance on music, which actually caused a sensation, especially in the ghost scene.[39] One observer suggests how unfamiliar this experience was—at least for those audiences who were more likely to attend Drury Lane than Astley's Circus. "The hurry and the perturbation of the scene were forcibly depicted by the agitated notes of the orchestra," the *Times* reviewer noted, adding that this "new adjunct to the interest of the drama was immediately felt by the whole audience."[40] One of the leading musical figures at Drury Lane was Michael Kelly, the Irish tenor for whom Mozart had written some of his comic roles. Kelly provided the music for *The Castle Spectre*, much of which he derived from existing sources. The *air parlant* for the ghost scene—a slow four-bar chaconne borrowed from an opera by Nicolò Jommelli and hauntingly sung offstage to the accompaniment of a guitar—achieved such an instant success that it was published as "The Favorite Movement . . . during the Appearance of the Ghost in . . . *The Castle Spectre*."[41]

Two years later Kelly adapted a large amount of music for Sheridan's *Pizarro* (Drury Lane, 1799) that included songs and marches. *Pizarro*, derived from an August von Kotzebue original and one of the most popular English plays of the next fifty years, contained many of the structural components of gothic melodrama, including a dungeon, a villain, and a rescue scene. But this was a "play with music" rather than a *mélo-drame* in the French sense. There is no evidence for music to accompany dialogue or action sequences, not even for Pizarro's confrontation with Elvira and Rolla in act 4, scene 3, or for Rolla's celebrated rescue of Cora and Alonzo's child. Nor does Charles Kemble's promptbook mention the use of any music in these places.[42]

Pizarro's significant contribution to the popular drama, however, lay in Kemble and Sheridan's specifications that the orchestra play music before each act that suggested events to follow. This was a powerful device, drawing on the full expressive range of the Drury orchestra. Perhaps Kelly did not feel up to this task, for he invited Johann Ladislaus Dussek, already an established composer and performer in London, to write the overture and the "characteristic pieces" to precede each act. Instrumental entr'actes had been in use for some time, as in some *opéras-comiques* of Grétry. Even in 1762 Henry Home (in his *Elements of Criticism*) had expressed the hope that the "music betwixt the acts" would be "gradually varied till it accord with the tone of the passion that is to succeed in the next act."[43] The device of the foreshadowing overture was certainly popularized in opera, most notably in Mozart's *Don Giovanni* (Prague National Theatre, 1787). But Home's expectations reached full fruition in Dussek's evocative curtain raisers. These included "Preparatory to Battle" to introduce act 2; "Triumph after Victory" to introduce act 3; "Despair" and "Dungeon" music to introduce act 4; and "Mournful"—foreshadowing the death of Rolla—and "Storm" to bring up the curtain in act 5.

Early English melodrama was nourished by a growing popular interest in history, especially its impact on recent conflicts such as those between the Ottomans and the West (*The Siege of Belgrade*), the Italian overthrow of French rule (*Rinaldo Rinaldini*), and the ongoing conflict with piracy off the North African coast. A reviewer of *A Tale of Mystery* in 1802 recalled what seemed to him an important melodramatic precedent in *Lodoïska*, produced at Drury Lane in 1794. Though based on Luigi Cherubini's *opéra-comique* of 1791, Kemble's version was an "English opera," adapted with airs, new dialogue, and comic situations not in the original. Kemble changed a few of the names, but the plot is essentially the same. The powerful Polish noble Baron Lovinsky, who has been ravaging Tartar lands to the east, has locked away the beautiful Lodoïska in the tower of his castle. Her lover, Count Floreski, enlists the help of the Tartars, storms the castle, and rescues her. In the last act the baron, hearing the drums and trumpets and clash of swords on his castle battlements, realizes that he may soon be overtaken. "What's Lodoïska now?" he laments. "Lost, lost to me forever! The helpless prize of some fierce, lawless savage. Horrible thought!" At this point, Kemble's text asks for a "martial symphony," referring not to sounds heard from an offstage band but to a *melos* played by the musicians before the stage. Though intended to be inaudible to the character, it certainly aided the actor in his delivery. "Where is her father?" the baron asks. "My friend, my benefactor? All bleeding, mangled, murder'd. Frightful image!" Another "martial symphony" accompanied the baron as he braced himself against his shield. "Hark! My soul's beat down, down to the very ground." And again the "martial symphony" resumed as the baron snatched his battle-axe. "The tempest swells, Floreski too, perhaps, directs the storm, thundering and fierce in arms." Realizing that he must fight to the death, the baron rushes off. Doors on the opposite side of the stage suddenly burst open, and the Tartars enter. (At this point the Tartar soldiers and the abducted female prisoners of the castle sing a chorus, this being an opera.)

Stephen Storace composed and compiled the music for Kemble's adaptation, drawing from the famous opera by Cherubini but also from other musical adaptations of this work of French historical fiction. The use of music here is clearly proto-melodramatic, though it functioned exactly as had Rousseau's *mélo-drame* with alternating speech and music for pantomime. The baron's lines inform us that he is on the brink of despair. But Kemble realized that the orchestra's intervention served as an actor's aide: it could reinforce the character's courage and steel his resolve to defend the castle.

Holcroft, Busby, and A Tale of Mystery

The author who first imported French melodrama into England, Thomas Holcroft, began singing as a boy, traveled as an actor in Kemble's company, where he studied acrobatics and fencing, then worked for another itinerant group of strolling players as "music," providing the "accompaniment to all songs, &c on his fiddle in the orchestra." Holcroft worked with composers such as William Shield and Michael Arne, in some cases translating and adapting Italian and French operas and plays, and became an actor for Sheridan's company at Drury Lane, where he played innumerable principal roles in the standard comedies, studied Shakespeare with ardor, and wrote several plays himself. Holcroft's play *The Road to Ruin* was a huge success in 1792 and established him as a leading figure in the theatrical life of London. While living in Paris in 1801 he witnessed the sensation surrounding *Coelina* and immediately crafted an English adaptation. Thomas Harris, the enterprising new manager-proprietor of Covent Garden, wisely foresaw profits ahead in the new form. Continuing in the tradition of having a musical piece follow the main legitimate fare, *A Tale of Mystery* opened in November 1802, as an afterpiece to a comedy by Frederick Reynolds. It was a decided success and ran nearly continuously for thirty-eight performances.

In the introduction to the published playtext Holcroft acknowledges the original French drama but credits his melodrama's success to the performers, the composer of the music, the scenic effects, and the dances. For Holcroft, as for Pixerécourt, the melodrama is not so much a play as an event, a spectacle for the eye and ear. Moreover, Holcroft had at his disposal the extraordinary Charles Farley, dancer and choreographer of *The Corsair* and other ballet pantomimes in the London theatres. Farley designed the costumes and sets, handled much of the staging, and also created the mute character of Francisco, the central mime role in the play. Others in the company were well-known names at Covent Garden. Henry Johnston played Romaldi, arguably the first melodramatic villain on the English stage. Louis Bologna created the folk ballet sequence in the second act. Thomas Busby was also known for having composed a musical drama for Covent Garden the previous year.

The complicated story is set in historical Savoy (around 1600). Holcroft made many revisions to the plot, converting Pixerécourt's three acts to two, simplifying the longer speeches, and shifting the emphasis from explanation to action. Stephano, the son of the noble Bonamo, is in love with Selina, Bonamo's soon-to-be-adopted niece and an orphan with a considerable inheritance. Bonamo learns that the wealthy and powerful Count Romaldi is coming to see him with an eye to arranging Selina's marriage to his own son. Recently given asylum under Bonamo's roof is a mute and disfigured beggar. In actuality he is not only Francisco Bianchi, Count Romaldi's brother, but also Selina's true father and knows that his brother was behind the attack that tried to silence him. The *mystery* of the story hinges on why Francisco will not reveal his secret and the nature of the animosity between the two brothers.

Holcroft used Pixerécourt's designation, calling it a "melo drame" (without the hyphen), the first appearance of this so-named genre on the London stages. Covent Garden allowed for spoken dialogue, so on the page *A Tale of Mystery* looks for all intents and purposes like a play. But it incorporates the crucial elements of Pixerécourt's genre, including a significant character whose thoughts and emotions must be conveyed solely through gesture and music.

Busby's pantomime and action music appears to be original. But he used the art of *melos*, consistent with the practice of linking musical affect to the dramatic passions, as Holcroft's musical descriptions reveal. "Music, to express discontent and alarm" to open the first scene. "Hunting music" for the entrance of Stephano. "Music: to express chattering contention" to prepare the entrance of Bonamo and Fiametta, the domestic. "Music to express pain and disorder" as Bonamo threatens to throw Fiametta out of the house. "Confused music" for the entrance of Piero, another servant. For the entrance of Montano, a villager: "Music plays alarmingly, but *piano* when he enters and speaks." Music continues under Montano's line "I beg pardon, good sir, but—." Then "Music loud and discordant at the moment the eye of Montano catches the figure of Romaldi, at which Montano starts with terror and indignation. He then assumes the eye and attitude of menace, which Romaldi returns. The music ceases." The dialogue continues for a few lines, before "Hurrying music, but half *piano*" as Montano exits. The published text continues at this level of detail. Even by just reading the script we can see that this is an intensely visual play. Affective music is essential for each character's entrance and for every minor turning point within the episodes.

Music to *The Tale of Mystery* was published in a kind of short score with melody and bass line only, as in the old comic tunes, but without numbers. The layout of the score resembles the Benda type of through-composed *mélodrame*. Each musical piece is prefaced by a text or visual cue and given clear specifications for tempo. (Also, the character of each musical piece corresponds precisely to Holcroft's specifications in the published version of the play.) Often additional visual cues are provided, and multiple tempo changes occur within continuous segments of pantomime underscoring. The score contains relatively few dynamics (often none at the beginnings of cues). The first act alone has nineteen instrumental accompaniments.

Midway through act 1 Romaldi and Bonamo inquire of Selina what she may know about the beggar. A servant introduces Montano, who begins to speak to Bonamo. The instant hostility between these two characters is intensified by the music. Then the music pauses.

> *Romaldi* (Returning his threatening looks): Sir!
> *Montano*: You here!
> *Romaldi*: Not having the honour of your acquaintance, I know not why my presence should please or displease you.
> *Montano* (to Bonamo, after a look of stern contempt at Romaldi): Good night, my friend; I will see you to-morrow. (Exits suddenly.) (Music)

After the hurry music, the measured phrases to assist Romaldi as he gathers his courage seem like operatic recitative. But instead of culminating in an aria, the action immediately continues, with a new character's entrance heralded by a few abrupt chords. A conclusive cadence in A-major momentarily dispels the tension as Malvoglio begins to speak. As Janet Shepherd noted in her discussion of this scene, Busby seemed to write music around Romaldi's dialogue, not being quite comfortable yet with having music played during such important lines.[44] In performance the actor would need to fit his questions into the short musical silences,

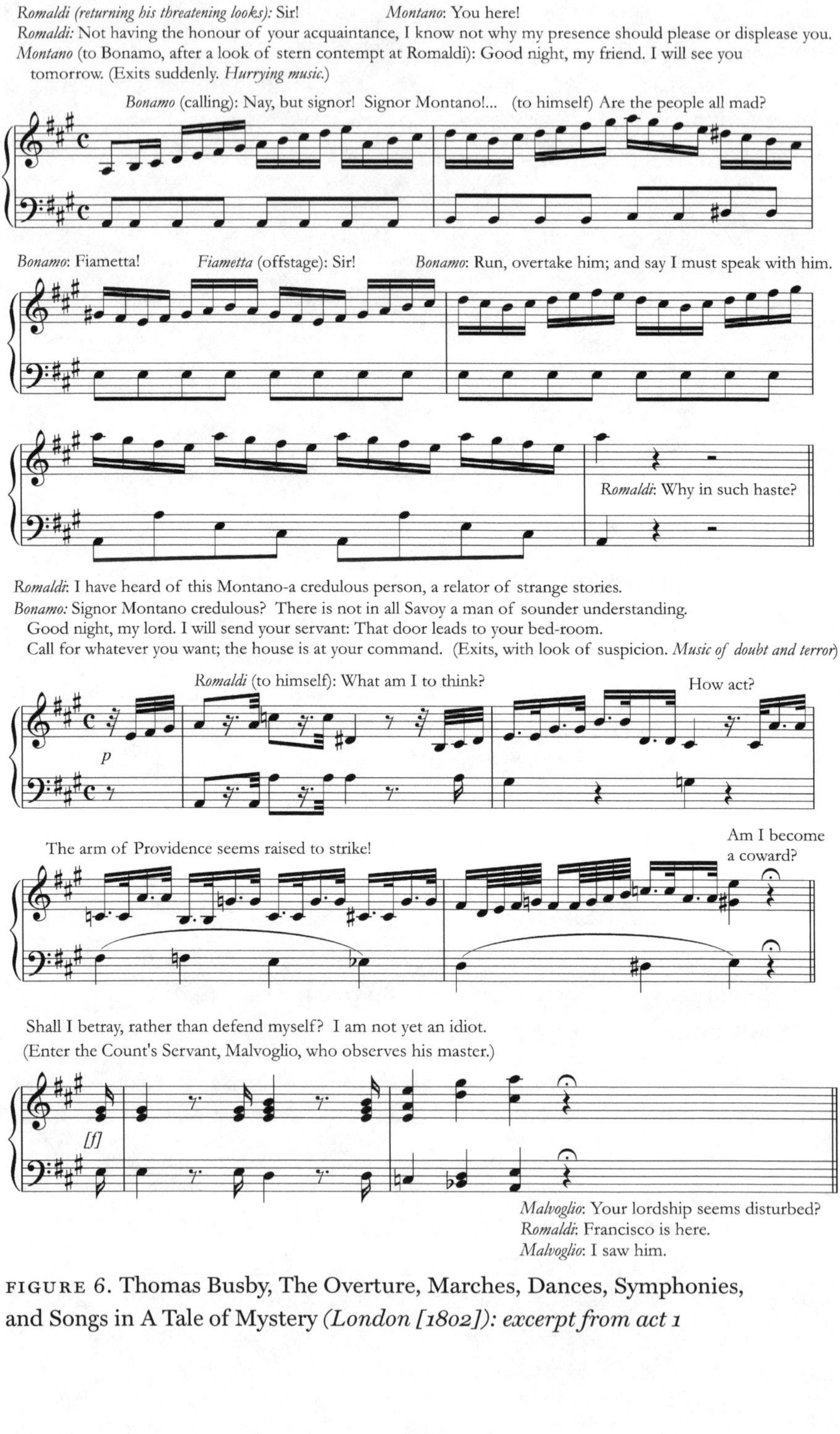

FIGURE 6. Thomas Busby, The Overture, Marches, Dances, Symphonies, and Songs in A Tale of Mystery *(London [1802]): excerpt from act 1*

while the orchestra leader would need to be careful of this timing. Occasionally actors do have to speak over the music—as in Bonamo's few lines above. But in this early stage of incorporating both speech and pantomimic music Busby leans toward their separation.

The climactic scene of act 2 takes place in a wild mountainous region. Romaldi, dressed in peasant clothes, attempts to escape amid flashes of lightning and thunder. The music was particularly effective in setting up the *quiproquo*. As one reviewer observed, "the trees are represented in actual motion from the storm which, with the accompanying music, is well suited to Romaldi's state of mind, whose dreadful guilt has made him a fit object both of earthly and divine vengeance."[45] But Holcroft's modifications to Pixerécourt's original encourage the audience, as Jane Moody notes in her analysis of this play, to perceive Romaldi not just as a criminal and cardboard villain but as a figure of pity.[46]

The final confrontation involves all the characters in an elaborate chase led by a group of "archers" (that ambiguously named army of royal protectors) and was acted out entirely to through-composed music. Romaldi's capture and the resolution of conflict between the characters would seem to signal a happy ending. But no victorious music affirms a fairy-tale conclusion. Bonamo replies to Selina's last pleas that Romaldi be shown mercy with guarded hope and dark uncertainty, and the curtain falls to eleven bars of solemn music in G minor. If any catharsis was experienced in the knowledge of the villain's imminent punishment, it was partly due to the tragic implications of the final music.[47]

Musical Sources for Melodrama in the Patent Theatres

The *Monthly Mirror* observed in 1808 that Holcroft's *Tale of Mystery* met with a "swarm of imitators." All these of course were limited to the patent theatres and remained relegated to afterpieces, following the main tragedy or comedy. The reviewer also complained that it was impossible to witness a single afterpiece "without having our nerves fretted to fiddle-strings."[48] Not all of these imitations sparked entirely original music, however. Holcroft's *The Lady of the Rock* (Drury Lane, 1805) had music "selected and composed" by the author's wife, Fanny Holcroft. The need to come up with music in very short order, given the huge numbers of melodramas crafted literally overnight (and many to formula), no doubt resulted more often than not in the assembly of available music, using stock passages from operas, pantomimes, and even purely instrumental compositions.

Still, it is possible to isolate works with original music, because scores to these would otherwise not have been published. The British Library holds the printed music to some fifty British melodramas and burlettas from 1802 to 1826. Among these is Busby's music for another English adaptation of Pixerécourt entitled *Rugantino, or The Bravo of Venice* prepared by Matthew Gregory Lewis for Drury Lane in 1805. Many other Pixerécourt adaptations followed, the two with greatest longevity being *Tekeli, or The Siege of Montgatz,* adapted by Theodore Hook with music by his father, James Hook (Drury Lane, 1806), and *The Forest of Bondy, or The Dog of Montargis* (Covent Garden, 1814), adapted by Thomas Harris with music by one of the leading composers of English opera at both Covent Garden and Drury Lane, the prolific Sir Henry Rowley Bishop (1786–1855).[49] Meanwhile British playwrights developed their own melodramatic plots based on history and legend with titles such as *The Blind Boy* by the Irish-born James Kenney (Covent Garden, 1807), *Timour the Tartar* by Matthew Gregory Lewis (Covent Garden, 1811), and *The Miller and His Men* by Isaac Pocock (Covent Garden, 1813).

The orchestras in the patent theatres that provided this music were often of a generous size. Covent Garden and the King's Theatre needed substantial orchestras, of course, for Italian and French opera. Charles Dibdin gives an account of approximately forty musicians in the Covent Garden orchestra in 1810 with as many as twenty-four strings (eight first and eight second violins), double winds, and a small battery of percussion (including piano).[50] Contracts for this same orchestra in 1818 under Henry Bishop indicate thirty-one paid musicians, nineteen of them string players.[51] Though no sets of orchestra parts have been found, manuscript full scores by Henry Bishop and others exist for some of the melodramas at the royal theatres that reveal details of orchestration.

Why did London music dealers publish so much original melodramatic music in its early years, unlike their French counterparts? First, melodramas performed at Drury Lane and Covent Garden were to some extent legitimized, high in tone and equal in standards of preparation to English operas. A melodramatic playwright whose piece was accepted at these two theatres (or at the Haymarket during the summer) could count on it being "done up in style." These theatres had wealthy patrons and could afford the best and most prestigious of the British composers. Because they could count on sales, publishers like Edward Riley in the Strand (from 1795) or Goulding and D'Almaine (1810 to 1834) were more apt to invest in typesetting the music to melodramas along with the operas and ballets of Thomas

Busby, James Hook, Matthew Peter King, John Davy, William Russell, William Ware, and especially Henry Bishop. Second, performing rights at London's patent theatres were extended to royal houses in York, Bath, Dublin, and elsewhere, and these same melodramas were soon taken up in the minor theatres of London, in the provinces, and across the ocean in America. Composers at this time were not entitled to royalties, so an initial fee from the theatre and sales of music were the only means to derive any profit from their work. For example, Matthew Peter King's melodramatic music to *Ella Rosenberg* (Drury Lane, 1807) was published immediately after it opened. Twelve years later King's music was still being used for productions of *Ella Rosenberg*, as an 1819 playbill from Edinburgh shows. (To give some idea of the currency of this music, a score was still being made available as late as 1882 by Samuel French in conjunction with performing materials for the play, including a set of parts for reduced orchestra!)

Also much to publishers' delight, melodramas were popular enough that musical excerpts were played outside the theatre. The overture from Busby's music to *A Tale of Mystery* was printed separately as a piano solo, presumably for enjoyment at home, and Busby himself arranged the peasant dance from the second act for a military band. Similarly, three country dances from *Ella Rosenberg* and a rondo for piano based on one of these were also published shortly after the play opened. For an extremely popular melodrama like *The Miller and His Men*, which also contained songs, rounds, glees, and other items more typical of an English opera, Goulding, D'Almaine, and Potter published a full piano score.[52] Perhaps the most internationally famous of such scores from this time is Carl Maria von Weber's music to J. R. Planché's *Oberon* (Covent Garden, 1826), for which the composer was paid £100 more than the author of the play. Still, Weber's orchestra parts remained the exclusive property of the theatre until the score was published, whereupon the composer, had he lived, would have been able to settle for a fee.

When musical scores of melodramas were published complete, as was the case with *A Tale of Mystery*, they were prepared as "practical editions," for piano only.[53] They could also be used in theatres where only a keyboard or small orchestra was available. Sometimes the scores were published with all musical cues in order, as they would occur in production. At other times, as in the case of *The Patriot, or The Hermit of Saxellen* (Royal Hibernian Theatre, Dublin, 1811), John Stevenson's score was published with the "melo-dramatic music" at the back, disconnected from the songs and choruses. Some piano editions occasionally provide clues for instrumentation. For one of the songs in *A Tale of Mystery* ("omitted in the representation," we are told) Busby requested first and second violin, viola, bass, two flutes, and two horns. The original orchestration was no doubt much larger for some of the grander moments in the score. We know, for instance, that there was a harp in *The Blind Boy*, since a Mr. Nicholson's playing on that instrument during the overture was mentioned in one of the reviews. As noted earlier, a few full scores in manuscript survive. Bishop's holograph for *The Miller and His Men* reveals that the orchestra consisted of seven woodwinds (flute, two oboes, two clarinets, two bassoons), five brass (two horns, two trumpets, one trombone), timpani, and full strings.

Three important British composers working in theatres besides Bishop were John Stevenson (1761–1833), Matthew Peter King (1773–1823), and John Davy (1763–1824). Both Davy and King were associated with James Kenney, an Irish-born playwright who specialized in comedies (such as *Raising the Wind*) but also wrote comic operas and was deeply interested in the new emerging vein of English domestic melodrama.

John Davy, an organist and violinist, began his theatre career playing in the Covent Garden orchestra. His first theatrical compositions were for Sadler's Wells, which have not survived.[54] When Davy composed for Kenney's 1807 melodrama *The Blind Boy* at Covent Garden, however, the score was immediately published. Kenney's text is rich in music cues, making it clear that he envisioned a drama infused with *melos*. Parenthetical notes such as "music expressive of affection" or "music expressive of violent agitation" abound on nearly every page. The published piano score shows that Davy adhered closely to these designations but, unlike Busby, numbered each of the music cues. For no. 2, "When Oberto appears," Davy composed "music expressive of joy"; for no. 3, "When Edmond appears on the bridge," Davy supplied "music expressive of fear"; and so on. This might seem to be rather obvious musical signaling, but it is not quite as it appears. Edmond is the blind boy (played by Fanny Kemble in the production). His first entrance is up on a hill, feeling his way with a cane. Ahead of him is an old rustic bridge that has given way. Oberto and Elvina ascertain the danger and are about to warn him. The "fearful" music at Edmund's first entrance is not for his character but rather for his perilous situation and the emotional states of the characters onstage who observe him. A reviewer noted that Mr. Davy's music "does him much credit" and observed that "the *melos* accompanying the piece was frequently very ingenious, [though] more solemnity would often have made it more appropriate."[55]

In the same year as *The Blind Boy*, Kenney wrote *Ella Rosenberg* for the great tragedienne Sarah Siddons. It was produced at Drury Lane, with music by Matthew Peter King, by now well known as the author of a treatise on thorough bass and composer of melodramas. The story takes place in a seventeenth-century Prussian military camp. Ella, a gifted young painter, is the wife of a young officer from a noble family beloved and protected by the elector. At the opening of the play, however, Rosenberg (played by Robert W. Elliston) has been missing for some time. He and his family's archrival, Colonel Mountfort (the villainous character played by Vincent De Camp), had crossed swords, after which Rosenberg was no longer heard from again. In view of the officer's extended absence, Mountfort begins to confiscate the Rosenberg family lands and places Ella under the protection of Officer Storm (played by John Bannister). As in the example of *Thérèse* (at the opening of this chapter), Kenney required music to convey the seriousness of tone and the underlying tragic implications as the villain laid each snare.

The music of *Ella Rosenberg* exists in full score, presumably in the composer's hand.[56] King's manuscript, which begins with a lengthy overture in the festive manner of Gioachino Rossini, is arranged according to "symphonies" as in Kemble's *Lodoïska*, a label applied to pieces that are purely instrumental rather than vocal. Most of these are indicated by sight cues and correspond to their position in the playscript.[57] The instrumentation is for five woodwinds (one flute, two oboes, two bassoons), five brass (two horns, two trumpets, one trombone), timpani, a full complement of strings (perhaps twelve or thirteen), and an onstage fife and side drums. The fife and drums provided fanfare for the scenes of the elector of Brandenburg, who serves as the benevolent agent in the play. (Davy, living near a military camp as a boy, had fallen in love with the sound of fifes played during roll call.)

At the opening of the play, Ella, despondent over her lost husband, makes her entrance to two horns, two oboes, and strings playing the first *melos* in E minor (a "naïve, womanly" key, wrote Christian Friedrich Daniel Schubart, a music theorist of the time).[58] According to an illustration in the published text, Siddons made her entrance in a state of grief, her face looking heavenward. The second *melos*—necessary to mask the villain's actual intent—begins sometime later and is titled "Mountfort shows the sketches." The villain has disguised himself as a Jew who has come to commission a painting. His entrance music consists of a four-bar *andante* in D major, the mildly cheerful tone serving to aid the villain's duplicity. The flute leads, quietly playing a sweet melody. Ella's line "Thank you for your favours" is penciled in toward the end of King's score, so we know that both characters spoke their dialogue while the music was playing. A rest follows, held by a fermata during which "Mountfort speaks." His line is an aside: "'Tis well, she does not know me." The music immediately continues with a meter change to three-four, as the disguised Mountfort pretends to interest Ella in some sketches that he has brought. Meanwhile Mountfort's cronies have crept in behind him and proceed to hide in the closet. At the visual cue "two men steal in" the unison strings begin their first note with a stinging accent and the tempo increases slightly (*moderato*). This continues for ten measures with a *crescendo*, then *piano* (presumably allowing enough time for the men to secure themselves safely in their hiding place), and then returns to the opening flute tune as Mountfort kindly asks Ella what she thinks of his ideas for a painting. While the first E-minor *melos* was single affect (Ella's grief), the second was fluctuating in affect, following the dramatic arc of the incident. Without the music the scene might have had overtones of farce. But King's score propels its audience in a different direction.

Affective and action music thus figured prominently in *Ella Rosenberg*. When Kenney's play was published a few months later, the *Monthly Review or Literary Journal* proclaimed that "whatever interest may have been excited by this piece, when aided by music and adorned by the decorations of the theatre, we are obliged to say that, without these helps, it is flat and insipid."[59] *Ella Rosenberg* may make for bland reading as a play, but the drama was theatrically successful, performed in theatres across the British Isles and in America for some fifteen years afterward. It was a success partly because affective music assisted in persuading audiences to focus on the tragic consequences of the situations rather than on the absurdity of their dramatic construction.

Several definitions of melodrama imply that music is added to a play to intensify a dramatic moment. Many details of the music undoubtedly were decided upon in rehearsal. But we should not overlook an intrinsic quality of melodrama as a work conceived both *for* and *in* music. In other words, the author—who after all was often the director in those days—decided exactly when and where music was to go when conceiving the play. Many manuscripts of early melodramas sent to the Lord Chamberlain's Office for review include liberal instructions for music. Some are found at a character's entrance, often telegraphing a state of emotion, but some are specified for scenes of conflict. As Kenney's published text for *Ella Rosenberg* (Fig. 7) illustrates, the author expected music to underscore a scene of confrontation as the villain Mountfort orders his guards to seize Ella while Officer

[Music.] *Enter Stephen and Conrad from the Closet.*

Ella (kneeling). Nay, then, I implore your pity.

Mount. It is too late!

Ella, in rising, attempts to draw Mountfort's sword and defend herself.

Mount. Secure her, I say!

Stephen and Conrad seize her and are dragging her off. Storm enters, hastily and intercepts them.

Storm. Ah! Russians, in my house—Stand off!

[Music.] *Storm fights with Stephen and Conrad and drives them off. Mountfort, in the meantime, seizes Ella. Storm, having dispersed his opponents, rushes between them.*

Ella. My protector!

Storm. Don't be frightened! Now, Sir. Why shouldn't you share the fate of your companions? Do you know that this house is mine?

Mount. Is it? Lower your tone, friend Storm, or I may chance to change your residence. Remember who you are.

Storm. I do—a greater man than you—the friend of suffering innocence—you are but the Governor of Molwitz!

Mount. You shall repent this behaviour.

Storm. Never! If you have poisoned the ear of my Sovereign, I've still an appeal to heaven, and here's the angel that shall be my advocate! Come near her, if you dare! Tho' I am doom'd to hobble on a shatter'd limb, I have still a sound heart and an arm strong enough to obey its dictates. I wish your Governorship would condescend to measure weapons with me.

Mount. (aside). This shall secure him. Insolent! I will not baulk you then. Come forth. You shall find me a fair enemy.

Storm. Have at you, then.

Mount. Follow me! *Exit.*

Ella (endeavoring to hold Storm). For heaven's sake!

Storm. I'm coming!—damme! I'll scratch you. [Music] *Exit, following Mountfort.*

Ella. Gracious heaven! Still accumulating calamities! Should the Captain fall? Dreadful thought! My friend, my protector, lost to me, and I the cause! Abandoned, perhaps, to the power of my persecutor. [Music.] *She falls into a chair.* Suspense is horrible! I'll fly to them. Still I may prevent them, and save—

Enter Christina, hastily.

FIGURE 7. Ella Rosenberg *(London: Printed for Longman, Hurst, Rees, and Orme, 1807): excerpt from act 1*

Storm (her protector) comes to her rescue. (The music cues are numbered as 3 to 6 in King's score.)

Most of the melodramas at the patent theatres in the first decade of the nineteenth century—like *Ella Rosenberg*—were historical costume dramas with ample opportunities for fight scenes and heroic rescues. Some of these dramatic devices, especially in the following decades, were cultivated in the minor theatres, whose managements drew large profits catering to audiences' appetites for noisy and fast-paced entertainment.

Timour the Tartar *at Covent Garden*

Not to be outdone, however, the majors responded with melodramas such as Matthew Gregory Lewis's *Timour the Tartar*. John Philip Kemble's production of *Timour*, directed and acted by the extraordinary Charles Farley, was a tour de force of pageantry, costume, spectacle, and brilliant cavalry horsemanship. The horses were virtual characters in the drama, providing an endless amount of delight to the audience. Matthew Peter King provided the music. His "Grand Cavalry March in *Timour the Tartar*" became almost instantly famous on both sides of the Atlantic. The plot involves the historical figure of Timour the Mongol warrior, who kills the Georgian prince of Mingrelia, usurps his throne, and holds the prince's son in chains. The escaped princess (Zorilda) returns in disguise to undertake her son's rescue.[60]

The musical pieces in the score are unnumbered. As in pantomime King relies almost exclusively on sight cues rather than text cues. He does have the occasional "symphony while the curtain rises," and the music that opens the second act is atmospheric in suggesting the moonlight streaming in through the window of Zorilda's chamber. Though we can only guess at the orchestration, the piano score reveals a considerable variety of music for this play. Many *melos* numbers are relatively short, from five to twenty-two measures. It has four character-entrance cues (not counting the big ceremonial marches) and two *melos* numbers specifically devoted to a unique passion ("Selima implores protection" and "Oglou expresses joy"). Several musical items are of the fluctuating type of *melos*: they underscore an entire incident ("Scene between Kerim and Selima"). The most substantial pieces are several stirring marches and the big combat scene in act 1.

The climax of the first act centers on the conflict between two of Timour's chieftains, Kerim and Sanballat, and their love for the same woman: Selina, a beautiful Circassian captive. The woman is secretly in love with Kerim and begs them not to fight. But their jealous feud is distracting the army, so Timour insists that they must end it one way or another. The two decide to resolve the dispute by formal combat. King's musical "combat" (like some of the battle pieces cited in chapter 1) consists of no less than sixteen subsections. The spectacular scene opens with a grand march for the entrance of Timour and the secretly avenging Zorilda—who magisterially ascends the throne—along with the army and the many spectators in the stands. At the sound of trumpets, each barricade is thrown open. Kerim and Sanballat enter on horseback from opposite sides with lances at the ready.

The "combat music" begins, divided into sections as shown in Table 1 below. The battle is a bloody and ruthless one. At a certain point the men have given up their horses—who are led away—and fight hand-to-hand. Sanballat has an advantage when Kerim loses his sword. But Kerim's horse leaps over the parapet, intercepts Sanballat, picks up Kerim's sword, and brings it to him. In a fit of anger Sanballat kills the horse. Empowered by a desire for revenge, Kerim drags Sanballat to his horse and "sacrifices him on the body." The crowd cheers as they descend from the stocks, with Timur crowning the victor and Selina embracing him. Despite the fermatas in the score, which allowed for the action to catch up, it was a minor miracle that all this could be timed to music, with a certain amount of the precision depending on the horses and their trainers.

King's music abounds in rhetorical devices, as can be seen in Figure 8. Downward-moving triplets suggest Kerim's collapse, the lightning quick upward dash clearly represents Kerim's horse leaping from his pen, Sanballat stabbing the valiant horse results in a wild orchestral outburst, and so forth.

The climactic battle scene in which Zorilda's son rescues her from the tower of the fortress and overcomes Timour with the help of his army was staged without music, though an engraving of this scene served as the cover illustration for the published score. Perhaps the intricate stage actions—the crossfire of the soldier's arrows, Zorilda's plunge from the tower, Agib's leap on horseback from the parapet—were too intricate for music to add yet another layer of complication. The sheer amount of noise onstage would probably have rendered the music pointless. As an eyewitness observed in the *Morning Chronicle*: "amidst the clattering of hoofs, the clangor of swords and spears, and the shouts of an enraptured audience, it is scarcely possible, or perhaps hardly worth while, for criticism to attempt to speak."[61]

Melodramas such as *Timour* were eventually produced in London's

TABLE 1. *Details of the combat scene in* Timour the Tartar, *act 1, scene 3*

Headwords over Music in the Published Score	Description of the Music
Kerim and Sanballat charge with lances.	*Allegro*. D major. 4/4. 19 mm.
[Kerim's] horse takes part in the combat.	Same tempo and key. 8 mm.
Sanballat is dragged to the ground.	*Presto*. 9 mm. (fermata)
Sanballat rises . . .	*Andante*, 3/4, 4 mm.
. . . and attributes the victory to the horse.	*Presto*. 3 mm. (fermata)
Kerim proposes single combat.	No tempo specified. 2/4. 7 mm. (fermata)
The horses are led off.	*Allegro*. 4/4. 8 mm. (fermata)
The fight begins.	*Presto*, G major. *Fortissimo*. 12 mm. (with repeats)
Kerim falls.	(See musical example in Figure 9)
Kerim's horse leaps and prevents Sanballat from advancing.	
The horse picks up the sword [and carries it to his master].	
Sanballat stabs the horse, who falls and expires	
Kerim disarms his rival.	*Allegro furioso*. D minor. 3/4. 22 mm. (with some repeats)
Selima embraces Kerim.	*Affettuoso*. D major. 3/8
(Etc.)	

minor theatres as well as in the majors, so surviving sources for music and text do not always agree. Some instructions in the musical score of *Timour*, for example, vary slightly from those in the playtext. In the published text, for example, Kerim kills Sanballat, while in the music Kerim merely "disarms his rival." Lewis observed that in the provinces the combat scene was enacted without horses while in London theatres the horses "were received with great favor by the public."[62]

FIGURE 8. *M. P. King,* Timour the Tartar *(London: Clementi and Co., 1811), 27: "The Combat" (excerpt). Reproduced by kind permission of the Syndics of Cambridge University Library*

A Final Comment on Sources

One prominent example of the sharp disparity between published texts and surviving music can be seen in *The Forest of Bondy, or The Dog of Montargis* (Covent Garden, 1814). Charles Farley's adaptation was made from Pixerécourt's melodrama. Henry Bishop's published score conforms to Farley's version, using the same character names and sequential ordering. The published text of *The Dog of Montargis*, however, circulated among minor and regional theatres in an adaptation by William Barrymore. Because this version changed characters' names and removed a considerable amount of dialogue, turning the melodrama into more of a *pantomime dialoguée*, it could not possibly be used with Bishop's music. Barrymore was a prominent actor at the Coburg Theatre. His version appeared there and at other theatres where censors would have been less tolerant of incendiary political and social attitudes represented in speech. Yet another adaptation by Henry Harris was staged in Dublin with music by Jonathan Blewitt, while *The Forest of Bondy* was performed at the Chestnut Street Theatre in Philadelphia with Bishop's music. In short, many discrepancies between sources of early nineteenth-century melodramas would need to be sorted out for any of these plays to be revived on anything like their original scale.

3

The Early Popular Drama in the Public Theatres

In the first decade of the nineteenth-century, melodrama, with its national heroes, class and ethnic conflicts, sensational scenic effects, and tuneful musical accompaniments, spread like wildfire, not just to the minor theatres of London but also to the regional and provincial theatres of Great Britain and Ireland as well as to theatres in the east-coast cities of the United States. When Holcroft's *Tale of Mystery* opened at the New-York Theatre in March 1803 and James Kenney's *The Blind Boy* opened in New York's Park Theatre in December 1808, they used the same music as the London productions, because American music dealers could easily acquire the published scores for these and make them available to theatrical managers. Within a few years new and original American melodramas sprung up, such as John Blake White's *The Mysteries of the Castle, or The Victim of Revenge* at the Charleston Theatre in 1806 and James Nelson Barker's *The Indian Princess, or La Belle Sauvage* at Philadelphia's Chestnut Street Theatre in 1808 (the only American melodrama from this time with a published musical score). The form even spread eastward from Paris and London into central Europe. In 1806 *La Belle Assemblée* observed that "the Germans have admitted melo dramas [*sic*] on their stage" with *The Enchanted Vale of Swetard*.[1]

Between 1800 and 1843 "melodrama" split into so many different categories (Maurice Disher describes over twenty different types in England alone) that I use the all-embracing category *popular drama* here to avoid confusion with the specific French varieties that evolved in the early years of the nineteenth century.[2] Many of the popular dramas produced in the first and second decade either leaned toward English-style operas (plays with set musical numbers) or were principally dramas with accompanimental music, which included the occasional (and omissible) song. The minor theatres of London "insert in all the pieces sent to the licenser a certain number of songs or choruses in each act," as a New York newspaper later noted. In other words, censors would not interfere with the repertory of the public theatres as long as the spoken plays were liberally sprinkled with music—usually between five and seven songs. The same article, however, then added: "these songs and choruses not being intended to be sung at all, of which the licenser is well aware."[3] This little dance between the reader of plays (usually an author himself such as John Larpent or George Colman) and the management of the minor theatres actually put the security of houses such as the Adelphi or the Olympic dangerously at the whim of the Lord Chamberlain, who could revoke the theatre's license for refusing to comply at any moment if someone complained. Theatres outside this jurisdiction, such as the East London or Pavilion in Whitechapel or the Surrey and Coburg theatres, both built south of the Thames, could still be taken to court.

Hence we find Robert W. Elliston mounting a production of *Macbeth* at the Surrey Theatre in October 1809, calling it "a ballet of music and action" so as not to threaten Kemble and Siddons, who were then producing a legitimate *Macbeth* at Covent Garden. The Surrey *Macbeth* had been melodramatized (as were other Shakespeare plays decades later by Samuel Phelps, Charles Kean, and Henry Irving, although for different reasons).[4] It was billed as containing most of the compositions of Matthew Locke but with a new overture "and other music" by Thomas Busby. The play was to be followed the same evening by the grand spectacle of *Love's Perils, or The Hermit of St. Kilda*, presented—as the playbill noted—"with new scenery, machinery, dresses, and decorations, particularly the broadside section of a Ship of War, her weighing anchor and setting sail." Stage music may have been interpolated to comply with the burletta restrictions; many actors and actresses liked to sing and dance, however, and audiences in the minor theatres found the relief of a song now and then highly pleasurable. It was also true that managers of the minor theatres went out of their way to make sure that plenty of music was announced in the advertisements and playbills.

In the early years of the minors, certainly during the 1780s, the burletta limitations were so severe that actors were forced to deliver their lines in a singsong style modeled on operatic recitative, and a keyboardist was kept at his post to pluck out a few occasional chords. It is difficult to imagine how this could have been improvised or to know when exactly the tradition died out. But reliable accounts by John Philip Kemble, Thomas Morton, and George B. Davidge concur that this was indeed how some minor theatres operated to avoid being shut down, even as late as 1810. But from 1802 on, it was the running emotive commentary played by the band of musicians—the persuasive auditory information in the instrumental accompaniment—that distinguished the new genre of the popular drama. The excessive amount of action music in the minor theatres may have eased the pressure on actors to intone in recitative. Some even called this type of music a "new adjunct" to the spoken drama. "A melo-drama is a species of dramatic absurdity with which our ancestors were unacquainted," noted an anonymous writer in the *Monthly Mirror* in 1808. "Formerly when a hero exclaimed 'I *can no more*,' he was carried off kicking and the curtain dropped. But the leader of the band now answers that observation by another. '*If you can't, we can*,' and the whole orchestra roars approbation."[5]

Given the licensing mandates in the early nineteenth-century London theatres—as well as the changing demographics of theatre neighborhoods and audiences—theatre managers had to be creative in how they handled the role of music in any dramatic genre. British as well as American playbills from this time almost always announced the genre of the play as well as its spectacular effects, and reviews and other eyewitness accounts make clear that audiences not only expected a play to develop and be resolved in accordance with its genre but also expected to hear specific types of music. Naval airs or hornpipes, for example, were essential in any "nautical burletta" given at the Surrey Theatre, patronized by sailors and dockworkers. The Adelphi in the Strand, in contrast, could count on a more fashionable and literate audience. Hence any "dramatic burletta" performed there in the 1820s and 1830s would invariably feature lyrical songs in the new Italianate style.

Similar links between theatres and types of music existed in New York as well. For several decades the Park Theatre ("Old Drury") attracted the highest class of audiences. In the 1820s and 1830s entr'acte features nearly always included excerpts from symphonies and operas. In the 1820s challenges to the Park's supremacy came from new theatres such as the Chatham Garden and the Lafayette, where managers incorporated more diverse dramatic and musical entertainment. The Chatham, for example, imitated Astley's Amphitheatre and featured musically accompanied equestrian shows, ballets of action, and serious pantomimes such as *Robinson Crusoe*. The Bowery Theatre, built in 1826, was designed as a fashionable rival to the Park; but as its neighborhood became more ethnically diverse, managers Charles Gilfert and Thomas Hamblin cultivated a working-class audience, with dramatic and musical entertainments reflecting this diversity. Interpolated ballads such as "Bonny Doon," "Jeremy Fickle," and "Hurrah for the Red, White, and Blue," for example, were sung to great applause in the late 1820s.[6]

The greatest challenge in this book is to discuss music for the early English popular drama in London's public theatres. Musical sources are practically nonexistent. We cannot rely on newspaper accounts, because London's critics were prejudiced against the minors and the best of them would not even attend these theatres. But we can turn to the so-called acting-editions that began to appear once a version of a play was successful. A good example of this distinctive format is Holcroft's *Tale of Mystery*. Pixerécourt's published text of *Coelina* is literary: it provides a clear description of each character, lays out the actor's lines and the basic action, and numbers scenes in the French style, according to characters' entrances and exits. *A Tale of Mystery*, however, abounds in various specific staging instructions, scenic cues, and music cues. One reviewer of the publication noted: "So numerous, and so minutely detailed [are the] instructions to the performers that the printed play seems rather addressed to the manager of a theatre than to the public at large."[7] This was indeed the point. Holcroft never intended his play to be read as literature. The text is a blueprint for performance, with each component part contributing to the whole. Even if we had no published score to corroborate we would still know exactly where music was placed. Moreover, Henry Tresham's illustrations were clues to important tableaux (picture poses) for the actors to strike at dramatic turning points in production. Most of the popular dramas for the early nineteenth century exist in the form of these acting-editions that publishers and dramatic agents made available for public and amateur performances. Among the most prominent are Cumberland's Minor Drama, Duncombe's Acting Editions, Miller's Modern Acting Drama, Richardson's New Minor Drama, and Turner's Dramatic Library in Philadelphia. They can make difficult reading for the uninitiated, but their explicitness—down to cut and color of the costumes, precise stage positions, meticulous transliteration of vernacular speech, and specifics as to instrumental *melos*—is a valuable key to interpreting melodramatic performance of this period.

The Royal Coburg Theatre

Though the melodrama in England took root in the patent theatres it did not take long for the minors to realize that the popular heroes of melodrama were a huge box-office draw for their local constituents. By the 1820s the matter had gotten out of hand, resulting in legal battles over repertoire between the minor and the majors, in part because of the vast amount of piracy in the theatre industry.[8] In January 1821, for example, Robert Elliston at Drury Lane had bought and produced *Thérèse, The Orphan of Geneva*, a play by John Howard Payne. By February the Coburg Theatre under the management of Joseph Glossop had staged a remarkably similar version of *Thérèse*. Elliston sued on the grounds that the play was stolen from him. He was right. Not only did Glossop and a young John M. Maddox admit to returning nightly to copy the entire play from the pit, but they brought their scene painter with them so that he could sketch the visual effects in the production.[9]

The Royal Coburg Theatre (later renamed the Victoria and eventually known as the "Old Vic") serves as a prime example of the early nineteenth-century popular theatre, whose early history still remains to be told. It was built in Lambeth, on the south side of the Thames, shortly after the completion of the Waterloo Bridge in 1817. The theatre was designed by a French-born architect and stage machinist named Rudolphe Cabanel, who used a crescent shape in the style of a Parisian secondary theatre. Built in an age before theatre safety laws, the original house could hold approximately 3,800 people. At the back of both the dress and upper circles were large saloons, the lower one elegantly fitted up with paintings of military victories and views of famous Italian marinas by John Thomas Serres, the house scenic artist. There was a shallow well for the orchestra in front of the stage, capable of accommodating thirty musicians and outfitted with some eighteen music desks, each with a lamp on either side fitted with a reflecting shade.[10] The stage itself was huge—conceived for spectacle—and the sheer size of the auditorium meant that actors needed to raise their voices and enlarge their gestures to be heard and seen at the back of the gallery.[11] The area surrounding the theatre had a reputation as a rough neighborhood. But because it was so close to the bridge, the theatre—outside the jurisdiction of London's licensing laws—at first attracted a "fashionable audience," many of whom came over from the city. Playbills announced that "extra patroles [*sic*] are engaged for the bridge and roads leading to the theatre, and particular attention will be paid to the lighting of the same." But this alone was not effective in drawing London playgoers, and the theatre quickly became a denizen for the locals. Lambeth parish in 1818 had a population of around 272,000, but it was still largely an industrial working-class area. Charles Matthews remembered the Coburg: "the lower orders rush there in mobs and in shirt-sleeves, applaud frantically, drink gingerbeer, munch apples, crack nuts, call the actors by their Christian names, and throw them orange-peel and apples by way of bouquets." When the gallery was full, with 1,800 persons, it could be a crowded and noisy place. The audience not only carried on among themselves but shouted back at the performers or even at the crew if the set malfunctioned. "Respectable West-enders," another source decreed, "would not have dared to enter the house without an unquestioned life assurance."[12]

An 1822 review of Henry M. Milner's *The Enchanted Castle, or The Sleeping Beauty in the Wood* gives some sense of the hurly-burly of a Coburg production from these years. It is worth reprinting in full.

> The galleries were thunderstruck at the noise—and to show themselves judges of fine acting, returned a deafening shout of applause—this, joined to what is technically termed behind the scenes, the "Crash," which was unceasingly and unmercifully worked in every scene, the hoarse trumpets, squeaking violins, and gruff bass of the musicians in the orchestra, who apparently enjoyed the storm, formed such a "*concord* of horrible *discord*," as completely "split the ears of the groundlings" and sent us home to our beds with an aching head, which we have scarcely yet got rid of. To all appearance Bedlam had broke loose. We really must beg of Mr. Milner to present us with something a little more rational . . . [than] "magic fires," "thunderbolts," "gushing waters," "subterranean fires," "fiery dragons," etc.[13]

The Coburg opened on 11 May 1818 under Joseph Glossop's proprietorship with a full evening of entertainment, beginning with the kind of sensational melodrama for which it would become famous.[14] This was *Trial by Battle, or Heaven Defend the Right*. The subject was inspired by a notorious court case that had concluded only two weeks before. One Abraham Thornton was accused of the murder of Mary Ashford by her brother. Ashford met Thornton at a dance, and they were seen leaving together. She was found drowned the next morning. Thornton was acquitted because the court could not find conclusive evidence for his role in her death. When her brother appealed, Thornton was again incarcerated. Resorting to a medieval option still on the English law books, Thornton challenged Ashford to a trial by combat (or judicial duel), which the court accepted. Ashford recoiled from such a solution, so Thornton was freed. (He quickly relocated to the United States.)

London must have been abuzz with suspicions about the case, and Thornton's audacity gave house playwright William Barrymore an idea. He would give the Coburg audience what the trial did not, an actual hand-to-

FIGURE 9. *"Royal Coburg Theatre as It Appeared on Opening Night, May 11th, 1818": detail from William Herbert and Robert Wilkinson,* Londina Illustrata: Graphic and Historic Memorials . . . , *vol. 2 (London: R. Wilkinson, 1819). Digital Collections and Archives, Tufts University Library*

hand combat between the two men (Fig. 9). The story would have to be moved to an earlier time, of course, so Barrymore fell back again on the gothic symbolism of castles and the aristocratic abuse of power. Thornton is now a baron, Ashford and her brother are peasants. The baron abducts the Mary Ashford character (Geralda) but instead of killing her—which would preclude a genuine happy ending—he kills her father. The brother discovers the crime and challenges the baron. Because none of the baron's knights will take up the challenge for him, he must fight the duel himself. He is killed in a climactic tournament sequence, and justice is served to shouts of victory. (Curiously, Sir Walter Scott's *Ivanhoe*, published the following year, culminates in a similar climactic trial by battle.)

This two-act play had at least forty music cues (not counting the opening "glee" and various trumpet flourishes). Each of these is carefully specified throughout Duncombe's published version, which includes a description of the costumes, a list of properties, and "the whole of the stage business."[15] Music brought characters on and took them off and appears in nearly every action sequence, including the abduction, the murder and false arrest, and several fight scenes (except, oddly, the final combat itself, though the artist's rendering shows the orchestra playing during this battle). In *Road to the Stage* (1827) Leman Thomas Rede helps us get a sense for music's complete integration in a melodrama such as *Trial by Battle*. Actors were expected to carry out their business to so many bars of music. Entrances and exits were frequently signaled merely by a change in the music's tune or affect. Sometimes actions needed to occur on a precise note. The actors were expected to learn the music and count the beats to coordinate their movements accordingly. "One visit to the Coburg Theatre," Rede counseled his actors, "will convince any skeptic how much effect is enhanced by attention to these minutiae. The things are indeed little, but the effect is great."[16]

Trial by Battle ran for several weeks, sharing bills with Barrymore's *Wallace, the Hero of Scotland*, the exotic fairy tale of *Alzora and Nerine*, a harlequinade, and various comic songs and other entertainments as oleos between the dramatic fare. When the winter season began in November, the Coburg playbill announced the names of the entire company, including the band. With violin in hand Thomas Hughes led an orchestra of nineteen personnel.[17] These consisted of nine strings (five violins, one cello, and three basses [no violas]), five woodwinds (flute, oboe, clarinet, and two bassoons), three brass (two players who doubled on French horn and trumpet and one trombone), a harpist, and a drummer. This is a reasonable number of musicians, although three double basses and two bassoons equaling a full quarter of the ensemble would certainly have resulted in the "gruff bass" heard by the reviewer cited above. Besides Hughes, a "Mr. Crouch" led the music for pantomimes, with Mr. Leclerq providing the choreography. In addition to the theatrical fare, the theatre also hosted sacred concerts during the Lenten season with guest leaders such as Montague (Monte) Corri and George Ware, William Ware's father. The orchestra was greatly augmented for oratorios and symphonic works (such as Kotzwara's *Battle of Prague*, typical of symphonic fare at the Coburg).

Shortly after the Coburg opened the *Theatrical Inquisitor* called it "the prettiest theatre in the metropolis . . . with the worst company we ever saw."[18] The Coburg was a stock theatre, which meant that it had a resident stable of actors and even house writers. The term "stock" in a dramatic sense goes back at least to the early eighteenth century, when it was used in reference to plays ("stock of plays"). By the early nineteenth century the term was applied to all aspects of a resident company, stock author, stock actors, stock tragedian, stock characters, and so forth. As was typical of most nineteenth-century stock theatres, the Coburg maintained a team of minor actors who were pressed into service for nearly every production. Prominent members of the company assumed the leading roles, including Mr. and Mrs. William Barrymore, Mr. and Mrs. Rowbotham, George B. Davidge (who was also actor-manager), a Miss Holland and Miss Watson, and a young John Cartlich. The Coburg also brought in "star" actors, as they were already called in the 1820s. These guest artists, such as Junius Brutus Booth in *Richard III* and Thomas P. Cooke re-creating his role of Long Tom Coffin in *The Pilot*, appeared for a single performance or a short run of a play. Many stock theatres featured local talent, and this was partly true of the Coburg as well. But several of the company assembled by Glossop and Davidge came from Drury Lane or Sadler's Wells or from Theatres Royal in Bath, York, and Edinburgh. Some actors remained at the Coburg for years. Some left after a season or two, such as the Barrymores, who went to New York to act at the Park and the Bowery theatres, or the Rowbothams, who went to Baltimore.

The scene painters and machinists also were thorough professionals. The Coburg Theatre's impressive 34-foot-wide by 92-foot-deep stage as well as the scenery, costumes, and properties "cannot be surpassed by those of any theatre in the kingdom," a reviewer noted.[19] Davidge made every effort throughout his tenure as actor-manager to attract more than local attention to the Coburg. His choice of overtly political and nationalist repertory (*Wallace, Napoleon Bonaparte*) and winning the patronage of the popular Queen Caroline were subversive maneuvers to overturn the economic and political monopolies of the Royal Theatres, as David Worrall convincingly argues.[20] In 1821 the Coburg installed its famous looking-glass curtain, made of sixty-three cut mirrors embedded in a gilt frame. It was regarded as one of the sites of London. In 1823 the New Surrey Theatre opened just a short distance away, and the Coburg responded in the spirit of competition, producing not only well-known melodramas such as *Timour the Tartar* in 1826 (with King's music) but also its own versions of current novels and plays, including Mary Shelley's *Frankenstein*. Perhaps the competition was at times *too* pressing, for the Coburg seemed to have had more than its share of accidents and tragedies. During a performance of *Timour* an actress was nearly crushed when a bridge collapsed under her horse. That same year an oil explosion in the machinery room killed one of the stage crew and maimed several others. After the last incident Davidge promised his wary audience that the theatre would switch to all-gas lighting (both Covent Garden and Drury Lane had already converted). By the early 1830s the *National Standard* recognized the Coburg as one of the very best theatres in the metropolis, but the neighborhood was still one of the worst.[21]

Though no music has yet been found for any original Coburg productions during the 1820s, a few surviving sources for *Frankenstein*, given in its first version by Henry Milner on 18 August 1823, suggest how it may have been integrated. The choice of topic reveals the sense of competition among the popular theatres, for a version of Shelley's novel had opened in July at the English Opera House (or Lyceum) in the Strand. There it was called *Presumption, or The Fate of Frankenstein*, adapted for that theatre by Richard Brinsley Peake and with music by resident leader John Watson. The audiences at *Presumption* hissed, hailed, shuddered, had nightmares, and yet returned to see it again.[22]

A review of *Presumption* conveys a fascinating aspect of theatre music at the time. It was produced as a musical play—no doubt for licensing reasons—with songs and choruses. Watson's music for these (which has not been found) is generally praised in the reviews. When it came to the melodramatic music necessary for the play, however, the *London Times* noted: "there were at least thirteen movements which we have heard in every melodrama for the last five-and-twenty years, not to speak of their occasional performance in operas, overtures, and between the acts."[23] Someone (perhaps Peake himself or T. P. Cooke, who handled much of the stage business) cobbled together bits of music in keeping with the *melos* of the moment for the considerable amount of action and pantomime music required for this adaptation.[24] Peake's musical demands are remarkably specific, such as the link at the opening of act 2: "The hurried music from the close of the first act to play in continuance until this scene is discovered." The author at times also requested that a character "speak through music." When Peake's *Frankenstein* was given at Covent Garden in 1830, the playbills stated that the music was by Watson, no doubt referring to the songs and choruses. The craftsman behind the compiled action and dialogue music remains a mystery.

The Coburg mounted its challenge the following month as *Frankenstein, or The Demon of Switzerland*. The cast was entirely from the stock, with Mr. Stanley as Dr. Frankenstein and "the most gentlemanly" and "much beloved" house favorite Mr. Bengough as the creature. Thomas Hughes provided the music. The managers of the Lyceum may have threatened to sue, for the Coburg put away its well-attended production after ten days, citing the manager's "pledge to the community to produce constant variety."[25] When it was revived three years later, Henry Milner prepared a thorough revision, mingling bits of Shelley's plot with a recent French melodrama from the Théâtre Porte Saint-Martin called *The Magician and the Monster. The Man and the Monster, or The Fate of Frankenstein* opened at the Coburg on 3 July 1826. Perhaps in part to upstage the Lyceum—or to acknowledge that no music had been lifted from the French version—the playbill for the Coburg *Frankenstein* announced: "the music entirely new by Mr. T. Hughes."[26]

The revised version was also designed for a "star," the inimitable O. Smith (Richard John Smith) as the creature. Smith acquired the "O" because of his close connection with the title role of John Fawcett's *Obi, or Three-Fingered Jack*.[27] Smith was undoubtedly the first true villain of the popular melodramatic stage and the model for generations to come. He began his career in pantomime, and Elliston brought him to Drury Lane late in 1824 to create the role of Samiel in Henry Bishop's adaptation of *Der Freischütz*. In a review of that production, the *Theatrical Observer* called him "the King of Terrors—the arch fiend."[28] "In parts of deep villainy," *Drama* noted, "where more depends upon gesture than declamation, Mr. Smith is clearly an unrivaled actor."[29] The *Lady's Magazine* dubbed him a "performer of mysterious and monstrous characters."[30] As Shelley's "unnameable" monster, listed in the playbills only as "(* * * * * *)," Smith was dressed in earthy tones with meaningful touches of color: a dark-brown Greek shirt heightened with blue as if to show his muscles, a closed vest, a broad black leather belt, and leggings of a very pale yellowish brown. Because the creature did not have the power of speech, Smith had to create the character entirely through mime.

In Milner's version, Dr. Victor Frankenstein (played by Mr. Rowbotham) is working in a palace in Sicily under the patronage of a noble. In scene 2 Frankenstein rejoices about the forthcoming night in which he plans to activate the monster. His servant Strutt (comic E. Lewis) has been shut out. With the help of another servant Strutt puts a ladder to the window of the pavilion so that he can spy on his master. A bright flash of light from inside frightens them off, and the scene moves to the interior of the pavilion. Frankenstein is found next to a table covered with a large cloth. The space is set up like a laboratory. At this point in both Duncombe and Lacy's editions—both "printed from the promptbook"—music is cued to begin. "Courage, Frankenstein," the inventor says. "Glut thy big soul with exultation. Enjoy a triumph never yet attained by mortal man." Music begins, as the doctor eagerly lays his hand on the chest of the figure to feel for breathing. "The breath of life now swells its bosom." *Music*. "As the cool night breeze plays upon its brow it will awake to sense and motion." Music continues as he rolls back the black covering to reveal a colossal human figure of a cadaverous livid complexion. It slowly begins to rise, gradually attaining an erect posture. Frankenstein observes with intense anxiety as the figure, eventually fully perpendicular, glares at him. "Merciful heaven! And has the fondest visions of my fancy awakened to this terrible reality? A form of horror, which I scarcely dare to look upon. Instead of the fresh colour of humanity he wears the livid hue of the damp grave." The scene continues, but no additional music cues are specified. The monster begins to move freely. Frankenstein is horrified and mistakes the monster's reaching toward him as aggression. He draws his sword to defend himself, but the monster grabs it from him and snaps it in two. Frankenstein rushes from the laboratory. The monster tries to follow him; finding himself vexed, he smashes the door from its hinges and goes out.

Scene 4 takes place directly outside the pavilion, as Frankenstein rushes out and locks the door behind him. In a short speech, Frankenstein is mortified that his years of planning and knowledge of science have only resulted in the kind of creature that would terrify anybody in its presence. A tremendous crash is heard—a genuine Coburg "crash"—as the monster breaks through the door of the pavilion. Frankenstein cries out: "He is here! I have imbued him with a giant's strength, and he will use it to pluck down ruin on his maker's head." Another music cue follows, as the monster approaches him with gestures of conciliation. "Do not approach me," Frankenstein warns. "Touch me and I will straightway strike thee back to nothingness!" The creature reaches out to him, but Frankenstein again misreads his curiosity and tries to stab him with his dagger. The monster knocks the weapon out of Frankenstein's hand and reaches down to fetch it. While he is momentarily lost in contemplation of its form, Frankenstein steals off. Realizing that he has been abandoned again, the monster wanders off in search of his creator.

What evidence do we have for the kind of music that Hughes might have fashioned for the laboratory scene? The placement of cues in the text seems to imply that music is required to change mood, expressing first Frankenstein's anticipation, then his excitement (perhaps even exaggerated to megalomania), and finally the joy turning to terror as the cadaverous figure rises. If the far more cultivated English Opera House audience would have shuddered and hissed, then surely the anxiety growing in the Coburg audience would have been intensely audible. O. Smith's reputation in demonic roles would have had audiences on the edge of their seats as he slowly rose from the table. Hughes would probably have had to increase the volume of his orchestra to ride the audience's murmurs and gasps. In addition, Milner's three specifications for music in the scene represent different types of dramatic cues. During the first two, before the monster awakens, Frankenstein speaks through the music (or the music continues to play under his speech). The third is more of an action cue, as the monster assumes lifelike characteristics and the creator's first reckoning with his creation takes place.

It is somewhat easier to envision music for the cue in scene 4. Milner's request for music here is clearly meant to humanize the monster, to encourage audiences to empathize with him and impart some qualities of tenderness and perhaps even wonder to this mute character. In Milner's version, the creature is born innocent. He learns hatred, jealousy, and murder through the hostile conditions into which he is repeatedly forced. His muteness, as Jane Moody so perceptively notes, "highlights the creature's capacity for intense feeling and psychological pain," emotions that must certainly have been partly communicated through music.[31] The doctor expresses a great deal of emotion through speech, whereas the creature is constantly in need of music to help interpret his bodily language. The creature's awakening in the Coburg *Frankenstein* represents one of the key moments in the development of the popular drama, particularly as the pervasive aspect of speechlessness so crucial to the first Covent Garden melodrama carries over into the popular theatres. Peter Brooks perhaps phrased it better than anyone: "Different kinds of drama have their corresponding sense deprivations: for tragedy, blindness, since tragedy is about insight and illumination; for comedy, deafness, since comedy is concerned with misunderstanding, failures of communication; and for melodrama, muteness, since melodrama . . . is about expression."[32]

Fitzball and Rodwell at the Adelphi

If the Coburg typified the performance of melodrama at this time in the public theatres, the Adelphi developed its own unique personality, beginning with the management of Daniel Terry and Frederick Yates in 1825, who were seen as the team that brought a civilized and refined character to the popular drama.[33] The theatre had first opened in 1806 as the Sans Pareil, built on the Strand (and sometimes also called by that name). In 1819 it was bought by playwright James Thomas Rodwell and stage manager Willis Jones, who redesigned the interior and installed a dazzling gas chandelier suspended from the center dome. Until it was remodeled again in 1858 it was known as an intimate house, where dramas could be acted less broadly than at Astley's or the Coburg.[34] As a minor theatre it was of course licensed for burletta, though Terry and Yates were able to get away with bending the rules: many of their productions were more like camouflaged spoken dramas. Like its Parisian counterpart the Porte Saint-Martin, the Adelphi eventually gained a reputation as a theatre in the West End of London specializing in melodramas of crime and passion. In the 1820s Terry and Yates gathered together a magnificent company of actors, including John Reeve, Tyrone Power, Mrs. Edward Fitzwilliam (Ellen Chaplin), and Ellen Brunton (who became Mrs. Yates). They also hired the services of three of the early nineteenth-century's most prolific melodramatic playwrights: Douglas Jerrold, John Baldwin Buckstone, and Edward Fitzball, who served as principal author.

Fitzball, labeled "the melodramatist of the macabre" by a recent biographer, began his theatrical career in 1820 by writing for the Surrey and then in 1825 started his long association with the Adelphi.[35] Between 1825 and 1840 the force of his imagination was imprinted on the English dramatic world through his plays. In his autobiography Fitzball credits several musicians with whom he worked over his career: William Hawes, Henry Bishop, Michael Balfe, William Vincent Wallace, George Herbert Rodwell (the playwright's brother), and Edward Loder.[36] The most important was undoubtedly Rodwell (1800–1852)—or George Herbert, as he sometimes billed himself in honor of the seventeenth-century poet. In fact, Fitzball and Rodwell might almost be said to be the first long-standing British playwright-composer team of nineteenth-century popular drama.

Whether melodramatic music in the theatres of the 1820s was cobbled together or whether it was announced as "entirely new," few sources have been located that allow us to investigate these claims further. A bit more evidence exists for Rodwell's theatre music, though surprisingly less than we would expect, given his prominence in the theatrical life of London in the 1820s and 1830s. Many of the songs that he wrote for plays were published and exist today in music libraries. They reveal his affection for the spun lyricism of the new Italianate *bel canto* style. But little else from the scores he compiled and composed for thirteen of Fitzball's twenty-four Adelphi melodramas seems to have survived.

The size of the orchestra in the Adelphi's early years, when songs were still a prominent feature of most productions, was large for a metropolitan minor theatre. Sometimes it equaled the scale of Drury Lane. On a playbill for Rodwell's *Valmondi, or The Unhallowed Sepulchre*, an 1824 "romantic burletta spectacle," the entire orchestra of forty musicians is identified by name. The first of these is William Russell, who on this occasion served as leader, with violin and bow in hand.

Fitzball and Rodwell began their collaboration with *The Pilot, or A Tale of the Sea* in 1825. They were famous with audiences throughout Europe and the Americas largely for their unique amalgamation of the "gothic" and the "nautical" melodrama. During the 1820s Fitzball and Rodwell produced *The Flying Dutchman, or The Phantom Ship* (1826), *The Red Rover, or The Mutiny of the Dolphin* (1828), and *The Floating Beacon, or The Norwegian Wreckers* (1829, original version for the Surrey in 1824).

The Adelphi was located within the jurisdiction of the Lord Chamberlain, so Fitzball was required to submit a copy of each play to the official licenser. The manuscript of *The Flying Dutchman* introduces the play as a "burletta in three acts." It was clearly intended to impress the reader as a musical piece; the first act contains choruses, dances, recitatives and arias, and a ballad for Lestelle Vanhelm, the starry-eyed heroine. Like Pocock's *The Miller and His Men* (Covent Garden, 1813), the work has a lot of music at the beginning—almost like an opera—and then devolves into a spoken play, with the exception of an invisible chorus at the end of act 2. Perhaps Fitzball did not expect the licenser to read much beyond the first act or so. In any case the cues for affective music remain consistent throughout the whole manuscript and are always double-underlined, perhaps so the licenser would not miss them. When the mysterious sea captain Vanderdecken delicately pulls Lestelle's letter from his pocket (in act 1, scene 3), Fitzball specified a "symphony on the harp." (This was simplified to "music" in the published version.)

The Flying Dutchman has retained a kind of mystique in the theatrical world, having been based on an old seafaring legend told in many forms and guises by sailors that had become known to English readers largely through a story in *Blackwood's Magazine* in May 1821. Vanderdecken, who was known to boast that he would have his way in spite of the devil, cursed the storms that prevented him from sailing around the Cape of Good Hope. When asked by the well-meaning crew of a passing vessel if he would be putting into port for the night, he roared that he would rather confront the storm till Judgment Day. He has never been seen since, except by sailors who sometimes spot his ghostly ship, known as the *Flying Dutchman*. Fitzball's play holds special significance for musicians because it served as a key influence for Richard Wagner's 1845 opera of that name. An advertisement in the *Theatrical Observer* on 11 December 1826 stated that Rodwell's music in *The Flying Dutchman* was to be published by Goulding and D'Almaine, but so far no copy has ever turned up. The only items actually printed were a duet, "'Tis the Hour," and Lestelle's ballad in act 2, "Return, O My Love." Nearly every review of the play remarked on the ballad, and people were known to swoon over it. As playwright J. M. Morton recalled years later:

> It used to be said that the perfection of music as allied to the drama was in *The Flying Dutchman*, but this probably arose from the fact that the musical numbers of *The Flying Dutchman* were all original and of exceptional beauty, while those of most melodramas were eclectic in nature and culled from the composers of all ages and climes. Thackeray worshipers will remember how that immortal reveled in the melodies of the *Dutchman* and grew sentimental over the loveliest ballad of the age, which Senta [*sic*] sings when she moans "Return, oh my love, and we'll never, never part." [Morton forgets that Fitzball's heroine was Lestelle, not Wagner's Senta.][37]

Fitzball's reputation as master of the macabre meant that as soon as his plays opened in one theatre others clamored to obtain them. *The Flying Dutchman* was performed in English-speaking theatres all over the world. It was staged at the Park Theatre in New York in 1827, only months after it opened at the Adelphi. John Ireland noted forty years later in *Records of the New York Stage* that it was still frequently revived.[38] We can only make some assumptions about Rodwell's music: much of the evidence—like the Dutchman himself—seems to have vanished. No doubt leaders at some houses were forced to cobble together appropriate music, as this was before theatrical agencies began to distribute such things. There seems to be no record that Goulding and D'Almaine circulated manuscript orchestra parts for unpublished theatre music. Later in the century, however, Samuel French owned rental rights to Fitzball's play and as late as 1882 listed band parts available to accompany it. Although no copy of this rental music has been found, a set of manuscript parts recently turned up for *The Flying Dutchman* produced by the theatrical company of Martin and Bella Golden, who toured the central and southwestern United States in the

1860s and 1870s. These parts include the music that Rodwell composed for Lestelle's "Return, O My Love" as well as music to fit the duet and choruses in the original, and all the cues for action music match up exactly with those in Fitzball's manuscript. The Goldens acquired much of their music from theatrical dealers in New York and Philadelphia, so this score probably is indeed a later-generation copy of Rodwell's music. With a small caveat to the reader, I move forward with this analysis on that assumption.[39]

The original cast of 4 December 1826 featured the versatile Thomas P. Cooke as Vanderdecken. Cooke was also responsible for staging much of the "melodramatic business" (which generally referred to any action that required musical accompaniment). Daniel Terry played Captain Peppercoal. Lestelle was played by Miss Boden, who had created the role of Elvina in Rodwell's opera *Valmondi* of 1824. Because of her youth and noted singing ability, she went on to play lyrical ingénue parts at the Adelphi, the English Opera House, and other theatres. In these early years she was known more for the sweetness of her singing voice than for her acting ability.[40] *The Flying Dutchman* ran uninterrupted to the end of the season—87 nights, which was nearly a record in those days. When the season started up in October, the play was on the boards again. It was revived in the fall of 1829, when O. Smith took over the role of Vanderdecken. While T. P. Cooke was unmatched when playing a British sailor, O. Smith was better suited to the Dutchman's dark demonic character. His bloodcurdling laugh at the end of the play, it was said, could be imitated but never surpassed. (Other changes in the cast included Mr. Butler as Coalpepper and Mrs. Fitzwilliam as Lestelle.)

The play takes place in and near an old fortress on the seacoast of South Africa. The first act introduces the main characters, particularly Lestelle Vanhelm, who is awaiting the arrival from Amsterdam of her intended, Peter Von Bummel, a lily-livered coxcomb she has never met. Lestelle is a romantic and melancholy young woman who thrives on ghost stories like that of Vanderdecken, a Dutch sea captain whose mysterious portrait hangs on the wall of the fortress. The legend among the sailors, which they probably told their daughters to scare them away from swabs, is that the Dutchman returns every hundred years in the hopes of luring a young bride to his cave beneath the sea. Lestelle's uncle, Captain Peppercoal, laughs the story off, although he admits that the old oak chest beneath a portrait of a shepherdess is said to contain the clothes of the Dutchman's wife. In the final scene of act 1, on board the ship carrying Von Bummel, the crew rescues a drowning man, who turns out to be the long-dead sea captain. We learned earlier in a scene with Rockalda, evil spirit of the deep, that the one condition of Vanderdecken's return to human life is that he must not speak to any mortal. Communicating entirely through gesture (and instrumental music), he is able to outsmart Von Bummel, steal his marriage license, and magically disappear. The men are horrified when they see him hovering above the water, his ghostly ship in the sky behind him (created at the Adelphi by the projection of an image from a magic lantern slide).

Act 2 opens with a comic scene followed by a scene in Lestelle's chambers. She confides in her maid Lucy her deep fascination with the old portrait and intones a mysterious ballad said to have been sung by Vanderdecken's wife when he failed to return from his journey. During the second verse the sea chest behind them eerily creaks open—visible only to the audience—and Vanderdecken emerges slowly. He listens intently to her singing. As the final gentle moaning of her song dies away, he accidentally lets the lid fall with a crash, startling the young women. Still undetected, the Dutchman vanishes. Lestelle and Lucy clutch one another in fear and scream at a sudden loud banging on the door. It turns out to be only Captain Peppercoal.

What follows is reconstructed in Figure 10. The musical insertions, placed into the text where they are cued, are from the violin-leader book (Golden Collection), where they are also numbered (L.D. refers to "stage left door," "left" from the actor's point of view).

Nearly all of these music cues accompany mimed action. Cue no. 17 brings on the Dutchman, who pretends to be the expected groom. The *melos* is confidant and formal. Cue no. 18 starts with an infamous *forte* "chord," an operatic alerting device that nearly always portends a change of mood or events. Here it signal's Vanderdecken's "start" (a physical gesture of recognition attributed to Garrick). The Dutchman is startled by Lestelle's resemblance to his long-dead wife. Suddenly the tuneful *melos* played by the clarinet is like a distant echo of her song, wafting across the centuries. No. 19 begins with an even more shocking chord, this time cutting off Lucy in mid-sentence. Vanderdecken realizes that he is about to be discovered, so with a magical wave of his hand—and some tumbling sixteenth notes—he transforms the portrait so that it resembles the hapless Von Bummel, soon to arrive. The maid instantly notices the change, and her reference to "Old Nick" betrays her lower-class superstitions. Then Peppercoal encourages Vanderdecken to speak, and the string shivering of no. 20 reflects the Dutchman's momentary panic. How can he escape detection? Can he possibly fool them all? With three silent gestures, accompanied by the three forceful statements in music no. 21 (*risoluto*), Vanderdecken unambiguously conveys his physical disability. Lestelle is taken aback. Peppercoal seems about to renege on his permission. With the dashing expectant opening of music no. 22, Vanderdecken improvises a way out of his predicament. To this surging music, he runs to the table and begins writing. When he hands the note to Peppercoal, the *melos* changes. Over soft and tiptoeing strings, the captain reads Vanderdecken's outlandish excuse. The groom's muteness is temporary, it seems, the result of an accident en route. The full orchestra lets loose a sigh of relief, and Peppercoal goes on to make a joke about it. Shortly afterward Smutta, a black slave, shows up with his heavy dialect and confuses everyone by introducing the real Von Bummel.

In some scenes the music cues are longer. Act 3, scene 2, for example, takes place in a dramatic setting: the mouth of a cave beneath a gigantic cliff, with the violent sea rolling in. The orchestra accompanies the opening of the scene with some forty measures of music (no. 35). Meanwhile Vanderdecken enters carrying the unconscious Lestelle and tries to revive her with a sprinkling of water. She awakens in fright and begs not to be taken further. The mysterious sound of Lestelle's ballad, played offstage by a ghostly flute and harp, stops the Dutchman dead in his tracks. Lestelle also seems almost hypnotized, which allows Vanderdecken to lead her into the abyss. After an intervening front scene at Coalpepper's fortress, the action returns to the interior of the cave, at the back of which is situated a large stone altar and a magic book. The sequence—Lestelle speaking, Vanderdecken miming—is entirely accompanied by music. Vanderdecken lays down his torch alongside the book and tries to persuade Lestelle to sign the marriage vow, but Lestelle refuses. When the book flies open to reveal Vanderdecken's name, Lestelle screams. Coalpepper's men arrive in the nick of time and engage the Dutchman in a furious sword fight. But though the men stab repeatedly at the abductor's bluish body, their attempts to kill him are in vain. The Dutchman begins to laugh maniacally at their consternation. Forgetting himself, he speaks for the first time, breaking his vow of silence and the spell that renders him in human form ("Music expressive of great bodily agony which he displays"). Looking at Lestelle pleadingly, he points to the magic book. Upon seeing this, one of the sailors grabs the torch and sets fire to it.

Fitzball's manuscript reveals that the music here should identify the Dutchman not as a villain but as a tragic figure. "Music—agony, rage, despair. Vanderdecken, after covering his eyes with his hands, fills up the music." When the Dutchman began to speak, continuous music was no

Peppercoal. [*Enters* L.D. *with a letter in his hand.*] Why, Letty, what's the matter with you: you shrieked out as if you had been—may my ship's anchors come home if your cheeks are not as white as the mainsail after a six months' bleach.

Lestelle. Oh, my dear sir, I've been so terrified.

Captain Peppercoal. What, another hobgoblin story, eh? It's like your thinking the ship's picture in the next room hoisted sail because the moon happened to shine on it, ha, ha! Nonsense—but away with all these moonshine fancies—he's come—ha, ha, ha! the dear boy—he's here.

Lestelle. He, who?

Lucy. Not the Flying Dutchman, I hope?

Peppercoal. No, no, the Walking Dutchman—here he is—here's Von Bummel's hand, sure enough; and here comes young Von Bummel, as like his father as water is to water. Hollo! Smutta! bear to leeward there! clear the gangway! [Music no. 17.
Enter Vanderdecken, shown in by Smutta, L.D.]

Welcome, my dear boy, how are you? how like old Von, to be sure. Well, what sort of a voyage have you had? —I'm afraid rough; you look as if you had been a little sickish, but it's all over now—here's Letty—here's your wife that is to be; look at her—isn't she a trimbuilt vessel, from keel to topmast, eh? [*Lestelle gets to* L.—Music no. 18.]

[*Vanderdecken starts at sight of Lestelle—he takes off his hat and bows to her.*

His eye wanders from her to the picture of the Shepherdess.]

Peppercoal. I see what you mean, why couldn't you speak; you fancy there's a bit of a likeness between that old picture and my Letty; I have heard that said before, though I don't know why it should be, but if you are fond of old pictures, I have plenty of them in this house.

Lucy. Sir, sir, if you talk of likenesses, the one there of the Flying Dutchman is exactly like—[Music no. 19.—*Vanderdecken, unperceived, stretches out his hand, and the portrait of himself changes to a resemblance of Peter Von Bummel.*]

FIGURE 10. The Flying Dutchman, *nos. 17–22. The Golden Family Collection, Working Men's Institute, New Harmony, Indiana*

Peppercoal. Ha, ha, ha! nonsense.

Lucy. But it was like him if Old Nick hadn't changed him this instant.

Peppercoal. Why, Letty, what are you doing there, twiddling up in a corner? Why don't you give the young man a little encouragement? And you [*To Vanderdecken*], why don't you speak to her—bring her to an anchor—Speak to her. [Music no. 20.—*Vanderdecken is somewhat disconcerted*—]

A thought strikes him, and he declares himself dumb. [Music no. 21.]

Lestelle, Lucy. Dumb!

Peppercoal. What does he say?

Lucy. He says he's dumb, sir!

Peppercoal. Oh, then that's what he meant by— [*Mimicks [sic] the action of Vanderdecken.*] Dumb! I didn't bargain for that; but, I say, the dispatches are as dumb as yourself on that subject. [Music no. 22.—*Vanderdecken runs to the table and writes, and gives it to Peppercoal.*]

Peppercoal. Well, come, that's not so bad; and as the women generally like all the talk to themselves, why, perhaps, it may be all the better in the end, and to-morrow shall be the wedding of yourself and Lestelle.

Lestelle. To-morrow, uncle! Uncle—

Peppercoal. Ay, to-morrow: a dumb husband will be all the better for you, and the sooner you're married, the longer you'll have all the talk to yourself; therefore, give me your hand, and give me yours. [*To Vanderdecken.*] You shall be spliced to-morrow morning.

[*A loud knocking is heard at* L.D. *as he is about to join their hands. Enter Smutta, hastily,* L.D.]

Smutta. Oh, massa, there's anoder Mynheer Von Bummer man vid blind old sailor man, and dam large a bear, massa.

Peppercoal. Another Von Bummel? why, there is but one Von Bummel, and here he stands.

longer necessary and sound effects took over. Loud stage thunder provided the counterpoint to his powerful curse: "Malediction! You triumph, but I go to my revenge. Tremble, tremble! The rushing waves which rise to welcome the return of Vanderdecken shall bury ye deep, deep in their unfathomed darkness. Burst, stormy clouds, and overwhelm them." Music resumed as he leapt onto the altar, which sank and vanished amid a flame of red fire. For this final sequence Rodwell wrote forty-eight bars of furious music (mostly in C minor and C diminished harmonies).

Fitzball's instructions for the character to "fill up the music" reveal the degree to which *melos* and drama were fused in conception. In a Fitzball-Rodwell collaboration, music was part of the form, rather than something to be added in rehearsal to facilitate stage business. Except perhaps for the opening chorus in the deep, Lestelle's ballad, and a duet, little of Rodwell's music elevates *The Flying Dutchman* to English opera status, if the sole discovered copy relied on here truly is Rodwell's music. But in terms of establishing the technique of crafting appropriate *melos* to fit both action and dialogue, Rodwell was an ideal match for Fitzball.

As for the rest of this composer's theatre music, the manuscript parts to Peake's *The Skeleton Lover* (Adelphi, 1830) have been preserved in the British Library, consisting of only fourteen short numbers in the style of the *Dutchman* excerpts.[41] Perhaps if more of his music and that of other English and American theatrical composers from these years could be found we would understand which aspects of musical style remained fixed and which changed as melodrama evolved from the historical romances and gothic yarns of the 1820s to the new topicality of the 1830s, an age of growing fascination with modern life and greater social engagement with issues of class difference and the criminal underworld. At this point we can only guess what Rodwell's music must have sounded like for later Adelphi dramas such as *Jack Sheppard* and *The Fortunes of Smike, or A Sequel to Nicholas Nickleby* (both 1839).[42]

Black-Eyed Susan *at the Surrey*

Douglas Jerrold was only twenty-five years old, and already thirteen years out of his boyhood service as a midshipman on the quarterdeck of the *Namur* in the royal navy, when he took his manuscript of his first nautical drama to Robert W. Elliston, manager of the Surrey Theatre. The Surrey was situated in Blackfriars Road, south of the Thames. The theatre, with its circus ring, had been around since 1779 as a site of burlettas and equestrian exhibitions.[43] In 1809 Elliston converted the space to a playhouse for spoken drama, although he could never get a legitimate license. In its early years the Surrey, as Michael Booth notes, "drew a considerable proportion of its patrons from sailors, Thames watermen, shipwrights, dock workers, and all those who lived on the river or sailed on it to the open sea."[44] Hence it became one of London's major venues—along with Sadler's Wells—for nautical pantomimes and burlettas. In the 1810s and 1820s the Surrey repertoire was similar to the Coburg's, except that under Thomas Dibdin's management they produced more melodramas of crime and intrigue as well as reworkings of older tragedies, dramatizations of novels (*The Vicar of Wakefield*, *Ivanhoe*, *Florence Macarthy*), pantomimes, and musical pieces. When Elliston resumed control in 1827, his hope, like Davidge's at the Coburg, was to expand its audience beyond the immediate neighborhood. *Black-Eyed Susan, or All in the Downs* opened on 8 June 1829. By its three-hundredth performance—in the days when most productions ran one to two weeks—Elliston had achieved his goal. "All London went over the water" to see this play, observed the *Gentleman's Magazine*.[45] A writer from the *London Literary Gazette* made a "shameful confession" that he would never think of visiting a minor theatre like the Surrey, fearing what he called the vice of vulgarity, but that he could no longer resist the enthusiasm surrounding Jerrold's long-lived drama and its production.[46]

Black-Eyed Susan was without doubt the most successful of all the British "nautical dramas" produced in the first half of the nineteenth century. Its uncomplicated plot was a model of concise construction: it had clearly defined characters with whom many in the audience could empathize, its subplots were kept to a minimum, it had stirring and recognizable music, and it was lavishly and carefully produced. Within five days the Coburg mounted its own version of the play. *Black-Eyed Susan* opened at Sadler's Wells in August, at New York's Park Theatre in September, and at the Charleston Theatre in December. By the end of November even Covent Garden added it to its boards as an afterpiece. Subsequent performances of the play drew crowds at nearly every professional theatre in the British Isles, Australia, and the Americas—for which the author received not a penny—and at performances by quite a few amateur groups too.

The main reason for the play's initial success was the actor and musician Thomas P. Cooke, who portrayed William, a midshipman in His Majesty's navy. Cooke brought to the role his reputation as one of London's leading melodramatic actors. A review of his silent portrayal of the creature in *Presumption* in 1823 praised his skill in pantomime: "the effect of music upon him is affecting and beautiful in the extreme."[47] As the hero in *Black-Eyed Susan*, the *Literary Gazette* called him "the best sailor that ever trod the boards" and observed an unusual degree of sincerity in his acting.[48] "Mr. Cooke's personation of the sailor is one of the cleverest things of the kind that has ever been exhibited," the *London Times* noted. "His singing and dancing are admirably in character, and the more pathetic parts of his acting irresistibly moving."[49] Eager to capitalize on the Surrey's success, Charles Kemble at Covent Garden in late November engaged Cooke for *Black-Eyed Susan*, which had to be given as an afterpiece. The star was brought over in a hackney coach each night, still wearing his blue jacket and white trousers and sweating from his performance on the Surrey stage.[50] For this version Jerrold shortened the play from three acts to two. By its two-hundredth performance at the Surrey it was eventually moved into the slot of afterpiece as well. (A review of *Black-Eyed Susan* from 1854 reveals that the nimble Cooke, even at the age of sixty-nine, danced a hornpipe that amazed audiences.)[51]

The music for *Black-Eyed Susan* was arranged and composed by Jonathan Blewitt (1782–1853), the London-born organist who had been working since 1813 in theatres and came to the Surrey from Sadler's Wells in 1828. A twenty-one-page piano score (undated) of Blewitt's music to *Black-Eyed Susan* was published in London by the firm of Clementi, Collard, and Collard, and the score is dedicated to Elliston. With a few exceptions, it probably represents the music as originally used, as the title page reads "as performed . . . at the Surrey Theatre." The circumstances of its publication are not known. In November George Bartley was stage manager at Covent Garden when Kemble added *Black-Eyed Susan* to the repertory. Elliston lent Bartley not only some costumes but also what he called Blewitt's "score." Presumably the music was not yet published: in a letter to Kemble sometime later, Elliston acknowledged the manuscript's safe return. Given the play's enormous popularity, it would have been shrewd of Bartley to have a copy made for future use. In fact Covent Garden may have been instrumental in getting Blewitt's score published, as no other play produced at the Surrey—or at any of London's minor theatres—is known to have enjoyed this distinction. (The score of *Black-Eyed Susan* seems to be missing many cues, especially in the first act, so it may reflect the afterpiece version.) Nevertheless, Elliston's account is one of the few pieces of evidence from this period to demonstrate how music for a specific play traveled between theatres.[52]

Duncombe's published playtext indicates that music in the Surrey production consisted "chiefly [of] selections from Dibdin's naval airs." Blewitt's score in fact uses many such tunes. But our focus here is on *how* they were used. In addition to indications in the printed text and the piano score, we have access to a handful of other musical sources. These consist of three sets of manuscript orchestra parts dating from the 1850s and 1860s and found in different theatre collections.[53] In terms of musical cues and actual notes these sources are close to identical, though they are continents apart (and allowing for differences in two- and three-act versions).[54] Unfortunately a copy of the *Black-Eyed Susan* music listed in Samuel French's rental catalogue of 1882 has not been located, but this clearly attests to the popularity of this play even at that late date. (Also, a famous burlesque on *Black Eyed Susan* by F. C. Burnand was first performed in 1866. It is evident from the description that French's music was in relation to the Jerrold play, not the burlesque.)

In order to appreciate the full communicative role of music in this melodrama it is essential to evaluate the connection between *Black-Eyed Susan* and Dibdin's naval songs. Charles Dibdin the Elder composed and performed these songs during a period of vast expansion of the navy between the 1780s and about 1805, a time when the British Tar became a figure of great national pride. By 1829, however, the navy had suffered a number of severe losses and Trafalgar was a fading glory. A simply drawn character like William (married to his childhood sweetheart), who saves the life of his captain while at war and can sing, dance, and play tunes on the violin, is just the sort of sailor idolized by Jerrold and perhaps many others, both seafarers and landlubbers who idealized the British navy. In act 2 William and his messmates return to English soil from the French wars, with the orchestra playing an instrumental version of "The Tar for All Weathers." As a long-standing function of the "talking tune," many in the Surrey audience would have recognized—if not hummed along with—the melody that went with "I sail'd from the Downs in 'The Nancy,' My jib! how she smak'd thro' the breeze!"

William, as played by T. P. Cooke, was both bold and naïve, charming and dangerous, thoughtful and impulsive. He represented an important model in British society, "the return of the wanderer or the prodigal to the fold," as Jeffrey Cox describes it. Sailors, then as now, could be a dangerous lot. The dramatic urgency in William's character and the poignancy surrounding the accidental circumstance of his indictment stem from the need of all returning soldiers to adapt to civilian life, after three years away at sea. Cox argues that a play like *Black-Eyed Susan* allowed "for the conversion of potentially revolutionary and at best nonsocial energy [as in the all-male world of the navy] into socially acceptable forms, roughly conjugal sexuality and work."[55] It seems that the enormously popular *Black-Eyed Susan* may have gone even further than that. It actually served better than any law or injunction to wedge this structure back into place. That is why the graceful, witty, *musical* William epitomized every sailor, even the impressed and violent ones, who might maul each other in the taverns and then go to cheer on their virtuous hero in the theatre. "What do you know of his moral character?" the president of the court-martial asks a sailor in the final scene. "A good deal" is his answer. "He plays on the fiddle like an angel."[56]

The action takes place in and around Deal, a fishing and mining town on the southeast coast, just north of Dover. Act 1 introduces most of the main characters, including Susan (created by an actress known only as Miss Scott), her avaricious uncle Doggrass (played by Dibdin Pitt), and the scheming Tom Hatchet (played by Mr. Yardley).[57] Susan makes her first melancholy appearance pining away for her husband while singing a verse of "All in the Downs," John Gay's well-known eighteenth-century ballad about Black-Eyed Susan and her Sweet William. (According to Disher, the play's original name was actually changed from *Sweet Poll of Plymouth* to accommodate this ballad.)[58] The wistful air, with its minor mode, has a somewhat antique feel next to Dibdin's all-major-key tunes. Doggrass demands that Susan pay the rent or face eviction. He has shady dealings with the villain Hatchet, who manages a smuggling ring down by the shore. Hatchet has designs on Susan; with his illegal cash he ostentatiously pays off her arrears and plans to capitalize on her gratitude, if he succeeds in persuading her that William is dead. At the conclusion of the act a marine sting operation manages to invade Hatchet's den of smugglers. Though Hatchet himself escapes, the fight sequence brings down the curtain to a rowdy action *melos*.

At the beginning of act 2 William's ship has pulled into port. Like the other sailors, he comes ashore hoping to find his wife dutifully waiting for him. As the women came on to greet their returning men, Blewitt's orchestra played the tune "The Standing Toast," with its textual allusion to:

> Some sweetheart or wife that he lov'd as his life
> Each drunk, while he wish'd he could hail her;
> But the standing toast that pleas'd the mo-o-o-o-o-st
> Was the wind that blows, the ship that go-o-o-o-o-oes
> And the lass that loves a sailor.

Susan is not among those waiting, however, having been misguided by Hachet. To a ruddy orchestral flourish derived from the tune, William exits to find her.

Except for the fight sequence, most of the music until this point had been drawn from well-known songs. The second scene of act 2, however, has several short original cues that Blewitt composed to fit the action. The act curtain rose on Susan's cottage without music as William arrives to find the place empty. He soon hears Susan's sobs and men's voices and withdraws to eavesdrop. The orchestra plays four mournful bars of "All in the Downs" as Susan enters. Hatchet has brought along one of his cronies, who poses as a sailor and is in the midst of relating how he saw her husband killed at sea. William can take no more and leaps to Susan's rescue to the accompaniment of three bars of heroic music (cue no. 7). To this "wrapping up" music, Susan falls joyfully into his arms. Another fight scene soon follows—a bold six-bar hurry in major (cue no. 8)—as police arrive and arrest Hachet. In reflection of his joy T. P. Cooke interpolated a well-known song to conclude the scene. "Bound 'Prentice to a Coasting Ship" was a contrafactum of James Sanderson's "Bound 'Prentice to a Waterman," first sung in *Sir Francis Drake* (Surrey, 1800), with new text written by Mr. Ensworth. As William and Susan exit, the orchestra burst into the tune of "Meg of Wapping" (cue no. 10). The scene quickly changed to a public house where the returning seamen are drinking and enjoying the company of several women, including Dolly, Susan's feisty friend and a favorite with the sailors. For this transition into the next scene, the "Meg" tune served—certainly for Surrey audiences of the day—as a typical song that sailors might have sung while swilling ale. In the following scene William and Susan join the sailors. William does his famous dance to the tune of "Sailor's Hornpipe" (no doubt with an encore or two).[59]

Returning from celebrations at the local tavern and full of liquor, Captain Crosstree forces himself upon the waiting Susan, with whom he is infatuated. William, not recognizing the inebriated captain, whose back is turned, comes to Susan's defense with drawn cutlass. His blow is not fatal, but it might just as well have been. It was a capital offense to strike a superior officer in His Majesty's service, with the penalty of death. The music cue for the captain's "you shall be mine" is a ten-bar hurry in C major (cue no. 16 in Blewitt). The *melos* is not threatening in tone (which would reflect Susan's alarm) but instead urgent and heroic, alerting the audience to William's ardent attempt at rescue. The last note (marked with a fermata) is held just

FIGURE 11. *Jonathan Blewitt,* Black-Eyed Susan, *no. 17 (London: Clementi, Collard, and Collard, undated). (f 15460.249.350) Harvard Theatre Collection, Houghton Library, Harvard University*

long enough for William to exclaim "The Captain!" and turn away horror-stricken. Instructions in Blewitt's score to "go on" urge the leader to segue to cue no. 17, an *adagio* in F major (Fig. 11).

The Dibdin tune here is "The Sailor's Return." While Susan falls on her knees and the sailors come to the captain's aid, the *air parlant* reminded the Surrey audience of the culminating line of "Bleak was the morn' when William left his Nancy":

> Sorrow's all a notion, Grief's all in vain;
> Sweet love, take heart, For we but part
> In joy, in joy to meet again.

The stately pace of the melody, played first *pianissimo* under dialogue and then again *forte* by the strings, complemented the stage action with a touch of irony (to those who knew the words) and added considerable poignancy as the drama reached its crisis. The key of F major—designated in nearly every theory treatise from the late eighteenth to the early nineteenth century as characteristic of "calm" (and in one case also "manly vigor")—intensified the pathos of William's acceptance of his actions and provided an important counterweight to the tragic force.[60] This is a wonderful instance of how a major-mode tune can intensify an underlying sadness when played in dramatic counterpoint to a serious turn of events, particularly one in which an innocent and beloved character is entrapped by fate. A performance of *Black-Eyed Susan* today with the original score could not possibly have anything like the effect that it would have had when these tunes (and their well-known words) were an intrinsic part of the audience's experience.

Many theatre historians have written about *Black-Eyed Susan*. But because musical sources do not factor into these studies I would like to complete this analysis by taking a fresh look at the final act through the lens of music. Act 3 in the original full-length version opened with a front scene on a street in Deal, in which we learn that Doggrass has acquired a mysterious packet directed to the captain. With Doggrass's exit, the orchestra plays a few bars of grim "horror" music: a bar of crescendo leading to three sustained diminished seventh chords. As borrowed from opera, the reserved and pointed use of this ambiguous harmony in melodramatic accompaniment came to symbolize a dramatic reversal of fate. Hence I refer to it as the "chord of reversal." This darkly foreboding harmony brought up the curtain on the admiral's stateroom, where the court-martial was in progress. A stately *adagio* in E-flat major followed William's sentencing and the admiral's cue "this court is now dissolved." It provided underscoring for the pantomime of the admiral coming down to shake hands with William, "who, after a momentary struggle, collects himself and is escorted from the cabin." Then came another street scene while the stage crew prepared the gun-room behind. The street parted to reveal William in chains, seated in front of his opened chest. William's "prison scene" was rife with music. The orchestra played the tune of "Tom Bowling: Poor Tom, or The Sailor's Epitaph," which it repeated several times during the scene. Other tunes were "The Sailor's Journal," played while the shackled William gave his possessions away to his shipmates; "The Watery Grave," as his shipmates took leave of him (just before Susan arrived); and a tender, moving melody (unidentifiable, perhaps Blewitt's own) for the lovers' farewell. This *adagio* (no. 22), about eighteen measures, is the longest cue in the score and may have underscored William's last speech to Susan.

After Susan's departure, sudden activity can be heard above on deck. It seems that cannon-fire brought afloat a body, identified as Susan's uncle, Doggrass. Music precedes the opening of the final scene—the planned execution on deck. While the orchestra plays a solemn march in C major, the curtain rose, the only sounds onstage being the tolling of the minute bell and shuffling feet of the crew's procession along the starboard gangway. As William is led on, the music changes to a slow "prayer" in triple meter (G major). The melody may be Blewitt's own or a sacred piece (it does not seem to be Dibdin's). The scene on the Surrey stage was certainly one of the most ceremonial moments in the entire history of English popular drama up to that time. As Louis James describes it: "All ranks of the navy from the Admiral down are represented, all admit that William is morally innocent. Yet the system demands that he must die, or the whole system is threatened. His friends must pull the rope."[61] As William is led before the Union Jack, he impulsively embraces it as the orchestra erupts in a bold *fortissimo*. Dibdin's "True Courage" rings out, with its known words:

> Why what's that to you if my eyes I'm a wiping?
> A tear is a pleasure, d'ye see in its way.

Using this noble tune at this moment was like turning on the tap, unleashing emotion among the most cynical souls. The comedian John Bannister admitted to being ashamed at having to pull out his handkerchief, and this scene is reported to have caused even rough Surrey bargemen to weep.[62] The music pauses momentarily for William to call out "bless you, bless you all!" and continues as the master-at-arms helps him up to the platform, where he goes to face death bravely. No sooner is the noose around his neck, however, than the orchestra breaks off abruptly. Captain Crosstree rushes on with the discovery of William's honorable discharge for having saved his life, which was issued some months earlier but which Hachet deliberately confiscated (and Doggrass was in the process of delivering when he was murdered). William was already a civilian at the time he struck the captain, so he was not answerable to maritime law. Though this extraordinary twist of fate might seem unduly contrived to us today, for audiences at the Surrey "the surprise it created was almost electrical."[63] Both William *and* the honor of His Majesty's navy are saved. As Susan is brought on and all cheer the sailor's reprieve, the orchestra erupts in a few bars of C-major chords over a *crescendo* tremolo to bring down the curtain. (In later productions it became customary instead to play a rousing strain of *Rule, Britannia!*)

Black-Eyed Susan may be one of the best melodramas ever crafted, a prototype for many to follow, and Jerrold's use of the form relied heavily on music to delineate its shape. Music was also necessary to persuade and reassure its audience, particularly as the sometimes farcical plot of villain and smugglers veered toward tragic realism—in situations all too familiar to many in the 1829 Surrey audience—and finally as the tragic force miraculously dissipated, imbuing moralistic tragedy with the satisfying catharsis of a fairy tale.

TWO

Propagating the Popular Drama

4

The Anglo-American Melodrama and Its Music

In early 1828 Francis Courtney Wemyss, actor and manager of the Chestnut Street Theatre in Philadelphia, tried to capitalize on the notoriety of James Fenimore Cooper's nautical novel *The Red Rover* by having Samuel H. Chapman prepare a dramatic version of it. The play opened on 21 February 1828, less than six weeks after Cooper's novel was first published in America. "Here was a field for manager, author, painter, and machinist," wrote Wemyss, "not forgetting the excellent music of Mr. Braun" (the Chestnut Theatre's resident orchestra leader). "Never in any theatre," Wemyss continued, "was a more successful piece produced, enabling us to act on the Tuesday and Thursday nights to five hundred dollars per night."[1] For his efforts as author and actor, Chapman received $20 per night as long as the play ran at the Chestnut.

Over the next eighteen months pirated versions of *Red Rover* opened in several cities in the United States and England, including at the Surrey Theatre, where Jonathan Blewitt is credited with writing the music.[2] Trying to protect his rights, Chapman had F. Turner publish *Red Rover* in Philadelphia "as performed in the London Theatres," stating that copies were sold at all "dramatic repositories" in the United States.[3] In addition to a few songs and choruses, Chapman's text contains dozens of cues for action music, including music for the novelty of a moving panorama against which some characters abandon a sinking ship and appear to sail to safety in a small skiff. Aside from a few individual songs, sung in productions in New York, Boston, and London, none of the stage music was ever published. If it were not for the music cues in Turner's edition we would have no evidence that any music other than the songs was ever required to produce this play.

The speed with which *Red Rover* traveled across the Atlantic reflects the expanding opportunities for playwrights, actors, musicians, and other theatre personnel as hundreds of new theatres sprung up across England and North America, in towns as well as major cities. The publication of the texts of Anglo-American popular dramas, particularly after the passing of the Dramatic Copyright Act in 1831, protected authors and facilitated the spread of performances among both professional and amateur stock companies. But what happened to the *music* of these plays? Its sudden disappearance in both print and manuscript suggests that it ceased to be integral to the new dramas. But other evidence tells a very different story.

In the early years of the popular drama English publishers often printed piano scores for burlettas and melodramas produced at the patent theatres. This is how composers such as Thomas Busby, Henry Bishop, Matthew Peter King, and Charles Horn were able to secure if not royalties (which did not exist for composers in those days) then at least an outright fee for selling their theatrical music, both songs and any newly composed melodramatic music. An eminent composer such as Bishop enjoyed greater and more lasting success. "The whole of the music" for George Colman's *The Law of Java* (1822) as well as for George M. Soane's *Faustus* (1825) and E. L. Blanchard's *Aladdin, or The Wonderful Lamp* (1826) was published in piano scores by the London firm of Goulding, D'Almaine, and Potter and was therefore available for performances for decades afterward.[4] Circumstances were far less propitious for other theatre composers. Take, for example, Charles Farley's *The Vision of the Sun, or The Orphan of Peru* (Covent Garden, 1823). A *London Times* reviewer observed that "the strains which accompany the action of the melodrama are . . . uncommonly pleasing."[5] Others must have agreed, for productions followed elsewhere, including Philadelphia in 1836 and New York as late as 1851. And yet of William Ware's music only one song was ever published, the sole means by which Ware would have received any compensation. Being asked to compose for melodramas performed at Covent Garden or Drury Lane in 1810 may have smoothed the path to publication, but no composer could count on such an advantage by the 1820s. The situation was even worse for the music directors at London's minor theatres. With the exception of *Black-Eyed Susan*, none of Jonathan Blewitt's musical scores to Surrey melodramas, for example, are known to have made it into print; nor did William Reeve's or William H. Montgomery's for Sadler's Wells, George Herbert Rodwell's or Alfred Mellon's for the Adelphi, James H. Tully's for the Olympic, or John Barnett's for the Lyceum.

The subject of music in the popular drama, at least in England, arose during an inquiry by the select committee of playwrights and politicians, who assembled in London in 1832 to review licensing laws for British theatres. When playwright John Poole was called upon to define the legitimate or regular drama, he said that it was "comedy and tragedy without any musical accompaniment." "If music is introduced as it is introduced into melo-drama," Poole clarified when pressed for details, the play "would cease to be regular drama." When the singer-composer John Braham was questioned about the musical styles for melodrama, he replied that Weber's music in *Oberon* (Covent Garden, 1826) had "improved the taste of the public very much." When asked why the old English ballads (presumably of the type used in plays like *Black-Eyed Susan*) were beginning to fall out of favor, Braham acknowledged a fast-growing interest in Italian music, even among those in the galleries who represented the middle and poorer classes and who had traditionally preferred such ballads.[6]

Italian music had become the rage, largely through Rossini's popularity. But German music also had an influence, particularly the early Romantic style of Weber, who was so wildly popular in England in the 1820s on both operatic and illegitimate stages. Hence the current tastes for music recognized at the 1832 committee hearings were solidified in the *melos* tradition, which spread through the stock system. This musical language incorporated the lyrical Italianate style of Rossini and Vincenzo Bellini, the folksy tunefulness and occasional horror-shroud typified by Weber's *Oberon* and *Der Freischütz*, the four-square sturdiness of the Anglo-Irish ballads, chanteys, and sentimental parlor songs, and—eventually—the delicate chromaticisms of Mendelssohn and the melodiousness of Daniel Auber and other early nineteenth-century French opera and ballet composers.[7] (Characteristics of American minstrelsy began to show up by the 1850s.) This mélange, in varying degrees, became the musical language of the nineteenth-century popular drama in both England and America. For most authors, actors, and managers—not to mention audiences—it was impossible to envision performances without this stylistic amalgam.

One reason why publishers may have stopped printing music to melodramas is that much of it may have consisted largely of compilation: part of the music original, part borrowed or adapted, and part drawn from stock material. It was unlikely that another theatre manager would be interested in paying for music that his or her own leader could just as easily provide.

Another possibility, however, is that competition among theatres forced music directors to become more protective of their work, keeping most of their manuscripts close to the chest and sharing them only as personal favors or on an exchange basis. Many theatres had heavy fines for such "leaks."

The Rules and Regulations of the Boston Theatre in 1854 under Thomas Barry specified that "no prompter, performer, or musician will be permitted to copy any manuscript or music belonging to the theatre." The penalty for doing so was fifty dollars, an astronomical sum (about eight hundred dollars in today's currency), especially in the days when infringements for missing lines or entrances cost an actor some twenty-five cents.[8] The Boston Theatre, like the Adelphi and other large theatres, contained its own music library: once a composer fashioned music for a play, the orchestra parts were preserved in case they should need to be loaned out or the play was revived.

Theatre Music and Copyright

When John Vandenhoff and his leader George Macfarren decided to use Mendelssohn's music for a production of Sophocles's *Antigone* at Covent Garden in 1845, they purchased what was available to them: printed chorus materials in English translation from the London firm of J. J. Ewer and a manuscript full score and set of orchestra parts, which the publishing firm had in its possession from the composer.[9] Mendelssohn had sold the piano score of *Antigone* to a Leipzig firm in 1842. When Ewer published the vocal score later that same year, Mendelssohn essentially settled on a fee for "all my copyright and interest, present and future,"[10] just as he would for his even more celebrated music to Shakespeare's *Midsummer Night's Dream*. Mendelssohn was always duly credited for the use of this elaborate score, which was standard in English and American productions throughout the nineteenth century and even in the first half of the twentieth century (not to mention in early cinema). But even while he was alive, he received no additional fees for providing score and orchestra parts, only reimbursement for the copyist. Had there not been publishers in Germany, France, and England to offer Mendelssohn a fee-in-exchange for printing rights, he would have had little to gain from the use of his music in performance. This was precisely the case for the leader-composers who wrote for the Anglo-American popular drama. Much of their music remained in manuscript, and the only fee that they ever received was their weekly salary from the theatre.

Composers of original theatrical music who felt deprived of their rights sometimes went after wily or unscrupulous managers. One Mr. Erskine, leader at the Surrey Theatre in 1825, brought a case against David Edward Morris, proprietor of the Little Theatre in the Haymarket, who engaged

Erskine to compose music for a play by Thomas Dibdin and then refused to remunerate the composer for his services when he decided not to produce the play. Erskine won damages of £80 in the suit, because he incurred a loss of time from his usual post at the Surrey to complete the project. But the case did little at the time to advance the cause for original theatre music.[11] It was not until the 1850s in Britain that music written for a specific production was determined to have enough commercial value to merit legal protection. This was Addison and Hollier's publication of a piano arrangement of "the whole of the music" of *Sardanapalus, King of Assyria*, composed by John Liptrot Hatton for Charles Kean's 1853 production at the Princess's Theatre.

What happened to all that manuscript music for popular dramas between the 1820s and the 1850s, especially for plays that remained in the repertory of many stock theatres? We have no easy answers to this, only clues. During the early growth of the popular drama from about 1800 to the 1840s a great deal of music resided in house. When Covent Garden burned in 1808, it lost what Henry Saxe Wyndham called "that vast collection of music." The English Opera House (Lyceum) also had a large collection; all the manuscripts of plays and the music were saved when it burned to the ground in 1830.[12] (This would probably have included John Watson's music to Peake's *Presumption* and other melodramas from that period.)

William Clapp tells how Ben Blaike, a combat fighter who had come to Boston from the London minor theatres, was always on the lookout for new melodramas. One day in 1829 Blaike came beaming into the green room of the Tremont Theatre "with a package as big as a tea-box." He handed the bundle to actress Mary Duff, requesting that she take the items home and read them. "What are they?" she inquired. "Eleven new melo-drams [*sic*], with all the music!"[13] The original music to melodramas traveled not only between cities but also across continents. In 1826 Junius Brutus Booth was managing the Chatham Theatre in New York. He wrote to George Holland, who was coming from London the following year as first comedian of the Bowery Theatre, to bring along a number of performing materials for plays. "The manuscript and music of *Paul Pry*, with *Faustus*'s music ditto—and book of *The Pilot*—the manuscript and ditto of a piece played some few years back at Sadler's Wells, call'd 'The Ghebers.'"[14] The music for *Faustus* had recently been published. But only three songs by Charles Horn from *Paul Pry* ever came out in print, and nothing at all from "The Ghebers" (*The Gheber, or The Fire Worshippers* [Sadler's Wells, 1818]). As Booth's letter implies, Holland must have transported to New York not just the texts of these plays (some published, some unpublished) but also hand-copied music, which Booth presumably gave to his orchestra leader John Davies to use in production. An article from the Charleston, South Carolina, *City Gazette* in 1828 reveals that the manager of the Charleston Theatre had obtained the manuscript of Fitzball's *Flying Dutchman* from the manager of New York's Bowery Theatre, noting also that the burletta "will be brought forward with the original music, scenery, dresses, [and] decorations."[15] In cases where such circulating music has been found, it is not unusual to see band musicians signing their names in different cities and theatres in which local musicians had been engaged. An undated set of surviving parts for music to Fitzball's *The Floating Beacon* (Surrey, 1824) is signed on the cover "J. B. Wright, Brighton" (Massachusetts, as Wright was a Boston prompter). But a musician in Philadelphia signed the viola part "John L. Mickley, Chesnut [*sic*] Street Theatre, 1852."[16]

At that time no laws protected composers against the free circulation of their music. Designs for Drury Lane in 1813 provided for a "music copyist's room," in which a leader or appointed scribe would make a usable copy of orchestra parts from a borrowed copy.[17] American copyright law of 1831 and English copyright law of 1833 (and its subsequent revisions in 1842, 1844, and 1848) do not account specifically for music written as part of a dramatic production. In England theatrical productions were "copyrighted" in the sense that the author's text was insulated against piracy once a play was produced. But according to peculiar British law, authors surrendered their rights once a play appeared in print. Adaptations of plays by subsequent managers were similarly protected in the sense that a version of an existing play—including its staging and scenic effects—was thought to have some originality and hence justified legal protection. It is not clear if this coverage extended to any music written for the play, as no legal challenges appear to have been recorded. Operas enjoyed a separate provision under the International Copyright Law, but music written for scenic effects and other stage business did not.

Two important court cases of 1859 and 1867 exerted a decisive impact on theatre music. In 1859 Hatton brought suit against Charles Kean, alleging that the music he composed for Kean's production of *Much Ado about Nothing* at the Princess's—which, unlike *Sardanapalus*, had not been published—was his own property and could be adapted or performed as he saw fit. The court interpreted this differently. It argued that Hatton was hired specifically to write music in support of a unique production ("as part of the general plan of the spectacle"), so the music was an inseparable part of Kean's design and hence protected as such by law.[18] The case set a precedent, for nearly all British theatrical music composed in the ensuing decades, written in response to unique dramatic situations and therefore identical with the circumstances of *Much Ado*, became the property of the manager and was generally filed with the promptbook and sides for future productions. It is largely for this reason that any of this music survives today, having been preserved with performing materials in a theatre's library or among a manager's personal papers. The survival rate is exceedingly low, however, for any manuscript theatrical music kept in composers' private collections, even those who wrote a great deal of theatre music, such as Isaac Collins, William H. Montgomery, and Alfred Mellon. No library seems to have acquired (or identified) manuscripts by these composers.[19] It was not until 1897 that *Hatton v. Kean* was overturned in English courts on the basis that Hatton's contribution required unique skills and a separately measurable level of originality, similar to those of an illustrator for a book.[20]

The second case, *Wallerstein v. Herbert*, reveals significantly more about music and the relationship between manager and composer. When George Roberts's version of *Lady Audley's Secret* opened at the St. James's Theatre in 1863, Ferdinand Wallerstein, the resident leader, composed all the theatrical music associated with that play, which included several sensation scenes, such as Lady Audley's setting fire to the Castle Inn at the end of act 2, scene 3. As Wallerstein was under contract to Frank Matthews, proprietor of the theatre at the time, his responsibilities—as the court document put it—were to "provide incidental music for dramas, when necessary, and such music he might either select or compose." When Wallerstein left his position at the St. James in 1864, he apparently left behind the orchestra parts of *Lady Audley*. Given the success of this adaptation of Mary Braddon's novel, Matthews planned a tour of the play to the provinces. He graciously obtained permission from Wallerstein to use his music. The problem began when Louisa Herbert, the star actress of the play, took over the management of the St. James's and wished to revive *Lady Audley* in 1867. Finding Wallerstein's parts in the theatre's library, she assumed that they were among the "properties" that she had bought and proceeded to use them. When Wallerstein learned of this, he brought suit against Herbert for the sum of twenty shillings royalties per performance.[21] According to the law summary ("Music as accessory to a drama"), the court held that the situation was no different from *Hatton v. Kean*, in that the music was an inseparable part of the play and was hence not an independent composition. The wording of Wallerstein's contract with the theatre at the time of the composition, the court decided, was sufficient evidence to grant Matthews as lessee of the theatre the right to use this music in all future productions of the play, and that right passed on to any managers under his license. It was incumbent upon the plaintiff, the court argued, to demonstrate that he retained an independent legal right to the music, which Wallerstein was apparently unable to do.

It took several decades before any composer could claim such rights to theatre music under international copyright law. The exception in the case of *Wallerstein v. Herbert*, as an American copyright lawyer finessed in 1879, was that Wallerstein had indeed written this music while in the discharge of his ordinary duties (to "provide incidental music"), but no express agreement had existed as to whose property the music itself should be.[22] The St. James's Theatre apparently had no separate budget for acquiring music, the court record showed, and it fell upon Wallerstein to shoulder the cost of copying parts for his orchestra. He therefore had every right to retain said music as his property. It was the "playing of the music and the *use* of the compositions," the American court asserted, and "not the property in them" for which the manager contracted and paid the composer. This clarification was helpful for composers of theatre music after about 1880 but, alas, it was too late for Wallerstein. An argument in his favor might have had a significant impact on the development and quality of music for the popular drama of the 1860s and 1870s: under the existing statute most composers had little incentive to write for the theatre.

The situation evolved slightly differently in the United States, although the result for theatre composers was roughly the same. Theatrical music generally resided in house unless the building burned down or was demolished, in which case it might have been rescued by the resident music director. All the orchestra music was lost in Philadelphia's Chestnut Street Theatre fire in 1794. But when the National Theatre in New York burned in September 1839 one account relates the effort to save promptbooks and music by throwing them down from windows, along with costumes and properties.[23] But some composers were shrewd enough to make copies for themselves. When James Hewitt died in 1827, "the whole of the theatrical music" was found in a box stored in his basement. This most likely contained his manuscripts, so its fate remained in his family's hands; it has now vanished.[24] When Henry Beissenherz accepted the position of leader for the Park Theatre in Brooklyn under Sarah Conway in 1865, perhaps he was familiar with *Wallerstein v. Herbert*. He agreed to Conway's terms "to furnish all the music required during the season" but added the clause "with all new music composed to remain my property."[25] This may have offered practical advantages to composers at the time, but it was not favorable to posterity. The music that Wallerstein retained for *Lady Audley's Secret*, like the rest of his theatre music, has completely disappeared. A copy of some manuscript arrangements that he sent to the Boston Theatre remained with that library's collection, which still exists today.[26]

The disappearance of so much theatre music written before the 1860s is frustrating, though it is easy to understand why composers would have wanted to safeguard their unpublished work. The U.S. Copyright Act of 1831 assured authors of plays and composers of songs and instrumental works of first *publishing* rights, but it was not until the American Dramatic Copyright Law of 1856 that this privilege was also extended to sole right of first representation. Moreover, an 1848 statute confirmed that an author or composer's work had no protection at all unless it was published or unless a manuscript copy was deposited and registered in the Library of Congress. Most theatrical music then was in manuscript and consisted mostly of separate instrumental parts, not full scores, so it therefore remained out of copyright. This is probably what motivated the composer and orchestra leader Robert Stoepel—like Hatton in England—to publish "Reminiscences of *Leah*" in 1863. This was a medley of five or six *melos* numbers written for the original production of Augustin Daly's *Leah the Forsaken* at Niblo's Garden.[27] It may speak to the salability of musical excerpts from a successful play that William A. Pond was willing to publish this, although the lithograph cover of Kate Bateman in her Leah costume no doubt had greater appeal to collectors of theatre memorabilia than the few pages of music inside. The sales of descriptive musical gems from plays such as *Sardanapalus* and *Leah* were rare, however, at least until the 1880s, when British composers began to publish keyboard selections or orchestral suites from their theatre music (see chapter 9). Until then most of the theatrical excerpts that found their way into print—and hence copyright protection—were songs and dances. Onstage waltzes or polkas performed in the course of the play were particularly marketable. George Loder and the music dealer Samuel Jollie were caught up in a legal battle in 1850 over one such number. *Jollie v. Jaques* appears to be the first music copyright case argued in the United States. Loder had arranged a German melody for a dance in the play *The Serious Family* at Burton's. It was immensely popular, and Jollie published it under that title. Jollie sued when someone else brought out another version of the same tune, but he and Loder lost the case.[28]

For many of these reasons, original scores (*melos* numbers composed, ordered, and designed for a specific play) either resided in a theatre's music library until that collection was liquidated or were removed by orchestra leaders who retained their own circulating rights. Copies left in the theatre were available to the manager (or licenser) of the theatre for future use. Mellon's original music for *The Green Bushes* (Adelphi Theatre, 1845), a wildly popular and frequently revived play, has vanished along with the Adelphi's entire collection. But a copy resided in the Grecian Theatre music library until that theatre was closed down and its collection dragged over to Drury Lane. Hence a version of Mellon's music survives. The same is true of *Under the Gaslight* and dozens of plays for which copies of orchestral parts were prepared for subsequent productions, reflecting this music's close and valued connection to the original melodramas for which they were conceived.

How Theatre Music Circulated: A Trans-Atlantic Industry

In his impressive study of Henry Irving, theatre historian Jeffrey Richards wrote: "Each theatre in Victorian England had a resident orchestra and musical director whose job it was to compose incidental music for the plays, select appropriate overtures and *entr'actes* from existing scores, and to conduct the orchestra."[29] Although this is a true statement (mostly consistent with the 1863 court's description of Wallerstein's duties), it can also be misleading because it relies on several assumptions. If music already existed for a given play, then the music leader was not obliged—perhaps not even expected—to compose new incidental music but might very well track down the existing music and secure it on loan, perhaps even making a pirated copy. For example, Robert Stoepel composed the original music to *Leah the Forsaken* when it opened at Niblo's Garden in January 1863 and is duly credited as such on the playbill. Yet according to the same playbill it was Harvey B. Dodworth who led the "orchestra and full chorus." Stoepel was at that time fulfilling his duties as music director at Wallack's. *Leah* was no more a "musical play" than other popular dramas of the time. It contained thirty-four *melos* numbers for the band, two choruses for the villagers, a dance, and an offstage organ over which Leah delivered her famous curse. Kate Bateman took Daly's uncopyrighted version of *Leah* to London, where she used it at the Adelphi in October. The French-born violinist Jules P. Rivière led the orchestra. Bateman again used Stoepel's music, as he is clearly credited on the playbill. Nine years later, when Kate and her father took over the Lyceum Theatre, they opened with *Leah.* Once again the playbills give major billing to Stoepel's music, even though the leadership of the Lyceum band had passed to J. Mallandaine. Stoepel himself was at that time in New York, though by now leading the orchestra at Daly's Fifth Avenue Theater. As late as 1881 Lawrence Barrett was using Stoepel's *Leah* score or a version of it—uncredited—on his national tour.

We have many such examples of music being reused from production to production. Thomas Baker was a long-standing orchestra leader at Laura Keene's Theatre in New York. An advertisement in the *New York Clipper* in 1864 announces the availability of "original music arranged by" Baker for a variety of melodramas, including *The Colleen Bawn, Jeanie Deans, The Marble Heart, The Seven Sisters,* and others. Purchasers, presumably orchestra leaders or managers of regional theatres, could obtain parts "for large or small bands" directly from Baker at the Olympic Theatre or at 52 St. Mark's Place, a private residence.[30] Some of this music was made available even to managers of small provincial theatres. An 1867 playbill for Edmund Falconer's *Peep o' Day* at the New Harmony Theatre (Indiana) heralds that "the original overture and the original music composed expressly for *Peep o' Day* will be performed by the leader F. Ossenberg." This wording leaves little doubt that "original" refers to the music that John Barnard fashioned for the Lyceum production in 1861, much of which was derived from well-known Irish tunes. This music is not among the Goldens' surviving collection of theatrical music, however, so we are left to assume that it was rented or borrowed from some professional agency and returned after the production. There are important exceptions to the borrowing of music, of course. No one used the music to Charles Kean's Shakespeare productions, which the manager seems to have carefully guarded. Nor did anyone later in the century appear to recycle any of the original music commissioned for play production by major theatrical managers such as Henry Irving, David Belasco, or Charles Frohman, as least not without a lawsuit.

An industry about which we know remarkably little sustained the production and acquisition of music for theatrical plays throughout much of the nineteenth century. We get some insight into this world from an interview with playwright Charles Reade, author of *Masks and Faces, The Courier of Lyons, It Is Never Too Late to Mend, Griffith Gaunt,* and dozens of other popular plays. His interlocutor from *Gentleman's Magazine* writes about a visit to Reade's *sanctum sanctorum* in 1882, just one year before the author's death:

> In a small room adjoining the library are kept the MSS., music, and sketches of scenes of the author's dramas. When Mr. Reade writes a play, he does his work in a most systematic manner. His original MS. is handed to his secretary, who makes a careful copy. This is revised by the author, and a fresh copy is made, with instructions for prompter and stage manager. Then the author has an interview with a first-class artist, and a set of sketches are made. These drawings are sent to the wood engraver or lithographer, for large posters or window-cards. Appropriate music is written by a competent musician, and several complete sets of the score are arranged. If the play is not printed, three or four prompt copies are made by the secretary, and the actors' parts are all written in a legible hand. When the piece is accepted, everything is in readiness as far as the author is concerned. Duplicates of MSS., band parts, models, and sketches of scenes are always kept in reserve, so that the piece can be played in several places at the same time.[31]

This remarkable account raises as many questions as it answers. Would all of this conceptual work of production, down to and including music, be prepared so well in advance without even knowing the cast or theatre? And who were the "competent musicians" to whom the composition of the music would have been entrusted? One source indicates that Reade's close friendship with author Tom Taylor and his wife, Laura Wilson Barker, led to her composing some of the music for his plays, anonymously of course. Another possibility was Edwin Ellis, for whose obituary Reade wrote that the leader "lifted scenes and situations for me and other writers scores of times, and his share of the effect never been publicly noticed." "When he had a powerful action or impassioned dialogue to illustrate," Reade said of Ellis, "he did not habitually run to the poor resource of a 'hurry' or a nonsense 'tremolo,' but loved to find an appropriate melody, or a rational sequence of chords, or a motived strain, that raised the scene or enforced the dialogue."[32]

Two items that must have come from this "small room," both a promptbook in the hand of one of Reade's secretaries (and autographed by him) and a neatly copied set of orchestra parts, exist in the Harvard Theatre Collection. *Dora*, a pastoral drama "with new scenic effects and appropriate music founded on Tennyson's poem," had opened at the Adelphi in 1868 and was printed in London by W. Clowes and Sons. Sometime later Reade sent a clean copy of the promptbook and orchestra parts to the Boston Theatre, where the play was given in the spring of 1873. The illustration in Figure 12 shows two pages from the "conductor" book. The music is typical of a mid-

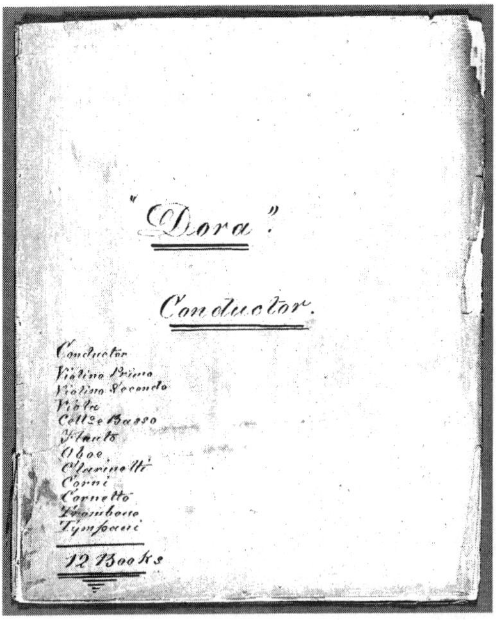

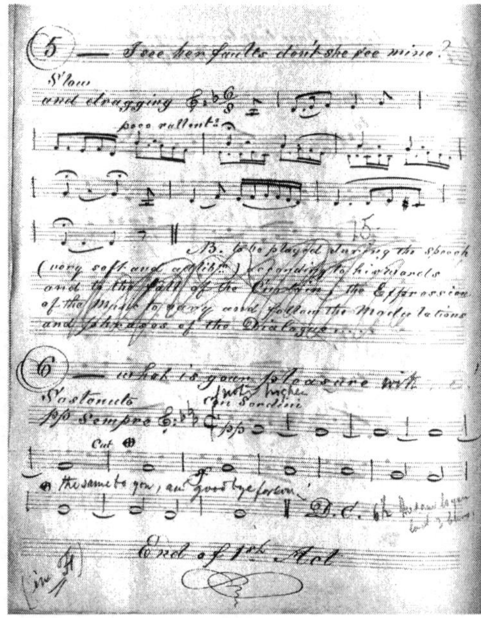

FIGURE 12. *From the orchestra music to* Dora. *MS Thr 554 (Box 7), Harvard Theatre Collection, Houghton Library, Harvard University*

century part for the violinist-leader, with each *melos* preceded by a number and a text cue, though this beautifully written "archive copy" is neater than most. The title page specifies twelve separate parts (which could be used by up to eighteen players), and the second page shows the last two cues of the first act. The small notes indicate to the leader the moving counterpoint in a different part. The fermatas over some notes allow for necessary pauses, should the action need to catch up. The added pencil markings on the score are typical of the kinds of changes that a local leader might make to parts that had been originally prepared for another theatre or acting company. So far these orchestra parts to *Dora* remain an exception. What happened to the rest of the music manuscripts of this prominent British author when the multiple copies were so carefully protected? The answer is still shrouded in mystery.

As to the fate of music for some other plays, a few choice clues sometimes turn up. An American theatrical firm by the name of Brooks and Dickson (44 W. 23rd St., New York) was going out of business in 1885. According to a *New York Times* article, it was auctioning off manuscripts, parts, music, scenery, properties, and "rights to produce" to secondhand dealers and theatrical people. Among the few items mentioned were the manuscripts, parts, and music to George Robert Sims and Henry Pettitt's melodrama *In the Ranks* (Adelphi, 1883). The brief article also noted that the actor J. B. Roberts acquired for fifty cents all the performing materials—including music—for a French play, *La charbonnière* by Pierre Decourcell and H.-J. Crémiux.[33] In another instance the ailing actor John McCullough held an auction sale of his performing materials. In addition to manuscripts of many nineteenth-century standards to be sold (*Ingomar the Barbarian*, *The Gladiator*) a newspaper article mentioned "the incidental music of a number of popular dramas."[34] McCullough must have felt it necessary to hold onto music for plays in which he was a star attraction and, as in the Reade case above, must have understood its value for subsequent productions. Similarly the actor Frank A. Tannehill, who frequently performed the villain Jagon in *The Stranglers of Paris* (by a young David Belasco, 1883), kept a copy of orchestra parts for the music composed by Giuseppe Operti for the original New Park Theatre production of the play. He presumably used these for his performances on tour throughout the United States.[35] A somewhat different type of case is found at the Adelphi for Benjamin Webster's 1864 adaptation of *The Workmen of Paris, or The Drama of the Wine-shop*. Though Jules Rivière led the Adelphi orchestra, the playbill assured the audience that "all the original music by M. Artus" would be heard. In this case Rivière must have brought Artus's music with him from Paris, where it had been composed for Adolphe d'Ennery and Philippe Dumanois's original at the Porte Saint-Martin. The music for this sensation drama was obviously considered not just an intrinsic part of it but a celebrated one.

This little-explored circulation of special dramatic scores composed throughout the nineteenth century merits serious study. Of course we might expect a high level of interest in using Mendelssohn's music for *Antigone* given the composer's cachet. Its choruses and under-dialogue music enhanced productions of the play in New York at Burton's Theatre in the spring of 1845 (with George Loder leading) and then again in London at Drury Lane in 1850. But evidence clearly shows that it was not just internationally famous composers whose music was so carefully protected and sought out. For example, when Dion Boucicault's *Flying Scud* opened in New York at Wallack's Theatre on 24 April 1867, with Edward Mollenhauer leading the orchestra, an ad in the *New York Times* tells us that the play included "the original music by G. Richardson." Richardson had composed all the *melos* numbers six months earlier for the first production at the Holborn Theatre in October 1866.[36] The music—precisely calculated, accurately timed, and interspersed with a few well-known tunes of the day—had originated with the author-director's concept of the play and was now a set part of it. Whether Richardson was compensated for the use of his music in New York, however, is unknown, which would have required a system of rights and permissions for such music that was not yet legally in place. Even as late as the 1890s many theatrical managers held on tightly to their musical manuscripts. When Henry Krehbiel wished to quote examples of William Furst's music from David Belasco's production of *Madame Butterfly* (Herald Square Theatre, 1900), the tunes had to be credited "by permission of Mr. David Belasco" and not the composer (or a publisher, as Furst's theatre music was never published).[37]

The form in which the orchestra parts for Boucicault's *The Colleen Bawn* were found among Oscar Barrett's music for the Grecian Theatre—each part bound with heavy protective covers, with quartos sewn in signatures, and an ink manuscript written in an extremely legible even beautiful hand—suggests that this was some kind of master or archival copy, like Reade's *Dora*. The parts were signed as "Property of James Weaver" and were hand-stamped "orchestral band office" at the rather posh address of 45 Howland Street, Fitzroy Square West. Weaver was a composer of light music and a theatrical manager associated with the Egyptian Hall, Piccadilly, in the 1860s. But by 1876 he was clearly involved in some way with the "band office," possibly as a distributor of theatre music. *The Colleen Bawn* was given at the Grecian in 1875, fifteen years after its first London performance at the Adelphi. A copy of Thomas Baker's music almost certainly resided in the Adelphi music room, from which a set may have been prepared for Weaver to lend to other theatres on authority of the Adelphi's managers Benjamin Webster and Frederick Chatterton. Or perhaps Weaver had even been one of the Adelphi copyists for a time or a *répétiteur*, which might explain his signature on an archive copy. Weaver could mark the archive copy as his "property," claiming that he had the right to loan the *physical parts*, not as artistic property. This set of parts might have been prepared by request of George Conquest at the Grecian. Weaver went on to lead orchestras at different theatres (the Royal Artillery, the New Olympic). None of his theatre music has turned up. But the *Colleen Bawn* parts presumably prepared by him remained in the Grecian Theatre library and hence became part of a collection that has survived intact.[38]

Rental of Theatre Music

The American actor Charles Farrar wrote of starting up the Boston Parlor Theatrical Company in 1868, hoping to establish a small repertoire of popular dramas. One of these was *Michael Erle, or The Maniac Lover*. An actor in the company knew of a street band of six players that he thought they could get cheap (for $45 of their $377 budget for three nights in the theatre). Initially the band was to fill up the intervals with musical oleos. But, as Farrar noted, "there were several places in *Michael Erle* where music was introduced." The tiny ensemble "managed capitally," and "an outsider would hardly have taken it for a street band."[39] He pointed out that they hired a local orchestra, however, when they took the play to Lyceum Hall, Milford. Farrar does not say what music the "street band" and the orchestra used to accompany *Michael Erle* and where they obtained it.

Samuel French's 1859 acting edition of *Michael Erle* provides a costume and properties plot, but no hint about the music. French's 1858 acting edition for James G. Burnett's *Blanche of Brandywine*, however, indicates that "terms of permission to perform this drama, together with sketches of scenery, music, and other information, may be ascertained by addressing Mr. Burnett, Laura Keene's Theatre." It is not yet known exactly when French, who began licensing plays in New York in 1846, and Thomas Hailes Lacy, who initiated this process in London in 1830, began to make music available as part of their loan materials. It is clear that Lacy was doing so by the 1860s: the eighth edition of their *Amateur's Hand-Book* (1871) mentions rental or purchase of band parts for dramas. The Samuel French catalogue of 1882 gives a full list of the plays with music available. How it acquired so much material from the earlier part of the century—and what subsequently happened to it—is unknown. None of the nineteenth-century music that I have found bears the stamp of Samuel French, so I can only presume that the company liquidated all of the theatrical music from this collection.

French hired Wentworth Hogg to manage the growing amateur rentals division, and in 1882 French's London office published Hogg's *Guide to Selecting Plays, or Manager's Companion.* This included a two-page list of "music to burlesques, operas, and dramas to loan." The repertory is exclusively English. The only "operas" listed are of the English opera variety (*Guy Mannering*, *Rob Roy MacGregor*, and so forth), and "burlesques" included those of Italian operas such as *Ernani*. No less than forty items for loan, however, are music for popular dramas. A list of these is so important to this study that it merits full repetition here. Though none of these items appears to have been preserved—or passed on to subsequent theatrical licensers such as Arthur Tams or Marcus Witmark—it is astonishing to think that as late as 1882 provincial companies would produce a seventy-five-year-old melodrama with its original music. The list of loan music for dramatic productions, by the way, is dropped in the 1899 and 1910 editions of the *Guide*, so French must have discontinued these titles.[40]

Here are the popular dramas on the 1882 list from Samuel French:

Anchor and Hope, 9 band parts
Ashore and Afloat, 10 band parts
Austerlitz, or Love and Honor, 7 band parts
Avenger (1835), 13 band parts
Black-Eyed Susan, full score and piano vocal score
The Blind Boy, 4 band parts
Blue Beard, piano vocal score
The Bride of Abydos, 6 band parts
The Bride of Lammermoor, 5 band parts
The Brigand, score and 3 band parts
Bronze Horse, band parts
The Bottle Imp (Stephenson), 1 and 2 violins, basso
Cataract of the Ganges (1823), 6 band parts
The Colleen Bawn, 8 band parts
The Cricket on the Hearth, 10 band parts
Dearer Than Life, 9 band parts
Deeds Not Words, 11 band parts
The Eddystone Elf, 6 band parts
Ella Rosenberg, 5 band parts
Exile, 4 band parts
Father and Son, 5 band parts
Gilderoy, 5 band parts
The Innkeeper's Daughter, 4 band parts
Jack Sheppard (songs in)
Joan of Arc, 4 band parts
Lady of the Lake, score and 5 band parts
Luke the Labourer (1826), 6 band parts
Macbeth, vocal score and 8 band parts
The Mariner's Compass, 15 band parts
Masaniello, 4 band parts
The Miller and His Men, 5 band parts

Nobody's Child, 9 band parts
Oak Chest, 9 band parts
Raymond and Agnes, 3 band parts
Robert Macaire, 4 band parts
Sardanapalus, "entire music"
Sister's Sacrifice, 11 band parts
Thérèse, or The Orphan of Geneva, 5 band parts
The Tower of Nesle, or The Dark Gondola (1832), 9 band parts
The Vampire, 4 band parts
Watch and Wait, 8 band parts
Wild Boy of Bohemia, 5 band parts
Willow Pattern Plate, 9 band parts

Were these plays for which music circulated because they were still popular and regularly performed in 1882? Some of these are obviously quite old plays. Jane Scott's *The Oak Chest, or the Smuggler's Sons and the Robber's Daughter* and Richard Peake's *The Bottle Imp*, for example, date from 1816 and 1828, respectively. It would be interesting to know if the "4 band parts" to *The Innkeeper's Daughter* were handed down from T. P. Cooke's music for the 1817 production. The music for *Macbeth* was almost certainly the Restoration period music attributed to Matthew Locke that still seemed to be de rigueur in many nineteenth-century productions, which was otherwise widely available in a published version.[41] It is curious indeed to see *Ella Rosenberg* on a list of performing materials from so late in the century, a play whose 1808 views on virtue versus villainy must surely have seemed rather old-fashioned by then. Also surprising is the apparent steadfastness of Payne's *Thérèse*, a classic melodrama first performed in London and New York in 1821 (see chapter 2) and sustained to much acclaim by Mary Duff and Edwin Forrest in the 1830s.[42] Spectacle melodramas like *Cataract of the Ganges* or *The Mariner's Compass* were standard mid-nineteenth-century fare at larger theatres. Wildly popular crime dramas like *Gilderoy*, *Luke the Labourer*, and *Robert Macaire* with their glamorous villains must have seen extensive amateur rentals, which would of course have meant a need for multiple copies of loan parts. It seems odd, however, not to find on this list titles such as *Mazeppa*, *Peep o' Day*, or *The Corsican Brothers*, which were among the most popular melodramas of the century. Successful as many of these plays were, I have been able to find only twelve sets from the forty titles on this list (five having been published and therefore preserved somewhere in a library), again, none bearing a Samuel French imprint.

Perhaps lending agencies such as French's and Lacy's kept only a small supply of dramatic music, especially because many small-town stock companies—like Farrar's itinerant group—would probably not have had orchestras large enough to handle the parts as written for their original venues. Several of the titles in the French's list seem to be available only in reduced orchestrations. Surely Davy's music for the *Blind Boy*, first performed at Covent Garden in 1807, originally had far more than four band parts. Similarly, Matthew Peter King's original music to *Ella Rosenberg*—which, as we have seen, survives in full score—shows a much larger ensemble than four parts could reasonably accommodate, unless one of them was a piano. Parts for *Dearer Than Life*, a Henry J. Byron play from the 1868, survive from the Selwyn Theatre, Boston. There Koppitz scored the music for twelve parts, but the music was available from French for only nine.

Conversely, the fifteen band parts listed for *The Mariner's Compass* seem exceedingly optimistic, given that even the orchestra for the first production of Henry Leslie's sensation drama at Astley's Pavilion in 1865 consisted of about sixteen players. Who could be in the position to rent parts for such an ensemble? A personally signed copy of the original orchestra parts to *The Mariner's Compass* by James H. Tully, Astley's leader, was sent to the Grecian Theatre, where a reduced set of seven parts was made in 1869, presumably by Edward Barrett.[43] There the music was played in an arrangement for at most ten musicians. Only the biggest melodrama houses capable of handling the special effects would have been able to produce *The Mariner's Compass*. And only first-tier theatres would have had an orchestra large enough to perform the music in its original format. Curiously, the 1882 list remains an intriguing but enigmatic document.

Of one thing we can be certain. By the 1880s many agencies in London and New York made dramatic music available to theatrical managers, who came from all over the country to obtain performing materials for local stock and amateur productions of various sizes. The 1882 Samuel French catalogue offers a tantalizing view of music that was still available at that time for traditional popular dramas. Perhaps someday more of this music and other music will be discovered that will answer some lingering questions about these scores, especially how and why they circulated and who rented them. Some of this music obviously held considerable value for theatrical managers, not only at the time it was written but also for decades afterward.

5

Victorian Theatre Bands and Their Leaders

The nineteenth-century theatre music that survives provides only a partial view of how this music sounded and the effect that it had on an audience's interpretation of the drama. Let us now turn our attention to the musicians who played from these pages and who constituted that anonymous and little-examined entity called the "theatre band."

In the heyday of the stock system in the nineteenth century (from the 1830s to the 1870s), most companies maintained some kind of orchestra. The model established in the 1820s by Hughes at the Coburg, Rodwell at the Adelphi, and Blewitt at the Surrey—an ensemble of about eighteen musicians (nine strings, eight winds, and percussion)—could only be upheld at the best urban playhouses. In London such ensembles might be found at Drury Lane, the Haymarket, Sadler's Wells, the Princess's, the Olympic, the Adelphi, the Lyceum, the Queen's, the Holborn, and the Prince of Wales's (Covent Garden converted to an opera house). In New York relatively large theatre orchestras were maintained at Niblo's Garden, the Winter Garden, Burton's, the Chatham (Purdy's), Laura Keene's, Wallack's, and the Fifth Avenue. Many of the plays examined in the following chapters were first staged in these theatres, so the makeup of their orchestras is an essential component of their sound world. Smaller theatres, such as the Standard, Pavilion, Britannia, and the Grecian in working-class East London and Mitchell's Olympic, Brougham's, and the Bowery in lower Manhattan, more typically maintained an orchestra of about eight to ten, though illustrations of these theatres may occasionally depict larger ensembles. In playhouses devoted to the spoken drama, a nucleus of salaried musicians might be supplemented for pantomimes, burlesques, extravaganzas, and operas. Most theatre managers realized that a balanced ensemble and a good leader greatly enhanced not only the production but the reputation of the theatre as well.

The quality of a British or American theatre band depended on the competency of its leader, who was responsible for hiring and paying the musicians.[1] Some leaders were trained in the classical traditions of German, French, and British conservatories, but the medium in which they worked also required knowledge of diverse musical styles. Orchestral programming between plays contained operatic overtures and potpourris, concertato numbers featuring various members of the orchestra as soloists, but also polkas, waltzes, and other popular dances of the day. Leaders were invariably men, but it was not unheard of toward the end of the century to find a woman leading the band in a regional or amateur theatre. By the 1830s most music directors had adopted a centermost position in the orchestra, and many still played first violin as well as leading with bow in hand.[2] Some took up the baton, though from a manager's point of view it was an impractical waste of manpower. Many leaders learned their craft by coming up through the ranks and passing traditions on from theatre to theatre, even across continents. Benjamin J. Deane was an English-born violinist who played in orchestras at the City of London, the Standard, and the Pavilion theatres from the age of seventeen (1839) before he went to New York in 1850. At Hamblin's Bowery Theatre he served as "second leader" under William T. Peterschen and then took over the leadership himself in 1860.[3] Some leaders maintained a close association with one manager or theatre, such as Thomas Baker with Laura Keene. The longest-known continuous music directorship of a theatre was that of the American-born Napier Lothian, who held this position with the Boston Theatre for forty years.[4] Some even juggled theatres: for example, Edward Mollenhauer in New York (Wallack's, Winter Garden, Niblo's Garden) and Robert Stoepel on both sides of the Atlantic (the Princess's, then Wallack's and the Fifth Avenue Theatre in New York, then back to London for the Lyceum). Besides leadership skills, a resident orchestra leader needed to possess innate dramatic sensibilities and an actor's sense of timing. "With what interest we used to look at Alfred Mellon," one observer recalled in 1894, "as he led the slow music in the orchestra when the Adelphi villain or adventurer was in the slow agonies of death!"[5]

In addition to a proficient and capable leader, who often composed or adapted much of the music, at least four other factors were responsible for the size and composition of bands in Victorian-era theatres: (1) the physi-

FIGURE 13. *Standard Theatre, detail.* Illustrated London News *(17 May 1845), 320*

cal limitations of space, (2) the percentage of overall production costs that a manager was willing to invest in the orchestra, (3) musical requirements dictated by the genre of play, and (4) a manager's taste and imagination in areas of musical style.

Theatre orchestras tended to be small compared with those in a nineteenth-century opera house or concert hall. Even at an average well-equipped theatre, money might allow for at best a nucleus of twelve musicians, usually including a quartet or quintet of strings and a few wind instruments. Such modest forces imply a relatively narrow range of color and volume, but some of the best leaders managed to work creatively within these limitations. As one critic observed of a theatre orchestra, "one good man" is equal to a "multitude of cheap fiddlers."[6]

A typical early Victorian theatre orchestra can be seen in an artist's rendering of the Standard Theatre (Fig. 13) during a performance of *The Conquest of Tartary,* an equestrian drama similar to *Timour the Tartar.* Not counting the leader, this orchestra includes about fourteen persons, apparently both male and female. They are seated on the audience level (and seem perilously close to the action onstage). Some of the musicians to the leader's right are still using the old type of face-to-face music desks (one of the violinists depicted in this sketch may well be Benjamin Deane).

At a theatre like the Standard orchestra space was precious. In theatres with an expanding pit audience, musicians might be crowded into a long and narrow allotment, having to spread out the full length of the stage lip. This made it difficult to hear from one side to the other and created a special challenge to achieve a satisfactory blend. Music—much of it in manuscript—had to be read in dim lighting. Music stands had placeholders for one candle covered with a tin shade on each side. This meant that reading depended upon the inconsistent glow of the flames (which sometimes also caused the music to catch fire). In the early days some spectators were allowed to sit in the orchestra; as late as 1871 musicians were sometimes asked to give up their seats to accommodate audience overflow.[7] Sinking the orchestra into a "well" (sometimes even called the "orchestra pen") became a feature of theatre design later in the century (Booth's Theatre in New York, built in 1869, was perhaps the first). Most orchestras were simply separated from the audience by a movable curtained railing. In some of the largest theatres in the days before stall seating (such as Drury Lane) the enclosure between the footlights and the first row of benches could be expanded to accommodate up to thirty musicians.

Playing in a theatre orchestra had its pros and cons. An established stock theatre offered job stability, because a band was often hired for the season. Pay was not great, however, especially before the organization of musical unions. And a fixed salary meant that musicians could be called for lengthy morning rehearsals and very long performances in the evenings, with only Sundays off.

Financial records that survive for early nineteenth-century theatres are sparse, but an 1840–1841 receipt book from the Tremont Theatre in Boston (comparable in size to the Standard) shows an orchestra of sixteen players, counting the director, and a weekly budget of $175 "for seven nights" of performances (Table 2). This was roughly equivalent to $4,500 in today's dollars, with the average musician drawing a salary of $250.

Table 2. Average Weekly Orchestra Budget, 1840–1841

Director (Thomas Comer)	$25
Musicians (2), @ $12	$24
Musicians (11), @ $10	$110
Musicians (2), @ $8	$16
	$175

Source: *Tremont Theatre, Drama and Receipt Records Book*, Houghton Library, Harvard.

The two higher-paid musicians, though unspecified, may have included a librarian and a *répétiteur*, whose additional responsibilities would have entailed running the music cues in staging rehearsals. The two lower-paid musicians may have been a drummer and trombonist, who were perhaps required mostly for the intermission music, as their roles throughout most popular dramas were traditionally small. For some weeks the Tremont receipts show only twelve musicians. The director's salary varied too, rising at times to $35 weekly but dipping to $9 in the summer (or about $220 today).[8]

No evidence before the 1890s seems to show that theatre musicians could expect "extras," such as a doubling fee for playing more than one instrument or for playing benefits and holidays. In an article on New York theatre orchestras of the post–Civil War period, John Graziano determined that many theatre musicians supplemented their income by playing for balls and other evening events and would often send substitutes to their posts in the theatre.[9] This practice—undoubtedly also found in London—must have been responsible for the frequent accounts of rag-tag or ill-balanced ensembles. Musicians who applied for theatre jobs, it was said, were usually those who did not get the opera or symphony gigs. But we cannot assume this to be universal, as the quality of musicians varied greatly between theatres and across decades. First-rank theatres in major cities could always afford to attract musicians of better caliber. During the heyday of its success in the 1850s Burton's stock theater in New York maintained a core of twelve musicians. A reviewer recalled not only that George Loder "did wonders with the number of instruments at his disposal" but that in terms of quality his orchestra "ranked next to that of Max Maretzek at the Italian opera."[10]

In 1864 a number of theatre orchestra leaders in New York, including Thomas Baker, Harvey B. Dodworth, Edward Mollenhauer, and Henry Wannemacher, were involved in forming the musical protective union. Despite an interim period where managers refused to comply with union wages, orchestra pay increased—and quality with it. In 1870 Olive Logan estimated that the weekly salaries of an orchestra of twelve to sixteen musicians at a New York stock theatre ranged from $18 to $30 per person (about $300 to $500 today). By then a leader could earn as much as $100 a week ($1,700 today), three times as much as the prompter and about the same as a good scene painter.[11] At these inflated prices, a resident leader and core of twelve musicians amounted to a significant outlay for a theatre manager.

Playbills and newspapers sometimes offered details for bands in New York's more fashionable theatres, like Wallack's, which maintained an orchestra "of first-class performers" (or so its playbill advertised). Statistics for orchestras at the Bowery, the Chatham, or Barnum's American Museum, however, are rare indeed. An engraving in *Frank Leslie's Illustrated Newspaper* for an 1865 production of Wilks's drama *A Roll of the Drum* at Barnum's—sketched from the wings—shows about nine musicians, but another six or so are almost certainly hidden behind the actors' bodies. The orchestra appears to be playing while the action is in progress. House lights usually remained on during the performance, as indicated by many nineteenth-century theatre illustrations (for example, see Fig. 21). Still, musicians had to read their parts by ambient light from house and stage. Not until the 1880s did orchestral musicians acquire stand lights when theatres consistently began to darken the house.

The makeup of orchestras sometimes reflected a manager's tastes and the class of audience that he or she wished to cultivate. John Stetson, for example, was a great lover of the cornet and always made sure that his theatres (the Globe in Boston and Booth's in New York) had a top-notch cornet player who was featured regularly during the entr'actes.[12] During the play itself some managers (such as Marie Wilton at the Prince of Wales's) would let house musicians sit for great lengths of time, preferring not to have music interfere with action or dialogue, while others urged the strings to shiver at the first portent of conflict.

A manager and playwright like Augustin Daly shrewdly managed the *melos* in his melodramas. At his Fifth Avenue Theatre, from 1869 to 1873, Daly's musical demands earned the admiration of Robert Stoepel, who led a well-polished ensemble of flute, clarinet, three brass, and seven strings.[13] After this theatre burned down, Daly remodeled an old space into a new Fifth Avenue Theatre, which he managed from 1874 to 1877. In an engraving from 1875 (Fig. 14), the players—still on the same level as the audience—all face the action onstage. The scene is the cathartic conclusion of Daly's *Pique*. Charles Fisher as the wealthy Matthew Standish enters left, holding aloft his rescued grandson, whose sham kidnapping turned out to be real. Fanny Davenport as the remorseful mother shrieks with joy. The eleven musicians under Harvey B. Dodworth seem to be playing full out in support of this tearful reunion. In using such a small band, Daly's musical imagination may well have been hampered by space. Or, like other theatre managers, he may have been stinging from the financial panic that caused the economic downturn in 1873. When he opened the new Daly's Theatre in 1879, he hired the seasoned Mollenhauer, who assured the manager that he could furnish an orchestra of sixteen good players for $280 a week.[14]

FIGURE 14. *Orchestra at Daly's Fifth Avenue Theatre: detail from engraving by J. N. Allan, 1875. Eno Collection, Miriam and Ira D. Wallach Division of Art, Prints, and Photographs, New York Public Library, Astor, Lenox, and Tilden Foundations*

Some later New York playhouses like the new Broadway Theatre, built in 1888, were designed to accommodate much larger ensembles. "Spectacle dramas" at the Broadway, such as *Ganelon* in 1891 and *Ben-Hur* in 1899, employed substantial orchestral forces with double winds, full brass (including three trombones), and at least fourteen strings. Drury Lane under Augustus Harris often employed an orchestra of twenty-eight, not only for pantomimes but for popular dramas as well. Even for large urban houses with a salaried orchestra, however, conventions associated with specific genres determined the size of ensemble. Herbert Beerbohm Tree, for example, produced a courtroom drama at the Haymarket in 1888 entitled *A Man's Shadow* that had two offstage band pieces (meant to be heard from the salon of a hotel) and only a few short melodramatic cues for a small body of strings. For the same director's production of Sydney Grundy's *Musketeers* (see chapter 10), a full orchestra accompanied the historical swashbuckler with nearly continuous music.

Few theaters in either New York or London, however, consistently maintained anything like the size of the Lyceum Theatre orchestra during the years of Henry Irving's management. In the late 1870s the Lyceum employed between twenty-six and thirty musicians (about nineteen strings),

FIGURE 15. *Prince's Theatre, Manchester: detail.* Illustrated London News *(27 November 1869), 528*

and Irving expanded the orchestra even further to match the lavish sets and costumes of *Faust* (1885) and *The Dead Heart* (1889).[15] When Irving brought the Lyceum company to New York in 1883, Henry Abbey, manager of the Star Theatre (formerly Wallack's), attempted to persuade him to use the house orchestra, then consisting of twelve musicians. Irving scoffed at this, insisting that his productions required an orchestra of forty. The local musicians' union stood behind Irving; he got his larger band, though compromising at thirty-five.

Some managers incorporated new and unusual instrumental colors into the orchestra, relative to a production concept. Charles Kean at the Princess's in the 1850s allowed Hatton to employ six harps for the Assyrian court in *Sardanapalus* and several medieval instruments for *Henry V*. It has proved difficult to find an image of the orchestra space at the Princess's. But an illustration from Manchester (Fig. 15) shows a comparably well-appointed theatre with a fairly generous and possibly expandable orchestra space. The illustrator depicted sixteen musicians, not counting the leader, whose raised and mounted music stand marks the center of the stage and the orchestra. Twelve musicians play traditional strings and winds. But Charles Calvert also requested the cithara, phorminx, and other "ancient Greek instruments" for *The Winter's Tale*. The band's supplemental members appear to be wearing traditional Greek dress.[16]

Orchestras for small-town theatres were of course a different matter. Classified ads for these often mentioned the "low pay." Hamilton Clarke discussed the instruments commonly absent in bands outside the major

FIGURE 16. *Star Theatre (Wallack's): orchestra and audience at* Uncle Tom's Cabin *(detail). The Museum of the City of New York/Art Resource*

British cities. "I do not suppose there are ten provincial theatre bands which can boast of a pair of horns, while in many instances there are to be found only one clarinet, one cornet, and very seldom either oboe or bassoon."[17] Clarke said that he knew of theatre bands that included only seven instruments: first and second violin, double bass, flute, clarinet, cornet, and euphonium. The problem with such an ensemble, he warned in his study of orchestration, was that it was top and bottom heavy, with most instruments playing either melody or bass. The inner parts, so crucial to establishing the harmony, were missing.

But London managers at the St. James's and Her Majesty's used large orchestras for their spectacles, as did David Belasco in America. Despite the size and timbral palettes of the urban theatre bands of the 1880s and 1890s, many theatre managers found the large model financially unsustainable after the turn of the century. William Archer and Harley Granville-Barker in their 1907 proposal for a National Theatre included a budget of twenty-four permanent orchestral musicians ("bandsmen"). But these liberal projections were surely reflective of earlier, more idealistic times.[18] Guides to play production in the early twentieth century—excluding, of course, huge playhouses such as Drury Lane, the Broadway Theatre, or the Hippodrome—usually acknowledge eight pieces in most first-class theatres. Orchestration manuals prescribe an ideal theatre orchestra of twelve but explain how many dramatic accompaniments can be achieved with as few as eight musicians.[19] This is exactly the number shown in the photograph from the Star Theatre in 1897 (Fig. 16), where leader Sidney H. Horner sits at the center, holding his violin. The orchestra space is greatly confined, especially considering that this is the same theatre where Edward Mollenhauer led an orchestra of about eighteen for James and Lester Wallack thirty-seven years earlier and Meredith Ball conducted an orchestra of thirty-five for Irving twenty-two years earlier.

Armed with some basic statistics on English and American theatre orchestras, we can now begin a closer investigation of how the music they provided interacted with the stage.

6

The Craft of *Melos* in Rehearsal and Performance

Nineteenth-century playgoers and critics prove notoriously inarticulate witnesses on the use of music in the popular drama. The best evidence is to be had from those with a stake in the process: the managers who staged the business and often selected (or rejected) music, the actors who negotiated music into their interpretation of a role, the prompters who recorded these developments in rehearsal, and the orchestra leaders whose job it was to please all of these people. Their decisions are preserved in the crucial documents of production. Besides orchestra parts (discussed in chapter 4) these include "acting editions" of plays, promptbooks, music plots, and actors' accounts.

The techniques of rendering a play in the nineteenth century could be as diverse and capricious as the playgoers themselves. Actors then as now worked within a prevailing atmosphere of competition, which undeniably led to ingenuity and originality. Still, the very concept of "stock" implied a "stability of artistic impulse and its accumulating traditions," wrote Edward Fuller. For this American newspaper editor, the vanishing stock theatre had been the "real school" for drama in the nineteenth century.[1] This was the tradition whereby each theatre had its own regular company of actors, supplemented with occasional visits of guest stars. Even at a fashionable urban theatre like the Adelphi in London, John Baldwin Buckstone wrote his plays for a strong company of stock actors, including Charles Selby, Charles Hudson, Elizabeth Yates, and Fanny Elizabeth Fitzwilliam. These players both influenced and were influenced by Buckstone's stock approach to drama and characterization (a tradition that lingered well into the early years of sound film, with a nucleus of actors assembled by directors such as John Ford and Orson Welles).

Music and the Role of the Mid-Century Actor-Manager

As we have seen, melodramatic authors typically conceived their popular dramas with music in mind. But the exact style and placement of music were often the result of a collaborative process and guided by the tastes and experience of a strong-willed actor-manager.

Shortly after taking over the management of the National Theatre in Boston in the early 1840s, John Cartlich had to play the role of "young Malfort" in Andrew Cherry's *The Soldier's Daughter*, an old-fashioned comedy that required no affective music. When he missed his entrance in a rehearsal he was alerted by J. B. Wright, the prompter. "That's your cue, Mr. Cartlich." "Well, where's the music?" the actor replied in his booming voice. "I can't come on without music. Mr. Holloway, please play three bars from the hurry in *Mazeppa*."[2] Meanwhile Wright, finding no indication for music in his promptbook, was justifiably flummoxed. Cartlich had begun his career as a tragedian in Richardson's fairground theatre, then acted minor parts at the Coburg, and finally became famous for creating the role of Mazeppa at Astley's in 1831. According to Walter Leman, he "was the concentrated essence of bucket-topped boots, smuggler's belts, big buckles, fighting swords, and pizzicato music." Cartlich had apparently never in his life acted without some *melos* to accompany him, if we trust Leman's account.[3]

Clearly, Cartlich came from a tradition in which a leading actor would be heralded by a signature tune, much as Garrick and Sheridan in the eighteenth century had used well-known operatic arias. What about Cartlich's choice? A "hurry" was a *melos* typically used for action sequences or some other stage imbroglio. By itself, it hardly seemed appropriate for a first entrance. Like their pantomimic predecessors, hurries in the popular drama were generally used to accompany some ongoing action, not to stimulate applause. Maybe the *melos* would have served as a kind of musical calling card, to remind audiences that the actor striding onto the stage in Georgian dress was none other than the great Byronic hero in the flesh. Other, more practical issues were raised here. First, in some large theatres a spoken cue could not always be heard backstage; but when the orchestra began to play, the signal for the offstage actor was unmistakable. Second, this episode took place during an early rehearsal for the play, perhaps even the only rehearsal, if the other actors were already seasoned in their roles. And yet the music director or his *répétiteur* is on hand.[4] As manager of the theatre

Cartlich probably inherited his orchestra leader, as he inherited the veteran prompter.[5] Still, how did he know that Holloway would be familiar with a specific *melos* in *Mazeppa*? The horseback-riding Cossack had been a stage phenomenon practically everywhere. But was that particular *melos* so well known in the theatre world? Perhaps Cartlich traveled with his own stack of music and therefore expected Holloway to rout it out in short order. Or perhaps Leman was confusing the Boston composer John Holloway with John Harroway (1810–1857), the English violinist and music publisher who led theatre orchestras in London.[6] Might Harroway have accompanied Cartlich to America?[7] If not, what were the odds that the leader would have had a copy of this *melos* handy, along with a stash of other theatre music on his stand? Finally, was "Mr. Holloway" alone at this rehearsal or did he have the band in situ—did the whole group suddenly have to scramble to pull out the requested number?

A larger-than-life personality such as Cartlich (who resembled Elliston in this regard) no doubt exerted a decisive controlling force over all aspects of production. It was a nineteenth-century actor-manager's job, after all, to choose the plays and the rest of the cast, coach the actors in their roles, and preside over rehearsals. (Cartlich was listed in some Boston advertisements as "Melo Dramatic Manager.") In the days before the reigning director, the manager was one of the principal actors of the company. Sometimes the acting manager was also proprietor, in which case he—or she, in the case of Marie Wilton or Laura Keene—was financially responsible for the success of a play. Some theatres had a separate stage manager, whose duties included the planning and construction of sets, lighting, costumes, and properties. In the stock theatre "manager" could refer to either or both sets of responsibilities.

Some managers of theatres, who came up through the stock system as actors, were trained in music. William Wood recalled John Henry, manager of the old John Street Theatre in New York, picking up a fiddle and jumping into the orchestra to help out during a performance. A very young Benjamin Webster (manager of the Adelphi from 1847 to 1870), when denied an acting post at his first audition in Croydon, inquired if there was room in the orchestra. The manager, suspicious, produced a violin, whereupon Webster proceeded to play a few bars of Giuseppe Tartini's "Devil's Trill" sonata.[8] He got the job. (Webster's father had been a violinist and dancing master in late eighteenth-century Bath.)[9]

In the nineteenth century a musical background was extremely useful for a manager, because plotting out and even selecting music were usually on his list of essential responsibilities. For example, John Coleman was manager of the Princess's Theatre when he decided in 1865 to produce Charles Reade's *It's Never Too Late to Mend.* Coleman took the company to Leeds, where they rehearsed and ran a short try-out before bringing it to London. Amid some controversy over the prison scenes, the play finally opened at the prestigious London playhouse. Coleman wrote: "When the play was produced on the 4th October, it was done with all my original business, music, *mise-en-scene*, etc.," though he expressed dismay that Reade managed to restore some controversial scenes that he had cut.[10] In other words, in this case it was the manager who claimed credit for working out the music, perhaps even concocting some of it. Several of the surviving instrumental parts for some of Samuel Phelps's productions (for example, *Virginius* and *Werner*) appear to be in his hand.[11]

Through music an acting manager could put his personal stamp on a production, though even this interpretive aspect was subject to change over the years. Phelps was manager of Sadler's Wells Theatre in 1844 when he staged the first version of his famous *Macbeth.* For this production he used the music attributed to Matthew Locke, written for William Davenant's Restoration version of the play. This included songs for the witches and other choruses and solos. In effect it turned *Macbeth* into a play with music. Furthermore, Phelps's promptbook for this production includes additional music cues that melo-dramatize the play. For example, at the end of the witches' scene in act 4, the margin of the promptbook reads "discordant music and then trap pull for sinking cauldron. A loud gust of wind."[12] (It was presumably up to the leader Isaac Collins and his band in 1844 to satisfy Phelps's request for "discordant music.") Several years later at the same theatre Phelps was in the midst of his famous Shakespeare revivals, during which his focus had shifted to an emphasis on Elizabethan performance style. As one playgoer recollected, "Shakespeare's text" did not mention music, so for this production there was not a note from start to finish. This would have been a performance to remember, as "Locke's music" was an almost continuous presence in *Macbeth* from the eighteenth through the middle of the nineteenth century. Phelps's purging of music was far from trendsetting, however. Many managers such as Charles Kean, Charles Calvert, Henry Irving, and McKee Rankin staged Shakespeare's tragedies using music like sound and lighting effects: to influence interpretation of the characters' emotional and psychological development. Such music-laden productions must have taken place to the great chagrin of the playgoer who recalled Phelps's unadorned approach with nostalgia.

Charles Kean was known to use quite a bit of music. In *Macbeth* he added "apparition music" for the appearance of Banquo's ghost. In very different ways from Phelps, however, Kean brought to his productions an almost archaeological sense for history. For *Henry V* he added an "historical interpolation" on Old London Bridge for which he requested onstage instruments such as cornetti, pipes, and tabor. Kean liked to exert control over music in addition to other aspects of production. One night prior to his management of the Princess's he was on tour in the United States, appearing in 1846 at the St. Charles Theatre in Mobile, Alabama. The opening play was Moore's *The Gamester*. At the close of this tragedy, the German-born leader of the St. Charles's orchestra—who was reportedly inexperienced but who had led the orchestra two nights earlier for Henry Placide in the melodrama *Thalaba, or The Destroyer*—had his orchestra play a piece of slow, solemn music to accompany Kean's death as Beverley at the end of the play. Apparently the leader did not know the difference between a tragedy and a melodrama. The observer makes it seem as if the leader, moved by the actor's pathos, was suddenly inspired to add some under-dialogue music. However it may have happened, the cue had most decidedly not been agreed upon in rehearsal. As soon as the curtain came down, Kean erupted in fury and ran to the orchestra. He started abusing the musicians, the theatre, and the management. To Kean, it was unconscionable that this final scene should be disturbed by anything so melodramatic as slow music. But perhaps the leader was more knowledgeable than the teller of this tale supposed. As noted earlier, it was this very scene to which David Garrick added the slow, solemn strains that moved Burgoyne to write about the powerful impact that such music could have on the English drama.[13]

The Acting Company in the Nineteenth-Century Stock Theatre

Other members of the company also had sharp opinions on when music should and should not be used. It was not uncommon in the early decades of the nineteenth century, James Cook wrote in 1841, for a couple of actors onstage about to engage in deadly combat to wink at the leader of the band, "expressing their wish for a strong chord."[14] Céline Celeste, the French actress who appeared at the Adelphi in 1832 in *The French Spy*, at that time had very little command of the English language. The multiple characters that she played in this melodrama had to be created largely through pantomime, and for this she relied upon an extensive amount of music. Each time a character would ask her a question she would respond in the language of gestures while music especially composed for her began to flow out of the orchestra. By this point, of course, English audiences were long familiar with the concept of muteness as an allegorical subtext of melodrama. Though this play about the recent Franco-Arabic conflict brought some of the kinds of misunderstandings between these two different linguistic cultures to public attention, Celeste in her double role as a French spy among the Arabs and an Arab boy among the French made rather complicated communication without language seem natural. "I am deliberately of the opinion that Madame Celeste could not act without music," wrote John M. Morton. "In her long life she never suffered greater pain and mortification than when an inattentive or incapable leader failed to take up his 'music cue.'"[15] Given the importance of the accompanying music, Celeste must surely have traveled with a set of orchestra parts containing these cues, though these have disappeared.

As we saw at the Coburg in chapter 3, stock theatres large and small maintained a "regular company," consisting of a range of actors who covered all the necessary lines of business based on their physical shape, personality, and vocal timbre. Numerous acting manuals in the nineteenth century discuss these character types. Among those listed in articles such as "The Theatrical World" in *Chambers's Journal* (1858) and "Actors and Their Remuneration" in the *San Francisco Bulletin* (1860) are leading men and ladies, heavy men and ladies, singing chambermaids or servants, juveniles, walking gentlemen and ladies, old men and women, light comedians, low comedians, utility actors and actresses, and character actors. Most of these were further ranked by salary as first, second, or third.[16]

We can see several of these lines in *Lost in London*, a mid-century domestic melodrama. Watts Phillips crafted his play in the early 1860s for the Adelphi company. But the first known performance was in New York at Wallack's in 1865 in a pirated version. The Adelphi followed two years later. Both of these were first-rate stock theatres. The play begins in a mining town in Lancashire. At the conclusion of act 1 (Fig. 17) the bearded miner Job Armroyd (leading man) ascends the coal mine in a lift with Tiddy Dragglethorpe (second leading lady or second comedian), who has come to inform him that the mine's wealthy owner, Gilbert Featherstone (heavy man), has managed to lure away Job's wife with promises of a luxurious life in London. The miners and his friend Jack Longbones (first utility man) support his determination to go in search of her.

The second act takes place six months later. Nelly Armroyd (leading lady) is living with Featherstone in a villa in Regent's Park, a wealthy dis-

FIGURE 17. Lost in London, *act 1, scene 3. Stock poster image in Stanley Appelbaum,* Scenes from the Nineteenth-Century Stage in Advertising Woodcuts *(New York: Dover, 1977), 44*

trict of London. In act 2, scene 3, Job finally locates his wife. In this picturesque exterior scene (Fig. 18), Featherstone has sent his wily servant Blinker (first comedian) on an errand. Job, pausing in front of the villa to listen to the lively dance music he hears from within, suddenly spies Nelly in the window. Blinker, returning, encounters the impassioned Job, who recognizes him and hurls him into the path of arriving guests (walking men and ladies). Featherstone does not appear in the image, but his butler Thomas (character or respectable utility man) is seen here at the top of the stairs restraining the footmen while Tops, the post-boy (juvenile), intends to light the way for Blinker. Each of these images represents the final tableau of the scene, with the actors momentarily frozen in a stage picture, hand gestures and all. (Is Thomas's restraining gesture to prevent the servants from intervening or to insist that Job not be allowed in?) The second leading lady is paired with the first comedian to provide the regional patois and comic business that serves to offset the play's tragic implications. Moreover, even

FIGURE 18. Lost in London, *act 2, scene 3*

a heavy man must on occasion be able to sing: Phillips has given Featherstone a song at the opening of act 2.

Though a characteristic *melos* was sometimes expected to be associated with a certain line, in the best of circumstances these were selectively applied. "Plaintive music," associated with a leading lady in distress since the eighteenth century, still served its identifying function; in fact the captive Nelly makes her act 2 entrance to just such a yearning *melos*. But it was also true that a misplaced or too-obvious *melos* could meet with ridicule. Even within the established conventions of a nineteenth-century stock theatre, the best actors and orchestra leaders managed to avoid rigid stereotypes.

Consider the nineteenth-century villain. The score that Edwin Ellis prepared for Adelphi's *Lost in London*, for example, contains no specific character music at all for Featherstone, who was initially played by Henry J. Ashley, a relatively young actor who took on leading roles in comedy in addition to heavy roles. (Charles Fisher, who played Featherstone in New York, was similarly versatile as heavy and comic.) W. J. Florence, an itinerant American actor specializing in heavy lines, took great care with his music and kept a set of orchestra parts to accompany his major roles. One of these was Obenreizer, the melodramatic villain of *No Thoroughfare* by Charles Dickens and Wilkie Collins. A twelve-bar *melos* indeed underscores many of Obenreizer's entrances, including his first. Working against convention, however, the *melos* does not signal the character's actual line of business; instead it is a pastoral *andante* in E-flat major, redolent of the Swiss mountains from which Obenreizer originates. The sweetness of this signature tune belies the actor's *ethos* in the play, which is cruel and ruthless.

J. B. Studley, the noted melodramatic villain who created the particularly nasty underworld character of Byke in Augustin Daly's *Under the Gaslight* (New-York Theatre, 1867), had no music at all for his entrances throughout the play, with the exception of his very last. In the final scene Byke appears on the moonlit balcony with the intent of breaking into the second leading lady's home and abducting her. A quiet but intense *pizzicato misterioso* accompanies his spooky entrance as Byke steals around the shadowy room and prepares his chloroformed handkerchief. Though the *pizzicato* quietly sustains a sinister mood for Byke's stealthy pantomime, it is worth noting that this tension-filled *melos*—unlike the ubiquitous Swiss tune for Obenreizer—was withheld until the last act. Whether the decision on this reserved use of music to minimize (or maximize) obvious lines of business was made by Studley, Daly, or the music director is unknown, but it was most likely a combination of the three.

Music and Management in the Nineteenth-Century Stock Theatre

Despite occasional reports of music leaders ad-libbing in performance—as in the *Gamester* example above—most decisions about music were made in rehearsal. Rehearsal time could be limited in a mid-century stock theatre with frequent changes in repertoire; even a new play might get as few as eight or nine rehearsals. Hence a popular drama would rarely be rehearsed without the orchestra leader, usually with fiddle in hand like the dancing masters of old. An experienced stage manager knew that music most appropriate for action and dialogue could best be selected or created by an ally who shared the manager's knowledge of the play and the company's actors. Even for a play with no songs, choruses, or dance music, a resident orchestra leader played a central role. In September 1836, for example, Macready was in Bristol and went to the theatre to find nothing ready for the rehearsal for *The Bridal*, a tragedy adapted by Sheridan Knowles from a Francis Beaumont and John Fletcher play with several cues for onstage music. “We waited an hour for the property man and for the leader of the band,” he recalled in his *Reminiscences*.[17]

An actor-manager like Dion Boucicault was so particular about his music that he demanded a number of staging rehearsals with not only the leader but the whole orchestra present. When he assumed management of the Winter Garden in New York in 1859, Boucicault decided to begin the season with two of his plays. *The Phantom* was a revision of an earlier play (*The Vampire*) produced in 1852. *Dot,* his adaptation of Dickens’s *Cricket on the Hearth,* was entirely new. Edward Mollenhauer was Boucicault’s resident music director. He was required to have his musicians present at any rehearsals requested by the manager. Mollenhauer composed all new music for *Dot,* according to the playbill. This information is not specified for *The Phantom,* so Mollenhauer (or Boucicault) may have had access to a copy of music originally prepared for the play in London. (Neither score has been found.)

A surviving fragment of a rehearsal schedule in Boucicault’s hand indicates that he asked for the full instrumental ensemble to be present at several staging rehearsals, The “full band” is double-underlined in Boucicault’s note.[18]

Thursday	Read *Phantom* at 1
Friday	*Phantom* at 11, *Dot* at 12½; music of *Dot* and *Phantom* at 2
Saturday	Full band
	Dot, 1st scene at 11
	Phantom, 1st act at 1
Wednesday	*Dot* without parts at 11½—full band (etc.)

Neither *Dot* nor *Phantom* is a play with music in the generic sense. But Boucicault was no doubt aware, like Macready in the earlier incident, that it was wasteful to rehearse the timing of any stage business without the participation of the leader or his *répétiteur*, particularly in the case of melodramas like these.[19] “Music” in Boucicault’s Friday slot probably referred to a dedicated session in which he went over details of both scores with his leader. Some actors, by the way, were still working from sides. It was not until Wednesday that the play was run completely from memory, with the full band again present.

Melodramatic playwrights like Boucicault often knew exactly where music would be most effective. It was ultimately the prompter’s job to make sure that the music fit with the stage. “If there is any particular movement or action, technically termed *business*, for you to perform,” instructed Leman Rede in 1827, “the stage-manager or prompter will explain it to you, and show you how to go through it.”[20] The act of re-creating the original business of a play was typical of many stock companies, and the prompter might be the one walking the actors through their roles. The manager might work out entrances and positions for a new play, in which case the prompter would follow the actors’ movements and keep a careful record in the promptbook.

During performances the prompter always sat on stage left at a small table. From there he could see both the actors and the audience through peepholes and signaled the curtain with a little bell that ran up into the flies. At his desk was also a chronograph used to time each scene and act break. Serving as the company clock, the prompter ordered the call-boy to retrieve actors in time for their entrances, notified the property man, turned gas jets up or down for lights, cued stage business and sound effects with a speaking trumpet and the orchestra leader through one of the long tin “speaking tubes,” whistled to alert scene changes, and “rang” in the curtain.[21] Both the speaking tubes and the prompter’s whistle for the rigging crew were borrowed from their use on a ship, which served as a model of management for the stage in many significant ways.

The prompter was captain backstage in a nineteenth-century theatre, which might play naturalistic drawing room comedy one evening and comic pantomime another (and perhaps both on the same night). A visitor backstage before a production of *Richard III* at the Chestnut Street Theatre in Philadelphia in 1842 noticed that “the prompter directed the carpenter to set the first act, pulled a bell-handle with ‘lights up’ engraved on it, and shortly after kicked the call-boy and told him to announce ‘second music’ to the green room.”[22] Toward the end of the nineteenth century, when electricity was wired in, the prompter at a major theatre would generally cue the leader with signal lights of different colors, although the speaking tube remained in use as late as 1918.[23] As if these duties were not enough, the prompter was expected to memorize the play or keep one eye on the promptbook, in case actors lost their way.

This backstage world is revealed to us in a fictional account of a melodramatic rehearsal in a novel by Albert Smith called *The Fortunes of the Scattergood Family*, serialized in *Bentley’s Miscellany* (London, 1844). Smith, who began his career as a surgeon, soon turned to dramatic adaptation for the Adelphi and other theatres and eventually was appointed dramatic critic

FIGURE 19. *Detail from Albert Smith,* The Fortunes of the Scattergood Family, *vol. 1 (London: Richard Bentley, 1845), opposite 138*

of the *Illustrated London News*. He was also a member of a semibohemian circle of writers including Douglas Jerrold, William Thackeray, Tom Taylor, and Dion Boucicault, who regularly met to discuss literature and the theatre.[24] Smith's fictional rehearsal is of a nautical drama at a "transpontine theatre" (south of the Thames), like the Coburg or Surrey. The play is by one Glenalvon Fogg, a "dramatic author."[25] The actors onstage are rehearsing in street clothes amid scenic disarray, while the leader and prompter are down in the orchestra busily "working out the music" (Fig. 19).

"The leader was shivering in the middle of the orchestra, exactly in his own light, which streamed in one long dusty ray from the back of the gallery over the sweepers, who were clearing away the orange-peel; and, violin in hand, was arranging what he termed the 'meloses'—the little bits of incidental music to come in when anything interesting took place. As the play was to be produced that night, of course none of the scenery was finished, so the stage was fitted up with half a drawing-room flat, and half a smuggler's haunt, with a ship's bulwark and cannons running across the front, and a grassy bank at the prompt entrance, which looked very like a portable bath in a green petticoat."[26]

Smith clearly understood the intimate collaboration between the prompter and orchestra leader. In performance these two needed to work together closely to assure the play's unbroken flow. The prompter in the illustration has what appears to be a chronograph in his left hand. On each music stand is an open book. On the right stand may be a promptbook, on which the prompter is intensely focused as he delivers the cues. On the left stand is probably a violin-leader book, presumably containing the numbered *melos* items. The fictional leader with his violin is patiently awaiting instructions as he absorbs information about lines and business, some of which the actors may be working through onstage. Both leader and prompter appear to be running through timings, with the music already in place. This may have been composed afresh or assembled from existing sources (or some combination of the two) or—if the play was not new—even acquired from another theatre.

This meeting between prompter and leader possibly takes place early in the morning, before the orchestra arrives (usually at ten). Perhaps important changes had been made since the last rehearsal, with some insertions or deletions. John Coleman, for example, tells the story of "getting up" Charles Reade's *Put Yourself in His Place* in 1870. It was slated to open at the Adelphi but was rehearsed for a trial run in Leeds, like the earlier *Never Too Late*. Rehearsals began only a week earlier. On the eve of the opening Reade, who was adapting the play from one of his earlier novels, still had not finished the last act. Finally the act arrived at midnight, and an exhausted Coleman "read through every part, and arranged the business and the music of every situation three times consecutively."[27] The orchestra leader would then have needed to copy out the parts for a rehearsal at ten the following morning, before which he may have had a dry run with the prompter, similar to the illustration. Coleman makes it clear, however, that this was a highly unusual situation.

Some directors planned their music cues well in advance. For the first production of J. Redding Ware's adaptation of *The Polish Jew, or The Sledge Bells* in 1872, Oscar Barrett dated his orchestra parts 26 February, a full week before the first performance on 4 March. His music was ready in plenty of time for rehearsal before opening night. The supposition that musicians might even have improvised in performance, as refuted by Sarah Hibberd and Nanette Nielsen, is based on modern notions and is completely "alien to the musical environment of early nineteenth-century theatre."[28] Even in the *Scattergood* novel, a combat scene in the ensuing rehearsal of Fogg's play goes badly, with the two actors unable to capture the forceful mood. "We had better try it over again to the music," grumbled the stage manager.[29]

Interpreting Documents of Rehearsal and Production

Once music was composed and agreed upon, the details were entered into a "prompt copy" of the play, which indicates exactly where music was employed and how it interacted with other aspects of production, such as staging, sound effects, and—as technology became more elaborate—special types of lighting cues such as calcium beams or cross fades. Our understanding of music in the nineteenth-century stock theatre is closely connected with this important document. For example, the Surrey Theatre produced a version of Dickens's *Oliver Twist* in November 1838. The adaptation was by George Almar, a comedian who also played the role of Toby Crackit. Within a year Chapman and Hall published Almar's version "correctly printed from the prompter's copy." This publication—designed for productions in other theatres—specified eleven music cues, along with scenic arrangements and the positions of characters in significant episodes and tableaux. Though *Oliver Twist* was given in innumerable versions in the United States and in England (after a ten-year ban was lifted in 1848), Almar's adaptation was the most popular. A promptbook of this play from the 1860s was very likely used for American productions starring E. L. Davenport and Lucille Western. It is a "window script," with leaves from the published text by Almar pasted onto larger pages, on which the stage manager has added many handwritten instructions. Not only are the music cues in Almar's original highlighted, but additional sound and music cues appear in the margins.

It would have been the prompter's job to prepare the promptbook in theatres where a play was first produced, and duplicates might have been made for productions in other cities. For example, the promptbook from an 1858 production at Niblo's Garden of *The Pope of Rome* (an adaptation of *Sixtus V, or the Broken Vow*, an earlier play from the Olympic in London) reveals how L. I. Vincent, the prompter, marked in specified indications for music, along with other technical requirements. The bound promptbook consists of a copy of Samuel French's printed version of the play, interleaved with blank pages on which Vincent has carefully written his notes in ink. "Music at rise," for example, and the indication "NOTA BENE" throughout are both followed by the symbol of a dot surrounded by a circle and the word "Music" (Vincent used the same symbol for other cues such as special sounds, lights, and curtain).[30] The printed text of *The Pope of Rome* contains no music cues at all, whereas instructions for music in Vincent's hand are written on nearly every page. The cues here are not numbered as they sometimes are in other promptbooks. In some cases Vincent specified music on the inserted page opposite (for example, "Organ Music [circle with dot]") and then drew a line to the position in the text where he had placed a corresponding circle and dot. Promptbooks served several functions, but the most important of these was as a master plan from which the prompter was to run the production.

The promptbook prepared by Mr. Jenkins for *Jack Sheppard*, a popular drama by John Buckstone given at the Adelphi in 1839, demonstrates how even the most basic indications for action and dialogue music may entail subtle shadings in application. *Jack Sheppard* was among the best of the class of subversive melodramas featuring a depiction of English criminal life and a popular working-class hero. The following scene occurs near the beginning of act 1. It is late at night in a "miserable room in a house in the Old Mint." Mr. Wood has accompanied home the destitute widow and infant child of one of his former workers, Tom Sheppard. The master has offered to adopt and raise the child. During their conversation the young woman remembers a key that Tom gave her to return to his master. Placing the infant in Mr. Wood's arms, she runs upstairs to fetch it. Mr. Wood is about to acquire a second baby. The following excerpt is from Chapman and Hall (ca. 1840), an edition "correctly printed from the prompter's copy":

> *Mr. Wood.* Poor thing, she's seen better days and better circumstances than ever she'll see again. Strange, I never could learn her history. My journeyman, Tom Sheppard, was always a close[d] file and would never tell whom he married; however, she was much too good for him and was never meant to be Tom's wife. (*Dandling the infant.*) Poor little thing!—I'll bring you up, and make a carpenter of you, eh! my little gimblet? Now, don't cry. Mrs. Sheppard, make haste, the baby wants you! Now, none of your tricks, you villain! What a time she's hunting for the key. Mrs. Sheppard, it's impossible I can

hold the baby any longer! (*Music, piano*) Holla! There's someone coming up stairs. Who can it be?—none of those rascally minters I hope. (*Music, forte.*)

(*Darrell, enveloped in a horseman's cloak, rushes on* L.D. *He glances hastily round the room—listens at the door—produces a child from beneath his cloak—places it in Wood's arms—takes off his cloak, and fastens it round Wood's throat.*)

Darrell. By heavens, you've an infant there already!

The scene continues, the last *forte* music cue presumably having ceased or abated at some point for the brief dialogue. Aggravated voices are then heard from offstage. Darrell hurriedly explains that those pursuing him are bent on killing the child, whereupon Mr. Wood offers to help him escape. Darrell removes one of the babies—the wrong one—while the two men exchange names.

Mr. Wood. You see that window—force it open. You can then step on the roof of some low houses, and gain the street. Quick, quick! (*Music. Darrell runs off. Sir Cecil enters, a drawn sword in his hand . . .*)

None of the three musical instructions here indicates the *melos*, though the context suggests some sort of continuous (or nearly continuous) nonthematic *agitato* hurry. The music's volume seems to be the author's immediate concern. At first it must be soft enough (*piano*) so as not to cover Wood's speech and also for Darrell's offstage footsteps to be audible to the audience as well as onstage to the actor playing Mr. Wood. Music aids characterization as well, or else Buckstone would not have asked that it be cranked up to *forte* for Darrell's entrance. But this dynamic was possible only because of a pause in the dialogue. The next few moments are taken up with hurried action and considerable stage bustle. Based on the limited information about music in the promptbook, Buckstone appears to have left the choices of *melos* affecting tempo, key, and mood to the music director.

A second important document regarding the placement of music in the Victorian popular drama is the music plot. Manuals such as *A Practical Guide to Theatricals* (1875) refer to the music plot along with the other "plots" prepared by the manager or prompter, such as a property plot or entrance plot.[31] For example, Frederick Wilton, manager of the Britannia Theatre in the 1860s, wrote in his diary for Tuesday, 15 September 1863: "Gave out Scene, Property, and Music Plots of *Fanfan the Tulip* last night, and

Wardrobe Plot this evening."[32] It was clear from an earlier entry that Wilton spent his Sunday at home working out these plots so that he would have them ready for the prompter at the next rehearsal. The music plot—usually written by hand—would have been a list of cues to instruct the orchestra leader on exactly what kind of music was needed and where. These lists were sometimes also called "directions for music," although the elements that specifically make them a music plot are that the musical numbers (1) are listed in the order they occur in the play; (2) must be executed precisely according to a word or visual cue; and (3) include some indication as to the *melos* and possibly volume of the music.

If we had the music plot to the *Jack Sheppard* sequence above, we might see something like this:

[cue]	[*melos*]
"hold the baby any longer"	Agitato, *piano*
	(*forte* at "rascally minters I hope")
"quick, quick!"	*Hurry*

In some instances the music plot might have been prepared before rehearsal, therefore reflecting an actor-manager's conceptual approach to production. In others it may have served as a record of the types of music decided upon in rehearsal if another leader needed to assemble appropriate music from stock. In either case these lists demonstrate that *melos* was typically engaged as a tool of interpretation and very often developed as part of the overall conception, rather than merely as an improvisatory item added at the last minute at the whim of a blustery actor or intrepid orchestra leader.

Let us try to reconstruct music and action from a surviving music plot. It was drawn up in connection with a production of James Pilgrim's *The Female Highwayman, or The Blighted Lily* at Purdy's National Theatre (the Chatham) in New York in 1851. The British-born author was at that time only twenty-six years old but already had a reputation in England and America for his *Limerick Boys* and would go on to write the often-performed *Robert Emmet*, a play about the famous Irish revolutionary. He also wrote plays for a number of star actors such as Maggie Williams and S. C. Chanfrau and enjoyed particular success at working-class houses such as the Bowery and managed small stock theatres such as the St. Charles. Although *The Female Highwayman* was revived at Purdy's in 1854 and again in 1857, the play was never published and circulated only in manuscript. Pilgrim's copy at the New York Public Library includes indications

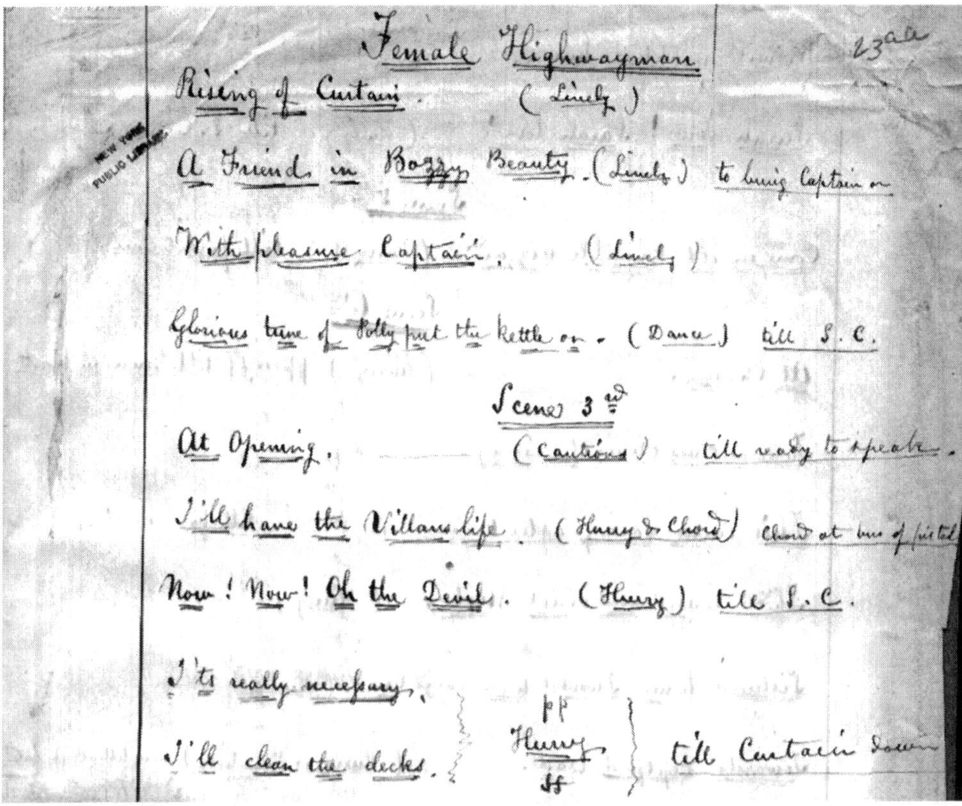

Female Highwayman 23a

Rising of Curtain. (Lively)

A Friend in Bozzy Beauty. (Lively) to bring Captain on

With pleasure Captain. (Lively)

Glorious tune of Polly put the kettle on. (Dance) till S.C.

Scene 3rd

At Opening. (Cautious) till ready to speak.

I'll have the Villains life. (Hurry & Chord) Chord at [illegible] of pistol

Now! Now! Oh the Devil. (Hurry) till S.C.

I'ts really necessary,

I'll clean the decks. pp Hurry ff till Curtain down

FIGURE 20. *Detail from* Female Highwayman *music plot. Billy Rose Theatre Division. The New York Public Library for the Performing Arts, Astor, Lenox, and Tilden Foundations*

for music throughout as well as a separate music plot (Fig. 20) prepared by the prompter ("C. Winter"). The plot consists of text cues that correspond to those in the play as well as indications specifying the character or affect of each *melos*. What did instructions such as "lively," "cautious," or "hurry and chord" say to a music director? If we examine these in the context of the play, as a leader of the time certainly would, a sense of balance and pacing in the melodramatic shaping of this nineteenth-century popular drama emerges with remarkable clarity.

Jenny Diver, the heroine of the play, was one of the most notorious criminals of eighteenth-century England, resorting to such clever tricks as positioning fake hands on her dress while her real hands were busy dipping into pockets of the people around her. A British dime novel entitled *Jenny Diver: The Female Highwayman* by "Pickpocket Jane Webb" published in

1850 presumably served as Pilgrim's source.[33] In this episode Jenny is disguised as a man in order to seek out Jack Splashton, another criminal and her lover of some years. She infiltrates his gang as a new recruit, apparently without being discovered.

A "rising of the curtain" reveals scene 1 in the London apartments of an actress, one of Jenny's childhood friends to whom she has gone to solicit help with her plan. There is no music for the scene change and opening at Black Bull Public House. The next music cue ("lively") is for stage business of Old Moll supplying the gang of thieves with liquor and for bringing on the "Captain," Splashton's new alias while in town. The next "lively" is again for stage business, and the scene ends with the gang dancing a reel to a well-known tune—a characteristic device for portraying the criminals as likeable "coves," as Pilgrim calls them. In scene 3 Jenny has secretly followed Jack, whom she finds wooing Alice Allcroft, the daughter of one of Lewisham's successful merchants, in order to gain her father's money. The scene opens with a *melos* labeled "cautious" as Alice, having snuck out alone, bemoans the fact that her suitor has kept her waiting, a negligence that seems too compromising for comfort. This is Alice's first appearance, and Pilgrim's choice for music is more in keeping with her current emotional state than with any expression of her innate character. The cautious ends just before she begins to speak. There is no music under her dialogue with "the Captain," nor for the arrival of Jenny, who remains hidden and whose violent asides reveal her mounting sense of betrayal.

When Alice and Splashton leave the stage, Jenny furiously rushes forward from hiding (still with no music specified). "My heart is crushed," she weeps, taking the stage. "My peace of mind is destroyed forever by a villain who swore eternal constancy to me beneath my mother's roof." She works herself into a vengeful frenzy. "I'll have the villain's <u>life</u>," she cries, this being the orchestra's cue for a "hurry and chord." Taking a gun from her coat, she aims it at Jack. Bozzy, one of Jack's cronies, dashes on and manages to stay her arm and prevent the shooting. Perhaps Pilgrim felt that agitated music was necessary to facilitate a character's rather instantaneous emotional escalation from hurt to murderous rage. But the chord itself was most certainly intended to coincide with Bozzy's intervention. The chord here serves as a crucial marker of dramatic reversal. The scene ends as Jenny shouts "oh the devil!"—the cue for the next music (another hurry)—as she presses her hands to her face in grief. Pilgrim expected the music to sustain the mood through the scene change ("till S.C.").

Throughout the entire music plot of *Female Highwayman* "lively, "hurry," and "chord" figure most prominently. "Slow," "bold," and "plaintive" occur less frequently. Some labels refer only to tempo, while others are more precise as to mood. At this point the cues have no numbers, which would have been assigned at the assembly stage and would have been essential in rehearsing the orchestra. Some prompters transferred these numbers into their promptbooks, while others did not. (By the 1880s and 1890s music plots were often typed, in many cases with the items already numbered.)

The most efficacious response to a music plot such as the one for *Female Highwayman* would be simply to plug in an appropriate *melos*. "It used to be formerly a matter of no little pride," observed a London critic in 1867,

> for a leader to be the fortunate possessor of a large collection of such small pieces, numbered and labeled:—"Slow music," "Mysterious music," "Dreamy music," "Thieves' *pizzicato*," "Creeping murderer's music," "Triumphant virtue music," "Hunting music," "Lively dreamy music," "Agitatoes [*sic*]," "Hurries," "Dying music," "Wild music," "Angel and demon music"—and all to be used at the fitting occasion.[34]

Similarly, orchestra leader Jimmy Glover wrote that mid-century itinerant musical directors "travelled with a book of 'agits,' i.e., *agitatos*, 'slows'—that is, slow music for serious situations—'pathetics,' 'struggles,' 'hornpipes,' *andantes*—to all which adapted numbers called 'melos' any dramatic situation was possible."[35]

This was exactly the method employed by the leader of a regional American company. Martin and Bella Golden toured standard melodramas throughout the central and southwestern United States in the 1860s and 1870s. They traveled with an orchestra leader—"J. M. Rodi" (Rodenbaugh) of Chicago, Illinois—and manuscript parts for a small local band of six players. For their production of Joaquin Miller's *The Danites* (1877), each musician had only one page of music with four generic *melos* numbers on it: no. 1, a mysterious, no. 2, a plaintive, no. 3, a lively (in 6/8), and no. 4, a hurry (in minor). Rodenbaugh used a music plot with text and sight cues to signal the musicians which of the four numbers to play. For example, the cues for the last act were:

23. Plaintive _____ till Curtain.
24. Plaintive _____ "no small potatoes." (till Piper is on stage)
25. Mysterious _____ "Confidence in her." (till Billy falls on stage)
26. Plaintive _____ "I might live hereafter." (till Billy is off)
27. Hurry _____ "he didn't know." (till all are on stage)

28. #Chord# _____ "you lie!"
29. Hurry _____ "what shall be done with them." (till all are off)
30. #Chord# _____ "a woman!"
31. Lively _____ "Glorious climate of California." (Till Curtain)

Each *melos* was therefore repeated multiple times throughout the play, which must have seemed rather tiresome to some listeners. A "chord" was specified only twice in the entire music plot, both times near the climactic end of the play where they would have heightened the sense of dramatic reversal, especially if played as diminished sevenths. The chords were not notated in the parts and would need to have been worked out beforehand in rehearsal. This approach typifies the most reductive application of *melos*, simplified for traveling companies where local musicians in small towns were speedily pressed into service. The technique was perhaps less a matter of dramatic exigency than one of minimizing musical mishaps with inexperienced and under-rehearsed players. For some of the plays the Goldens performed in larger theatres in prominent cities, such as *Enoch Arden* (1866), J. M. Rodi used more extensively written out orchestra parts, some even borrowed from major theatres in Philadelphia and Boston.[36]

Set music for plays like *Enoch Arden* (and the many other examples in chapter 4) reveals that Victorian-era theatre music was far more complex in practice than the simple instructions for "agitato" and "hurry" imply. By this time the actors' needs for *melos* had evolved into a common practice, requiring two distinct kinds (and both often within the same play).

The first is a simple thematic *melos*, a lyrical eight-bar tune reminiscent of a folksong or parlor ballad. Technically its function—as it had been since the beginnings of melodrama—was to promote empathy. Often indicated with repeat signs (or written instructions to "repeat until" some text or visual cue), it could be replayed as necessary until an actor had made his points or the dramatic situation had been played out (see the discussion of *The Green Bushes* at the end of this chapter). Such lyrical tunes might appear only briefly to introduce certain types of characters (essentially as signature tunes) or might linger while serving to accompany a crucial sequence of dialogue (under-dialogue music). The prominent role of the thematic class of *melos* in Victorian-age melodrama, which inevitably contained such a strong moral core and message, was partly to maintain and reinforce the social order. Though tunes such as plaintives, for example, may sound overly honeyed to modern ears, their simple melodies and balanced structure made them easily memorable. Their comforting harmonies, so typical of nineteenth-century sentimental songs, put audiences at ease in their expectations that a higher order was at work.

The second kind of *melos* is gestural or nonthematic and breaks with this social ideal. Though these may also fall into eight-bar patterns (such as hurries, for which actors needed to hear clear phrases or count beats), they are far more likely to consist of an uneven number of bars and to lack the tunefulness of the thematic *melos*. The irregular metrical features of such a *melos* (Byke's creeping *misterioso*, for example) suggest anarchy, and this kind of broken musical punctuation is more likely to underscore scenes of conflict in which the social order is threatened.

In addition to these two kinds of single-affect *melos* numbers, some music directors prepared "through-composed" numbers, combining *melos* items and building in stop-gaps to help coordinate the orchestra with the developing conflict onstage.

Examples from two important plays demonstrate how varied *melos* technique actually was in the best of circumstances. The 1864 promptbook for *Oliver Twist* contains twenty-seven numbered music cues. None of these are songs or dances. Four of the music cues functioned specifically to bring up the curtain or open a scene. (Some scenes opened with no music.) Seven cues were located internally, that is, initiated by an action or line of text and also concluded with a specific line or action or entrance of a character. Five cues were designed to close a scene, initiated by a line of text or action and played "till end of scene" or "till curtain." Eight cues were initiated by some action at the closing of a scene and continued as a "bridge cue," covering the scene change and carrying through to the opening of the next scene. There were four chained (or segue) cues, meaning that music halted momentarily for some action or line only to follow almost immediately with the next numbered cue. Finally, two through-composed musical numbers played through an entire scene, the first during Sikes's moonlit episode on the bridge just before he returns home to murder Nancy (which was followed by a segue cue) and the second in the subsequent scene, when Fagin is captured. Not surprisingly, music cues followed one another more closely in the final scenes of the play, during the falling action. (Indeed, in Almar's printed text, ten of the eleven specified music indications are in the last two acts.)

Given Davenport and Western's detailed promptbook of *Oliver Twist*, they may have arrived in Boston with their own set of orchestral parts. If so, leader Charles Koppitz did not have access to this music (or chose to disregard it). Koppitz composed the exact number of cues specified in the promptbook: twenty-seven. He used very few thematic *melos* numbers, no surprise given that most of the play takes place in London's social underbelly, where music of an irregular and anarchic nature was more effective for the dark plot twists. Of the nonthematic cues, five were tremolos, three of these functioning as under-dialogue music. The single *pizzicato* occurs near the end of act 2 when Toby and Sikes stealthily abduct a bound Oliver from the Brownlow residence. This *pizzicato* is part of a longer cue: the music eventually erupted into a full-blown *allegro fortissimo* in the final moments of the act.

Given the many different adaptations of *Oliver Twist,* music written for one production might not work for another. This is clearly the case in George Aiken's adaptation of *Uncle Tom's Cabin,* made famous by the touring Howard family. H. J. Conway prepared a different version for the Boston Theatre in 1852, which P. T. Barnum purchased for his American Museum in 1853.[37] The Conway promptbook contains thirty music cues, not counting several interpolated songs. Some of the cues in the promptbook specify the *melos* ("lively music," "hurried music," "plaintive music," "music *agitato*," "negro music," "march," "mock minuet," and so forth). Three of the cues are dances. Seven open an act or scene (establishing cues). In addition to many internal and closing cues, two closing cues specified a "picture" or frozen tableau. One sequence even included a panorama, a continually unfolding backcloth against which actors moved and music played.

The orchestra parts prepared by Thomas Comer survive to corroborate the evidence in the Conway promptbook. They include twenty-nine numbered cues; the interpolated songs are unnumbered. Some scenes involved rather more extended music than the promptbook alone would seem to indicate. (A lengthy medley, for example, accompanied the panorama.) In the scene at the Inn where the escaped slave Eliza and her tiny son are hiding in hopes of securing safe passage to Ohio, only one music cue is specified in the promptbook. The parts indicate that this is actually two segue cues. Drover John, who originally was assisting the slave trader, has had a change of heart and runs back to help Eliza. At his line "we must break through" music cue no. 7 began as he smashes the window. This consisted of just a *fortissimo*-sustained tremolo and three sharp chords. This music is emphatic in the sense that it was crafted to emphasize specific visual information. It is morally indifferent and conforms to no specific categories of *melos.* After John shouts to Eliza to jump, the strings began a *pianissimo* "hurry," cue no. 8, which functioned as a kind of vamp. This continued as the slave trader and his cronies broke down the door and stumbled over one an-

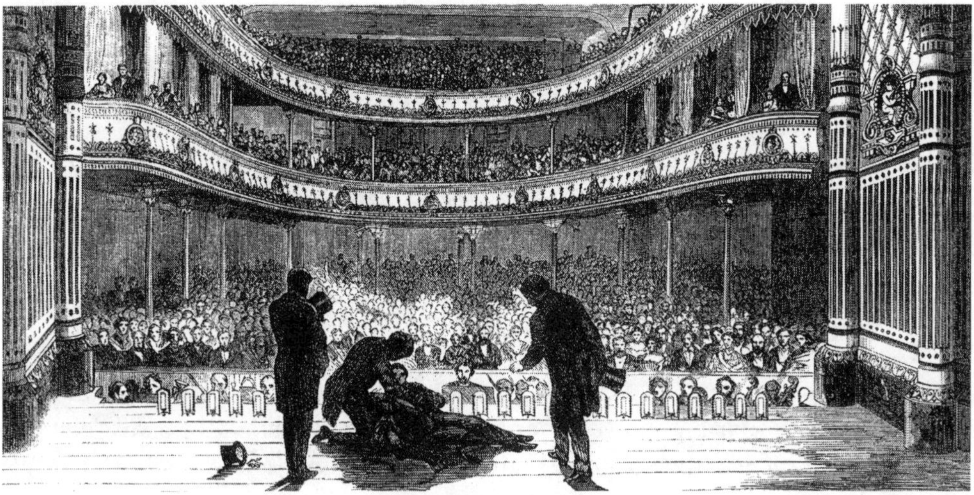

FIGURE 21. *Holborn Theatre: detail.* Illustrated London News *(13 October 1866), 372*

other into the room. The promptbook instructs them to freeze in this position as a tableau. Moments later (possibly after applause) the scene closed and the vamping cue no. 8 continued "til change and characters on." This action or nonthematic music was repeated as necessary—long enough to allow for Eliza to escape and the traders to be caught empty handed—until the new scene opened to the sound of wild dogs barking and the traders' voices shouting ominously from offstage.

Thomas Comer's music remained integral to the Conway version of *Uncle Tom's Cabin.* This single set of parts was in use for over twenty years. The evidence for this is found in handwritten notes penciled in by the musicians, who sometimes added their names, cities, theatres, and dates. These same parts were still being used, as one bass player noted, for Mr. and Mrs. Howard's "three-week's engagement" in the "centennial year" of 1876.

The Actor's Relationship to the Orchestra

The best nineteenth-century actors relied on the band as an ally, as a watchful mediator between stage and audience. The close relationship of actors, leader, musicians, and audience is clearly evident in a sketch from the stage of London's Holborn Theatre in 1866 (Fig. 21). We see George Richardson at his slightly elevated center position, surrounded by his orchestra, who accompany the outcome of a duel scene in Boucicault's *Flying Scud.* From the actors' perspective, the musicians provide a cushion of sound into which—or *through* which—they deliver their lines. The musicians, with bows in motion but their faces turned toward the stage, clearly observe the action. They hear their cues and understand how their music relates to the situation.

Attentive theatre musicians could of course be expected to have some flexibility should something go wrong. But once music was established in rehearsal, actors generally arranged their business to accommodate it. One mid-century actress spoke a bit about this process. First, lines must be delivered in such a way as to set up the *melos*. "If it is a *music cue*," she writes, the line "must be given out with emphasis, in order that the band may be certain to hear you." (Manuscript band parts almost always contained the text cues in all parts, not just the leader books.) This practical necessity may have unintended consequences for an actor's interpretation of the role. This actress, without identifying the play or the theatre, goes on to describe an incident in which a desperate character is about to commit suicide and how his delivery was affected by the music cue. "This pistol, then, shall end my sufferings!" the actor decrees. "Wife—children—friends—adieu, for ever! Yet—hold! Let me fasten first the cottage-door." The actress points out that "the sense of this speech would evidently require the emphasis to be laid on the words 'for ever.' But as the action of stealing up the stage on tiptoe and turning the key in the lock requires the accompaniment of *pizzicato* music, the [word] 'cottage-door' must be loudly emphasized, and thrown—figuratively, I mean—at the orchestra."[38]

The artificial result of bellowing a cue to a sleepy band leader would have been drawing attention to the entrance of the music, a convention that may have been imperative in some theatres but would have been laughable for audiences at a theatre such as the Holborn. The technique is straight out of burlesque and seems highly inappropriate to a stock drama. Still, this recollection of a *pizzicato* once again implies that a melodramatic character must have timed his actions to music and, even in this dire circumstance, retained a certain balletic grace as he moved intently toward the door.

The same actress recalled playing the part of a mute boy who is brought onstage as a witness to a murder. In rehearsal she identified the perpetrator to the extreme left of all the other actors onstage. But the manager suddenly shouted to stop.

> I learned that I had to "fill out" thirty-two bars of expressive music by taking each individual separately down towards the footlights, making a careful examination of his or her features and dress, shak-

ing my head to the spectators that he or she was not the criminal, and winding by arrival in due time—at the end of the thirty-two bars of music—at the extreme left hand, and seizing the murderer by the throat just as the orchestra was ready with a powerful chord and the gallery with cheers and plaudits.[39]

The actress who wrote these words chose to remain anonymous, so unfortunately her experiences cannot be corroborated. From the description, the mute role sounds like one that Celeste would have played, given the extended pantomime. The reference to "thirty-two bars" is noteworthy: most actors, when they discuss melodramatic music, seem to refer to a *melos* in numbers of bars, usually consisting of phrases of even length (such as "four bars," "eight bars," "sixteen bars," or "thirty-two bars"). It is very likely that these lengths developed because actors found them easier to count, much like dancers, who learn their steps according to the pattern of symmetrical bars in a phrase. As we have seen, melodramatic cues could be any length, even an odd number of bars. But when actors needed to time their action to music, it helped to have the music structured in easily recognizable chunks.

We can see how actors would have to negotiate existing music in a scene from the second act of John Buckstone's *The Green Bushes* (Adelphi, 1845). The music was by Alfred Mellon and was used for productions of *The Green Bushes* for decades afterward. In this action sequence the actors have some control over the timing of events in the music. Buckstone's play begins in 1745 during the time of the Irish rebellion. Connor O'Kennedy (created by Charles Selby) is forced to leave his wife and daughter and flee to America to avoid arrest for secretly recruiting an army for the Irish brigade. The second act opens several years later in the interior of a log cabin "in the valley of the Mississippi." This is Connor's new home, where he now lives in domestic bliss with Miami, a half-French half-American Indian woman (a role written for Céline Celeste). In an episode later in the act Connor is alone after Miami goes off to hunt. He pulls out a letter that has recently reached him from Geraldine, his Irish wife. In a long monologue, during which he reads bits of the letter, we learn that Connor's desperate wife is coming in search of him. While his attention is fixed on the paper in hand, a tattered and worn Geraldine (created by Mrs. Yates) appears alone upstage, unaware at first to whom the cabin belongs. She advances to a gallery running along the back of the open cabin and spies the back of a human figure. When she recognizes her husband, she rushes to him and falls at his feet with a loud cry. Startled and confused, Connor pulls away at first then comes to her aid.

Geraldine's arrival was acted to music. Connor's long soliloquy took place unaccompanied. As he finished his last line, however, music began. During the ensuing pantomime the actors must have remained attentive to the music but were also partly in control of its pacing. The stage directions for Connor read: "*He sits with his glance fixed steadfastly on the letter.—Low music.*" The strings shimmer in tremolo, while the solo violin leads with the lovely melody of a talking tune, a version of the Irish pentatonic ballad "The Green Bushes" (Fig. 22). To this music, Connor falls deeper and deeper into nostalgic reverie, such that he is oblivious to Geraldine's approach. The directions continue. "*Geraldine, pale, her dress torn and scarcely able to support her steps, appears on the gallery,* R.H." (stage right, on the actor's right hand). The actress must find a different motivation for the shimmering music. Perhaps the reminiscence of the tune symbolizes the steadfast love that led her over the thousands of miles. Or perhaps the tremolo helps her to depict physical weakness or a sense of fear and dread at what may lurk ahead in the wilds of America.

The tune is marked with a repeat sign in the parts, which means that Geraldine—unlike the unnamed actress quoted earlier—is not physically restricted by its sixteen bars. If she took longer, the leader was free to circle back until the moment of recognition. Geraldine lets out a cry, which startles Connor, but it is the visual cue in the orchestra parts—"when Geraldine falls"—that prompts the leader to break off the tune and signal the orchestra to skip forward to a *forte* chord of reversal. The stage directions then read: "*Connor starts up; the letter falls from his hand; he looks in amazement on the form at his feet. He raises it from the earth. Geraldine's eyes meet those of Connor.*" Connor may have used the brief musical silence to come to Geraldine's aid, or both actors may have held the moment in a picture. The orchestra, led by the clarinet and strings, then accompanies the tender reunion with four quiet bars of sweet and melting music, which brings the *melos* to a gentle close as natural dialogue resumes.

Unlike action or pantomime sequences such as this, dialogue scenes with accompanying music needed more care and attention. Many Victorian actors and actresses seemed to appreciate that music could help them shape the emotional arc of a monologue or a dialogue sequence, a studied technique of delivery that was often called "speaking through music."[40] This may at times have vexed some leaders as well as confused audiences, especially in the early part of the century. (In the earliest decades of *mélo-drame*, as we saw, playwrights assumed the music would pause during speech and resume when the action required it.) Under-dialogue music could be diffi-

The music continues. — [Geraldine] crosses gallery and descends, opens the door L.H. p., and advances silently. Connor, still intent on the letter, does not hear her. She regards him with a fixed gaze. Her eyes wander to the letter, then again to his face, when she utters one loud cry, and falls prostrate at his feet.

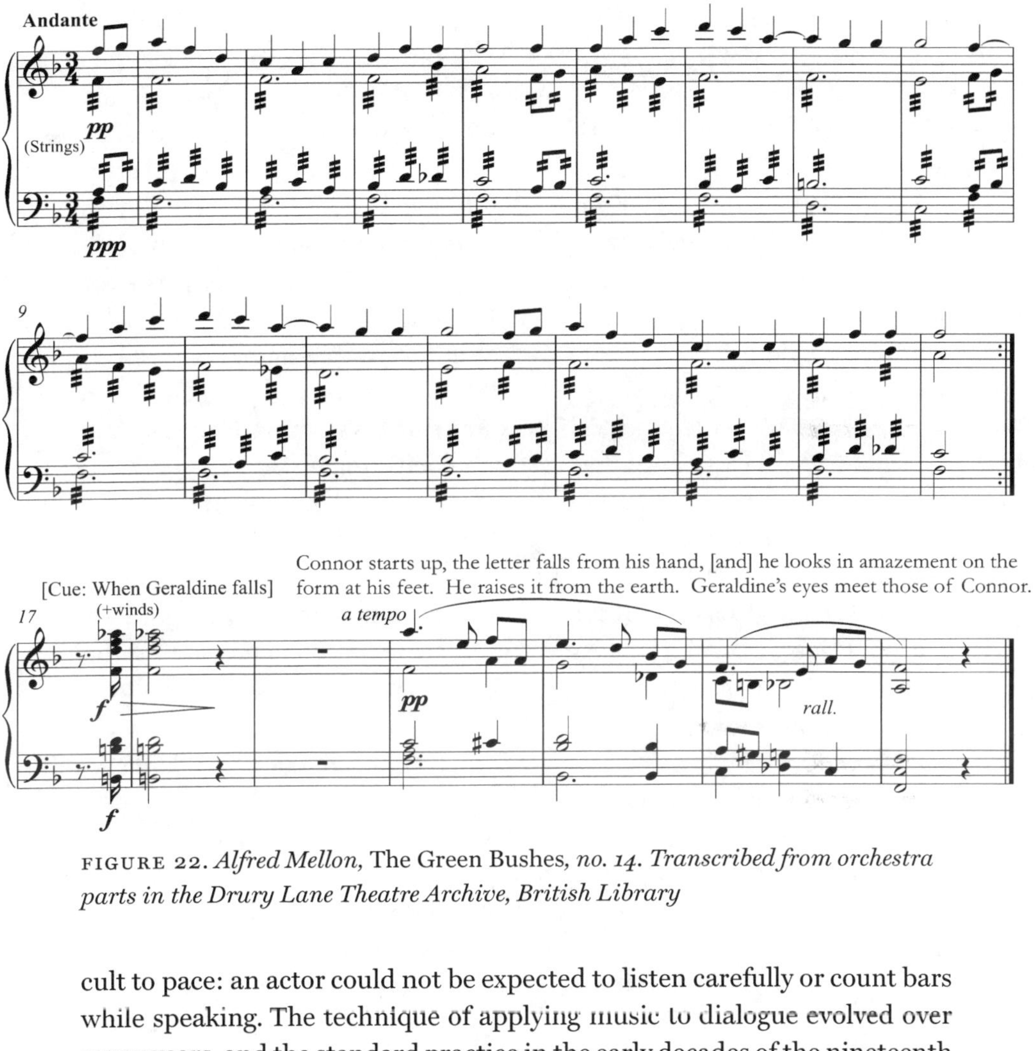

FIGURE 22. *Alfred Mellon,* The Green Bushes, *no. 14. Transcribed from orchestra parts in the Drury Lane Theatre Archive, British Library*

cult to pace: an actor could not be expected to listen carefully or count bars while speaking. The technique of applying music to dialogue evolved over many years, and the standard practice in the early decades of the nineteenth century (such as we can determine from the minuscule fragments of information) was for the band to play quietly enough so as not to interfere with the spoken lines. Leaders had to immediately shush their ensembles to *pianissimo* the moment anyone began talking. In *Jack Sheppard*, as we saw, Buckstone specified dynamics to cue the leader when to play softly. There are many reports of audiences being frustrated at not being able to hear or understand dialogue, which sometimes led to musical passages being stricken out or played so softly that they might as well not have been played at all.

Let us take a dialogue sequence in which the actors had to deal with precomposed music. This scene is from the end of act 1 of *The Corsican Brothers, or The Vendetta,* one of the most famous melodramas of the century, first staged and acted by Charles Kean (Princess's Theatre, 1852). Louis and Fabien dei Franchi are twins joined by uncanny telepathic powers. They swear that if one should ever be near death, he would appear in spirit to alert and summon the other. Louis dies in a duel with a jealous suitor in Paris while Fabien is attending to local business at the family estate in Corsica. The play featured the sensational device of having one actor play both brothers. The duel—seen from two different angles—forms the climactic conclusion to both acts 1 and 2, to give the impression of taking place simultaneously.

Fabien has just settled a local dispute and is in his study by dim light talking with his guest Alfred. Earlier that day, Fabien relates, he experienced a sharp, sword-like pang in his chest, a sign of his brother in distress. When his mother enters, holding a candle, Fabien breaks off his story, not wishing to alarm her. As she exits to show their guest to his room, the orchestra begins to play music no. 11, a short lyrical *romanza.* In Charles Kean's promptbook, a dramatic lighting change occurs with the music to prepare for the spookiness of the scene to follow ("Put Wing Lights quite down. Side Boxes and Chandelier ½ down"). Fabien, deeply worried about his brother, calls his servant Griffo and explains the mysterious signal. "I looked at my watch; it was ten minutes after nine." At this point music no. 12 begins (a nonthematic *melos*). The eerily oscillating strings sustain a deliberate tension under the dialogue. "Look," Fabien cries, suddenly noticing the standing clock. It has stopped at the same moment as the watch. Madame, returning, says that she noticed the incorrect time and confirms that the clock was recently wound. To Fabien, this is the second warning. As he bids his mother good night, the violins relax to an oscillation between two neighboring tones while the lower strings creep through slowly changing chords. Before she exits, Madame blesses her son in the hopes that providence will avert some evil. She goes out through the right-hand door flat, closing it after her. The texture of the music then thins to a violin tremolo on a single note, lingering only until Madame is safely out of earshot. In a more animated tone, Fabien directs Griffo to ready a horse in order to dispatch a letter to Louis in Paris. The orchestra follows immediately with music of a more rhythmic and agitated nature while Fabien takes off his jacket, sits at a small table down left, and begins to write his letter.[41] (The famous sensation of the vision scene with the "Corsican trap" and "ghost theme" then follows.)

This sequence consists largely of dialogue involving three characters who speak in a fairly natural pace. The music projects a worried, mysterious tone (Fig. 23).

The orchestra leader here is given no ad-libs or repeat signs, so the music must play through exactly as written. A tempo must be chosen to establish an appropriate air of mystery, and the actors must time their lines to the music so that Madame dei Franchi has exited by the arrival of the fourteenth bar. This is not quite as difficult as it sounds. The opening music flows and lacks any obvious markers. But after Fabien's line "'tis a second warning," the double basses enter on a very low and ominous G natural. After this point Madame—who is close enough to the bass players to hear this note—is free to continue with her next line, which keeps the rest of the sequence on track. As Fabien and Madame bid one another good night, the previously flowing music is now marked by changing chords in half notes then whole notes and finally comes to rest on a single chord (G minor). The final tremolo (with fermata) allows the leader time to be sure that Madame is completely offstage. And a sharp actor playing Fabien can leap into his next line before the leader cuts off the tremolo.[42]

Not all instances of "speaking through music" required such precise coordination, of course. But reports on how music was actually negotiated, especially in monologue and dialogue sequences, are extremely rare, especially given how frequently nineteenth-century actors insisted on musical accompaniment.

For insight into how actors and orchestra leaders of the time handled this process we can turn to the Covent Garden production of *Antigone*, staged by John Vandenhoff in 1845 for his daughter Charlotte. The plan (see chapter 4) was to use all the music that Felix Mendelssohn had written in 1841 for a German production of the play. While preparing the music, George Macfarren wrote to the composer for advice. "I am very glad that [the *Antigone* music] is in your hands," Mendelssohn answered, "because it wants a musician like you to make it go as intended—quite as a subordinate part of the whole, as a mere link in the chain of the poem, and yet perfectly clear and independent in itself."[43] The composer also offered several valuable interpretive tips. "Let the succession of dialogue and music be as rapid as possible, indeed quite without the least interruption or pause."[44] Regarding the tight connection between music and dialogue, he added, "after the last chord of the wind instruments (G-natural) Antigone begins to speak

Fabien. Look! Look!—the clock—it points to the same hour, although it must be close on midnight—the clock has stopped.

Madame. (*returning*) Yes, I noticed it before. The clock stopped this morning, and without apparent cause.

Fabien. This morning! They must have forgot to wind it up.

Madame. On the contrary, it was wound up the day before yesterday.

Fabien. There's no mistaking this; 'tis a second warning.

FIGURE 23. The Corsican Brothers, *no. 12. Transcribed from orchestra parts in the Folger Shakespeare Library*

while the chord is still kept"; "Kreon must . . . begin to speak while the chord E-flat is hardly given, and it must be kept during the first words." He then offered perhaps the most valuable bit of advice, which not only Macfarren but dozens of the best leaders in the Victorian theatre after him must surely have followed. "In the melodramas, [i.e., *melos* as opposed to sung numbers] where the words must go together with the notes . . . do not let the actress take the tempo of our music (as I heard them do lately at Dresden), but let the flutes accompany *her* tempo of speaking, which is also not difficult if the flutes will follow you *and* her." The composer was insisting on the natural inflection of the actor's spoken voice, with the *melos* assuming

Madame. What say you, Fabien?

Fabien. Nothing, nothing. Good night.

Madame. Bless you, my son. Good night. If evil hovers over us, may Providence avert it.

[*Exit* Madame la Contessa Savillia dei Franchi, *door*, R.H. *flat*.]

Fabien. To horse! to horse! Griffo, lose not a moment.

a flexible and yielding quality that could only be obtained through careful rehearsal. Mendelssohn also assumed, as did most theatre orchestra leaders at the time, that the musicians could fully see and hear the actors that they were accompanying.

Would that every music director in the melodramatic theatre had learned this technique. Alas, many clearly did not. By the 1860s there was already a great deal of criticism of music covering up or interfering with dialogue. This was less obvious, perhaps, in melodramas of action. But as the popular drama began to focus more on character and psychological development—particularly in the 1870s—it was essential that audiences catch every word. The best playwrights, managers, music directors, and actors continued to refine the process and arrived at solutions that were not just practical but often thrilling.

7

Music, Suspense, and the Sensation Drama

As Charles Reade, Dion Boucicault, Henry Leslie, Edmund Falconer, and others were to demonstrate, with a well-crafted and well-cast popular drama and a suitable musical score all that was needed was the cachet of sensation to draw audiences to the theatre like pins to a magnet. Using new developments in stagecraft and technical wizardry, near-instantaneous communication among all aspects of production, and increased musical participation, the "sensation drama" emerged with full force in the 1860s. Many of the elements, of course, were present in earlier popular dramas. But the sensation drama offers an opportunity to examine a new role for music: building or increasing suspense. The popular drama—with its emphasis on action—took on new levels of intensity.

Audiences and the Taste for Sensation

As they had earlier in the century, sensational plots centered on the most shocking news events or social issues of the day. We begin with a review in the *London Times* on the morning of 27 June 1854. The critic expressed considerable dismay over a new melodrama that he had seen at the Princess's Theatre. He called *The Courier of Lyons* (in which Charles Kean assumed the roles of two look-alikes) a "startler," bordering on the offensive, with its extremes of character forces beyond the pale. "The authors, having clapped on the shoulders of one actor a miracle of human virtue and a monster of human depravity, have reveled in their means of producing excitement." The reviewer complained that the play had no moral message. "What ethical instruction can one gain from a story about a man who is guillotined merely because he looks like another?"[1] Dutton Cook, equally disturbed by what he called the low taste of mid-century British theatrical audiences, used *Courier of Lyons* as an example:

> The crimes of the cut-throat Dubosc are not held to be by any means too horrible for achievement in the presence of the audience. Certainly there is rather a slaughter-house air about certain of the incidents, such as the stabbing of Jeanne . . . and the brutal murder of the postilion and guard of the mail coach. But the purveyor of melodrama feels himself bound to thrill his public, to make their blood curdle and their flesh creep, by any expedients that may occur to him.[2]

The term "sensation drama" today evokes an era of elaborate stage effects—explosions and train wrecks, perhaps, or some timely rescue from a sinking ship. An 1867 playbill for *The Mariner's Compass* at the Royal Amphitheatre in Leeds, for example, states that the performance is "illustrative of the hair-breadth escapes and life-sacrificing perils of the sailor's life, and replete with the most sensational situations and startling effects."[3] The notion of mere audience titillation—effect for effect's sake—is a key component of many melodramas of the mid-nineteenth century, even as they continued to embody one of popular drama's most enduring functions: to highlight some social ill or injustice. It would be difficult to say whether audiences at the City of London or the Bowery Theatre flocked to performances of *Oliver Twist* because of its lurid depiction of London's social underbelly or for the thrill of seeing such "realistic" effects as Sikes's grisly onstage murder of Nancy. Even at a middle-class house such as the Boston Museum, the murder scene with Lucille Western as Nancy and E. L. Davenport as Sikes was known to strain nerves to the breaking point, and some audience members were reported to have gone into hysterics or run screaming from the hall.[4] Though the term "sensation drama" did not come into standard use until 1860, the amount of action, lurid detail, and mounting suspense in *The Courier of Lyons* identifies it as a prototype of this class of popular drama.

"Sensation"—as produced by the timing of a precisely calculated visual effect—had been around in the theatre since the earliest melodramas of Pixerécourt. Even some of the earliest British melodramas and proto-melodramas such as *Tekeli* and *The Castle Spectre* had been described in these terms. Many plays since the 1830s resorted to graphic detail with an appeal to sordid tastes and prurient interests. Take, for example, *The String of Pearls* (Britannia, 1847), the first known stage rendering of the story of the murderous barber Sweeney Todd. Why, then, did the term "sensation drama" attain standard usage only in the 1860s with plays such as Dion Boucicault's *The Colleen Bawn*? One explanation is that as dramas of gritty realism—which had been "sensational" in their lurid effects since the 1830s in working-class playhouses like the Coburg or the Bowery—moved into theatres like the Princess's, Drury Lane, and even the Adelphi, the sordid and the prurient were to some degree legitimized, at least in middle-class consciousness. Moreover, these playhouses had the financial resources to produce overwhelmingly effective scenery and stagecraft. For these audiences, a literate class reared on contemporary literature, theatrical sensation reflected the journalist spirit of the age. As Arthur Hobson Quinn described it, looking back from 1925: "There are times when we wish neither our souls exalted [as in tragedy] nor our weaknesses exposed [as in comedy]. We wish to have our attention caught, held, kept by interesting situations and capable dialogue, and we wish to have above all that element of suspense which is the heart and soul of melodrama."[5]

Suspense is conveyed partly in the writing and partly in the enactment. And nothing aided suspense, stage managers soon learned, like the right music at the right time. When James W. Wallack as Nathan, an apostate Jew in Augustin Daly's *Leah the Forsaken* (1863), described the menace of persecution in his terrifying speech, the taut, march-like *misterioso* that built under his rising voice had the same hair-raising effect as a would-be assassin who slowly wraps and tightens the murderous cord around his fist. Such requirements for music highlight the significant difference between sensation dramas of the mid-nineteenth century and the far more "legitimate" social dramas. Sensation dramas such as *The Courier of Lyons*, Boucicault's *The Poor of New York* and *Flying Scud*, Daly's *Under the Gaslight*, Henry Arthur Jones's *The Silver King*, Belasco's *The Stranglers of Paris*, and Reade's *Gold!* all relied heavily on mounting suspense and affective music. In comparison, social dramas such as Boucicault's *London Assurance*, Reade's *Masks and Faces* and *Drink*, Tom Taylor's *Our American Cousin*, and T. W. Robertson's *Caste* required little, if any, music.[6]

Sensation scenes did not always depend on music, however. The sensation header at the end of act 2 in Daly's *Under the Gaslight* (1867), with its famous rescue scene from the railroad tracks just before the train rushes by, used only dialogue and sound effects. The roar of the train was created offstage by several wind machines and the impact of multiple hammers drumming on a heavy iron sheet. In fact music did not even enter *after* the rescue to bring down the curtain. The only instructions to the musicians were "*tacet* for railroad business till end of act."[7] Naturally, given our own conditioning in the age of sound film, we might automatically assume that music was always used for such heightened dramatic effects onstage. But we would be wrong to base our interpretation on burlesque and vaudeville versions—which poked fun at these types of sensations by exaggerating them—and later silent film adaptations, where music would have been a necessary replacement for missing dialogue and sound effects. Not all of the scenes explored in this chapter are as emphatic as rescues from burning buildings or railroad tracks. But they were all sensational in one form or another: the dramatic pacing of the act usually built up to these scenes, and the highly physical business and stagecraft often required precise coordination with specific music.

The Courier of Lyons *at the Princess's and the French Influence*

The Courier of Lyons as produced by Charles Kean at the Princess's Theatre in 1854, with its focus on lurid detail and mounting tension, was an important prototype of the sensation drama that Boucicault would bring to full fruition in a few years. The Princess's had been in existence for some twenty years when Kean, son of Shakespearean actor Edmund Kean, and his wife, Ellen Tree, assumed the management in 1851. While it was perhaps the lavishly designed and costumed productions of Shakespeare that won them lasting fame, the Princess's became known for "gentlemanly melodrama" such as *The Corsican Brothers*.[8] This elegant style developed partly from Kean's skills as a Shakespearean but also from his incorporation of new French techniques. English dramas had long been adapted from French originals, of course. What was new was a whole generation of authors, playwrights, and actors who had grown up in the melodramatic theatre, who were deeply familiar with its signs, and who were gradually coming under the influence of French "realism," both the "historical realism" of Victor Hugo, Honoré de Balzac, Paul Féval, Prosper Mérimée, and Alexandre Dumas père, and the French literary realism of Stendhal (Marie-Henri Beyle), Eugène Sue, and Alexandre Dumas fils. Balzac's characters, for example, negotiated moral ambiguities that would have been unthinkable in the Manichean worlds of gothic or domestic melodrama.

The new relevance of French melodramas, however, does not really explain why they suddenly seemed to overwhelm the English stage. The reason most often given is that English dramatists could not earn much from an original play. Instead British theatre managers sought adaptations from

French dramas, particularly those that had proved successful abroad and would assure packed houses. Such adaptations, as Dion Boucicault duly observed, could be tossed off in a few days, unlike an original play, which was labor-intensive to write and risky to produce.[9] Benjamin Webster, manager of both the Haymarket and the Adelphi theatres in 1844, hired the young, bilingual Boucicault to go to France just to find good plays and adapt them for his theatres. Webster produced four of these in 1846 alone. The next few years saw a frenzy of adaptations. The first crest of the French wave occurred in 1848. Paris was in the throes of a revolution leading to the restoration of its monarchy. Dumas and Boucicault were managing the Théâtre Historique at the time, which packed up its company and moved to London to ride out the political disturbance. Their production of a two-evening version of *The Count of Monte Cristo* was a disaster, partly because the company had set up in Drury Lane: protesters rebelled against the "occupation" of a hallowed English domain. The second crest came in 1852 with the International Copyright Law. The changes were to protect the rights of foreign authors in Great Britain but excluded "fair Imitations or Adaptations to the English Stage of any Dramatic piece . . . published in any Foreign Country."[10] The new law, much to the outrage of Bulwer-Lytton and other English playwrights, only further encouraged the adaptation of foreign novels and plays. Both Samuel Phelps at Sadler's Wells and Charles Kean at the Princess's were adamantly devoted to producing "native drama," leading with the plays of Shakespeare. But Kean soon realized that the big moneymakers would be the latest French sensations. To this end he hired Boucicault in 1850 as house dramatist: his job was to search out new French dramas, write new plays, and adapt old ones.[11] Boucicault brought with him his unique insights into the kind of melodramatic music that he had seen move Parisian audiences to rage and to tears.

The Princess's Theatre, located on Oxford Street in Norrington Square, had opened in 1840 and was known principally for English opera and English-language versions of European operas.[12] Upon assuming the management, Kean, who was also a fellow of the Society of Antiquaries, shifted the repertoire toward historical drama and Shakespeare, both produced in the spirit of an almost archaeological attention to historical accuracy. He also produced several comedies and no less than ten new melodramas, both original works and free treatments of French plays: *Pauline*, *The Vampire*, *The Duke's Wager*, *The Corsican Brothers*, *Anne Blake*, *Faust and Marguerite*, *Marco Spada*, *The Courier of Lyons*, and two of Douglas Jerrold's last plays, *St. Cupid* and *A Heart of Gold*. Several of Kean's historical dramas—such as Angiolo R. Slous's *The Templar* and an adaptation of Casimir Delavigne's *Louis XI*—could also be classified as melodramas by their treatment. As Kean managed a stock company, old favorites ran in alternation with new productions.

Along with these melodramas came French styles of acting. Charles Fechter had caused a sensation in *Les frères corses* (The Corsican Brothers) at the Théâtre Historique in 1850 and as Armand Duval in *La dame aux camélias* (The Lady of the Camellias). The intensity of these dramas was enhanced by smaller performing spaces, concentrated lighting effects, more direct and sincere delivery of lines, and a more nuanced approach in the use of music. Fechter is quoted as saying that in *La dame aux camélias* (1852) he "endeavored to cause the footlights to disappear and to bring the spectator in direct communication with [the play's] characters." Kean, not to be superseded by these French actors, went to Paris and observed Pierre Mathieu Ligier in *Louis XI* and Fechter in *Les frères corses*. "He took it all in," wrote Boucicault, "and returned topfull of the character and the methods of the French actors."[13]

Kean's production of *Pizarro* at the Princess's typifies this new physical style. He was playing Rolla (one of his father's roles), an Inca hero who escapes from the Peruvian temple with Cora's child. "Instead of the old-fashioned mode of cutting down a rustic bridge that looked as if arranged for the purpose," John W. Cole wrote, Kean "swung himself by the pendent branch of a tree across a tremendous chasm and, being mortally struck by the musketry of the Spanish soldiers in the passage, was seen staggering through the rocks and glades until he disappeared in the distance, the effect of perspective being carried out by a duplicate figure of smaller size, which gave rise to endless conjectures and arguments as to how this optical delusion could be contrived."[14] It was this kind of technical ingenuity that led to the tremendous London success of *The Corsican Brothers*, with its unique movable stage trap, vanishing walls, and the *coup-de-théâtre* of having the same actor appear as two similar characters.

One of the long-standing requirements of popular dramas, especially prominent in the new melodramas of crime, was that they enact some true story or event. The period drama *The Courier of Lyons* is based on a notorious French case of wrongful execution. At least two adaptations had already been made for London theatres, by Lewis Phillips at the Standard and by Edward Stirling at the Marylebone. Not one to be sidelined by these attempts, Kean turned to Charles Reade to help him prepare a version that would again allow him to portray two characters, this time complete strangers in an infamous case of mistaken identity. The play opened at the Princess's on 26 June 1854. Leading the orchestra was Bertram Isaacson, who had come to Kean with some ten years of experience as leader and composer at the Grecian Theatre under Thomas Rouse.

The story was based on an incident that occurred in France in the 1790s. Three men artfully planned and executed an attack on the mail coach heading from Lyons to Paris. They brutally murdered the courier and his postilion and confiscated a known treasure carried aboard. Joseph Lesurques, an honorable citizen who unfortunately resembled the leader of the gang, was tried and executed in his place. Only later was the actual murderer discovered and brought to justice. The case was discussed in the press for years afterward, finally reaching the Théâtre de la Gaïté as a play in 1850. (The Lesurques family gave their permission for playwrights Eugène Moreau, Paul Siraudin, and Alfred Delacour to use the innocent man's real name, which further sensationalized the event.) It was produced in two versions, one with a happy ending conforming to melodramatic conventions, in which Lesurques was rescued in the nick of time. This is the version that Reade adapted for the Princess's.

Kean's sensational conceit, of course, was to play both Dubosc the murderer and the innocent man, characters of extraordinarily different mien.[15] Though the characters never actually meet, to the amazement of the audience they *just miss* each other in their comings and goings throughout the play. And in the final arrest and rescue scene, Kean astounded his audience by having both characters onstage at the same time. "The piece is one of rapid and exciting action," wrote Fanny Kemble. "The interest . . . never flags and rises gradually to the conclusion, keeping the audience in an agony of suspense to the last moment."[16]

The scene of the attack occurs at the end of act 1. Suspense had already been building to this moment through the characters' pointed references to time and audible clock strikes. The audience learns in scene 1 that the attack will occur that night at eight. Throughout the act the clock strikes noon, three, six, and finally eight, the fatal hour.

The following description is derived from the dialogue and stage directions in Kean's promptbook and Isaacson's manuscript score.[17] Scene 2 opens at an inn on the outskirts of Paris at five o'clock. It is one of Kean's "double scenes": both the inside and outside of the inn are visible, allowing the audience unrestricted access to information only partially known to the characters themselves.[18] The innkeeper Jerome, Lesurque's elderly father, is seated by the fire. Facing mounting debts and virtually no patrons, he has decided that he must sell the inn. Music cue no. 6 is a pastoral duet for two French horns in C major over a rocking string accompaniment. These sixteen bars establish the rural scene and reflect the mood of the pensive innkeeper. The music concludes when Jerome rises and exits onto the street, coming down front. He is about to head off to post the sale in a nearby village. Joliquet, his young servant, warns him not to travel alone after sunset. Jerome brushes the concern aside, reminding the youth to be sure to have some food and special brandy for the mail carrier and his coachman, who are expected around eight P.M. Jerome leaves, and Joliquet prepares for the carrier's arrival. "I'll watch him from the right side of the door" signals music cue no. 8.[19] As evening gradually descends the apprehensive Joliquet goes into the darkening inn, shutting the door behind him. The music sustains the opening mood: clarinet and solo cello play a gentle duet over a string accompaniment (now in G major).

During the closing bars of the music Joseph Lesurques enters up right, wearing a cloak. He has come in disguise with a plan to help his father keep the inn. His loud knock frightens the boy. Lesurques cheerfully claims a broken spur on his boot and waves some money at Joliquet, who opens the door. "Well come in then" is the cue for music no. 9, a cheerful 2/4 tune in B-flat major. The promptbook notes: "Joliquet opens drawer in table and gives him a bit of string [to repair the boot] then lights a candle." When Lesurques orders a bottle of vintage wine, the young servant lights another candle, which he uses to descend a stairway into the cellar. Lesurques seizes the moment to slip furtively into his father's room and plant a large bag of money with a note attached. He then makes a hasty exit, returning in the direction he came while a nearby clock chimes six. Meanwhile Joliquet emerges from the cellar, singing to himself a quirky unaccompanied tune ("A boy on a very dark night lost his way").[20] Joliquet sets the bottle on the table. He is surprised to discover no one there ("gone out again?"). Less than a minute after Lesurques has slipped out, Dubosc arrives upstage right with his three accomplices for the setup and robbery. Their entrance music (cue no. 11) begins with a two-bar unison phrase played *forte* by the lower winds and strings as if announcing the arrival of a somewhat weighty character (Fig. 24). Its nervous string tremolos and marked difference from Lesurques's music serve to mislead the audience into assuming that Dubosc is an entirely different actor.

Meanwhile, Joliquet comes out of the inn holding the wine and surprises the man that he thinks is Lesurques. He does not see the others who are hiding. The music shifts from the broad lyrical opening—the first four mea-

FIGURE 24. The Courier of Lyons, *no. 11, beginning. Transcribed from orchestra parts in the Folger Shakespeare Library*

sures in the example above—to some breathless sixteenth notes, reflecting both men's startled responses. With a menacing tone, Dubosc jokes that a single bottle of wine will not be enough for four men. As the three accomplices emerge from the shadows the youth grows visibly agitated. Music cue no. 12 begins *pianissimo*, and Joliquet runs inside and down into the cellar while the men hurry after him. The accomplices drag the heavy table over the cellar door, trapping the boy. He cries out, but the men silence him with threats. The next scene is tense and without music: all the lights are extinguished except for a red glow from the fireplace (the house lights were dimmed as well). Pulling out their long-blade knives and pistols, the criminals wait and listen for the distant sound of the horses and the bell on the mail coach. At one point Dubosc silences the others, thinking that he hears a faint tinkling. This is the cue for music no. 12½, which begins like a gentle breathing in the strings (Fig. 25).

"It is only the wind," one of the men replies. The promptbook specifies "bells distant, L.H." Dubosc jumps up. "To your places," he shouts to his accomplices. The eight-bar *agitato* repeats while the bells of the post-horses and the cracking of the postilion's whip grow louder and louder. The rest of the scene involved precise coordination by Isaacson, his orchestra, and the actors. As the "wind music" continues, the scavenging Dubosc comes

FIGURE 25. The Courier of Lyons, no. 12½, mm. 1–3.

running out of Jerome's room with the bag of money that he has discovered. "What is this?" he asks, reading the label. "'Money restored!' How honourable we are!" He secretly hides the bag in his pocket. Meanwhile the promptbook asks the soundman to increase the effect with "bells nearer and whip." Fouinard, one of Dubosc's men, rushes in, giving the signal for the courier's arrival. As he and the other accomplices rush to their hiding places outside, the shivering "wind music" breaks off and a cornet fanfare—the post-horn—signals a tempo change to a quickstep (Fig. 26).

A short coda brings this galloping music to a halt as the mail coach draws up alongside the inn (Reade's instructions specify that "[t]he horses smoke").

Music stops briefly for the next exchange. The postilion and courier descend from the coach calling for "Father Jerome." They are surprised to find a stranger in his place. Dubosc is ready with the expected brandy, however, and one taste convinces the courier that it is the right stuff. The postilion goes out around the shielded side of the inn to tend to the horses. Suddenly he begins screaming for help, the signal for music no. 13 (Fig. 27). His body is heard falling heavily to the ground.

No. 13 is a long through-composed cue consisting of sixty measures of

FIGURE 26. The Courier of Lyons, *no. 12½, mm. 9–16*

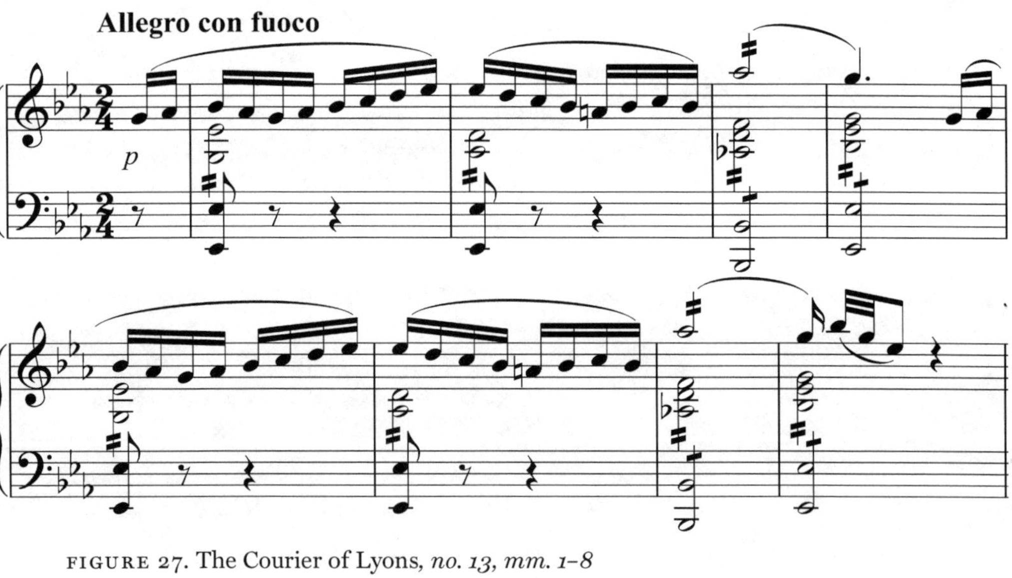

FIGURE 27. The Courier of Lyons, *no. 13, mm. 1–8*

FIGURE 28. *Sensationalizing violence in the popular drama: "Scene from . . .* The Courier of Lyons *at the Princess's Theatre."* Illustrated London News *(8 July 1854), supplement: 17*

changing instrumentation and musical gestures, each synchronized to stage action as well as sound and lighting effects. The business that follows here is encapsulated and paraphrased from the promptbook.

The courier drops his glass and runs to the postilion's defense. Meanwhile Fouinard climbs on top of the mail and his accomplice Choppard cuts the side of the bag away, releasing a tumbling array of parcels and letters. Finding the iron box, he hands it down to the waiting Dubosc, who breaks it open. The courier, realizing too late what is happening, tries to stop the men, but Dubosc pulls out a gun and shoots him. He collapses (Fig. 28).

After grabbing their share of the loot, the accomplices disperse like the wind in different directions, one of them taking the postilion's horse. As Dubosc is rummaging through the courier's pockets, Jerome, the old innkeeper, suddenly returns. Hearing the trapped boy's cries, he realizes that something is wrong. Jerome grabs Dubosc, and a struggle ensues. Jerome is wounded by a gunshot from Dubosc's pistol, but not before getting a good look at him and reacting in horror at what seems to be his own son.

The music is almost entirely in E-flat major, and the effect is more of a heroic action cue than a villainous *agitato*. The opening seven bars under-

FIGURE 29. The Courier of Lyons, *no. 13, mm. 28–40*

score the courier's attempt to rescue the postilion, while the accomplices go to work. The second section, built around a brisk string gesture, accompanies the seizure of the mail. The next section functions as a kind of *stretto*—an intensification through repetitive musical gestures that rise in pitch and volume—while the mail is released, the box is found and broken open, and the courier is shot. Then the full ensemble plays *forte* (still in E-flat major) as Dubosc sends his men scattering. But from this point the changes in the music are quicker and more deliberate. The first of these is a repeated seven-bar athematic and asymmetrical *melos*. An ascending motive explodes in a diminished-seventh chord—the melodramatic chord of reversal—that undoubtedly was intended to alert the audience to Jerome's return and fateful recognition (Fig. 29: the chord is in measures 5 and 6).

The orchestral agitation continues while the two men struggle. This turbulent music is the dramatic high point of the act, with alternating bars of string *agitato* and explosive brass and wind outbursts.[21] The contrast between dynamics and texture accompanies the struggle, the second shot, and Dubosc's escape. A few measures of coda, played *fortissimo* by the entire ensemble, ensue immediately after Jerome's stunned recognition ("My son!") and accompanies the quick act drop. Meanwhile, according to Kean's promptbook, "the moon shines fitfully" as Joliquet—yet another witness—peeks out from the cellar on the proceedings, his face "white as death."

The Courier of Lyons is a "wrong man" type of melodrama that influenced later plays (and the film melodramas of Alfred Hitchcock). Kean's tour de force also inspired other prominent tragedians to play Dubosc-Lesurques, including Hermann Vezin, Henry Irving, John Martin-Harvey, and Bransby Williams. *The Courier of Lyons* had a clear-cut villain, an outsider whose motives were blatantly ruthless. Villainy resided closer to home, however, in the new sensation dramas of the 1860s.

Boucicault: The Original Master of Suspense

The arrival of a new "sensation school" of drama was typified by an announcement in the *New York Herald* for the production of Dion Boucicault's *Pauvrette, or Under the Snow* at the New Bowery Theatre, stating that "an avalanche is part of the scenic effects."[22] Sensation dramas, like sensation novels of the time, usually hinged on some morally ambiguous plot development. This provocative device was hardly new, as we saw when a shocking murder case in 1818 was immediately translated to the Coburg Theatre in *The Trial by Battle*, although the action then had to be removed to an earlier time to avoid censorship.

By the 1850s playwrights like Dion Boucicault and Charles Reade seemed to be neck and neck in their search for theatrical sensation. They both found it at the same time with Eugène Nus and Édouard Brisebarre's *Les pauvres de Paris*, produced in Paris in 1856. Reade was so tied up with lawsuits over pirated copies of *Courier* and his other plays that he never did get his version to the stage. But Boucicault's *The Poor of New York* opened at Wallack's Theatre on 8 December 1857 and was without doubt the kind of success that put him at the forefront of prominent dramatic authors for the next twenty years, his only rivals in terms of numbers of performances being Tom Taylor and Augustin Daly. *The Poor of New York* turned a French melodrama into something new, at least for New York. The play put the city on the stage: Union Square and its vendors, street-theatre, the nightlife, the opera house and its patrons, the recent stock market crash and the hardship it brought to both upper-class and lower-class New Yorkers, the personal tragedies of the destitute, the sensation of an apartment building on fire and the community's efforts to rescue the victims, and so on. Boucicault created an image of New York that would influence literary and dramatic successors such as O. Henry, Damon Runyon, and Frank Capra.

The Poor of New York rode the crest of a wave of sensationalism that began in journalism. As the *New York Clipper* urged in 1858, "sensation stories are the feature now in the newspaper world, and we do not see why sensation plays should not meet with equal success."[23] Much has been written in recent years about the growth of sensation literature in Victorian England, with the genre fomented by novels such as Wilkie Collins's *The Woman in White* in 1860 and Mary Elizabeth Braddon's *Lady Audley's Secret* in 1862. Harriet Beecher Stowe's *Uncle Tom's Cabin*, of course, was an obvious antecedent. In his book *Victorian Sensations* Michael Diamond traces the rise of sensationalism in England to the 1840s and 1850s, focusing on the increase in lurid crime, the newspapers' graphic interest in prurient detail, and the stoking of controversy.[24] All three are manifest in the prosecution and execution of several notorious criminals, including the Mannings, hung in 1849 for the murder of the wife's lover. Several infamous trials occurred, including the case of mass poisoner William Palmer in 1856 and the even more sensational case of the lovely twenty-one-year-old Madeleine Smith, who supposedly fed arsenic to her pestering lover in 1857 to eliminate evidence of their sexual relationship and to free herself to marry into a higher station. All of England was focused on the outcome of the Smith trial when Boucicault had his villain Gideon Bloodgood in *The Poor of New York* set fire to a populous tenement house in order to erase evidence of his shady dealings there.

The rescue of people from a burning building in an age before municipal fire stations created a stirring public event. But burning buildings were not the main public spectacle. Madame Marie Tussaud had already proven with her Chamber of Horrors that in the new public space of the nineteenth century the gruesome always attracted large crowds. Diamond explains that beginning in the 1840s public hangings (of the Mannings, for example) were sensational events, attended by tens of thousands of ill-behaved and drunken people. A disgusted Thackeray and Dickens sought petitions to repeal capital punishment in England. The masses would have their sensations in one way or another, whether in tracing the day-to-day developments in a grisly murder trial, shouting out to an endangered heroine or especially nasty villain during a melodrama, or (for the better educated) quietly reveling at home in the crime and punishment that played a central role in serialized literature. Sensation novelists were responding to the moral ambiguity in all crime and the "appeal to fear," as Walter C. Phillips put it, that had recently gained momentum in sensational journalism.[25] The Mannings, William Palmer, and the young Madeleine Smith were "normal" and not at all in the classic villain mold, which made their crimes even more frightening. Such fears led to the rise of evangelism-as-theatre with preachers such as Charles Spurgeon in 1856. They also led the Lord Chamberlain's Office in the late 1850s to censor any plays with an undue emphasis on vice. And these same fears were the foundation upon which novelists such as Dickens, Reade, and Collins built their characters. As a critic in *Blackwood's* described it in 1862: "A writer who takes boldly in hand the common mechanism of life, and by means of persons, who might all be living in society for anything we can tell to the contrary, thrills us into wonder, terror, and breathless interest . . . has accomplished a far greater success than he who effects the same result through supernatural agencies . . . or violent horrors of crime."[26]

These kinds of subjects for the stage met with plenty of criticism from dramaturgs, but Boucicault remained unfazed. He liked to tell a story of being at a dinner party early in 1866 when he was asked whether the literary quality of a dramatic work had anything to do with its success. He said that he would settle the matter by writing three new plays, "one a society drama, relying primarily on its literary treatment, the second a domestic drama, and the third a sensation drama." He informed his friends that he would produce these simultaneously, "and I guarantee that the success of each shall be in the inverse ratio of its merits."[27] Whether the story is apocryphal or not is irrelevant. Within the span of just fourth months (July to October) Boucicault wrote and produced *Hunted Down* (a society drama), *The Long Strike* (a domestic drama), and *Flying Scud* (a sensation drama), which was the one that raked in the cash.

James Hurt refers to Boucicault's plays as "that extraordinary confusion of art and opportunism."[28] Given his unparalleled success for nearly half a century on the British and American stage, much has been written about Boucicault's entanglements with journalists, his dramatic formula, his approaches to adaptation, his characters, his acting, and his influence. But Boucicault's use of music in his plays merits a full study in itself. It is unfortunate that music cannot be found for *The Poor of New York*. A reconstruction with its original music would allow a remarkable comparison with later depictions of New York on the stage and in film. Given that the play was produced in literally dozens of cities in America, England, Ireland, and Australia (under various local names, such as *The Poor of Boston* and *The Poor of Manchester*), perhaps such music awaits discovery someday.[29]

Often turning to the five-act French form rather than the traditional three-act form of the popular drama, Boucicault followed *The Poor* with one sensation drama after another for New York, most notably, *Jessie Brown, or The Relief of Lucknow* (a play about the recent mutiny in India), *The Octoroon* (about race relations on a southern plantation), and the first of his so-called Irish dramas, *The Colleen Bawn*, all before he returned triumphantly to London in 1860. *The Octoroon* opened at the Winter Garden Theatre in December 1859 and featured two sensation scenes: the slave trade at the end of act 3 and the fire on the riverboat at the end of act 4. The anonymously composed musical score consisted almost entirely of hurries, *agitatos*, and tremolos, with virtually no thematic material or known quotations. The only recognizable tune was "Jeanie with the Light Brown Hair" at the rise of the first curtain. Presumably this served to establish a relaxed atmosphere of gentility on the plantation.[30] The fourth act opens along the Mississippi River with the docked steamer *Magnolia* about to depart. In the course of the act the Indian Wahnotee, previously accused of murder by McClosky (a villain in the Gideon Bloodgood mold), is caught and about to be tried. The young mulatto boy murdered in the second act was actually Wahnotee's inseparable companion, and tensions still run high over this unresolved crime. The existence of a photographic plate capturing an image of the murder proves McClosky to be the true culprit. (In 1859 few would have known the actual chemical process involved in making a photograph, so Boucicault took considerable dramatic license with time.) McClosky escapes onto the deck of the ship, but the men lock him in the boiler room. There he overturns barrels of turpentine and sets fire to them. He intends to leap overboard and swim to safety, but Wahnotee wrestles him to the ground. The agitated music begins as some ladies on deck casually approach the captain asking when they are expected to depart. Shouts are heard below as the first flames begin flickering out of the hatch. The music is a long melodramatic *agitato* (fifty-four bars) beginning with tremolo strings, chromatic upward and downward motion, wavelike, over two measures, followed by a quick lightning-like wind figure. This gesture repeats until the chromatics take over, their up and down motion becoming more persistent and tempest-tossed. The music, like the scene, builds dramatically to accompany the spreading fire, the panic onboard, and the fight on deck between the two adversaries. Though Wahnotee's tomahawk is knocked out of his hand in the fierce struggle, he wrestles McClosky's bowie knife from him and stabs the villain to death with it. Almost simultaneously the steamer's engine catches fire. The ship explodes, with passengers still attempting to escape. The final visual moment was the tableau of a tragedy frozen in time. The agitation in the orchestra quickly subsided and came to rest on a somber minor chord.

Boucicault initially achieved only mixed success with *The Octoroon*. Some audiences may not have been ready for the social even-handedness in its treatment of racial injustice. Northern sympathizers were annoyed that the play did not take a firm enough stand against slavery, even as it underscored the social evils of racism. But at the height of the Civil War Mark Twain found it a remarkable piece, "very peculiar in its construction, and so shrewdly balanced that it has met with as much success in the extreme South as in the extreme North—as much éclat in London and in Dublin as in New York, in Boston, or in Mobile or New Orleans."[31] What dramatic author could hope for so much?

The Colleen Bawn

Boucicault's next sensation was *The Colleen Bawn* (Gaelic for the "Fair-Haired Girl"), which opened in New York in March 1860 at Laura Keene's Theatre. The author and his wife, Agnes Robertson, starred in the two leading roles in the play. Six months later the couple began the longest run in English history up to that time with *The Colleen Bawn* at the Adelphi Theatre under Benjamin Webster's management. As biographer Richard Fawkes described it, this was the play for which Boucicault had been searching, "artistically and financially."[32] It was also the first play to which the term "sensation drama" came to be attached. Here, as H. Barton Baker described it, "the actor and the author are subordinated to the scene painter, carpenter, and property man, and the situation is made to depend upon scenic instead of imaginative effects."[33] Although music was often left out of such descriptions, the New York and London productions were loaded with music, both sung and instrumental. In a sense the play *began* with music. Before Boucicault had written a single word, he sent Laura Keene a book of Irish melodies, with some marked for Thomas Baker to score for orchestra.[34]

Boucicault took his idea from a novel by Gerald Griffin. The Irish had experienced a stage characterization in both England and America similar to blackface minstrelsy. They served as figures of burlesque—mistrusted, pugnacious, lazy drunkards—and the butt of jokes.[35] Ireland was known largely as a backward country. Boucicault's purpose in writing this play, he announced before the curtain on opening night, was partly to reveal the unexplored field of Irish history and romance.[36] He certainly knew his audience. Even a Dublin newspaper gushed effusively about Boucicault's portraiture of Irish life, acknowledging that "we can well imagine the charm it must have possessed for the Irish in America, who are, by their very position, more Irish than their countrymen at home."[37] Once the Lenten season was over, New York's considerable Irish population flocked to see the play.

Critics at first were not so welcoming. The *New York Times* acknowledged that while Boucicault was considered a leading representative of "the French school," the play relied too much on antique contrivances such as actors in "talky" front scenes to allow for behind-the-set carpentry work, eavesdropping of all the principal characters, and the wrong delivery of important letters.[38] Nevertheless, one critic called it "the most intense drama of the season." Another said that it was a work of "startling originality."[39] The *Spirit of the Times* noted that the drama was "full of thrilling interest and keeps the audience on tip-toe of expectation and attention from beginning to end . . . The piece itself has some defects, but the acting, the music, and the scenery are perfect."[40] And the Boucicaults' performances in London in September took the city by storm. "For a very long time so decided a sensation has not been made at any London theatre," wrote the *London Times*.[41] *The Colleen Bawn* ran continuously at the Adelphi for seven months. The Boucicaults left briefly to open the play in Dublin then returned to the Adelphi in April, whereupon the *Times* observed: "the excitement that lasted from September to March was renewed with all its violence, and *The Colleen Bawn* promises once more to fix the attention of the town. Everybody has been to see it already, and from the aspect of the Adelphi last night we may infer that everybody intends to see it again."[42] (Queen Victoria and Prince Albert saw *The Colleen Bawn* three times.)

Moreover, the production was lovely to behold. The *New-York Daily Tribune* noted the beauty of the scenery, painted by John Thorne and Minard Lewis, and specifically identified "The Lakes of Killarney by Moonlight" and "The Water Cave."[43] The London production employed different scene painters (Pitt and Thompson) as well as making some cast changes. But the promptbook and music used for both Laura Keene's and the Adelphi productions were identical copies, so this discussion applies to both productions.

As with *The Courier of Lyons*, the subject matter of the novel and play is based on an actual incident. In 1819 the body of Ellen Hanley, the sixteen-year-old daughter of a rope maker of Garryowen, washed ashore on the banks of the River Shannon. The lovely peasant girl had been secretly married to Lt. John Scanlan, a man of some fortune from nearby Ballycahane Castle. Scanlan eventually tired of her and wished to marry the heiress of Castle Chute. He hired Stephen Sullivan, a servant, to do away with his wife. Sullivan bludgeoned her to death and threw her bound body into the river, and the two men were caught by soldiers trying to escape. Scanlan's trial ignited fires of indignation because the Irish at the time were just beginning to demand justice from the ruling class, represented by men like Scanlan. Both Scanlan and Sullivan were hung in 1820.[44] Boucicault depended on just this kind of gruesome background—and its peculiar similarity to the recent Madeleine Smith case—for his drama. Despite this sensationalism, in Boucicault's adaptation the characters were so skillfully drawn and the construction was so artful that the play enjoyed an almost continual presence on the English-speaking stage for some twenty years.

An elaborate six-part overture to *The Colleen Bawn* by Thomas Baker was published separately by Lafleur in Paris.[45] It includes several Irish tunes that do not occur in the play itself (such as "The Irish Washerwoman" and "Believe Me If All Those Endearing Young Charms"). Baker was the music director at Laura Keene's at the time of the first performance. Though the surviving orchestra parts bear no signature, both the New York and London playbills credit him with the composition and arrangement of the music.[46] Baker (ca. 1820–1888) was born in England and was a prodigy on the violin. He studied at the Royal Academy of Music in London and came to America in 1853, playing in Louis Antoine Jullien's orchestra. He began his conducting career by leading English opera at Niblo's Garden. It was his eight years as Laura Keene's musical director (1855–1863) that established his reputation as one of the city's leading musicians, resulting in the successful publication and sale of a great deal of music, primarily arrangements of popular and folk music.

Both the New York and London playbills also note that the score is laden with Irish melodies (Fig. 30) and specify no less than fourteen (and the score uses a few others not named). Baker treated these like talking tunes, quotations of well-known songs where known lyrics would have contributed an additional layer of meaning. Unlike Blewitt's use of preexisting tunes in his music to *Black-Eyed Susan*, where each *melos* is largely a complete quotation, the Irish melodies in *The Colleen Bawn* are paraphrased or spun out for mood and atmosphere ("pleasantly pathetic," as one reviewer

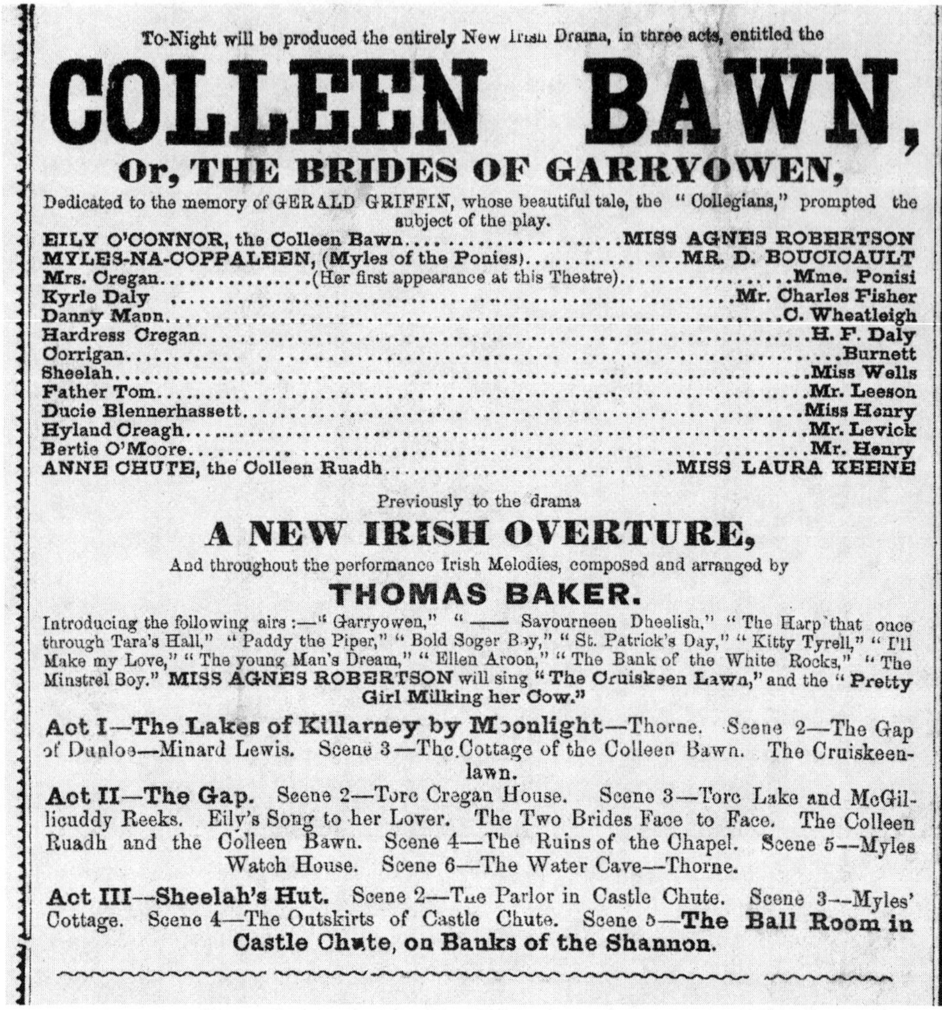

To-Night will be produced the entirely New Irish Drama, in three acts, entitled the

COLLEEN BAWN,

Or, THE BRIDES OF GARRYOWEN,

Dedicated to the memory of GERALD GRIFFIN, whose beautiful tale, the "Collegians," prompted the subject of the play.

EILY O'CONNOR, the Colleen Bawn.......................**MISS AGNES ROBERTSON**
MYLES-NA-COPPALEEN, (Myles of the Ponies)..............**MR. D. BOUCICAULT**
Mrs. Cregan...............(Her first appearance at this Theatre)..................**Mme. Ponisi**
Kyrle Daly ....**Mr. Charles Fisher**
Danny Mann..**C. Wheatleigh**
Hardress Cregan..**H. F. Daly**
Corrigan..**Burnett**
Sheelah..**Miss Wells**
Father Tom..**Mr. Leeson**
Ducie Blennerhassett..**Miss Henry**
Hyland Creagh..**Mr. Levick**
Bertie O'Moore..**Mr. Henry**
ANNE CHUTE, the Colleen Ruadh................................**MISS LAURA KEENE**

Previously to the drama

A NEW IRISH OVERTURE,

And throughout the performance Irish Melodies, composed and arranged by

THOMAS BAKER.

Introducing the following airs:—"Garryowen," "—— Savourneen Dheelish," "The Harp that once through Tara's Hall," "Paddy the Piper," "Bold Soger Boy," "St. Patrick's Day," "Kitty Tyrell," "I'll Make my Love," "The young Man's Dream," "Ellen Aroon," "The Bank of the White Rocks," "The Minstrel Boy." **MISS AGNES ROBERTSON** will sing **"The Cruiskeen Lawn,"** and the **"Pretty Girl Milking her Cow."**

Act I—The Lakes of Killarney by Moonlight—Thorne. Scene 2—The Gap of Dunloe—Minard Lewis. Scene 3—The Cottage of the Colleen Bawn. The Cruiskeen-lawn.

Act II—The Gap. Scene 2—Tore Cregan House. Scene 3—Tore Lake and McGillicuddy Reeks. Eily's Song to her Lover. The Two Brides Face to Face. The Colleen Ruadh and the Colleen Bawn. Scene 4—The Ruins of the Chapel. Scene 5—Myles Watch House. Scene 6—The Water Cave—Thorne.

Act III—Sheelah's Hut. Scene 2—The Parlor in Castle Chute. Scene 3—Myles' Cottage. Scene 4—The Outskirts of Castle Chute. Scene 5—**The Ball Room in Castle Chute, on Banks of the Shannon.**

FIGURE 30. *Detail from undated playbill for* Colleen Bawn, *Laura Keene's Theatre [1860]. (bpf TCS 65) Harvard Theatre Collection, Houghton Library, Harvard University*

referred to them).[47] Sometimes the tune would emerge clearly, and audiences might recognize a fragment of "The Last Rose of Summer" or "Cruiskeen Lawn." But just as often the Irish sources were woven into a through-composed musical fabric. Memorable bits of tunes became motives that transformed some *melos* numbers into miniature compositions. Moreover, rhythmic ostinatos provided the taut foundation upon which the principal actors timed the buildup of suspense. The orchestration consisted of about sixteen players: flute, oboe, two clarinets, bassoon, cornet, trombone, percussion, and the usual four string parts, each doubled.[48] Baker's use of his small orchestra is quite sophisticated. The strings do not just play tremolo, they shimmer, sometimes very high in register, as if Baker is using instrumental timbres to add highlights to the lustre of the scenic backdrop of Thorne's moonlit lake, which plays so important a role in the story.

For this first of his Irish dramas, Boucicault returned to the standard three-act form of the popular drama. The action takes place in Killarney at the end of the eighteenth century. Hardress Cregan, a young man of considerable means, although just about to lose his estate due to a lien on his family's property, has secretly married Eily O'Connor, a beautiful and kind-hearted peasant girl (played by Agnes Robertson). Hardress's mother assures her mortgage-holding attorney, Mr. Corrigan, that her son's marriage to Anne Chute, the daughter of a wealthy landowner, will settle the matter. But Anne is already in love with Hardress's college friend Kyrle Daly, who loves her in return. Through a conversation with Danny Mann, a somewhat shady boatman, Anne is misled to believe that it is Kyrle who sails across the lake each midnight to meet Eily, not Hardress. In the play's exposition Boucicault highlights the relationship between two different classes of Irish: the rich, linked by both nobility of breeding and nobility of character, and the poor, who speak with a brogue and whose moral boundaries are far more ambiguous. The play is enlivened and complicated by two imaginative poor characters. The servant Danny Mann—inadvertently the villain of the story—was disfigured in his boyhood through an accident with Hardress but nevertheless remains fanatically devoted to him. The second is Myles-na-Coppaleen (played by Boucicault), an outlaw bootlegger with a big heart who has loved Eily all his life and now looks after her like an older brother. Myles is a descendant of the melodramatic comic foil, though his combination of folksy humor and heroic action puts him on equal footing with the actual protagonist. In situations when nineteenth-century melodrama is often described in hyperbolic terms, it is interesting that the *Era* at the time observed that the character of Myles was "utterly devoid of . . . exaggeration."[49]

Eily lives on Muckross Head in a small cottage that Hardress has set up for her. Her closest friend is Sheelah, Danny's mother. They rely on the kind assistance of Father Tom, the parish priest, and Myles. In their first scene together we learn from Eily that the college-educated Hardress is ashamed of her manners and her use of "confounded Irish words." Eily resolves to change herself to please him. But Myles tells Eily that he wishes Hardress would "lave me yer own self and take away wid him his improvements." Myles has brought Father Tom some of his homemade whiskey. While Tom and Sheelah drink, Eily leads them in several verses of "Cruiskeen Lawn," accompanied by the orchestra. The song serves to bond these characters to one another as a peasant class, for its haunting minor-mode tune invokes an ancient Celtic flavor. Hesitating, Eily mentions that Hardress has forbidden her to sing any "ould Irish songs" because of their vulgar words. "Father Tom will give ye absolution," Sheelah assures her.

Hardress arrives, clearly troubled. He has come to the realization that the only way to save his mother from poverty is to destroy any evidence of his marriage to Eily so that he is free to marry Anne. This declaration is the exciting force that initiates the rising action. They argue over the marriage certificate, which Eily keeps safe in her bodice. They were practically children at the time of their marriage, with no witnesses but Danny, so the certificate is Eily's only legal protection. Yielding to Hardress, she reluctantly surrenders the paper. Myles has been listening secretly to their conversation. He is outraged and comes to Eily's defense. When Myles snaps his fingers in a prearranged signal (also the cue for music), Father Tom and Sheelah emerge from hiding, whereupon the embarrassed hero throws down the paper. The first act ends with Hardress leaving in anger, threatening never to return unless Eily rids herself of the "vermin" that hang around her, while Father Tom makes Eily promise never to surrender that document. Baker's through-composed *melos* sustains the tension to the fall of the curtain.

As already mentioned, some of the characters have songs associated with them. Myles makes his first entrance singing (unaccompanied) and closes that scene with the song "Oh, Limerick is beautiful." Notably, only the peasants or lower-class folks sing in the play. Even Father Tom is first presented singing "Tobacco Is an Injun Weed" while he enjoys his pipe. Though the land-owning characters do not sing, the Irish tunes in the orchestra seem to represent their thoughts and feelings. At the same time, Baker's rendering of the tunes judiciously avoided obvious Irish sentiment. The songs are never played "full out" with luscious accompaniment. Even in quoting "The Last Rose of Summer" Baker studiously avoids any hint of nostalgia. Already in the first scene the tune is linked with Hardress's love for Eily. When Eily's signal of the three lights in her window causes Hardress to extinguish his light and set out to join her, Danny's line "that's my gentleman" initiates the tune again, which shimmers in the strings as Hardress comes running down to the boat.[50] Significantly, the tune of "The Last Rose" is only heard when Eily is referred to, never when she is actually onstage. Its straightforward and "sincere rendering" aids in reinforcing Hardress's innocence, which comes into question later in the play. The tune bodily associated with Eily is "A Pretty Girl Milking Her Cow." She actually sings this melancholy melody in act 2, but the orchestra plays it earlier. It is the main tune to underscore Eily and Hardress's confrontation over the marriage document at the end of act 1.

The complication continues in act 2 with a far more serious misunderstanding. Danny, sensing Hardress's anguish, makes the offhand suggestion that his master's problems would be solved if only something accidentally "happened" to Eily. Hardress is shocked. With no sign of contrition, Danny says that they would never have to discuss the matter: if Hardress changed his mind, he would only have to send one of his gloves; Danny would understand what needed to be done. Hardress threatens Danny if he should ever so much as mention the subject again. Alone, Danny admits that it would take a great deal for him to harm such a "darlin' creature." But his love for Hardress is so great that he would do anything to save his master. Meanwhile a shady attorney has admitted a long-standing attraction to Mrs. Cregan (and, no doubt, her property). He suggests that she marry him to save her land and home. Hardress approaches his mother to explain about Eily, but he cannot bring himself to confess that they are actually married. Mrs. Cregan is shocked that her son would even consider marrying such a "poor, lowborn, silly, vulgar creature." But her son's despair is too much for her. Vile as the attorney may be, she admits that she would probably marry him to save them both.

Hardress is sickened over the whole business. His dilemma is further complicated: Anne, who thinks that Kyrle has betrayed her, has now decided to marry him after all. When Mrs. Cregan is alone, Danny comes to her, offering to do anything to help the "ould family." He suggests that maybe Eily can be persuaded to go to America for Hardress's sake, sparing them any humiliation before the wedding. He offhandedly mentions "another way," a meaning that Mrs. Cregan fails to understand, and adds that the master need only send his glove. "He'd know the manin' of that token, and so would I." Baker's *melos* begins here. Puzzled, Mrs. Cregan goes to look for Hardress. Finding his gloves in the hall and thinking that Danny's offer was to have Eily sent off to America, she picks one up and brings it back to Danny. The orchestral strings shiver in a minor mode, while the cellos and double bass several times pluck out an ominous two-note warning. Mrs. Cregan's simple misunderstanding (the melodramatic *quiproquo*) sets in motion Danny's plans to murder Eily.

The important "sensation scene" occurs at the climax of act 2. The scene's impact can best be felt by examining it in context. Baker's musical score suggests that he thought in terms of unifying the six continuous scenes through key, themes, and musical character. The first scene opens in a mountain pass. The curtain music is in E minor. It is a slow *allemande*, with the winds playing the melody and the strings playing an agitated internal figure. It is quite short, and Baker composed the fade-out by the thinning of musical activity in the last few bars. Hardress, distressed over his situation with Eily, enters with Danny, who makes the fatal suggestion. As Hardress exits, the opening *allemande* repeats to close the scene and bridges the almost instant change to a room in Mrs. Cregan's house. Anne Chute is waiting in a riding outfit. When Kyrle arrives they have an exchange rife with innuendo and befuddlement. Anne still thinks that it is Kyrle who goes nightly to his lover but refuses to call him on it. Once the confused young man leaves, Anne makes it clear that she intends to ride around the lake to investigate the cottage on Muckross Head. With her departure, Mrs. Cregan and Hardress enter. The *melos* is in D minor, a surging melody in a moderate 6/8 played in the middle winds and strings, while the upper strings play a fast-moving counterpoint, perhaps suggestive of wind. The agitated figure could allude to Anne's flight, while the surging melody serves to bring on Hardress and his mother. They are expecting the attorney Corrigan, who arrives on cue, hoping to receive his answer from Mrs. Cregan. She is just about to consent when Hardress interferes and angrily throws Corrigan out. Still undecided about his predicament, Hardress leaves sadly. The Irish tune "I'll Make My Love" begins in the flute and oboe, but Baker transforms this major-key air into minor, keeping D minor as the "key of the scene." The tune is sparsely played, and the lower strings—in canonical fashion—answer the oboe heavy-heartedly. After five bars, the *melos* comes to rest on a simple D-minor chord.

Danny appears at the window just at that point and climbs through. In his exchange with Hardress's mother, he offers his solution to remove Eily from the picture. As Mrs. Cregan goes to fetch her son, the strings softly begin to play "A Pretty Girl Milking Her Cow"—a melancholy tune by now associated with Eily's forlorn situation. The ten bars of the quivering melody in G minor, harmonized with *divisi* strings playing *tremolando*, manage to build a considerable amount of tension, especially as Mrs. Cregan returns with the glove over the bass *pizzicati*. The music comes to a dead stop. "Take her away," Mrs. Cregan urges Danny before leaving. Danny stops to make a final solemn point: "He shall never see or hear again of the Colleen

Bawn." No music whatsoever follows this ominous line and the separating flats that reveal the exterior of Eily's cottage. The strange silence leaves the audience without any emotional commentary. Sheelah and Eily are discovered quietly knitting and chatting. Eily has sent Hardress a letter by way of Myles, but Sheelah doubts whether he will ever return. Eily tries to dispel these fears by singing "Pretty Girl Milking Her Cow" accompanied by the orchestra (again in the key of G minor, as hinted at in the previous scene). The words serve as an allegory for the simple and sincere circumstances in which she and Hardress met and fell in love.[51]

After Sheelah's exit, Anne arrives. During their encounter Anne is taken by Eily's beauty and her gentle sincerity. She confronts her assumed rival with the signals, the late-night trysts, and the unsigned letter that she has brought with her. Anne is mortified to learn that Eily and her lover are already married. But never once is Hardress's name mentioned, so Anne leaves thinking that they have been discussing Kyrle. (This is the kind of exchange that only a skillful melodramatist like Boucicault could bring off, with the help of two brilliant actresses like Anne Robertson and Laura Keene.)

Danny arrives and tells Eily that Hardress has agreed to join her tonight in a secret place, a cave on "Divil's Island." Danny will meet her later on the bank of the lake with his boat. "There's no moon tonight," he tells her, "an' no one will see us crossin' the water." Music begins. The woodwinds play four bars of the opening of "The Harp That Once through Tara's Halls" in B-flat major as Eily tells Danny that she will go down to the little chapel by the shore and pray until he comes. Watching Eily go into the cottage, Danny is suddenly overwhelmed with the awfulness of what lies ahead of him. "I'm wake and cowld! What's this come over me? Mother, mother, acushla," he cries out, as the music abruptly shifts back to G minor. The cellos wail in their high register as Sheelah comes running out. Against the cello melody, the violins play an agitated figure and the lower strings again punctuate ominously with *pizzicati*. Lasting just eleven bars, the music modulates downward through some Phrygian coloring—the bleakest and most mysterious harmonies so far in the act—and comes to rest on a D-minor chord as Danny grabs the bottle of spirits and collapses into a chair. The scene changes quickly without music, with only the sound of an approaching storm.

Anne is heading home on foot, the thunder having frightened off her horse. Along the way she meets Myles (singing to himself again), who cheerfully offers to fetch the animal. When it begins to rain, Myles wraps his coat around Anne to keep her warm. As he does so, the orchestra begins to play. The music—a miniature "storm piece"—begins in a quiet agitated B-flat major with a descending chromatic bass figure that tries to drag the mode down to D minor. High tremolo violins descend quickly in chromatic thirds, conveying an effect of wind in the trees. Two quick flourishes in the high woodwinds, piccolo, and percussion suggest the crack of lightning, while the bass drum rolls thunderously. The storm music lasts just under a minute. But as Anne and Myles go off together, moments before Eily arrives at the spot designated to meet Danny, the last six bars consist of slowly moving chords, with the low strings tremolo, and come to rest on an A-major chord. Danny arrives, moody and tanked with liquor. Eily is apprehensive but departs with him as planned. The remainder of this scene is taken up with Myles and Anne's return on foot, Hardress's concerned arrival (the horse galloped home without its rider), and Anne's immediate offer to marry him. The most important plot development here is that Myles hands Hardress Eily's letter, which says that he would "never again be troubled" by her if she did not hear soon from him.

The fifth and sixth scenes are continuous. Myles is outside his cabin singing an unaccompanied "Brian O'Linn." He is about to go down to his whiskey still, which he keeps in O'Donoghue's stables, coincidentally in the same water cave where Danny is taking Eily. As Myles exits, the orchestra begins its sad boat song in D minor. This bassless *melos* opens with an agitated sixteenth-note figure in the middle strings, alternating between string groups and played *pizzicato*—an unusual orchestral effect—while the violins play a high melody in tremolo (Fig. 31).

The melody does not appear to be a known Irish tune but has the character of an old seafaring ballad, shifting between C-sharp and C-natural in the melody, depending upon whether it is ascending or descending. This adds greatly to the mood and the tension, which is intensified by the agitation of the inner strings. The scene revealed during this music is Thorne's beautiful and mysterious backdrop of the water cave. After nine bars the music reaches its ominous cadence on a single note: D. Myles has a short soliloquy, just long enough to describe his still and to explain his rifle, which he uses occasionally to hunt otter for his supper. Then he disappears up a rock. As Danny and Eily arrive in the boat, the music resumes. This is a broad lyrical statement of "Kitty Tyrrel" ("O Blame Not the Bard"), played warmly in F major by the clarinet. The second violins, however, maintain an inner agitated figure, similar to the previous *melos* but now *arco* instead of *pizzicato* and more chromatic. The smoothly moving clarinet melody, so familiar and

FIGURE 31. The Colleen Bawn, *no. 8, mm. 1–4. Transcribed from orchestra parts in the Drury Lane Theatre Archive, British Library*

gentle, suggests an eerie calm, over which the lower strings (violas and cellos) play a figure, a half note followed by four sixteenths, that repeats identically eleven times (Fig. 32).

The insistence of this repeating rhythmic pattern—an ostinato—adds to the tension of the approaching boat and the sense of expectation. The music comes to rest on an ambiguously open fifth (F and C). The conversation in the boat turns violent, with Danny accusing Eily of ruining Hardress's life (Fig. 33). He demands that she hand over the marriage certificate. The strings, *divisi* and tremolo, begin an agitated melody in A minor while the lower strings tensely exchange a short *pizzicato* motive. The music continues under the action, with dialogue cues written over specific measures in the violin leader book. "While I live I am his wife," Eily says firmly, leading to a fragmentary reminiscence of the tune "Pretty Girl." The orchestral texture grows thicker. "Then you have lived too long," Danny replies, raising his voice over the full instrumental ensemble.

The alcohol in Danny has caused him to lose all his inhibitions. As he shouts "take your marriage lines wid ye to the bottom of the lake" over a sustained A-minor chord, Danny pushes Eily from the rock backward into the water as all the upper strings play a quick upward flurry to a *fortissimo* explosion of the full orchestra—with timpani roll—on a powerful dimin-

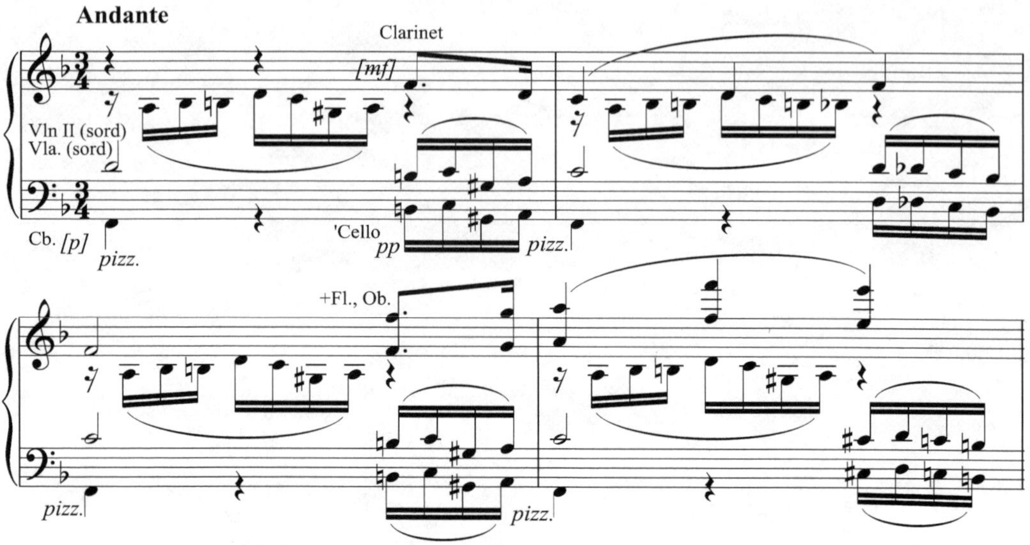

FIGURE 32. The Colleen Bawn, *no. 9, mm. 1–4*

ished seventh. This is a much-expanded "chord of reversal," a complex and elaborately textured orchestral moment (Fig. 34).

A sudden increase in tempo, with just the strings and winds playing *pianissimo*, continues this agitation as Eily begs Danny not to kill her. She clings to the rock, while the upper violins and flute sing out a passionate melody. Danny repeatedly shoves Eily back into the water. As she sinks, the music stops on a dominant seventh chord on B, followed by a brief musical silence ruptured by the sound of Myles's gunshot. His "otter on the rock" on this dark night turns out to be Danny, who tumbles into the lake. Myles comes running down, not realizing that he has just shot his friend. A furious orchestral *fortissimo* in E minor accompanies Myles's descent. He leaps onto the rock, just in time to see Eily's hand rising up out of the water. When Myles yanks off his waistcoat and makes his famous dive into the lake, the instrumental texture abruptly thins out. The high violins play tremolo on a single tense note, while the oboe leads off with the "Cruiskeen Lawn"—their bonding tune. Only nine bars of this remain until the end of the act, with a few instruments joining cautiously. As Myles rises up out of the water with Eily across his left arm, the orchestra concludes with a somber plagal cadence in minor (A minor to E minor) as the curtain falls. The final music has no romantic grandness or sense of heroism. The audience presumes

FIGURE 33. *Detail from sheet music cover, "The Colleen Bawn Waltz" (ca. 1861). Artist: J. Brandard. Special Collections, Templeman Library, University of Kent, Canterbury*

FIGURE 34 *(above and opposite).* The Colleen Bawn, *no. 10, mm. 4–21*

that Eily has been saved. But Baker's music ends the act reflectively on a note of quiet tragedy.

The "sensation" in this scene was of course due in part to the haunting beauty of the set and in part to Boucicault's headfirst dive into the water. The exquisite blue gauze that represented the lake was a completely new effect—the ripples were caused by the movements of some twenty small men and boys beneath it. Agnes Robertson also played her drowning struggles with graphic verisimilitude, sinking down into a trap and then being forced up again above the gauze. Myles first tried to pull out the body, recognized the clothing, then tore off his jacket before diving into the water to bring up the unconscious Eily (Fig. 35).[52] Some critics objected to this level of realistic detail. "Too really horrible," one newspaper wrote.[53] Another commented: "We are inclined to doubt the good taste of executing so repulsive a murder upon the stage . . . The shaking woman can be seen, fainter and fainter, clearer and clearer, as she descends."[54] Yet the account above surely awakens the sense in every reader that Baker's music, so carefully crafted to the drama, must have heightened an effect that could only be partly achieved visually. Audiences needed to hear the threat of the storm, feel the movement of the water and the tense approach of the boat,

FIGURE 35. *Detail from sheet music cover, William Forde, "The Colleen Bawn Quadrille" (ca. 1861). Artist: Thomas Lee. Special Collections, Templeman Library, University of Kent, Canterbury*

sense Eily's mounting fear and Danny's surging strength, and identify with Myles's quick action. The music artfully assisted these sensorial changes from moment to moment.

In some ways the third act of *The Colleen Bawn* is even more remarkable than the second, with its moving encounter between the dying Danny and his mother, the town's reaction to Eily's supposed death, and the taut confrontation that occurs in the final scene as Hardress and Anne's wedding is about to take place. But the climactic scene of act 2 and its vivid use of elaborate music set a standard to which every sensation drama afterward would be compared.

Boucicault's Influence

As the reigning "master of sensation" in the 1860s Boucicault produced one thrilling piece after another, influencing other dramatists and in turn borrowing back from those he influenced. The tower scene in *Arrah-na-Pogue*

(1864), for example, was undoubtedly inspired by Charles Fechter's production of *The Duke's Motto* (Lyceum, 1863), in which the dashing hero saves the duke's infant from sword-wielding brigands by grabbing the child and scampering up a rope. Successful as *Arrah-na-Pogue* was in its initial run at Dublin's Theatre Royal, Boucicault did not consider the last act climactic enough, so he cut the duel and heightened the sensation by having Shaun (played by the author himself) scale an ivy-covered prison wall. Like *Colleen Bawn*, *Arrah-na-Pogue* had music profusely scattered throughout, this time by W. C. Levey. One newspaper called the score "a galaxy of sweet Irish melody."[55] While one of Levey's thrilling melodies soared in the strings, a tower of immense height sank into the stage as Shaun climbed. Grasping the vines, Shaun hid from the soldiers, who appeared with torches and daggers leaning out various windows. When *Arrah-na-Pogue* opened in London at the Princess's Theatre in March 1865 (again with Levey's music), the Irish tunes were noted in the reviews. Some, like "The Wearing of the Green," were still controversial because of incendiary links with the Fenian rebellion. Charles Reade, curious as to *Arrah*'s enormous success, was sitting in the audience. As noted, Reade was as much a trained musician as a playwright and novelist. He was perhaps among the few to notice the degree to which Levey's underscoring contributed to the sensation header in the final scene.[56]

Boucicault sometimes built his plots around famous locales and events. For instance, he brought the first horse race to the stage with *Flying Scud, or A Four-Legged Fortune*.[57] This "sports play" was commissioned for the opening of the Holborn Theatre on 6 October 1866. The choice of subject was opportunistic: the new theatre was built on the site of the stable yard of the old post office, and the entrance to the stage was from "Jockey's-fields." The opening of the theatre, the *London Times* wrote, "caused an immense excitement in a district which, though populous in the extreme, has never been enlivened by dramatic entertainments," or at least not since Elizabethan days. The house "was crowded to excess with an audience determined to be gratified by the new building and the new piece." A writer from *Bailey's Magazine*, "not usually disposed to dramatic criticism," found the play a temptation that he could not resist. "The audience on the night of our visit was of a most miscellaneous description, ranging from members of the Jockey Club to cardsellers and touts." He wrote of their "breathless attention" throughout the entire evening (see the image of the Holborn audience at this play in Fig. 21 in chapter 6).[58]

Like Myles-na-Coppaleen, Nat Gosling, the hero of *Flying Scud* (played by George Belmore), also sings while he works, though unaccompanied by the orchestra. Boucicault established a tradition in his plays—later imitated by Irish dramatists all the way up to film director John Ford—of having the good characters sing or play instruments, while the bad guys are decidedly unmusical. The Holborn's orchestra director George Richardson composed all the music, which included an overture, a song ("The Jockey's Lament"), and forty-eight *melos* numbers, some of which incorporate a well-known melody.[59]

The horse race that concluded the second act featured all the sounds, noises, and crowd cheers of an afternoon at Epsom Downs, while the orchestra played an action *melos*, a rollicking *allegro vivace* in 12/8. The audience members at the Holborn knew that the "small cloud of horses" that they could see moving along the track were made of frosted cardboard, but no one voiced disappointment. The music galloped, the crowd cheered, and the excitement, wrote one reviewer, "was scarcely less intense . . . than that attending a real event."[60] As Nat and his steed—who had been drugged by the villain—pulled ahead of the challenger the grandstand went wild, waving hats and handkerchiefs. At the climax the orchestra burst into the well-known "Drink to Me Only with Thine Eyes" as shouts of "Flying Scud wins!" brought the race to an exciting finish.[61] Within a year *Flying Scud* was produced at Wallack's, where it created a similar sensation, and then at the Adelphi in 1868. It continued to be mounted in other theatres across England, Australia, and North America.

Boucicault's unique sense of dramatic construction, precise calculation of business, and elaborate musical accompaniment presented an obvious challenge to his competitors in the melodramatic genres. His influence can be discerned in many stage adaptations of sensational novels (*It's Never Too Late to Mend*, *Lady Audley's Secret*), historical romances (*Monte Cristo*, *The Hunchback of Notre Dame*), and French adaptations (*The Red Pocket Book*, *The Two Orphans*) as well as in original Anglo-American melodramas by authors such as Edmund Falconer (*Peep o' Day*, *Eileen Oge*), Henry Leslie and Nicholas Rowe (*The Orange Girl*, 1864, and *The Mariner's Compass*, 1867), Augustin Daly (*Under the Gaslight* and *A Flash of Lightning*, 1868), J. Redding Ware (*Death Trap*, 1870), Henry Pettitt with Paul Meritt (*The World*, 1875), and Henry Pettitt with G. R. Sims (*In the Ranks*, 1883).

Like *The Colleen Bawn*, Leslie and Rowe's *The Orange Girl* featured a dramatic rescue, this time by the principal female character. The play was first produced in 1864 at the Surrey (under the management of Richard Shepherd and James Anderson). Though this still-popular transpontine theatre burned down the following year, the anonymous music survived, largely because the orchestra parts for *The Orange Girl* were copied out and used for productions at the Marylebone Theatre in 1865 and the Grecian in 1866.[62] As for most popular dramas of this period, the complicated plot is nearly impossible to abbreviate.

The main action unfolds in Ashburton, Devon, and features a famous geographical location, the mythic Loggan Stone on the Tarn in the Druid Valley of Dean Burn. The sensational rescue occurs at the end of act 1. In a prologue Jane Grierson, a young orphan who supports herself by selling oranges in the streets of London, is at the bedside of her older sister, who lies dying. The sister, entrusted by her dead husband to his brother's care, has been severely abused and deserted and her own child taken from her. One of the lodgers is a young engraver, John Fryer, with whom Jane is in love. Seven years later Jane and John are married, living in Devon, and are raising a little girl who has mysteriously come into their lives. Meanwhile the wicked brother has now acquired a large estate and has a steward named Uriah Underwood, who in earlier days was one of John Fryer's associates and who knows that Jenny, the little Fryer girl, is actually his master's niece and therefore heir to his estate. He plans to do away with the girl by luring her to the Frozen Tarn at midnight. It is nearly twelve o'clock on New Year's Eve as Uriah arrives to cut a fissure in the frozen lake. The entire scene, from its mysterious opening until the rescue at the end, is accompanied by one extensive through-composed piece of music (music cue no. 10 occupies five pages of the violin 1 leader book). At the opening the *melos* is tense, but the swirling chromatic movement also suggests the bitter wind that blows across the lake. Accompanied by this atmospheric music Uriah descends onto the ice in search of a vulnerable spot. Each blow of his crowbar is synchronized with music (*fortissimo* string tremolos), an effect that harkens back to one of melodrama's earliest devices. After Jenny arrives, the strings play quiet nonthematic and tense music under the dialogue sequence. The orchestra comes to a stop as distant bells begin to peal in the New Year. A chime tolls midnight just as Jenny, coaxed onto the lake, falls through the fissure. The music immediately resumes, *allegro assai agitato*, as Jane Fryer appears at the top of the hill. Thinking fast, she grabs a branch and begins trying to dislodge the massive Loggan Stone, which first totters, rocks, and then slips forward and falls with a headlong crash onto the ice, cracking it wide open. With the full orchestra now roaring, Jane leaps into the icy water and is able to pull the fainting Jenny to safety. The furious music culminates with a *fortissimo* minor chord. This intensity is brought into sharp relief with an abrupt change to gentler music in 3/4 time. This nonchalant music ushers on some casual passersby, who quickly assess the situation. As these strangers rush to Jane and Jenny's aid, Uriah escapes.

The Legacy of Sensation

Dion Boucicault gradually turned his attention to other types of plays. But sensation continued to be mounted on a large scale by several of the most prominent producers of the late nineteenth century. Among these were Augustus Harris at Drury Lane, Wilson Barrett at the Princess's, and the Frohman brothers, David Belasco, and Augustus Thomas in various New York theatres. Popular dramas such as *The Lights o' London* and *The Silver King* earned their managers a tremendous amount of money (and both plays have music surviving). But a hunger for sensation also drove the repertory at the newly emerging popular-priced theatres, through which melodrama in the late nineteenth century acquired a rather tawdry reputation. Plays such as *The Power of Money*, *The Great Diamond Robbery*, *The Convict's Daughter*, *From Rags to Riches*, and *White Heather* in the fifty-cent houses (with their matinees for twenty-five cents) packaged sensation at affordable prices, no doubt with a cheap music budget to match.[63] So far no special music has been discovered for any of these late nineteenth-century offshoots of the sensation melodrama, whose characters remain associated in our minds with stock music. In the meantime, however, we have the model of a popular drama like *The Colleen Bawn*, whose moods were reflected through the prismatic hues and constant variations of a well-planned musical accompaniment.

THREE

Transforming the Popular Drama

8

Melos in Crisis

Despite the widespread success of sensation and audiences' fascination with spectacle in an age of fast-growing technological developments, the popular drama—and the music long associated with it—underwent stunning diversification in the last third of the nineteenth century. In cities and towns across the English-speaking world stock companies continued a varied repertoire, of course, with old and new favorites. In major urban centers such as London and New York, the emphasis was on new plays, sparked by the opening of new theatres, the growing competition among managers, and the increased mobility of many playgoers. A rising middle class with expendable income resulted in an expanding range of entertainment options. Variety provided an alluring alternative to the legitimate theatre in New York, as did the rise of extravaganzas and "light opera" following the sensational run of *The Black Crook* at Niblo's Garden in 1866. American popular music thrived in the minstrel show and variety theatre, especially in a city like New York, which in the last half of the nineteenth century became a nexus for the popular music industry.

The growing numbers of music halls and casinos were luring audiences in London, especially younger ones, away from traditional theatres. By 1870 London had no less than eighteen music halls. Some, such as the Alhambra and the Royal Holborn, sported exceptional orchestras and enterprising leaders. (The Alhambra eventually became known for its very clever comic ballets under the baton of Georges Jacobi.) As the old minors had done earlier in the century, music halls were seeking permission to perform dramatic repertory as well.[1] In 1866 a select committee met in Parliament to update theatrical licensing laws, which had not fundamentally changed since 1843. Some of the debates pertained to morality, such as how much (or rather how little) ballet dancers in burlesque theatres and music halls were allowed to wear. A relaxation of old laws threatened to hasten audience defection from the regular theatres. Some managers relied heavily on the new law's "free trade" clause, which allowed them to hire music-hall artists as part of an evening's entertainment. The new licensing freedoms also had serious implications for actors, who no longer needed to be bound professionally by their lines of business. Though the *Era* in the 1860s still contained ads for first old men, low comedians, and singing chambermaids for "theatres and music-halls in every part of the kingdom," it was becoming increasingly unlikely, complained Benjamin Webster, that an actor would be content to distinguish himself in a career as a walking gentleman at Drury Lane when he could play Hamlet in an east London theatre and be paid more for it.[2]

At the beginning of the 1870s the stock theatre was largely the functioning model on both sides of the Atlantic. Many major theatres still maintained house authors or adapters, such as C. H. Hazlewood at the Britannia, Paul Meritt and Henry Pettitt at the Grecian, T. W. Robertson at the Prince of Wales's, and Robert Buchanan and G. R. Sims at the Adelphi. Still, the rules by which stock companies in major theatres would formerly "get up" a standard play—with the expected music—were quickly changing. "Those were the transition days in the professional theatre," Augustus Thomas recalled, writing with fifty years of hindsight.[3] Thomas was referring to the endangered stock traditions of local theatres and the new system that gradually seemed to be replacing them, featuring major theatres tied up with long runs of a single play and touring combinations with star actors that threatened to put many regional companies out of business. London managers increasingly sought the next play and actor that—through a run of a hundred nights or more and guaranteed bookings for a tour—would naturally reduce overhead and potentially yield enormous profits.

In an article for the journal *Dark Blue* in 1871, Tom Taylor, author of *Our American Cousin* and dozens of plays popular on both sides of the Atlantic, complained about this mania and the detrimental effects on playwrights and audiences. Taylor's major concern for the future of theatre—at least for England—was that modern practices did nothing to foster permanence as the old patent system had, in terms of either the reputation of the theatre or standards in dramatic writing. Star actors are like comets that burn brightly and then go out, Taylor warned, while great plays contribute to a growing stellar system. The *Era* replied to Taylor's criticisms, labeling him a sentimentalist in his glorification of the old days. But Taylor could claim one uncontestable truth. A "long run" in London catered to a metropolis with a population of 3.5 million people, not counting a hundred thousand nightly visitors from the country who came to the city looking for amusement. In Taylor's youth a playhouse largely reflected the character of its neighborhood, so stock companies varied the repertoire in accordance with the playgoing habits of local audiences. That practice was quickly disappearing.[4]

Part of this was due to the explosion in theatre building during these years, even in small towns. In central London alone no less than twelve new city theatres were erected from the mid-1860s to 1900 and four existing playhouses were remodeled. A cluster of theatres in the West End—including the old Adelphi and the Princess's—catered more to star power in the 1870s than theatres in the East End did, but the socioeconomic differences in audiences for these theatres grew less apparent over time, given how easy it was for people to travel between them. In addition to Drury Lane and Covent Garden (since rebuilt and given over to opera and ballet), the ten theatres of the West End tend to dominate British theatrical histories about the later nineteenth century. For many visitors to London these buildings were close to each other and centrally located. It is true that managers of West End theatres such as the Lyceum and the St. James's (situated in an aristocratic quarter) strove to attract a more educated class of playgoers. This allowed these managers and their music directors to develop dramatic music that catered to the tastes of a public that was not only trained in some aspect of music performance but might just as well attend the opera or symphony. Clement Scott referred to the critical audience for Irving's *Charles I* (Lyceum, 1872) as "the art-world of London."[5] Histories of British theatre that focus on the West End obviously privilege the success of long-running plays, the newly developing cult of the author, and the prestige accorded to stars.

In 1870 each of London's twenty-four theatres still maintained a somewhat distinct identity. The Lyceum under the Batemans appealed to diverse audiences with melodramas adapted from the French. Theatres like the Gaiety catered to London's businessmen, and the Royalty and the Strand served as reigning homes for smart burlesques. (W. S. Gilbert and Arthur Sullivan's first collaborative success, *Trial by Jury*, premiered at the Royalty in 1875.) Comparable theatres to the north, east, and south—such as the old Surrey, still going strong—maintained a repertoire of stock plays that catered largely to local clientele, including a variety of entertainments other than the popular drama. The Britannia in Hoxton under Sarah Lane still reveled in sensation melodramas but was also known for its glittering pantomimes. By the late 1870s, though, an organizational principle that had driven the stock theatres—a company of actors with a leading actor-manager and occasional guest stars (not to mention a resident leader-composer)—had begun to disintegrate, at least in large urban centers. Beyond London's principal theatres, the stock system struggled to survive. And as theatres and music halls proliferated, "stage music," rather than being composed or compiled from the stock of a resident music director, could instead be rented from Lacy's and London music publishers such as Lonsdale, Metzler (later Chappell), or White and Sons.[6]

In New York at least twelve new theatres were built between 1869 and the mid-1870s, by which time the theatrical district had moved uptown to Union Square. The equivalent of London's West End was the junction of Broadway, the Bowery, and Fourteenth Street, a district that its residents called the Rialto. For some thirty years it was recognized as the hub of theatrical activity. Its businesses were monopolized "by costume houses, scenery shops, manufacturers of stage properties, theatrical printers, stage photographers . . . and shops that sold the latest foreign and domestic scripts."[7] Among the businesses located there were agents such as Taylor's Theatrical Exchange, publishing houses such as the *Dramatic Mirror*, *Dramatic Times*, and *Freund's Music and Drama*, theatrical lending agencies such as Samuel French and Marcus Witmark, as well as music publishing houses such as William A. Pond and Gustave Schirmer. Theatrical managers from all over the country only had to come to the Rialto to find all their repertoire and performing materials for the coming season.

No doubt the single most destructive influence threatening the stock system in America, however, was the financial panic of 1873 and the economic depression that followed. Between 1873 and 1876, as Peter A. Davis has demonstrated, the number of stock companies in the nation's major cities declined from over fifty to less than twenty, with several major repertory theatres in New York converting to variety entertainment in order to survive the economic downturn.[8] The upsurge in companies sent out on the road to make the most of a successful play partly accounts for the increased centralization of the dramatic industry in New York as well as the shift in dramatic repertoire.

As late as 1879 the *Atlantic Monthly* still observed two distinct classes of theatres in New York.[9] Wallack's and the Union Square Theatre (managed by A. M. Palmer) each sustained a strong stock company with an even distribution of skills and a dedicated orchestra leader, like Henry Tissington, who had come up through the ranks.[10] The other class consisted of companies with reigning stars, such as Booth's, the Fifth Avenue Theatre, the Lyceum, and the Grand Opera House. The musical directorship seemed to change hands frequently, depending upon the management. Stars not only contributed to the prestige of New York theatres but also organized their own combinations, intended to bring quality productions to theatres and "opera houses" that sprung up across the country.

As might be expected, the popular drama continued to be the bread and butter of both stock and star companies, with French-derived plays like Daly's *Frou-Frou* (Fifth Avenue Theatre, 1870) and Hart Jackson's *The Two Orphans* (Union Square Theatre, 1874) sustaining phenomenal successes and long runs. Touring combinations, sometimes rival ones, brought these plays to towns large and small. Melodramatic favorites such as *Camille, East Lynne, Mazeppa, Ingomar the Barbarian, Leah the Forsaken, Oliver Twist, Uncle Tom's Cabin*, and *Under the Gaslight* proved to be money-makers that outlived the economic depression. One combination assembled under Lawrence Barrett and Edwin Booth brought such standard melodramas as *The Duke's Motto, Monte Cristo, No Thoroughfare*, and *Rosedale* to many cities. Barrett got much of the music that he used from New York managers or agencies (who in some cases got them from London managers). Hence, for his touring production of *Rosedale* in the 1870s, Barrett was still using the original music written by Edward Mollenhauer in 1863 for Wallack's Theatre. Arthur Tams, an agency begun in 1870, also loaned music to theatrical companies. Parts for orchestras of about twelve musicians were available from Tams as late as the 1890s for old favorites such as *Camille* and *The Streets of New York* and newer plays such as Hall Caine's *The Christian*.[11] As in England, provincial and touring companies continued to book such staples of the popular drama well into the next century.

With major urban centers like London and New York teeming with dozens of theatres and regional playhouses numbering in the thousands, the need for music in the various types of repertoire was never so great. Hence it would be absurd to reduce the use of music to a single universal practice. Some new plays (such as Paul Meritt and Augustus Harris's *Youth* at Drury Lane) incorporated a huge amount of music, while others (such as Leonard Grover's *Our Boarding House* [Park Theatre, 1877]) used very little. For the traditional repertory of popular dramas a theatre might use set or preexisting music (perhaps received directly from the copyright holder of the play or a theatrical agent), the theatre's music director might fashion a new score, or music might be done away with entirely or managed by a single individual at a cabinet organ or piano, as no doubt was the case in many smaller houses or amateur theatre groups.[12]

Changing Melos

In London new approaches to stagecraft and dramatic writing that had a decisive influence on the use of music became evident in the 1860s. Consider, for example, a performance of Henry J. Byron's *Dearer Than Life* at the Queen's Theatre in 1868. Byron was known principally for his theatrical burlesques. His "quiet domestic drama" may qualify as a melodrama by today's standards, but at the time—at least according to one eyewitness—it lacked many qualities presumed to be associated with the genre. J. L. Toole played the upper-middle-class protagonist Michael Garner, who at the climax of act 2 discovers that his entire life's savings have been wiped out. He assumes (incorrectly) that this was due to his son's indiscretions. But in fact his son's unscrupulous associate Bob Gassitt (a role created by the young Henry Irving) had been siphoning off the accounts. The *melos* accompaniment that traced Garner and his family's slide into poverty in act 3 added such a "powerful effect" to the situations that it was criticized in the *Daily News*.

> Mr. Toole's pathos is not increased by the tremulous performance of Mr. Wallerstein's admirable and admirably conducted band, and there is much absurdity in hearing broken-down tradesmen—and more broken-down paupers—speaking huskily through music. Mr. Byron's play has neither burglary nor murder in it, and it is a pity to waste such powerful effects on crimes that never go beyond embezzlement.[13]

In other words, without the pantomimed action required by a robbery-in-progress or a sensational murder attempt, affective music no longer seemed necessary. For this West End theatre critic, the musical language of *melos* had become too limited in its associations. Newer plays, with characters reflecting more middle-class values and concerns, had limited use for such music.

A popular dramatist such as Tom Taylor requested much less affective music. In *Ticket-of-Leave Man* (Olympic, 1863)—one of his most widely performed plays—he specifies hurried music as the criminal Dalton attempts to escape the detectives at the end of act 1 (essentially in pantomimed action). But most of the music required for *Ticket-of-Leave* and other Taylor plays is "source music," performed either by the actors onstage or by some invisible but identifiable characters offstage, such as music from an adjoining parlor.[14] Taylor occasionally requested a concerted musical number, such as Emily singing "The Maniac's Tear" onstage during the last act of *Ticket-of-Leave*.[15] Byron did something similar in *Dearer Than Life*, though he turned the practice on its head. The concerted number is "An Honest Man," which Garner's guests use to toast him and his wife in the second act. But when Garner discovers the stolen money (aided by a nervous *melos*) at the end of the act, from the next room comes a reprise of his cheerful guests singing "An Honest Man." Without changing the character of the tune itself, its *affect* has turned from sincerity to bitter irony.

This new use of music is reflective of the "contemporary spirit" brought to the presentation of "contemporary subjects" that managers everywhere were beginning to emulate, as Pierce Egan observed in 1870, even in theatres that were traditionally home to stock repertory.[16] This was decidedly the practice adopted by T. W. Robertson in his plays, especially those premiered at the Prince of Wales's Theatre under the Bancrofts. Robertson's plays are generally comedies, in the more legitimate sense of the term. But it is useful to consider his use of music, because these intimate "talking dramas" served as an important influence on subsequent English-language popular drama. Like Taylor and Byron, Robertson would also occasionally introduce a musical performance, as in the political satire *Society* (1865), when Sidney is asked by his club members to sing one of his favorite roasting songs. But Robertson's placement of a song was always with the purpose of integration.

For example, *Ours* (1866) explores British patriotism during the recent Crimean War. The play was loaded with music, a great deal of it designed as realistic backdrop. Fife and drums play "British Grenadiers." An offstage military band plays first "Annie Laurie" and later "The Girl I Left Behind Me" to the cheers of troops marching off to war. But Robertson also cleverly planted a tune in the onstage music, requested the orchestra to render it as a reprise, and then threw it right back onstage with a change of mood and meaning. This was a borrowed air from Jacques Offenbach's *opéra-comique La chanson de Fortunio* (1861), translated into English. In a scene in the park near the end of the first act the young captain Angus MacAlister has an intimate conversation with his sweetheart, Blanche Haye. He recalls being fascinated with a song that he heard her sing recently at a soirée and asks if she will sing it for him now. She does, but without the orchestra (also excusing the lack of accompaniment). In act 2 Blanche is in her parlor, struggling with her feelings about Angus leaving for the Crimea. She sits down at the piano and tries to sing the song again, this time accompanying herself, with Angus gently leaning over her shoulder. But she can barely get through the first strophe and eventually breaks down in tears.

As act 3 opens in the Crimea, the orchestra for the first time renders the Offenbach air. As the scene opens on a rude hut, with snow blowing outside, Angus (bearded and in muddy boots) is discovered seated at a table, reading a letter from Blanche by candlelight. The orchestra quietly plays the romantic *chanson*, interrupted by distant bugle calls. When Angus and Blanche are united at the end of the play, a passing brass band plays exactly the same tune, though it is now invigorated and recast as a march. This is not coincidental, we soon learn. Blanche is startled by the music. "I think I've heard that march before," she says to the sergeant. "It's Captain MacAlister's March," he proudly informs her. Angus has asked the bandmaster to arrange the tune. Blanche is overwhelmed by this symbolic token of his love. The Offenbach melody has become a character in the drama. Though this same march brings the play to a rousing finish, the audience has heard it evolve: Blanche's joy becomes the main focus, intensified through the dynamic transformation of a melody. Robertson's avowed technique was to avoid sentimentality, so he carefully eschewed music that would add anything of a maudlin character to his situations. Even in the case of a theme that would serve to unite the lovers, he was careful to justify its existence. He used a similar device in *School* (1869), a modern version of the Cinderella story. Here the *air parlant* was taken directly from Rossini's *Cenerentola,* a melancholy tune already well established in English theatrical culture. Bella, the protagonist, first sang the song early in the performance, before Robertson had the orchestra play it as a curtain tune or as underdialogue music.

In fact the orchestra itself was so seldom required for most of Robertson's plays that in September 1869 Marie Wilton and Squire Bancroft redesigned the Prince of Wales's Theatre and removed the enclosure entirely, seating the musicians backstage. The stated intent of the reconstruction was to put in permanent stalls and allow for more comfortable space between aisles, but Marie Wilton revealed in her autobiography that abolishing the ordinary position of the orchestra was her "pet project." This was apparently the first time that anything like this had been tried, so naturally it generated much controversy and discussion. Despite its banishment to the wings, however, a reviewer from the *London Times* said that the orchestra was "perfectly audible."[17] Such a move was only possible in a repertoire that no longer required an immediate form of communication between the orchestra leader and actors: that is, genres without pantomime accompaniment or synchronized dialogue underscoring.

Most histories of British theatre agree that by 1871 the enormous success of Robertson's plays and their naturalistic manner, not just at the Prince of Wales's but in the many theatres in which they were subsequently produced, had exerted a decisive impact on both the writing and performance of new English-language plays. As historian Daniel Barrett observed, audiences were struck by the author's reliance on dialogue, character, and *mise en scène* rather than sensation to arouse interest.[18] Robertson meticulously oversaw the staging of his plays. Like Byron and Taylor, he was careful and deliberate in his choices for music, realizing the value of a well-placed tune or song as part of the story-world of the play. The next generation of English playwrights, including W. S. Gilbert, G. R. Sims, and even George Bernard Shaw, were all directly influenced by this new style of drama with its limited and focused role of music.

Robertson's plays were also promoted in the United States by Lester Wallack, McKee Rankin, and others and clearly influenced American playwrights of the time, most notably Augustin Daly. Daly began to build less music into his popular dramas, even in those adapted from French plays, which might have had more music in the original. Plays such as *Frou-Frou* (1870) and *Divorce* (1871), both at the Fifth Avenue Theatre, used very little nonsource music (based on evidence in the surviving orchestral parts). The musicians may have slipped away for much of the act, returning in time to bring down the curtain and continue with interval fare. (This was not possible in the rebuilt theatre, however. See Fig. 14 in chapter 5.)

One argument supporting the Bancrofts' removal of the orchestra is that many audiences in the 1860s were beginning to grouse about the involvement of *melos* in the drama. Some protested when music was badly played, of course, preferring no music at all. Others voiced disapproval when music was emotionally or characteristically inappropriate. Still others criticized it for being too loud or too active. Some found the musicians' movements and their stand lights to be distracting in an age of darkening theatres. And some complained about the increasingly old-fashioned and hackneyed style of the music. By 1882 the old style of *melos* accompaniment to the popular drama was too much for one annoyed reviewer in Milwaukee, Wisconsin:

> In [Joaqin Miller's] *The Danites*, when Nancy Williams is telling Sandy how the Mormons have killed all her family and are laying for her, to cut her open with a scythe, the orchestra commences low, gets excited with their terrible recital, and before she gets through talking

every fiddler is playing for all that is out, and the audience can only tell by the movement of her pale lips covered with foam whether she is telling the story of her wrongs or has got the hydrophobia. In all plays where there is any deep mystery the orchestra gets in its work right where it should be asleep.[19]

As plays in the 1870s and 1880s relied more on dialogue than on action to elucidate plot, *melos* seemed to get in the way instead of being helpful to both actors and audience. In the world of contemporary dramatic writing and performance, music was no longer necessary in its decades-old role as the suturing tool of a hybrid genre. No longer could a respectable author resort to a fairy-tale solution and rescue the heroine in time. No longer could a villain be "foiled" through a series of errors, as in melodramatic construction. Authors of popular drama, fluent for nearly ninety years in the genre's hybridity and three-act design, were forced to choose between legitimate comedy and tragedy, which was often devised in four or more acts. For comedies, only stage (or source) music or the occasional action "hurry" was generally required. It was in the modern tragedy, on the popular stage now called merely a "drama," that instrumental music still served a meaningful purpose, when it did not interfere with the dialogue.

How were theatre managers in the 1870s to respond to these changing tastes in music and drama? They had several possible options. If the play was not a tragedy or drama, they could dismiss the orchestra or put it out of sight, as the Bancrofts had done (obviously the most extreme solution and the one least imitated). They could change the nature of the orchestra enclosure (deepen the well, build it further under the stage, put a cover over it, and so forth). Managers could insist that the orchestra play as quietly as possible. They could use less music, especially any that underscored dialogue, or cut any music that had been written for a dialogue scene in previous productions. Finally, managers could work collaboratively with music directors who were creative enough, if time and money allowed, to find solutions for a more nuanced and coordinated relationship between the actors and the orchestra.

The architect of Booth's Theatre, built in 1869, sank the orchestra well below the first row of stall seating. When Lester Wallack moved into his newly built third theatre in 1882, veteran Thomas Baker retired, voicing his objections to being "stuck under the stage."[20] Many theatre orchestras were forced to play so softly that they were nearly inaudible. Under such conditions the quality of the musicians hardly mattered. Also, a great deal of music was cut, as can be seen in orchestra parts from the time with numbers stricken through with blue pencil. We turn again to J. M. Morton, who was eyewitness to the disappearing *melos* and the loss of a tradition:

> I have lately visited many theatres in New York and London, and find the great art of theatrical music almost extinct. Society plays and comedies pass through their tedious course without a note of "suggestive music," without a bar of "hurry," and without a solitary "chord" to announce the sudden arrival of the rightful heir or the missing relation. Of course it may be urged that music is inappropriate to comedies, which are pictures of real life. This I maintain to be stuff [and nonsense], and declare that melodrama, with its romantic episodes, its perspiring virtues and adequately punished villainies, is quite as true to nature as the chivying of other people's wives among French flats, or the flirtations with other people's husbands in cafés and gardens, which seem to be the staple of "modern comedy."[21]

Morton wrote this just before the popular drama experienced a remarkable revitalization in the early 1880s (as we will see later in this chapter). But until then *melos* maintained an unsettled and precarious position.

Keeping in mind both aesthetic issues of music fitted to the play as well as economic and social conditions of the changing life of the theatre and its audiences, let us visit three theatres in the 1870s. Each tried to re-create itself in order to survive as a home for the popular drama, but only one managed to do so.

A Theatre in Transition: The Grecian

When Benjamin Oliver and Clarissa Ann Conquest purchased the property of the Grecian Saloon on City Road in northeast London in 1851, they were inheriting a tavern (still fondly called the Eagle), a ballroom, a pleasure pavilion and gardens, an outdoor dancing area, and a theatre that seated about 2,000 people. This enterprise had been the brainchild of Thomas Rouse, a Mason and builder who converted the old Shepherd and Shepherdess teahouse into a "free and easy" and then into a center of amusement largely for the working-class public living east and north of the city. In the 1840s Rouse—who had been involved in drafting the 1843 theatre laws—gained a reputation for producing some of the best English and French light opera in London. Benjamin Conquest was principally an actor. His wife, Clarissa, had been a successful ballerina, beginning as a child dancer at the Coburg. The Conquests' focus was therefore on performances of ballet, melodrama, and comedy. Clarissa immediately set up a training school for young dancers, and her influence can be seen in the number of *ballets d'actions* produced at the Grecian in the 1850s and 1860s (such as Cesare Pugni's *Star of the Rhine*) as well as the increasing importance of dance in the pantomime. Under Benjamin's management the Grecian company excelled in popular dramas such as John Buckstone's *Flowers of the Forest*, Walter Banks's *Dred*, Henry Leslie's *Mariner's Compass*, Dion Boucicault's *Arrah-na-Pogue*, William E. Suter's *A Life's Revenge*, and old classics such as *Pizarro* and *Macbeth* (with singing witches). By the mid-1860s the standard of performances had risen to a professional level comparable to London's better theatres. The *Reader* magazine called the Grecian "a very elegant little theatre" where both "tragic and comic muses" graced the stage.[22]

The Conquests worked hard to expand Rouse's devoted local following. They had to bear indictments by temperance critics such as Arthur J. Balfour and James Ewing Ritchie, who attended East End theatrical events already disposed toward great suspicion. Balfour objected that the pleasure gardens attracted many young people who were "plied with drink." He was displeased by the number of "females of a certain description" as well as the types of songs that he heard performed there.[23] Ritchie found the habitués to be mostly young men, not just locals but also men from eastern and northern suburbs, who listened to "indifferent songs," witnessed "inferior dramatic performances," and associated "with the refuse of the other sex." Nor did he have much good to say about what he called the "domestic part" of the audience: "fat old women with their baskets filled with prog, the pursy old tradesmen that drop in to smoke a pipe, and the various tribes of gents and bagsmen on their way home from the city."[24] The *Reader* came to the defense of the working-class youth who packed the Grecian in the evenings, who were not just attracted to the comic songs in the saloon, the open-air dancing, and the chance to brush with middle-class business types. They were also extremely susceptible to both the comedies and tragedies presented there. "They strongly take the side of virtue in distress, though an energetic villain does somewhat excite their admiration."[25]

The Conquests' struggle to bring citywide respectability to their establishment led to their imaginative pantomime-extravaganzas. For the Christmas season of 1857 *Peter Wilkins and the Flying Indians* featured their twenty-year-old acrobatic son, George. The Conquests were among the first to use chest harnesses and high-wire rigging, and audiences were delighted at their amazing leaps from spring traps and weightless flights through the air. Another of Benjamin's specialties was to make himself up into various grotesque versions of animals, such as crabs, spiders, or flying fish. A *diablerie* of fantastic creatures became a standard feature of the Grecian pantomimes throughout the 1860s and 1870s. And the pantomimes were chock full of music. *Dick Whittington* in the Christmas season of 1868–1869 contained seventy-seven musical numbers.

The musical directorship of the Grecian changed hands in 1870. General musical director William Edroff died, leaving his son Andrew to direct the bands in the ballroom and on the outdoor platform. Edward Barrett, however, had been the leader of the theatre orchestra. Barrett's son Oscar took over music for the dramas and pantomimes in 1870. Oscar literally grew up at the Grecian, as a boy helping his father with arrangements and rehearsals. At the age of nineteen he took a job at the Theatre Royal, Southampton, in 1866. His involvement in fashioning the music for the Christmas pantomime must have been exceptional, for in the span of three years he was invited to prepare pantomimes at theatres in Newcastle, Liverpool, and Glasgow and served as the music director at the Prince of Wales's in Glasgow after the theatre was rebuilt in the fall of 1869. During these years of apprenticeship in the stock theatre Oscar Barrett had become familiar with a wide variety of mid-century theatrical repertory and had written music for a number of plays, including Maria Lovell's *Ingomar the Barbarian*. Barrett adopted the system of leading with a baton, like an opera conductor, rather than with the violin as his father had. Oscar came to the Grecian as music director at the age of twenty-three. He held that post for ten years, while at the same time writing, composing, and even directing the lavish annual Christmas pantomimes at the Crystal Palace in Sydenham.

The management of the theatre was soon to pass into George Conquest's hands, for Clarissa had died in 1867, followed by Benjamin in 1872. As his parents had done, George ran the Grecian like a stock theatre, with frequent changes of repertory and bills that generally included a drama, followed by an hour-long interval of dancing in the ballroom or gardens, and concluding with a comedy or musical piece. Under George the theatre developed a strong company of actors, all adhering closely to their lines of business. J. H. Clynds was the hero of sensation dramas. Emily Miller was the ingénue and George Sennett the melodramatic villain. The children of George Conquest and his wife were dancers and acrobats, playing flying insects and other creatures in the pantomimes.[26]

George Conquest had been sent to France as a boy and was well educated in French language and theatre. He could be quite experimental in his tastes, even producing *Romeo and Juliet* in modern dress in 1874. In the late 1860s the Conquests employed the services of two men, Paul Meritt (Maetzger) and Henry Pettitt, who began as ticket takers and front-end managers and quickly became house authors.[27] With George's collaboration they adapted novels and French dramas and in the 1870s wrote original plays that came to be known somewhat ironically as "Grecian dramas," alluding to the theatre's penchant for domestic intrigue. Rather than relying solely on well-known repertoire, as in the 1860s, the Grecian generated new plays in the 1870s. These dramas, with titles like *Dead to the World*, *Snatched from the Grave*, and *Sentenced to Death*, were written expressly for Clynds, Sennett (who, like O. Smith, excelled in deep-voiced and shady characters), and others with colorful stage names, such as Lizzie Mandlebert, Alice Denvil, and Minnie Inch. George Conquest usually reserved the comic parts for himself, and accounts describe him as keeping his audiences in stitches.

Schriften, the One-Eyed Pilot (April 1877), one of the "romantic melodramas" by Conquest and Pettitt, was loosely based on the story of the Flying Dutchman. In this version of the legend, before his disappearance Vanderdecken had thrown overboard his treacherous pilot, the traditional villain of the play, who will stop at nothing to get even with his old captain. Oscar Barrett composed thirty-three music cues for this three-act drama "full of action and incident." The orchestra consisted of his usual ten players: flute, clarinet, cornet, euphonium, drum, violin 1, violin 2, viola, cello, and bass (he may have actually had twelve players, doubling each of the violins). The principal motive for *Schriften* opened the play (Fig. 36). This mysterious and haunting music sets the mood for the story. Its descending opening gesture suggests the fall from grace of the ultravillainous title character (played by Sennett) and the anguish of the wandering Vanderdecken (played by George Gillett). Conquest and Pettitt's play taps into long-standing structural formulas for melodrama. The treatment of the ghostly sea captain serves in part as a resurrection of the gothic style of Edward Fitzball. As a "Grecian drama" it fulfills the dramatic requirements for its working-class audience: a villain in the position of power seeks to destroy the moral fabric of a community and is overcome by the virtuous hero.

Barrett's score for *Schriften* was entirely original and particularly effective in characterization and in scenes of dialogue accompaniment, most of which are through-composed pieces. Vanderdecken has a wife and son (played by Alice Denvil and William James). A locked cabinet in the family house is said to hold a secret to a fortune. The widow Vanderdecken has

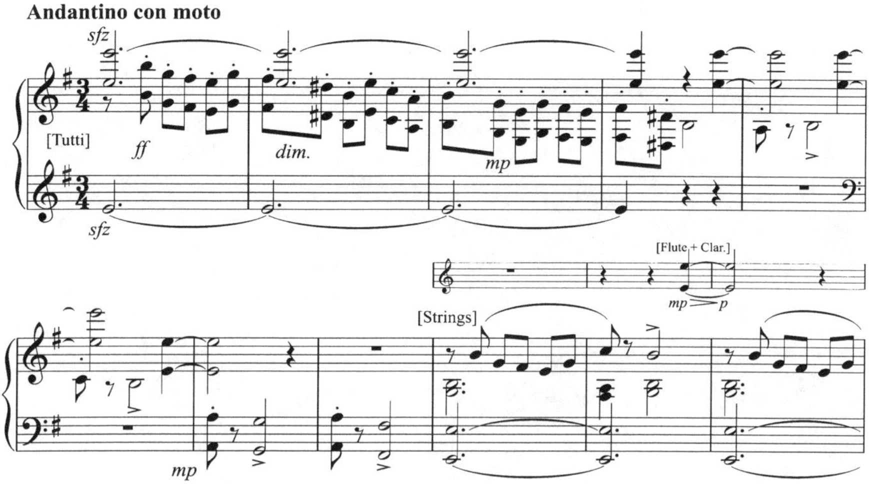

FIGURE 36. *Music to* Schriften, *no. 1, opening. Transcribed from orchestra parts in the Drury Lane Theatre Archive, British Library*

refused to open it, afraid that this may lead to losing her son as well. One dark and stormy night, at Philip's persistence, she finally relents and decides to tell him that it contains a map to the buried treasure. In the middle of the widow's story, the shutters suddenly blow open. The ghostly captain appears through the window.[28] The example here is a reconstruction from the parts with lines and cues taken from the promptbook (Fig. 37). This scene passes through a variety of tones and moods. The music changes with each one of them. First are the ascending *pizzicati* for the pantomime of Vanderdecken's entrance and his family's stunned shock. Second are the stern solo strings as the Dutchman begins his tale, measuring his phrases against the music.[29] Third is the shimmering string chorale as the Dutchman refers to the Holy Relic. Fourth are the solo strings again as the Dutchman quotes the prophecy. At the climax the strings play an anguished tune as a father appeals to his son's better spirit. Finally, unison strings bring tonal closure as the worn sea captain solemnly delivers his instructions. In addition to the nuanced handling of the under-dialogue music, something else is different here. Barrett's music reflects the continental influence of composers of the chromatic and national schools. While his music for traditional contemporary class dramas such as *Dead to the World* is simpler, the mythic undertones of the Dutchman story allowed him to experiment with the more chromatically inflected harmonies of Frédéric Chopin, Franz Liszt, and Richard Wagner.

FIGURE 37 *(above and opposite). Music to* Schriften*, no. 6*

In 1877 Conquest again enlarged the theatre. The plans of architect J. T. Robertson kept much of the old building, converting parts of it into storage and dressing rooms. For the opening of the new Grecian in 1877 (built to "nearly the size of Drury Lane"), Barrett expanded the orchestra for the Conquest and Pettitt musical-drama *Bound to Succeed, or A Leaf from the Captain's Log*. He used eight winds and a larger string section—even writing *divisi* for the second violins and violas—as well as an ensemble onstage.

that in defiance of the storm and the seas, of lightning, of heaven or of hell, that I would gain my point—even tho' I beat about the raging seas till the day of Judgement—my oath was registered in heaven. The hurricane burst upon the ship.

The canvass flew into ribbons, the seas swept over us. A voice cried in my terror stricken ear: "In living Judgement shalt thou beat about these seas—a spirit hovering twixt life and death—until upon the deck of the Phantom Ship—thy son shall place the Holy Relic in thy hands—

and thou shalt shed one tear of deep repentance on the Holy wood. *Then* shall thou rest in peace."

Philip my son, by one of those pitying spirits, whose eyes rain tears for mortal crimes,

am I permitted to appear and tell these how to end my fearful doom.

Philip: And I will save you, father, tho' I be lost myself. By the Holy Relic I swear it.

Vanderdecken: In yonder cabinet thou wilt find the packet, which tells thee how and whereere to find the treasure. It is there.

FIGURE 38. *Interior of the Grecian Theatre. Oscar Barrett and his orchestra.* London Journal *67, no. 1717 (5 January 1878): 5*

A fairly detailed orchestra can be seen in Figure 38, which even depicts Oscar Barrett in the act of conducting, with both arms outstretched.

Profits from the pavilion, outdoor dancing, and saloon, however, did not rise to match the expense of the new theatre. Not long after the opening George Conquest and his family curiously abandoned ship. They floated for a few years, eventually ending up at the Surrey. Perhaps George saw the end nearing. The Grecian, like other local stock theatres, was also losing its audiences to the many music halls springing up in the area, and pleasure grounds were becoming anachronisms. Conquest could not even hold his leading actors, as many began to defect for better prospects in West End theatres. Barrett also left in 1880 for the greener pastures of Drury Lane, where he went on to produce enormously successful fairy-extravaganzas with Augustus Harris, the most internationally famous of which is no doubt *Cinderella* in 1885. Barrett lived a long and rich life (1847–1941) and managed several theatres in the early decades of the twentieth century with his son, also named Oscar. In 1882 the Grecian had been sold to Gen. William Booth, who used it as the headquarters for the Salvation Army. In 1901 the entire enterprise was torn down.

A Theatre in Transition: The Lyceum

The Lyceum Theatre in Wellington Street had been managed by Charles Fechter from 1863 to 1867. The dashing French-trained actor produced both traditional fare such as Bulwer-Lytton's *Lady of Lyons* and new popular dramas. The greatest of these was *The Duke's Motto* (1863), a swashbuckling costume melodrama starring Kate Terry as the leading lady and Fechter sword fighting his way to chivalric victory. The comic actor John Brougham made the adaptation from *Le Bossu*, a French play about an early eighteenth-century French captain who impersonates the hunchbacked Aesop in order to avenge the death of his friend at the hands of a tyrannical Spanish prince and his band of sword-wielding ruffians. *The Duke's Motto* was in one sense an ideal melodrama, bringing the genre back to its eighteenth-century roots in Audinot's spectacular productions at the Ambigu-Comique. The Lyceum's music director in 1863 was William H. Montgomery, who composed a nearly cinematic score of seventy-one numbers. (This same music was loaned to New York for productions there.) Despite having a play that was obviously a blockbuster for the company—though pirated in theatres across the country—Fechter lost money in this changing theatrical milieu because he could produce no successful long run to follow. That was achieved once H. L. Bateman took over the Lyceum in 1871, beginning with the 151 successive performances of *The Bells*, another French adaptation that incidentally helped to secure the career of Henry Irving, known until that time largely as an actor of villainous roles.

Theatre historians and Irving biographers have lavished a great deal of attention on *The Bells*, so its discussion here need only be brief. The French version, *Le juif polonais* (The Polish Jew) by Émile Erckmann and Alexandre Chatrian, was written in the mold of a sensation drama, not necessarily because it relied on fast-paced action or quick escapes but because it was based on a true story. This was a grisly murder of a wealthy Jewish merchant by a poor Alsatian miller, who then burned the body and managed to elude detection for fifteen years until he eventually went insane from guilt. A traditionally melodramatic version by F. C. Burnand appeared in England at the Alfred Theatre (Marylebone) called *Paul Zegers, or The Dream of Retribution*, in which the murder and guilt were only a dream from which the miller eventually awoke—hence the happy ending. Leopold Lewis, by profession an attorney, was fascinated by the legal implications of the story and made his own adaptation that preserved not only the hallucinations but also the miller's death at the end.

Bateman was not interested at first. But Irving saw the play as a great vehicle for a star actor. He could play Mathias in the *Doppelgänger* mold of Dubosc and Lesurques (in *The Courier of Lyons*), though here the two were rolled into one character. The protagonist embodied both hero (the loving husband and father) and villain (the innkeeper who murders for money). As we have seen, in popular dramas from the 1780s to the 1870s the villain, the fallen hero of tragedy, served as nemesis to the hero-protagonist, with whom audiences were meant to identify and who generally triumphed in the end. In *The Bells* (as in *Eugene Aram*, a subsequent Irving success) this distinction is blurred. The audience comes to know the hero in one guise, only gradually realizing that a monster lies within. With this role Irving attained a persona that George Taylor called "master of the pathological."[30]

The plot itself focuses on the wedding of Mathias's daughter Annette, whom he is determined to shield from his guilty past. In the original Erckmann and Chatrian kept their audience guessing as to the connection between the missing Jew and Mathias's wealth, confirming it only in the dream-trial in the last act. Lewis sets up the suspicion before Mathias even enters, and the hallucinatory vision-scene added at the end of act 1 reveals how Mathias committed the murder that stormy winter night. He stole the gold and threw the body in a fiery kiln. The Lyceum audience was therefore given an unrestricted view of Mathias's crimes. This allowed them to follow the progression of his guilt, while the other characters remained in the dark. Unlike Mathias and the audience, they were oblivious to the mysterious ringing of sleigh bells, the sound that appears to emanate from the guilty man's troubled conscience.

In melodramatic style, Lewis loaded his text with specifications for music. He indicated frequent chords, for example, during the vision scene. Bateman hired Étienne Singla, who had provided the music for the first production at the Théâtre Cluny in Paris in 1869, to adapt his score for Lewis's version (J. Mallandaine led the Lyceum band, however). Irving jettisoned much of the extraneous music that was associated with the French original and which had been replicated in the version performed at the Grecian Theatre in 1872, such as the splendidly evocative spinning music at the opening of the play and the eerie underscoring for the unsettling "ghost story," the family's conversation about the unsolved murder that occurs just prior to Mathias's entrance.[31] Music to *The Bells* survives only in parts that Irving used in his later touring productions, by which time he had made many changes. Perhaps Irving realized that much of Singla's music preserved the flavor of the old stock villain from which he was trying to distance himself. In the scaled-down version Irving retained the source music as an outward sign of a normal life—the *Lauterbach* waltz played at the wedding, for example—but limited the orchestral *melos* solely to chart Mathias's inner consciousness, his guilt and fear of detection. (Irving's touring version of *The Bells* has been published by David Mayer and the music faithfully reconstructed by Stephen Cockett.)[32]

The music cues—exclusively of the "single-affect" variety—anchor the two sides of Mathias's personality, a haunting *misterioso* heard at his entrance (the "guilt *melos*") and a recurring theme for his tenderness toward Annette. Even the dance music played by the band onstage turns to mockery, as Mathias is again haunted by the sound of the infernal sleigh. Against the whirling joy of the music he throws his arms in the air and screams "the bells! the bells!" All the revelers are at a loss except his wife, who begins to suspect not guilt but madness. The effect was anempathetic: the cheerful waltz was disturbingly indifferent to Mathias's mounting anxiety. The "wrong music" was far more terrifying than if the "guilt *melos*" had returned.

Before the beginnings of experimental psychology in 1879 little was known about such phenomena as guilt-complexes. The most mysterious music imaginable was a suggestion of that dim and fearful world called the "unconscious." The portion of Singla's music that Irving retained was used in this way, reserving the shivering *melos* for those instances when Matthias is pulled away from reality and plunged into a fearful state of emotional trauma. The *tremolo misterioso* under Matthias's vision at the end of act 1 (and again in act 2) once more conjures up that central resonance in the melodramatic imagination alluded to since the beginnings of melodrama, which here reveals its true origins. Mathias is brought to justice only in his own mind and exacts his own punishment by dying of remorse. But the "vision scenes"—like the scene in the *Corsican Brothers*, performed behind a scrim of gauze—remained some of the most stirring theatrical experiences of the time.

The Bells marked the beginning of Irving's emergence as a potent force in the late nineteenth-century theatre. As he demonstrated again in his interpretation of W. G. Wills's *Charles I* (October 1872), Irving insisted on characters with psychological depth. Perhaps this was one of the reasons why the Lyceum was able to replicate the long-running success of *The Bells* in subsequent productions. Despite a weak George Belmore as Cromwell, *Charles I* ran intermittently for 180 nights. Written in the vein of Shakespeare's histories, Wills's text specified only "soft music" for the first-act drop, which was probably provided by J. Mallandaine, still leading the orchestra. Though there is no hint of it in the text, Percy Fitzgerald recalled "an old French air of a plaintive cast" that shadowed Irving's depiction of the unhappy protagonist.[33] *Charles I* was briefly suspended for *Leah the Forsaken* with Kate Bateman in March 1873, by which time Robert Stoepel (coming over from America) had replaced Mallandaine in the orchestra. H. L. Bateman and his daughter must have thought a great deal of Stoepel for more than just his *Leah* music: he remained as orchestra leader until Bateman's death in 1878. Kate Bateman even went to bat for him when her father and Irving decided to reject Charles Villiers Stanford's commissioned score to *Queen Mary* for something more appropriately functional by Stoepel. Wills followed his *Charles I* in 1873 with *Eugene Aram*, a play based on the murder poem that Irving liked to recite. Stoepel continued to provide music for Irving in *Richelieu*, *Hamlet*, *Macbeth*, and *Othello*, as well as increasingly lavish productions such as Casimir Delavigne's *Louis XI*, Alfred Lord Tennyson's *Queen Mary*, and melodramas such as Percy Fitzgerald and W. G. Wills's *Vanderdecken* and Robert Buchanan's *Corinne*. He also led scintillating entr'acte music, which no longer consisted of the ubiquitous dance numbers and cornet solos. With an orchestra expanded to twenty-four musicians Stoepel led overtures by Richard Wagner as well as instrumental selections from the operas of Charles Gounod and Giuseppe Verdi. It was clear not only from Bateman's and Irving's emphasis on psychological and historical melodramas but also from Stoepel's orchestra selections that the Lyceum was already catering to a wealthier and more educated audience.

Throughout H. L. Bateman's management until his death, every aspect of production, set painting, costumes, lighting, and music would be focused toward overall dramatic and structural unity. Irving carried that forward when he assumed the management in 1878 and went on to lead one of the most successful theatrical enterprises of the century (see chapter 9). Until the end of his life, however, Irving always pulled out *The Bells* when he needed a quick moneymaker.

Edwin Booth, eminent Shakespearean, gradually returned to the stage, in the wake of his family's humiliation after his brother John Wilkes Booth assassinated Abraham Lincoln. After the Winter Garden burned down in 1867, he struggled to raise the funds to build a new theatre on 23rd and Sixth Avenue. Given his plans for a solid granite building and plush interiors Booth found himself faced with expenses totaling a million dollars. The house could seat 2,000 and featured upholstered stall seating, three large gold-gilt boxes on either side, and three galleries. The stage was designed without wings: all scenery was intended to "sink and rise" on hydraulic lifts. The theatre opened in February 1869 with *Romeo and Juliet.* Mary McVicker, Booth's second wife, played opposite him. Mark Smith, also a stage manager, was Friar Lawrence. The leader of the orchestra was veteran Edward Mollenhauer, who came over from Niblo's Garden. The orchestra in the first season consisted of twenty-four players, some of whom also taught at the Mollenhauer brothers' short-lived conservatory of music.

Booth's intention was to foster an American love for Shakespeare and the legitimate theatre. He would cater largely to an upscale audience—given the expenses he hoped to recoup—while also appealing to a business class of visitors to this fast-growing center of finance. Shakespeare figures prominently in the theatre's first years. Booth starred in *Othello*, *Hamlet*, and *Richard III*, among others. One of these was Booth's own adaptation of *Julius Caesar*, an odd choice given that Edwin had last acted in this play with both of his brothers in 1864, at the height of the Civil War. The subject of assassination still weighed heavily on the national conscience. At his new theatre Booth repeated his role of Brutus, which was less than enthusiastically received. A bluff and beefy Henry Bangs played Marc Antony.[34] The star of the production, however, was Lawrence Barrett, a sensitive and poetic actor that Clara Morris once described as "the man with the hungry eyes." (He appears to be unrelated to the Barrett family of Grecian and Drury Lane fame.) Cassius, the lean and choleric instigator of the rebellion, was a role that Barrett largely owned in New York, Boston, and on tour across America for almost twenty years.[35] This *Julius Caesar* lasted eighty-five performances, a significant run. The set and realistic backdrops by William Voigtlin for the opening public square in Rome, as John Ripley put it, were designed "as a breathtaking introduction to an age in which architectural splendor reflected the grandeur of human ideals."[36]

Shakespeare was not necessarily big box office at the time. For the theatre to succeed financially Booth booked in fare more typical of the eclectic tastes of the age. This included standards such as *The Iron Chest* and *Lady of Lyons*, melodramas such as *The Marble Heart* and *Enoch Arden*, comic afterpieces such as *A Regular Fix*, and new successes from London, such as W. G. Wills's *Man o'Airlie*, brought over from the Princess's as a vehicle for Lawrence Barrett, and even *The Bells*, with James W. Wallack portraying the haunted Alsatian. Other visiting stars in the theatre's first years performed *Guy Mannering* (Charlotte Cushman), *Rip van Winkle* (Joseph Jefferson), *Leah* and *Mary Warner* (Kate Bateman), *No Thoroughfare* and *Ticket-of-Leave-Man* (W. J. Florence), the wildly successful *Fanchon, the Cricket* (Maggie Mitchell), and even comic sketches such as *Solon Shingle* by the inimitable John E. Owens. Dozens of other stars made guest appearances at the theatre. At first Mollenhauer provided serviceable music for many of Booth's productions, except when guests such as Mitchell or Florence brought their own music with them.

In 1873 the *New York Times* published an article on the quality of theatres in New York. Wallack's and Booth's were singled out as having attained a standard of dramatic performance hitherto unknown in the United States. Although acting was not always at a consistently high level, the *Times* wrote, taking all things together—"acting, costumes, scenes, and other accessories, the thoroughness of rehearsal and stage business, the quality of the orchestras, and the comfort and elegance of the auditorium"—Booth's (along with Wallack's) had definitely raised the bar on overall production values.[37] Despite this reputation and the attraction of star actors, Booth could not manage to remain above water financially, even with his brother Junius's help. Perhaps adhering to the old stock approach to repertoire—rather than gambling on a new hit play—was his undoing. These were short-term gains but long-term losses, as star salaries drained the coffers. Sadly, in 1874 the Booth brothers took a pass on Hart Jackson's adaptation of *The Two Orphans*, which might have saved their theatre. This melodrama was immediately snapped up by A. M. Palmer, who produced it with gorgeous costumes and scenery at the Union Square Theatre and made a fortune from one of the great successes of the nineteenth-century American stage. By the fall season of 1874 the Booth brothers had given up their lease. A. M. Palmer and Henry Jarrett assumed the management. With the Union Square booked up with a long run of *The Two Orphans*, they were free to focus their energies on trying to save the more upscale enterprise still known as Booth's Theatre.

One of the first things that Jarrett and Palmer did was aim for a hit that would also uphold the ideals on which the company was based. For this they turned to Dion Boucicault, commissioning a play in which John McCullough could act in something other than his gladiator tunic. For the occasion Boucicault penned one of the first Civil War dramas, *Belle Lamar*. It included both fictional as well as historical characters, such as Stonewall Jackson (created by the brilliant character actor Frank Mackay). Given the associations with this theatre, the play may have been Boucicault's attempt to draw on the Booth family name to establish an American national drama. The plot concerned the trial of a Confederate woman who tricked a Union officer into betraying his army's plans. For *Belle Lamar* Michael Connelly, who had replaced Mollenhauer as music director, provided both source tunes such as "Tenting on the Old Camp Ground" and *misteriosos*, lyrical *andantes*, and *andante tremolos*, most of which underscored dialogue scenes.[38] The play featured none of Boucicault's infamous sensation headers other than a Union and Confederate battle over a bridge near the end of the play while the orchestra stormed repeatedly through "When Johnny Comes Marching Home." This, by the way, was one of the earliest instances of using this dynamic Civil War tune as an accompaniment to dramatic action. *Belle Lamar* ran only as long as the house was papered, according to Townsend Walsh. It was criticized for being more "a series of incidents" than a well-constructed drama befitting the seriousness of the subject.[39]

When Booth designed the theatre, he included an enclosure for an orchestra that could accommodate up to thirty musicians. This space was literally a well. He sank it below the level of the audience stalls so that he could move a portion of the orchestra directly under the stage and move the front row of stalls closer to the actors. This meant that musicians playing at the rear of the ensemble could no longer see or hear what was happening onstage. Sometime during Jarrett and Palmer's management, the lip of the stage was extended forward. This "buried" even more of the orchestra, allowing only the head of the leader and perhaps the scroll of a double bass or two to be seen.

The effect was psychologically detrimental for the musicians. It meant that their role was reduced to a mere mechanical one, with little possibility for any emotional investment in the product. Mollenhauer most probably led the orchestra playing his violin. But by about 1875 it was no longer practical for the leader—elevated in order to see the stage—to be a performing part of the ensemble. He was now a conductor, a mediator pure and simple. Sarah Bernhardt made her first appearances in America at Booth's in 1880. During rehearsals for *Camille* the frustrated actress cut several of the orchestra cues because musicians had difficulty coordinating them with the stage.[40]

Jarrett and Palmer tried booking itinerant companies into the theatre. One of these was the company of George Fawcett Rowe, who brought his production of Andrew Halliday's *Little Em'ly* to Booth's in late 1874 after a successful run in Boston. Halliday, an English journalist and playwright of burlesques, was also a master of the adaptation. His five-act version of Dickens's *David Copperfield* (Olympic, 1869) had been a huge success in London, praised even by Dickens, and Rowe was touring it to different cities and delighting audiences with his Wilkins Micawber. *Little Em'ly* was followed by a spectacular production of *Henry V*, staged for George Rignold. Shrewdly observing the impact that spectacle had on audience draw, Jarrett and Palmer decided to revive *Julius Caesar*, this time without Booth. They added new backdrops, new costumes, and an additional 100 supernumeraries for the crowd and battle scenes. E. L. Davenport replaced Booth in an antiheroic interpretation of the role.[41] Bangs returned as Mark Antony, and Lawrence Barrett once again provided star power as Cassius.

In addition to the amplification of spectacle, Jarrett and Palmer decided to add new and more prominent music. For this they hired Giuseppe Operti, leader of the orchestra for the famed *Black Crook* at Niblo's Garden. Operti brought a certain prestige factor to the theatre. Born in Italy in 1824, he sported the title of "Pianist to Victor Emmanuel II, King of Italy." He arrived in America around 1869 to lead the music at the Tammany Theatre and in 1870 went over to Niblo's. His publication record until his death in 1886 includes many songs as well as a few comic operas and burlesques.

Perhaps Jarrett and Palmer were aware that in France some principal and secondary theatres were turning to prominent nationally known composers such as Gounod and Bizet to provide theatrical music. A national theatre in New York should similarly have a prestigious leader and composer at its helm. But qualified American candidates for this position were few and far between. A class of professional artisans was still in charge of theatrical music in 1875. William Withers, Mark Hassler, and Frank A. Howson were perhaps among the best of the recent generation writing for the Boston/New York/Philadelphia stock circuit. There was as yet no national composer to whom an enterprising American manager could turn. Jarrett and Palmer gambled on Operti.

Some of the *melos* numbers used through the play may have been Mollenhauer's music from the earlier production, especially those underscoring

Cassius's speeches, which were closely linked to Barrett's interpretation of the role. Given the prominence of stage spectacle in this play, it is no surprise that Operti also contributed a significant number of fanfares and other "public" music, along the lines of those established by Charles Kean two decades earlier. Since the days of Garrick—and certainly since Elliston—Shakespeare's tragedies had been interpreted as popular dramas, with similar styles of acting and music as in the great melodramas of the day. Some of this had changed since the advent of Kean and Phelps, of course. The use of *melos* seems to have diminished, particularly in dialogue scenes. *Julius Caesar* embodies both the public and private spheres. The public sphere in this production was amply represented by music, some of it drawn from well-known compositions.[42] The private sphere was not, however, at least not in the first half of the play. No music accompanied such obvious melodramatic moments as the soothsayer's warning or Calphurnia's foreboding as she urges Caesar not to attend the Senate that day.

Booth had divided the play into six titled acts ("The Assassination," "Before the People," and so forth). Jarrett and Palmer added a final tableau: a "cremation scene" in which Brutus's soldiers erect a pyre for his body and dramatically set it alight. Several small but crucial scenes were deleted.[43] What remained focused the action around the conspirators and their plight. Caesar and the revelation of his character dominate the first three acts, but Brutus almost certainly comes across as the play's protagonist or tragic hero. In him, Coppélia Kahn remarked, "the contradictions embedded in his culture are set at war."[44] In the first half Brutus emerges as the architect of the conspiracy. In the last acts Brutus's world crumbles around him while Antony and Octavius's armies grow ever more victorious. The orchestra parts include twenty-eight cues. The first two-thirds of the play contains only seven of these, all in some sense reflecting the public ethos of imperial Rome. (There was no music for either of the famous forum speeches, only a weighty funeral march with brass band and bass drum as Caesar's body was brought in.) In contrast, the last two acts, which take us into the private world of the play's disillusioned characters, have twenty-one music cues.

Let us turn to Cassius's suicide scene, as Lawrence Barrett played it, with Operti leading the music (whether written by him or carried over from the 1871 production). In the preceding tent scene neither Cassius and Brutus's confrontation nor the appearance of Caesar's ghost had any music. Lucius's melancholy song was sung to light orchestral accompaniment. Only at the end of the scene did the orchestra move into the role of commentator by playing an instrumental version of Lucius's song, while the page clutched his master in devotion. This aided in setting the tone for the impending tragedy in the next act. Without an intermission the scene changed to the battlefield at Phillippi, with the orchestra bringing up the curtain with a rousing piece heard for the first time in the evening. It was labeled in the parts as "Antony's March." "Act 6" contained the most elaborate and most complex mix of music in the play, including music that focused solely on the orchestra (scene change, no. 25). *Melos* items worked inconspicuously to underscore action and dialogue (nos. 20–24 and no. 26), and public music had a precise visual or aural reference in the play. The public music included intermittent fanfares and trumpet calls—some of them referencing the Roman music from the first act—and several reprises of "Antony's March" that brought formal unity to the Phillippi act.

ACT VI: THE PLAINS OF PHILLIPPI

SCENES: PARLEY BEFORE THE BATTLE. THE BATTLE.

DEATH OF CASSIUS AND OF BRUTUS

"Nature might stand up and say to all the World, This was a man!"

	Booth	First Folio (1623)	Music
16	Act VI, i	V, i	"Antony's March" (ethos of Rome; suggests preparations for military battle)
17	Act VI, i	V, i	Fanfares
18	Act VI, i	V, i	"Antony's March"
19	Act VI, i	V, i	Fanfares and March (to suggest offstage army)
20	Act VI, i	V, i	Agitato, fight music
21	Act VI, i	V, i	Plaintive (Cassius)
22	Act VI, i	V, i	Adagio (Cassius's suicide)
23	Act VI, i	V, i	Martial Music (for Brutus's entrance and discovery of Cassius's death)
24	Act VI, i	V, i	March (Dirge)
25	Act VI, ii	V, v	Scene-change music
26	Act VI, ii	V, v	Adagio (Brutus's resignation & suicide)
27	Act VI, ii	V, v	"Antony's March" (for arrival of Antony and his army)

The melodramatic music of nos. 20 to 23 was nearly continuous. This was Lawrence Barrett's big scene: Cassius's capitulation and death. As soon as the offstage battle was established with the no. 19 march, Brutus crossed the stage, fighting off Antony's and Octavius's hotly pursing guards. This stage fight was accompanied by an *agitato* (no. 20), during which Cassius enters in pursuit of a standard-bearer. He kills him, seizes the eagle, and comes down center to plant the Roman emblem into the ground. As the battle recedes into the wings, the *melos* changes to a plaintive in slow march tempo (no. 21). Trebonius enters with news that Brutus's soldiers have been defeated as Antony's troops advance. Pindarus also runs in, warning Cassius not to return to his camp because Antony has overtaken it and set it ablaze. Hearing victorious shouting and drumming offstage, Cassius mistakenly thinks that Titinius, his friend and messenger, has been captured. With Antony's army closing in, only one option is left to him: to take his own life. The *melos* changes again (no. 22). Under Cassius's final speech, a muted solo violin sings out a tender melody accompanied by a soft combination of tremolo and *pizzicato*. Cassius is resigned to defeat and asks his servant to hold his sword so that he may run upon it. Without wavering from its regretful tone, the sweet melody continues under Cassius's death, as Pindarus gently lowers the lifeless body to the ground and respectfully covers his master's face with the toga.

Trebonius and Titinius enter, find Cassius's body, and fall to their bended knees in tribute. Cue no. 23 is more characteristic music, as Brutus and his soldiers arrive and discover their dead friend. These consecutive cues, though private and introspective in tone, managed the pace and deeply enhanced the emotional impact of the scene. With no. 24, however, the music moves onto another level. When Brutus orders Cassius's body lifted and born away, Operti's orchestra, modest as it was, burst into a tragic but stately dirge in C minor. This was an almost operatic moment. The production made much of this ceremony—unlike Shakespeare. The stage directions for the bearing of the body and the scene change are extensive, with a wistful Brutus left behind as the cortège moves off. Present-day audiences might hear the *melos* under Cassius's death scene as sentimental, but it conveyed an important subtext for the actors and audiences at the time: dignity rather than dishonor; humility rather than ambition; and perhaps above all a pervasive sense of regret for a lost cause.

For the remainder of its short life, Booth's Theatre led a schizophrenic existence. After Jarrett and Palmer gave up the lease, it housed several seasons of operas in the late 1870s, first Italian opera under Clara Kellogg and then French *opéra bouffe* under Jacob Grau. Various visiting companies had a go at it, including an *Uncle Tom* combination, until John Stetson took it over in 1881. Engaging William Withers (formerly of Ford's Theatre in

Washington) as his musical director, Stetson tried to uphold the theatre's reputation as a temple of high art, producing legitimate dramas and opera until the theatre closed in 1883, fittingly, with Helena Modjeska in *Romeo and Juliet*, the same play with which it had opened. The building was sold to R. H. Macy, who converted it to the department store for which his name is now famous.

Melos *and a New Generation of American Managers*

A glance inside these three stock theatres serves to show that the development of nineteenth-century theatre music was closely tied to the fate of the theatres with which it was associated. Hence we must consider the historical implications of Bateman and Irving's ability to succeed at the Lyceum while the managers of a theatre such as Booth's could not. Bateman and Irving appealed to the tastes of an affluent and well-educated audience at a time when the cultural institutions that supported the British Empire were in the ascendancy. It was a greater challenge for an entrepreneurial New York manager to sustain a stock theatre of this type in a post–Civil War economy. The audiences that might have attended Booth's were caught up in some of the most dramatic economic, social, and cultural changes in New York's history. The building of the Metropolitan Opera in 1880 and the growth of a major symphony orchestra in the city—to cite just two significant examples—skimmed off the cream of New York society. For New York's fast-growing immigrant class, the vaudeville houses provided music in affordable packaging. The phenomenal metamorphosis of burlesque and the comic skit created a new star class of entertainers, with Tony Pastor's Fourteenth Street Theatre ultimately leading the way. Finally, the rise of the American musical, nourished in its early years by the streams of vaudeville and ethnic theatre, served as a distinctively American answer to English opera. In the midst of these musically oriented genres it seemed that America's home-grown play would be neither melodrama nor modern comedy but another hybrid that developed from mid-century melodramas (like those of Boucicault and Daly) and minstrel-variety shows with their songs and dances. The most popular of these in the 1870s was the "Mulligan Guard" series of sketches by Edward Harrigan and Tony Hart, which eventually culminated in the full-scale production *The Mulligan Guard Ball* (Theatre Comique, 1879).

Vaudevilles such as *The Mulligan Guard* had no need for affective music (or at least we have no surviving evidence of it).[45] Some of the new hybrids did specify the occasional *melos*, but the orchestral parts seem to have disappeared while the published songs survived. One important example is *The Old Homestead*. The play grew out of a sketch acted by Denman Thompson, an experienced stock actor, who created the character of the wide-eyed rube Joshua Whitcomb. In January 1887 Thompson and George Ryer's full-length dramatic version began a successful run at Tony Pastor's Theatre. Given that it originated on a variety stage, it is not surprising that the play contained a great deal of music in the form of songs, vocal quartets, hymns, and fiddle tunes (T. B. Harms published a selection of these in 1889). The published text includes one "cue for sympathetic music *pp* [*pianissimo*] in orchestra." This was to run under a scene between Whitcomb and a young hobo, Jack Hazard. The hungry man asks the old farmer for some food. As he talks about his hard luck, the music begins. Joshua, aided by the persuasive *melos*, is increasingly taken in by the fellow's tale of woe. Alcohol led him into this life, the young man admits, and a hobo's world is fraught with peril. When Jack reveals that he has a mother still living in New York, Joshua offers the young man ten dollars if he will give up drinking and buy himself a train ticket to see her. At Jack's "ten dollars, eh?" the music abruptly stops. Was the *melos* being truthful or manipulative? Did it stop because Jack's mind was suddenly thrown into reverse at the magnitude of the kindly gesture? This is left to the viewer's interpretation, as is the close of the scene. While an unseen vocal quartet begins to sing "Oh Where Is My Boy Tonight," the old farmer watches the footsore youth depart with his small fortune. Will it lead him to his mother, or will he use the money to buy more booze?

Vaudeville and successful hybrids like *The Old Homestead* appeared to controvert the traditional musical strategies of the popular drama, even spelling their demise. Efforts to capture the "contemporary spirit" on the stage seemed to be turning away from long-established techniques of the melodramatic theatre. For over a decade *melos* and the dramatic aesthetics that it supported had been in peril. By the late 1870s it seemed as if the popular drama itself, with its intrinsic moral universe, was about to be downgraded to a merely provincial or eccentric form of diversion.

Miraculously, however, the old form received a totally unforeseen jolt of fresh professional energy. The first sign of this in the United States was in the remarkable successes of the Madison Square Theatre, managed first by James Steele Mackaye and then by the Frohman brothers, Gustave, Daniel, and Charles. This beautifully remodeled theatre opened in 1880 with Mackaye's *Hazel Kirke*, a heartfelt melodrama starring Effie Ellsler that ran a staggering 486 nights. Though orchestra parts have not been found, French's performing edition (published nineteen years later) specifies fifteen music cues to assist the action and dialogue. Charles Frohman's genius was in immediately establishing several exchanges that would open *Hazel Kirke* in different parts of the city—and cater to different types of audiences—while also touring nationally. As many as fourteen "*Hazel Kirke* Companies" toured at one time, each with its own cast and each traveling with a musical director whose job it was to hire local musicians, at least in the early stages of Frohman's tours.

Charles Frohman had begun his career as a boy in New York in burlesque and minstrelsy. Although Frohman was opposed to the idea of a "national theatre," he and his brothers nevertheless managed to promote a rising generation of new American playwrights, including Mackaye, David Belasco, Bronson Howard, William Gillette, and even British-born authors like Frances Hodgson Burnett. Charles Frohman was also a brilliant "play doctor." He resurrected a failed Civil War drama, for example, that Bronson Howard had written some years earlier. Though obviously influenced by T. W. Robertson's *Ours*, the play had great potential, Frohman realized. So in 1889 he brought out Howard's *Shenandoah* at the Star Theatre. A topic thought too fraught to be enacted onstage was now a long-running success. The *Dial* later wrote that more Americans had seen *Shenandoah* than any other American play except perhaps *Uncle Tom's Cabin*.[46] The drama was rife with music: bugle calls taken directly from Civil War field manuals, onstage bands playing period music, and well-known Civil War tunes played by the orchestra for the rise and fall of the curtain.

With the financial gains from *Shenandoah*, Frohman founded the Empire Stock Theatre Company, promoted in the *Clipper Annual* in 1893 as "the finest stock theatre in the world." Frohman proved that the critics of the 1870s were too hasty in celebrating the demise of melodrama and the systems that supported it. The stock theatre was not dead, just in need of restructuring. Until the end of his life Charles Frohman (along with his brother Daniel) put his faith in the great melodramatic tradition that he inherited. In fact he brought it to a level of financial and commercial success unimagined by his predecessors. He could be intolerant of overacting; but as for the genre itself, he famously asked: "What is melodrama? Life itself is melodrama, and life, put upon the stage only seems untrue when it is acted melodramatically—that is, unnaturally."[47] By the end of the century, in connection with the theatre syndicate that he helped found, Charles Frohman owned or controlled half of New York's best theatres and was beginning to invest in London theatres as well. He was responsible for promoting actors such as Maude Adams, John Drew, Julia Marlowe, Ethel Barrymore, and many others to stardom.

Much of the music that Charles and his brothers used for their productions has evaded discovery. No doubt they held a tight rein on all their performing materials, as they worked closely with attorneys to be sure none of their plays circulated in pirated copies or were illegally produced. The right music, correctly chosen and correctly placed, could save a weak play and improve a good one. Music, like the acting script itself, equaled money. Perhaps someday a cache of materials will be found in a warehouse. Until then we must rely on the few scores known to be associated with Frohman's productions, all of which have been found in either the R. H. Burnside Collection (removed from the old Hippodrome Theatre) or the David Belasco Collection, both now residing at the New York Public Library. Examples from the 1880s provide some insight into Charles and Daniel Frohman's use of music during this transformative decade.

David Belasco was one of the manager-playwrights that the Frohmans brought to New York. All three brothers had met him around 1881 while Belasco was still a young director at the Baldwin Theatre in San Francisco. For over a decade Belasco had acted, stage-managed, led tours, revised and authored plays, and then directed for various San Francisco companies. He developed close connections with some of the leading actors of the day. Like Frohman, Belasco was steeped in the melodramatic tradition. He spent his teenage years in "one of the most vicious, turbulent, and perilous cities in the world," wrote William Winter, where he loved to visit murder sites and deliver "shockers" (grizzly poems and recitations) in San Francisco's many saloons and dives.[48] In 1873 Belasco served as an amanuensis for Dion Boucicault, transcribing his play *Forbidden Fruit*. Between 1875 and 1880 Belasco prepared promptbooks "of almost every play that was successfully produced in San Francisco." Belasco's revisions for the Baldwin Theatre productions of Boucicault's *The Octoroon* and his own *American Born* (an adaptation of a Pettitt and Meritt "Grecian drama") led Daniel Frohman to hire him as a stage manager for the Madison Square Theatre.

When Belasco arrived in New York in 1882, the reigning heir of the French adapted drama was still Augustin Daly. Belasco at first followed in these footsteps, attacking New York with *The Stranglers of Paris*, a play that he derived from a French novel and had already produced the previous year at the Baldwin. Charles Frohman was convinced that the play could be a moneymaker, though he thought it too relentlessly grim and advised

Belasco to add some humor. Unable to find an available theatre, Frohman remodeled an old skating rink, calling it the New Park. He hired Giuseppe Operti to write the music for this sensation melodrama, which consisted of twenty-eight cues for an orchestra of twelve musicians. Most of the music was geared toward characterization of the play's central villain, Jagon, the stalker and strangler. Belasco's stage direction had already developed a reputation in San Francisco for its "atmosphere." Act 6 in *Stranglers* opens at sea in the moonlight, on a convict ship carrying Jagon and other chained prisoners to New Caledonia. Operti wrote some grand and exquisitely beautiful "sea music" in A-flat major, with the strings gently surging upward and downward in 6/4 time. (This music bears a startling resemblance to Sinbad's sea music in Nikolai Rimsky-Korsakov's *Scheherazade*, written six years later.) The entire escape scene, from the moment Jagon steals another prisoner's jacket to the time when soldiers fire upon him as he floats away from the boat on a barrel, was acted to music. *Stranglers* did not achieve the hoped-for long run in New York, but it was quickly taken up by others and was a popular play on tour to theatres throughout the United States.[49]

Though Belasco's output reveals his powerful affinity for melodramatic construction, he was also a proponent of what he called a "new style of acting" to replace melodramatic methods. Winter and other contemporaries assure us that Belasco's "natural" and "quiet" acting had long been practiced by some of the best actors in New York. Belasco was its latest and most ardent advocate. Like Robertson and others in the new school of stage direction coming from London, Belasco was also meticulous in attention to production detail, musical as well as visual. In 1888 he was developing an acting school at the New York Lyceum Theatre with Steele Mackaye and Henry C. De Mille when Daniel Frohman invited him to write a starring vehicle for Edward H. Sothern. Still at a somewhat insecure stage of his writing career—at least as far as a New York premiere was concerned—Belasco collaborated with De Mille. The result, *Lord Chumley*, was produced by Frohman at the Lyceum. In some respects the plot largely rehashed older reliable melodramatic devices. But the witty dialogue, observed the *New York Times*, "flashe[d] through the play elusively like heat lightning on a summer night."[50]

Daniel Frohman had brought in Charles Puerner as orchestra leader for the Lyceum the previous year. Puerner, born in Norfolk, Virginia, in 1859, was probably best known for some rather bland comic operas such as *The Robber of the Rhine* (written with Maurice Barrymore). For a time he also led the orchestra at Tony Pastor's Fourteenth Street Theatre. Writing for about twelve musicians, Puerner provided the music for *Chumley* as well as for *The Charity Ball*, Belasco's next play at the same theatre. The only mention of music anywhere in the published text of these works is for source music onstage, but they also included a considerable amount of action and dialogue music.[51] It was evident that Belasco and the Frohmans were hitting on a successful formula when both plays ran over 200 nights.

Lord Chumley was modeled partly on the comedies of Tom Taylor and Henry Byron. E. H. Sothern, who admittedly preferred to be acting Petruchio, refused at first to take on a character so similar to Dundreary, the role made famous by his father in Taylor's *Our American Cousin*. In the end, however, he brought to Chumley a scintillating and irresistible charm. Other characters become entangled as the plot reveals several disparate situations: the retired and wealthy English general Alan Butterworth, his son Hugh (a somewhat reckless lieutenant), his daughter Eleanor, the villain Le Sage (a suave French gambling racketeer who has designs on marrying Eleanor), and Blink (a professional thief). In *Lord Chumley* Belasco and De Mille, like Boucicault in *Flying Scud*, brought the farcical construction of melodrama into the foreground. Unlike the leading males of mid-century gentlemanly melodrama, Chumley is a complete antihero. His best friend takes advantage of him, and even the girl he loves thinks that he is a booby. He probably would have let the burglar get away with the money too, had it not been for an ironic twist of fate.

This crisis hinged on the exploitation of a newfangled invention, pistol-shaped cigarette holders, which came into fashion in 1887. Chumley uses one of these to light his pipe while relaxing in the parlor at the Butterworth home, to which he was invited for dinner. In the preceding scene Hugh Butterworth confides in his friend that he has lost the £1,000 that his fellow officers had managed to raise for the widow of a fallen comrade. He cannot admit to them that he was swindled out of this money in a gambling bout, during which he was too drunk to recall what happened. Le Sage, the swindler (Herbert Archer), is a temporary guest in the Butterworth home and plans to use this money to blackmail Hugh into endorsing his marriage to Eleanor. The general graciously offers to place Le Sage's envelope in his safe, not realizing its contents. He turns over the task to his son, but the preoccupied young man leaves the safe door open. Meanwhile it grows dark outside. Chumley smokes in a chair up left by the window and inadvertently falls asleep.

Blink (played by George Backus) has just completed a five-year prison sentence thanks to Le Sage. He has heard that the swindler is in town and

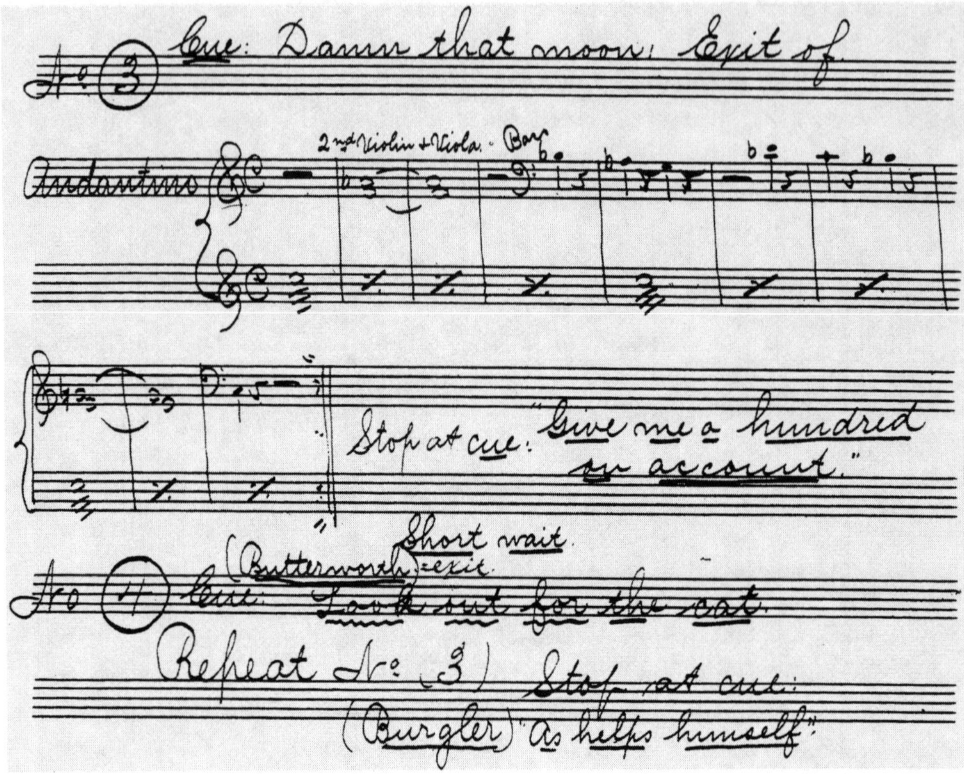

FIGURE 39. *Conductor book to* Lord Chumley, *"Set no. 1." Belasco Collection of Incidental Music and Musicals. New York Public Library*

has traced him to the house to get even. As Blink enters, music no. 3 (a *misterioso*) begins. Blink pounces on Le Sage the moment he enters the darkened room. He tries to blackmail the Frenchman, but the two are surprised by Butterworth, who peeks into the room briefly to call his guest to dinner. Butterworth just misses seeing Blink, who has slipped behind a curtain. As the general goes out with Le Sage, his line "look out for the cat" is the cue for music no. 4, a repeat of no. 3 (Fig. 39). Blink emerges cautiously from behind the curtain and looks around the room, not seeing Chumley. He is surprised to find the safe door open and removes the envelope, which he discovers is full of money.

The *misterioso* that Puerner composed for this scene evokes the eeriness of the moonlit room, but its abruptness also supports the comic situation that follows. The first violins play tremolo on one note while the other strings fill out an F-minor chord. The cellos and bass play just three short descending *pizzicati*, followed by a pause then another three *pizzicati*. The harmonic movement of the whole *melos* is an F-minor chord resolving to a C-major chord (in bar eight). Puerner had found a way to add an extra layer of meaning to a *misterioso* by drawing on known devices—tremolos and *pizzicatos*—and combining these with the suggestion of a plagal cadence, oddly miscast in the minor mode.[52] The overall effect is both creepy and tongue in cheek. What could be easier to rob than a wide-open safe? As a reviewer noted, "There is fun in Mr. Backus's quiet caricature of the stage burglar."[53]

The repeating *misterioso* is also ten bars long, as opposed to the usual *melos* lengths of four, eight, or sixteen bars, lending a feeling that something is not quite right.

Just as Blink is about to pocket the money (cue: "as helps himself"), Chumley wakes up and surprises him. He inadvertently lifts up his lighter, which the burglar thinks is a real gun. Seeing the reaction, Chumley suddenly swells with bravado and takes advantage of the situation. He gets the envelope from the burglar and extracts details about Le Sage's shady past. The scene of attempted burglary, instead of spilling over into melodramatic parody, actually sparkles with wit. Chumley keeps his nerve and outsmarts the villain to a comic finish. His heroic success is almost entirely accidental (and, of course, he gets the girl in the end). As one reviewer noted, *Lord Chumley*'s characters "are either in the picturesque shadow of melodrama or the bright light of bustling farce. The two elements are felicitously commingled."[54]

Belasco's *Chumley* represents only one of the many ways in which the popular drama transformed itself in the 1880s, especially through the controlling vision of the director-producer. We must now turn to the most influential of these transformations concerning music: Henry Irving's extravagantly picturesque melodramas in London, leaving Belasco and the Frohmans' triumphs in the 1890s for another study.

9

Nationalism, "Prestige Music," and Irving's Lyceum

In August 1879 a writer in London's *Saturday Review* observed that "the departure of the fashionable world is commonly the signal for the armed bandit to step forth from his hiding-place."[1] In other words, melodrama survived solely as entertainment for the British lower classes during the summer months. But just as it had in New York, the form was about to receive an unexpected jolt of new life. Critics did not know what to make of the broad appeal of fast-moving spectacles like Augustus Harris's *The World* at Drury Lane, swashbuckling revivals like *The Corsican Brothers* at the Lyceum, and new sensation dramas like Wilson Barrett's *Lights o' London* at the Princess's. The most outstanding difference from their American theatrical counterparts was an unmistakable improvement in the quality of the music. Henry Irving may not have been the sole pioneer behind this effort. But as "melodrama" grew upwardly mobile in the 1880s, Irving's productions at the Lyceum set a new standard. Not since the days of Kean at the Princess's had melodramas been enacted with the same degree of seriousness and technical polish as a Shakespeare history. Lyceum audiences—which included the best-educated classes of Great Britain—grew to expect productions that were sonically as well as visually beautiful.

Since the late eighteenth century, managers such as Audinot, Kemble, and Pixerécourt had generally relied on skilled practitioners to provide music for their popular dramas rather than on composers whose music would compete with the actors for attention. But by the 1860s (see chapter 8) the stylistic amalgam that had long served as the musical sound of the Anglo-American popular drama had grown stale. Enterprising managers were looking for fresh alternatives. One unpredictable development occurred on the continent, where some of Europe's most famous composers began to write music to support the drama. Besides prestige and national recognition, these composers brought more progressive harmonies, colors, and instrumental effects to melodramatic music (influences that we have already seen in Barrett's *Schriften* and Operti's *Julius Caesar*). Significantly, publishers began to realize that such music had appeal beyond the medium for which it was created and were more willing to invest in the costs of printing and distribution with a famous name attached.

Concert and operatic composers had previously been drawn to the spoken drama, of course. But most realized, as Mendelssohn did, that little money was to be made in composing incidental music, other than fees offered by publications. Additionally, composers with strong musical personalities did not feel especially welcome in the theatre, given most actor-managers' insistence on music's subordinate role in the popular drama. Early Romantics whose names are associated with well-known incidental music—all Germans: Ludwig van Beethoven, Carl Maria von Weber, Felix Mendelssohn, Giacomo Meyerbeer—remained the exceptions. By the early 1870s even the famous German theatrical troupe of the court of Saxe-Meiningen, which began to attract attention for electrifying stagings of classics by Shakespeare and Schiller, relied only on a sparse smattering of affective *melos*, provided for them by house musicians such as Wilhelm Reif.[2]

In the 1870s the standard procedure in the best London and New York theatres was to have music prepared by an experienced but flexible leader, someone accountable to the actor-manager in charge. Among such artisans prominent in London's West End theatres were W. C. Levey at Drury Lane and the Princess's, Edwin Ellis at the Adelphi, Ferdinand Wallerstein at the Queen's, Meredith Ball at the Prince of Wales's, and Robert Stoepel at the Lyceum. None of these can be said to have enjoyed national, much less international, fame as composers. Publishers took no interest in their theatre music, and their names do not even appear in standard music encyclopedias. When these leaders were singled out in reviews, it was usually to express some gratitude for their "appropriate music," the "excellent selection" of overtures and entr'actes, or the musicality and technical polish of their bands.

But theatre critics, as we have seen, are generally unhelpful in their assessments of music. They tended to illuminate the worst while leaving the best in the shadows. Let us take two examples from Drury Lane in 1873. Productions at the Drury had recently "risen greatly in the social scale," according to Edward Walford, and were beginning to rival the operas at Covent Garden.[3] William Charles Levey (1837–1894) was in charge of the orchestra. For a revival of William Thomas Moncrieff's *The Cataract of the Ganges* in March, a reviewer in the *Musical Standard* claimed that the music was all by Auber. In a prompt letter of rebuttal, Levey wrote that aside from Auber's overture to *Le cheval de bronze*, credited in the program, he himself had composed all the incidental music specially to fit the play.[4] Later that year the Drury mounted Andrew Halliday's adaptation of *Antony and Cleopatra*. Levey, with a "greatly augmented" orchestra, composed extensive music to accompany the addition of a "Roman festival" and for the Battle of Actium, which accompanied a spectacular fight at sea.[5] The entire production was on a gigantic scale, and audiences were treated to Cleopatra in her burnished barge sailing down the Cydnus River to the accompaniment of Levey's music. These were spectacles, a newspaper observed, in which the actors were merely "aids and vehicles of the scene-painter and the costumier."[6] Not a single review acknowledged the music—not even the previously erroneous *Musical Standard*—though the advertisements and program clearly identified Levey as composer. Under such circumstances why would anyone aspire to write music for the drama—even for Drury Lane?

One young British composer arrived at this profession by a circuitous route. Arthur Sullivan was a student in Leipzig in 1860 when he set about writing music for an imagined production of Shakespeare's *Tempest*, patterning his score after Mendelssohn's *Midsummer Night's Dream* with overture, entr'actes, and several sung pieces interspersed with dialogue. Though portions were first performed in Leipzig, the entire score was given in concert at London's Crystal Palace in 1862 and again the following year by the Hallé Orchestra in Manchester.[7] News of this must have reached Charles Calvert, the brilliant and imaginative actor-manager who was just about to take over the Prince's Theatre in that city. Calvert or his musical director, the veteran Wallerstein, obtained Sullivan's permission to use his *Tempest* music in 1864. According to reliable reports, it was Wallerstein who adapted the score to fit the reduced orchestra and Calvert's staging, even supplementing Sullivan's music with traditional *Tempest* pieces by Thomas Arne and Henry Purcell.[8] Sullivan's composition was a concerted work. Once brought into the theatre it was reconfigured to the needs of the production, much as theatre music had been for a century or more. Perhaps because of this experience, it would be a long time before Sullivan would write incidental music on the scale of his *Tempest* score. In 1871 Calvert invited him back to Manchester for *The Merchant of Venice*, for which the young composer hastily crafted a masque with a few pieces and a song. Some reviews noted the quality of the music, and J. B. Cramer of London published the score that same year as a piano duet. But Sullivan had begun his relationship with John Hollingshead at the Gaiety and would soon leap to national acclaim in another theatrical genre entirely.

European Theatres and the New "Prestige Music"

East of the channel, however, many of Europe's most famous (non-German) composers—Charles Gounod, Georges Bizet, Jules Massenet, Pyotr Tchaikovsky, Edvard Grieg—suddenly began to write music to accompany the spoken play. The trend began in 1871, when Charles Gounod was living in London to escape the horrors of the Franco-Prussian War. He had been commissioned to write music for Ernest Legouvé's *The Two Queens*, a sacred drama starring Adelaide Ristori.[9] When he learned that French censors had cleared the rights, he completed several instrumentals, songs, and choruses and one short *mélodrame* (as it was labeled). Like Sullivan's *Merchant of Venice* masque this was largely "incidental music," of course. But the significance of Gounod's participation at the Théâtre Ventador in 1872 could not have escaped notice by someone like Alphonse Daudet, who was then completing his tragic drama *L'Arlésienne* for Léon Carvalho, manager of the Théâtre du Vaudeville. Carvalho, a professionally trained musician and singer as well as a stage director, invited Georges Bizet to compose the music. *L'Arlésienne* was an odd sort of play about a woman to whom the characters constantly refer but who never makes an appearance. For this Bizet provided an elaborate score that contained no less than fifteen *mélodrames*, in addition to its now-famous instrumental pieces and a few choruses. Well-known composers had written *mélodrames* to underscore concert narrations or poetry readings but rarely to accompany actors in the popular theatre. The publisher Antony de Choudens printed Bizet's music complete, including the *mélodrames* in their entirety, with the spoken lines spaced out more or less evenly above the notes. For decades afterward these served as a model for British composers of theatre music.[10]

That same year the Théâtre de l'Odéon invited Jules Massenet to provide music for *Les Érinnyes* (The Furies), Charles Marie René Leconte de Lisle's tragedy based on Aeschylus. The score originally contained only one *mélodrame* (a "dolorous muted cello solo" to accompany Electra as she poured the libations over her father's grave), but Massenet added several more for a revival in 1876.[11] These three prominent invitations heralded a decisive shift, both in the aesthetics of production and in the nature of popular theatre. In the mid-nineteenth century the popular drama was a "people's drama," focusing largely on social and ethnic concerns. With the rise of nationalism—not only in France, but across Europe—each country began to pursue its representative voice in the arts. Many theatres turned to native drama in a show of national pride. The end of the Franco-Prussian War, for example, gave rise to a renewed interest in symbolic national figures. In 1873 Jules Barbier's play on Joan of Arc was brought to the stage of the Gaîté with actress Lia Félix.[12] Befitting the importance of a "national drama," manager Maurice Boulet engaged Gounod, certainly France's greatest living composer, to provide the music. Like the Ambigu, the Gaîté was a theatre along the Boulevard du Temple specializing in sensational pieces.[13] Gounod lent this verse drama a period feel by weaving through the score a hint of plainchant as well as the tune of a medieval French *ballade* (H. L. Bateman and his leader Mallandaine had already tried this device the previous year in *Charles I*). The Gaîté's audiences were thrilled and moved, especially by Joan's vision scene at the end of act 1, with special lighting effects and Gounod's chorus and orchestra rising to *fortissimo*. The play was reportedly "sold out" for three months.[14] It was revived later, most notably for Sarah Bernhardt, and Samuel French made loan materials—including music for "4 band parts"—available as late as 1882 (see chapter 4). *Joan of Arc* is not an opera, as some mistakenly refer to it.[15] What made it "operatic" was what the French called *musique de scène*: music added to the play by way of songs and choruses.[16] What made it "melodramatic theatre" were the three large sequences of dialogue underscoring and several instrumental pieces that enhanced the picturesque quality of the production.

Gounod conducted a concert version of *Joan of Arc* in London in early 1874 at St. James's Hall. Though this was reviewed as a bit of a novelty, British orchestras began to play more theatre music. Among the most exceptional was the set of excerpts that Bizet had fashioned from his theatre score. The *L'Arlésienne* suite became so internationally famous that it led to several unsuccessful attempts in London and New York to revive Daudet's play.[17] Bizet's distinctive suites seemed to bring new respectability to theatre music. Clear testimony of this was a revival of Beethoven's music for Goethe's *Egmont* in 1874 at the Crystal Palace—rarely performed complete in England—with actor Lin Rayne supplementing the missing drama with newly written narration.[18]

Bizet died in 1875, but Massenet went on to accept invitations to compose for the popular drama. Three of these works were adapted from well-known novels: *La vie de Bohème* at the Odéon in 1875, *Notre-Dame de Paris* at the Théâtre des Nations in 1879, and Jules Verne and Adolphe d'Ennery's *Michel Strogoff* at the Théâtre de Châtelet in 1880 (successfully adapted in London and New York). Unlike his *musique de scène*, however, Massenet's music for these genuinely popular dramas remained only in manuscript. Presumably it was so closely tied to the action and dialogue that publishers felt that it had little independent commercial value.

Whether it was cause and effect or a "fortunate simultaneity"—to borrow a meteorological expression—managers in other countries began to turn to nationally recognized composers to enhance the status of dramatic performances in a way hitherto unknown. For example, Josef Kolár's historical play *The Jew of Prague* opened in 1871 with music by one of Bohemia's leading composers, Zdenek Fibich, who also wrote music to Czech productions of *The Public Servant* (1876) and *Dora* (1877). In 1873 the Moscow Maly Theatre staged Alexander Ostrovsky's *The Snow Maiden* and turned to Pyotr Tchaikovsky, who composed twenty-one numbers, including two short but crucial sections of dialogue underscoring.[19]

But without doubt the most influential link between a major composer and the national drama took place in Norway. In 1874 Ludvig Josephson, the newly appointed Swedish manager of the Christiania Theatre in what is now Oslo, determined to bring a Norwegian repertory to the theatre. First came the success of Bjørnstjerne Bjørnson's *Sigurd Jorsalfar* with music by the country's most famous composer, Edvard Grieg. Then followed *Peer Gynt*, Henrik Ibsen's unwieldy and satirical verse play consisting of some forty scenes. Written in 1867, the work was already a widely read "national drama" but was believed to be unperformable. Josephson and his strong troupe of actors defied the skeptics with an imaginatively staged production in February 1876, starring Henrik Klausen as Peer. With Grieg's music, *Peer Gynt* ran for over a year and was both a dramatic and musical sensation, with productions soon following in Germany and elsewhere. This was some of the most elaborate music ever written for a spoken play. Grieg had access to a full orchestra with all its possibilities of colors. The instrumental effects were narrating devices in themselves. The audience could almost smell nature blossoming into life in the "Morning Mood" prelude and feel the surging of waves in the musical tumult accompanying Peer's shipwreck. Grieg's music rarely attempts to illuminate Ibsen's "inner drama," as an opera might. Instead it is atmospheric and pictorial.[20] Grieg also composed music to extensive passages of dialogue, all of which demonstrate a mastery of dramatic nuance and pacing, with no ad-libs or "repeat until necessary." Instead of simply labeling these accompaniments as *mélodrames* (as Bizet and Tchaikovsky did), Grieg gave each a title, such as "Peer Gynt and the Boyg" or "The Death of Asa." The melodramatic music ranges in scope from a fast action scene, as Peer is hunted by the trolls (no. 10), to a lengthy under-dialogue love sequence in the Moroccan act between Peer and the Bedouin's daughter Anitra (no. 20). The entire final scene of the play, Peer's return to his village and his reunion with Solveig, was staged to through-composed music that ebbed and flowed with the action and dialogue.[21] Like Bizet, Grieg fashioned two orchestral suites out of his score, which quickly became staples of the concert repertory.

The *Peer Gynt* music was exceptional in its range of mood and color, not to mention the international prestige that it brought to both the composer and the play. This could not have escaped the attention of British managers like H. L. Bateman and Henry Irving, who—as George Godwin and others observed at the time—were clearly bent on raising the status of the Lyceum to that of a national theatre.[22] In 1876 they turned to Charles Villiers Stanford to compose music for the first staged production of Tennyson's historical drama *Queen Mary*. This was to feature Kate Bateman as Princess Elizabeth and Irving as King Philip, both of whom had a hand in revising the play. The story of the incidental music has often been told from the standpoint of Stanford's biographers, who portray Bateman and Irving as the enemy, so additional facts need to be illuminated here. Tennyson had indeed recommended Stanford for the job. Though still relatively young and, like Sullivan, recently returned from studies in Leipzig, Stanford had a reputation as a prodigy and had also studied under W. C. Levey's father, Richard M. Levey, who for many decades served as musical director of Dublin's Theatre Royal. But Stanford had a hard lesson to learn when it came to writing for the drama. First, he composed the music from a published copy of Tennyson's play and naïvely expected to deliver his completed score at the beginning of stage rehearsals.

Meanwhile Bateman and Irving had made heavy cuts to a play that they saw as essentially literary. Out went the character of Thomas Cranmer entirely, and one of Stanford's entr'actes served as a musical portrait of the archbishop. In addition, Stanford had written three other elaborate entr'actes and an overture, no doubt with an eye to salvaging these in a separate concert suite. Robert Stoepel was still music director at the Lyceum and had prepared his own music during rehearsals of the play. Stoepel was a theatrical craftsman of the old school whose *melos* technique was finely honed in the French boulevard theatres, under Boucicault and Kean in London, and under Lester Wallack and Augustin Daly in New York. Stage music should be affective and topical, Stoepel understood; it should enhance but not draw too much attention to itself. Moreover, he asserted, the intervals between the acts were a time for audience relaxation and socializing, not for grand orchestral statements. Kate Bateman agreed with him. Stanford quotes her in a formal letter of complaint that he fired off to Tennyson, alleging that the Batemans disliked his music. They had never commissioned an overture and entr'actes, Bateman retorted, reminding Stanford pointedly that "music for a play" meant music to be performed "while the curtain is up."[23] Aside from two songs that furthered the action, most of what Stanford wrote was obviously composed principally for listening and was "on too large of a scale" for the theatre and the production, as Bateman pointed out. Even with an orchestra of thirty musicians the audience could not be expected to give the music much attention anyway. So Stanford's score was rejected, though that did not deter him from later composing incidental music for plays at Drury Lane, Covent Garden, and even once more at the Lyceum.

Meanwhile Charles Calvert again lured Arthur Sullivan to Manchester, this time to provide music for a sumptuous production of *Henry VIII* in 1877. Sullivan came up with only four pieces, and orchestra leader Frederick Stanislaus provided additional "historical music" throughout the play. Sullivan's march and pageant music—though in no way on the atmospheric scale of *Peer Gynt* or even his earlier *Tempest*—were recognized in all the reviews, not only in Manchester but in Liverpool and other places that Calvert's production toured. Sullivan's "incidental music" for *Henry VIII* appeared in a concert at the Crystal Palace in October 1877.[24] No doubt the dramatic efforts of the younger guard of Sullivan and Stanford must have impressed Irving. As soon as he assumed the management of the Lyceum in 1878 he released Stoepel—who went over to join Wilson Barrett at the Court Theatre—and hired Hamilton Clarke, a well-established young organist and composer then in his thirties, to take on the role of orchestra leader. Irving's decisions for the 1879–1880 season heralded a shift not only in the way music was employed in the major theatres but also in terms of reformulating the popular drama as high art. In the same spirit of competition evident in artistic decisions throughout this book, we can view Irving's increasing attention to the quality of theatre music over the next ten years in part as his reaction to the continental influence.

Irving's Approach to Music in Shakespeare and the Popular Drama

A great deal has been written about Irving's spectacular and expensive productions at the Lyceum. One of his first acquisitions was Ellen Terry, who acted Pauline to Irving's Claude Melnotte in *The Lady of Lyons* in April. Other prominent actors that the magnetic Irving attracted to his strong stock company were William Terriss, George Alexander, Johnston Forbes-Robertson, and Edward Gordon Craig. During the later Bateman administration Irving began to assemble a team of some of London's finest set designers to enhance the visual splendor of the productions. Hawes Craven, a scene painter, had been at the Lyceum on and off since 1863 and had become "artist-in-chief," working with William Telbin and other designers, not to mention architects, book illustrators, and landscape painters, to complete all of Irving's elaborate sets and canvases. By the time of *The Corsican Brothers* in 1880, Irving employed a backstage crew of ninety carpenters and fifteen property men, according to Percy Fitzgerald, and a crew of thirty men operated gas and calcium lights until electricity was installed in 1892.[25]

Irving also modified the Lyceum's orchestra space. Many theatres during the 1870s in both London and New York were decreasing the size of their orchestra wells or pushing them further under the stage in an effort to bring the audience into more intimate contact with the actors. Irving did exactly the opposite. His plans included carving out an enlarged space for the musicians—which cost him some audience seats—and bringing them forward to a position of greater visibility. This not only increased the orchestra's presence in the hall but also enhanced its prestige. The new orchestra space even allowed the Lyceum to be loaned out on occasion to opera companies. For the opening production of *Hamlet*, Clarke used the full ensemble of thirty musicians, but he experimented with orchestra seating, as one reviewer noted. For the overture and entr'actes, the musicians were all in their usual places. Once the curtain went up and the dialogue began, however, they moved to a position beneath the stage.[26] This is admittedly something of an odd exercise: it would require thirty musicians to shift places some ten times throughout the evening. In any case it seems that the idea was soon abandoned. Clarke and others leaders learned to manage the volume of sound with appropriate dynamics and textures.

Though Hamilton Clarke claimed that Irving had no ear for music, the actor-manager had gleaned much from the many musical directors that he had worked with in the past, including Ferdinand Wallerstein at the

St. James's and the Queen's and of course Robert Stoepel during his seven years at the Lyceum. In his review of Bateman's *Vanderdecken* in 1878 Clement Scott—one of the first British theatre critics to take music seriously—noted that Stoepel's music, while mostly an amalgam of recognizable bits, had been very effective in "imparting value" to the production in a way that he had not noticed before.[27] Up to that time a pointed phrase from the orchestra, like limelight, could help focus audience attention. But like the soft colored mediums in Irving's lighting plot, scene-setting music must correspond to the delicate play of gaslight upon the set and assume a more blended, shaded quality, nuanced in timbre and texture. Critics could convey their impressions of the vivid atmosphere of Irving's lighting and Hawes Craven's evocative scene paintings for *Vanderdecken* and other Lyceum productions, but they obviously had no words to describe the musical atmosphere. Scott's comments hint that this kind of musical value was unprecedented. To this end Irving worked carefully with Clarke to design instrumental entr'actes—played as the house lights were lowered and just before the curtain went up—that would immerse audiences in the mood of the scene to follow, much as the act preludes of Wagner, Verdi, and Bizet did for their operas and Grieg's preludes did for *Peer Gynt*.

Clarke established the generous proportions of the Lyceum orchestra, which consisted of six first and four second violins, two violas, two cellos, two basses, two flutes and two clarinets, a single oboe and bassoon, two cornets, two horns, one trombone, one percussionist, and one harp.[28] This was even augmented on various occasions. For *The Corsican Brothers* (adapted from Boucicault and Kean's version), which ran over 200 nights, Clarke expanded his orchestral palette to thirty-five players, including three trombones. Clarke—who was later remembered as "perhaps the greatest master of instrumentation in the kingdom"—composed a medley overture that incorporated all the themes used in the drama and, near the end, dramatically showcased the famous "ghost theme," known by then to nearly every English playgoer.[29] The effect was electrifying. Perhaps inspired by this success, Irving banished the practice of playing irrelevant interval music and from then on insisted on music that would establish an appropriate atmosphere for the act to come. Percy Fitzgerald vividly recalled Clarke's many "picturesque overtures." This was a crucial formulation given the increasingly artistic direction in which Irving was headed and the integral role that music would play in the overall concept.[30]

Before Clarke left the Lyceum in 1881 he composed the music for W. G. Wills's *Iolanthe*, Tennyson's Roman drama *The Cup*, and *The Merchant of*

Venice and *Othello*. He returned to the Lyceum periodically to provide other music. Irving must have realized that he needed a conductor more than a composer when he engaged Meredith Ball (ca. 1838–1915). Ball was hired on the strength of his work at the Queen's for Wallerstein and his reputation for leading the infamous backstage orchestra for the Bancrofts at the Prince of Wales's in the 1870s. He remained the Lyceum's musical director for seventeen years. Ball worked with Irving to help him achieve his goals, which in many cases involved commissioning major composers to write for the drama. The first of these—and the closest comparison to Gounod in France—was Sir Julius Benedict, brought in for *Romeo and Juliet*. Benedict's musical pedigree goes back to Weber himself, with whom he studied. He had led the music for the last years of Charles Matthews and Mme Vestris at Covent Garden. Moreover, Irving must have remembered Benedict's melodramatic music to accompany H. G. Bell's grizzly poem "The Uncle," which he narrated in 1849 while still a student of elocution.[31]

Irving's *Romeo and Juliet* was on the most lavish scale imaginable. One reporter wrote that productions of even the most eminent Shakespeareans—Charles Kean, Edwin Booth, and the Saxe-Meiningen Company (which astounded London audiences in 1881)—were "eclipsed far and away in the gorgeous, and at the same time artistic, setting." Irving had become an "illustrator of poetic pictures," wrote the reviewer; critics everywhere assailed him for having "subordinated the art of the actor to that of the painter, the musicians, the costumer, and the stage manager."[32] For someone like Benedict, who had been perhaps England's most performed and internationally known composer at mid-century, the return to the limelight was particularly significant. Journals like the *Musical World* took notice and observed how Benedict's beautiful and appropriate music "stimulated the imagination of the spectator."[33]

Ball led the orchestra, and mood setting was one of its key roles. Ellen Terry remembered that Benedict's music, instead of attempting to "reflect the passionate emotion of the drama," conveyed "a great deal of Southern joy."[34] Some reviews commented on the poetic use of the choir and orchestra to assist the lighting transitions and to suggest the passage of time. One of these was the continuous sequence from the night of Juliet's taking the draught to the morning, when a small group of carolers arrived to awaken the young bride only to find her seemingly lifeless body lying peacefully on the bed.[35] Irving had something special in mind for *Romeo and Juliet*, for he was convinced that a good musical score by a known composer would greatly enhance the play's "business aspect," as his manager Bram Stoker put it, as well as its artistic value.[36] Irving must have sensed the possibilities of commercial interchange (and value enhancement) if music from a currently running production came to be played by an orchestra in a concert hall (like the Bizet and Grieg suites) or sung and played at home. Like today's media tie-ins for film and television companies, such plugs would reach wider audiences and reflect value back to the production and the theatre. Though circulation is difficult to measure, Benedict's "Wedding Carol" (with words by Francis Hueffer) was privately published, possibly for sale in the local music shops. Frank Chappell of G. Metzler and Co. of London published two pieces from Benedict's score for piano solo, the "Sarabande" and the "Minuet."[37]

Irving continued in this fashion at the Lyceum, alternating popular dramas and classical dramas such as *Werner* with Shakespeare. When it came to bonafide melodramas like *Robert Macaire* (1883), Irving was not above using the standard approach to *melos*, at least according to Weedon Grossmith, who on one of the company's tours waited backstage for his entrance as Jacques Strop.

> Meredith Ball . . . had started the grotesquely sensational music for Robert Macaire's entrance. Irving threw back the lapels of his ragged blue coat, gave a twist to his snuff-box to see that the creaking lid was working all right . . . I watched him from the wings as he swaggered on to the bridge. Oh, what a reception he had! I thought it would never finish. Then the music changed to a quick *tremuloso*—my cue—and Macaire waved his stick, and on I came with a rapid run![38]

While a traditional *melos* would suffice for signature and action tunes, Irving was particularly sensitive to the way it could interfere with dialogue. Instead of just cutting it out, as some managers did, he worked with his music directors to find the right timbral balance between the speaking voice and instruments. Many composers seemed to resent writing music to accompany dialogue. When required to, they generally wrote for strings alone, simply because the *legato* of bowed instruments was less likely to interfere with the dentals and fricatives of human speech, as a woodwind or brass instrument certainly would. Again, Irving had learned a great deal from Ferdinand Wallerstein, who in 1877 wrote an editorial in the *Era* regarding criticism of under-dialogue music. The problem of the orchestra covering up the speaker was not just one of volume, Wallerstein pointed out, but also a problem of texture. Having heard the speech of a deep-toned actress completely obscured by an accompanying melody played on the viola, Wallerstein identified the problem in the similarity in range between voice and instrument, which would have been alleviated had the orchestral melody been placed higher than the actress's speaking voice (for example, played by a violin).[39] Louis Calvert, son of the Manchester director, was eyewitness to the way Irving handled the problem. The actor stopped one day during rehearsals of *Werner* (1887) to ask Ball to prepare some music to accompany one of his speeches. At the next rehearsal they gave it a go, but Irving was not pleased with the result. So they tried it without the flute, then without the cornet and trombone, and finally removed all the instruments except the strings. An expressive melody played on the violin seemed to irritate Irving, who asked that it be removed too. This obviously unnerved Ball, who felt that his music was compromised by the loss of melody. But Irving knew, as Calvert observed, that "the secret of writing music to accompany the voice" is to remember that "the voice takes the place of the melody."[40]

When it came to historical or classically inspired pieces, Irving's munificence expanded to meet the challenge. Otto Devrient had produced a famous *Faust* in Weimar in 1876, for which composer Eduard Lassen wrote an extensive original score. For his production of W. G. Wills's *Faust* (1885), Irving brought back Hamilton Clarke to help Ball fashion similarly elaborate music. The period flavor would be conveyed visually by the costumes and the imitation of Albrecht Dürer in the set designs. But the music, like Irving's sophisticated lighting plot, would establish a gothic tone, situate the location in late medieval Nuremberg, and carry audiences through the shifting moods of the scene. It was compiled almost entirely from well-known works, such as Schubert's *Erlkönig*, Adolf Marschner's *Vampire*, and various *Faust* compositions by Louis Spohr, Hector Berlioz, Peter Josef von Lindpaintner, and Eduard Lassen. Theatre composers had recycled well-known music before, but never with such an obvious attempt to draw attention to the pieces themselves. Aside from a few original character preludes by Clarke, the *Faust* music was a genuine compilation score. Accounts reveal Irving's exactitude with the *Faust* music: the orchestra supposedly sat through some "eighty rehearsals" in preparing for the opening. (This surely must be an exaggeration. But even after the opening performance Irving called the orchestra to yet another rehearsal; when the musicians threatened to walk, Irving called their bluff by vowing to install a Mustel organ in their place.)[41]

For *Macbeth* in 1888 Irving turned to Arthur Sullivan, who by now was internationally famous as the composer of scintillating operettas with W. S. Gilbert. Sullivan also had a reputation for his Shakespeare music, given the many excerpts that were frequently played on concert programs. Drama and music critics' reactions to Sullivan's elegant and haunting music for the Lyceum *Macbeth* reflect the sea change in British attitudes toward theatre music. The brooding Macbeth theme and the strange music for the witches' scene, so different from the delightful tunes in Sullivan's comic operas, proved to be just as unforgettable. His dramatic overture thematically incorporated these themes, like the great tragic overtures of Hector Berlioz and Robert Schumann. Although much of the Lyceum audience whispered or hunted for seats while Ball led the overture, it was soon recognized as a major piece of theatre music and was performed by conductors and symphony orchestras throughout England.

In addition to enhancing character, Sullivan's music brought a great deal of atmosphere to the production. Many English audiences were still used to "Locke's music" and singing witches for *Macbeth*—controversial as they could be—so Irving and Sullivan's rethinking of the tone came as something of a shock. Act 3, which consisted of the planning and execution of the murder of Banquo, began with a prelude featuring a weird march in 5/4 that continued into the opening scene. Bram Stoker, ever the attentive eyewitness, wrote that the music had "a barbaric ring" to it that seemed "to take us back and place us amongst a warlike and undeveloped age."[42] Stoker's observations make it clear that the actors and crew were as affected by this as was the audience. Sullivan and Irving constantly made adjustments to the music in rehearsal to achieve the right tone, as Stoker vividly describes. The entire first scene of act 4—when Macbeth goes to the witches for advice—was accompanied by through-composed music, with atmospheric passages and dialogue underscoring amounting to some thirty pages of orchestral score.[43] One observer wrote that the incantation was "introduced by an *andante maestoso* of a singularly weird character, and that character [was] well sustained throughout the scene. As each apparition [rose] from the cauldron the strains of the orchestra emphasize[d] its nature in an individual and striking manner."[44] Sullivan also incorporated many unusual timbral effects, such as the ethereal sound of two solo harps when Macbeth gives instructions to the murderers. In act 1, scene 6, when Macbeth is showing King Duncan the grounds of the castle, Sullivan had the strings play tremolo while two French horns answered one another antiphonally, one in the orchestra and another entirely behind the scenes, lending the production sonic as well as visual depth.[45] By the time of Irving's *Macbeth*, whole articles in journals were devoted to discussion of the music.[46]

Irving's integration of elements in production set a standard that other managers not only in England but also in the United States would soon begin to emulate, as a result of the company's three American tours in the 1880s. "The conductor of every theatre tries to be another Meredith Ball," wrote Stephen Fiske, the American playwright and manager. Thanks to Irving, American audiences now "listen to the musical accompaniments and appreciate them."[47] Music, along with lighting and set design, as Irving explained in his lecture at Harvard University in 1885, must be employed "with strict regard *to the production of an artistic whole* in which no element shall be unduly obtrusive [emphasis mine]."[48]

The Dead Heart *and Popular Drama as Art*

The year 1889 marked the centenary of the French Revolution. In the spirit of giving new life to old melodramas like *Werner* and *The Courier of Lyons*, Irving turned to Watts Phillips's *The Dead Heart* (Adelphi, 1859), a tale of the Revolution with a hero that resembled Dickens's Sidney Carton (and with a similar ending). With Telbin's massive sets, Craven and his team's evocative canvases, and Irving's subtle lighting and meticulous attention to the detail of over one thousand costumes, the production at the Lyceum brought this vivid period in history to the stage in a way that dazzled and thrilled audiences. Nearly every review used the word "picturesque," suggesting Irving's obsession with historical accuracy, even down to the set designs, drawn from book illustrations such as the *Tableaux de la Révolution*. Frederick Widmore, shrewd critic for the *Academy*, criticized the lack of genuine dialogue and the play's emphasis on action and visual stimulus, which he found to be the fault of melodrama generally. "There is point after point," Widmore observed, "now of energy, now of revenge, and now of gentleness."[49] And yet Irving abandoned some standard melodramatic techniques, such as the obligatory frozen tableaux. Incidents and scenes blended seamlessly into one another.

To help provide a musical background to equal the gigantic scale of his imagination, Irving turned to Georges Jacobi. The German-born composer had studied at the Paris Conservatoire and for two years conducted at the Bouffes-Parisiens. A refugee from the Franco-Prussian War, Jacobi assumed the role of leader and composer for the Alhambra, an upscale music hall for which he is known to have composed over one hundred ballets. Following in the steps of Montgomery's "action score" to *The Duke's Motto*, Jacobi composed what critics alluded to as nearly continuous music. One passionate theatregoer wrote that the music "kept awake in one's mind" the spirit of that revolutionary age. In combination with Irving's "wild figure" and minute but intense lighting effects—such as the gray beam on the executioner's axe—music "showed the dramatists of today what melodrama might be."[50]

The British change in attitude toward theatrical music that took place in the late 1880s is evident in an interview with the composer and the music critic of the *Pall Mall Gazette* (probably Vernon Blackburn). The article referred to the music as "one of the chief features" of the play. In Jacobi's own words,

> there is the opening movement . . . light, melodious, and well-marked, intended to reflect the spirit of the garden scene which ends with the graceful dance. And of course there is the undercurrent of mystery in it to accompany the ominous beginnings of the Revolution . . . Then, of course, there is the usual musical accompaniment to the dramatic action of the play, the music having to be set to the [spoken] words in many places as carefully as in an opera.[51]

Jacobi also described the process of creating the music. After meeting with Irving and carefully going over exact specifications for where and how much music there should be, the composer retreated to Herne Bay with a prompt copy of the play where he spent three weeks drafting his score. Using full sheets of orchestral manuscript paper, he wrote at the piano on two staves at the bottom of the sheets then spent the afternoons filling out the orchestration. Much of the music was completed before the first rehearsals began. But unlike Stanford's *Queen Mary*, it was written in accordance with the concept of the production. Jacobi created his theatre music in his private workshop, at a keyboard, unlike some leaders of old with their fiddles, who later fleshed out ideas that had been improvised first in rehearsal. Jacobi certainly could have used this method, for he was an excellent violinist, had studied with Charles-Auguste de Bériot in Brussels, and played first violin in several opera orchestras in Paris and London.[52] But his role was complete once he turned over his manuscript to Meredith Ball, who—after making minor alterations—led the orchestra in rehearsals and performances.

Jacobi's score contained thirty-eight long through-composed melodramatic cues, not counting preludes, overture, and entr'actes. We focus here on the prologue and the opening scene of act 1. Robert Landry (played by Irving) is an energetic young sculptor with revolutionary ideals who is engaged to Catherine Duval, the beautiful daughter of a wine merchant.

Catherine (played by Ellen Terry) has inadvertently attracted the attention of the Count de St. Valéry, an unscrupulous nobleman (played by William Haviland), whose confidant is the Abbé Latour, a crafty and Machiavellian plotter. Latour (acted with great relish by Squire Bancroft) devises a devious plan for St. Valéry to win Catherine. He should first send Catherine flowers and love poetry and then gain entrance to her chamber at night, to compromise her reputation with Landry. The count follows this advice. When Catherine cries for help, Landry comes to the rescue, only to find her in the count's arms, with the verses addressed to her lying on her table. As he is about to defend her honor a file of soldiers enters the room, accompanied by Latour, who has obtained a *lettre-de-cachet* for Landry's arrest on the grounds of creating songs intended to humiliate the king's mistress. This concludes the prologue. Eighteen years elapse, during which Landry's heart eventually "died" while his body was confined to the dark recesses of the Bastille. In the meantime, however, the count and Catherine were married and had a son (played by a young Gordon Craig). Arthur, the son, was about seventeen years of age on 14 July 1789, the day when the Bastille was stormed and Landry, among other dazed prisoners, was freed.

The clearest way to get an overall sense of the music's role in the production is to see the cues laid out. The prelude began solemnly with woodwinds alone in a strong chorale-like motive, foreshadowing the powerful character of the Abbé Latour. The strings are added gradually to enrich the tone. The sudden sound of a small band from onstage anticipates the cheerful mood of the opening scene. Then the orchestra was to have reprised the solemn prelude to contrast with this cheerful music. But Jacobi's plan was changed in rehearsal. The orchestra entered again with no. 1, a rumbling of a stirring march in the basses and cellos, as the curtain rose on a view of Paris during the rule of Louis XV. The gardens of the café were brilliantly lit. In an opening song with conspiratorial overtones, a band of drinking revelers—the "gray brothers" in the original play—poke fun at extravagances of the monarchy. Latour and St. Valéry arrive in time to catch the end of the song. Latour knows full well that Landry, a member of the group, is its author. The first scene of the prologue consists of almost continuous music: three stage pieces (the drinking song, a military band, and a small onstage ensemble) and several long passages of dialogue underscored by the orchestra. The only direct musical association established in the first scene is Latour's ominous chorale, sounding menacingly in the underscore as Latour hatches his plot. In general, the music for *The Dead Heart* is affective, dramatic, and anticipatory, as revealed in the list of musical cues.

Prologue
Prelude (*Moderato*), Played by the orchestra before the curtain rises.
Band onstage (behind scenes): Passepied (*Allegretto*)

No. 1	Orchestra (*Allegretto*)	Curtain. Opening of scene 1 at the Café. 1771. Action, Song and Chorus
No. 2	Band on stage (*Allegretto*)	Under dialogue. Latour and St. Valéry discuss Landry
No. 2½	Band on stage (*Allegretto*)	Under dialogue. Latour learns of St. Valéry's infatuation with Catherine
No. 3	Orchestra	Under dialogue. Latour discusses his plan with St. Valéry to remove Landry from the scene
No. 4	Reprise of Song and Chorus	
No. 5	Band on stage (*Allegretto*)	Robert Landry enters
No. 6	Passepied (musicians in the café)	Light-hearted interlude. Landry and the royal hairdresser Toupet compare differences and similarities in their "art"
No. 7	Orchestra (*Allegro non troppo*)	Under dialogue. Latour and St. Valéry overhear Landry making some comments against the monarchy. Music continues for entrance of Catherine, who is accosted by the two men
No. 8	Orchestra (*Allegretto*)	Under dialogue. To shake their melancholy, the people ask Catherine and Landry to lead them in a dance
No. 9	Dance (*Allegretto*)	Segue

Prologue (*continued*)

No. 10	Orchestra (*Moderato*)	Change of scene
		No music for scene 2
No. 11	Orchestra (*Andantino*)	Opening of scene 3 in Catherine's bedchamber. "Catherine's Theme" (solo flute with winds)
No. 12	Orchestra (*Allegro agitato*)	Under dialogue for confrontation between Catherine and St. Valéry; Catherine calls for help and Robert arrives
No. 13	Orchestra (*Allegro non troppo*)	Climax and conclusion of scene. Latour arrives with guards and official orders to have Landry arrested (repeats the agitated music of No. 7)

Act 1
Overture: "The Dead Heart"
(played by the orchestra during the set change)

No. 14	Prelude (*Moderato*, then *Allegro*)	Opening of act 1, scene 1. July 14, 1789. The Storming of the Bastille Action cue. Alarm bells on stage. Battle music ("firing of guns and cannons"). Shouts of the liberators. Bells
No. 15	Orchestra (*Allegro*, then *Andante*)	Under action and dialogue. Prisoners brought out of the Bastille, Landry among them

Act I (*continued*)

No. 16	Orchestra (*Andantino*)	Under dialogue. The liberators try to jog Landry's memory of Catherine. Return of "Catherine's Theme" (French horn with strings)
No. 17	Orchestra (*Allegro*)	Under dialogue and end of scene. Landry's memory returns, and he is overjoyed. (Alternates between a march in 4/4 and "The Carmagnole" in 6/8)

The third scene opens with Catherine alone in her bedchamber. Here is the first presentation of a theme associated with her (no. 11), played by the flute with string accompaniment. During this scene she receives St. Valéry's verses. Eventually the count himself arrives, having stolen in through her window. When Catherine angrily insists that he leave, cue no. 12 begins, an *agitato* based on a motive derived from Catherine's theme. This crescendos for four bars during the confrontation, at which point the orchestra breaks off, leaving a tremolo in the lower strings while Landry's unaccompanied voice is suddenly heard offstage, singing the refrain from the play's opening song. The rest of no. 12 is tightly composed, with dialogue and music alternating or occurring simultaneously. The orchestra halts to allow the brass and lower winds to sustain three tense chords as Landry breaks into the room. An intense "display of power" follows, as the *Era* described it. "The dissolute Count stood face to face with a foe splendidly defiant, magnificently resolute."[53] When Landry draws his sword, the agitated music of no. 13 begins. Irving did not have the chance to demonstrate his sword-fighting prowess before they were interrupted, however (that was reserved for the climactic scene of the second act in the dramatic confrontation with Latour, one of the most talked-about stage fights of the decade).

As the curtain fell on the prologue, the orchestra immediately launched into the delayed overture. Its length (nine minutes) was necessary to allow Irving to transform himself from the passionate young sculptor to the aging, bearded, haggard prisoner. The overture is in seven clearly defined parts, which, as Jacobi himself described them, “foreshadow the events and passions of the play.”[54] The overture introduces and weaves together several revolutionary songs from the period, including Étienne-Nicolas Méhul’s “Chant du départ” (written in 1792) and “The Marseillaise.” The final section of the overture was a turbulent march that began in A minor, increased in tempo and intensity (and also dramatically shifted up a half step to B-flat minor), and concluded with a grand Berliozian finish in B-flat major. Few of the hundreds of actors, extras, and scene carpenters getting ready backstage could have failed to note that the curtain was shortly to rise on the reenactment of a significant event in French political history.

After a slight break as the audience applauded Maestro Ball and the orchestra the music resumed. This time it was a soft march in E minor with a prominent side drum playing a sharp militaristic rhythm. *Lloyd’s Weekly Newspaper* described what the audience saw:

> The great state prison is built entirely along the prompt side with a sloping platform. Through the central gateway at the back, affording a glimpse of the old city beyond, pours the tumultuous mob, the women, with all kinds of uncouth weapons, being even fiercer than the men. In vain is the resistance offered by the soldiery. A cannon is brought to the gates, and as the outer portal is demolished the wild cheer of victory rises above the roar of determined conflict. Then comes a brief hand-to-hand fight, but the Bastille is already won . . . the officials come out under the shelter of a flag of truce.[55]

Jacobi’s music reflects a great deal of dramatic flexibility in terms of mood and tempo. A few passionate tunes ring out and cornet fanfares crackle through the noise, while most of the orchestra keeps up a sense of *agitato*. Music and the complex stage action were closely synchronized. In a few places in the score stage directions line up with where the orchestra should be (“alarm bells onstage”), and in other places it has bars with repeat signs so that the orchestra would not outrun the stage on nights when the action took longer. Meredith Ball had to keep a sharp eye on the stage as he cued his busy musicians.

The music ends as soon as the Bastille is taken, superseded by cheers from the crowd. It resumes as the prisoners are brought forth. The tempo begins optimistically but quickly changes to a more subdued *andantino* with Legrand’s line “it’s like opening a grave.” Landry is seen and recognized by some, and the citizens try to jog the confused man’s memory. This is the cue for music no. 16. The name "Catherine" seems to provoke a glimmer of recognition, and the musical reminiscence of Catherine's theme is now transformed (as she herself has been). It is played by an elegant and stately French horn rather than by the high, breathy flute of the prologue. As Landry's memory returns—and his desire for revenge is unleashed—the orchestra surges and concludes the scene with a rousing version of "The Carmagnole." Aided by this thrilling music, the excitement of the screaming crowds spread to the spectators, as the *Era* noted, "who roared their applause as the tableau curtain fell and shut from view as grandly impressive a spectacle as has ever been witnessed on the stage."[56]

Into the 1890s

No further proof of the dramatic and economic effectiveness of first-class music and the spoken drama was needed after Irving's *Dead Heart*. The transformation begun on the European continent a decade before had fully taken root at the Lyceum and was also being imitated by Augustus Harris at Drury Lane, Richard Mansfield at the Globe, George Alexander at the St. James's, Beerbohm Tree at the Haymarket, and many others. If that wave had not quite reached the United States, this was likely due to the lack of nationally recognized American composers in the 1880s who could assure that theatre managers would be paid back at the box office. McKee Rankin was probably the only American producer at the time who emulated Irving's "artistic whole" with its added value of music. For his expensive production of *Macbeth* in San Francisco in 1885 Rankin employed a fifty-piece orchestra and a large choir to render Edgar Stillman Kelley's elaborate original score. Though this production remains historically important for both dramatic and musical reasons, it is probably a good indication of the attitude of American theatregoers, the drama and music critics, and the major theatrical financiers that Rankin was never able to secure the backing to stage his *Macbeth* in New York, which he insisted required Kelley's full musical component.[57]

But many playgoers in London, Henry Irving seemed to recognize, were now as sophisticated in musical matters as they were in the dramatic arts. And the Lyceum had attracted the cream of this society, for whom the inspired music brought more than just additional cachet to the productions. One music critic wrote of Hamilton Clarke's score to Irving's *Much Ado about Nothing* in 1891 that he could not judge whether it would be considered "good" or "bad" music if performed in a concert hall, but as theatre music it literally "doubles the value of the play."[58] This was a strong endorsement indeed.

Ellen Terry recalled a frustrated Clarke throwing up his hands in exasperation at Irving's musical requests only to realize later, after trying them, that the suggestions were right on the mark.[59] But Irving was not always intransigent about his musical instincts, and a composer with equally strong dramatic instincts could occasionally persuade him against his better judgment, even to the point of substantially altering the tone of the play. That was the case with Sir Alexander Mackenzie, previously orchestra leader at the Theatre Royal, Edinburgh, and now principal of the prestigious Royal Academy of Music. Mackenzie and librettist Francis Hueffer had attracted considerable interest with their two Wagner-influenced "lyrical dramas" written for the Carl Rosa opera company in the 1880s. In 1890 Irving commissioned Mackenzie to write the music for *Ravenswood*, Herman Merivale's adaptation of Walter Scott's historical novel *The Bride of Lammermoor*. The composer received a copy of the play with Irving's notes and music plot and set about preparing a great deal of music. Perhaps to intensify the romantic ache of this melodramatic tragedy, Mackenzie wrote in many dark flat keys—B-flat major and D-flat major are the brightest of these, with many cues in F minor or B-flat minor. A "Funeral March" and a "Storm" were lengthy pieces within acts, and the entr'acte to act 2 was a character piece depicting Lucy Ashton, the doomed heroine.

Mackenzie completed most of his commission prior to the trial and error of rehearsal. Several accounts of Irving's rehearsals report that the director asked "Mr. Ball" for one type of music but then changed his mind. For *Ravenswood*, however, Irving met with the composer a full two months before the opening in September to work through the score. The only other person present for this meeting in Irving's study was his assistant manager, H. J. Loveday. Irving listened quietly while Mackenzie played an overture-prelude, three entr'actes (two quite long), and twenty-three melodramatic cues. When the composer had finished, Irving complimented him on his work and said that his only reservations were about the ending. It did not capture the right atmosphere. Irving's idea, according to Austin Brereton, his secretary, was that the last scene—after Lucy's death—should show Edgar, the master of Ravenswood, lost in a waste of quicksand and bathed in a cold glare of moonlight, with shivering music capturing the mood of his desperate situation.[60] Instead, as Mackenzie describes it, "I had the *love motive* which runs through the piece in a triumphant burst." When Irving asked the composer what he meant by this obviously inappropriate music, Mackenzie explained that the lovers were not tragically severed, as in *Faust*, but rather were to be joined in death. Irving promised to give the matter some thought. The next morning came a surprising letter:

> Dear Mackenzie: You were right after all. Faust does, we hope, get to Heaven in the second part—and Edgar and Lucy, I am sure, go together. At all events your music will certainly send them there, and the moonlight—the sea—I shall change to the breaking of the rising sun. Sincerely yours, Henry Irving. 15th July, 1890.[61]

Mackenzie was even more amazed at the final dress rehearsal, when he heard Ball leading his entire score nearly intact, only one of the melodramatic numbers having been cut. Within a month the *Ravenswood* overture and entr'actes were played in concert at the Norwich Festival. Within a year the music publisher Novello brought them out in a piano four-hands edition (Novello later marketed the "Lucy" prelude for piano solo too). Mackenzie agreeably returned to the Lyceum in 1898 for *Manfred* and in 1900 for *Coriolanus*.

Irving had yet another new idea for *Henry VIII* (1892), to be enacted with meticulous historical accuracy. He wanted music that was not merely poetic but directly suggestive of the Tudor period. So he turned to Edward German, who was then musical director at the Globe. German had studied at the Royal Academy of Music in the early 1880s and earned his living by fiddling for Drury Lane pantomimes and playing second violin in the orchestra at London's Opera Comique, where he participated in the premieres of several Gilbert and Sullivan operas. Richard Mansfield at the Globe hired the young German and gave him an orchestra of twenty-eight top-notch players, including three from one of London's most prominent wind quintets (much to the aspiring conductor's delight).[62] German had earlier written music for a production of *Antigone* at the Wimbledon School, and his theatre experience served him in good stead when it came to providing the music for Mansfield's *Richard III* in 1889. Critics took notice, including Sir George Grove, who observed how everyone had commented on the music's "appropriateness, grace, and vigour." Following one of the performances, Mansfield gave a supper at which the critic Joseph Bennett stood up and toasted the art of "music wedded to the drama," saying that the *Richard III* music was perhaps the best example he had known of the art. Among the guests that night were an impressive array of actors, authors, critics, and theatrical managers, including John Hare, Joseph Hatton, J. Comyns Carr,

J. L. Toole, Max Orell, Beerbohm Tree, and Davenport Adams. This was a turning point in the young German's life, for he not only went on to become one of England's most famous composers but was known principally for his theatrical music. Novello published the overture for *Richard III*. Sometime later even a "Selection from the Incidental Music" was available for sale.[63]

Even before *Henry VIII*, German's theatre music attracted a lot of attention in the musical world. Bernard Shaw's friends advised him to go hear *Richard III* specifically for the music, "with its *leitmotivs* after Wagner's plan." Shaw was not impressed, at least as far as the comparison went. He outlined the principal theme of German's overture (C-D-E-flat-D-C then G [a longer note]) and acknowledged that whenever Richard entered the bassoons honked out the motive in the low register. A leitmotiv it was certainly, Shaw said, but hardly after Wagner's plan.

> What Mr. Edward German has done is this: having had about 22 players at his disposal, he has wisely written for the old Haydn-Mozart symphony orchestra—two flutes, two oboes, two clarinets, two bassoons, two horns, drums, and strings: no trumpets or trombones. He has also necessarily economized in the strings by doing without cellos. For these hardly Wagnerian forces he has written an overture and a series of intermezzos, all pretty and well put together, but none presenting a single point of novelty. The style is the style of, say Max Bruch—that is, everybody's style, Gounod's, Bizet's, Mendelssohn's, Verdi's, all styles *except Wagner's*.[64]

We can probably excuse some of the hyperbole in this assessment, as Shaw generally had very little good to say about any theatrical music whatsoever. But the point is well taken. By his later operas Wagner had demonstrated that referential themes and motives could be woven into a fabric of considerable musical and psychological complexity. Jacobi had attempted this in his score to *The Dead Heart* (about which Shaw was, characteristically, silent). The refrain of Landry's seditious song and Catherine's tender theme are transformed throughout the score in ways that would probably only be, at best, felt by audiences rather than distinctly heard. Such music, while dramatically effective at a subconscious level, did not require extensive musical development, as Wagner did in his music dramas. The "motives" that Edward German used were more like "reminiscence themes," as they are often called in early Romantic opera, rather than the fragmentary threads called leitmotivs in the mature Wagnerian sense.

For Irving's *Henry VIII*, German composed an overture, act preludes, marches, a set of dances (that went on to become one of the most performed British concert pieces of the era), and a few songs. As David Russell Hulme has shown, Irving sent German some traditional sixteenth-century airs that he hoped the composer would weave throughout his score. Though German avoided obvious quotation, he promised the director (in an unpublished letter) that the music "will have the necessary touches of old English colour in keeping with the play."[65] Hulme notes that this distinctive "old English" sound lent German's music a national tone that distinguished him among late Victorian composers. The music was tunefully memorable as well as effective, and German's suite of *Henry VIII* music was taken up immediately by orchestras. But the composer could not have had more discerning listeners than those at the Lyceum Theatre in 1892, Clement Scott duly noted. "Never before in our memory has the old Lyceum contained such an exceptionally brilliant audience as assembled last night to see the glories—histrionic, musical, decorative, and spectacular—of Mr. Henry Irving's last and unexampled Shakespearean revival."[66]

When Irving revived *Romeo and Juliet* in 1895, he and Johnston Forbes-Robertson, who oversaw the production while Irving was on tour in America, decided against reusing Benedict's music from 1882 and invited the now-famous German to write new music. German composed a nearly cinematic score, thick with themes and motives.[67] Like Grieg, German also titled each cue, setting a precedent that would become standard practice in the early twentieth century with the advent of sound film. Novello published a "Selection of Themes" from German's score that has to be the most substantial potpourri of music for a single play published in the nineteenth century. Prepared, like the *Henry VIII* dances, for the amateur pianist, the selection contained "Curtain Music, "Peter Theme," "After the Street Fight," "March," "At Capulet's Reception," "Juliet Theme," "Love Theme," "Nurse Theme," "Marriage Music," "Romeo's Departure," "Paris at the Tomb of Juliet," and "Death Theme." Like the selections from twentieth-century film scores that were provided for amateur pianists, these evocative titles helped musicians to envision specific episodes in the production as they rendered the music at the keyboard.

King Arthur *and Popular Drama as Pageant*

In an age of Victorian monumentality Irving raised the popular drama to a level of dignity and prestige formally granted only to Shakespeare. He had come a long way since his Methodist mother rejected him because he went on the stage or the time when his wife left him on opening night of *The Bells*, a tawdry waste of his talents in her opinion. Jeffrey Richards has offered the compelling argument that Irving struggled his whole life to make an actor's career respectable. In achieving this goal he lifted his musicians and the rest of his artistic staff up with him.[68]

With *The Dead Heart* and *Ravenswood* Irving reached the apex of the musico-dramatic genre that had begun a century earlier in the French boulevard theatres. As Wagner symphonized opera, Irving effectively legitimized melodrama, raising it to the level of a fully integrated art form. By using already established symphonic and opera composers, however, Irving moved further and further from melodrama's roots as popular entertainment. These spectacles were now becoming tragedies with music, even pageants in some cases. By all accounts his production of Tennyson's *Becket* (1893) was a huge success. Charles Villiers Stanford returned to the Lyceum to provide an extensive musical score (which remains unpublished).

But *King Arthur* (1895) was symptomatic of the pitfalls of the fully integrated art form. J. Comyns Carr fashioned his mythic drama in four acts and a prologue specifically for Irving, and Arthur Sullivan returned to provide a musical score full of Victorian majesty. Though *King Arthur* ran for an entire season at the Lyceum (105 performances) and was taken on tour to the United States, it was heavily criticized for its use of blank verse, its weak dramatic construction, and even Sullivan's "sugar-stick" coating (to quote Bernard Shaw).[69] The play was loosely based on Thomas Malory and Lord Tennyson, but Carr focused his drama almost exclusively on the tragic consequences of Queen Guinevere's affair with Lancelot, Arthur's favorite knight. Irving played the king; Ellen Terry, Guinevere; and Johnston Forbes-Robertson, Lancelot. Arthur Sullivan's most elaborate theatrical score for the Lyceum was written to complement the pre-Raphaelite settings, designed by Edward Burne-Jones. The only music available was published by Novello after the run of the play, a concert-cantata in five movements. The analysis here is based on the complete score, which survives only in manuscript like Mackenzie's *Ravenswood* and Stanford's *Becket*.[70] Sullivan's music for Carr's four-act drama consists of twenty-eight music cues, nearly all of them lengthy action and dialogue underscoring.

The play began with a prologue ("Excalibur"). Clement Scott, sitting in the audience on opening night as usual, found himself completely immersed in the mood of Sullivan's "exquisite" overture then saw the curtain rise on the Magic Mere in the faint glimmer of early dawn. "All is dreamy, fantastic, mysterious. The music, always suggestive, never pronounced, helps the imagination."[71] Some compared the opening to Wagner's *Rheingold.* To the sound of a mysterious chorus of spirits, Merlin (played by Sydney Valentine in a long white beard) has led the youthful Arthur to the place where he knows that he will find his sword Excalibur. In the bluish light of the lake Arthur also sees the vision of a beautiful woman, his future queen. Eager to possess the sword and capture Guinevere, Arthur goes toward the mere, from which a spirit rises. The Spirit of the Lake (played by Maud Milton) intones "The Chant of the Grail," a solemn speech in rhyming couplets. "Arthur, England's chosen lord, Fear not Fate but take thy sword." To accompany these twenty-three lines of text, Sullivan composed a shimmering tremolo in the strings (played by the violins in their lower range). This continues while the spirit speaks. The strings modulate fluidly through gorgeous harmonies, not too obtrusively. Just after the shimmering begins, a solo violin heralds a rising nine-note "Excalibur motive," a phrase sung earlier by the spirits ("Fashioned by no mortal hand"). The motive coincided with a ray of light aimed directly on the jeweled sword. At regular points in the spirit's prophecy, every two bars or so, the solo violin plays a version of this magical motive. The only other activity is an inverted echo of the sword motive, mirrored portentously in the cellos and double basses. Though distinct, the motive is low enough to be out of the range of the actress's speaking voice. Moreover, occurrences of the Excalibur motive—each slightly different in pitch and character—were equally spaced so that the actress could situate her lines between them, even using the violin's sweetness to color her delivery. With Irving's forward orchestra at the Lyceum, the actress had no problem hearing the musicians and could freely exercise the craft of speaking through the music.

Sullivan demonstrated that under-dialogue music when deftly handled could be both atmospherically beautiful and dramatically effective. To get some sense of the amount of music in this score, following is a list of cues for act 1, titled "The Holy Grail," which takes place in the Great Hall at Camelot.

Once the Great Hall was revealed and the prelude ended there was no music for the opening dialogue among four of Arthur's knights. Sir Gawaine informs Lancelot that Arthur has assembled a fellowship to depart that evening. When Lancelot asks: "[O]n what quest?" under-dialogue music begins (no. 9). Lancelot questions whether the Grail can ever be found. Kay tells the story of Percival's discovery of this holy relic, as the hall darkens. When he gets to the fellowship—"and close upon this hour"—there is a flash of lightning and thunder, and the orchestra segues into the Grail music as a

Act 1

No. 8	E-flat major, 6/8	Prelude. *Andante*
No. 9	C minor, 4/4	Cue (Lancelot): “Bound on what quest?” “dialogue through”—strings only (repeat)—at cue (Kay): “And close upon his hour” *segue* into next section featuring violin solo
No. 10	E-flat major, 6/8	cue (Mordred): “So did the king.” (Morgan LeFay): “Ah truth. So did the King.”
Unnumbered		Flourish on Stage at Flag Signal (2 Cornets, 2 Horns, 3 Trombones)
No. 11	E-flat major, 4/4	Cue: “Back to that heart that once did seem its home”—for chorus with harmonium—begins with tenors and basses: “Look not to thy sword . . .”
No. 12	(same)	Cue: “Love speaks at last. Love will be obeyed!”—“twice through”
No. 13	C minor, 4/4	“The Chant of the Grail”—cue: “Put on my sword”—full orchestra—Segue no. 13½
No. 13½	(same)	Similar to above, but just strings (*sordini*). Swell at “Glad return”—dim at “Lancelot’s entrance”
No. 14	(same)	Cue (Arthur): “Stand forth and speak”—under dialogue: “All shall seek the Holy Grail. All and all save one shall fail . . .”
No. 15	E-flat, 4/4	*Andante alla Marcia, ff* triumphant. Cue: “I do thy bidding. Lancelot stay”—with chorus: “Look not to thy love . . .”

slanting ray of bright light reveals a vision of a maiden bearing the shining cup. Much of the act used music in a similar way, running in subordinate fashion under a long dialogue sequence in order to culminate in some visual moment for which the music moves into the foreground.

Later in the act Guinevere tries to persuade Lancelot not to join the quest, but the infatuated knight—who cannot tell Arthur the real reason why he wants to leave the court—is adamant. Arthur is confused and turns to Merlin for advice. As the wizard steps forth, the orchestra started to play (no. 14). This passage in C minor begins quietly with the strings. Like the Spirit of the Lake Merlin speaks in musical rhythm, and the strings move in lockstep with him, obviously meant to impart mythic import to his prophecy: "All shall seek the Holy Grail, All and all save one shall fail." The strings then pause for silence as Arthur replies in prosaic, unmusical speech. "Nay, leave thy riddles. Shall he go or stay?" As Merlin resumes intoning his rhyming verse the strings also resume, marking the rhythm of his text, note-to-word. "Fate doth not answer yea or nay. Love shall bid him go or stay!" As Arthur replies, the strings once again pause for a small bit of unrhymed colloquial dialogue.

Arthur. Say on. What is this love that bids him go?
Merlin. I can but read the words that Fate hath writ.
Arthur. Then we have done with Fate. Go, get thee hence and never more shall that dark face of thine pass, like a withered shadow, through these halls!

Merlin then delivers four more rhyming lines of prophecy, again marked by the strings. After Merlin intones his last couplet ("He Pendragon's son shall slay, That is born with the May!"), the wizard retires. Irving's light cue here couples the dimming of the hall with a rising intensity of the sunset beyond the castle, a reminder of the imminence of the fellowship's departure. The orchestra plays a short postlude to accompany Merlin's exit and to lend formal closure to his scene. After a tranquil pause on a C-major chord (the sunset resplendent), the dialogue of Guinevere, Arthur, and Lancelot resumes naturally.

Like *Joan of Arc* at the Gaîté and *Peer Gynt* at the Christiania, *King Arthur* at the Lyceum bore all the outward signs of national drama with music by an important national composer. But it also represents a flawed attempt to raise the rhetorical component of the drama to the poetic level of the settings, costumes, lighting, and music. The music's job here—along with the lighting—was to impart a large part of the mystical atmosphere.

In this it succeeded. But it also bore some of the responsibility for going down a path that was essentially a dead end for the popular drama. While Irving and his company were pursuing this vain quest, authors and managers on both sides of the Atlantic would soon hit on the successful commercial formula, proving that costume dramas could once again also be popular dramas.

10

Melodrama and Glamour at Century's End

In 1890 Charles M. Skinner, American writer and editor of the *Brooklyn Eagle*, wrote a piece for the *New York Dramatic Mirror* on drama and "musical accompaniment."

> A musical accompaniment to a theatrical performance gives delicacy, feeling, and finish to the acting, softens the voices of the actors, intensifies the emotional effect of their deeds and speeches and impresses them more deeply on the memory. For one, I have never attended a stage performance that was not the better for music. It has been my fortune—sometimes it was a misfortune—to see a number of familiar plays in provincial theatres where trust-worthy orchestras were not to be had, and invariably I have been struck with the lack of grace and pathos in scenes that were affecting in the city houses. The acting was the same. In the musical accompaniment was the glamour of the city representation.[1]

Rarely can we find such a cogent and comprehensive explanation for why theatrical managers and directors such as Henry Irving, Herbert Beerbohm Tree, George Alexander, Richard Mansfield, Wilson Barrett, Charles and Daniel Frohman, Marcus Klaw and A. L. Erlanger, David Belasco, and others used not less but rather more music for their productions in the 1890s and even into the twentieth century. The key here, the astute Skinner observed, was to be found in the big city theatres. For only in major urban centers could managers afford a large and proficient orchestra to match the overall professional caliber of the production. These managers—who anticipated the dream machine of the 1920s silver screen—knew that audiences who patronized the popular theatre at the end of the century expected four things, to quote Romain Rolland: a mingling of pleasing and painful emotions, true realism in production values, the presence of evil but with the hint that good will prevail, and to get their money's worth from an evening's entertainment.[2] The best managers knew the power of music to help fulfill these expectations. Exquisite and well-placed music lent their productions a kind of glamour far beyond the playgoing experience of most out-of-town visitors. It also did not hurt that this musical glamour—like the expensive costumes and sets—could help catapult their actors into stardom.

Given how much theatre music from this period survives, prospects for future research are ripe. We can see from the examples here that even at the end of the nineteenth century music for the popular drama continued to fulfill its long-standing role of providing moral authority while also serving to glamorize evil (a medieval devil, the mesmerizing Svengali, the plotting Milady de Winter and Cardinal Richelieu) and heroism (a dashing D'Artagnan and a doomed Japanese prince and princess).

Herbert Beerbohm Tree at the Haymarket

Henry Irving had raised music to an equal level with other production values for both the popular drama and Shakespeare. His influence is evident in the career of Herbert Beerbohm Tree, a character actor turned director. Tree had taken over the Haymarket Theatre in 1887. Earlier that same year he visited Bayreuth, where he heard three of Wagner's music dramas, including *Tristan* and *Die Meistersinger*. He found them "an intoxicating delight," according to his wife.[3] In trying to emulate the Lyceum Theatre's eye-beguiling and ear-bathing productions, he too hired prominent composers to prepare scores for his productions. In the early years Hamilton Clarke wrote the music for *Partners* and *The Pompadour* (both 1887), George Henschel (his Bayreuth traveling companion) for *Hamlet* (1892), Hubert Parry for *Hypatia* (1893), and Edward German for Henry Arthur Jones's *The Tempter* (also 1893). In a speech to the newly formed Musical Directors' Association in 1899 Tree claimed that music was "invaluable for assisting the imagination and in attuning the audience to sweet melancholy, to fairy mirth, or to the storm and stress of tragedy." But for many older uses of *melos* he seemed to agree with the more modern tendency to renounce music "to mark the entrance and exit of a star" or "as an accompaniment to dialogue."[4]

The Bancrofts had remodeled the interior of the Haymarket Theatre in 1879 when they took it over, and one of the architectural modifications was to create a gold picture-frame proscenium, the bottom of which hid the orchestra so that it was submerged under the stage. The space could accommodate thirty or so musicians, but it was a dark hole, making the musicians completely invisible. As one architect put it, "the first row of stalls is within three feet of the footlights."[5] This encouraged greater intimacy between actors and audience, of course, but many visitors to the theatre in the 1880s found it peculiar to have the orchestra hidden, especially as opera was also performed there (including Wagner).

Most writings about Tree focus on his work as a Shakespearean or his later founding of the Royal Academy of Dramatic Arts. But it was in the popular drama—and the glamour surrounding its increasing use of technical magic—that the actor first managed to overcome his physical weaknesses: a plain face, a high tenor voice, and a slight lisp. Despite these ordinary qualities he brought the melodramatic villain to new heights of dramatic intensity, as, for example, when he played the devil in *The Tempter*.

The Tempter is a somewhat unsettling piece, somewhere between spectacle drama and historical tragedy. Loosely based on the Faust legend, it takes place in the fourteenth century and concerns a young prince Leon of Auvergne, who is headed to England to marry Lady Avis, the daughter of the Earl of Rougement. The marriage has been arranged between two warring provinces in the hopes of securing peace. But the devil is a very real threat in this medieval world and in flesh-and-blood form plans to prevent a marriage that would cheat him out of the bloodshed, pestilence, and famine of the Hundred Years' War. In the end, of course, he succeeds, but not before pushing the resilience of human beings to extraordinary limits. The play has no heroes, because everyone suffers the consequences of the devil's intervention. Alfred Stephens, an Australian playgoer in London, called it "a satirical study of human nature under temptations, hitting slyly at the crude conceptions of popular theology."[6]

Jones wrote his play largely in verse, and some reviewers poked fun at the archaic language. But many also found it dramatically effective, observing Jones's craft as a playwright and his deep sense of humanity in the creation of interesting characters. Also credited were the fine performances of Tree's company, Joseph Harker and Walter Hann's ravishing sets, costumes by L. and H. Nathan, and Edward German's integral and highly theatrical music. Rehearsals began in late August at the Princess's Theatre while the stage of the Haymarket was being excavated to accommodate the sinking ship in the first act. Opening night was three and a half weeks later on 20 September. Carl Armbruster, a conductor long associated with promoting Wagner's music in England, was hired to lead the expanded orchestra.

Sources for *The Tempter* include three annotated promptbooks (one for the stage manager, another for lights, and another for the composer), a lengthy handwritten music plot, sections of music manuscript in full score, the violin leader book, and all the orchestra parts as played and marked up by the musicians. Tree turned to German largely because of the success of his *Henry VIII* music for the Lyceum. His practical experience of working at Drury Lane and the Globe served him in good stead for *The Tempter*, for his music, like Tree's concept of the play, seemed to evolve in rehearsal. As noted earlier, Hamilton Clarke and Meredith Ball at the Lyceum often prepared a library copy of the full score once the music was set. But only portions of *The Tempter* music are in full score, and Armbruster must have led the orchestra from the first violin leader book. All the documents suggest that the musicians worked under the extraordinary pressure of a tight deadline. The extant manuscript score contains a lot of shorthand notes to the copyist to "copy out in full" or "make two copies" of such and such a number.

Aside from the overture, entr'actes, and the long opening storm scene, which is through-composed in score format, the many individual *melos* numbers appear as separate items. German composed a unique *melos*—with a unique orchestration—for each character and situation, and these were reprised periodically. For the entry of the Earl of Rougement and his party, for example, German wrote a short march, a moderate walking piece in D major that imparts a penitential mood to the small weary band. This he labeled simply "number 5." Later in act 2, when these same pilgrims arrive at the Canterbury guesthouse, the orchestra repeated this music. At that point in the promptbook, however, "number 5" actually appears as music cue no. 15. This process—which was obviously established in rehearsal—allowed certain cues associated with specific characters, moods, or dramatic developments to be reused in identical form throughout the play. Such repetitions are not extensive but substantial enough, for example, that orchestra "number 9," written to sound like a vesper hymn in the first act, is repeated for promptbook music cues nos. 12 and 21. At first this might seem confusing, especially in a case like orchestra "number 9," which is immediately followed by no. 27, whereas orchestra nos. 10 and 11 are missing entirely. Obviously German must have composed music for both missing cues but decided in rehearsal that no. 27, composed originally for the last act, would be more effective if first heard here in place of the old no. 10, providing an emotional foreshadowing of events and situations to come. By the time the orchestra parts were copied out, the decision about the ordering of items had been finalized, because they follow sequentially in the parts.

A two-page music plot of thirty-seven cues with consecutive numbers was drawn up (now pasted inside the cover of German's copy of the score). This was likely prepared for Hugh Moss, the stage manager, who would have entered the final numbering into his promptbook.

German's music figures highly in reviews of the play, and music periodicals carried articles devoted to the *Tempter* score, some calling it "powerfully dramatic" and "exquisitely melodious."[7] Even Joseph Joachim, the famous German violinist, thought the music "exceptionally fine" for a stage play.[8] Tree allowed German to score for an ample body of strings, full double winds and brass (two cornets, two horns, three trombones), harp, and two percussionists. German's overture grandly set the tone for a spectacle drama and integrated important themes from the play. The music also included three titled preludes, played before each subsequent curtain: a "Bacchanalian Dance," a "Berceuse," and, before the tragic last act, a "Dramatic Interlude." Aside from the storm music, these are the only pieces that use the full forces of the orchestra simultaneously. German assigned a yearning theme to the principal heroine, Lady Avis. For the love scenes between the prince and Lady Isobel, strings underscore their dialogue with tender romantic music. (It resembles the music for the young lovers in Verdi's *Falstaff*, an opera that had premiered six months earlier.) To the devil German allotted several *melos* numbers associated with the various manifestations in which he appears: one for the steersman, one for the soldier, one for the minstrel, and one for the friar. The evil motivations of these characters are consistently expressed through menacing or mysterious musical effects—diminished-seventh chords and arpeggios, roaring chromatic scales, ominous pedal tones, and agitated string tremolos.

The play begins, like the *Tempest*, in a storm at sea. A ship carrying Prince Leon (played by Fred Terry) is attempting to cross the channel. In a bolt of lightning, the devil appears at the steersman's wheel. He manages to sink the ship but does not intend to dispense with Leon just yet. The devil rows the unconscious prince to shore in a small boat. The scene changes to an inn on the road to Canterbury. A steward to the Earl of Rougemont has just arrived to seek accommodations for his master, the Lady Avis (Helen Tree), the Lady Isobel (Julia Nielson), and other pilgrims on their way to the shrine of St. Thomas. The earl has seized the estates of Carmyne in France belonging to Isobel's family and by the decree of the church is doing penance for his wrong. Upon arriving at Canterbury, Avis plans to celebrate her wedding with Prince Leon while Isobel resolves to become a nun. Meanwhile the devil, attired as a soldier, enters the inn with the dazed and exhausted prince, who has little memory of the night before. The devil speaks in glowing terms of Isobel but tries to plant suspicions about Avis. The prince, not having heard of Isobel and not having seen his intended bride since they were children, is persuaded by the soldier's suggestion to conceal his identity for a time so that he may judge the two ladies for himself. He agrees to masquerade as a squire.

The following is a close transcription of the music plot for act 1, the original of which is in the Herbert Beerbohm Tree Theater Music Collection at the Boston Public Library. The numbers on the left do not correspond to the final numbering of cues but instead reflect Tree's original text or visual cues for where music should stop and start. Dynamics are almost always specified, but never tempo or musical characterization. The additional numbers on the right of the plot were added once the music was already composed, given the references to the "double bar" and various out-of-order cue numbers (no. 27, for example). This was the conductor's instruction sheet as to how German's *melos* numbers would fit to the stage. "Wind A" and "Wind B" in the opening storm music refer to two separate musical cues. There are indications here for the conductor ("signal 2 fingers"), who probably also gave the "curtain bell" to the prompter.

Act I. Overture, then

1) Opening No. 1. Curtain bell (page 7) at double bar: *pp*

cue: Look at this boiling pit! —	Wind A (signal 2 fingers)
cue: I've kept my row! —	Wind A
cue: We're in Gold's hands! —	Wind A and strings *ff*
cue: Low crash of thunder —	Wind B, then strings *pp* (signal for B, first)
cue: Nearer! Awake old thunder —	Wind A
cue: Lash and chafe —	Wind A
cue: I pronounce destruction good —	Wind B and strings *ff*

After about 4 bars more go back to the beginning of No. 1 (signal spread-out hand) and at double bar go to No. 2 (signal 1 finger), give curtain bell 2 bars before 9/8. Continue 9/8 until Drogo down in front. —

2) cue: See that all is made ready — No. 3 *pp*, crescendo at exit Drogo (once only)

3) cue: I'll hide me somewhere till they've gone their way: — Chord (celli and basses) at once

4) cue: You'll find me a merry easy Master: — No. 3 *f*, then *pp* while Devil says: Judge her before you marry her, then *f* again. Once through then immediately No. 5 until Lady Isobel is down in front.
5) cue: To see your holy uncle butter Heaven. Watch him!: — No. 6 about 10 bars, till beggar falls.
6) cue: I'll scourge ye! I'll scourge the devil out of ye!: — No. 5 once
7) cue: Come Isobel, 'tis near vesper time, come!
    1) As devil turns toward Isobel: — Chord!
    2) Devil follows Isobel; when behind her: — Chord!
    3) Cue: and footfalls of some great event to come: — Chord, followed closely by No. 9, stop when Isobel off.
8) cue: Under the thick oppression of stagnant air: — No. 27 *mf*, crescendo at the words and ride on circling whirlwinds, keep *f* until the words: Choruses reverberant, then suddenly *pp*; crescendo again at: more clamorous than cymbals, keep *f* till: and wails unending, then die away *pp*.
9) cue: after: Thy pardon, ha! Ha! Exit Sir Gilbert. When Isobel sinks down on bales and as Devil approaches her: Chord!
10) cue: What kind of man! He is the top of . . . No. 11½ *ppp* through speech, stop at his lips speak honey.
11) cue: The Prince is here tonight! Where? [Promptbook differs from the published text: Within the house playing my Squire. This is he]: — No. 11½ *pp*, crescendo to *ff* at: and mine! Until Curtain down 2nd time.

The opening storm sequence was truly frightening. Rarely, noted the *Era*, have "the horrors of shipwreck . . . been so awfully depicted." Some of this realism was aided by German's musical design, which is remarkable and without precedent (foreshadowing techniques used by experimental composers half a century later). Armbruster began the act by leading the pit orchestra in the tumultuous storm music, with musical devices based on motives that will eventually be linked to the devil. After eighteen bars of *allegro agitato*, the curtain rises on the deck of the prince's ship in the storm. The orchestration at first thins out somewhat so that the sailors' shouting to one another can be heard. It is eventually reduced to just strings. The violins and violas play tremolo on sustained chords while the basses and cellos play ascending and descending chromatic scales, suggesting the rise and fall of the sea. The *agitato* strings continue under the master helmsman's orders—shouted over the wind—and into his dialogue with the prince, who comes up on deck to assess the situation. At key points in what follows, however, German has two interpolations, written for woodwinds and brass. Interpolation "A" consists of roaring "wind" music, a swirling effect in the flutes and clarinets and a quick chromatic scale downward. Interpolation "B" consists of "lightning" music, beginning with an ominous augmented triad sounded by the brass, while oboes, clarinets, and cornets play slowly rising chromatic thirds to explode in powerful chords emphasized by the trombones and piccolos, followed by a sharp roll in the timpani. This innovation allows the strings to continue the background of turbulent "sea" music, while the effect of confusion is intensified at key moments by cutting in—thus overlaying—the whirling "wind" or "lightning" music, with no intent at synchronization. Armbruster kept time with the strings—making gradual dynamic modifications too, according to the parts—and signaled the wind groups at the appropriate cue lines. The resulting dissonance between the musical elements is impressively suggestive of the chaotic natural elements of an actual storm. The wind music occurs three times during the opening tumult. The third time the gusts are so strong that the steersman is swept overboard. With a flash of lightning the devil appears in his place, the first cue for the "B" music.

The strings continue the sea music along with the backstage sound effects as the sailors' frantic efforts to save the ship prove futile. With the ship sinking, they turn on each other in desperation, egged on by the devil. At the devil's line "Curse! Mutiny! Blaspheme!" Armbruster signaled the orchestra to jump to no. 2—a sudden increase in tempo—just as the devil crashes the ship onto the rocks, hurtling men into the water. Roaring for a few furious bars the orchestra erupted into a *maestoso*—victory for the devil and the musical climax of the scene. The orchestra then calmed down gradually, while cries and groans from the drowning men emanated in the darkness. "A lurid dawn slowly spreads over the scene," writes Jones, and there are only a few short quiet bars of calm music as the audience catches a glimpse of the devil rowing the small boat in the distance against a copper sky, the sea strewn with corpses.[9] Without any pause the orchestra then moved smoothly into a gentle *allegretto* in 9/8. In two bars of music the Haymarket stage was completely transformed into the courtyard of the inn.

The music plot for the next scene contains numerous requests for a "chord" of punctuation (see nos. 3 and 7 in the plot). Though it is perhaps surprising as late as 1893, Tree clearly wanted the villain to be identified with this long-standing melodramatic tradition. German gave Tree something rather unusual, however. The first instance occurs when the prince learns that his betrothed is to arrive that evening. "I'll hide somewhere till they've gone on their way," he says, ashamed of his bedraggled attire. The devil (as soldier) stays him instantly with his hand. "Hearkee," he says, "you've not seen the Lady Avis since you were children?" The lower strings—violas, cellos, and basses—bow a thickly voiced A-minor triad with a hairpin crescendo, like a groan. Instead of being the stinging gesture typical of the obvious chord of reversal, the effect was more felt than heard, like a subtle allusion to the manipulative wave music from the storm. Tree and German must have added this effect at a late stage, because it is not copied into the original parts but penciled by the musicians wherever it was needed. What a writer for the *Pall Mall Gazette* called "the twanging chord that signals the Tempter's approach" appeared often enough that the simple device rose to the level of a thematic reference.[10]

Later in the act Rougement's party arrives. This is the no. 5 walking music in plot number 4 above. The devil, now disguised as a gentleman scholar, tries to ingratiate himself with them, especially with Isobel, whom he plans to entangle with the prince. With cue no. 6, the earl has gone into the inn up left. Avis follows, calling from the door: "Come, Isobel, 'tis near to vesper time." She goes into the inn, and Isobel intends to follow. Here is the sequence of action, dialogue, and music:

ISOBEL	PROMPTBOOK NOTES
"No," she says, hesitating, "I'll stay here and take the evening air."	She goes up R. to bench.
"What is it so disquiets me tonight?"	Isobel falls down bashfully.
"Breathes and o'erhovers, drives about my spirit . . .	The devil follows her, a menacing chord.
. . . with unimaginable dreads and hopes. . .	Isobel then comes down R. and crosses in front of arch.
. . . and footfalls of some great event to come?"	The devil crosses down R. and comes down behind her, another chord intensifying his approach.
"Shadow me softly, angel of my future!"	Isobel turns and looks at the devil then turns to exit up L.

The devil's threat lurks in his physical presence and in the ominous chord. As Isobel turns to go (apparently not sensing the invisible fiend), music no. 9 (still part of cue 7) begins. This consists of a sustained pedal A in the strings (violins playing tremolo), a cymbal roll, and woodwinds playing the snakelike "tempter" theme from the overture. Leaning against the arch and resting his chin on his left hand, the tempter closely watches the innocent Isobel until she exits into the inn.

The devil's monologue that immediately followed (music cue no. 8) is a stunning sequence of dialogue-underscoring. It reveals just how much had changed in theatre music in recent decades. The pilgrims begin to sing the vesper hymn inside the chapel. "How wooingly this Isobel doth lend her soul unto its ruin," the devil says, moving toward the center. "Oh thou desire of every eye! Beauty incomparable!" The devil contemplates loveliness in women, his tone becoming coarser and more vehement. At his line "to ache and pant under th' intolerable, thick oppression of stagnant air" the orchestra began (music no. 27). This music is lyrical, passionate, yearning, reminiscent of Wagner's Isolde waiting for her Tristan. Though softly at first, it gradually started to cover the offstage hymn. The devil continues:

> Then, to suddenly snatch thee to awful heights, breathless, unbearable; to buckle thee all shuddering to my side, and ride on circling whirlwinds boisterous . . . [the orchestra grows louder] . . . intoxicate with bedlam mirth, midst loud ascending choruses reverberant, th' eternal music that lost spirits make, sweeter than dulcimers, more clamours than cymbals . . . [here the orchestra is at its loudest point, the actor at the apex of his rhetorical intensity, the vesper hymn completely obliterated] . . . groans, howls, gnashings of teeth, desires, despairs, tears, shrieks, and wails unending.

At these climactic words the orchestra and chorus suddenly and abruptly stopped. A long, hollow, and frightening stillness followed, into which the devil quietly spoke one simple phrase: "This is thy lot, Lady Isobel." And in an inexorably grim silence he turned and exited through an arch upstage.

Tree gave several of the devil's speeches music, but only the final one, delivered after the powerful scene of the death of Isobel and the prince, surpassed this level of intensity. The devil's last speech is triumphant, even as he admits that "my hate is vain and futile, as all else that Thou hast made." After his last line—the only time he refers to the existence of God—the music disintegrates and the devil vanishes, leaving a fallen oak tree in his place. The only sound left is the gently blowing wind against a long quiet roll on the timpani. Finally, a delicate harp and strings begin the "dawn" sequence as the first streaks of light appear in the sky. The dawn music continues under the concluding cathartic scene. As the prior takes Avis into his arms to comfort her, the unaccompanied voices of grateful pilgrims ring out from the church.

The Tempter ran only for about fifty performances, but the extensive surviving performing materials allow a glimpse into the practices of a theatre dedicated to the melodramatic tradition, even carrying it to another level. In an article on Tree's 1908 production of *The Merchant of Venice,* John Ripley observed that Tree's promptbook—compared with those of Edwin Booth, E. H. Sothern, and others—was a virtual plot for a live soundtrack, "in which sound becomes a dynamic rather than a passive adjunct to picture, a tool for making precise sociopolitical comments."[11] He added that Tree's most important audio innovation was his use of music as a structural device. It was evident that Tree brought this sensibility to his productions as early at *The Tempter.*

Svengali, a Modern Villain

With the ultimate villain under his belt, Beerbohm Tree turned his attention to Svengali, that diabolical creation of George Du Maurier that Paul Potter had transformed into a play for A. M. Palmer in New York. The play was set in bohemian Paris. Potter somewhat toned down the ghastly anti-Semitism in the portrayal of the bearded man "from the mysterious East." But as the artist Taffy describes him to the naïve Trilby just before his entrance—a quotation taken directly from the novel—"Svengali walks up and down the earth seeking whom he might cheat, betray, exploit, borrow money from, make brutal fun of, bully if he dared, cringe to if he must—man, woman, child, or dog—he's as bad as they make 'em."[12] Tree immediately bought up the rights and secured a young and unknown actress named Dorothy Baird to play the part of Trilby O'Ferrall, the artist's model who dares to pose nude. Svengali has taken a fancy to her and decides that he will turn her into a great singer, even though she is completely tone deaf.

Tree gave a typed list of musical pieces that he wanted to include to twenty-year-old Raymond Roze, who would become his long-standing music director. Unlike the *Tempter* music, this was to be a compilation score, consisting entirely of preexisting (and fairly well known) music. Some of the tunes were already specified in Potter's play and in the original novel: the folklike song "Ben Bolt" for the unaffectedly girlish Trilby, the *romanza* from Schubert's *Rosamunde* music, a Chopin impromptu for Svengali (Chopin for a Viennese Jew?), and a Schumann art song, "Nussbaum," to signify Trilby's “transformation” into a real singer. Other specified music included a few topical French songs, “Messieurs les étudiants,” “Plaisir d’amour,” and “Au claire de la lune,” helping to set the scene as Paris in the 1850s. Potter had added a few others, “Annie Laurie” and “The Last Rose of Summer,” perhaps meant to emphasize the origins of Trilby’s English-Scottish circle of friends. Some prominent stage music was also included: a few quadrilles for the dance scene on Christmas Eve, the organ playing Adolphe Adam’s “Cantique de Noël” from the Church of St. Nicholas, and, for the Cirque des Bashibazouks in act 3, a “gypsy band” (a few strings and cimbalom) playing some “Hungarian National Music,” for which Tree and Roze selected a czardas and a Hungarian Dance by Johannes Brahms. Thus *Trilby* included a great deal of music. Though all the songs derived from other sources, they were tightly integrated into the play.

In his music instructions Tree also specified what Roze should provide for entr’actes.[13] Between acts 1 and 2 he wanted the Chopin piece arranged for orchestra. Between the second and third acts he wanted a fantasia on the theme of “Ben Bolt.” And for the last entr’acte he wanted a medley of “Trilby” airs. The tone of the entr’actes was strictly middlebrow, without any symphonic interpretation of the characters or situations (à la Stanford or German). No “leitmotivs” were to be invisibly woven into a symphonic fabric to provide audiences with a moral compass.

In fact Tree asked the conductor, Adolph Schmidt, to play the cheerful *Rosamunde* overture before the first curtain, as if purposely to mislead audiences about the amoral situations that the play explores. Roze must have found this a bit too alienating, however, because the program for the opening night included his own “Trilby Overture,” based on themes from *Rosamunde* and the tune of “Nussbaum.” Schmidt also managed to squeeze in other symphonic works during the entr’actes. (Mikhail Glinka’s “Kamarinskaya” and the prelude to the third act of Wagner’s *Lohengrin* were completely out of place: was this allowance based ultimately on the types of audiences that Tree wanted to attract or on Schmidt’s desire to educate the theatregoing public musically?)

In a memorandum at the bottom of his music notes Tree wrote: “incidental music from Berlioz and Rubinstein accompanies certain scenes of Svengali.” In the end, however, Roze did not write much “incidental music” of this kind. The hypnotic music was generated almost entirely onstage, first by Svengali himself—or, rather, by Roze playing the piano offstage while Svengali went through the motions—and second by Svengali’s violinist-friend Gecko, whom he accompanies on the piano in *L’Adieu*, a sentimental melody thought at the time to have been by Schubert (a tune nearly as popular in France in the 1850s as "Full Moon and Empty Arms" from Sergei Rachmaninov would be a century later). The Berlioz music turned out to be an offstage band playing the "Rakoczy March" from *The Damnation of Faust*, but no music of Anton Rubinstein appears in the orchestra parts (which, though unspecified, was presumably to have been from his 1871 opera *The Demon*).

Svengali's business in the artists' studio in act 1 was something of a tour de force. During the "piano scene" with Trilby and her bohemian friends, Svengali reveals the insidiousness of his aestheticism as he begins to manipulate the hapless young woman. The *Globe* called the scene "a triumph for the actor" and noted that Svengali ran to the piano and "whilst playing tender melodies mocked at poor Trilby, devised mischief against little Billee, and vaunted his own importance." As Tree played him, Svengali "fascinated instead of repelled."[14] Roze prepared a detailed piano score from which he played in the wings, complete with full text and indications for precise visual and textual alignments.[15] The scene was so effective that audiences believed Tree was actually playing the piano and often asked him at parties to render one of the tunes.[16] In actuality Tree played only a few sets of improvisatory arpeggios or "preludes," as the promptbook calls them. Svengali's arpeggios are in fact the tool by which he exerts his hypnotic power.

"Svengali, give us some music," Taffy asks. "Trilby has a touch of neuralgia." Svengali laughs harshly. "Ah ha, la grande Trilby. I will make music for you and take away your pain and keep it myself. I have brought my friend Gecko with me, he shall make music too—he plays the violin like an angel. I play like an angel." Kicking Gecko, he adds: "We are two angels." Trilby replies coyly, taking a cigarette from her purse: "You carry your wings inside for convenience." Svengali pretends not to hear her. He moves to the piano and begins to demonstrate his prowess with some elaborate scales and arpeggios. "I know what you English like," he suddenly bursts out, hunting for the right tune. He plays a bit of "Annie Laurie," laughing sinisterly. Each upbeat to the tune is grotesquely accented. After only three bars he breaks off. "Last Rose of Summer—Bah!" He plays only a few bars of that before he loses interest and then quickly modulates to a dominant seventh chord on F. This leads into a sublime rendering of the *Rosamunde* music, which he continues to play, entranced, while he carries on a conversation with Trilby (Fig. 40).

Trilby has never heard the tune before and in fact does not even recognize the composer's name. "Schubert was a countryman of mine," Svengali

FIGURE 40. *Svengali playing the "Rosemunde" of Schubert. Illustration by George du Maurier from his novel* Trilby. Harper's New Monthly Magazine *88 (1 December 1893): 177*

says, "and made music just like me," a point that he drives home by suddenly adding a long rolled chord under his last three words. "He was a perfect gentleman, just like me," Svengali emphasizes, adding another rolled chord. He resumes playing the sweet music of *Rosamunde* as if nothing happened. "Don't know him," Trilby says, puffing on her cigarette. "Never heard his name." "That's a pity," Svengali replies. "He had talent—just like me." At this point Svengali rolls an even wider chord at the piano. But then his fingers begin to tug delicately at the first few notes of the *L'Adieu*, a prearranged signal for Gecko to pick up his violin. While the two musicians render the haunting melody, Taffy half leans on the sofa, according to the stage instructions. Billee, in love with Trilby, sits on a chair near her, and Laird continues painting at his easel. The violin carries the tune sweetly, while the piano part glides up and down the keyboard athletically. Svengali even takes a few opportunities to stage glances at Trilby under each of his raised arms. There is a long pause at the end of the playing. Suddenly Svengali breaks the mood of reverie by launching into a raucous "Messieurs les étudiants." "You like this better?" He laughs, adding grotesque accents to the popular student song and varying the dynamics wildly.[17] "Much better," Trilby says, coming over to the piano. "Was that also written by a countryman of yours?" Svengali, tearing his hair, retorts: "Ach, heaven forbid, no—no!" He then suavely rolls a long chord from the bottom to the top of the keyboard, a diminished seventh (that long-standing chord of reversal), only to come crashing down ferociously on an ominous F#–C–F# tritone in the lowest range of the piano. Schizophrenically Svengali resumes improvising sweetly, turning to Trilby. Smiling, he asks, "Are you fond of music, mademoiselle?"

The scene continues in this manner. Svengali eventually convinces Trilby to sing. She chooses "Ben Bolt," an English ballad, although it is immediately evident to everyone except Svengali that she has a terrible voice. Near the end of the act Potter requested that the orchestra be used in a way rarely allowed during the play. Trilby and Billee got into an argument earlier, and he stormed out. Trilby turns to Laird to explain how she and Billee are expecting to be married and—in tears—how she plans to be a good wife to him, when the orchestra quietly begins to play the melody of *L'Adieu*. It is obvious that the orchestra for one rare occasion has taken on Svengali's persona, for the tune serves to manipulate her into his clutches. (A different reading may argue that by stealing Trilby away from Billee and putting her on the stage Svengali is trying to save her from the tedium of bourgeois married life.)

Trilby exhibits a new relationship between music and drama that is increasingly evident in the 1890s. While the variety of music used in this play would seem to differ greatly from the concept of the "artistic whole" embodied in the original symphonic theatre scores by Jacobi, German, Sullivan, and others, music in general is just as important a presence, both in terms of quality—nearly all the music is recognizable to the audience, even that from the standard classical repertory—and in the integrity and relevance of each number to the ideas in the play and Tree's conception.

So far music has not been found for A. M. Palmer's production of *Trilby* at the Garden Theatre in New York, though a playbill indicates that the orchestra indeed played Schubert's *Rosamunde* and the Chopin impromptu. Wilton Lackaye may have been the first to portray Svengali on any stage, but it was Tree who created the indelible portrayal that would survive into the twentieth century.

When Beerbohm Tree opened his new theatre Her Majesty's in 1897, he began to produce plays that afforded him heroic roles. Shakespeare plays featured prominently, and the first of these was *Julius Caesar*, for which Raymond Roze provided an elaborate original and thematic score. Roze (1875–1920) was French-born, the son of opera singer Marie Roze. Trained musically in Brussels, he was something of a prodigy both on the piano and with the baton. The eminent orchestra conductor Henry Wood may have questioned the young man's tenacity to study composition seriously, but he later programmed two of Roze's theatrical overtures, *Sweet Nell of Old Drury* and *Antony and Cleopatra*. Roze was only twenty-one in 1897 when he became music director for Her Majesty's Theatre, and many of his scores received excellent reviews. *Punch* found the music for his *Rip van Winkle* (1900), for example, "effectively dramatic and of the greatest assistance to the action." Several reviewers praised the "exquisite incidental music" for *Julius Caesar* and other plays. Bernard Shaw's opinion of the *Julius Caesar* music, however, was that it "missed the Roman vein rather badly." If Roze was going to imitate other composers (the soldiers' chorus from *Faust*) he might at least have found his inspiration in the great Greek-themed overtures of Gluck, Shaw groused.[18] Despite the lack of Shaw's imprimatur, the *Julius Caesar* music was later given in concert at Drury Lane. Roze's opera *Joan of Arc* (1913) enjoyed twenty performances at Covent Garden.[19]

Roze came to Her Majesty's at a time when there was a sudden burst of interest in the historical melodrama. Irving's arty efforts like *King Arthur* even then were beginning to seem staid and old-fashioned. But when Clement Scott saw Lewis Waller's gracefully athletic D'Artagnan in *The Three Musketeers* at the Globe Theatre, he wrote that "the old brigade rubbed their eyes with delight, for it seemed as if old times had returned again, with their spirit, vivacity, and admirable elocution. As for the youngsters, they were not ashamed to own that there was something after all in romantic drama when led by a young actor. No more dawdling, no more pauses, no more irritating atmosphere of depression and dullness."[20] Waller was making a sensation all over London in this fast-action drama, which astonished Scott and many less sentimental critics as well.

Dozens of English-language versions of Dumas's novel had occupied theatres a few decades earlier. During the 1890s, however, the educated West End playgoers that Irving managed to enthrall in the 1880s turned to the new drama of Henrik Ibsen, Gerhart Hauptmann, and Maurice Maeterlinck. Theatrical managers in both London and New York who specialized in spectacle, like George Alexander and Charles Frohman, were well aware of this new trend. Suddenly, however, it was possible for a novel like Anthony Hope's *The Prisoner of Zenda* (1894) to become an international craze. For teenaged to adult readers, *Zenda* brought chivalry back into vogue. Managers realized that they could reap profits with big historical melodramas, if they were staged with lots of action and brimming with exciting music. As a play *Zenda* had a spectacular theatrical run in New York in 1895 as produced by Frohman and was taken up the following year in London by George Alexander at the St. James's. *Zenda* was a sensational swashbuckler, with a fictional court, a deposed king, and even a charismatic villain, Rupert of Hentzau, who escapes in the end to return in the sequel named after him.[21] Add to *Zenda*'s popularity the additional success of Edmond Rostand's *Cyrano de Bergerac* in 1897, and it comes as little surprise that at least five versions of *The Three Musketeers* opened within the year. The two outstanding ones were Henry Hamilton's for the Metropole (carried over to the Globe) and Sydney Grundy's for Her Majesty's. Both versions toured extensively in the United States. E. H. Sothern starred in Hamilton's version, while James O'Neill promoted Grundy's version.

The critics were nearly unanimous in their assessment of Grundy's version as a series of pictures rather than a well-rounded drama with fully fleshed-out characters. *Musketeers* made its mark as spectacle, wrote an eyewitness in the *Academy*, rather than as drama.[22] Grundy's play was never published. The only typescript available—in the old microcard series *English and American Drama of the Nineteenth Century*—is essentially a draft script and includes none of the elaborate stage business that was used in London and New York. In order to fit Roze's music to the staging we must turn to the surviving promptbooks for this information.[23]

Tree mounted a gorgeous and expensive production and assembled a fine cast, even managing to get Waller to give up his run at the Globe to play the Duke of Buckingham. The most significant actors were Helen Maud Holt (Mrs. Tree) as Queen Anne of Austria, Cora Brown-Potter as the deliciously evil Milady de Winter, Franklin McLeay as the ruthless Cardinal Richelieu, Norman McKinnel as the conspiring Rochefort, captain of Richelieu's guards, and a winning team for the three musketeers: Gerald du Maurier, Louis Calvert, and Frank Mills. Backdrops were painted by Walter Johnson, and "the tremendously heavy scene plot" was designed and built by William

Telbin, Joseph Harker, and Walter Hann. To coach the extensive sword-play, Tree hired Alfred Hutton, captain of the queen's dragoon guards. Raymond Roze composed all the music and led the orchestra.

The drama is laid out in ten tableaux and takes place at the time of Louis XIII. The queen of France has indiscreetly given her admirer, Lord Buckingham, a diamond necklace presented to her by the king. Richelieu, who has been scheming for the queen's downfall with the help of Milady, slyly urges the king to request that his consort wear this necklace at a ball. Thanks to the gallantry and dash of D'Artagnan and his comrades (Athos, Porthos, and Aramis), the necklace is recovered in time, much to the cardinal's chagrin. Grundy's version begins with a stormy prologue that reveals the incident leading to Milady's hatred of the queen. But in the true spirit of the popular drama the play ends happily, with the king and queen reconciled and Milady merely banished for her treason instead of executed.

Roze's orchestra for *Musketeers* was large: thirty-six musicians. When he prepared a list of the "band required" to accompany a duplicate set of parts sent to New York for the opening at the Broadway theatre, he listed "six first violins, four second violins, three violas, three celli, three bassi, two flutes, one oboe, two clarinets, two bassoons, two horns, two cornets, two tenor trombones, one bass trombone (in G), one harp, one tympani, and one drum set." The score contains a substantial thematic overture and thirty music cues, many of them very long. The first violin part alone is fifty-six pages. The cues are all of the through-composed variety, some of them bringing a scene to its climactic conclusion, some bridging the scene change and even carrying on into the opening of the next scene. Some are character-entrance cues: for example, no. 5 for the entrance of Milady and no. 9 for the queen (who is "returning from Vespers"). These were characteristic pieces, to be sure, but Roze cleverly used colorful orchestration to complement the splendor of the richly brocaded gowns worn by both actresses.

Tableau 3 opens on the imposing grand quadrangle of the Louvre. In this scene D'Artagnan first encounters the three musketeers. In the second tableau he has made an enemy in Rochefort but has been spared at the request of Milady, who realizes that she might have use for him. The king questions D'Artagnan, only to discover that the youth has gotten into trouble with several of his musketeers as well, each of whom awaits a duel with him that afternoon. After the king departs, the musketeers—mostly in jest—challenge the awkward youth, who nevertheless puts up an expert fight. This "mock battle" (for Athos, Porthos, and Aramis, anyway) occurs without music. But Rochefort and the cardinal's guards have been observ-

FIGURE 41. The Musketeers, *no. 13, mm. 2–10. Transcribed from orchestra parts in the Herbert Beerbohm Tree Theatre Music Collection, Boston Public Library*

ing from a distance. As they move in to arrest the duelers for breaking the peace, music begins for the real fight. Here are the directions from Tree's promptbook:

> D'ART flings himself on Rochefort, going round and round him, fighting. Athos engages two of the guards—D'ART wounds Rochefort, who falls. Athos has dropped upon one knee, but still defends himself—D'ART attacks one of his adversaries. Athos rises and hurls himself upon the other, whom he drives back. In the upshot, the Guards are all struck down, a musketeer standing over each.
>
> *Rochefort*. [supporting himself on one elbow] "A truce!"

Roze's wonderfully picaresque music for the fight, cue no. 13, began with the cellos leading off in minor mode in what is to become the "musketeers motive" (Fig. 41).

After their triumph over Rochefort the musketeers swear allegiance with D'Artagnan joining ("all for one and one for all"). Without a break, the music reaches a victorious climax (Fig. 42).

This scene "was calculated to stir the blood of the most sluggish person," wrote Arthur Lawrence.[24] The exultant music comes to a blazing finish as the curtain falls, which allowed the audience to applaud the satisfying realism of Alfred Hutton's masterfully coached sword fight.

Before the applause could die out, the orchestra launched into the frolicsome musketeer music again, this time bridging into lengthy scene-

FIGURE 42. The Musketeers, *no. 13, mm. 76–83*

change music (nos. 14 and 14½). The music transitions gradually from the heroic "all for one" character to a darker mood. Finally, out of the shadows of tremolo and other gloomy chords, a new anguished theme emerges (Fig. 43).

It is the next evening, in Milady's chambers. As the curtain rises, the music has taken on a warmer glow, the murky timbre of lower clarinets and bassoons suggesting ominous dealings ahead. Rochefort and two guards emerge through a secret panel. Once the guards have secured the two main entrances to the room, the cardinal himself appears. The music continues to flow, and Richelieu enters to muted string chords that slither through troubled, murky harmonies (Fig. 44).

The slow, eerie procession of chords carries on as the cardinal asks Rochefort how his wound is doing. The captain replies that it smarts, but only for revenge. The cardinal requests that he not be interrupted. With a salute and a signal to the guards to exit, Rochefort slips out through the panel. Without a change in the character of the music, Milady enters, wearing a low-cut dress with only a kerchief covering her shoulders. She curtsies to the cardinal, who motions her to a seat. Finally, the chords fade out unobtrusively as the two begin to converse ("I have grave news from England").

Throughout their serious discussion of Buckingham and the Protestant threat to France, the orchestra has been silent. At the conclusion of their talk, during which the cardinal has given her a document (private orders to assassinate Buckingham), he taps at the panel. Rochefort emerges. "In

FIGURE 43. The Musketeers, *no. 14½, mm. 36–43*

FIGURE 44. The Musketeers, *no. 14½, mm. 50–62*

case of accident," the cardinal instructs him, "you will remain here with your guards. But interfere on no account unless Milady calls. If you have any news I shall be in my cabinet." Rochefort salutes as the cardinal exits through the panel, leaving Milady alone. At this point the orchestra begins cue no. 15 (entitled "Love Scene" in the parts). The cello solo and murmuring strings—though lyrically romantic—are obviously establishing a mood that is disingenuous (Fig. 45).

Some unspecified business with incense occurs, then Milady rings for her servant. "Show in D'Artagnan," she orders. As the music continues, Milady puts away the document in a casket containing a long slender poignard, which she fingers for a moment before returning it to its place. The servant reenters with D'Artagnan, now wearing a musketeer's tabard of blue velvet. "Welcome, chevalier," Milady addresses him admiringly and then says to her servant: "I am at home to nobody—observe—to nobody." The servant nods and exits. D'Artagnan speaks one aside, "I am in luck's way," and then comes forward a bit awkwardly. At this point the music again fades imperceptibly into silence.

The unaccompanied scene that followed was among the most effective dialogue sequences in the play. The beautiful and refined Milady first manipulates the impetuous D'Artagnan into falling in love with her. Then she inveigles him into avenging her "betrayal" by agreeing to kidnap the Duke of Buckingham, who, she now insinuates, poses a dangerous threat to the queen as well. D'Artagnan is taken in by all of this and vows to find Buckingham with the help of his musketeers. Milady, suddenly unsettled, is mistrustful of these men (knowing that Rochefort reported them to the cardinal yesterday) and denounces one of them as a drunkard. D'Artagnan comes to his friend's defense, even sharing his secret knowledge of Athos's past (his mysterious wife branded as a criminal whom he hung up to die). Milady is of course that same branded woman. Her startled cry alarms Rochefort, who peeks in just long enough to be noticed. The confused D'Artagnan engages in a tangle with the lady to reach the secret panel, when her kerchief falls open to reveal the brand. Their struggle brings them over her casket. Milady quickly reaches inside for her weapon and tries to defend herself with it. Her cries for help signal music cue no. 16, a tremolo with the cellos leading off with an agitated minor-mode version of the musketeer motive.

All is becoming clear to D'Artagnan. As Rochefort flies to the rescue, the young musketeer fights his way upstage, managing to fling the captain's sword from his hand. D'Artagnan reaches the window, at which point the

FIGURE 45. The Musketeers, *no. 15, mm. 1–12*

musketeer music freezes on a tremolo-sustained diminished seventh—the chord of reversal. With an "*au revoir*, Milady," D'Artagnan leaps from the window. The orchestra immediately launches into music cue no. 16½—a victorious rendering of the musketeer theme—while an enraged Milady rushes to the window and hurls the poignard after him. D'Artagnan's offstage laughter assures us that she missed. The rousing music plays on as the curtain falls and continues through the long scene change into D'Artagnan's lodgings (tableau 5).

The Musketeers ran only a few months. But Tree took it on tour and sold the rights to Theodore Liebler and George Tyler in New York for an opening at the Broadway Theatre in March 1899. The Broadway was one of the larger New York theatres, in terms of both the stage and orchestra. It would host William Young's dramatization of *Ben-Hur* with a live chariot race later that year. For the Liebler *Musketeers*, Raymond Roze's music was retained more or less intact, although the leader of the Broadway Theatre was Richard Maddern, who led the performances. A few of the music changes were significant. For example, in the dialogue scene with Milady and D'Artagnan, the Liebler promptbook says "music through all this." There is no extra music cue in the Liebler set of parts, so the musicians may well have repeated no. 15 or perhaps returned to some of the mysterious scene-change music. Some of Roze's cues in the Liebler parts are also marked out in pen. These may have been cut in the New York production or perhaps may have been simplified for local orchestras during the national tour. In any case, when *Musketeers* opened in Boston in January 1900, the program announced "exactly as played in London and New York."

Belasco and a Modern Melodrama of Japan

By the time David Belasco produced *The Darling of the Gods*, he had written or directed plays for seventeen New York theatres. Though nearly every aspect of his life in New York exemplified the mystique and glamour of the modern stage, Belasco was devoted to the popular drama and to entertaining "the great mass of people of moderate means." He hoped to thrill his audiences, to get them "emotional, quivering, frightened."[25] But instead of relying on journalistic sensationalism his goal was to find the uncanny in simple, natural, even beautiful things. In 1902 he also got a theatre of his own. He had just produced the monumental *Du Barry*, an eighteenth-century French costume extravaganza on the scale of Irving's *Dead Heart*. Using antique Bourbon furniture and props, hundreds of costumes for a cast of 200, and candle lighting to imbue the stage with period romance, Belasco astounded his audiences and set fashion trends, even as he shocked them with the amorality of life at the decadent French court. William Furst, with whom Belasco already had a long association, provided an equally elaborate score, consisting of both original music and period pieces. *Du Barry* was carried over from the Criterion. On 3 December the Belasco Theatre featured its first new production, *Darling of the Gods: A Drama of Japan*. Leading the orchestra in the theatre's sunken pit, Furst again provided the music.

Darling gave Belasco and John Luther Long a chance to correct some of the errors that they had made in their earlier collaboration, *Madame Butterfly* (1900), which by all accounts was not a success. Blanche Bates, who had created Cho-Cho San, returned as the princess Yo-San, a character of greater dimension. Though Belasco still retained some use of pidgin English, he dispensed with the misplaced attempt at dialect that mars the earlier character. The cast of *Darling* included over forty solo parts, as well as imperial soldiers, geisha girls, maids-in-waiting, heralds, acrobats, and many other supers.

Belasco's only published version, in *Six Plays* (1928), does not represent *Darling* as performed in 1902. His manuscript and original prompt copy have not been found. But the Tree Collection (Boston) has a set of five promptbooks prepared by him (signed "property of David Belasco") and sent to Beerbohm Tree for performances in London. A secondary interleaved promptbook in the University of Toronto Library may have been used on one of Belasco's touring productions. Moreover, William Furst jotted down pages of instructions to his English counterpart on timings and sight cues. The following information on dialogue and action is derived from these.

The play takes place about 1876, during the Japanese Meiji Restoration. This is the period of the "sword edict," when the emperor seized control by confiscating the weapons of the samurai, the military nobility of preindustrial Japan. The production (three and a half hours long) was structured in five acts and ten scenes or "pictures," as Belasco called them. The *Washington Post* called it "probably the most elaborately costumed play ever produced in America."[26] The depiction of Japan was extravagant and wildly Orientalist. A Japanese audience member described the settings as "cluttered." Though the central historic conflict was correctly represented, this observer wrote, very little else about the play reminded him of his country.[27]

The princess Yo-San, "darling of the gods," is betrothed in childhood to a nephew of Zakkuri, the evil minister of war (played by George Arliss). As a young woman she falls in love with Prince Kara (Robert T. Haines), now leader of a group of ten samurai outlaws who refuse to comply with the emperor's edict. Kara is invited as a guest of Yo-San's father, the prince of Tosan (Charles Walcot), but he is wounded in a skirmish with Zakkuri's guards. The resourceful Yo-San hides him in her apartments and nurses him to health. Her indiscretion is discovered by one of Zakkuri's spies. Although she swears "Before Shaka, God of Life and Death," that she has not seen Kara, the outlaw is captured and condemned to torture and death. Like Victorien Sardou and Giacomo Puccini's villain in *Tosca*, the treacherous Zakkuri horrifies Yo-San with the torture chamber and promises life and freedom for her lover if she will reveal the whereabouts of his loyal comrades, thus sealing her own fate and Kara's. Zakkuri ambushes the outlaw band and murders Kara's samurai. Kara himself commits hara-kiri. After a thousand years in the Japanese equivalent of hell as punishment for her betrayal, Yo-San is permitted to join her lover in paradise, where he awaits her with outstretched arms.[28]

In his youth William Furst (1852–1917) moved from Baltimore to San Francisco, where he eventually became director of the orchestra of the Tivoli Theatre. There he began his association with Belasco, for whom he provided music at the Baldwin Theatre and who brought him to New York. Furst became a conspicuous and increasingly admired orchestra leader, beginning with Belasco's *The Girl I Left Behind Me* (1893) at the Empire Theatre, after which he wrote music for dozens of Belasco plays. Charles Frohman, realizing Furst's dramatic gifts, teamed him up with playwright and actor William Gillette to produce a revised *Secret Service* in 1896 that proved one of the most successful American dramas of the decade. *Munsey's Magazine* wrote that in *Darling of the Gods* "the ear is kept on the alert by William Furst's music, never insistent, always appropriate."[29] Another reviewer wrote: "The music was an extremely artistic invention . . . It was saturated with the atmosphere of the play. It interpreted rather than embellished the action."[30] Brander Matthews, who described the "brooding mystery" of the production, wrote that "the accompanying music is almost incessant, but so subdued, so artfully modulated, so delicately adjusted to the action, that perhaps a majority of the audience was wholly unconscious of the three Japanese themes which had been insisted upon again and again."[31]

Furst prepared no less than seventy-three music cues for the five-act drama. The pit orchestra was large: full strings and winds (including English horn), four French horns, two trumpets, three trombones and tuba, harp, and timpani as well as a percussion group of woodblock, cymbals, and celesta. In addition, a number of instruments were required to mimic the Japanese instruments onstage. Audiences *saw* a biwa, shamisen, koto, tsudzumi, and fuye, but they *heard* a guitar, two mandolins, a harp, a drum, and a flute. Furst prepared a piano score (presumably for rehearsal rather than to lead the orchestra, because it has no instrumentation marked). The violin leader book includes a rare new addition to melodramatic scoring: complete metronomic indications for all tempos.

Act 1 opened with an unnumbered orchestral prelude played before the curtain. With the music change to a solemn *maestoso* in 5/4 (no. 1), the curtains parted to reveal a drop scrim, upon which was painted a shrine of the Buddha of Kama Kura with the sacred mountain in the background. As the backlights came up, this faded into a garden in the yashiki of the prince of Tosan (no. 2 began at the fade, leading with the first playing of the "Yo-san theme," see Fig. 49). The scrim remained in place until details of the garden lit by the sunset came into view and then rose. Setsu, Yo-san's maid, was alone onstage. A long pantomime to music for solo flute and strings followed. Specifying the measure numbers in the music, Furst's notes to the conductor began:

Mm. 1–10 Setsu discovered R, arranging flowers in basket
Mm. 11–16 Yo-San enters across bridge with armful of flowers, goes straight to Setsu and gives them to her
Mm. 17–23 Yo-San goes to bush no. 1, plucks single Iris, takes it to Setsu
Mm. 24–34 Yo-San then goes to bush no. 2, busily engaged plucking flowers
Mm. 35–40 A butterfly flies from bush no. 3. Setsu calls Yo-San's attention to it. Yo-San turns and sees it

It continued this way on two sheets of paper through 119 measures of music. Catching the butterfly in her hand, Yo-San realizes that she has accidentally crushed it (at this moment Furst cleverly combines Yo-San and Prince Kara's themes, foreshadowing the tragic outcome). Distant thunder rolls ominously. Yo-San, frightened, grasps Setsu as the thunder grows louder. While the flute and strings blithely carry on with the delicate pantomime music, the two women hear Kaëde's voice calling offstage. This imposing lady has come for Yo-San's lesson in manners. As the evening light grows darker, Yo-San and Setsu run off. The curtain closes.

The pantomime music comes to an end, with the cue for the stage band (no. 3). This is music heard from the palace interior, played by a flute, a guitar, two mandolins, and a harp. The curtains part in dim light to reveal the banquet room, decorated for the "feast of a thousand welcomes." The shadowy forms of servants are seen moving against the flicker of lanterns. Lantern-bearers and torch-bearers enter, gradually filling the room with more light. A soft blue moonlight comes up outside, revealing the misty courtyard gardens and stone steps leading to the palace. The stage is gradually and radiantly illuminated first with blue calciums and then with foot and border lights.

The offstage music continues throughout the next sequence. The prim Kaëde is perturbed not to find her young charge waiting for her. Yo-San eventually enters hurriedly. While they are preparing for the lesson, Shusshoo, the major domo, arrives to set the places for the prince and his guest of honor: Kara, the outlaw samurai. After Shusshoo finishes his inspection, he goes off. With soft gongs, the music changes (no. 4). The prince of Tosan is heard in an anteroom, greeting his guests, while Yo-San peers off, shocking her maid by counting the men she sees with great wonder. She then looks among the cushions, seeing the parchment cards for each guest. "Prince Kara," she reads, not realizing that this is the young man she fell in love with three days earlier on Hakone Mountain. The offstage band finishes its music.

Kaëde tries to get the lesson going. Yo-San's betrothed, Tonda-Tanji, is expected to call shortly. Yo-San is too excited to focus. In the distance they suddenly hear a young woman singing (no. 6). This is Rosy Sky, a geisha who has come to entertain the guests (her song is based on an actual geisha melody). Once she arrives, a lighthearted scene ensues, involving the three women and their maids. It begins without music. Yo-San seems ignorant of the geisha life. Each of Rosy Sky's frank admissions shocks Kaëde but fascinates Yo-San. "You must be a good girl," Yo-San deduces innocently, putting her arm around Rosy Sky, "to be dedicated to love." With Kaëde's "reprehensible!" delicate *faux* Japanese music (no. 7) crackles up from the orchestra with percussion—woodblock, cymbals, and celeste. The change in the character of the music suggests a different side of Yo-San: she is a woman of forceful determination. She ushers Kaëde away as unfit for love. As the music fades, she moves in close to Rosy Sky. They discuss face painting and engage in "kissing practice." Their delicate play continues until Kaëde re-enters, warning that Yo-San's father is arriving with Zakkuri. As Rosy Sky rushes off, trumpet and trombone fanfares are heard offstage.

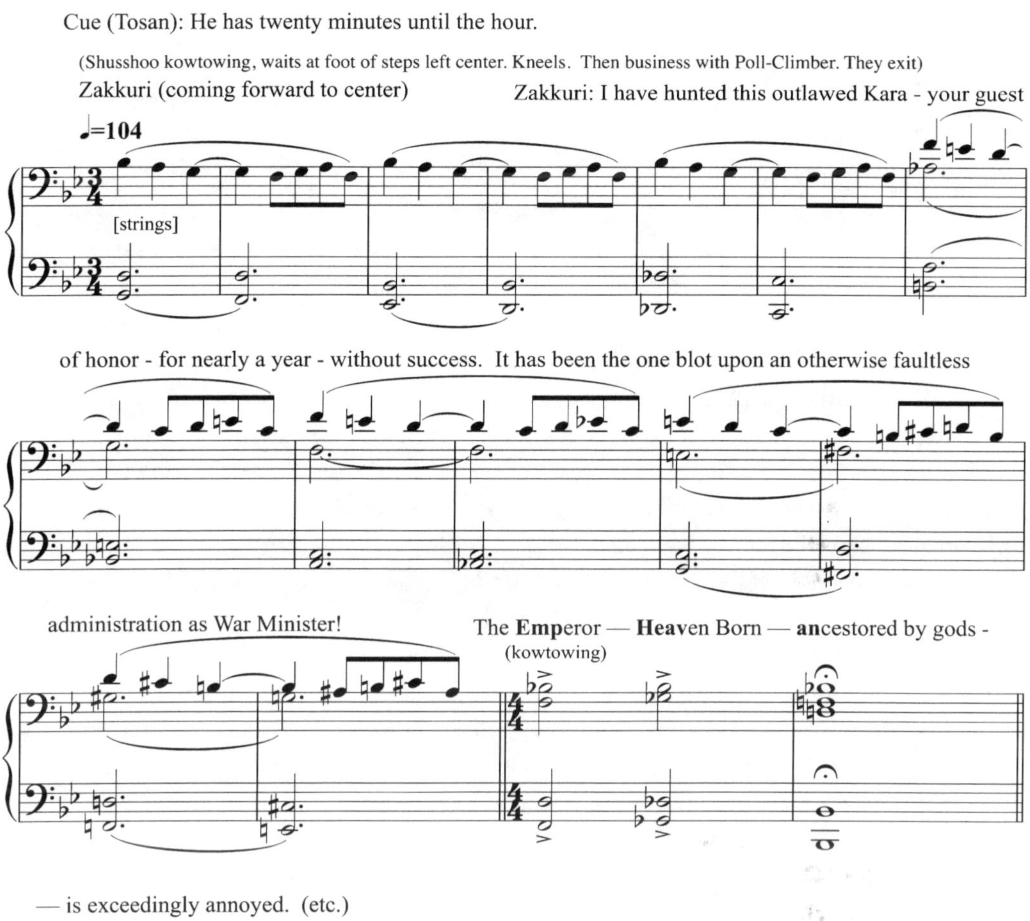

FIGURE 46. The Darling of the Gods, *no. 8. Transcribed from orchestra parts in the Belasco Collection of Incidental Music and Musicals, New York Public Library*

Yo-San's father, a man of regal bearing, enters, closely followed by Zakkuri (without music). Music no. 8, an under-dialogue *melos*, begins when Tosan turns to Zakkuri, referring to Kara (Fig. 46). As Zakkuri pauses to bow at each of his three pointed references to the Imperial Meiji, the orchestra pauses with him. This sly obsequiousness sets the tone for the focused dialogue to follow, without music. Tosan makes evident his unsympathetic views of the emperor and his admiration for Kara and those brave traditionalists who resist the tyrannical edict. Though Zakkuri has the authority to arrest anyone for such a treasonous assertion, he chooses to ignore the comment because he is aware that Tosan serves as a useful decoy. In a forceful aside Zakkuri turns to his guards and quietly orders them to wait and kill Kara before he enters the palace.

As Kaëde arrives to inform Tosan that his daughter is ready for the second visitation with her betrothed, onstage music begins again (no. 10), this time to accompany Tonda-Tanji, who makes his entrance in mid-song. He sings in a high falsetto and accompanies himself on a shamisen (played offstage by a mandolin). Tonda-Tanji is a dandy of Japan and wears a large lotus flower. Zakkuri greets him somewhat reluctantly as "exquisite and highly scented nephew." The watchman formally announces the entrance of the exalted princess Yo-San, as a lone oboe begins to play offstage. Over this instrumental solo the prince informs Zakkuri that the couple are to decide the hour of their marriage. Six girls enter carrying three large figured and transparent screens. The orchestra begins to play Yo-San's theme (no. 11), while the girls open the screens to make a private room for Yo-San. The princess enters in a state kimono glittering with gold embroidery, holding a fan between herself and the men with a great show of modesty. When she is enclosed within the screens, the music stops.

The dialogue between Yo-San and Tonda-Tanji begins without music. It is apparent that Yo-San does not think much of her betrothed. Some of her comments embarrass her father, who makes excuses to Zakkuri for the lack of maternal influence. The dialogue underscoring begins at this point, and the orchestra accompanies the rest of their scene (nos. 12, 13, and 13½). Yo-San naïvely confesses to having met a brave young man with whom she has fallen in love. Her description of the man produces a stern glance of recognition between her father and Zakkuri. Tonda-Tanji asserts that he too can be brave. He vows to fight and kill the outlaw that his uncle seeks. Yo-san laughs this off. Music no. 14 begins as the girls disassemble the screens and Yo-san prepares to leave. The orchestra is gently playing the "Yo-San theme" but is immediately halted by a gong and the offstage band (no. 15), which greets Tosan's arriving guests with boisterous music. As they enter, acrobats perform onstage to the lively dance number.

Meanwhile Zakkuri's guard has come in to say that his men have successfully ambushed and killed Kara. Zakkuri has no sooner greeted the news with joy, calling the outlaw a coward, than offstage trumpets announce the honored guest's arrival. Shusshoo rushes off to greet him, while a roll of drums is heard off right. The orchestra quietly begins no. 16, a noble march that grows in volume and intensity (Fig. 47). The guests are hushed with amazement as servants appear, strewing paper addresses of welcome. Shusshoo reenters, calling out: "The honorable guest of a thousand wel-

FIGURE 47. The Darling of the Gods, *no. 14*

FIGURE 48. The Darling of the Gods, *no. 19*

comes! His Highness, Kara, Prince of Chosu!" The prince appears in splendid regalia, evoking a murmur of admiration among the guests. Zakkuri is choked with rage. Advancing, the outlaw samurai firmly eyes the guests, whom he knows to be his enemies. Arriving downstage center at the *fortissimo* chords, he turns to Tosan. With a *maestoso* fanfare of trumpets—now onstage—he stretches out his hands and proudly offers his katana and daisho, which Tosan gives to Shusshoo to put on the sword-rack.

The next sequence leads to the climax of the act. Kara, we learn, has been seriously wounded in the ambush but is feigning excellent health, trying not to reveal to Tosan and his guests that he is actually bleeding to death. More lively dance music for tumblers and the geishas (nos. 17 and 18) only serves anempathetically to heighten the mounting tension: first as Kara falters in front of the guests and second as Yo-San enters unseen and recognizes him as her beloved. In the light of a golden shower of fireworks, the guests go out into the lamp-lit garden, while Kara informs his host that he must leave. Tosan knows that this means the young samurai's death. Respectfully bidding Kara "sayonara," Tosan exits. Meanwhile Tonda-Tanji detains Kara with a cup of wine, bragging that he plans to kill him the moment he steps out of the palace. Kara takes the cup, the cue for music no. 19 (Fig. 48).

During this solemn and ceremonial *misterioso*, played by only two instruments onstage, Zakkuri alerts his guards that Kara will be leaving shortly and exits. All the guests have dispersed into the night, so Tosan's servants gradually extinguish lights and draw a screen of silk across the room. Eventually—to the persistent sound of the taut *misterioso*—the only light in the hall is the moonlight and candlelight emanating from Yo-San's lantern. She

FIGURE 49. The Darling of the Gods, *no. 20*

observes Kara carefully, undetected. With a groan, he lets his sword fall. Realizing that he cannot survive another attack, he decides to kill himself. Yo-San moves toward him, gently calling his name. As she lifts the lantern up to reveal her face, music no. 20 begins (Fig. 49). The muted strings play a fragment of Yo-San's delicate theme.

Kara is too weak to do more than collapse near the sacred shrine. Yo-San reminds him that she gave him her soul on Hakoné. Kara tenderly affirms this. "I know a secret way," Yo-San says, calling on Inu, her faithful eunuch. Meanwhile music no. 21, an exact reprise of the tense *misterioso*, begins as Yo-San observes one of Zakkuri's spies lurking in the garden. "Put out the light!" she whispers. Inu helps Kara to hide behind a sliding *shoji*, where the princess is sure that he will be safe. With only the moonlight illuminating Yo-San, who quietly observes the moving shadows outside, the act ends with the sound of the softly throbbing music. As the curtains slowly close, the orchestra begins no. 22, transitional music that develops the English horn's mysterious "danger theme" of no. 21 into an interlude. The second act followed without an intermission.

The Darling of the Gods ran 182 nights, toured to several major cities, and was revived the following year for 64 performances. Drawing on Yo-San's theme music, the entertainment entrepreneur Sol Bloom published sheet music advertised as "The Story of David Belasco's Great Drama Told in Song." Blanche Bates appears in costume on the cover, but Furst is not mentioned, only the "arrangers." When *Darling of the Gods* was staged in Washington, however, an unidentified author in the *Washington Post* devoted an entire article to Furst's music. Here is the description of the last act:

> Then follows the war march of the Samurai . . . [with] a stirring, patriotic theme. It swells to full volume as Kara leads the forlorn hope up the rocky staircase against Zakkuri's musketmen. The curtain music

> is thematic in character, at the same time descriptive of the battle, interspersed with the clash of swords and the cries of the wounded. Kara's death march follows in slow, impressive measure. The music is continuous to the end of the play. It is heard during the death scene of Kara and Yo-San at the River of Souls, with its weird effect changing as the curtain rises on the Meido, or Buddhist first heaven. The harp solo is particularly effective during Yo-San's ascent to Kara. At the last embrace, Yo-San's theme is softly taken up and swells to crescendo at the final curtain.[32]

Any discussion of Furst's theatre music—notably for productions of *Madame Butterfly* and *The Girl of the Golden West*—has served largely to provide a context for Puccini's operas. In such comparisons the music to Belasco's plays seems less developed. But most of this music was never designed to stand on its own. Relying on simple melodies richly harmonized and luxuriously orchestrated, Furst's music was meant to help glamorize Belasco's productions, thereby making them even more irresistible to audiences. As good theatre music, it added characteristic value and a degree of "truthfulness" to the acting, costumes, lights, setting, and sound effects. In keeping with the technical polish so typical of the big London and New York theatres, music helped integrate these components into an artistic whole, recalling Irving, "in which no element shall be unduly obtrusive." This was music that brought a host of new techniques, colors, and moods to the popular drama. But it was also deeply rooted in the melodramatic traditions of the past.

CONCLUSION
The Legacy of Melos

Melodramatic theatre, as this book demonstrates, emerged out of pantomime and the intersection of legitimate theatrical traditions in the last two decades of the eighteenth century. Staging and music were bound tightly together in this new form, and the conventions established in London's minor theatres infused the Anglo-American popular drama as it branched outward (and upward) into domestic, crime, sensational, historical, romance, national, western, and other subgenres. By the first decade of the twentieth century the popular drama had attained unprecedented levels of prestige, glamour, and commercial success. The basic criteria identified in chapter 1 were still distinctly present in Tree's *Musketeers* and Belasco's *Darling of the Gods*: (1) some connection to a "true story" or historical characters, (2) a folk hero or outlaw as protagonist, with a formidable rival (= villain), (3) a clear moral message and happy ending, (4) considerable use of special effects, and (5) music to chart the emotional and moral terrain and to underscore the villain's errors. In the 1920s a new generation of modern playwrights arrived to challenge nineteenth-century conventions of the popular drama. But the three-act melodramatic form proved incredibly resilient. It thrived in the new popular media, especially in the narrative platforms of film, radio, and television.

At the dawn of the twentieth century the concept of "melodramatic music" varied widely. In most provincial stock theatres the musical language seemed not to have evolved a great deal since the old days of Buckstone's *Jack Sheppard* and Davenport's *Oliver Twist*.[1] But a major transformation had been evident in "high-class" Broadway and West End theatres since the 1870s, especially in terms of length of cues, musical styles, instrumental timbres, and manner of application. For George Alexander's production of *Paolo and Francesca* at the St. James's in London (1902), leader Percy Pitt followed the Irving model. He provided musical themes for each of the principal characters as well as four motives that served to reinforce the main "dramatic themes" throughout the play. Others followed the model established by T. W. Robertson. In Eugene Walter's *The Easiest Way* (Stuyvesant Theatre, 1909), an onstage organ grinder cranked out an insipid ragtime tune in the last scene, with the mechanical rendition objectifying the heroine's collapse into the seedy world of New York's Tenderloin.

Many actors still believed that music—whether from the orchestra or onstage—helped them to hold an audience's attention. Playwrights and directors still used music to highlight the structure of the play, clarify situations, and emotionalize characters and conflicts. Most audiences still expected moral orientation from the music. Critics claimed that Charles Frohman's production of *Notre Dame* (Daly's Theatre, 1901) failed to overcome Paul Potter's weak dialogue. But the final sequence of Esmeralda about to be burned at the stake and her dramatic rescue by Gringoire did not disappoint the audience. Frank Howson's orchestra accompanied the action with nearly continuous music, resembling the musical pantomime for the rescue of Dorothée at the Ambigu-Comique in 1780. Of course some critics continued to complain about the overuse (or misuse) of music, as they had for decades. Arthur Symons, for example, objected to the music in Alexander's *Paolo and Francesca*. This same literary critic, upon hearing actor Ernst von Possart narrate *Enoch Arden* with Richard Strauss's powerfully atmospheric accompaniment, considered this latest development in the fusion of dialogue and music "a step further along a downward path."[2] But as late as 1910 the drama critic Clayton Hamily wrote in his *Theory of the Theatre* that "a running accompaniment of music, half-heard, half-guessed, that moves to the mood of the play, now swelling to a climax, now softening to a hush, may do much toward keeping the audience in tune with the emotional significance of the action."[3] This opinion was certainly shared by Percy Cross Standing, who wrote a lengthy article in 1906 on all the best "composer-conductors" in the London theatres.[4] And by the 1920s and 1930s this idea came to dominate the aesthetics of major Hollywood film producers, who insisted on musical accompaniment for exactly these reasons.

Until about 1914 the popular drama on the stage was in a continual state of expansion, alongside vaudeville, the musical review, and operetta. Any discussion that would do justice to this medium from the 1890s to 1914 goes far beyond my own research and would require a book in itself. Though some American and British director-managers abandoned melodramatic music during this time—apparently following "the custom of most European theatres"—many held onto the conventions.[5] To offer just one instance, consider the Hippodrome Theatre in New York. Frederic Thompson and Elmer S. Dundy built this huge enterprise in 1905, and R. H. Burnside was stage manager. Arthur Voegtlin invented the amazing scenic effects. The music director from 1905 to 1915 was Manuel Kline, who had begun his career with Belasco. Kline provided scores for such dramatic spectacles as *The Battle of Port Arthur*, *The Earthquake*, *At the Court of Cleopatra*, and many others. One reviewer observed in 1912:

> Everything at the Hippodrome goes by music cues. It may be a certain strain, a blare of a trumpet, a beat of the drum, a shake of a tambourine. To the audience it is just a part of the music played by the orchestra. But to the army of performers and stagehands, 700 strong, it is a series of signals. Even the horses know their music cues. You can stop the human actor from responding to theirs, but a horse seems to regard his as a command that must be obeyed no matter what happens.
>
> At the cull of every scene, when in an ordinary theatre the signal would be for the curtain to fall, the Hippodrome has instead a music cue which means "lights off!" Instantly every light in the house except the red ones marking the exits goes out.[6]

In their traditional linking of music and spectacle, Voegtlin and Kline were indebted to the precision effects devised back in the days of Philip Astley at the Amphitheatre, to the sensational battles in Kemble's *Timour the Tartar*, and to the breathtaking horse race in Boucicault's *Flying Scud*.

Some managers discovered added benefits in using a compilation score, which had gained in prominence since the 1890s. English stage music had been "compiled" since the days of Restoration theatre, of course. But both the conveniences and the advantages of such a method can be seen in a more recent example from around the turn of the century. For their American touring production of Shakespeare's *Coriolanus* in 1901—the same year that Henry Irving produced *Coriolanus* with a big original score by Alexander Mackenzie—Charles B. Hanford, R. D. MacLean, and Odette Tyler used music drawn from well-known classical and light-classical works. The "score" was compiled of printed materials from the 1880s and 1890s, all arranged for theatre orchestra: "The Gladiator," a concert march by H. O. Wheeler (for the opening and for Coriolanus's early Roman scenes), Felix Mendelssohn's "Spring Song" (for the women's scenes), Louis Moreau Gottschalk's "The Dying Poet" (for Coriolanus in the military camp and for some of his later scenes), Moritz Moszkowsky's "Serenade" (for the collusion of Brutus and Sicinius), Gounod's "Queen of Sheba March" (at Coriolanus's renouncement of Rome), Gounod's "Ave Maria" (as a curtain tune for the scene in Antium), Chopin's "Funeral March" (following Aufidius's decision to join with Coriolanus against Rome), and Beethoven's "Funeral March" (to underscore Aufidius's final speech after Coriolanus's murder).[7] Such an approach was common on both sides of the Atlantic to attract middle-class audiences to more serious theatrical fare with music that they were likely to know and appreciate. In a paper on music to English stage plays, Norman O'Neill, leader at the Haymarket Theatre, complained about this "barbarous" technique. He found it intensely distracting when some melody by a well-known composer was used to underscore action or dialogue. "Let us rather have the old type," O'Neill submitted, "the constantly repeated and insignificant eight-bar phrases."[8]

Despite these various approaches to music, it has been possible to examine the three stages of the nineteenth-century popular drama in a single book because they relate to one another so logically. But the threads that held the popular drama together—inevitability of construction, narrative closure, moral certainty—began to unravel in the 1910s. At least three developments at this time exerted a decisive impact on the use of melodramatic music. The first of these was the economic effect of the First World War on theatres, which brought significant changes in repertory and production style. Elaborate sets and large musical ensembles seemed extravagant in such times, if not financially impossible. Some theatres were reduced to using no music at all or perhaps at best a piano or organ if the type of play warranted musical accompaniment. The war years also decisively ushered in modernism and the avant-garde, which rebelled against the bourgeois trappings of theatrical illusion—the exaggerated "dream world" of the melodrama. Finally, the widespread appeal of modern dance styles and jazz, particularly in the 1920s, rendered old-fashioned the traditional use of melodramatic music and the sentiments that it was meant to affirm.

But as it had in the 1880s, the popular drama (and its music) experienced a surprising regenerative boost, this time from the cinema. The first wave occurred in the 1920s cinema palaces, with their elaborate musical accompaniments. The second wave followed in the 1930s, specifically in the large Hollywood film studios, with producers' insistence on full orchestras and an entire musical staff of composers, orchestrators, and arrangers. And the waves have been coming ever since—in the magnificent Cinemascope epics of the 1950s and 1960s (such as Anthony Mann's *El Cid*), in the breathtaking fantasy epics of the 1970s and 1980s (the *Star Wars* and *Indiana Jones* series), and in the *Lord of the Rings* series in the 2000s.

Music was absolutely indispensable, of course, in the photoplay, the multiple-reelers of the silent film era. Many of the formulaic accompaniments came directly from music publishers, who acquired them from musicians who had worked in the theatre. For example, Al Henderson, actor, singer of light opera, and orchestra leader, had his personal collection of original *melos* numbers published in New York and London by M. Witmark in 1901.[9] "No more is it necessary to ask: what shall I play while the 'heavy' and the 'hero' are dueling?" an ad promises, as if no such music had ever before been available.[10] Henderson's collection is an important one because it marks the transition from stock theatrical music of the nineteenth century to stock music for silent film, of which Witmark was a noted publisher. Selections include several livelies, hurries, *mysteriosos* [*sic*], tremolos and muteds, and martials as well as combats, *pizzicatos*, and other character pieces. One of the *andante mysteriosos* is a sweet tune in F major over a *pianissimo* tremolo, reminiscent of the ever-popular "Ghost Melody" from *The Corsican Brothers*. The collection was published in three formats—full orchestra, small orchestra, and piano—and was marketed as "valuable for minstrel afterpieces or any style of dramatic entertainment." By 1915 Witmark, in tandem with Carl Fischer, had enlarged this collection to vast proportions.[11] But by that time these editions were being produced more for films than for plays and were advertised as such in *Moving Picture World*. "Don't try to force any one kind of music on all your pictures," advised Clarence Sinn to what must have been thousands of movie house pianists and organists. "It is a good idea to have enough of this in your repertoire so that you don't have to constantly repeat yourself for scenes of similar character."[12] When organist Bob Mitchell accompanied *The Vanishing American* at its premiere in 1925 he relied on a fluid compilation of formulaic *melos* pieces such as hurries and plaintives, some improvised bits that "played through" the action, and well-known tunes appropriate to the situation.[13]

The theatrical technique of a compilation score also led the way to a more reliable and commercially successful approach to silent film accompaniment: using "prestige music" to enhance the glamour of the new medium. Adolph Zukor, president of the Famous Players Film Company, admitted that his model for the cinema was not vaudeville but the artistic and high-class theatrical productions of Charles and Daniel Frohman.[14] Control of the new medium required preparing musical instructions for dramatic accompaniment—like the theatrical music plots. Film studios began to distribute "cue sheets" in 1909 to aid the organists, pianists, or orchestra leaders responsible for providing music at each theatre. Many of these specified middlebrow fare: current popular tunes and familiar classical works. The cue sheets for silent film differed most from the music plots in their need to provide continuity, because—like *Dorothée*, *Robinson Crusoe*, and other serious pantomimes of the late eighteenth century—films like Zukor's *The*

Prisoner of Zenda (1913) required a nearly steady flow of music from start to finish.

At nearly the same time, advertisements in newspapers such as the *Kalem Kalendar* announced "Special Music for *Arrah-na-Pogue*" (1911), in which the Irish airs of Boucicault's original play were still being adapted to suit the photoplay "by an experienced composer" (W. C. Simons). *Moving Picture World* promoted "Daly's Version of *Frou Frou*" (1913) with "special musical accompaniment prepared by the Tams Music Library." For British screenings of the American film *The Mystery of Edwin Drood* (1914), Herbert H. Hainton composed and published a score that included titles such as "melos no. 1" and "melos no. 2." Surprisingly, while some prominent composers between 1900 and 1914 were writing music for the stage, very few made the transition to cinema. The most famous, of course, is Camille Saint-Saëns, who set a high tone with his score to *The Assassination of the Duke of Guise* (Société Film d'Art, 1908). The most important leader-composer to bring his experience with the popular drama to the screen was William Furst. Because of his reputation with Belasco, he was hired in 1916 to prepare a lengthy score for *Joan the Woman* by Cecil B. DeMille, who believed that every "important picture" should have a score "specially composed to tell its story."[15]

By the 1920s the major film theatres of New York, London, and other cities were beginning to resemble the large urban theatres of the late nineteenth century, with their substantial orchestras. In 1922 studios began to produce cue sheets with thematic incipits from which regional music directors could identify the *melos* of the cue and perhaps find a suitable substitution. The format had already existed informally in the theatre world. One unnamed actress at the Boston Theatre in the 1880s, for example, left behind a manuscript copy of her thematic music plot for *Fanchon, the Cricket*. Using similar thematic cue sheets, the organist or pianist for a silent film could make his or her own selection of music. In the 1920s both systems were in use, as they had been in nineteenth-century theatre: the largely original score and the largely compilation score. For Carl Laemmle's *The Hunchback of Notre Dame* (1923) the studio distributed a thematic cue sheet with a compilation of different mood and characteristic pieces so that organists in movie houses could accompany the picture appropriately. For the 1926 Paramount release of *Old Ironsides*, a full orchestra accompanied screenings in major cities such as Chicago and New York with a score of "original themes" by J. S. Zamecnik and Hugo Riesenfeld.

Photoplays were essentially pantomimes with music. Radio, with its mix of dialogue, music, and sound effects, was the first real beneficiary of the practices investigated in this book. Commercial radio in the 1920s and 1930s followed two paths: those of vaudeville or variety (with comic skits and musical numbers) and the radio play (enactments of popular dramas with an organ or a live orchestra providing background music). *The Eveready Hour*, the *Philo Vance* mystery series, and many small acting companies engaged for dramas by local radio stations in the United States and Britain used music interspersed throughout. By the 1930s the flow of money from advertising combined with technological advances in recording resulted in elaborate setups for actors and studio orchestras. Weekly series such as *The Lone Ranger*, *Cavalcade of America*, and *Lux Radio Theatre* regularly employed affective music to signify characters, to establish period and location, and to bridge sequences.[16] While radio dramas reproduced only the sounds of stage action, in many ways they resembled the nineteenth-century popular drama more closely than either silent or sound cinema, particularly in the way actors spoke their lines through live music.

Nevertheless, sound film inherited and adapted many musical conventions from the popular drama, especially when it came to creating atmosphere, defining genre, and articulating dramatic form. Beginning in the early 1930s—once music could be mixed in with dialogue and sound effects after the editing of the film—studio cue sheets again resemble the music plots of the nineteenth century: music stops and starts, initiated by some key word, action, or sound effect, and ends or fades out when it no longer serves its affective or structural purpose.[17] When and how music was to be used again became a matter of the director's taste, as it often was in the nineteenth-century popular drama.

Important musical differences among these changing media can be demonstrated with one example: Charles Reade's *Never Too Late to Mend*, which first appeared as a novel (1856) and then in several dramatized versions. Studios in England, Australia, and the United States produced five silent films based on this story between 1911 and 1926. All five versions would have required nearly continuous music. In the early two-reelers lasting only twenty-two minutes, music naturally would be needed to make the most of a character's few moments onscreen and quickly set up the conflicts. In 1937 George King produced a full-length sound version. This film contained only a smattering of music, provided anonymously (and possibly drawn from stock). Charles Reade's hero, an English farmer, has struck gold in Australia and returned a rich man. In Reade's play (Princess's, 1865), the hero recounts the incident in which the villain drugged him and stole his bank notes. The sound film actually shows this incident. The villainous squire—unctuously portrayed by Todd Slaughter—carries out his delicate maneuvers while accompanied by soft *pizzicato* music. Despite all the villainy afoot throughout the film, this is the only place where the producers decided to incorporate a *misterioso* cue. Like the music for Daly's Byke in the last act of *Under the Gaslight*, this distinctive *melos* is reserved for the one place where it serves a structural purpose—to alert audiences to the villain's *quiproquo*. In this pantomime sequence the villain is committing the final error that will lead to his downfall.

Similarly, Charles Chaplin, ever sensitive to music's dramatic effects, fashioned a great deal of it for his silent films. But in the scoring of his sound film *Monsieur Verdoux* (1947) he selectively employed only one *misterioso*. There it entered quietly as a macabre *pizzicato* for the bigamist's failed and humorous attempts to murder the latest of his many wives. The effect is almost identical to Charles Puerner's tongue-in-cheek *misterioso* for Blink's botched robbery in Belasco's *Lord Chumley*.

In the nineteenth century extended musical underscoring came to prominence in the sensation drama (*The Colleen Bawn*, *The Orange Girl*) and was harmonically and timbrally enriched in the more lavish orchestrations used by Irving, Frohman, Tree, Alexander, and others. As the quality and quantity of music in nineteenth-century melodramatic theatre varied from house to house (and from production to production), so did the quality of music in twentieth-century melodramatic film. With the advantage of enormous budgets, Hollywood studios of the 1930s established an irresistible linkage between music and storytelling. The legacy of *melos* resided in the "half-heard, half-guessed" musical references, the "swelling to a climax," and "keeping the audience in tune with the emotional significance of the action." Given the imprimatur of this tradition by Alexander Korda, David O. Selznick, John Ford, Michael Curtiz, Alfred Hitchcock, Orson Welles, and other producers and directors, composers such as Max Steiner, Alfred Newman, Erich Wolfgang Korngold, and Franz Waxman spun out melodramatic music to extraordinary lengths.

Selznick and Hitchcock, for example, were very particular about music in their films. But we can see how closely linked they were to the melodramatic tradition in their collaboration on *Spellbound* (1945). Surviving studio records, as Nathan Platte has demonstrated, show music notes with Hitchcock's specific requests for a "hurry" or a "misterioso" and Selznick's insistence on a "chord" of punctuation. Out of these basic and now centuries-old directives, Miklos Rozsa fashioned a beautiful, haunting, and largely original score. But even here, as Platte reveals, the end result involved a degree of compilation. For several prominent cues Selznick and his music editor incorporated stock or music previously written for other films.[18] For these producers, the affect of music was ultimately more important than stylistic coherence.

Throughout the history of melodramatic theatre, music directors responded to actor-managers' shorthand instructions as they "composed and arranged" music to complement the drama. The practical language to describe *melos* that evolved in nineteenth-century promptbooks and music plots may seem formulaic, but in many instances the actual music—not to mention the dramatic effect when combined with compelling acting—often went far beyond merely fulfilling stereotypical expectations. Competition drove innovation and creativity, as I have argued in this 150-year coverage of a tradition. Furthermore, the late eighteenth-century marriage of music and melodrama could not be suppressed, even in the complex moral universe of the twentieth century. On the contrary, this powerful heritage of the nineteenth-century stage has continued to define the emotional and moral registers of modern storytelling. Even twentieth-century plays that needed no music when staged acquired a musical voice on the screen. The kinds of music may have changed (for example, in the more frequent use of popular songs in film to replace *melos*). But *melos* is nevertheless represented in a seemingly endless flow of music in the "background" of almost every conceivable type of film and television narrative in the last eighty years. The nineteenth century developed a sophisticated (and often complex) use of music to deliver melodramatic theatre. This achievement, however modified in its accommodations to new technologies, has remained foundational to the aims and methods of those who write, direct, and produce dramatic entertainment.

NOTES

INTRODUCTION

1. Charles Dickens, *Sketches* (Leipzig: Tauchnitz, 1843), 111. Thomas Frost observed in 1825 that the orchestra of "Richardson's Theatre" consisted of "a band of 10 performers." *The Old Showmen and the Old London Fairs* (London: Tinsley Brothers, 1874), 266.

2. Laurence Hutton, *Plays and Players* (New York: Hurd and Houghton, 1875), 21–22.

3. Allardyce Nicoll identifies all sixty-six genres in *A History of English Drama, 1660–1900*, vol. 4 (Cambridge: Cambridge University Press, 1930), 246–247.

4. In 1853 playwright James Robert Planché parodied some of the principal genres. The genres of tragedy, comedy, burlesque (parody), English opera (sometimes also called "semi-opera"), ballet, pantomime, hippodrama (or equestian drama), and spectacle were all represented by characters in Planché's "Camp of the Combined British Dramatic Forces" in *The Camp at the Olympic* (London: Olympic, 1853). Parody cited in Michael R. Booth, *Theatre in the Victorian Age* (Cambridge: Cambridge University Press, 1991), 196.

5. *New York Evening Post* (25 June 1821): 3. Collins's ode was written in 1746.

6. For more on the late eighteenth-century term "characteristic," see Richard Will, *The Characteristic Symphony in the Age of Haydn and Beethoven* (Cambridge: Cambridge University Press), 4–11.

7. Perhaps the ambiguity of this term is more fully illustrated by its derivation "incidentally." When someone starts a sentence with this word, what follows is rarely inconsequential but often of utmost interest and importance and usually provides a telling bit of convincing evidence.

8. Martel's classification numbers (ML3860 for "incidental music" and ML3861 for "melodramatic music") are no longer used. "Theatrical music" (songs for plays) is now ML2000 and "theatrical melodrama" ML2050.

9. The tradition of inserting songs in the commedia dell'arte goes back at least to the sixteenth century, according to eyewitness accounts. See Martha Farahat, "Villanescas of the Virtuosi: Lasso and the *Commedia dell'arte*," *Performance Practice Review* 3, no. 2 (Fall 1990): 121–137.

10. See Curtis A. Price, *Music in the Restoration Theatre* (Ann Arbor: UMI Research Press, 1979). For "music within the drama" (1665–1713), Price identifies several categories, such as "melancholy music," "music for comic effect," "music for soliloquies," "music for discoveries," "music for love scenes, eulogies, and hunts," and "music for change of scene." He observes, however, that in most instances music "is

introduced to entertain the play-going courtiers rather than to deepen the effect of the drama" (3). See also W. J. Lawrence, "The English Theatre Orchestra: Its Rise and Early Characteristics," *Musical Quarterly* 3, no. 1 (January 1917): 9–27. A sample of a Curtain Tune (used presumably for the storm at the opening of the play) can be seen in *Matthew Locke, Incidental Music: The Tempest* [Duke's Theatre, 1674], in *Musica da Camera*, vol. 41, ed. Peter Dennison (London: Oxford University Press, 1977), 9–12.

11. Compare early editions in John Bell's collection *British Theatre* of *George Barnwell* (vol. 5, 1776) and *Douglas* (vol. 20, 1780) with the same plays in Frederick Fleischer's one-volume *British Theatre* (1828) (quotation).

12. Adolf Bernhard Marx, *Allgemeine Musiklehre* (Leipzig, 1839), 255; trans. G. Macirone as *General Musical Instruction* (London: Novello, 1854), 93.

13. Ibid., 92.

14. *Era* (11 December 1853), 16.

15. John Lawrence Toole and Joseph Hatton, *Reminiscences of J. L. Toole*, vol. 1 (London: Hurst and Blacett, 1889), 71.

16. *Dwight's Journal of Music* 33, no. 6 (28 June 1873): 47.

17. "Musical Chit-Chat," *Dwight's Journal* (29 September 1860), 215.

18. Franklin Peterson, "Studies in Modern Opera," *Monthly Music Record* 23, no. 276 (December 1893): 267; Richard Wagner, *Über das Dirigieren*, translated by Edward Dannreuther as *On Conducting* (London: W. Reeves, 1887), 18.

19. In his *Dictionary of Music* (1768, translated by William Waring; London: Printed for J. French, 1775), 229. Jean-Jacques Rousseau uniquely defines "melos" as "sweetness of melody" and claims that it derives from the Greek word for honey.

20. Charles Burney himself cites this definition in a footnote in his *General History of Music*, vol. 1 (London: Printed for the Author, 1776), 436. Andrew Barker, *Greek Musical Writings* (Cambridge: Cambridge University Press, 2004), 156. Barker's translation of Aristoxenus is found in the footnote to the first line of *Elementa Harmonica*, Book 1, p. 126. Francis Haskins Eyles Stiles, "An Explanation of the Modes of Tones in the Antient Graecien Music," *Philosophical Transactions*, vol. 51, part 2 (London: Royal Society of London, 1760), 733. For a major nineteenth-century music historian's views on Greek *melos*, see August W. Ambros, *Geschichte der Musik*, vol. 1 (Leipzig: F. E. C. Leuckart, 1862), 347.

21. J. M. M. [John M. Morton], "About Music Cues," *Music and Drama* 3, no. 1 (8 July 1882): 4–5.

22. *London Times* (22 June 1830), 6.

23. Jim Davis and Victor Emeljanow, *Reflecting the Audience: London Theatregoing, 1840–1880* (Iowa City: University of Iowa Press, 2001), 8.

24. "The Drama," *New Monthly Magazine and Literary Journal* 30, no. 118 (October 1830): 423.

25. "Melodrama," *All the Year Round* 21 (9 November 1878): 440.

CHAPTER 1

1. John Burgoyne, preface to *The Lord of the Manor* (1781), xiii–xiv.

2. Kalman A. Burnim, *David Garrick, Director* (Pittsburgh: University of Pittsburgh Press, 1961), 94.

3. Burgoyne, preface, xiii.

4. Garrick's account books for Drury Lane at times show payment to an instrumental ensemble of as many as twenty-one musicians. See George Winchester Stone Jr., "The Prevalence of Theatrical Music in Garrick's Time," in *The Stage and the Page: London's "Whole Show" in the Eighteenth-Century Theatre* (Berkeley: University of California Press, 1981), 117–118.

5. Marian Smith, "Borrowings and Original Music: A Dilemma for the Ballet-Pantomime Composer," *Dance Research* 6, no. 2 (Autumn 1988): 9.

6. A secondary musical allusion in this example is the line *dans les champs de la victoire*, which was a popular French folksong that would come to serve as a political anthem during the Revolution. "Dans les champs de la victoire" is listed in Conrad Laforte, *Le catalogue de la chanson folklorique française* (Québec: Les Presses de l'Université Laval, 1977), vol. 6 (*Chansons sur des timbres*), p. 84.

7. I have not been able to locate any of the music used in cases of noted readings of *The Passions* ("Mrs. Barnes will recite Collins's *Ode on the Passions*, with appropriate music," in the *Evening Post*, 25 June 1821, 3). Published musical works on Collins's *Ode* (in the eighteenth century by Benjamin Cooke, William Hayes, and others) are all cantatas.

8. See Aaron Hill, *Essay on Acting* [1746], published in vol. 1 of *The Works of the Late Aaron Hill* . . . (London: Printed for the benefit of the family, 1754); Henry Siddons, *Practical Illustrations of Rhetorical Gesture and Action*, 2nd ed., "Adapted to English Drama from a Work on the Subject by M. Engel, Member of the Royal Academy of Berlin" (London: Printed for Sherwood, Neely, and Jones, 1822); and Leman Thomas Rede, *A Guide to the Stage, or How to Enter the Theatrical Profession, Obtain an Engagement, and Become an Actor; Founded on and Partly Taken from Leman Rede's Book* (1832; later reprints by Samuel French).

9. On Diderot and the actor's control of the passions, see Joseph Donohue, "Actors and Acting," in Kerry Powell, ed., *The Cambridge Companion to Victorian and Edwardian Theatre* (Cambridge: Cambridge University Press, 2004), 29.

10. Paul Ekman, "An Argument for Basic Emotions," *Cognition and Emotion* 6 (1992): 169–200; and Dylan Evans, *Emotion: The Science of Sentiment* (Oxford: Oxford University Press, 2001), 1–30.

11. James Burgh, *The Art of Speaking*, 3rd ed. (London: T. Longman and J. Buckland, 1772), 13.

12. Johann Jakob Engel, *Ideen zu einer Mimik* (1785), 2nd ed., in *J. J. Engel's Schriften*, vol. 7, *Mimik*, part 1 (Berlin, 1804), 18 (my translation).

13. Gilbert Austin, *Chironomia, or A Treatise on Rhetorical Delivery* (London: T. Cadell and W. Davies, 1806), 214.

14. James Beattie, *An Essay on Poetry and Music as They Affect the Mind* (written in 1762) (Edinburgh: William Creech, 1778), 147.

15. Specific affects of music as links to particular emotional states are discussed by philosophers René Descartes and Athanasius Kircher in the seventeenth century and theorists Mattheson and Batteux in the eighteenth century, among others. René Descartes, *Les passions de l'âme* (1649); Kircher, *Musurgia universalis* . . . (1650); Johann Mattheson, *Der vollkommene Capellmeister* (1739); and Charles Batteux, *Les beaux arts réduits à un même principe* (1743).

16. Marc-Antoine Charpentier, *Régles de composition* (ca. 1692). Reproduced, with other examples, in Rita Steblin, *History of Key Characteristics in the Eighteenth and Early Nineteenth Centuries* (Rochester: University of Rochester Press, 1996), 30–40.

17. Mattheson, *Der volkommene Capellmeister*, p. 127, §45 (II, 4), trans. Dietrich Bartel and cited in his "Ethical Gestures: Rhetoric in German Baroque Music," *Musical Times* 144, no. 1885 (Winter 2003): 18.

18. Jean-Philippe Rameau's *opéra-ballet Pigmalion* was performed in Paris at the Opéra in 1748. A Viennese *ballet d'action* was staged by Gasparo Angiolini at the Käntnertor Theater with music by Joseph Starzer.

19. Horace Coignet, *Pygmalion: Scène Lyrique*, ed. Jacqueline Waeber (Geneva: Éditions Université–Conservatoire de Musique, 1997).

20. See Edgar Istel, *Jean-Jacques Rousseau als Komponist seiner lyrischen Scene Pygmalion* (1901; reprint Walluf bei Wiesbaden: Sändig, 1973); Emilio Sala et al., *Pygmalion* (Milan: Ricordi, 1996); Jacqueline Waeber, "*Pygmalion* et J.-J. Rousseau," *Fontest Artis Musicae* 44, no. 1 (January–March 1997): 32–41; Gerhard Sauder, "Rousseau und das Melodram," in *Musik als Text* (Kassel: Bärenreiter, 1998); Raymond Court, "Le *Pygmalion* de Rameau et le *Pygmalion* de Rousseau: Un mythe au défi d'une révolution esthétique," *Analyse Musicale* 35 (March 2000): 68–71; Jacqueline Waeber, *En musique dans le texte: Le mélodrame, de Rousseau à Schoenberg* (Paris: Van Dieren, 2005); and Erik Leborgne, "Le fantasme de l'artiste et sa dramaturgie: Le *Pygmalion* de Rousseau," *Europe* 84, no. 930 (October 2006): 71–86.

21. Boyce's music is in the Bodleian Library, Oxford University. It is printed in appendix A of Randy L. Neighbarger, *An Outward Show: Music for Shakespeare on the London Stage, 1660–1830*, Contributions to the Study of Music and Dance, no. 27 (Westport, Conn.: Greenwood Press, 1992), 234–238.

22. My numbering follows that of the version edited by Jacqueline Waeber. See Jean-Jacques Rousseau and Horace Coignet, *Pygmalion: Scène lyrique* (Geneva, Switzerland: Geneva Conservatory of Music, 1997).

23. Waeber notes that in one oboe part the musician wrote in "Repeat no. 26 at end": ibid., p. 25.

24. Rousseau's text was published with Coignet's complete music in an edition

by Emilio Sala (Milan: Ricordi, 1996). On the music to *Pygmalion*, see Waeber, *En musique dans le texte*, 17–27. The Viennese composer was Franz Aspelmayr.

25. John D. Drake, "The Eighteenth-Century Melodrama," *Musical Times* 112, no. 1545 (November 1971): 1058–1060. For a fuller discussion of the evolution of the term "melodrama" from 1770 to 1800, see Emilio Sala, "Mélodrame: Définitions et métamorphoses d'un genre quasi-opératique," *Revue de Musicologie* 84, no. 2 (1998): 235–246.

26. The musical incipits of this melodrama—all in full orchestration—are included in José Subirá, *El compositor Iriarte* . . . , vol. 2 (Barcelona: Consejo Superior de Investigaciones Científicas, Instituto Español de Musicología, 1950). Sala, in the introduction to his edition of *Pygmalion* (xv), says that "Spain was experiencing the frenzied *melologos* vogue."

27. The text was adapted from the libretto of a tragic cantata by Heinrich Wilhelm von Gerstenberg.

28. David Joseph Buch, *Magic Flutes and Enchanted Forests* (Chicago: University of Chicago Press, 2008), 268.

29. Sala, "Mélodrame: Définitions et métamorphoses d'un genre quasi-opératique," 236.

30. Francesco Galeazzi, *Elementi teorico-pratici di musica*, vol. 2 (1796), quoted in Steblin, *History of Key Characteristics*, 110.

31. Johann Christian Brandes, *Sämtliche dramatische Schriften* (Hamburg, 1790), vol. 1, p. xxvii, cited in Jan van der Veen, *Le mélodrame musical de Rousseau au Romantisme: Ses aspects historiques et stylistiques* (The Hague: M. Nijhoff, 1955), 58, n. 2.

32. Unlike the operas of the time, which still clung to eighteenth-century dress, Thomas Bauman notes that *Ariadne auf Naxos*, "at Duke Ernst II's personal stipulation, used a natural, flowing Greek robe for its heroine, lending persuasive visual realism to its violent emotions, just as historically accurate costuming did at the same time for Goethe's *Götz von Berlichingen* at Berlin and Hamburg": Thomas Bauman, *North German Opera in the Age of Goethe* (Cambridge: Cambridge University Press, 1985), 155. Benda's reduction for strings was published privately in Leipzig in both German and French (ca. 1780).

33. Benda's melodramas also had a significant influence on the subsequent German popular theatre. See Fritz Bruckner, "Georg Benda und das deutsche Singspiel," *Sämmelbände der Internationalen Musikgesellschaft* 5, no. 4 (August 1904): 571–621.

34. See Emilio Sala, *L'Opera senza canto, il mélo romantico e l'invenzione della colonna sonora* (Venice: Marsilio, 1995), 43–54.

35. Roger Fiske, *English Theatre Music in the Eighteenth Century* (London: Oxford University Press, 1973), 232.

36. Fiske, *English Theatre Music*, 67; and Anne Dhu Shapiro [McLucas], "Action

Music in American Pantomime and Melodrama, 1730–1913," *American Music* 1, no. 4 (Winter 1984): 51.

37. The scenario is adapted from "Account of the New Pantomime of Harlequin Dr. Faustus," *London Magazine, or, Gentleman's Monthly Intelligencer* 35 (December 1766): 676.

38. Ibid. The music was published as *The Songs, Tunes, and Dances in Harlequin Dr. Faustus, for the Harpsichord, German-Flute or Violin, Composed by Samuel Arnold* (London: Welcker, [1766]). The published score numbers each comic tune, although the numbers in this score do not always seem to follow the order of the synopsis. Either the synopsis of the pantomime is incorrect or the ordering of the items was changed for publication. My deduction is that more music must have been used during the pantomime than in the piece Arnold published. Perhaps these were repetitions of other numbers or borrowed tunes, and Arnold may have rearranged them in "suite" order. Without further research, it would be difficult to decide conclusively.

39. Robert H. B. Hoskins, "The Pantomimes and Ballets of Samuel Arnold," *Studies in Music* (Australia) 19 (1985): 81. For another example, see "The Lyon" in Shapiro [McLucas], "Action Music in American Pantomime," 52.

40. "A Christmas Tale," *Monthly Miscellany* 1 (January 1774): 28. Walpole quoted in Ralph G. Allen, "Irrational Entertainment in the Age of Reason," in G. W. Stone, *The Stage and the Page: London's "Whole Show" in the Eighteenth-Century Theatre* (Berkeley: University of California Press, 1981), 98. Dibdin relates his account of working with Garrick, which was unpleasant. He felt ill used and considered *The Christmas Tale* to be largely "a vehicle for the display of scenery and rich decorations." "Charles Dibdin," *Tinsley's Magazine* 13 (December 1873): 544.

41. A copy of the published score of *The Christmas Tale* is in the British Library. It contains only the songs (and one march), with no other stage music.

42. Jean-Georges Noverre, *Lettres sur la danse et sur les ballets* (Lyon: chez Aimé Delaroche, 1760; my translation), ix; quoted and translated by Deryck Lynham, *The Chevalier Noverre: Father of Modern Ballet* (London: Sylvan Press, 1950), 141.

43. Quoted in Daniel Heartz, "From Garrick to Gluck: The Reform of Theatre and Opera in the Mid-Eighteenth Century," *Proceedings of the Royal Musical Association*, 94th Session (1967–1968): 112.

44. Noverre, *Lettres sur la danse*, 24–25.

45. For an excellent study of some of these ballets with musical detail, especially *Médée et Jason* (1770), see Edward Nye, *Mime, Music, and Drama on the Eighteenth-Century Stage: The Ballet d'Action* (Cambridge: Cambridge University Press, 2011), 194–207. Nye also notes (4) that the annotated musical scores of eighteenth-century *ballets d'action* survive only in manuscript and reproduces samples in his book.

46. James Frederick Mason, "The Melodrama in France from the Revolution to the Beginning of Romantic Drama, 1791–1830" (Ph.D. diss., Johns Hopkins University, Baltimore, 1912), 13.

47. Glyndwr Williams, *The Death of Captain Cook* (Cambridge, Mass.: Harvard University Press, 2008), 78–79.

48. *The Death of Captain Cook*, apparently adapted from a French "serious ballet," had already been produced in 1789 at the Haymarket with Carlo Delpini in the title role.

49. "Pantomime," *Town and Country Magazine, or Universal Repository of Knowledge, Instruction, and Entertainment* 21 (March 1789): 101–102.

50. Review of the Berlin performance by Johann Friedrich Reichardt, *Musikalisches Magazin* 1 (1782): 52. The London account is in *Weekly Entertainer, or Agreeable and Instructive Repository* 1, no. 25 (23 June 1783): 593–594. The two orchestras in London were led by separate conductors, Wilhelm Cramer and Johann Peter Salomon. The detailed breakdown from the score can be found in Richard James Will, *The Characteristic Symphony in the Age of Haydn and Beethoven* (Cambridge: Cambridge University Press, 2002), 266–267. Such "combat pieces" or "battle music" grew in popularity in the late eighteenth century. A few of the most influential of these were Ignazio Raimondi's *Battle* (1785), Franz Kotzwara's *The Battle of Prague* (1788), and Jan Dussek's very timely *Naval Battle and Total Defeat of the Grand Dutch Fleet by Admiral Duncan on the 11th of October, 1797* (1797). The growing need for such intensity to be enacted in sound was in evidence in the many programmatic orchestral works played in London theatres in the 1790s. In the ballet pantomime *Oscar and Malvina* at Covent Garden 1791, for example, William Reeve composed a battle sequence in several movements that included skirmishes, attacks, even "groans of the wounded." Descriptions in Reeve's musical score, *Overture to Oscar and Malvina, with the Highland March and Battle Pieces* (London: Longman and Broderip, 1791).

51. David Charlton, "Revival or Survival?" (review of a recording of *Richard Coeur-de-Lion*), *Nineteenth-Century Music* 2, no. 2 (November 1978): 159.

52. The Angelos subsequently established an academy in Soho Square, where they taught the art of broadsword even to members of the British cavalry.

53. Rochefort's manuscript score is at the Bibliothèque Nationale, Paris, VM6-142. I am grateful to Frà Richard Divall for his help in obtaining details from this score.

54. Henry Saxe Wyndham, *Annals of Covent Garden Theatre from 1732 to 1897*, vol. 1 (London: Chatto and Windus, 1906), 248.

55. Edward Walford, *Old and New London: A Narrative of Its History, Its Peoples, and Its Places*, vol. 6, revised ed. (London: Cassel and Company, 1880), 404.

56. Emilio Sala, "Musique et dramatisation dans la 'Pantomime Dialoguée': Le cas de *L'Homme au masque de fer* (1790)," in Jacqueline Waeber, *Musique et geste en France de Lully à la Révolution: Études sur la musique, le théâtre et la danse* (Bern: Peter Lang, 2009), 218.

57. Mason, "The Melodrama in France," 15.

58. Sala, "Musique et dramatisation dans la 'Pantomime Dialoguée,'" 218.

59. Jane Moody, *Illegitimate Theatre in London, 1770–1840* (Cambridge: Cambridge University Press, 2000), 21.

60. Complete introduction reprinted in Richard Brinsley Peake, *Memoirs of the Colman Family* . . . , vol. 2 (London: Richard Bentley, 1841), 255.

61. Thomas Dibdin, *The Reminiscences of Thomas Dibdin*, vol. 1 (London: H. Colburn, 1827), 189–190. Dibdin says that Davy was working in a provincial theatre and was brought to London by a "Mr. Hughes," presumably Thomas Hughes.

62. The blue flame was not an entirely new device but "was managed with more complete effect than at the winter houses." *Monthly Mirror* 7 (1799): 369.

63. This "New Prelude" was anonymously published for piano solo in London by H. Pace in 1795.

64. J. C. Cross, *Rinaldo Rinaldini, or The Secret Avengers*, in *Circusiana, or A Collection of the Most Favourite Ballets, Spectacles, Melo-drames, etc., Performed at the Royal Circus, St. George's Fields*, vol. 2 (London: Printed for the author by T. Burton, 1809), 117.

65. In addition to dozens of songs, Reeve entered for copyright at Stationers' Hall several of his "musical entertainments" created with Cross at the Haymarket in the 1790s as well as a "grand serio comic romance" entitled *The Caravan, or The Driver and His Dog*, given at Covent Garden in 1803.

66. "Theatrical Journal," *European Magazine and London Review* 40, no. 2 (August 1801): 120–121.

CHAPTER 2

1. Morton interview in the 1832 *Report from the Select Committee on Dramatic Literature*, item 3952 (London: House of Commons, 1832).

2. *Freytag's Technique of the Drama: An Exposition of Dramatic Composition and Art* (1863), trans. Elias J. MacEwan (Chicago: S. C. Griggs and Co., 1895), 114–140.

3. Peter Brooks, *The Melodramatic Imagination: Balzac, Henry James, Melodrama, and the Mode of Excess* (New Haven: Yale University Press, 1976), xi–xiii.

4. The *olla podrida* quotation is from "Theatre Royal, Covent-Garden," *Monthly Mirror* 2 (December 1807): 441. Unknown author in *Analectic Magazine* (4 August 1814), section 4, 171.

5. Thomas Busby, *Dictionary of Music* (London, 1806), s.v. "Melo-Drama"; Frederick Corder, "The Leit-Motive, Its Use and Abuse," *Musical World* (24 July 1886), 467.

6. Victor Emeljanow, *Victorian Popular Dramatists* (New York: Twayne Publishers, 1987), 11.

7. Schlegel called these *Noth-und-Hülfs Dramen.* "Treatise on the Study of Romantic Poetry" (1800), trans. E. J. Millington in *The Aesthetic and Miscellaneous Works of Friedrich von Schlegel* (New York: H. G. Bohn, 1849), 281.

8. Alan Reynolds Thompson, "Melodrama and Tragedy," *Proceedings of the Modern Languages Association* 43, no. 3 (September 1928): 811, 813. See also Robert Bechtold Heilman's *Tragedy and Melodrama* (Seattle: University of Washington Press, 1968).

9. "Remarks on *The Slave*," *Amusing Chronicle: A Weekly Repository for Miscellaneous Literature* 2, no. 20 (1 February 1817): 70.

10. Eric Bentley, *The Life of the Drama* (1964) (New York: Applause Theatre and Cinema Books, 1991), 205.

11. Richard LeGallienne, "The Stage Life of Wilson Barrett," unpublished ms. (ca. 1900), 78.

12. Propp developed a compelling theory of functions in fairy tales with the return of the hero, his pursuit, and his rescue, sometimes followed by further sequences in which the hero must prove himself to be recognized. Vladimir Propp, *Morphology of the Folktale*, trans. Laurence Scott, 2nd ed. (Austin: University of Texas Press, 1968).

13. Jessica Milner Davis, *Farce* (London: Methuen, 1978), 43–46.

14. Ibid., 46.

15. All of the theatre music that I have found contains not one example of music to accompany a spoken farce. Playbills never mention music in connection with spoken farce unless it is a song, even though they may identify a composer for the melodrama. Also, accounts from orchestra leaders and musicians suggest that during the farces they had no music to play.

16. "Melodrame" in the *Oxford English Dictionary* quotes the 1818 entry in Lady Morgan's diary: Sydney Morgan, *Passages from My Autobiography* (1859), 212.

17. Samuel Phelps used "Locke's music" in productions of *Macbeth* at Sadler's Wells from 1844 to 1861, as did Charles Kean at the Princess's in the 1860s. Some actors' handbooks note that players are often called to the stage to sing the "choruses in *Macbeth*."

18. "A Tale of Mystery: A Melodrame by Thomas Holcroft, Esq.," *Monthly Mirror* 14 (November 1802): 338.

19. The eight influences that Hartog identifies are the decline of the tragedy, the *comédies larmoyantes* (tearful comedies) of Pierre-Claude Nivelle de La Chaussée, the theories of Diderot on the bourgeois dramas of Sedaine and Beaumarchais, the *Traité du Théâtre* of Louis Sébastien Mercier, the influence of Rousseau's *Pygmalion*, the *pantomime dialoguée*, the novel, and the German theatre. Willie G. Hartog, *Guilbert de Pixerécourt: Sa vie, son mélodrame, sa technique, et son influence* (Paris: Librairie Ancienne, Honoré Champion, 1913), 67–68. I am inclined to agree with James Frederick Mason, who asserted in his 1912 study of melodrama that Rousseau's *Pygmalion* and the "feeble attempts" by imitators actually bore little responsibility for the later development of the popular melodrama: Mason, "The Melodrama in France," 25–26.

20. René-Charles Guilbert de Pixerécourt, "Mélo-drame," in *Le Livre des cent-*

et-un, vol. 6 (Brussels: Louis Hauman, 1832); translated by Daniel Gerould and Marvin Carlson in *Pixérécourt: Four Melodramas* (New York: Martin E. Segal Theatre Center Publications, 2002), 311. Also discussed in Paul Ginisty, *Le mélodrame* (Paris: Louis-Michaud, 1910), 52–53.

21. Pixerécourt's comments quoted in *Théatre [sic] Choisi de G. De Pixerécourt*, vol. 1 (Nancy: Chez L'Auteur, 1841), li.

22. Sala examines this transition and these *mélo-drames* in considerable depth and detail: Emilio Sala, *L'Opera senza canto, il mélo romantico e l'invenzione della colonna sonora* (Venice: Marsilio, 1995), 23–70.

23. Norma Perry, introductory notes to R. C. Guilbert de Pixerécourt, *Coelina, ou L'Enfant du mystère* (Exeter: University of Exeter, 1972; my translation), 28.

24. The orchestra for Quaisain's music for *Le jugement de Salomone* (Ambigu-Comique, 1802) was much larger. This is a more operatic work with many sung numbers and a full chorus, however, so the ensemble may have been expanded for that purpose. The source for the music in *La forêt* is Joann Élart, *Catalogue des fonds musicaux conservés en Haute-Normandie*, vol. 1 (Le Havre: University of Rouen, 2004), 138. This source (265–266) also lists the instrumentation for a surviving set of anonymous parts for a production of Pixerécourt's *Le pelégrin blanc*, given in Rouen at the Théâtre de la République in the fall of 1801, only six months after its Ambigu-Comique premiere. The surviving parts are unfortunately incomplete and consist of violin 1, violin 2, viola, basso, piccolo, flute 1, oboe 1, clarinet 1, and horn 1. The source for *Jugement de Salomone* is RISM (Répertoire International des Sources Musicales).

25. Information on Quaisain and others is derived from Ginisty, *Le mélodrame.*

26. Brooks, *The Melodramatic Imagination*, 89.

27. Quoted and translated in O. G. Brockett, "Pixerécourt and Unified Production," *Educational Theatre Journal* 11, no. 3 (October 1959): 182.

28. Amaury Duval in *Observations sur les théâtres* (Paris: De l'Imprimerie des Sciences et Arts, 1797).

29. "Golden Age of the Boulevard," *Drama Review* 18, no. 1 (March 1974): 27.

30. F. W. J. Hemmings, *The Theatre Industry in Nineteenth-Century France* (New York: Cambridge University Press, 1994), 113–114.

31. Criticism of music in melodrama by Jules Janin, quoted in Gustave Vapereau, *Dictionaire universel des littératures* (Paris: Librairie Hachette, 1884), s.v. *mélodrame* (p. 1370).

32. Ginisty, *Le mélodrame*, 15.

33. William Dunlap adapted *The Judgement of Solomon* for the New York Theatre in 1803 as *The Voice of Nature*, with music by the immigrant composer Victor Pelissier. Only a few bits of ceremonial pieces from this music remain, published in Karl Kroeger, ed., *Early Melodrama in America, Nineteenth-Century American Musical Theatre*, vol. 2 (New York: Garland, 1994).

34. Sala reproduces a sample page of manuscript full score in *L'Opera senza canto*, 85.

35. In 1817 the Ambigu orchestra consisted of two flutes, two clarinets (still no oboes), two bassoon, two horns, timpani, four first violins, four second violins, two violas, two cellos, and two basses. Ginisty even lists the musicians in the orchestra by name: Ginisty, *Le mélodrame*, 218, n. 1.

36. George Taylor, *The French Revolution and the London Stage, 1789–1805* (Cambridge: Cambridge University Press, 2000), 1–30.

37. James Frederick Mason, "The Melodrama in France from the Revolution to the Beginning of Romantic Drama, 1791–1830" (Ph.D. diss., Johns Hopkins University, 1912), 20–21.

38. Jeffrey N. Cox, *Seven Gothic Dramas, 1789–1825* (Athens: Ohio University Press, 1992), 30–31, n. 27.

39. One exception is Aubrey S. Garlington in his article "'Gothic' Literature and Dramatic Music in England," *Journal of the American Musicological Society* 15, no. 1 (Spring 1962): 48–64.

40. Cited in Ernest Bradles Watson, *Sheridan to Robertson: A Study of the Nineteenth-Century Stage* (Cambridge, Mass.: Harvard University Press, 1926), 353.

41. The chaconne was from Jomelli's opera *Fetonte* (1768). Daniel Heartz wrote that this D-minor *Larghetto* in 3/4 was actually part of the overture, except the curtain went up on the chaconne to reveal a mysterious scene of priests "who circle an altar with lighted torches in hand": *Music in European Capitals: The Galant Style, 1720–1780* (New York: W. W. Norton and Co., 2003), 475. Simon McVeigh also observed that "Jommelli's Chaconne" was a popular piece in London at this time in *Concert Life in London from Mozart to Haydn* (Cambridge: Cambridge University Press, 1993), 141. Thomas Lyon published the chaconne as *The Favorite Movement [by N. Jommelli], Performed . . . during the Appearance of the Ghost . . .* (London: L. Lavenu, 1798).

42. Kelly's score for *Pizarro*, like those for other burlettas and English "operas" produced at Covent Garden and Drury Lane, was published (but only what would later be called the "incidental" music, the songs and stage music). Kemble's edition of *Pizarro* is published in *The John Philip Kemble Promptbooks*, ed. Charles Shattuck (Charlottesville: University Press of Virginia, 1974).

43. Henry Home (Lord Kames), *Elements of Criticism*, vol. 3 (Edinburgh: A. Kincaid and J. Bell, 1762), 283–284.

44. Janet Shepherd, "The Relationship between Music, Text, and Performance in English Popular Theatre, 1790–1840" (Ph.D. diss., University of London, 1991), 70. Shepherd includes many handwritten transcriptions from Busby's score for her analysis of *A Tale of Mystery*.

45. "A Tale of Mystery: A Melodrame by Thomas Holcroft, Esq.," *Monthly Mirror* 14 (November 1802): 338.

46. Moody, *Illegitimate Theatre in London*, p. 91.

47. As Moody put it: "The final pantomimic scene of *A Tale* therefore resists spectators' desire for moral judgements. Indeed, what fascinates Holcroft about melodrama is the genre's capacity to encode such contradictions": Moody, *Illegitimate Theatre in London*, 91.

48. *Monthly Mirror* 4 (July–December 1808): 256–257. For an extensive list of early nineteenth-century melodramas, see William S. Dye, "A Study of Melodrama in England from 1800 to 1840" (Ph.D. diss., University of Pennsylvania, 1919).

49. Nearly all music relating to nineteenth-century British theatres surviving in the British Museum is from early in the century and consists of arias, songs, choruses, and dances. Some forty-seven of these—sometimes called burlettas, sometimes "grand MeloDramas" or "operas"—qualify as early nineteenth-century burlettas, among them Michael Kelly's *The Africans* (Covent Garden, 1808), Matthew Porter King's *Ella Rosenberg* (Drury Lane, 1807), James Hook's *The Fortress* (Haymarket, 1807), Henry Bishop's *The Knight of Snowdoun* (Covent Garden, 1811), and John Davy's *Rob Roy MacGregor* (Covent Garden, 1818). Most of Bishop's burlettas are bound in twenty-seven volumes and were compiled ca. 1810–1836, according to British Library records.

50. "Orchestra.—Director, leader of the band, 6 or 8 first violins, 6 or 9 second violins, 2 tenors, 2 cellos, 3 or 4 double basses, oboe and flageolet, 2 flutes, 2 clarionets, 2 horns, 2 bassoons, trombone, trumpet and bugle, pianoforte, bells, carillons or small bells, and kettledrums, music copyist and assistants, and an attendant to lay out music, etc." Quoted in Henry Saxe Wyndham, *The Annals of Covent Garden Theatre*, vol. 1 (London: Chatto and Windus, 1906), 336.

51. "Covent Garden: Memoranda of Agreements, 1818" (manuscript ledger book at the British Library).

52. See David Mayer's study of Henry Bishop's music for *The Miller and His Men* in "Nineteenth Century Theatre Music," *Theatre Notebook* 30, no. 3 (1976): 119–120.

53. The new category of music to accompany a stage play seemed confusing to some library cataloguers. The Library of Congress catalogued *The Overture, Marches, Dances, Symphonies, and Song in the Melo drame [sic] Called A Tale of Mystery* as a "Monologue with music."

54. For more detailed biographical information on John Davy than is found in the *New Grove Dictionary of Music*, see "John Davy, the Celebrated Composer," *Mirror of Taste and Dramatic Censor* (1 March 1811), 157–158.

55. "Theatre Royal, Covent-Garden," *Monthly Mirror: Reflecting Men and Manners with Structures on Their Epitome, the Stage* 2 (December 1807): 441–443.

56. British Library, Add. Ms. 31767. Subsequent playbills at other theatres recognize music by M. P. King, even as late as 1819 at the Theatre-Royal, Edinburgh.

57. King eventually stopped numbering the symphonies, of which there are nearly thirty. The last at the end of the play, simply called "Last Symphony of Joy," is in D major and ends like the overture.

58. Christian Friedrich Daniel Schubart, *Ideen zu einer Ästhetik der Tonkunst* (Vienna: J. V. Degen, 1806).

59. *Monthly Review or Literary Journal* 57, no. 4 (London, 1808): 99–100.

60. In her analysis of this play, Jane Moody says that Lewis portrayed Timour as "a Napoleanic bogeyman." "Throughout the play," she notes, "characters refer to Timour using Napoleanic epithets such as 'usurper' and 'tyrant.'" Also, "Timour depicts an oriental world characterized by physical peril and spectacular ideological confrontation": Jane Moody, *Illegitimate Theatre in London, 1770–1840* (Cambridge: Cambridge University Press, 2000), 100–101. She includes an illustration of a toy theatre for *Timour.*

61. The *Morning Chronicle* eyewitness is quoted in Louis F. Peck, *A Life of Matthew G. Lewis* (Cambridge, Mass.: Harvard University Press, 1961), 104. Two years later Covent Garden produced Pocock's *The Miller and His Men,* an enormously long-running play and one of the first sensation melodramas in that it employed the use of the new invention of gunpowder. This play (with its music) has been extensively analyzed by both Janet Shepherd, "The Relationship between Music, Text, and Performance"; and David Mayer, "Nineteenth Century Theatre Music"; Jane Moody argues that *Miller* initiated the excuse for producers of melodramas to blow things up: Moody, *Illegitimate Theatre in London,* 28.

62. M. G. Lewis, *Timour the Tartar* (London: Lowndes and Hobbes, 1812), unnumbered page.

CHAPTER 3

1. "Miscellanies: Germany," *La Belle Assemblée* 1, part 1 (1806): 51. *Swetards Zaubertal,* by Emmanuel Schikaneder with music by Anton Fischer, was first produced in Vienna at the Theater an der Wien.

2. Maurice Willson Disher, *Blond and Thunder: Mid-Victorian Melodrama and Its Origins* (London: Frederick Muller, 1949). Some of Disher's categories of melodramas that originated in the London minor theatres from 1800 to 1843 (the titles of which may predate this period) were still in the repertory: virtue triumphant (*Richard the Lionhearted, Paul and Virginia*), mystery and terror (*Raymond and Agnes, The Castle of Montval*), the moral hero challenged (*The Mountaineers, The Iron Chest*), dramas of democracy (*The Fall of the Bastille, The Purse, or The Benevolent Tar*), tuppence colored, meaning appealing to younger audiences who buy and decorate illustrations of the actors and actresses (*Tekeli, or The Siege of Montgatz, The Miller and His Men*), domestic versus demonic (*The Lear of Private Life, The Vampire*), dramas of oppression (*Deaf and Dumb, or The Orphan Protected, The Jew of Lubeck, or The Heart of a Father*), crime exultant (*Jonathan Bradford, The Clerk of Clerkenwell, Sweeney Todd*), industrial unrest and tempting providence (*The Factory Lad, The Mutiny at the Nore*), highly moral and instructive (*London by Night, The Drunkard*), the femme fatale (*The Tower of Nesle, or The Chamber of Death, Mary Glastonbury*), and class-conscious dramas (*The Green Bushes, Lilian, the Show Girl*).

3. "The English Drama," *Spirit of the Times* (September 26, 1840), 10, 30.

4. Similarly, the *Morning Chronicle* reported on 8 January 1820 that "*Richard the Third* was melo-dramatized expressly for the Coburg, with additional musical scenes and an immense reduction of matter by Mr. Moncrief."

5. *Monthly Mirror* 4 (July–December 1808): 256–257.

6. Statutes in 1829 are clear about the need for a theatre management to apply to the mayor annually for a license. On the repertories of these theatres, see Bruce A. McConachie, *Melodramatic Formations: American Theatre and Society, 1820–1870* (Iowa City: University of Iowa Press, 1992); and Rosemarie Banks, *Theatre Culture in America, 1825–1860* (Cambridge: Cambridge University Press, 1997).

7. *Annual Review, or Register of Literature* 1 (January 1802): 692.

8. This subject of play piracy occupied a great deal of the discussion in the parliamentary *Report from the Select Committee on Dramatic Literature* (1832).

9. George Raymond, *Memoirs of Robert William Elliston, Comedian*, vol. 2 (London: John Ollivier, 1846), 257.

10. Thomas Allen, *The History and Antiquities of the Parish of Lambeth* (Lambeth: J. Allen, 1827), 302.

11. George Rowell wrote of newly built minor theatres such as the Coburg: "Many effects would be lost in a larger theatre with an audience of 3000, especially when the gradual disappearance of the apron-stage forced the actor farther and farther within the scene . . . Also, actors were more and more chosen for their acrobatic abilities, rather than their histrionic gifts." George Rowell, *The Victorian Theatre, 1792–1914: A Survey* (1956), 2nd ed. (Cambridge: Cambridge University Press, 1978), 22.

12. Edward Walford, *Old and New London: A Narrative of Its History, Its Peoples, and Its Places*, vol. 6, revised ed. (London: Cassel and Company, 1880), 394–395 (including Matthews quotation).

13. *Drama (Theatrical Magazine)* 3, no. 1 (June 1822): 47.

14. Glossop secured a license for "music, dancing, and other entertainments of the like kind," as Davidge later verified before the 1832 Select Committee on Dramatic Literature.

15. The text for the "glee" that opened the play and was so prominently announced in the playbills was included in the Duncombe edition. But it is stricken out of a surviving promptbook from the 1830s. Lacy's publication of the play in the 1840s leaves it out entirely.

16. Leman Thomas Rede, *The Road to the Stage, or The Performer's Preceptor* (London: John Smith, 1827), 62–63.

17. "T. Hughes" is listed as leader during these years at the Coburg. This is apparently a different person from Richard Hughes, who was musical director at Drury Lane during the 1830s. Neither of these is to be confused with H. Hughes, playwright and actor at the Adelphi.

18. "Royal Coburg Theatre," *Theatrical Inquisitor* 12, no. 71 (June 1818): 453.

19. "Coburg Theatre," *Theatrical Inquisitor* 14, no. 82 (May 1819): 398.

20. David Worrall, *Theatric Revolution: Drama, Censorship, and Romantic Period Subcultures, 1773–1832* (Oxford: Oxford University Press, 2006), 196–217.

21. "Royal Victoria," *National Standard of Literature, Science, Music*... 2, no. 24 (15 June 1833): 381.

22. *London Magazine* 8 (September 1823): 322.

23. Anonymous review, *Times* (29 July 1823), 3.

24. When T. P. Cooke staged *Florence Macarthy* in 1819 at the Surrey, the appropriate tunes were "selected from Irish Melodies and other national authorities by T. P. Cooke." *Theatre, or Dramatic and Literary Mirror* 1, no. 13 (12 June 1819): 203.

25. Playbill for *Frankenstein* (28 August 1823) in the microfiche collection entitled *Playbills and Programmes from London Theatres, 1801–1900* (Cambridge: Chadwyck-Healey, n.d.).

26. The relatively sparse number of music cues that ended up in the Duncombe edition of the 1826 published text may not reflect the number actually used in the production, which only an existing promptbook from the Coburg could verify.

27. Though often called a melodrama in modern sources, *Obi* was actually a play with songs.

28. "Drury Lane Theatre," *Theatrical Observer* (13 November 1824), 1.

29. "Memoir of O. Smith," *Drama* 7, no. 7 (April 1825): 223.

30. *Lady's Magazine* (November 1829): 610.

31. Moody, *Illegitimate Theatre in London*, 94.

32. Peter Brooks, "The Text of Muteness," *New Literary History* 5, no. 3 (Spring 1974): 549.

33. Ernest Bradlee Watson, *Sheridan to Robertson: A Study of the Nineteenth-Century Stage* (Cambridge, Mass.: Harvard University Press, 1926), 355.

34. As Watson put it, "this more intimate and domestic type of melodrama, with marked realistic tendencies, came to be known as the 'Adelphi Drama.'" Ibid., 355.

35. Larry Stephen Clifton, *The Terrible Fitzball: The Melodramatist of the Macabre* (Bowling Green, Ohio: Bowling Green State University Popular Press, 1993). It is difficult to believe, however, that Rodwell, so important to Fitzball's success as a dramatist, merits not a single mention in this only full-length study of Fitzball.

36. Edward Fitzball, *Thirty-Five Years of a Dramatic Author's Life*, vol. 1 (London: Newby, 1859), 54.

37. John M. Morton, "Fiddlers and the Play," *Theatre* 1 (1886): 449. Morton continues: "By the way, if this [tune] didn't furnish Arthur Sullivan with the theme of his famous and beautiful waltz song, which Mable sings in *The Pirates of Penzance*, then I am a Dutchman."

38. John N. Ireland, *Records of the New York Stage, from 1750 to 1860*, vol. 1 (New York: T. Morrell, 1866), 517. For a fascinating study of Fitzball's play in South Africa, see J. Q. Davies, "Melodramatic Possessions: *The Flying Dutchman*, South Africa, and the Imperial Stage, ca. 1830," *Opera Quarterly* 21, no. 2 (Summer 2005): 496–514.

39. The Golden Family Collection is preserved at the Working Men's Institute, New Harmony, Indiana. It includes their promptbooks, orchestra parts, playbills, and correspondence. The parts for *The Flying Dutchman*—like most of their music—have no attribution. I have corroborated the parts against available English sources, such as the published song "Return, O My Love" and other evidence of Rodwell's musical style.

40. On "Miss Boden," see "The Adelphi," *La Belle Assemblée* 30, no. 194 (November 1824): 223. On her reputation as a singer, see her reviews at the English Opera House, including *Theatrical Observer* 1736 (3 July 1827): 2.

41. J. Q. Davies has examined Rodwell's music to *The Skeleton Lover*. See "Musical Souvenir: London in 1829" (Ph.D. diss., University of Cambridge, 2005), 215–218.

42. Rodwell's score to Fitzball's *Lord of the Isles*, an "operatic" adaptation of Sir Walter Scott's work (Covent Garden, 1834), was published in vocal score by D'Almaine. The score contains none of the affective/melodramatic music requested in the published playtext, however. The possibilities are that this score was published for use at home, that it was for the personal enjoyment of musical patrons, or that it circulated to theatres where melodramatic music would be supplied by the local leader in production.

43. James Grant, *The Great Metropolis*, vol. 1 (London: Saunders and Otley, 1837), 84–86.

44. Michael Booth, *English Melodrama* (London: H. Jenkins, 1965), 102–103.

45. Obituary for Douglas Jerrold in *Gentleman's Magazine*, new series 3 (July 1857): 92–94.

46. "Surrey Theatre," *London Literary Gazette* 663 (1829): 654.

47. *London Magazine* 8 (September 1823): 323.

48. "Surrey Theatre," p. 654.

49. *London Times* (1 December 1829).

50. William Thornbury and Edward Walford, *Old and New London*, vol. 6, *The Southern Suburbs* (London: Cassell, 1893), 370.

51. A frequenter of Sadler's Wells, "Mr. T. P. Cooke," *Theatrical Journal* 15, no. 734 (January 1854): 6.

52. The incident is related by Cab Cye in "Elliston and the Ass's Head," *Olio, or Museum of Entertainment* 9 (London, 1832): 86–87.

53. Copies of the piano score are at the Victoria and Albert Museum (Enthoven Collection) and at the Houghton Library, Harvard University (now available online at the Houghton site: http://pds.lib.harvard.edu/pds/view/17456364). The three theatre collections are the William Seymour Collection at Princeton University, the Boston Theatre Music Manuscripts at Harvard University, and the Drury Lane Theatre Archive at the British Library. The Seymour Collection also includes a "music plot" for *Black-Eyed Susan* used by E. L. Davenport.

54. Perhaps a copied set of parts was brought over from England by E. L. Davenport, who acted the role of William in 1851 at the Haymarket and subsequently pro-

duced *Black-Eyed Susan* in 1854 at the Broadway Theatre in New York, and was handled by his prompter, William Seymour. In any case there is clearly a history of continuity between the original Surrey production and later productions in New York, even if the precise relationship may never be known.

55. Jeffrey N. Cox, "The Ideological Tack of Nautical Melodrama," in Michael Hays and Anastasia Nikolopoulou, eds., *Melodrama: The Cultural Emergence of a Genre* (New York: St. Martin's Press, 1996), 169–176.

56. John Timbs, *A Century of Anecdote from 1760 to 1860*, vol. 2 (London: R. Bentley, 1864), 228.

57. The "Miss Scott" at the Surrey could not possibly have been Jane Scott, who would have been fifty at the time and in any case had retired from the theatre in 1819.

58. Maurice Willson Disher, *Blood and Thunder: Mid-Victorian Melodrama and Its Origins* (London: Muller, 1949), 143.

59. One of the old sailors sings a few verses of "Black-Eyed Susan," accompanied by the orchestra, before Captain Crosstree enters to inform the men that their ship is to set sail again in the morning. William and Susan enter, again to the tune of "Meg of Wapping." William lifts the sailor's spirits by telling them stories and dancing to the tune "Sailor's Hornpipe." William danced the hornpipe with Miss Barnet, the principal house dancer.

60. See these key characteristics compared in Rita Steblin, *History of Key Characteristics in the Eighteenth and Early Nineteenth Centuries* (Rochester: University of Rochester Press, 1996). The characteristics for F-major, for example, are Georg Joseph Vogler, 1778 ("good for dead calm"), Francesco Galeazzi, 1796 ("majestic"), Christian Friedrich Schubart, 1806 ("complaisance and calm"), E. T. A. Hoffmann, 1814 ("consoling"), Heinrich Weikert, 1827 ("gentle, complaisant, and calm"), W. C. Müller, 1830 ("pleasant cheerfulness"), William Gardiner, 1832 ("rich, mild, sober, contemplative"), August Gathy, 1835 ("fitness, manly vigor, calm, serenity"), and Hector Berlioz, 1843 ("energetic, vigorous").

61. Louis James, "Taking Melodrama Seriously: Theatre and Nineteenth-Century Studies," *History Workshop: A Journal of Socialist Historians* 3 (Spring 1977): 156.

62. John Adolphus, *Memoirs of John Bannister, Comedian*, vol. 2 (London, 1839), 257–258; Cye, "Elliston and the Ass's Head," 87.

63. "Surrey Theatre," *Harlequin* 1, no. 5 (13 June 1829): 36.

CHAPTER 4

1. Francis Courtney Wemyss, *Theatrical Biography, or The Life of an Actor and Manager* (Glasgow: R. Griffin, 1848), 129–130.

2. "Surrey Theatre," *London Times* (8 September 1829), 2.

3. Title page of Samuel Henry Chapman, *The Red Rover* (Philadelphia: F. Turner, 1828).

4. *Faustus* (Drury Lane, 1825) by George Soane, also author of *Masaniello*, was

called a "musical romance." The music was a composite affair, composed by Bishop, Horn, and Cooke. Some of its tunes were immediately parodied in a Planché extravaganza. It opened in New York in 1827 at the Chatham Theatre.

5. *London Times* (1 April 1823), 3.

6. *Report from the Select Committee on Dramatic Literature* (London: printed privately for the House of Commons), 94, 192–193.

7. Indeed perhaps the earliest *Allegro misterioso* ever published was by a Frenchman, Henri-Montan Bertini. This piece, number 9 in *Caprices Études* (1836), is discussed in an article in the *Allgemeine Musikalische Zeitung* (1 June 1836).

8. Mona Rebecca Brooks, "The Development of American Theatre Management Practices between 1830 and 1896" (Ph.D. diss., Texas Tech University, 1981), 156.

9. Edward Buxton secured a manuscript score and parts from Mendelssohn from Ewer in 1843 with the intent of performing *Antigone* in concert with the Philharmonic Society. Mendelssohn advised against this, saying that his music needed the drama. The actual arrangement between them was 10 guineas upon receipt of the score and an additional 20 guineas to be paid should the work be performed (and choral parts sold). I am grateful to Peter Ward Jones of the Bodleian Library, Oxford, for this information.

10. Quoted in Felix Moscheles, ed. and trans., *Letters of Felix Mendelssohn to Ignaz and Charles Moscheles* (Boston: Ticknor and Company, 1888), 67.

11. "Law, Court of Common Pleas," *Examiner* 892 (7 March 1825): 156; and Thomas Dibdin, *The Reminiscences of Thomas Dibdin . . .* (London: H. Colburn, 1827), 2:236–237.

12. Henry Saxe Wyndham, *The Annals of Covent Garden Theatre*, vol. 1 (London: Chatto and Windus, 1906), 327. Information on the Lyceum fire is from A. E. Wilson, *The Lyceum* (London: D. Yates, 1952), 51.

13. William Warland Clapp, *Record of the Boston Stage* (Boston: James Munroe and Co., 1853), 263.

14. Quoted in William Winter, *The Jeffersons* (Boston: J. R. Osgood, 1881), 73–74.

15. *City Gazette and Commercial Advertiser* (1 February 1828), 3.

16. This set of orchestra parts to *The Floating Beacon* is in the New York Public Library.

17. Benjamin Dean Wyatt, *Observations on the Design for the Theatre Royal, Drury Lane . . .* (London: Printed for J. Taylor at the Architectural Library, 1813), 57.

18. *Hatton v. Kean*, 97 Eng. Com. Law (7 C. B. N.S.) 268. Commentary by Edward S. Rogers, "The Law of Dramatic Copyright," *Michigan Law Review* 1, no. 2 (November 1902): 109. See also a transcript of the case in *Era* 1103 (13 November 1859).

19. One rare exception is the manuscript score to *The French Spy*, composed principally by Edward Woolf, father of playwright Benjamin E. Woolf and for many years leader at the Pavilion Theatre. The score, which Woolf must have brought with

him from England when he relocated to the United States, now resides in the library of the New England Conservatory of Music, Boston.

20. *Petty v. Taylor* (1897), cited in E. J. Macgillivray, *A Treatise upon the Law of Copyright . . .* (London: John Murray, 1902), 63. *Hatton v. Kean* was being used as a precedent as late as 1912. See *British Ruling Cases from Courts of Great Britain, Canada, Ireland, Australia, and Other Divisions of the British Empire*, vol. 2 (London: Lawyers' Co-Operative Publishing Company, 1908), 93–110.

21. *Wallerstein v. Herbert*, 15 L. T. N.S. 364, on ap. 16 Id. 453. The incident is also related in "Music as Accessory to a Drama," *Illustrated Police News* (22 June 1867). See additional details in "Wallerstein v. Herbert," *Orchestra* 8, no. 192 (1 June 1867): 150–151.

22. Commentary by Eaton S. Drone, *Treatise on the Law of Property in Intellectual Productions in Great Britain and the United States* (Boston: Little, Brown, 1879), 252–253.

23. "Destruction of the National Theatre, New York," *American Miscellany* (26 October 1839), 82 (reprinted from the *Weekly Herald*).

24. John Tasker Howard, "The Hewitt Family in American Music," *Musical Quarterly* 17, no. 1 (January 1931): 29.

25. *Brooklyn Eagle* (28 December 1865), 2.

26. A single leader part of fourteen cues has been found at the Harvard Theatre Collection, Houghton Library, for *Lady Audley's Secret*. But this was found among manuscripts of the Boston Theatre, so there is no way to identify this unsigned music as Wallerstein's. It is for a five-act version of the play, which probably indicates that it is not. If Wallerstein's music is ever discovered, it will probably be among the papers of Louisa Herbert, not in a music collection. Different music to this play is inevitable, given the various types of productions that it underwent. While *Lady Audley's Secret* with Wallerstein's music was being performed at the upscale St. James, a different version of the play could be seen at the Britannia Theatre across town in the working-class district of Hoxton. The Britannia would have had a much smaller budget for music, which leads me to conclude that the accompanying melodramatic music would have been more generic and provided by the leader of the theatre, who is not credited on the playbill.

27. Other "selections" from music to stage plays were occasionally published, although they are hard to find. I have seen a published selection of music from Belasco's production of *Darling of the Gods* (1902).

28. *Reports of Cases Argued and Determined in the Circuit Court of the United States for the Second Circuit* (1852), 618–628.

29. *Sir Henry Irving: A Victorian Actor and His World* (London: Hambledon and London, 2005), 242.

30. "Thomas Baker's Popular Orchestral Music," *Clipper* (9 July 1864), 103. In another case the 1860 Samuel French edition of Joseph S. Jones's *Captain Kyd, or*

The Wizard of the Sea states that "the original music incidental to Capt. Kyd . . . can be obtained on application to the publisher of the drama [William V. Spencer], 128 Washington St., Boston."

31. W. Lynd, "An Author at Home," *Gentleman's Magazine* 253 (July–December 1882): 362–363.

32. Charles Reade, "A Dramatic Musician," *Musical Standard* 15, no. 748 (30 November 1878): 342–343; reprinted in Charles Reade, *Readiana: Comments on Current Events* (London: Chatto and Windus, 1881), 28–31.

33. *New York Times* (13 March 1885), 8.

34. "McCullough's Property's for Sale," *New York Times* (27 October 1885), 2.

35. This set of parts was donated to the New York Public Library, and the information on Frank Tannehill was received in a phone interview with his granddaughter on 31 May 2010. The circumstances under which Tannehill was able to use Operti's music for *The Stranglers* while on his tours are unknown. These productions may have been produced by Frohman.

36. *New York Times* (25 April 1867), 5.

37. Henry Edward Krehbiel, *A Second Book of Operas* (New York: Macmillan, 1917), 189.

38. Several collections of theatre music have survived, the most valuable being what appear to be the complete holdings of a theatre library. One of these is from the Grecian Theatre, containing a large portion of the music used at that theatre from 1851 to 1882. At that point, when the building ceased to be a theatre, the music library was brought over to Drury Lane. Another is the entire collection of the Boston Theatre from 1851 to the 1920s. A third is the Herbert Beerbohm Tree Theatre Music Collection, stemming from Tree's management of the Haymarket from 1887 and Her Majesty's from 1897 to 1916. The fourth is the David Belasco collection of music manuscripts, which contains not only music used in Belasco productions but also music associated with Charles and Daniel Frohman as well as Theodore Liebler and George Tyler. A few holdings, such as the Florida Boucicault collection and the Tams-Witmark collection, contain only a few sets of parts to nineteenth-century popular dramas, unlike the four collections cited above, which are extensive.

39. Charles Alden John Farrar, *Amateur and Professional Stage Life* (Jamaica Plain, Mass.: Jamaica Publishing Co., 1882), 125.

40. They may have been thrown out or perhaps remain undiscovered in a warehouse somewhere.

41. See "Mr. Bellew's *Macbeth*" on the ubiquity of the Locke-ascribed music in the nineteenth century. Only Samuel Phelps, in his Sadler's Wells' production of 1847, eschewed not only Locke's music but any music whatsoever. See the review of Phelps's production in *Theatrical Times* (2 October 1847), 11; and a discussion of the *Macbeth* music in *Pall Mall Gazette* (23 March 1870), 6, col. 5.

42. The William Seymour Theatre Collection at Princeton University has a copy

of string parts to *Thérèse*. There are no markings on these to indicate that they were rented or purchased from Samuel French.

43. Both sets of parts for *The Mariner's Compass* are in the Drury Lane Theatre Archive. The first is a clean and unused copy signed by Tully and includes ten orchestral parts: violin 1, violin 2, viola, cello and bass, flute, clarinet, cornet (two players), ophicleide, trombone, and timpani. This was undoubtedly the orchestration used in the original production, which would have amounted to a minimum of sixteen players, with double-stand strings in addition to the leader. It is surprising to see Tully using the ophicleide, an instrument popular in French wind ensembles that was gradually replaced by the tuba. The second set consists of a reduced orchestra of seven parts, presumably made from the former master or archive set. Edward Barrett, who was leader in 1869 when the Grecian first produced this play, dropped the violas, the clarinet, the ophicleide, and the trombone. He could have doubled the violins and bass, totaling about ten players.

CHAPTER 5

1. The term "leader" in modern parlance—in the United Kingdom, at any rate—refers to the concertmaster. The term is a holdover from the days when these musicians would both play and lead the orchestra, as most generally did prior to the 1860s in theatrical productions.

2. During the first half of the nineteenth century theatrical leaders in major theatres in France, England, and the United States were almost always violinists, who would play along with the musicians during performances for practical as well as economic reasons, cueing with the bow as necessary.

3. "Knight of Bow and Baton," *New York Times* (6 October 1878). Many other accounts of the two positions exist. At the St. Charles's Theatre in New Orleans in 1846, for example, Auguste Waldauer, who would later lead the opera and conservatory in St. Louis, served a "secondary position . . . of *repétiteur*" to C. H. Mueller, the actual leader. Noah Miller Ludlow, *Dramatic Life As I Found It: A Record of Personal Experience*... (St. Louis: G. I. Jones, 1880), 640.

4. Lothian took over as music director of the Boston Theatre from Charles Koppitz in 1867 and remained in that capacity until 1907.

5. "On Some of the Old Actors," *Gentleman's Magazine* 276 (January–June 1894): 170.

6. "Between the Acts," *Saturday Review of Politics, Literature, Science, and Art* 66, no. 1716 (15 September 1888): 321–322.

7. W. J. Lawrence, "The English Theatre Orchestra: Its Rise and Early Characteristics," *Musical Quarterly* 1, no. 3 (January 1917): 27. Simon Hassler's orchestra in 1871 moved onto the stage due to the especially large audience clamoring to see John Sleeper Clarke's appearances at the Walnut Street Theatre. *Philadelphia Inquirer* (6 February 1871), 7.

8. The *Tremont Theatre Drama and Receipt Records Book* for 1834–1843 is in the Harvard Theatre Collection, Houghton Library (MS Thr 751). Dollar comparisons are based on statistical information in Lawrence H. Officer and Samuel H. Williamson, "Purchasing Power of Money in the United States from 1774 to Present," MeasuringWorth (2011): http://www.measuringworth.com.

9. John Graziano, "Invisible Instruments: Theatre Orchestras in New York, 1850–1900," in John Spitzer, *American Orchestras in the Nineteenth Century* (Chicago: University of Chicago Press, 2012), 109–129.

10. John Thornbury, "Players and Playgoers Twenty-Five Years Ago," *Galaxy* 21, no. 5 (May 1876): 588.

11. Olive Logan, *The Mimic World and Public Exhibitions: Their History, Their Morals, and Effects* (Philadelphia: New-World Publishing, 1871), 89.

12. August Pitou, *Masters of the Show* (New York: Thomas Y. Crowell, 1914), 118–119.

13. "It is very pleasing to me to find that you appreciate so well the efforts I have always made in trying to satisfy you." Unpublished letter of Stoepel to Daly, 17 June 1872, Folger Shakespeare Library, Washington, D.C.

14. Unpublished letter from Mollenhauer to Augustin Daly, 31 July 1879, Folger Shakespeare Library.

15. Advertisement in the *London Times*, 30 December 1878, cited in Alan Hughes, "The Lyceum Staff: A Victorian Theatrical Organization," *Theatre Notebook* 18, no. 1 (1974): 14. "Instrumentarium" was the word used to describe the size of the orchestra for *Ravenswood* by one of Henry Irving's music librarians. This is a common scientific and musicological term, used in medieval and Renaissance studies to refer to the "collection of instruments."

16. It is difficult to say for sure whether these four are invited musicians or part of the regular orchestra but in costume. The *Daily News* (17 October 1864) reported on the Prince's Theatre's opening that the orchestra consisted of "about twenty performers," though this might have been an expanded group because of Arthur's Sullivan's large score for *The Tempest*.

17. Hamilton Clarke, *A Manual of Orchestration: Designed Especially to Enable Amateurs to Follow Intelligently the Performance of Orchestral Music* (London: J. Curwen and Sons, 1888), 11–12. By the 1890s Frederick Corder found the "septet band" common to many English theatres, consisting of first and second violin, double bass (no viola or cello), flute, clarinet, cornet, and drums. Frederick Corder, *The Orchestra and How to Write for It: A Practical Guide . . .* (London: Curwen, 1894), 84.

18. W. Archer and H. Granville-Barker, *A National Theatre: Scheme and Estimates* (London: Duckworth, 1907), 63.

19. Gaston Borch, *Practical Manual of Instrumentation* (Boston: Boston Music Company and Schirmer Books, 1918); and Arthur Edwin Krows, *Play Production*

in America (New York: Henry Holt, 1916). Krows argued that "a representative first-class American theatre usually maintains eight pieces" (381). Most theatres in America did not fit his "first-class" category, however, and his assessment of the size of a theatre orchestra around this time is fairly optimistic. It had long been a requirement in the *Constitution and By-laws of the Musical Mutual Protective Union* that a touring theatrical company must hire music directors who were also pianists (as opposed to the more traditional violinists), in case some of the local unions could not muster any sort of band at all for the production. John R. Commons, "Types of American Labor Unions: The Musicians of St. Louis and New York," *Quarterly Journal of Economics* 20 (May 1906): 430–431.

CHAPTER 6

1. Edward Fuller, "The Theatrical Renaissance of Shakespeare," *Lippincott's Monthly Magazine* 45 (January 1890): 98.

2. Walter Moore Leman, *Memories of an Old Actor* (San Francisco: A. Roman, 1886), 149–150. It seems that a Mr. Friedman was actually the leader of the orchestra at the National Theatre, Boston, in the early 1840s. J. Holloway, an American prodigy violinist (born 1811), was leader at the Tremont Theatre starting in 1839. Perhaps Leman remembered incorrectly, or perhaps Holloway was doing extra service as a *répétiteur* or "second leader."

3. Ibid.

4. A "Mr. [Max] Friedheim" is cited in newspapers as the music director at the time. Holloway may have been a *répétiteur*.

5. "Mr. Wright, the prompter . . . may be almost said to have been born and brought up in this establishment, having begun at the bottom and worked his own way up to where he now is." *Boston Courier* 14, no. 1659 (16 March 1840): 3.

6. Harroway had even published one song for a *Mazeppa* production.

7. This might also be the same Harroway who ran a theatrical and musical agency with B. S. Fairbrother in London.

8. The Henry recollection is in William B. Wood, *Personal Recollections of the Stage* (Philadelphia: H. C. Baird, 1855), 25. The Webster incident is recounted in Dutton Cook, *On the Stage: Studies of Theatrical History and the Actor's Art*, vol. 2 (London: Sampson Low, Marston, Searle, and Rivington, 1883), 102–105.

9. For many actors, playing a musical instrument formed a part of their training, as in the case of Thomas Holcroft. Similarly, the young George Rignold, while traveling through the English provinces with his father's company in the early 1850s, would act bit parts during the play and then run down to the orchestra to fill in on the violin during the entr'actes. Frederick Warde, *Fifty Years of Make Believe* (Los Angeles: Times-Mirror Press, 1923), 156.

10. John Coleman, *Charles Reade As I Knew Him* (New York: E. P. Dutton, 1903), 208.

11. Parts in the Folger Shakespeare Library.

12. The information on Phelps's promptbooks comes from Albert S. Weiner, "Samuel Phelps' Staging of Macbeth," *Education Theatre Journal* 16, no. 2 (May 1964): 130. The observer discusses the 1847 *Macbeth* sans "Mr. Bellew's *Macbeth*," *Pall Mall Gazette* (London) 1594 (23 March 1870).

13. Ludlow, *Dramatic Life As I Found It*, 630.

14. James Cook, *The Actor's Note-Book* (serialized in vols. 1–6 of *Odd Fellow*, 1841), 63. Cook used this example to criticize the practice, according to Alan S. Downer: "Painters and Painted Stage: Nineteenth-Century Acting," *Papers of the Modern Language Association* 61, no. 2 (June 1946): 546–547.

15. J. M. M. [John M. Morton], "About Music Cues," *Music and Drama* 3, no. 1 (8 July 1882): 4.

16. *Chambers's Journal of Popular Literature, Science, and the Arts* 238 (24 July 185): 52; and *San Francisco [Evening] Bulletin* 10, no. 51 (6 June 1860): 1. See also William Pleater Davidge, *Footlight Flashes* (New York: American News Co., 1866): 171–178.

17. *Macready's Reminiscences and Selections from His Diaries and Letters*, vol. 2 (London: Macmillan and Co., 1875), 50.

18. Undated fragment in the Boucicault papers, Special Collections, Tampa Campus Library, University of South Florida.

19. "Every day a melancholy man called the *répétiteur*," wrote George Augustus Sala of the rehearsal of a pantomime, "takes his station on the stage, which is illumined by one solitary gas jet." The *répétiteur*'s thankless job, of course, was to keep time for the dancers and mimists to rehearse their steps. As Jerome K. Jerome and others noted, a fiddler was usually present for staging rehearsals of melodramas as well. George Augustus Sala, *Gaslight and Daylight, with Some London Scenes They Shine Upon* (London: Chapman and Hall, 1859), 30.

20. Leman Thomas Rede, *A Guide to the Stage, or How to Enter the Theatrical Profession, Obtain an Engagement, and Become an Actor; Founded on and Partly Taken from Leman Rede's Book* (New York: Samuel French [1827]), 5.

21. Some of this information derived from Anna Cora [Mowatt] Ritchie, *Mimic Life, or Before and Behind the Curtain* (Boston: Ticknor and Fields, 1856), 279–280. Ritchie describes "a speaking-trumpet, through which the prompter directs the musicians." Actor John Drew tells a story of playing a prank on the conductor when he was a boy. "Somehow we did not take ourselves very seriously in the days at my mother's theatre [the Arch Street in Philadelphia]. I can remember one night it seems now the humor of a very youthful schoolboy filling the speaking tube which ran from the prompter's box to the orchestra leader with face powder. Just as the orchestra was about to play the overture I lured the prompter from his place and then blew through the tube as the leader answered the signal. A very pale and much whitened orchestra leader received a great laugh from his men and the people sit-

ting down front. As three or four other young people in the company were accused in turn, I had to own up. The calling down that I got from an infuriated manager-mother had better be left to the imagination." John Drew, *My Years on the Stage* (New York: E. P. Dutton, 1921), 37–38. See also Davidge, *Footlight Flashes* 147, who takes the reader backstage at a theatre in chapter 15.

22. "Uncle Sam" (anonymous), "The Play behind the Scenes," *Ainsworth's Magazine* 1 (London, 1842): 157.

23. Charles Elwell French, *Six Years of Drama at the Castle Square Theatre: With Portraits of the Members of the Company* (Boston: C. E. French, 1903), 48; and Edward Renton, *The Vaudeville Theatre, Building, Operation, Management* (New York: Gotham, 1918), 296.

24. Richard Fawkes, *Dion Boucicault: A Biography* (London: Quartet Books, 1979), 42. Smith was also a playwright. His adaptation of Dickens's *Cricket on the Hearth* was given at the Lyceum under the Keeleys in 1845.

25. "Glenalvon" was a lead character in Home's tragedy *Douglas*.

26. Albert Smith, *The Fortunes of the Scattergood Family* (originally serialized in *Bentley's Miscellany* 1 [1844]; London: Richard Bentley, 1845), 132 (illustration opposite 138).

27. Coleman, *Charles Reade As I Knew Him*, 313.

28. Sarah Hibberd and Nanette Nielsen, "Music in Melodrama: 'The Burden of Ineffable Expression?'" *Nineteenth Century Theatre and Film* 29, no. 2 (Winter 2002): 32. Hibberd and Nielsen staged Jane Scott's melodrama *The Old Oak Chest* at Exeter and workshopped various approaches with live musicians.

29. Smith, *The Fortunes of the Scattergood Family*, 139.

30. Boucicault's manuscript promptbooks for two of the earliest plays that he prepared for Kean at the Princess's—*Pauline* (1851) and *The Vampire* (1852)—both show extensive markings for music within the body of the script and are often double-underlined. In *The Vampire* several cues are marked in the border as "Music" (circled) with a squiggly line down the side of the text (presumably indicating that the music should continue) until the indication of a circle intersected with a Swiss cross, which is explained: "à cette signe la musique cesse" (at this sign the music ceases). (This is in French, so the hand might be Boucicault's.) An extensive music cue, for example, occurs in act 1, Music 4, which begins on page 12 of the manuscript and runs for the rest of the page and all of pages 13 and 14 until the dramatic end of the scene, where the sign occurs.

31. "An Old Stager," *A Practical Guide to Theatricals* (London: Thomas Scott, 1875), 70.

32. Jim Davis, ed., *The Britannia Diaries: 1863–1875* (London: Society for Theatre Research, 1992), 66. *Fanfan the Tulip, or A Soldier's Fortune* was an adaptation by W. E. Suter from a French drama by Paul Maurice and was also given that year at the Princess's.

33. An American version was published in DeWitt's series in 1860, and an American Confederate soldier noted reading this "trashy novel" in 1865. Jenny Diver is not to be confused with Bella Starr, the "female Jesse James" of the American West.

34. "Bashi Bazook," "London Theatre Orchestras," *Musical World* 45, no. 36 (7 September 1867): 621–622.

35. *Jimmy Glover: His Book* (1911), 240–241, cited in David Mayer and Matthew Scott, *Four Bars of "Agit": Incidental Music for Victorian and Edwardian Melodrama* (London: Samuel French, 1983), 1. Mayer and Scott reproduce one such collection of manuscript *melos* pieces by Alfred Cooper.

36. In the Golden Collection at the Working Men's Institute, New Harmony, Indiana, is a book of music cues for several plays, including *The Danites*. The collection also includes more elaborate original music—arranged in six parts—for plays such as *The Flying Dutchman*, *The French Spy*, *Enoch Arden*, and *The Two Orphans*. Rodenbaugh's address in a *Clipper* announcement of the Golden Troupe in 1883 is given as Chicago, while his address in the 1890 *Clipper Annual* is Rochester, New York.

37. Conway's promptbook is at the Harry Ransom Center for the Humanities, University of Texas, Austin; Thomas Comer's music, in a set of orchestra parts, is at the New York Public Library Research Division in the collection of theatrical agent R. H. Burnside and was rescued from his warehouse in the Hippodrome Theatre before its destruction. The parts were used and many hand-dated with the years 1852, 1854, 1868, and 1876.

38. "Behind the Curtain," *Chambers's [Edinburgh] Journal of Popular Literature* 348 (1 September 1860): 131. I find it strange that the actress never reveals who she is in this article or gives any specifics as to theatre or production.

39. Ibid.

40. Instructions for "speaking through music" show up early. J. Pattie's 1838 edition of David Webster Osbaldiston's *Naomi* in the Modern Stage series contains several.

41. For a detailed analysis of this scene, based on the promptbooks of Kean and others, see Barry Yzereef, "The Art of Gentlemanly Melodrama: Charles Kean's Production of 'The Corsican Brothers'" (Ph.D. diss., University of Victoria, 1995), 114–128.

42. The playbills for the Princess's *Corsican Brothers* list Richard Hughes (brother of the old Coburg orchestra leader Thomas Hughes) as music director. No composer is mentioned, and the author of this music remains anonymous, despite the number of times that it was copied (five sets of *Corsican* parts are known to exist). Robert Stoepel, who took over from Hughes, was often credited with writing the "Ghost Melody," but when asked directly he resisted confirmation.

43. Mendelssohn to George Alexander MacFarren, in Henry C. Banister, *George Alexander Macfarren: His Life, Works, and Influence* (London, 1892), 183.

44. Karl Mendelssohn-Bartholdy, *Goethe and Mendelssohn (1821–1831)* (London:

Macmillan, 1872), 129–131. All of the following Mendelssohn quotations are from this source.

CHAPTER 7

1. *London Times* (27 June 1854), 12, col. B.

2. Dutton Cook, *Nights at the Play: A View of the English Stage* (London: Chatto and Windus, 1883), 339–340.

3. Copy of playbill found at the Discovering Leeds website, at the Local and Family History Library, Leeds City Council, Leeds, England.

4. John S. Kendall, *The Golden Age of the New Orleans Theatre* (Baton Rouge: Louisiana State Press, 1952), 513.

5. Arthur Hobson Quinn, "In Defense of Melodrama," *Bookman: A Review of Books and Life* (June 1925): 413.

6. The acting version of these plays rarely mentions any music cues. A set of orchestra parts used for *Masks and Faces* at the Haymarket in the 1880s has the orchestra play only six short *melos* numbers in the entire play.

7. Set of orchestra parts for *Under the Gaslight* in the R. H. Burnside Collection, New York Public Library. These are signed and dated "J. C. Kenney, 1876."

8. It can be argued that this style was already implicit in the newer plays of Edward Bulwer-Lytton and John Westland Marston.

9. Richard Fawkes, *Dion Boucicault: A Biography* (London: Quartet Books, 1979), 52.

10. John Russell Stephens, *The Profession of the Playwright: British Theatre, 1800–1900* (Cambridge: Cambridge University Press, 1992), 102–103.

11. Fawkes, *Dion Boucicault: A Biography*, 69–70.

12. John M. Maddox produced classical dramas with actors such as Charlotte Cushman and Edwin Forrest. But the theatre was known principally as an "English opera" theatre, under the musical leadership of Edward Loder. Some of the operas produced there were Balfe's *Geraldine, or The Lover's Well* (August 1843), Balfe's *The Caste of Aymon* (November 1844), Loder's *The Night Dancers* (October 1846), Rodwell's *The Seven Maids of Munich, or The Ghost's Tower* (December 1846), Loder's *Robin Goodfellow, or The Frolics of Puck* (December 1849), and Macfarren's *King Charles II* (October 1849).

13. Kate Field, *Charles Albert Fechter* (Boston: James R. Osgood and Company, 1882), 41; Dion Boucicault, "Early Days of a Dramatist," *North American Review* 148, no. 390 (May 1889): 592–593.

14. John William Cole, *The Life and Theatrical Times of Charles Kean*, vol. 2 (London: R. Bentley, 1859), 188, 191–192.

15. In the spirit of competition, the Adelphi produced Benjamin Webster's adaptation of *The Courier of Lyons* on 15 July 1854, with Leigh Murray playing both roles. No composer is credited on the playbill.

16. Quoted in Cole, *The Life and Theatrical Times of Charles Kean*, vol. 2, 110.

17. The promptbook is at Princeton and the score is at the Folger Shakespeare Library.

18. The technique had already been tried as early as 1833 for a murder scene in *Jonathan Bradford* at the Surrey. When it was used at the St. James's Theatre in 1851 for a classical drama, *Valeria*, a critic said that the stage technique "lowered the play to the dull level of a melodrama." W. J. Lawrence, "Some Stage Effects: Their Growth and History," *Gentleman's Magazine* 265 (1888): 91.

19. No cue no. 7 is marked in the score or mentioned in the promptbook; perhaps it was eliminated in rehearsal.

20. Perhaps Isaacson originally wrote music to accompany him and also for the brief action beforehand. In any case cue no. 10 is also missing from the score and was presumably cut.

21. Some textures and harmonies of this cue reveal the influence of Hector Berlioz, which suggests that Isaacson may have derived some of this music from the original French stage music. I have not investigated the music for the Gaïté production of *Courier* and do not know if it even exists, so I am unable to draw any conclusions about the relationship between the two scores.

22. *New York Herald* (2 March 1863), 8.

23. *New York Clipper* (1 May 1858), 14.

24. Michael Diamond, *Victorian Sensations, or the Spectacular, the Shocking, and the Scandalous in Nineteenth-Century Britain* (London: Anthem Press, 2003).

25. Walter C. Phillips, *Dickens, Reade, and Collins: Sensation Novelists* (New York: Columbia University Press, 1919), 1.

26. Mrs. Oliphant on "sensation novels," cited from *Blackwood's* in Diamond, *Victorian Sensations*, 189–190.

27. Dion Boucicault, "Leaves from a Dramatist's Diary," *North American Review* 149 (1889): 234; cited in Richard D. Altick, "Boucicault Stages Mary Barton," *Nineteenth-Century Fiction* 14, no. 2 (September 1959): 129–130.

28. James Hurt, "Dion Boucicault's Comic Myths," in *When They Weren't Doing Shakespeare: Essays on Nineteenth-Century British and American Theatre* (Athens: University of Georgia Press, 1989), 253.

29. When Boucicault died in 1890, his third wife (then age twenty-six) kept a trunk of his manuscripts, which included music. After her death in 1956, the trunk mysteriously ended up at the University of South Florida. The plays for which Boucicault retained some if not all the music were *The Long Strike* (Lyceum, 1866), *The Shaughraun* (Wallack's, 1874), *Belle Lamar* (Booth's, 1874), *The O'Dowd* (Adelphi, 1880), *The Amadan* (Boston, 1883), *The Jilt* (London, 1885), and a few fragments of a violin-leader part for *The Colleen Bawn* (Laura Keene's, 1860). Additional music to Boucicault plays, such as *The Octoroon* and additional sets of *The Colleen Bawn*, has since been located at Harvard and the British Library. With respect to *The Poor of New York*, the Templeman Library, University of Kent, has a set of parts entitled *The Streets of Brighton*. These were meant to accompany a production of the play

in that city by Andrew Melville and may have been used as late as 1928. Similarly, the "Arthur W. Tams Music Library" in 1895 loaned out music to *The Streets of New York*, but this consisted of the simplest of *melos* tunes that were obviously composed in that decade.

30. Stephen Foster, living only a few blocks from the Winter Garden Theatre, probably received not a penny for the song's use. The musical score for the Adelphi production in 1861 has different music, but the opening use of "Jeannie" is the same.

31. *San Francisco Daily Morning Call* (3 July 1864).

32. Fawkes, *Dion Boucicault: A Biography*, 118.

33. H. Barton Baker, "The Old Melo-drama," *Belgravia: A London Magazine* 50 (March to June 1883): 331–339.

34. Letter quoted in Dion Boucicault, "Letters from a Dramatist's Diary," *North American Review* 149 (August 1889): 231; and cited in Townsend Walsh, *The Career of Dion Boucicault* (New York: Dunlap Society, 1915), 71.

35. See Stephen Watt, "Irish American Drama of the 1850s: National Identity, 'Otherness,' and Assimilation," in Rachel M. McNair and Margaret M. Mulrooney, eds., *Fleeing the Famine: North America and Irish Refugees, 1845–1851* (Westport, Conn.: Praeger, 2003), 99.

36. *New York Times* (31 March 1860), 8.

37. *Freeman's Journal and Daily Commercial Advertiser* (30 March 1861), [3].

38. *New York Times* (31 March 1860), 8.

39. *New York Times* (7 April 1860), 5.

40. *Spirit of the Times* (21 April 1860), 132.

41. *London Times* (11 October 1860), 6.

42. *London Times* (30 April 1861), 12.

43. *New-York Daily Tribune* (30 March 1860), 8, sec. 8.

44. The original incident is related in Fawkes, *Dion Boucicault: A Biography*, 115–116.

45. A copy is included with the Drury Lane manuscript parts.

46. The music used at both Laura Keene's and the Adelphi (and in other productions) survives in three known sets of performance materials: fragments of a violin 1 book in the Boucicault Collection in Florida; a set of manuscript parts from the Boston Theatre dated 1863; and a complete set of clean, apparently unused or archival manuscript parts in the Drury Lane Theatre Archive, originally received from the "orchestra band office" at Fitzroy Square. The Drury Lane Theatre Archive part and the set at the Boston Theatre (Houghton Library, Harvard) use identical music as in the Tampa fragment. The "band office" first violin part matches those in the other two sources.

47. *Albion: A Journal of News, Politics, and Literature* 38, no. 13 (31 March 1860): 151.

48. A set of parts at the Boston Theatre includes a part for two cornets instead of one. Samuel French's list of available Music for Loan in 1882 lists only eight band

parts for *The Colleen Bawn*. This may have been one of Baker's versions for "small bands" mentioned in chapter 4.

49. "It is utterly devoid of that exaggeration which has been found 'ere now to have affected the stage representation of similar characters, and for its fidelity to nature and vividness of colouring it must be pronounced a model worthy of all future imitation." *Era* 1153 (28 October 1860).

50. For a discussion of music in this scene, see my essay "Music for the Theatre: Style and Function in Incidental Music," in Kerry Powell, ed., *The Cambridge Companion to Victorian and Edwardian Theatre* (Cambridge: Cambridge University Press, 2004), 86.

51. The sheet music of this song, "as sung by Agnes Robertson in Boucicault's drama," was published by John J. Daly, New York, in 1860.

52. Three different versions in three different promptbooks are compared in Lisa Cooper Warren, "Boucicault and Melodrama Onstage: The Evidence from Nineteenth-Century Advertising Illustrations from Staging, Blocking, and Costuming" (Ph.D. diss., University of Georgia, Athens, 1984), 109–116.

53. *London Times* (11 October 1860).

54. *Lloyd's Weekly Newspaper* 930 (16 September 1860).

55. *Orchestra* 3, no. 59 (November 1864): 101.

56. Charles Reade, "A Dramatic Musician," *Musical Standard* 15, no. 748 (30 November 1878): 342–343; reprinted in Charles Reade, *Readiana: Comments on Current Events* (London: Chatto and Windus, 1881), 28–31. Music for *Arrah-na-Pogue* has been found in three sources: two sets in the Oscar Barrett papers of the Drury Lane Theatre Archive (British Library) signed by W. C. Levey, a set of orchestra parts in the New York Public Library signed by Frank A. Howson, and an unidentified violin 1 part in the Seymour Collection at Princeton University.

57. "Scud" is a nautical term meaning "to run before a gale with little or no sail set." A British schooner named *Flying Scud* was seized in 1863 off the Texas coast during the American Civil War. A mine in Australia was named "Flying Scud" in the late 1860s. And in 1892 Robert Louis Stevenson and Lloyd Osbourne named a British brig in *The Wrecker* the *Flying Scud*.

58. *London Times* (6 October 1867); "Our Van," *Bailey's Magazine of Sports and Pastimes* (January 1867): 314.

59. The music was acquired by the University of Wisconsin, Madison, as part of the Tams-Witmark Collection. The eight orchestra parts (some bearing a "Holborn Theatre" title page) are incomplete; a few wind parts seem to be missing. These parts were copied for use at Wallack's Theatre and by George Belmore on his America tours of the play.

60. *Newcastle Courant* (12 October 1866), 2.

61. Boucicault duplicated this sensation in *Formosa, or The Railroad to Ruin* (Drury Lane and Niblo's Garden, 1869), a play about a famous boat race. The music was again by W. C. Levey.

62. The orchestra parts for *The Orange Girl* are now in the Drury Lane Theatre Archive, British Library.

63. For a dramaturgical study of these plays (though with no mention of music), see Lewin A. Goff, "The Popular Priced Melodrama in America, 1890 to 1910, with Its Origins and Development to 1890" (Ph.D. diss., Case Western Reserve University, 1948).

CHAPTER 8

1. "Theatres and Music Halls, *Orchestra* 6, no. 146 (14 July 1866): 245.

2. "Theatrical Licenses: 1," *Fraser's Magazine for Town and Country* 75, no. 445 (January 1867): 89.

3. Augustus Thomas, *The Print of My Remembrance* (New York: Charles Scribner's Sons, 1922), 88.

4. Tom Taylor, "The Theatre in England: Its Shortcomings and Possibilities," *Dark Blue* 1, no. 6 (August, 1871): 746–754. Several of the problems that Taylor pointed out were the high cost of stars' fees and the expense of "startling effects, and under-rehearsed weak actors in supporting roles, especially on tours." The *Era* response (27 August 1871) was "Mr. Tom Taylor and the Modern Drama."

5. Quoted in William Clement Scott, *From The Bells to King Arthur: A Critical Record of the First-Night Productions at the Lyceum Theatre from 1871 to 1895* (London: John MacQueen, 1896), 26. Scott often referred to Lyceum stage settings as "picturesque."

6. Advertisers in *The Era* and other periodicals from this time note "Hirers-Out of Stage Music" and list the following: "French, S., 89 Strand, W. C.; Lonsdale, C., 26 Old Bond Street, W.; Metzler, Great Marlborough Street, W. C.; Robinson, W., 369 Strand, W. C.; White & Son, 337 Oxford Street, W."

7. John W. Frick, *New York's First Theatrical Center: The Rialto at Union Square* (Ann Arbor: UMI Research Press, 1985), 2–3.

8. Peter A. Davis, "From Stock to Combination: The Panic of 1873 and Its Effects on the American Theatre Industry," *Theatre History Studies* 8 (1988): 5–6.

9. "New York Theatres," *Atlantic Monthly* 43, no. 258 (April 1879): 455.

10. An obituary for Tissington wrote that "he could be depended upon invariably to score work of serious merit for his very small orchestra with taste and judgment. He was proud of his chair in the Union Square Theatre and did not resign it to Mr. Solomon for the run of *Pepita* without a pang of regret." *Theatre* 1, no. 6 (26 April 1886): 159.

11. The Tams-Witmark Collection at the University of Madison, Wisconsin, only seems to have a set of loan parts for these two plays. Each is bound in Tams folders and stamped "Furnished by Arthur W. Tams Music Library, 109 W. 28th St., New York." *Camille,* dated 1894, includes many musical quotes from Giuseppe Verdi's *La Traviata.*

12. "When the Richmond Theatre [in Surrey] was first opened by Mr. Russell a

good band was engaged, with Mr. Berry at its head. But as time wore on and the receipts fell off, the number of instrumentalists gradually decreased, until at last Berry with his piano was the sole survivor. *He*, however, never deserted his post. In hot weather or cold, with salary or without, there he sat, night after night, thumping away at his instrument, with untiring energy and a cheerfulness which nothing could depress" (the theatre closed in 1884). Frederick Bingham, *A Celebrated Old Playhouse: The History of the Richmond Theatre* (London: Henry Vickers, 1886), 40.

13. "Drama, New Queen's," *Daily News* 6766 (9 January 1868).

14. These restrictions actually harken back to the way theatrical music was used before the eighteenth-century application of *melos* by Garrick and others.

15. *Ticket-of-Leave* is a protest drama against society's mistreatment of ex-convicts. "The Maniac's Tear" is listed in an 1868 Adelphi production as an "original song composed by Mrs. Tom Taylor," though J. H. Tully was leading the orchestra.

16. Pierce Egan, "Minor Theatres of London," *Atlantic Monthly* 25, no. 149 (March 1870): 297–298.

17. Squire Bancroft and Marie Bancroft, *Mr. and Mrs. Bancroft On and Off the Stage* (London: R. Bentley, 1888): 135–136; review in *London Times* (13 September 1869), 8.

18. Daniel Barrett, *T. W. Robertson and the Prince of Wales's Theatre* (New York: Peter Lang, 1995), 216.

19. "Agony Music in Theatres," *Times Picayune* (New Orleans) (3 December 1882), 2; reprinted from the *Milwaukee Sun*.

20. *Music and Drama* 1, no. 1 (7 January 1882): 7. See also "A Notable First Night," *New York Times* (5 January 1882), 5.

21. J. M. M., "About Music Cues," *Music and Drama* 3, no. 1 (8 July, 1882): 4–5.

22. "The Theatres," *Reader* 6, no. 106 (7 January 1865): 20.

23. Quoted in James Ewing Ritchie, *The Night Side of London*, 2nd ed. (London: William Tweedie, 1857), 220–221, 224–226.

24. Comments by J. E. Ritchie in *The Night Side of London* (1857), quoted in Frances Fleetwood, *Conquest: The Story of a Theatre Family* (London: W. H. Allen, 1953), 99.

25. "The Drama," *Reader* 5, no. 111 (11 February 1865): 177.

26. George Sennett Jr. came to E. L. Blanchard's attention at eleven years old playing a flying acrobat in *The Flying Dutchman*, the pantomime of 1869.

27. The theatre's library, recalled Erroll Sherson, contained an extensive collection of French plays from which Meritt and Pettitt derived many of their dramas. Erroll Sherson, *London's Lost Theatres of the Nineteenth Century* (London: John Lane, 1925), 22.

28. The text and stage directions are taken from a manuscript copy of the play deposited in the Lord Chamberlain's plays, British Library.

29. As Percy Fitzgerald remembered, many a British actor in the popular drama

followed the Parisian model of timing his speeches to music—"measuring his phrases"—rather than having the music pause for him. Quoted in David Mayer, "The Music of Melodrama," in David Bradby, Louis James, and Bernard Sharratt, eds., *Performance and Politics in Popular Drama: Aspects of Popular Entertainment in Theatre, Film, and Television, 1800–1976* (Cambridge: Cambridge University Press, 1980), 50.

30. George Taylor, *Players and Performances in the Victorian Theatre* (Manchester: Manchester University Press, 1989), 152.

31. Several excerpts from the Grecian production exist in the hand of Oscar Barrett in the Drury Lane Theatre Archive, British Library.

32. Stephen Cockett, "Acting with Music: Henry Irving's Use of the Musical Score in his Production of *The Bells*," in Rachel Cowgill and Julian Rushton, eds., *Europe, Empire and Spectacle in Nineteenth-Century British Music* (Aldershot: Ashgate Press, 2006), 235–248.

33. Percy Hetherington Fitzgerald, *The World behind the Scenes* (London: Ayer Publishing, 1881): 285.

34. According to George C. Odell, Antony was a "part to which [Bangs's] muscular figure and his bluff, hearty style were particularly adapted." Odell's *Annals of the New York Stage*, vol. 9, *1870–1875* (New York: Columbia University Press, 1937), 144.

35. Morris quoted in Burton E. Stevenson, *American Men of Mind* (New York: Doubleday, 1910), 172. It is largely because of Barrett's later tours around the United States and the preservation of his library that several items that Mollenhauer prepared originally for Booth's Theatre survive in the Harvard Theatre Collection.

36. John Ripley, *Julius Caesar on Stage in England and America, 1599–1973* (Cambridge: Cambridge University Press, 1980), 121.

37. *New York Times* (29 January 1873), 4.

38. The music survives in the Dion Boucicault Theatre Collection at the University of South Florida, Tampa.

39. Papering the audience for *Belle Lamar* is found in Townsend Walsh, *The Career of Dion Boucicault* (New York: Dunlap Society, 1915), 23. Criticism is discussed in Charles E. L. Wingate, *The Playgoers' Year-Book for 1888* (Boston: Stage Publishing Company, 1887), 21.

40. "It is next to impossible to extract a really satisfactory accompaniment from never so well drilled an orchestra," wrote one of the musicians, "unless the members there-of—not to speak of the conductor—are placed in active personal sympathy with either the singers or actors." "The Orchestra at Booths: A Protest against the Censure of Critics Generally and of Actors in Particular—The Sub-Stage Arrangement," *New York Herald* (30 November 1880), 4.

41. Davenport, in his antiheroic interpretation of Brutus, was said to carry a certain "weariness about the stage." O. E. Bunce, "Julius Caesar at Booth's Theatre," *Appleton's Journal* 15, no. 357 (22 January 1876): 115.

42. In fact several newspapers announcing the new production mention this music specifically. It was to consist of an original overture by Operti entitled "S.P.Q.R.," Gounod's "Triumphal March," and Saverio Mercadante's "Elegia funebre" for the final scene.

43. Gone are Artemidorus's warning to Caesar, Portia's second scene in which she tries to get a message to Brutus, the sequences set in motion by Antony's forum speech (including the scene of Antony and Octavius preparing their list of compatriots to be executed), and others.

44. Coppélia Kahn, *Roman Shakespeare: Warriors, Wounds, and Women* (London: Routledge, 1997), 105.

45. See a reconstructed edition of *The Mulligan Guard* by Katherine K. Preston, *Irish American Theater: The Mulligan Guard Ball* (New York: Garland, 1994). Preston said that the original only included four songs and that more songs were eventually added with subsequent revivals. There is no surviving overture and no evidence of affective melodramatic music.

46. *Dial* 45, no. 532 (16 August 1908): 78.

47. *New York Clipper Annual for 1893* (New York: Frank Queen Publishing Company, 1893), 152; Isaac Frederick Marcosson, *Charles Frohman, Manager and Man* (New York: Harper, 1916), 305.

48. William Winter, *The Life of David Belasco*, vol. 1 (New York: Moffat, Yard, and Company, 1929), 21–22, 84.

49. One of the touring Jagons, Frank A. Tannehill, held onto his copy of the orchestra parts, which is how they came to the New York Public Library, as a gift from his granddaughter.

50. "Mr. E. H. Sothern's Success in *Lord Chumley*," *New York Times* (21 August 1888), 5.

51. The *Lord Chumley* orchestra parts are for conductor, violin 1, violin 2, viola, cello, basso, flauto, clarinet, two cornets, two horns, trombone, and drums. Some of the brass instruments were also used onstage.

52. A plagal cadence is a closing progression from the subdominant to the tonic, usually written in roman numerals: IV to I.

53. *New York Times* (26 August 1888), 2.

54. Ibid.

CHAPTER 9

1. "The Theatres," *Saturday Review of Politics, Literature, Science, and Art*, 48, no. 1243 (23 August 1879): 239.

2. Wilhelm Reif (1832–1890) was a clarinetist and composer. Adolph Aber, commenting on scores that he examined from the Meiningen productions, wrote that they "enthalten nur die in Schauspiel unmittelbar geforderte Musik, meist in Musikstücken von wenigen Takten Umfang" (contained only music directly called

for in the playtexts, most encompassing a few bars each). *Die Musik in Schauspiel* (Leipzig: M. Beck, 1926), 64.

3. Walter Thornbury and Edward Walford, "Chapter 28: Drury Lane Theatre" in *Old and New London: A Narrative of Its History, Its People, and Its Places*, vol. 3 (London: Cassell, Petter, Galpin, and Co., 1878), 227.

4. *Musical Standard* 4, no. 451 (22 March 1873): 178.

5. "Antony and Cleopatra," *Examiner* 3426 (27 September 1873); and "Drury-Lane Theatre," *Era* 1827 (28 September 1873). No trace of Levey's music has yet been found.

6. "Antony and Cleopatra," *Pall Mall Gazette* 2685 (23 September 1873).

7. Michael Ainger, *Gilbert and Sullivan: A Dual Biography* (Oxford: Oxford University Press, 2002), 39.

8. "Manchester," *Orchestra* 54 (8 October 1864): 20. The use of other music is noted by F. G. T., *Reader* 4, no. 95 (22 October 1864): 522.

9. *Memoirs and Artistic Studies of Adelaide Ristori*, trans. G. Mantellini (New York: Doubleday, 1907), 69.

10. Theatre composer Norman O'Neill later wrote that *L'Arlésienne* was "one of the most perfect examples of the play with music . . . Quite extraordinary sympathy for the emotions through which the characters are passing is shown in the music which accompanies the dialogue." "Music to Stage Plays," *Proceedings of the Royal Music Association* (21 March 1911), 92.

11. Demar Irving, *Massenet: A Chronicle of His Life and Times* (Portland: Amadeus Press, 1994), 68.

12. In 1871 the Paris Conservatoire's Prix de Rome required its competitors to write a vocal setting of Joan's heroic speech from Barbier's play. See Annegret Fauser, "Gendering the Nations: The Ideologies of French Discourse on Music (1870–1914)," in Harry White and Michael Murphy, eds., *Musical Constructions of Nationalism* (Cork: Cork University Press, 2001), 75.

13. We have seen this kind of mixed repertoire of melodrama/national drama before, when the Coburg produced Jerrold's *Mutiny at the Nore* in 1830.

14. Régine Pernoud and Marie-Véronique Clin, *Joan of Arc: Her Story* (New York: St. Martin's Press, 1999), 239. E. Gérard published a "vocal score" for *Jeanne d'Arc* in keeping with the spirit of disseminating French nationalist music.

15. Detailed information on the production can be found in James Harding, *Gounod* (London: Stein and Day, 1973), 179.

16. The term *musique de scène*—identified in G. Hartmann's 1876 edition of the complete score of *Les Érinnyes*—is now commonly translated as "incidental music." Before the 1870s, however, the term in France had a more specific meaning, according to the *Dictionnaire de l'Académie française*, vol. 2 (1843). Examples of *musique de scène* given there are *musique d'église*, *musique de bal*, *musique militaire*, and so forth, all genres that would have emanated from on or behind the stage.

17. Revivals of *L'Arlésienne* took place at the Duke of York's in 1888 and at New York's Broadway Theatre in 1897 (with no less than Agnes Booth in the leading role). None lasted more than a few performances.

18. Ebenezer Prout attended this performance and provided an analysis of Beethoven's music to the play, "Crystal Palace Concerts: Beethoven's *Egmont*," *Academy* (14 March 1874), 301–302. The idea of creating *Zwischenrede*, newly written speeches to connect incidental music in concert performance, was first tried by Friedrich Mosegeil in 1821. See Elizabeth Paley, "*Zwischenrede für Zwischenacte*: *Egmont* and the Melodramatic Supplement," *South Atlantic Quarterly* 104, no. 1 (Winter 2005): 79–97.

19. P. I. Jurgenson's published score of 1898 leaves out the dialogue for the melodramas and treats them as purely instrumental pieces. Tchaikovsky returned to the legitimate stage in 1886 by providing some remarkably delicate music—featuring a harp—for a scene from Ostrovsky's *The Voyevoda* and again most notably with the Mikhailovsky Theatre's French-language production of *Hamlet*, staged in St. Petersburg in 1891. Tchaikovsky reorchestrated his previously written concert overture for the theatrical version, to which he also added seventeen numbers. This score is liberally seasoned with *mélodrames*. When Tchaikovsky's *Hamlet* music was published the following year, the spoken text was again left out. Even the text cues are missing, so it would be impossible to determine what speeches or dialogue these *mélodrames* were intended to accompany without access to the original performing materials.

20. Gustav Kobbé (review of some piano rolls of Grieg's *Peer Gynt* music), *The Pianolist: A Guide for Pianola Players* (New York: Moffat, Yard, and Co., 1907), 105–106.

21. Grieg's stage music was not published until 1919 and then published by C. F. Peters in a German translation (incomplete).

22. George Godwin, "The National Theatre Question," *Theatre* (December 1878): 346–352.

23. Cited in Jeremy Dibble, *Charles Villiers Stanford: Man and Musician* (Oxford: Oxford University Press, 2002), 77.

24. A useful overview of Sullivan's stage music has been compiled (and perhaps authored) by Marc Shepherd and can be found online at http://gasdisc.oakapplepress.com/sullinci.htm.

25. Percy Fitzgerald, "The Lyceum Staff: A Victorian Theatrical Organization," *Theatre Notebook* 18, no. 1 [1974]: 11–17.

26. "*Hamlet* at the Lyceum," *Era* (5 January 1879), 12.

27. Clement Scott, *From The Bells to King Arthur: A Critical Record of the First-Night Productions at the Lyceum Theatre from 1871 to 1895* (London: John Macqueen, 1897), 140.

28. J. F. R., "Music in Theatres," *Monthly Musical Record* 25, no. 296 (1 August 1895): 169–172.

29. "Incidental Music," *National Observer* 13, no. 323 (26 January 1895): 295.

30. Percy Hetherington Fitzgerald, *Henry Irving: A Record of Twenty Years at the Lyceum* (London: Chapman and Hall, 1893), 109–110.

31. David Mayer, "Parlour and Platform Melodrama," in Michael Hays and Anastasia Nikolopoulou, eds., *Melodrama: The Cultural Emergence of a Genre* (New York: St. Martin's Press, 1996), 221.

32. "Mr. Irving's Newest Work," *New York Times* (26 March 1882).

33. "Music for *Romeo and Juliet*," *Musical World* (25 March 1882), 181; reprinted from the *Daily News*.

34. Ellen Terry, *The Story of My Life: Recollections and Reflections* (London: Hutchinson and Company, 1908), 209.

35. See, for example, "Mr. Irving's Newest Work," *New York Times* (26 March 1882), 3.

36. Bram Stoker, *Personal Reminiscences of Henry Irving*, vol. 1 (London: Macmillan, 1906), 95.

37. Benedict's seventy-five-page manuscript score to the overture is at the Folger Shakespeare Library.

38. Weedon Grossmith, *From Studio to Stage: Reminiscences of Weedon Grossmith* (London: John Lane, 1913), 175–176.

39. "Music at the Play," *Era* 2011 (8 April 1877).

40. Louis Calvert, *Problems of the Actor* (New York: Henry Holt, 1918), 222–223.

41. Edgar Shelton, "Victorian Memories," *Music and Letters* 29, no. 1 (January 1948): 7. Shelton tells this story to demonstrate how insensitive Irving could be to time wasted by Clarke and his musicians. Shelton does not say whether the issue was resolved and the orchestra members attended rehearsal the following morning.

42. Stoker, *Personal Reminiscences of Henry Irving*, 111.

43. Irving published his adaptation of *Macbeth* (London: Nassau Steam Press, 1889) with a four-page preface that includes a discussion of Sullivan's music in the play. The full score used by Ball at the production is at the Harry Ransom Center, University of Texas at Austin.

44. *Birmingham Daily Post* (1 Jan. 1889), 5.

45. Kenneth DeLong recently made an elaborate analysis of Sullivan's music to Irving's *Macbeth*: "Arthur Sullivan's Incidental Music to Henry Irving's Production of *Macbeth* (1888)," in Richard Foulkes, ed., *Henry Irving: A Re-Evaluation of the Pre-eminent Victorian Actor-Manager* (Burlington, Vt.: Ashgate Publishing, 2008), 149–184.

46. See especially "The Macbeth Music," *Era* (26 January 1889).

47. Stephen Fiske, "The Irving Influence in America," *Theatre* 27 (1 February 1896): 77.

48. Cited in Jeffrey Richards, *Sir Henry Irving: A Victorian Actor and His World* (London: Hambledon, 2005), 217. Irving repeated this in his article "The Art of Acting 1," *English Illustrated Magazine* 22 (July 1885): 650.

49. Frederick Widmore, "The Stage. *The Dead Heart* at the Lyceum," *Academy* (12 October 1889), 243.

50. "Mus in Urbe," *Musical World* 69, no. 40 (October 1889): 691.

51. *Pall Mall Gazette* 49, no. 7654 (28 September 1889): 4.

52. Georges Jacobi (1840–1906) had played first violin at the Opéra Comique and later at the Grand Opéra Paris then conducted at the Théâtre des Bouffes for Jacques Offenbach. In England he had been first violin at the Royal Italian Opera, Covent Garden, before taking the position at the Alhambra. In addition to composing some one hundred ballets he also wrote about twenty comic operas. Information from an obituary in Brampton Hunt, ed., *The Green Room Book* (London: Sealey Clark, 1906), 183.

53. *Era* (5 October 1889), 8.

54. *Pall Mall Gazette* 49, no. 7654 (28 September 1889): 4.

55. *Lloyd's Weekly Newspaper* 2446 (6 October 1889): 4.

56. *Era* (5 October 1889), 8.

57. A full account of the development of Rankin's production and Kelley's music over the course of the 1880s can be found in David Beasley, *McKee Rankin and the Heyday of the American Theater* (Waterloo, Ontario: Wilfrid Laurier University Press, 2002), 211–218. As had Stanford and Jacobi, Kelley wrote a good chunk of his music before *Macbeth* went into rehearsal, but the action and under-dialogue music was crafted together with the actors and director.

58. Mus in Urbe [pen name], "Much Ado about Nothing," *Musical World* (10 January 1891), 34–35.

59. Ellen Terry, *The Story of My Life: Recollections and Reflections* (New York: McClure Company, 1908), 168.

60. The account of Mackenzie and Irving is told with slightly different wording in Bram Stoker, *Personal Reminiscences of Henry Irving* (London: William Heinemann, 1907), 337; and Austin Brereton, *The Life of Henry Irving*, vol. 2 (London: Longmans, Green, 1908), 293.

61. Alexander Mackenzie, "Sir Henry Irving and Music: Some Reminiscences," *Musical Times* 46, no. 753 (1 November 1905): 714–716.

62. "Edward German: A Biographical Sketch," *Musical Times* 45, no. 731 (1 January 1904): 20–24.

63. Ibid., 22. The *Richard III* overture was available for performance before Novello engraved it in 1902. German himself prepared the "selection," which was published in 1890 by Edwin Ashdown.

64. George Bernard Shaw, "Richard Orchestrated," *Star* (23 March 1889), reprinted in *Shaw's Music: The Complete Musical Criticism in Three Volumes*, vol. 1 (London: Bodley Head, 1981), 586 f.

65. David Russell Hulme, "Orpheus with His Lute: Sources of Edward German's Music for the Victorian and Edwardian Drama," *Brio* 37, no. 2 (Autumn/Winter 2000).

66. Scott, *From The Bells to King Arthur*, 333. When Beerbohm Tree produced *Henry VIII* in 1910 he invited German to revise his well-known score.

67. An extensive analysis of German's music to *Romeo and Juliet* was published in the *Musical Times* (1 October 1895), 673. His complete musical score is still unpublished.

68. Richards, *Sir Henry Irving*, 401.

69. George Bernard Shaw, "*King Arthur*, a Drama in a Prologue and Four Acts," *Saturday Review of Politics, Literature, Science, and Art* 79, no. 2047 (19 January 1895): 93–95. The complete text of *King Arthur*, a copy of the Lyceum program book, and reviews may be found at http://www.lib.rochester.edu/camelot/carr-dh.htm.

70. There are two known copies of Sullivan's full score, one at the Harry Ransom Center, University of Texas, Austin, Texas, and the other at the Pierpoint-Morgan Library in New York City.

71. Scott, *From The Bells to King Arthur*, 374.

CHAPTER 10

1. Charles Skinner, "The Musical Accompaniment," reprinted from the *Dramatic Mirror* in *Musical World* (19 July 1890), 572–573.

2. In *The People's Theatre*, trans. Barrett H. Clark (New York: Holt, 1918), Romain Rolland was paraphrasing an article by Georges Jubin, "Le théâtre populaire et le mélodrame," *Revue d'Art Dramatique* 2 (1897): 972–976.

3. Helen Maud Tree, "Herbert and I," in Max Beerbohm, ed., *Herbert Beerbohm Tree: Some Memories of His Art* (New York: E. P. Dutton, 1920), 45.

4. "Beerbohm Tree on Music," *Era* (3 June 1899).

5. "The Haymarket Theatre," *British Architect* 13 (13 February 1880): 75.

6. A. G. Stephens, *A Queenslander's Travel-Notes* (Sydney: Edwards, Dunlop, 1894), 171–172.

7. Percy Notcutt, "Musical Notes," *Theatre* (1 October 1893), 232.

8. Recounted by Arthur Collins in Brian Rees, *A Musical Peacemaker: The Life and Work of Sir Edward German* (Windsor Forest, UK: Kensal Press, 1987), 82.

9. Henry Arthur Jones, *The Tempter* (London: Macmillan, 1898), 9. This beginning scene was apparently a technical disaster on opening night, when most of the reviewers were present. Presumably the kinks were ironed out over the next performances.

10. "The Incidental Music of *The Tempter*," *Pall Mall Gazette* (26 September 1893), 3. It would be interesting to know what other creative solutions orchestra leaders came up with throughout the century to respond to a manager's need for a dramatic chord of punctuation.

11. John Ripley, "Sociology and Soundscape: Herbert Beerbohm Tree's 1908 *Merchant of Venice*," *Shakespeare Quarterly* 56, no. 4 (Winter 2005): 391–392. Ripley includes sample pages of the promptbook.

12. George Du Maurier, *Trilby* (New York: Harper and Brothers, 1894), 59. For more on Du Maurier and Potter's character, see George Taylor, "Svengali: Mesmerist and Aesthete," in Richard Foulkes, ed., *British Theatre in the 1890s: Essays on Drama and the Stage* (Cambridge: Cambridge University Press, 1992), 93–110.

13. The music plot for *Trilby* is in the Tree Collection, University of Bristol.

14. *Globe* (31 October 1895), clipping in the Tree Collection, Bristol.

15. This score exists intact in the Tree Collection of Theatre Music, Boston Public Library.

16. On one occasion, inevitably, Tree stopped "playing" while Roze kept going. But the technique was otherwise extremely effective.

17. Roze did not bang out the bass in a different key, as Du Maurier has Svengali do in his novel.

18. Quoted in Malcolm Sterling Mackinlay, *Antoinette Sterling and Other Celebrities* (London: Hutchinson, 1906), 212; "A Regular Rip!" *Punch* 118 (20 June 1900): 434. A glance at Roze's entr'acte for act 3 reveals only a superficial relationship to the Gounod work; perhaps an allusion to the conspirators as "soldiers" was intentional.

19. Roze obituary in *Musical Herald* (1 May 1920), 224; Henry Joseph Wood, *My Life of Music* (London: V. Gollancz, 1938), 63; *Punch* 118 (20 June 1900): 434; Shaw's review of *Julius Caesar* (22 January 1898), reprinted in George Bernard Shaw, *Dramatic Opinions and Essays*, vol. 2 (London: Brentano's, 1907), 408.

20. Clement Scott, *The Drama of Yesterday and Today*, vol. 2 (London: Macmillan, 1899), 353.

21. *Zenda* even offered Sothern and Alexander the old *Corsican coup* of role-doubling, playing both the kidnapped king and the hapless impostor who is mistaken for him. The New York *Zenda* supposedly had music by Frank Howson, while Walter Slaughter provided a new score for London. Neither has been found. A set of parts for *Zenda* in the Lawrence Barrett Collection, Houghton Library, is unsigned.

22. J. F. N., "The Three Musketeers," *Academy* 1384 (12 November 1898): 260–261.

23. Tree's promptbook is in the Bristol Theatre Collection and is corroborated by the Liebler set of promptbooks at the New York Public Library. As for Grundy's play, reviews were contradictory. A reviewer in *Life Magazine* was disappointed that Grundy could not "tell a connected story and hold the attention of some one besides the gallery gods." *Life* 33, no. 851 (23 March 1899): 232–233. In stark contrast, the *Saturday Review* credited "the marvelous skill and ingenuity" that Grundy displayed "in telling a clear story, while he managed at the same time to include a very large number of the leading incidents." *Saturday Review* 86, no. 2246 (12 November 1898): 630–632.

24. Arthur Lawrence, "The Idler at the Play," *Idler: Illustrated Magazine* 14, no. 6 (January 1899): 805.

25. Herbert Bergman, "David Belasco's Dramatic Theory," *University of Texas Studies in English* 32 (1953): 110–122.

26. *Washington Post* (23 November 1902), clippings file, New York Public Library.

27. Unidentified author, "A Japanese Play Criticized by a Japanese," *Critic* 41, no. 1 (January 1903): 70.

28. This synopsis is an embellished version from Craig Timberlake, *Bishop of Broadway: The Life and Work of David Belasco* (New York: Library Publishers, 1954), who has written a plot synopsis of model concision.

29. "High Water Mark for Belasco," *Munsey's Magazine* (1903): 786–787.

30. "*Darling of the Gods* Sets New Mark in Pictorial Drama," unidentified article, New York Public Library clippings file.

31. Brander Matthews, "The Art of the Stage Manager," *North American Review* 178, no. 567 (February 1904): 257.

32. "The Music in *The Darling of the Gods,*" *Washington Post* (23 November 1902), 39.

CONCLUSION

1. See, for example, music for Andrew Melville's productions at the Metropole Theatre, Birmingham, and the Grand Theatre, Brighton, held in the Templeman Library, University of Kent, Canterbury.

2. Arthur Symons, "Music in the Theatre," *Academy and Literature* 63 (June/December 1902): 68. This essay is reproduced in Symons's book *Plays, Acting, and Music* (London: Duckworth, 1903).

3. Clayton Meeker Hamily, *The Theory of the Theatre, and Other Principles of Dramatic Criticism* (New York: Holt and Co., 1910), 110–111.

4. Percy Cross Standing, "Chiefs of the Orchestras," *Crown* (24 May 1906), 60–61 (includes photographs of Howard Talbot, Walter Slaughter, Paul Graener, Herman Finck, Clarence Corri, and Frederick Rosse).

5. "Theatre Orchestras," *New York Times* (18 October 1907), 10.

6. "Shifting Scenes in the Dark," *New York Sun* (14 January 1912), 2.

7. Orchestra parts acquired from Charles B. Hanford at the Folger Shakespeare Library, Washington, D.C. Many were Carl Fischer publications.

8. Norman O'Neill, "Music to Stage Plays," *Proceedings of the Royal Musical Association* (1910–1911): 88–89.

9. Information on Al Henderson from "*The Mikado* for Polish Relief Fund," *New York Times* (28 July 1915); and Al Henderson, *The Witmark Incidental Music* (London: M. Witmark and Sons, 1901).

10. Frank Dumont, *The Witmark Amateur Minstrel Guide and Burnt Cork Encyclopedia* (Chicago: M. Witmark and Sons, 1905), [161].

11. Henderson, *The Witmark Incidental Music*, no. 68, title page. The 15-page volume of *melos* items in *The Witmark Incidental Music* that I was able to see at

the George Eastman House, Rochester, New York, was numbered 68, which implies that it was part of a much larger series.

12. Clarence E. Sinn, "Music for the Picture," *Moving Picture World* (11 October 1913), 144.

13. Conversation between Bob Mitchell and myself, Los Angeles, October 2007.

14. Adolph Zukor, "Famous Players in Famous Plays," *Moving Picture World* (11 July 1914), 186, quoted in Sumiko Higashi, *Cecil B. DeMille and American Culture: The Silent Era* (Berkeley: University of California Press, 1994), 7–8.

15. "Special Music for *Arrah-na-Pogue*," *Kalem Kalendar* (22 December 1911), 6; "Daly's Version of *Frou Frou*," *Moving Picture World* 18, no. 11 (13 December 1913): 1288. *The Autobiography of Cecil B. DeMille* (1959; reprint New York: Garland, 1985), 135.

16. In his article "Background Music for Radio Drama," composer Boris Kremenliev identified four categories of music "used in the presentation of the unseen drama." He called them signature, curtain, bridge, and background. *Hollywood Quarterly* 4, no. 1 (Autumn 1949): 76.

17. For a more detailed comparison of theatrical and film melodrama, see Michael V. Pisani, "When the Music Surges: Nineteenth-Century Theatrical Precedents for Film Music Style and Placement," in *The Oxford Handbook to Film Music*, ed. David Neumeyer (Oxford: Oxford University Press, 2014).

18. Nathan Platte, "Music for *Spellbound* (1945): A Contested Collaboration," *Journal of Musicology* 28, no. 4 (Fall 2011): 418–463.

INDEX

Theatre locations are in either London or New York, unless otherwise specified. An asterisk indicates an illustration, musical example, or table.

STUDIES IN THEATRE HISTORY AND CULTURE

Actors and American Culture, 1880–1920
By Benjamin McArthur

The Age and Stage of George L. Fox, 1825–1877: An Expanded Edition
By Laurence Senelick

American Theater in the Culture of the Cold War: Producing and Contesting Containment
By Bruce McConachie

Athenian Tragedy in Performance: A Guide to Contemporary Studies and Historical Debates
By Melinda Powers

Classical Greek Theatre: New Views of an Old Subject
By Clifford Ashby

Czech Theatre Design in the Twentieth Century: Metaphor and Irony Revisited
Edited by Joseph Brandesky

Embodied Memory: The Theatre of George Tabori
By Anat Feinberg

Fangs of Malice: Hypocrisy, Sincerity, and Acting
By Matthew H. Wikander

Fantasies of Empire: The Empire Theatre of Varieties and the Licensing Controversy of 1894
By Joseph Donohue

French Theatre Today: The View from New York, Paris, and Avignon
By Edward Baron Turk

A Historiographical Guide to Theatrical Performance in Ancient Athens
By Melinda Powers

The Jewish Kulturbund Theatre Company in Nazi Berlin
By Rebecca Rovit

Jews and the Making of Modern German Theatre
Edited by Jeanette R. Malkin and Freddie Rokem

The Making of Theatrical Reputations: Studies from the Modern London Theatre
By Yael Zarhy-Levo

Marginal Sights: Staging the Chinese in America
By James S. Moy

Melodramatic Formations: American Theatre and Society, 1820–1870
By Bruce A. McConachie

Meyerhold: A Revolution in Theatre
By Edward Braun

Modern Czech Theatre: Reflector and Conscience of a Nation
By Jarka M. Burian

Modern Hamlets and Their Soliloquies: An Expanded Edition
By Mary Z. Maher

Molière, the French Revolution, and the Theatrical Afterlife
By Mechele Leon

The Most American Thing in America: Circuit Chautauqua as Performance
By Charlotte M. Canning

Music for the Melodramatic Theatre in Nineteenth-Century London and New York
By Michael V. Pisani

"Othello" and Interpretive Traditions
By Edward Pechter

Our Moonlight Revels: "A Midsummer Night's Dream" in the Theatre
By Gary Jay Williams

The Performance of Power: Theatrical Discourse and Politics
Edited by Sue-Ellen Case and Janelle Reinelt

Performing History: Theatrical Representations of the Past in Contemporary Theatre
By Freddie Rokem

The Recurrence of Fate: Theatre and Memory in Twentieth-Century Russia
By Spencer Golub

Reflecting the Audience: London Theatregoing, 1840–1880
By Jim Davis and Victor Emeljanow

Representing the Past: Essays in Performance Historiography
Edited by Charlotte M. Canning and Thomas Postlewait

The Roots of Theatre: Rethinking Ritual and Other Theories of Origin
By Eli Rozik

Shakespeare and Chekhov in Production: Theatrical Events and Their Audiences
By John Tulloch

Shakespeare on the American Yiddish Stage
By Joel Berkowitz

The Show and the Gaze of Theatre: A European Perspective
By Erika Fischer-Lichte

Stagestruck Filmmaker: D. W. Griffith and the American Theatre
By David Mayer

Strange Duets: Impresarios and Actresses in the American Theatre, 1865–1914
By Kim Marra

Textual and Theatrical Shakespeare: Questions of Evidence
Edited by Edward Pechter

Theatre and Identity in Imperial Russia
By Catherine A. Schuler

Theatre, Community, and Civic Engagement in Jacobean London
By Mark Bayer

Theatre Is More Beautiful Than War: German Stage Directing in the Late Twentieth Century
By Marvin Carlson

Theatres of Independence: Drama, Theory, and Urban Performance in India since 1947
By Aparna Bhargava Dharwadker

The Theatrical Event: Dynamics of Performance and Perception
By Willmar Sauter

The Trick of Singularity: "Twelfth Night" and the Performance Editions
By Laurie E. Osborne

The Victorian Marionette Theatre
By John McCormick

Wandering Stars: Russian Emigré Theatre, 1905–1940
Edited by Laurence Senelick

Writing and Rewriting National Theatre Histories
Edited by S. E. Wilmer

THE LIFE OF ALBERTA HENRY

Colleen Whitley

The University of Utah Press
Salt Lake City

The Defiance House Man colophon is a registered trademark of The University of Utah Press. It is based on a four-foot-tall Ancient Puebloan pictograph (late PIII) near Glen Canyon, Utah.

Library of Congress Cataloging-in-Publication Data

Names: Whitley, Colleen, 1940- author, interviewer, editor. | Henry, Alberta, 1920–2005, interviewee (expression)
Title: The life of Alberta Henry/Colleen Whitley.
Description: Salt Lake City : University of Utah Press, [2019]. | Includes bibliographical references.
Identifiers: LCCN 2018051869 (print) | LCCN 2018053079 (ebook) | ISBN 9781607816942 () | ISBN 9781607816935 (cloth : alk. paper)
Subjects: LCSH: Henry, Alberta, 1920–2005. | Civil rights workers—Utah—Biography. | Women, Black—Utah—Biography.
Classification: LCC E185.97.H448 (ebook) | LCC E185.97.H448 W47 2019 (print) | DDC 323.092 [B]—dc23
LC record available at https://lccn.loc.gov/2018051869

Errata and further information on this and other titles available online at UofUpress.com.

Printed and bound in the United States of America.

She was one of those people of stature who need only one name. When anyone said, "Alberta would like to meet with you," people knew who she was and what that meeting would likely be about. It would be about justice, opportunity, community and caring. . . . She was never a role model for just blacks but was a role model for Americans of every color and creed.

—"Alberta Henry," *Deseret News*

CONTENTS

INTRODUCTION

In 1972 Alberta Henry was hired as a minority consultant for Salt Lake City School District. She took that job just as the tensions of both the civil rights movement and the women's liberation movement were being widely acknowledged and hotly debated. And she was in the thick of both battles. Some people felt deep respect and affection for her while others felt something close to hatred. She acknowledged that her own approach did nothing to ease those feelings: "I don't sugarcoat anything. In fact, I don't know how to do that. I didn't like myself very much in those days, but I had a job to do. I usually wasn't very nice."[1] Carolyn Kemp, member of the Salt Lake City School Board at that time and later the first woman to serve as its president, fully understood the problems Alberta faced: "She was black and a woman. If she'd been nice, they'd have chewed her up and spit her out."[2]

I first met Alberta in October of 1998 when I was working on *Worth Their Salt, Too: More Notable but Often Unnoted Women of Utah*. I had wanted to include her in the first *Worth Their Salt* book published two years earlier, the result of several years of work by twenty people fascinated by remarkable women who had done great things but who were by then pretty much forgotten.[3] My proposal to include Alberta, however, was firmly squelched at the initial planning meeting for the project on the grounds that she was much too political.

I argued, "We've got Esther Landa, for crying out loud. How much more political can we get?" Those good historians pointed out that Landa was long since retired but Alberta was still president of the Salt Lake City Chapter of the National Association for the Advancement of Colored People (NAACP) and a member or officer in dozens of other organizations, and was still in the thick of civil rights negotiations—often dealing with people who weren't even aware of their own prejudices. So I reluctantly conceded the point.

By the time *Salt, Too* got under way, however, Alberta had turned the reins of leadership of the NAACP over to her protegee, Jeanetta Williams, and was no longer in the midst of every political and civil rights action in the area, even if she was still well aware of issues and holding very strong opinions. I insisted she was fair game. An out-of-state author with local ties volunteered to write an article on her, and I was satisfied—at least, I was until a year later when that author suddenly called and said she could not finish the work. Worse, her call came one day after another author had fallen through on Edith Melendez, a Hispanic linchpin in the Utah Democratic Party. Melendez was the only other woman of color who had survived earlier attrition, so I was looking at a lily-white slate of subjects, and the first draft was due at the press in a month. I knew I could not ask anyone else to jump in that fast, and I did not want to lose Alberta Henry a second time, so I called her, explained the situation, and she said simply, "Come on over. Let's see what we can do."

Two days later I was in her kitchen, where she was scrambling through the Bible, looking for a particular verse, which I happened to know. We bonded over Acts 3:6, Peter's command to a lame beggar, "Silver and gold have I none; but such as I have given I thee: In the name of Jesus Christ of Nazareth rise up and walk."[4] I didn't know then how unusual it was for someone to know where to find a verse in the Bible when Alberta did not. And as I think about it now, telling people to "rise up and walk" was exactly what Alberta Henry had spent her life doing.

Once we had settled Peter and the lame beggar and she had told me that everyone just called her Alberta and I told her to make me Colleen, we held our first recorded interview. When we concluded, she led me into the living room and showed me a large pile of papers, scrapbooks, newspaper clippings, and notes stacked on, under, and around her coffee table. She said they were all of her papers and I should take them and return them when I was through. I questioned her sanity. She said a lot of people did that. When I suggested her papers belonged in a university library, she said she would consider that. She did. Alberta's records are now housed in the J. Willard Marriott Library at the University of Utah.

I took her records—they filled the entire trunk and most of the back seat of my car—and went to work copying them in my office at Brigham Young University. I spent more than eight hours over a hot copy machine. I could have spent eight years to accumulate so much material without them, and then I would never have found the personal letters Alberta had included. When I returned her records the next week, we settled into the conversations that became the basis of the article for *Worth Their Salt, Too* and for this book as well.

Alberta said she would like this book to be her own autobiography. We set out to make it that: her words in the text with notes from me providing context, like identities of historical events or individuals. Unfortunately, death was quicker than we were, so it was not completed before she moved on. Consequently, I have tried to do the next best thing. All of Alberta's statements from our recorded interviews and extensive conversations, in person and by telephone, appear in one font, as do any quotations by Alberta from newspapers and interviews other than mine, the latter with quotation marks and citations. The rest of the book, including all quotations from sources other than Alberta, is in the same font as mine.

The organization of the book is essentially chronological, but given Alberta's extensive involvement in so many organizations at the same time, deciding where to include many pieces of information became a lot like waltzing with an octopus. While she was working with the Salt Lake City schools, for example, she was also involved in the NAACP, the Democratic Party, Model Cities, Altrusa Club, her church, her family, and at least two dozen other organizations. I've occasionally included endnotes to connect those items to further context in other chapters. I have also added occasional asides, especially when it is necessary to know the look she had on her face or the tone in which she made a given statement. She could be quite dramatic. And funny.

The historical context for her life and actions comes from published sources or those papers Alberta let me copy, but much of it comes from people who were kind enough to grant me interviews. Helen Sandack, for example, charmingly described their first meeting, Alberta's interview for the only job she ever applied for in Utah. Mrs. Sandack explained that she immediately hired Alberta as a maid after her baby, Artie Sandack, crawled into the room and Alberta picked him up. Watching her interactions with baby Artie, she knew Alberta would fit very well into their family. Then she added, "Alberta became my very best friend."[5] Donald Thomas, who became the superintendent of Salt Lake City School District in 1973 and one of Alberta's strongest allies, was most gracious in an extensive interview and in answering subsequent questions by telephone. Alberta's brother, David, confirmed Alberta's memories of life in Topeka, and he added a few more she hadn't mentioned. Her daughter, Julia, recalled her own involvement in many of her mother's good works from the time she was a child until just before her mother's death. Stuart Reid talked about first meeting Alberta when she decided to approach the LDS Church about community relations; Reid became both her good friend and a board member of the Salt Lake City Chapter of the NAACP. Reverend France Davis remembered working with Alberta on a range of projects from the time he first met her in the early 1970s until just before her death, when she was a volunteer at Calvary Baptist Church. Many other people—family members, neighbors, academics, religious leaders, students she helped—graciously provided information from their personal interactions with Alberta over her years in Utah.

Alberta's life spanned an important and turbulent period in U.S. history. She was born in a sharecropper's shack in segregated Louisiana in 1920, moved to semi-segregated/partially integrated Topeka, Kansas, in 1924, and arrived in mostly white/mostly Mormon Salt Lake City in 1948, just as the relationships among races and ethnic groups in America were beginning to alter more radically than they ever had before, even at the end of the Civil War.

During and immediately after World War II Americans had come to recognize both the depths and horrors of racial discrimination, not only through seeing what Hitler's ethnic cleansing had done to Jews, Gypsies, and others he despised, but also through witnessing how Americans were treating our own minorities: Japanese Americans were forced into relocation centers for the duration of the war. Black soldiers had to eat outdoors, sitting on the floor of railroad platforms while white German and Italian prisoners of war ate inside sitting at tables in the dining rooms. In 1954 the Supreme Court decision in *Brown v. Board of Education of Topeka* made many of us aware of legalized segregation in the Southern states, and then we looked around and recognized the less formal but still hurtful discrimination in our own neighborhoods. That recognition helped most of us understand the need for the civil rights movement of the 1960s and 1970s.

While the violent verbal and often physical responses of Southern politicians like George Wallace and police officers like Chief Theophilus

Eugene "Bull" Connor to legal requests and peaceful marches shocked the rest of the nation, national heroes like Medgar Evers, Martin Luther King Jr., and A. Philip Randolph led the effort to make all of us full citizens of the same country. Able as those national leaders were, and dramatic though their actions often were, the civil rights movement succeeded largely because local leaders like Alberta Henry took up the cause at home. They informed their friends and neighbors of the de facto segregation and often total discrimination in their own backyards. They worked in the trenches—school board meetings and city councils and individual homes, usually without the blaze of television lights—to end segregation in housing, seating in theaters, and access to schools, restaurants and dozens of other areas, segregation often invisible to the majority of the population. The Southern Colored Codes provided clear targets, but the lack of formal codification in areas like Utah presented an entirely different and often more difficult target.

Because Alberta's life began in an era of overt bigotry and ended after most legal distinctions had been eliminated, even though individual prejudices remain, this book will use a range of racial references, particularly in quotations. Some simply reflect the polite terminology of the specific times: "colored" then "Negro" then "Black" then "African American" and occasionally back to "Black" with or without the capital *B*. In this book any such references will appear as they do in the quotations and in the text simply as "black" and "white" regardless of the designation at the time in question. Since this text is based as much as possible on direct interviews and personal papers, all of those forms will appear, as will an occasional racial slur or epithet. Alberta didn't react to them; she even quoted them herself at times, so I figure that if she could tolerate them, we'll live with them when they show up here and then move on to more important issues. Alberta would have expected nothing less from us.

Similarly, Alberta grew up speaking what would have been called at that time "American Negro dialect" (subsequently called African American English, Black English, Black Vernacular, Black English Vernacular [BEV] or Black Vernacular English [BVE], and Ebonics). Both politeness and political correctness became issues for everyone during her lifetime. However, as she lived in Utah and assumed a public presence, she became more cognizant of her own language. When she spoke to me about her work in Salt Lake City School District, for example, her grammar was precise. When she was talking, joyfully or angrily, about her childhood, her style becomes far more casual and grammatically colorful. I have not attempted to remove any of that color with needless emendations.

At the end of the book are three appendices, which provide insights into Alberta Henry's life and what she viewed as her mission. Appendix A is a timeline of her life in the context of events in the history of the world and the state of Utah. It also contains a list of her affiliations and honors. Appendix B contains a small sample from the hundreds of students aided by the Alberta Henry Education Foundation with their subsequent successes. Appendix C is a complete copy of An Act in Relation to Service, the law passed by the 1852 Utah Territorial Legislature legalizing slavery.

I am deeply indebted to a great many kind and gracious people who provided information and insights on both the state of our state and Alberta's impact on it. First, of course, is Alberta herself, who was generous with her time and her records, and who became a really good friend. Her daughter, Julia Lebya, and granddaughter, Patrice Sawyer, provided invaluable perspectives and affectionate insights, as only family members can. Neighbors, friends, and colleagues from work in various areas and organizations graciously granted me interviews, providing stories and opinions not otherwise available. Alberta introduced me to Jennifer O'Neal, who was completing her master's degree at Utah State University with an excellent thesis on Alberta Henry, and my neighbor Tiana Freimann shared her outstanding senior thesis for the University of Utah about the juxtaposition of the LDS Church and African Americans.[6] Both of these good women helped me in several areas. Finally, John Alley of the University of Utah Press has provided his customary excellent advice and guidance, while my resident user-friendly software, my husband, Tom, has shown great patience and support with computers and much more. I am deeply grateful to all of them.

CHAPTER 1

UP FROM THE FLOOR

Alberta Henry was born into a racially segregated nation, despite the promises of the Fourteenth Amendment. "Black" and "white" did not simply refer to newspaper pages. Most of the Northern and Western parts of the country enforced segregation by custom rather than law and the separation usually extended only to specific businesses or neighborhoods. Public buildings and schools were usually available to anyone, but some accommodations were closed to blacks or to other races, and in some cases, to whites. Nonetheless, racial bigotry was a constant presence and sometimes it became highly overt. "The growth of bigotry and intolerance in America was stimulated by the rebirth of the Ku Klux Klan after 1915. . . . From beneath their burning crosses the hooded leaders of the Klan exhorted all true Americans (native born, white, Protestant) to unite against Negroes, Roman Catholics, Jews, Orientals, and all foreigners."[1] For example, in Indiana in 1924 Governor Ed Jackson and the "majority of the state's House of Representatives [were] all nominated and supported by the Klan."[2]

Louisiana, where Alberta was born, however, was a bastion of the Old South and the Klan was regarded as simply another civic organization. Blacks were firmly segregated by law, restricted to specific neighborhoods, schools, restaurants, even restrooms and drinking fountains. The policy was designed not just to separate the races but to debase people of any color except white. Segregation was upheld by the United States Supreme Court decision in the 1896 case of *Plessy v. Ferguson*.[3]

The *Plessy v. Ferguson* case came in response to a law passed by the Louisiana State Legislature on July 10, 1890. The law required railroads to supply separate cars for "whites" and "coloreds," in the polite parlance of the time. Its first test came on September 1, 1891, when a group of influential blacks in New Orleans formed the Citizens' Committee to Test the Constitutionality of the Separate Car Law. On February 24, 1892, Daniel E. Desdunes, a light-skinned black man, boarded the whites-only coach on the Louisville and Nashville Railroad. A conductor asked him to move to the colored coach; he refused and was arrested. The court dismissed the charges against Desdunes but could not rule on the constitutionality of the law itself since his ticket was for a destination outside Louisiana. The federal court ruled that since Congress controlled only interstate travel, no single state law could apply to a train that crossed state lines. That left individual states entirely free to impose restrictive laws within their own borders.

On June 7, 1892, Homer Adolph Plessy set out to provide a test case carefully designed to meet the necessary constitutional requirements. Plessy purchased a ticket in New Orleans on the East Louisiana Railway to Covington, just within the Louisiana borders. Covington was little more than a trading post, but it did contain a United States post office, which Plessy listed as one of his intended stops. Soon after the train began to move, Plessy, who was seven-eighths white, took a seat in the whites-only car. He told the conductor, J. J. Dowling, that he was by definition of Louisiana law "a colored man" and Dowling asked him to move to the colored car. When Plessy refused to move the conductor summoned Chris C. Cain, a private detective, to arrest him, carefully citing the Louisiana law. I suspect, as do others, that both incidents were set up, not only by blacks seeking freedom, but also by the railroad companies, which were greatly inconvenienced by the requirement that they attach two separate cars to each train even when there were not enough passengers to fill one.[4]

The *Plessy v. Ferguson* case eventually worked its way up to the United States Supreme Court, where Plessy's attorneys argued that the law violated the constitutional rights granted former slaves in the Thirteenth and Fourteenth Amendments. Those amendments outlawed slavery and granted full rights of citizenship to "all persons born or naturalized in the United States." Plessy's attorneys also noted inconsistencies in the Louisiana law that allowed exceptions; black nurses, for example, could accompany their employers and patients in the whites-only cars. The justices, however, were swayed by the state's arguments that separation did not necessarily mean discrimination and that while the amendments had granted legal equality, they did not guarantee social status. The Supreme Court came to the conclusion that separate but equal in terms of facilities and service was constitutional and denied Plessy's claims.[5] Justice Henry Billings Brown stated, "In the nature of things it could not have been intended to abolish distinctions based upon color, or to enforce social, as distinguished from political, equality, or a commingling of the two races unsatisfactory to either."[6] Ironically, the only dissenter was Justice John M. Harlan, a former slave owner.[7]

This decision cemented the concept behind the legal and systematic segregation of the races in both public and private facilities throughout the South for the next sixty years.[8] States in the South responded to the decision by enacting a host of Jim Crow laws, which dictated the operations of virtually every business and service in the South and were designed to keep colored citizens from advancing in any way. In theory all services were "separate but equal"; in practice those services provided nonwhites were almost always inferior, if, in fact, they worked at all.[9]

Alberta's father had grown up under that system and he knew nothing else.

Daddy, James Hill, was not a slave; his father was. He was born on the reservation in El Reno, Oklahoma.[10] *James worked on a sharecropping farm owned by Henry Nowell in Housten, Cado Parish, Louisiana.*[11] *We lived in a shack down in there. It was a shack—call it what it was. Two rooms. Two little rooms, a kitchen and everybody slept, some in the kitchen and some in the other room, on a sharecropping farm.*

Sharecropping was a system of farming that evolved after the Emancipation Proclamation went into effect throughout the South at the end of the Civil War. A condition in the lease required the sharecropper to purchase his own and his family's needs—seed to plant, tools to use, even clothes to wear and food to eat—through a company store where the value of all products bought and sold was determined by the owner. Moreover, sharecroppers could only sell their harvest through that same company store where the landowner controlled the price. Neither Alberta nor I had ever heard of a case where that system worked in favor of the sharecropper.

Beyond that, segregated schools for black children, and even the rural schools designed for the children of white sharecroppers, were at best inadequate. The extremely poor education virtually guaranteed that most sharecroppers faced difficulty if not impossibility in tallying the numbers for themselves. That lack of decent education restricted them to only the most menial jobs, keeping them in shackles as strong as any forged for slaves.[12] Since education was abysmal if not denied altogether, the former slave could not even question the amounts, so he inevitably found himself deeply in debt at the end of each season. Hence, the option to move forward from such a life was virtually obviated by the fact that the debt simply grew larger every year. The system was designed to create what W. E. B. DuBois called a "slavery of debt."[13] For all of his life James Hill reflected the submissiveness required of blacks in the Deep South, much to his wife's and Alberta's distress.

Alberta's mother, Julia Ida Palmer, had come from a very different background. Her parents, John Jackson and Susie Williams Palmer, had moved their family from Louisiana to Kansas City when Julia was eight years old. While Kansas had some segregation—both legal and de facto—it also had a large black population with access to businesses and decent schools, both integrated and segregated. Julia was able to attend school through the eighth grade so she could both read well and handle math. Consequently, she was aware of options—both legal and social—beyond those available in Louisiana.[14]

My mother, Julia Palmer, was part Native American. Grandmother Susan Palmer Barnes was an Indian-looking lady and she was a spiritualist. She lived in Kansas City, so my mother went to school there. I think she was in about the eighth grade and then on the way from school one day, she was dragged in an alley and raped. My mother never talked about it, but my grandmother would tell me. She said that when she found out there was nothing she could do after Mother was raped, she took her back to Louisiana, to Shreveport, where Mother's grandmother, my great-grandmother, lived.

Daddy and Mother got married, and my older sister, Rosetta Martin, was born in 1917.[15] *And for the babies, [Mother] would say, "Jim, it's time," and he would run across the field and get the midwife, Maggie Rattler. Maggie Rattler was the midwife for all of us. When he went to get her, Mother would put the sheets and blankets on the floor and got ready to have a baby in the kitchen because the stove was right there for hot water and the kids were in the other room in the little shack. It was a shack, nothing but a shack, but it's all the privacy she had.*

Nevada [pronounced NevAda] was born one year four months and two days before I was, June 12, 1919, and you didn't hear me say she was born in that two-room shack. When Nevada was born, Mother got real sick, she turned yellow and Daddy had to take her to a hospital. It wasn't a big hospital, because they couldn't go to the big hospital, but it was a little, old, dinky hospital that blacks could go to because they couldn't go to the white hospital. So the doctor came out, and said: "She's got yellow jaundice. We can either save her or the baby. But we cannot save both of them." They would try saving the child, if Daddy wanted it.

Daddy said, "I can't—wait a minute." And he went and got Susie Barnes, my grandmother, who was a spiritualist. Grandmother went in and said: "You leave both of them alone. Don't worry about her. I'll take care of her." And then she went out into the hills and the fields, got a whole bunch of herbs and stuff, mixed them together and mashed them up and made some kind of a salve, went in the hospital room and locked the door, went in there with Mother and rubbed her all down with it. I think Grandmother stayed for two or three days without letting the people come in, because she said they didn't know what they were doing. She said, "They don't have enough training and I'm putting you in the hands of the Lord and I'll do it," because she believed, oh, did my grandmother believe. For three days she applied this to Mother, and after those three days the yellow jaundice was gone and Mother was able to have Nevada, but Nevada was born very weak. The yellow jaundice, whatever it did, it took its toll upon her. But anyway, she saved Mother.

I was born at five o'clock in the morning on October 14, 1920. I came out squealing. I had two sisters, Rosetta and Nevada; they did not have a name for me, so there was a peach tree out in the yard, so she said, "We'll just call her Alberta." They never worried about me when I was little because before I was eight months old, I started walking and clapping.

David is one year and one month and one day younger than I am. November 15, 1921.[16] *He and I were like twins. When we went to school and the girls would pick on him, [he had] curly hair and everything, or if the boys would step on him,*[17] *well then, they had to fight me. We've always been close. If anything happened to one of us, the other one would be right there.*

These are the things Mother told me about me. Mother would have to go out in the fields to pick the cotton with Daddy, so they could make a little bit of money. Rosetta was supposed to watch us. Rosetta was three years older than I am, so when I was two, she was five, and she was supposed to watch Nevada and me. Mother had a great-big tub she put clothes in, and she washed the clothes with a wood fire under there. She'd come in and take a stick and push the clothes up and down. She made our dresses, the little tiny pinafore white dresses for Nevada and me because we were the same size. I'd run up there and say, "These are mine!" And I'd run up there again, and one time Rosetta wasn't watching and I ran up too far and got my foot in the fire. Mother could hear me clear across the field, hollering. And so they whipped Rosetta, because she was supposed to be watching us not letting us get close there.

She said another time, she was out in the field and she heard all of us hollering, not just me, but Nevada and Rosetta. And we were running and cowering by the door. She ran in and there was a snake. She grabbed one of the hoes and chopped its head off.

I was stunned that a snake could get into the house so easily, but Alberta dismissed it as just part of life in a sharecropper shack. It was not the difficulties in housing that sent the Hill family out of Louisiana, however. Since Julia had been raised and attended school in Kansas, she could do the math when they bought and sold things in the company store.

They would shop at Henry Nowells's store and buy all the material and the groceries and the stuff to plant the cotton and at the end of the term they would take it in.

"Mother had come out of Kansas City and she had went to school and she could read and write. I got all my knowledge of learning and doing those things from my mother. She could figure and add, and when they would go buy things at the store, the store that the man owned, she would put the prices and things down.

"Then, when they would bring the cotton in, the sharecropper [owner or store manager] would say, 'Well Jim' (they didn't talk to women) 'that's a pretty good crop you got there, but you still owe me.'"[18]

And Mother would say. "No, we don't." Now I've still got Mother's writing. Even when she was ninety she wrote, because she went to school and she loved figuring and adding. She kept accurate bank statements and records. And she said, "I've got it down." And they would look but they wouldn't talk to her.

And Mother said, "Oh no. The figures are—"

And he [Nowell] said, "Boy, you better keep that gal quiet or we are going to lynch her."

Mother said, "I will not be quiet."

I get that from her.

Alberta's brother, David, agreed, describing their mother as much like Alberta, "aggressive, authoritative, and usually right."[19]

They would say to my dad: "Shut up that gal, now, boy. You better make sure she keeps her mouth shut because she's going to get lynched down here."

That's when Mother decided that she couldn't send her kids to school [in Louisiana]. My oldest sister, Rosetta, was going on five and she said, "I want my kids to have an education," and there was no education there—Daddy didn't have any; Daddy couldn't read or write—she taught him how to write his name so he could sign checks, but my mother did all of the business, paying bills and finding a place to move to.

So what she did was move us all back up to Topeka, I think in 1923 in the dead of the winter. I was two, not quite three when we moved—came on the train to Topeka at night, raining—dismal introduction to Kansas. Daddy didn't want to move but Mother said that she was going to Kansas so he had to come too, because she was not going to keep her mouth closed and be lynched down there.

Julia was probably right about the money in this case, but so were the men who said she might be lynched if she stayed in Louisiana. Lynching of blacks was common in the states of the former Confederacy. From the end of Reconstruction to the 1950s, for example, investigators have documented over five hundred such lynchings in Mississippi alone.[20] Between 1890 and 1996 "nearly 3,500 lynchings have been documented, even though lynching a person was a capital crime in many of the states in which they occurred."[21] That number doubtless does not include all the lynchings that actually occurred.

Julia was also right in thinking her children would be better educated in Kansas than they would in Louisiana schools, and for her returning to Kansas meant familiar territory. For the Hill children it meant not just better education but far wider access to activities and opportunities than they could ever have known were possible in Louisiana. But for James Hill the move to Kansas took him to a society very different from the one he had always known.

CHAPTER 2

MOVING ON UP

The Hill family's move to Kansas doubtless altered the course of the children's lives. While Topeka was not entirely open to minorities, the levels of segregation and discrimination were far less severe and definitely less codified than in Louisiana. Louisiana, like most of the states of the former Confederacy, applied the *Plessey v. Ferguson* case with a vengeance, mandating segregation in nearly every area of life—neighborhoods, schools, churches, recreation, restrooms, even where specific races were allowed to sit on buses. Education for black children was minimal at best. Those restrictions on social interactions and job opportunities bred in children a supposition of failure. As Horace B. English would testify in the case of *Brown v. Board of Education*, "There is a tendency for us to live up to, or perhaps I should say down to, social expectations and to learn what people say we can learn, and legal segregation definitely depresses the Negro's expectancy and is therefore prejudicial to his learning."[1]

While de facto segregation in the North and West was enforced by custom rather than edict and did not regulate every aspect of life, it still exercised a denigrating effect on those groups targeted for negative discrimination. Private clubs and businesses could "reserve the right to refuse service to anyone." That phrase could include reasonable requirements like wearing shoes or shirts but could also enforce exclusion of specific races, religions, or ethnic groups. Neighborhoods were usually segregated by realtors rather than regulations. The attitude in Kansas, however, was schizophrenic. The state had elements of both legally enforced and de facto segregation as well as areas where various races and ethnic groups lived together amicably. The duality stemmed from the state's history and would in time affect the entire nation: During its original settlement by whites, the territory became known as "Bloody Kansas," a border state where battles ensued, both verbal and physical, between settlers from the South who wanted it to be a slave state and those from the North who wanted it kept free.

As the Reconstruction period following the Civil War ended in the South and the evidence grew that the region would become increasingly hostile to blacks, many former slaves and their families began to leave for the North and West. Kansas was one of the prime areas for that exodus in the 1870s. There was still homesteading land available, and railroads connected Kansas with the South. Black agents, including the legendary Benjamin Singleton, helped many former slaves move North. Born into slavery in 1809, Singleton escaped to the North and saw Kansas as the new Canaan—a place of freedom—and termed himself the Moses of the Colored Exodus. He traveled into the South, persuading blacks to come North and homestead. Many did, most of them displaced plantation workers who had become little more than peons under the Jim Crow laws. The largest group, the Exodusters, arrived in 1879–80, many settling in Topeka. Singleton continued his work of relocation into his sixties, by which time his white hair had people calling him Pap. Most of those migrants did well and stayed, though some returned to their former homes.[2]

As Kansas moved into the twentieth century, even though slavery had long since been outlawed, some citizens still advocated restrictions on blacks while others were little concerned with making distinctions. Some institutions, like schools or public buildings, were segregated while others nearby were integrated. Consequently, people could see options and possibilities in Kansas that were impossible in the Deep South but not so readily evident in other parts of the country, the kind of elements blurred in simple de facto segregation. But there were also specific laws they could fight, like a hook to grab and pull the structure down. Kansas's mixed segregation/integration laws revealed such a range of elements that citizens of Topeka would in time be forced to recognize and help to end segregation throughout the country.

For Julia Hill the move to Kansas was a homecoming, despite some difficulties.

When we came to Kansas—nowhere did we record it—came from Louisiana into Kansas, and she was pregnant, twice, she lost two sons. We never even talk about them because, miscarriage or something, but they say it was probably the weather, because Kansas was cold in '23. I mean, they don't have cold weather no more like they used to have cold weather.

But it was not the much-colder weather that bothered James Hill. It was a difficult transition to a society he neither knew nor understood. He had lived almost his entire life in a state that required abject servitude and submission from blacks and he could not entirely adjust to the far less rigid mores of racial relations in Kansas. One of the things that disturbed Alberta most was the way her father moved to let white people pass him. Although the sidewalk might be wide enough to accommodate all of them, he would step off the curb and down into the gutter when white people came toward him. She told him again and again, even after she was an adult, that he didn't have to do that, but it never seemed to register. She recognized that such deference had been drilled into him all his life and he simply couldn't shake it, but it still bothered her enormously. He carried it among the other legacies of stark segregation, but he did find employment in Kansas to help support the family, initially with the Morrell Packing House but later it was primarily yard work for white families because he did know gardening well.

Daddy would do whatever he had to do and go out in his garden. He always had a garden because you could get him out of Louisiana, but you couldn't get Louisiana out of him. Later on when we got bigger, after we had gotten almost grown, he went to work in the governor's yard, in all the rich people's yards, doing the lawn work. When the new governor got inaugurated, he had pictures with him. They invited him to put his suit on and his hat and he would be sitting there. When he died, he had two electric lawn mowers. Before then, on the WPA they gave the men the brooms and the shovels that they leaned on.

And when Daddy wasn't working, Mother would go out and she would be worried, and I would say to Mother: "Don't worry about it. The Lord will provide."

And I still say that, even today, and that's why I don't care too much about money. I have the money. I don't spend it, but the Lord will provide.

Alberta and her siblings were all young enough to make the transition more readily. They grew up with more freedom and far better education than they could have known in Louisiana, but they quickly learned that society and their parents expected good behavior.

Topeka wasn't that segregated. You didn't ride in the back of the bus, but we had a black theater. We had black policemen. We had black fire department people, black postman. But where Kansas sat and the fight over whether it would be slave or free had a lot to do with it. And the Southerners were there so they naturally had some of those black codes of the South. And you could marry whoever you wanted. It wasn't like Utah that had the miscegenation law, but it was surrounded by states that did. . . .

My mother did not talk much, she said something only when it was necessary to correct you and make it accurate. Mother did not talk very much, but she had opinions—and she was always right.

If you talk back, if you said a dirty word, if you broke anything, the neighbors could whip you. We lived in a black neighborhood in North Topeka, and then they would tell your mother, and you got another whipping. You got two whippings. You could not be disrespectful. I think it was a good thing when it wasn't abuse, because most of the time you deserved it.

Rosetta, my oldest sister—she's the one that Mother had when she was raped in Kansas City and Grandmother took her down South, so she was really my half sister—when Rosetta was little, she was beautiful. She looked not like we did because we were real dark. When I was about five, Daddy used to buy us black coats and hats, because he didn't want us to get them dirty. And our faces were black, so you didn't know where our faces started. Rosetta would tell people that she wasn't black, that Mother had adopted her.

Rosetta was a belligerent sort of a child, stubborn, rebellious. She did not like authority, Mother said. Daddy didn't have a relationship with her because she wouldn't pay attention to him, so Mother had to—my poor mother—she had to do all things at home and see about a job. I'm so glad I was not my mother, because she really had a hard time. Rosetta was supposed to stay at home and take care of us when we were young, but she had boys come in the house. She would lock us out of doors. And we'd come home or during the summer we'd be outside and she'd have boys in the house and we'd run up to the trolley, wait on the trolley to tell Mother, David and I. Nevada wouldn't say anything; she would just sit and look, but we would tell Mother.

Rosetta was really pretty; she looked like a Spanish girl. She really was pretty and made eyes at the boys. She didn't go to school to learn; she went to socialize. The girls didn't like her, so they would gang up and wait for her on one of the corners and then they'd jump on her. And Mother [would] come home and she was crying and showing what they'd scratched on her. Mother said: "OK. I'm telling you this once. You know how to fight. You don't let anyone jump on you. You will take care of yourself. Start swinging." Mother was a fighter. "Swing your hands and do whatever you have to do."

Well, instead of doing what Mother said, she took a little knife with her. And when they jumped on her she cut one of them. The rest of them ran, [that was] the only reason she didn't cut more of them, so they couldn't put her in jail because the gang [had] jumped her.

Rosetta never was around very much, but they had a lot of problems with her and when she got older they had to send her out to KVS, Kansas Vocational School, because she wouldn't mind. KVS was on the outskirts of town, and you could see the pictures of all the girls that they sent from all over the state, some from out of state, that their parents could not really handle. And it didn't cost a whole lot, but Mother had to pay it to keep her out there, so Mother would work. But when they sent her out there, Rosetta ran away and joined a fair at the fairgrounds. And then she got married and it lasted thirteen minutes or something. Mother laughed about that.

Alberta particularly remembered an encounter with Rosetta during the Christmas when she was about ten or eleven.

We'd wake up every Christmas to an apple and an orange and a thing. You always got an apple and maybe an orange and a little ten-cent toy like a little doll that you could pull the arms and legs off, with no clothes on, so you could make clothes. Mother had a sewing machine and I made clothes to go with that little doll. David would get one of those little cars that the wheels would come off of it; never got anything big. And all I ever wanted when I was little was a bicycle. I loved to ride bicycles.

Mother had made a Christmas sock and laid it under the little, scruffy Christmas tree, if there was one. Daddy and Mother would wait to the last day and everybody done bought the Christmas tree and they probably could give one away free. And we would sometimes pop popcorn and we would string it and put it on the tree because we didn't have Christmas ornaments. Until once Daddy went to work to clean up a drugstore and they gave him all of that stuff after Christmas that wasn't sold. And Mother put it in a box and saved it so then we felt like we were really blessed because that Christmas we had some little, some of the little balls were broken, but we had icicles to throw on there.

And I just believed in Santa Claus. The Christmas when I was little, I guess until I was about thirteen or fourteen, I still believed I could hear Santa Claus. I could hear the reindeers and I could hear Santa up there saying something; I always thought that Santa Claus was there, regardless, until, I guess I was eleven. Rosetta got mad. "No Santa Claus."

"Oh, yes, there is a Santa Claus—Santa Claus. Oh, yes, there is a Santa Claus."

"Come here." And Mother had one of them great big trunks, you know, those traveling trunks? You open them up like that [standing on the end and opening into two large compartments]. On one side you hang the clothes; the other side had drawers. She went to Mother's trunk. Well, that's where she [hid the presents].

We told her what Rosetta had done. Mother whipped Rosetta and she whipped David and I and Nevada for believing there was a Santa Claus. We were old enough to know better. That was the last of that. So no more of the Christmases did you believe in Santa. You knew you wasn't going to get anything, but I thought sometime there would be a package of gum in there, which was exciting. We didn't have money for that. And sometimes there would be a candy bar—that was exciting. I always thought everything was exciting. Mother never got used to me saying: "Oh, this is exciting. This is great." I still do it, too. The little things are exciting. But the Lord will provide.

Alberta was closest to David of all her siblings, partly because they were close in age but mostly because both Rosetta and Nevada distanced themselves with their own specific behaviors—Rosetta with her rebellion and Nevada with her illness. So Alberta would confide in David far more than she did in her sisters. She told him, for example, her tactic for avoiding a most unpleasant weekly ritual commonplace in many American homes at the time imposed on children to maintain good health.

The thing I remember the most every Friday night, when you came home, you got castor oil. You had to be cleaned out so we took castor oil every Saturday. Daddy would give us this big tablespoon and we would take it. I always had this in mind: How do you get by? How do you make shortcuts? How do I get by not doing things I don't want to do? So I learned when he gave it to us to put it up under my tongue, and say: "Mother, can I go to the bathroom? Can I go to the toilet?" We didn't have bathrooms; it was an outhouse out there.

And she would say, "Yes, go ahead, dear." And I'd go out and get almost to the toilet and I'd spit it out.

Now that went real good and I was telling David about it and my sister heard, and she said, "I want to learn how to do it."

I said, "No, I don't think you can; you have to be real strong." I was just telling David because David and me are like twins.

So we went, next Friday, here it come. "Mother, can I go—" but Nevada got hers before me, and she said, "Mother, can I go [spitting sound]" and out went the castor oil.

And she said, "Why didn't you swallow that?"

And you know what she said, don't you? "Alberta said you didn't have to. You could do it like—"

That was the end of that. Daddy would give it to us, and Mother would stand right there. "No, you can't go to the bathroom. Open your mouth. Let's see. OK. Now you can go." Spoiled it right there.

That outhouse later provided David with an opportunity to demonstrate just how much he loved Alberta. She told the following story with great enthusiasm, broad actions, and drama, changing her voice for David's lines. We both ended up giggling like little schoolgirls while she was describing what happened.

"I was brought up in the church, because Mother always made us go. I was raised Baptist in the Church of the Living God. We had to stay all day with Grandpa, and Grandpa would always tell us what he wanted. We couldn't even look in a barber shop, because men were getting their haircut, we couldn't go to a ball game, and you couldn't go to a theater—none of those things. But you had to walk in the way of the Lord."[3]

Even then when I was little, every Sunday we had to go to church. I hated it because you had to wear a hat. I could stand the dress as long as I could get it off when I got home. A little organdy-like dress and the hats were the same thing. Now, we had outhouses—didn't have telephones but you had outhouses. And we came from church this one Sunday in the summertime and you know how kids are playing and running around before you had to go in the house. I said I had to go to the bathroom. And when I got up off the thing to wipe myself, the hat fell down. And I came out crying: "David! David! David! Mother's going to kill me. David. My hat."

And "Oh, Alberta. It done fell down in there. What do you want me to do? I'm not going to—"

"But David—David." Now, you want to know how close we are, well, you may not know if you've never been in outhouses, but you can always lift the seats up on the inside, and he lifted up and he climbed down in there. And he got my hat and said, "Here." And was trying to hand it up, and I said, "I'm not going to—un-huh, I don't want that." And Nevada by this time had run in the house—old stool pigeon, 'cause we always was getting into something—and she was the tattletale. Told Mother and Mother came out. David was coming out from in the toilet, all with the stuff all on him, mad at me 'cause I wouldn't take the hat because I didn't want to get that stuff on my hands. Mother whipped both of us, but David had to stand outside and she stripped his clothes, naked right outside there, turned the hose on him and poured water, going back and forth to the house to get him clean because he couldn't come back into the house with those clothes on. After he got out, she put the clothes down in the tub. But we both got whippings and we got grounded. That's the truth.

David loves telling that one: "After I made the supreme sacrifice to go down there, just for her . . ."

David obviously loved and admired Alberta, and still did when I met him years after this incident. He said: "She was very brilliant, a very brilliant girl. She made just about all As, when she was going to school. We thought that was great and I was quite jealous of her getting those As. I'd get one once in a while." He noted that they played "marble games and I played jacks with the girls when I was a little fellow."[4] But play was not their only occupation. Julia Hill wanted to make sure her children knew how to work and how to do chores properly.

Mother would write lists. Mother would work and I'd come home from school and she had a list—"Alberta, Nevada, David. David, slop jar." He was to empty and clean that, sweep the walk off. The chores, wash dishes and so and so was to dry and put them up. You knew which day you were supposed to wash them. And [Mother] would stick them up on those cupboards so that you could read them. They were yellow. When I was packing up Mother's things, I ran across one or two of them and I laughed so hard. And she said, "Why are you saving them?"

I said, "Those are my heritage. I inherited this."

But anyway, I had this thing. There had to be a better way to do things. I would come home and you would sweep. Now, we didn't have carpet like this but you had a rug. Where did you sweep the dirt at? Real quick [sweeping motion under the rug]. Then you wash the dishes. When it was my turn to dry them, you'd wash them and we had a stove with an oven and you wash and rinse them and put them in there and they'd dry and they'd come out—now, you know, that's smart.

At least I thought so. Saturday morning, six o'clock in the morning, Mother didn't work. She would go and take all the dishes out of those cupboards. Not just the ones we had, but every one of them. Wake us up. We'd wash them all. Do you know why? If you're smart you would know that once you put them in the oven, when the water dried, it dried to the center and leave a white spot. She wouldn't tell us that; she told me after we got grown. If she'd had told me then I could have wiped those spots. I finally learned that you can't short-cut.

She said, "You are going to learn how to do things and do them right." My daughter [Julia] right now can iron perfect shirts—anything you give her, because I taught her how to iron. Mother taught me, but I hated it because shorts, pillowcases, handkerchiefs—if there was a wrinkle or a crease in them, they got wet down again, rolled up, and you had to do them again until Mother looked at them, inspected them, and there was no wrinkles in them. They were ironed just as straight because Mother used to have to take in washing and ironing. Even if it was the family, if it was mine, if it was Daddy's, it didn't matter. "You didn't half do things, Alberta, come on now. You had to learn to do things straight."

It helped because I learned how to do everything, and I learned how to do them just right. I could just remember one time. I never did like to cook. It's OK. But Mother's going to teach you. So one day I said Mother likes greens. So I went out in the field and I thought that these look like some of the things that Mother had. Wild greens. I used to know some of the names of the wild greens. Grandmother could bring the greens in and she could and I thought I could. And I put them in a pan and cooked them. Mother came home and dumped them out and she had to throw the pot away, because it got green whatever it was I cooked. She said, "You really can't do the greens, Alberta, because only expert people who know how."

Did you ever cook dinner and rice and stuff that's stuck in there? We'd put water in and put them out on the back porch. We were soaking them. Mother would come home and wake you up late at night. "You don't soak them that long. You have to do them now. You do it right. I know you all didn't do it." But I was trying to get out of doing something, because the next day might have been Nevada's time to wash and then she would get that pot that I had left out there.

Alberta wanted to be a boy because boys were allowed do many more things than girls, because boys did not face the same restrictions as girls. As the children grew older, both they and their mother looked for jobs outside the family. Julia found one for David that proved particularly lucrative for Alberta, even though she was a girl taking a job that was usually reserved for boys.

Mother got him a paper route because there was always someone who wanted money. He did not like it. So I said, "Mother, I want it. Can I have it? Can I? Oh, Mother!"

So Mother said, "OK." They let me do anything. I started when I was in elementary school, the time Joe Louis was fighting.[5] *And I would go and I would read the whole paper, and then I would go out—and, oh, I made so much money because I'd say, "You all got to buy it because it tells in here where black folks [are]." And I had a gift of gab, so I could stand up and talk to these people, right?*

Nobody who ever met Alberta Henry would question that statement.

The Kansas City Call, *the* Chicago Defender, *and the* Pittsburgh Courier. *Those are the three papers I used to sell. Those were all black papers—black advertisers about hair grease and so and so. But everything about them was black. I used to read all of them and then I could go and say, "If you buy this one you can do this . . ."*

Anyway, when Joe Louis was fighting, I would bet them—Mother didn't know this—I would bet them that Joe Louis was going to win, and they had to pay me—the papers were about ten cents, no more than ten cents—you have to pay me double if he won. But if he lost, then I would have to pay them double or they would get a free paper. They would get it for two times.

I made a mint. Until Max Schmeling.[6] *Until he [Louis] lost. And I went broke. All that they had owed me in the past, I had to quit betting. I don't know how*

I got by Mother with that. But that was what the deal was: they didn't have to pay. I had to pay to get the papers, but I had socked the money I had won away; I couldn't give that to Mother. I could only give her what the papers was, but not the money I won. And I didn't have nothing to spend it on, so I had socked it away. So I did get through with that one, but I said, Thank God Joe Louis didn't lose too many times; I'd been wiped out.

And in the summertime I [would] get to selling papers and come by the schoolhouse and on the school grounds the old men would sit with the checkerboard and the domino board.

I used to love to play dominos and checkers. My daddy had taught me how to play dominos. Slap them bones down there. And I would imitate my daddy. He loved that. I could beat him and he made me stay up half the night so he could beat me one game. And then I could go to bed. And then I'd go on the school ground, you know those old men sitting on the school ground, with a checkerboard or something sitting there. "Come here, girl." I'd beat them and laugh. It was my voice and my cockiness that I think got them and they'd want another game.

"Come on over here and play."

I said, "I better get home because I'm going to get a whipping if I don't—"

"Come on. You beat us the last time and you laughed."

That's the only reason why they wanted to play me was because when I beat them, I made such a charge out of it. "Ha, you don't know how to play the game."

"Come on." You know how they do.

I'd sit down and start playing. I'd beat them.

"One more game."

I almost always had a whipping every day for not coming home. It didn't do much good because I never did learn time. Mother was trying to teach me when you are supposed to be home for dinner, you come at that time because the family ate together: we sat down; dinner was being served. And when I would look up, it would be dark. So why rush? Since I knew I was going to get a spanking anyway. She was trying to teach me time.

But it had its effect, because when I run meetings, I want them to be on time. Time was stressed in my family. Right now if someone is going to pick me up, I'm all dressed, sitting downstairs then I go out and stand so nobody ever has to wait on me. If I am going to go pick up somebody with my car, I am time conscious because that's what Mother had in mind. Every committee that I have run—and I have been chairman of the NAACP, U.S. Commission on Civil

Rights, I would say about fifty different organizations—I was strict about time because they always say CPT, Colored People Time.[7]

So it did do some good.

Alberta's and David's childhood play came to an abrupt end, however, when he stood up to their eldest sister.

When I graduated and went to junior high, David was still in elementary school. He came home for lunch one day because it was just down the street. Rosetta was there and she had somebody there, so she wouldn't let him in and he pushed the door open and got in anyway. He was sitting in the kitchen eating and she said, "I thought I told you to stay out." They had a fight and he whipped the daylights out of her and then he got scared because in those days [boys] didn't hit girls. He thought Mother was going to get him and that's why he ran away from home.

David was fifteen when he ran away with two boys, one white and one black, that he knew from his elementary school. The black boy came home when he got hungry, and the white boy was picked up by the police and brought home. David, however, did not return. Alberta remembers her mother aging as she worried about him. It was the middle of the Great Depression, so David worked in a variety of menial jobs during that difficult period: janitor, shoe shine boy, picked strawberries in Louisiana, and went to California where he boxed under the name of Davie Milo. "It was the name that I used because the truant officer would stop me and then he couldn't find out I was a runaway."[8]

Mother always had a candle burning in the window. From the time he left, every night she burned a candle. When we used to live by the railroad tracks and every time hobos would come, we had to feed them. She said: "Somebody is feeding my son. Somebody is looking after my son, so I will do this."

We did a whole lot of things trying to find David. We heard from some fellow [who] had heard that David was in Los Angeles. Some railroad man or somebody that I had met said he heard that my brother was there and [he had written] to him at some number and I sent a letter to this address that the man said that David might get it. Nevada had got married but Nevada had had a spell [illness] and they put her in the hospital. But I had wrote to him and hoped he got the letter and told him about Nevada being in the hospital.

David was seventeen or going on eighteen and I was in Topeka High when he came home. Mother and I lived on Kansas Avenue. He came back to the door and knocked on the door. I opened the door and didn't know who he was. He said, "Hi, Sis" [spoken in a very low voice]. And he was a kid when he left in elementary school.

But after he come back home, if a policeman was walking down the street David wouldn't walk off the street for daring to bump him. He was hot [in trouble with the law] when he came back, but then he changed. He got married and went back to school and a whole bunch of stuff.

David had missed his family and was glad to get back to them. While he was still young and gone from home, Alberta had particularly missed her brother, not only because they had been so close, but because it left her home with only Nevada. Both David and Alberta agreed that their younger sister had some difficulties from her birth and was generally frail. They weren't sure whether her inability to do chores or help around the house stemmed from those problems or from their father's constantly calling her a "poor little thing." They both recognized that he treated Nevada far differently than he did the rest of the family.

When David ran away, so he wasn't home, and Mother put Rosetta into Kansas Vocational Training School, it was just Nevada and I. Nevada was Daddy's favorite. She looked just like him.

I would say, "Daddy, it's time for Nevada to wash the dishes or sweep the floor."

Daddy would say, "Oh, you go ahead and do it, the poor little thing." That got embedded in me. Daddy never paid attention to me because I was one of those self-sufficient kids, but "the poor little thing," that's Nevada. We got in the habit of saying "the poor little thing."

Mother would say, "Nevada, it's your time to do the dishes."

"I don't feel like it."

Daddy would say, "Poor little thing. She can't do them. Alberta, you have to."

And I got so I hated for anyone to say "poor little thing." I could hear my dad saying "poor little thing." Whatever Nevada needed or whatever was "poor little thing," he would get her. He would bring things home for her but never anything to me. That's how much difference he had between my sister and me. He never whipped us; he whipped me, but he never whipped her. But he didn't have nothing to say to me most of the time.

Mother always instilled upon me to be independent. She would show me how to do things, so therefore I knew how to do everything, even though I would try to find shortcuts, but I still know how to do them.

Money was tight for the family, even with both parents working. James worked two jobs and Julia worked as a maid in a hotel. They economized at home, eating from the garden and canning food for the winter. Alberta vividly recalled how quickly she went through clothes and how their father would talk to them about making things last.

We'd get ready to go to church, but being a tomboy, my socks would have a hole in them, so naturally, I would put Nevada's on. And Nevada would holler, "Mother, Alberta." Mother never did come in there and take them off. Everything that was torn and had holes in them, they had to be mine. And I'm just wondering if sometime didn't Nevada have an accident or something. But it didn't matter, Mother never even bothered to look. "Alberta, take them off."

Every time Daddy was going to buy some shoes, he would sit us all down and say, "Now you know your daddy and your mother, things was hard. We ain't got money to keep doing this. Now me buying you these shoes, they got to last you, you know. Now I don't want you to go out." Now I've been sitting up there listening to this speech: "Shut up. I'd rather have a whipping," I'm saying to myself, but I never heard hardly a word he said until he said, "I don't want you to, you hear this? I don't want you to go out kicking rocks and cans." What do you think is the first thing I did? Found the closest rock and can. Minute I got out of there.

But he would always—at least ten minutes talked real slow now, "Your mother and I—you know we don't have much money." But anyway, these loafers—he wasn't going to buy any more shoes, so when the loafers started getting a hole in them, he had a shoe lass. It has the shape of a foot and then he would get some sole and then he'd cut it around there. And then the top was all bruised, so he'd painted them house green. And he made them so heavy I couldn't hardly lift my feet they were so embarrassing going to high school that I wouldn't socialize with anybody. I had to walk near the railing against the wall to kind of pull myself up.

Alberta didn't comment on the color of the shoes, but she pulled a face not unlike the one she made when she talked about the outhouse.

A different pair of shoes became the center of a far more hurtful incident she vividly recalled from her childhood.

Nevada was weak from her birth and she tried to play the games we did. Then when we about seven or eight and running outside, she was trying to follow the rest of us kids and she couldn't run fast enough. She was going across the street, and there wasn't as many cars in those days; just a few white folks had cars, but car came and hit her and knocked her over on the side. I had to stay out of school until Nevada got better, because Mother had to go to work. Somebody had to be there, and I was always the one to stay home. Mother brought me back my lessons from school.

We were both in elementary school at that time, but when Nevada got a little better and went back to school, I was in junior high, and Nevada was in elementary because she had been out of school for over a year. But she never was quite the same.

So when she graduated from grade school, I was graduating from junior high school. Daddy went down and bought her real thin stockings kind of like silk, and a dress, a real nice-looking dress and the shoes with a little bit of heel to go with it. Me, some flat loafers, service weight, the kind you put the pennies in, and I could use them for school shoes, and one of those bargainy-looking dresses that kids wear on Easter.

Mother said, "Don't worry about it, because the Lord will bless us." It was Mother got us up every Sunday God sent around, took us to church because her father was the minister there, whether Daddy went or not. She said: "The Lord will bless us. Never mind. You graduated and I'm proud of you. I'd like for one of my kids to graduate." That was my mother: always low-key but knew how to get things done.

I said: "I'm not going if I have to wear those things, dingey-looking dresses, because I'm too old. I'm graduating, going on to high school, and I'm not going to wear them." I didn't weigh but fifty some pounds. I was real skinny, real short. Had to pin skirts up on me but anyway, I wasn't going.

So Mother said, "Don't worry about it." So she waited until the day of my graduation and when Daddy went to work, she got off of work and she got me and she took me to a beauty shop. My hair was in braids and I wanted a marcel, with the waves in it. Now it wasn't going to stay, but because I was graduating from junior high school, getting ready to go to high school, and while I was there she went to the store and got credit on the account they had and bought me one of the same kind of dresses [that her father had bought for Nevada]. Now, those dresses were not silk; they were rayon but they wasn't the little kid things.

And [Mother got] the shoes with that little teeny bit of heel. I couldn't hardly walk on them because I'd never had one on before. I had to hold on [to the furniture]. She said, "Walk around in them because you got to remember when you go up there, not to put your left hand out, put your right hand out to get your diploma." I said, that's right; I got to remember that, but I had to hold on to something to learn to walk with a little bit of heel. Then when we left there, we went to the school to graduate; and we rushed, we just got there in time for me to graduate.

And she kept saying, "Don't put your left hand out, put your right hand out when you receive your diploma." Because I always put my left hand out. I felt so good. I went up there and I had to hold on to walk in those shoes but I felt like I was really grown up.

When I got home, my daddy found out what Mother had done and went and closed out that account, closed it out and never let her get anything on that account,[9] *which she paid most of the time. But she couldn't get anything in her name. I can't believe that.*

My mother said, "Don't worry about it. I'll work him. Whenever you need anything, I'll just buy it for you." She didn't like it because he played favoritism with everything—everything was Nevada, nothing with me. But that didn't [usually] bother me, because I had too much to do, too many things to see and too many places to go to be worrying about little stuff like that.

Because Mother had got me these other shoes with a little bit of heel, come Sunday I had to wear these loafers. I had to wear them the first year I went to high school and I was the most embarrassed thing. We lived in North Topeka, but Topeka High was clear across town. Mother and them didn't have enough money to pay for me to ride the trolley, so I had to walk across the trestle where the trains went. I didn't have girlfriends because I went with the boys, four or five different boys including Vernon Turner and Clean McCord, always come by the house and got me because we had to go over a railroad track and the trusses where the freight trains ran across. So if a train was coming, they would grab my books and they would run ahead, and get on the side and stay there, then I had to jump down in a hole while the train passed overhead. Any time you go by you see a train track you see things down in the ground, there's a place that you can jump. The train will go over you; the tracks are there. So I would jump in the pen there and wait. And then I'd start to get up and they'd "No. No. Another one." Because another one would be coming. "Stay there," they'd say. And I'd stay there until the other went by. And then they'd say, "Come on, but hurry." Then I'd get up and I'd run. But that's the way I got to school, because it was about ten miles, but by going across the track it was shorter. These boys were the ones that I ran with. I didn't have no girlfriends, because when I got to school and I was so ashamed of my feet that I'd walk up against the wall. "Hello" [in a very quiet voice] with my head down, me and those penny loafers with green house paint on them.

Nevada, when she got about fifteen or sixteen, she had a boyfriend, Harold Moore. We lived in North Topeka, and he lived on the west side of the town. He would come over and they would sit on the porch or sit in the house and they didn't look like they ever said anything, but she never went with anybody else and I don't think he had either. They would sit on the porch, and they didn't talk that much. I guess they did say something to each other, because they did get married and were married for fifty years almost. They stayed married until she died in 1980. No children. But he kept going and he had a stroke and he walked with a walker. He went on till he finally died.

Harold, her husband, did everything for her, took her every place. She never had to do anything that she did not want to do. If not that the Lord had blessed her just to have a husband that loved her and his friends that he had, they took her under their wings and all those years, she didn't die until January of 1980. She hadn't quite got to her sixty-first birthday, 'cause she was born in June. Now that's a long marriage, right? That's a long life. We never hardly seen her, but any time I was coming home, Harold brought her over to spend that day, the whole day with us.

And she never—even when I would go home to see Mother, she would come over and sit the whole day, I would cook, and Mother said, "Now Nevada, when we would get through—I'd done all this cooking and everything—you go wash dishes." She would run to the bathroom and stay a long time, and Mother would say, "I'll do them." From force of habit, because we knew she wasn't going to do it.

Alberta was fond of Harold because he took good care of her sister. But even as a very young man courting her sister, he had won Alberta's heart. He understood that the tomboy who loved sports really loved his bicycle. It opened avenues for her that would otherwise have been closed.

He came clear across the big part of the town, and he would come with his bike. He would come over, even after I got to junior high school and after I graduated and went to high school, he would come over from the east side and they would sit on the porch. And he would ride his bicycle so I could ride it. I would just wait because he would let me ride his bike as long as I wanted as far as I wanted. I loved for Nevada's boyfriend to come because when I said I had too many places to go, he would say, "Take the bike." And he never told me when to come home.

I'd take the bike and a tennis racket, go play tennis—I won the tennis championship in Topeka just before I came to Utah. I loved all sports. I would go out and I'd play hard and then ride the bike some more, ride everywhere I wanted to ride—because I never had a bike. I never had anything when I was coming up—any kind of toys was bought for me. I didn't like dolls. I guess Mother worried whether I was going to turn out to be a boy or a girl because I played football, basketball, tennis, all kinds of sports. I could tackle, wore guards on my legs; I could run.

When I was growing up, I was a tomboy. I loved wearing David's clothes. I did not love wearing the dresses and things, but on Sunday, you had them. You had a Sunday shoes, hat, and when you wore it, you came home and you hung it up. You took them shoes off and you put on your everyday shoes that ones you went to school with, but you did not wear the Sunday shoes. Then when they wore out, the Sunday shoes became the everyday shoes, and they would buy [new shoes] once or twice a year, Easter and something other time, you got shoes, but I was so hard on shoes.

Big kids wouldn't play with me because I was so small, they called me Little Bit, Half-Pint, Lefty, all those things. They'd come over and tell my mother they were going to look out for me. Now, I was the same age as most of these people, but I was just little. So I always had to play with smaller kids because I was so small, but I would follow the boys.

"I wanted to always be young, because it was more fun to play basketball, football. Oh, I would tackle them just like a man. My mother worried: was I going turn up to be a women or a girl? If a boy tried to kiss me, I would beat him up. Then, I'd run and tell Mother, 'Now Mother, he tried that snoopy stuff—' (that's what I called it, snoopy stuff). 'I ain't got time for that.'"[10]

Hubert Stoval was one of the first fellows that used to come and play with us when we got to Kansas in 1923. We went to school together, and I'd go over to his house and wake him up and his grandmother would let me go in. She would let no other girls in, but I was one of the boys. I played football, basketball—tackled like a man, a natural man.

Playing with the boys, of course, meant she was often invading David's territory, and fond as he was of her, that sometime caused problems.

[Mimicking the voice of a disgruntled boy] "Here she come David."

[Mimicking David] "Oh Lord. Do she always have to be there?"

I would be here and I'd be following them everywhere. They'd go steal watermelons or go climb a peach tree or apple tree. Who'd you think be up there right along with them?

Mother used to make tea cakes. They are nothing but flour, sugar and a little vanilla and a little baking powder—a shortening bread. And she would cut them then she would put them in jars and put them up on the cupboard. Those old houses [had no built-in cupboards] just a room and you could buy those cupboards that you set in there. If you didn't watch, they would tip over on you, so sometimes they'd put boards in the front part so they wouldn't tip over. Then when she would give them to us, and all the kids in the neighborhood—ahhh! Sometimes when all them were gone that she had given us, we'd want another one.

David tells this lie. He said: "I went in there with Alberta. She pushed the chair over, climbed up, stepped up on top of the counter, had her hand down in the cookie jar, Mother walked in and caught her and whipped me." That's the way David tells that story.

David admitted to the story, but said it wasn't a lie.

I always got whippings because I was always the instigator, even as a child—still am, but was I really an instigator! I could think of the most delicious things. Every time they wanted to go to a show or to a ball game or anything, and the kids in the neighborhood, they would come down and they would have me go talk to their parents and David then would have me talk to Mother. And Mother would say, "No, I've already told you."

"But Mother—Mother—but Mother." You know by the time I got through talking I done wore her down and to get rid of me, she was going to say yes. And then I'd go to their [other children's] parents and "My mother has . . ." and, oh, I could make it sound like Mother had embraced this idea, that we would all be together, no problem because we couldn't get in trouble because we would look after each other. And their parents would [sound of exasperated consent]. I wouldn't lie, just embellish.

When I was younger, going to school I used to do acrobatic stunts. In fact, I did acrobatic stunts on the stage. I was so little then. I could bend all the way back and go back and pick up a handkerchief, do somersaults, put my legs around my head. So the teachers would get me when they had programs, used to take me to their sororities, myself and Martha Patterson. But when I graduated from junior high, I quit doing acrobatic stunts.[11]

And we roller-skated. They had a place they called Tenth Street. And it was a dance hall. And then they closed it up and made it a skating rink. And we would slip off and go roller-skating at the rink and keep watching on a watch to be home, because we were always supposed to be home by nine o'clock. But that was the best thing—just being a kid, just being a kid, no shoes on, barefoot, walking through the fields. I can remember us stealing peaches, climbing up in the tree, and the neighbors hollering at us, but they knew we were going to do it because all kids before us and after us did it.

And I could run. We were in elementary school when a fellow came from the college there and he watched us on the playground. L'Jean Napue and I were the fastest things there. [He] thought that L'Jean and I were so good that we would be good for the Olympics. I didn't even know what the Olympics were then. So he came and took us out to the country and had us run. He said that we had the potential of being able to go to the Olympics. That sounded good. He set us down and he told us what the Olympics was and he worked for the city or something in the recreation department. And he would come and get us every day in the morning, for one hour before school. He said to be in the Olympics: "You have to practice. I'll come by. And you have go home, be in bed by eight thirty, you have to get up an hour and a half before school and go out and run, after school, after you've done your homework, you go run again. You have to cut out all parties." No going to parties. And you know what? And we were young then. We were going out to the skating rink. No thoughts of boys. You just have to talk to your mother about the things that you could eat and everything and run. And we said: "No thank you. Forget it." Get up in the morning before school? No fun? You have to be dedicated to go. That was the end of him. No parties, no skating late at night, be in bed? Come on.

As you can see, I was a happy child. That was fun. A glorious life. I never wanted to grow up. It was no fun. Never wanted to leave Mother. My mother would do things for me. Whatever my mother needed, I would do. Never slacked on it because my mother was the greatest. But I wanted to be a kid and I was always getting something wrong.

I wanted to be able to run. In school one time I was running real fast—and we wasn't supposed to be running in school—so we got in trouble about that. You know how you play and somebody hit you and you run push the door, and my hand went through the glass. It clean cut my hand. The scar is right there.

We were out on the Fourth of July at the park, waiting on them to serve the food, and the boys used to come and light firecrackers, and just to throw them near us girls and we'd squeal and move, well, they throwed one up under us and I couldn't get out of the way so it took a chunk out back there [pointing to her backside] so at school I had to sit like this [half off the chair] and I've got a scar right back there.

Watching baseball, the pitcher throw the ball and the fellow swung at the pitch and the bat slipped out of his hand and hit me on the head and knocked me out. Had to run and get Mother. And every time they used to take x-rays in that spot and wonder what it was, but it never slowed me down. I just kept going. I don't know why, but I had a mind that don't ever stop. As I got older I couldn't go climb up the trees like I did and follow the boys.

Alberta's love of sports spanned her whole life. At McKinley Elementary she participated in school with the Lawn Fete Girls' "Gala Day," which included "tennis, croquet and horseshoes during the day and a ball game in the evening."[12] As an adult, she participated in one of the black tennis tournaments, being spotted number one in the women's division when the event was announced.[13] But her high activity level sometimes caused problems in the classroom. Today I suspect she would be labeled "hyperactive" or "ADHD."

In grade school I couldn't sit still. I moved around and Mother would go to school and say to the teacher, "She's hyper, and give her something to do." So they would have me, like a messenger, go around and go down to the office and take reports or I could go down into kindergarten and look after the kids because my mother said, "Give her all you have the rest of them, give her everything she has to have and know, but test her just like you do everyone else, because she retains." And they would do that and they found out that I could remember and I could recite: "Fourscore and seven years ago our fathers brought forth a nation conceived in liberty and dedicated to the proposition that all men are created equal," I could remember that from way back in elementary school. But I could remember those things and so they did not give me any trouble.

The only trouble we had was when the teacher, I think it was the third grade, was going to change me to being right-hand from left-handed. She put soap on it, hit it every time she went by, and put the left hand behind you so you couldn't use it. And then I started stuttering. And here goes Mother again, Bible in hand, she tackled that teacher with these words in the Bible: "In two places God called these left-handed people, one was a king, there was a bad king and he wanted a good king, so he raised up a left-handed, and in another he raised up seventy, it's in the book of Samuel, he raised up seventy men, left-handed to go out and do a special job. So people who are left-handed are special. And I don't want you changing her. She's stuttering because you are going against God's will." And she left me alone and I quit stuttering. I marvel when I look on the television and I see that past president Bush was left-handed, Clinton was left-handed, Ross Perot was left-handed. So I remembered that really well.

All of the Hill children attended McKinley Elementary, which was segregated. McKinley was in an old building, and both Alberta and David noted that schools designated for black children always had secondhand books, hand-me-downs from the white schools. By the time they reached the age for junior high school, however, three of the Hill children had essentially pulled themselves out of the public schools. Rosetta had been put in the Kansas Vocational School, a sort of reform or rehabilitation school, David had run away from home, and Nevada was simply "too poor a little thing" to face the rigors of junior high school. Only Alberta attended Curtis Junior and Topeka High, which were integrated. In the upper grades, Alberta learned to channel her activity into sports and settled down in classes. She did very well in both.

Junior high and high school were integrated, but you [minority races] didn't belong to the pep club or the glee clubs or anything, and when they had the graduations, graduation was all the same. You had to walk in the same line, but if you had prom or anything like that, it was separated.

But I never had any trouble. All the white boys and the girls—they just loved me. And I could tell the dirtiest—well, maybe not the dirtiest—but I could really tell stories. And then the white girls would get mad and wanted to take up with me. So I just thought I was Queen of the May because the boys wouldn't let nobody bother me.

One of the things I loved was history. I still love history. We learned about Abraham Lincoln freeing the slaves. We learned about Marcus Garvey going back to Africa and some of the people he took some people back with him.[14] *I'm trying to remember since I learned so much since I've been here; I'm trying to separate them: Frederick Douglass and the peanut man—George Washington Carver.*

Everybody had to learn about the peanut man. But at that time they didn't have a whole lot of books, but these black teachers had a way of getting the black history. They went to conferences and they might have learned something when they went to a black college.

And I used to go to the library and read all of the things because we didn't have books at home. That's why I knew about Utah. I was fascinated with Utah, but I don't know why. This is the strangest thing. You think about this, now: I had heard about the Mormons and I read about the grasshoppers and the seagulls—and to me this was exciting. I was fascinated with how many grasshoppers it was and I could see people with brooms and things trying to stamp them out—and of course, I imagine I embellished it a little bit in my mind—and then about the seagulls coming in. I thought that was so marvelous about what the Lord had done. I found all the books about them planting and all these grasshoppers coming and that fascinated me. I wrote a paper for history and got an A. So how was I to know that years later the Lord would send me out here, at least some place I had some knowledge of?

And when we had to write [that] paper, they said I could be on a debate team, but they didn't really want me because all of them were white and I was the only one that was black. So they let me be on there sometimes. Kansas wasn't a slave [state] but it was a border state. If they were at home, fine, but if they were going away from Topeka High School, no. So I finally had to get off from there because Mother said she did not think that was right.

Alberta found inequality in the sports she loved, too.

The boys' team was mixed [races], but they didn't have a girls' team. You just played basketball and different things in the gym when you had to go to gym. But they didn't have separate things for girls in those days.

I played with the basketball team at school in the summer. That was from the city park and this black man got the team together. And that was fine with me because the girls were all going behind the schoolhouse, putting makeup on, and talking about boys. Mother had to sign up because I was old enough. They needed a lefty on the team, and I was a hustling player. I used to travel with the team. We were all black, and we'd go play all-white teams because there weren't many other black teams. We'd go out of town to little Kansas towns to play, and some of them had signs "Darkie, don't let the sun go down on you."[15] *You could play, but you'd be scared to win. And then you had to be sure that everybody was together so you could get out of town in a hurry, some little old town down in Kansas that had a ball park, but you were going to get run out. That was for any darkie went by there, past there, don't stop, don't try to buy no house, no place to live, don't try to get a job, don't let the sun go down on you. So that would scare us. We'd have to play real fast because we knew better not to try, not to win, so we just played.*

Alberta could deal with the inequalities and injustices of segregation through junior high and high school largely because her mother, who dealt in realities, and her grandmother, who dwelt in a more spiritual realm, had helped her understand the realities of those issues, unfair though they were when she was still in elementary school.

They had one [elementary school] in each part of town, and ours was McKinley. The one that Linda Brown went to was Buchanan where the Supreme Court ruling came [Brown v. Board of Education of Topeka]. And the north, south, east, and west, each one of them had junior high schools, but then only one Topeka High School. All of us from north, south, east, and west, when we came together, we had to go to that one high school.

All of us [Hill children] went to McKinley Elementary but only I went to Curtis Junior High in Topeka. It was integrated and Topeka High was integrated [because] they didn't have money enough to build but one high school for all—the whole town. But that was the funniest thing. You were always in segregated schools in elementary but the minute you graduated, you were popped into the same group of kids you had fought with all your young lives because they didn't have enough money to segregate the junior highs and the high school in Topeka.

They had separate elementary schools on each part of town: Black school was here and white school was there. It was all black at McKinley, and a real, real old school. And a few blocks down the street, the brand-new school for all white kids. One time the black teachers decided we ought to visit to quit the fighting outside.

We would go out of our way to pick fights with the white kids. But then when they got to the junior high school, they didn't have money enough to build two schools, so these kids that you fought with, there you were in school with them. And most of them had a hard time, except me. And you can wonder why I didn't. I could tell the dirtiest jokes [said with a wonderful, wicked grin]. I could remember them. And the kids would come around me and say, "Say something." I would say something crazy, like I would say, "You sound like the Sigma Phi monkey. The Sigma Phi monkey, you know what he did? No, you don't know. He said to the lion one day, you big bad dum—dum—dum—dum." Those boys, they loved me and when the girls would try to attack me—white girls, they'd be all together, because some of them I had fought with, and I loved to fight in those days. The white boys said, "Don't lay a hand on her." They would not let nobody jump on me. So I had a good sailing.

When you're kids, you're just going to fight. And [when] we would go home, you'd go out of the way so you could encounter some white kids so that you could fight. They did the same thing. And so the teachers wanted to stop that. They couldn't ask them [white kids] to come to the black school, because it was run down. So, they had our parents dress us up so they sat us down in each of the rooms and said: "Now when we go to visit, we'll have a slight program. And I want you all to be perfect little kids. And you had to stay in line. I don't want nobody to use no kind of language and you will smile and you will sit and you will be . . ." all this stuff. We listened. You know how kids will listen to them. All that sounds really good.

So we went and we looked at the playgrounds when we went, and we'd get mad. Little kids, you know when your stuff is not right. We got in the school going down the aisles to go to the room. The white kids were all sitting over here; black kids sit on this side. That was what it was supposed to be back in those days. And we was going by the white kids said, "Nigger, nigger, nigger." [rasping sound] "Nigger, nigger, nigger."

We were told we were not to say anything and not to talk back. Now how could I possibly go down there and not say nothing? And I walked down and saw that no teachers were looking I said: [whispering] "Poor white trash. Poor white trash." And did you know they heard me. And did you know the teacher came and sat beside me while we were there, and when we got back, I was grounded for three or four—I don't remember whether it was a week or a few days whatever it was—I couldn't go out on the playground and play. That was the punishment for disobeying the order.

Years later, Alberta would remember that visit and talk about it in a short speech titled "Two Worlds, Two Cultures."

"Sorry, we do not serve negroes, sorry, we do not rent or sell to blacks. Sorry, we do not hire blacks, sorry, your children can not attend this school.

"Poverty, prejudice, and discrimination, were my black heritage the day I was born into this beautiful world of God's. I, like most blacks, lived in two worlds and

two cultures. My black world to me is real, warm, and filled with love, understanding, and compassion for all mankind. My parents believed so much in God, they taught me to love not hate. My second world offers me a second-class citizenship. It is white, cold, and hostile, with a double standard. There is an invisible sign that warns all blacks that poverty, and discrimination, is their way of life.

"When did I become aware of that invisible sign? It's hard to say, for in my black world I was never told of the double standard. Our friends and neighbors were all black, and everyone was poor but happy and willing to share. I knew that my family loved me for I was their precious darling. Not black or white. The elementary school and teachers were black, so my education, discipline, and training was just a continuation of home, black orientated. It was here in school those first years that the invisible sign became visible. At last I was aware of my second world, a world where I was different. The new world was like all the books I read. The people were white like the picture in my history books. Everything I read was white, even the posters on the wall. On rare occasions I read about Africa, then I would see black natives, but I did not identify with them.

"One day we went to visit a school several blocks from our school, in a very nice neighborhood. The homes were well kept and the school was almost new. How I wished that I could have gone there, if only to play on the playgrounds.

"The rooms were spacious and wide compared to our over-crowded rooms. There were new desks and books in the room we were asked to wait in. Soon we were marched into the auditorium where all the blacks sat on one side as though they had leprosy. All through the program you could hear whispers from the white side, 'NIGGER,' 'dirty black niggers.' From the black side came the response, 'Dirty, poor white trash.' Invisible sign was no longer invisible, it was a reality.

"This was my initiation into my second world, the day I began seeking answers to my questions, 'Why?' I learned 'why' by experience, not from what I was told. I knew why we were poor, why the clothes I wore were hand-me-downs, and why the school I attended was so poorly equipped. Poverty, I could take for it is no sin to be poor, but prejudice and discrimination is a deadly sin. It is too late for me to see the great change to one world and one culture for all people, perhaps my children, perhaps our children will live in a world that Christ envisioned many, many years ago."[16]

At the time of that visit to a white school, though, Alberta was angry about the discrimination (and worse) it represented, but her mother was much more realistic.

Now, when I went home and I told, of course the teacher sent the note to my mother to let her know. And I sat down, and I said, "Mother, why was it that nothing happened to the kids that called us niggers as we were going down there, and snigger and laugh and point? And why were we told not to say nothing." I think that's discrimination. Well, we use the word discrimination [now]. I said, "It's not fair. It's one-sided."

Mother sat down—and that's what my mother is really good at—to explain to me that was the kind of a world that we lived in, and the reason why we left Louisiana, because she wanted us to get an education. If we had of went to school down there, it would have been worse. That's what she told us. I don't know why I can remember that: "If we had of stayed, but here we have to mind whatever the teachers say. Do you understand Alberta? Really, your teacher is the boss, and I send you to school, so you have to mind."

But you know, I never did understand. But she wanted me to understand. Why could I not understand?

My grandmother understood. My grandmother was a spiritualist. She told Mother to leave me alone because I was going to be a leader. I was going to do certain kind of things. Grandmother somehow knew.

My grandmother had a real impact on my life, more than my mother did, really. My grandmother, when she would come up to Topeka, we would go places and go to church together and she would tell me because she said I might pick up some of her spirituality.

Every summer, Mother had to go to work, and we got to go to Kansas City, 2052 North Hallock. We spent the summer down there with Grandmother and then come back home. She lived in an old house. And she slept on the floor. She didn't believe in beds. And she didn't believe in water in the houses. She had a well in the back where we had to go out and a couple of us primed it and then we'd pump.

The airport that they built, the first airport was where Grandmother lived. They bought [her] land. We were sending her money and she would go out and buy oil and food and give it to people down in the street. We thought she was paying the taxes and Mother came in and found that she wasn't, so they took the land from her because she hadn't paid taxes.

Buying food for other people doubtless reflects Grandmother Susie Barnes's great sense of charity. Much as Alberta loved and respected her grandmother, she acknowledged that it was her mother who watched out for her constantly, especially as she grew older and encountered more of the realities of society, both racial inequities and social improprieties. She even came to appreciate all that discipline.

One of the friends got pregnant and we were told that we could not play with her; we could not go over to her house. She had a baby; he had water on the brain; he had a big head. So we'd slip over there against the rules with Mother not knowing. We figured she wouldn't find out. And when the baby died, he didn't live but a few months, and they had a funeral. The funeral home was a few blocks from high school and we figured we could slip out during the gym time, go to the funeral, and slip back in, and we would be clocked absent from that one class. And when we got through with the funeral—it was a short one because the baby was just a little teeny baby—and we were on our way back, who did we run into just before we got back to school?

My mother. She had been to the hairdresser that was two doors from the funeral home. I made up a lie: "Oh, Mother, we're supposed to be out on the gym. We're supposed to be out walking or doing something." I know she didn't believe me; she knew I was lying, but she never said anything. But one other time, I remember when she caught me and she said: "I want you to remember when I'm asking you about these things, remember this: your mother was a girl once, too. I want you to remember this."

I was seventeen, almost eighteen and I came home from school, my last year in high school, and I told you I didn't have no girlfriends, just all these boys, but finally Frances and all of them asked me one time if I'd go with them. I felt so thrilled these girls would ask me to go with them.

"Where are we going?"

"Going down to Laurence, Kansas. The football team is coming there from Oklahoma to play." Laurence, Kansas, is like twelve or fifteen miles outside of Topeka, it ain't that far. Frances was going with some man. You know, there is always some older man with good-looking cars that goes around the school and picks up people. Well, Frances was the one and she said, "Well, he's going to pick us up, and it's going to be four of us are going, and you've never been with us, so I thought maybe you'd like to go."

I didn't live far from her. Her daddy worked for the post office, and they were better off; we were the poor ones, if you want to call "poor trash." We were the poor ones because our family was on welfare. So she had all the finest things, but her father and mother did not want her running with any of us, going over to skate, or neat things we did. We'd go to parades and come right back home, but she wasn't allowed to because she came from this family. But when she went to high school, that was clear across town, they would take her, but they couldn't stay there with her. She used to come home on the bus. Once they go to high school the parents lose control. And I walked, so I always was free. My mother never knew I was going walking, so it didn't matter. I was going to get home sometime.

Anyway, it sounded so exciting—it did, and I went with them. Now you know them boys—little old scrawny high school girls, the football players didn't pay no attention to us. But we'd holler "Oooh you're good looking" and squeal and holler. He brought us back home, he let us off at school, but school was over, and I walked home from school. And I came in and Mother was at home, and she said, "Where have you been?"

I said, "To school" [nonchalant tone], and I was putting my books down and taking my coat off.

And she said, "Where you been?"

And I said, "School." Now, if I'd have been smart, I'd have listened to her tone, but I wasn't smart.

She said, "I said, where have you been?" [measured cadence]

You know how you pretend. "I said I've been to school."

And she backhanded me. My mother was a little woman. Oh, and I picked myself up across the room in the corner down on the floor. "When I ask you something, you will [tell the truth]."

I was sitting there thinking, now how did she know that? You know how your mind works when you do wrong, you know what I'm thinking sitting up there? My mother never has hit me ever since I've been a grown but I must have done something really bad. I wonder how she knew that. I really shouldn't have done that, but I sure had a good time. I wonder how she found out.

Now, the class that I didn't go to, my homeroom teacher's class, I wasn't there. The white teacher that was there, she liked me—everybody liked me at school, because I was friendly, and I was there every day, hand in all my lessons, but I had never been absent. The teacher said: "Where is Alberta? She's not here today." She looked at the clock. She got off, got in her car, and on the way home she went by my house, and she said to my mother, "Is Alberta sick?"

My mother said, "No."

She said, "Well, she wasn't at school today."

Mother said, "I sent her to school."

"Well, I missed her."

Mother said, "You did. OK, let's plan right now before she gets here." She said, "What can we do?"

She [the teacher] said: "Well, you can have her come an hour early every day and she can dust my room and empty the trash and put the books up in order and whatever. You can tell her whatever you want but I'll expect her in my classroom an hour before school."

Now that's how my mother knew. Who would have thought white people had paid that much attention to any of us? And all of a sudden when I decide to do the wrong thing, can you believe that? She didn't act like I was special or anything, never treated me any different than anyone else in the room. But how was I to know? But you know, I never played with [tried to trick] her again.

I went every day—every day! In fact, I think that's why I like school right now. And then she would have books there and she would ask me, she would let me take them home to read. She said, "I read this here at school." Some of them were black [history] books, and they didn't have any of them [in the school]. She'd got them from the library. That's how I learned, because they didn't teach about black history in any of the schools, except when we were in elementary school. We got a whole lot of it because they were black teachers, black principals, black social workers.

My graduation from Topeka [High School] was June of 1939.[17]

CHAPTER 3

A WIDER WORLD

Alberta's attitude about what she might do after graduation reflected the general feeling of the time: educated women of any race could be nurses, teachers, or secretaries. All others would be limited to relatively minor jobs in sales or factory or domestic work, if they got any job at all. Julia, however, had other ideas and found a way to put them, and Alberta, into action.

When I graduated from high school Mother said, "What do you want to do?"

Now, there was a lady that lived around the corner and her name was Lagerberg. She had met Mother at the bus stop and she said, "Do you think she would like to come over and watch my son and just do light things around the house while I work?" She wanted someone to be with their son and to do dishes and pick up and vacuum and stuff like that, no heavy stuff, but mostly to be there with Jimmy.

And Mother said, "I'm quite sure she would until she goes and does whatever it is she's going to do."

I never had talked about that, what I was going to do, because I never figured that when I went to work that I would really work, mostly baby-sitting. So I went to work sitting Jimmy Lagerberg. We'd go for walks or we used to play. They had a ping-pong table down there, and we would play and laugh and I would sweep or run the vacuum. Didn't have much to do because mostly it was just to be with Jimmy. They were paying me fifty cents a day, and I didn't have nothing better to do. And then while I was doing it, that's when they sent the papers out and Mother filled them out to go to the YWPA, the Youth Works Project Administration.

The Works Project Administration was the largest organization created by Franklin D. Roosevelt's administration under the Emergency Relief Appropriation Act to relieve poverty and create jobs during the Great Depression of the 1930s. While the WPA's best known projects included building roads, dams, and national parks, it also had programs to train people in various lines of work.

Racial discrimination existed even in this federal program. "Nationally, the average WPA wage in 1936 was fifty-two dollars a month, but in the deepest southern states, it was as low as twenty-three dollars a month. And since the prevailing scale of pay for blacks in the South was lower than for whites, Negroes refusing a three-dollar-per-week private job might be denied WPA eligibility, while whites were not."[1]

The WPA was set up specifically for young people looking for job training. During her time in the WPA Alberta honed those qualities of leadership and innovation she had shown in school and would display far more when she came to Utah.

The boys went out in the forest and fixed the trees and things, but the girls, we went into a home in Topeka. [It was housed in Topeka because] Topeka was the capitol. All of the girls whose parents were on welfare from all over the state would come and spend two weeks at the YWPA and then we'd go home, and then another group would come and spend two weeks and then you'd go back after their two weeks was over. Then they would bring different ones in. Some of them came from off the farm, and they didn't have the benefits we had [in the city], so you got to meet kids from Salina and all the rest of the little places around. I think we got paid eighteen dollars for those two weeks. I always took my money home and gave mine to Mother, and she would give me two or three dollars back, because I always did take care of my mother.

They had you learn how to cook, sew, clean the house, make the beds, wash the linen, go to the store, shop—all those things you went to learn, and then they found out what your aptitude was. I did not like to cook, so all I had to do was find one or two of them to do my chores and switch with them. I could wash dishes up a breeze so I would trade with some of the other girls and wash dishes. I still love to do dishes.

You had to pick a career or profession that you wanted to learn more about to do. And a lot of people wanted to learn how to be chefs or cooks. A lot of the girls wanted to work in hotels or motels. Mine was catering. There was a catering group, a black catering group that catered to the governor and the legislators and the senators. Because we were a WPA training group, they didn't have to pay for us so they were glad for us to come. And every time I'd go I'd get to learn more. I learned who all the big shots were. And they thought I was neat because I was little and small and could do all the things they asked. So I got a good training from just going out with that group. And I got to go away from the program but was still being paid.

Galenda French was the director. She was a little wiry woman, small like me but not so much meat on her. But she knew everything. That's why I consider myself another Galenda French because I act like her sometimes. And she loved to play table tennis. She would play the different girls and they would let her win, but not me. If she going to play me she'd better win it, because I was going to win. So she was always coming to get me to play with her when she wanted to play—and how I could con her. My mind was working overtime. She would call and have me come down, and the only way she could beat me was if I would let her, and I would never let her.

The kids would say, "Let her win so she can give us—"

I said, "No, she's going to have win the best way she can."

So I was always the head chica,[2] *the leader to go talk to Galena French about whatever we had that they disapproved of, because it was supposed to be a democratic kind of a thing. They never could win, if it was the rules of the house, you would pull out the rules. And I always knew the rules so I never would question them on that, but I would take the girls' complaints even though I knew they couldn't win, but they felt that they got a fair shake.*

I was always somebody's advocate. Even in elementary school, when they picked on some ugly girl or some girl that was poor—nobody got in more fights than me. I guess I'm crazy, but I'd go in and take up for them and I wouldn't let up. Even then Mother said she had a hard time with me because the teachers would say, "She wasn't involved," but I said I had to take care of it because they all were picking on her and they were calling her names.

Everything I have done seemed to be leading up to doing the things I am doing in Utah. It's a funny thing because Mother mentioned the same thing.

But when the girls did something at the center against somebody else, we would short-sheet their beds. But my bed was never short-sheeted. I was the leader. And Galenda French knew it, because the other girls would do whatever I said. So she said we were going to do something and I said, "We don't want to do that." Whatever it was that she said we were going to do and I said we weren't. It must have been something that wasn't quite kosher.

She said, "You will do that."

I said, "We'll go on a strike." I don't know where I got all that strike stuff. It was something I had read. And she said, "You'll be suspended." She sent me home.

And I said, "That's fine with me."

And Mother said, "Now what did you do? Alberta, I have taught you—"

I said, "But Galenda French was wrong."

Mother said, "Now what are you going to do?"

I said, "I'm going to sit here and wait because she's going to come after me and you're going to have to tell me that I have to go back because I'm not going back, but you're going to have to convince me that I have to go back."

"What makes you think that she's coming?"

"Because she don't have anyone there to keep the girls in line."

Mother knew me too well. It wouldn't be long. It wasn't but a few days, here come Galena French. "Now I intend to be easier on you, Alberta, because—"

I said, "I'm not coming back."

She got scared, and I wasn't coming back because they got evaluated. That was a federal program and you got evaluated and you had to put in that they [the clients or the students] did this, this, and this. You had to record those things. And if the girls didn't do them, it was her job. But I would say to the girls, "We're going to do this. Come on."

"We're going to do, why?"

"Because if you want to have fun," I can always say we're having fun, right?

She came and my mother sat there like this [assuming a firm posture, straight back, stern look]. "You know you're supposed to be a child of God." She could always throw that on me. "Your grandmother."

So I did go back and finish the program.

But the girls all liked me, and sometimes when the teachers would go to bed, we wanted to go to Twin Lakes—that was a night club out there where you could go and you could dance and slip back. I learned how that we could go downstairs and over the washing machines. There was a window that opened out and you climb through there and the boys would go tiptoe, and Galenda French was never going to wake up, so she wouldn't know, and we'd go partying out of there, four or five of us. And we'd get back in the car, we'd come back, slip back in, close that window down, jump into bed laughing to ourselves. We never got caught.

It was fun for a while, but one of the girls that went with us told Vivian who was with the other group on the other two weeks. Vivian lived down the street from me and I knew her all my life; we called her Newton. The other girl said, "Find out from Alberta how they got to go and slip out." You see, it's OK as long as you do things and nobody knows about it. So I told Vivian. They went out and they got out fine and they went to Twin Lakes.

On the way back, I don't know who was driving their car, they had to pass a cemetery. They had an accident and got thrown halfway over the fence into the cemetery and they got back in the car, the car could still run, and they came back, but she got bumped in her side. They came back and they climbed through the window. They didn't get caught, but a few weeks later, Vivian had to be at home and I wondered why. They said she was bleeding internally. I thought it was probably from the accident but we couldn't tell anybody that they had went. And I worried about it a long time till I met her sister; I was telling her and she said she knew about it because Newton had told her about it and when she was at the doctor. She asked about it but the doctor said no, she had just bumped her side. It didn't have nothing to do with the accident. Tuberculosis was in the family, and I found out later that's what she had. But she died and we all went to the funeral and I never can remember crying so hard. Any time you sing "Precious Lord," I'd start crying because I would think about Newton.

Alberta herself would be involved in an accident, one she felt certain her grandmother had predicted. Susie Barnes was noted for her spiritual nature and for her ability to predict someone else's nature—even, occasionally, predict specific events. The one Alberta recalled most vividly happened in Topeka while she was working in the YWPA.

Grandmother had already told Mother to keep that girl [Alberta] out of cars and Mother said, "I don't have no trouble with that because we don't have no car. Nobody we know has no car."

Another of the girls at the YWPA, Georgia—I think her last name was West—came from a little town, and she would stay over at my house until her parents came after her. So, Georgia and I wanted to go out to KVS, Kansas Vocational School, where they were playing football, and the boys from Oklahoma or something were going to be there. Now, they didn't even know we were alive, but we wanted to go. So I told Mother we were going.

We were going down to catch a bus, and as we walked to the bus, [we met] two of our friends that we knew had a car, which was rare [for nonwhites] in those days, a Ford, a little Model T Ford. They said they were going out, and so did we want a ride? So Georgia got in and the other fellow got in and I sat on his lap.

A drunk driver came out of nowhere and Milton, who was driving the car, pulled to the curb, said: "What's wrong with this fellow? Look at him! Look at him!" And I looked up just as he hit us. He came all the way to the curb and hit us, and glass broke in my face.

The fellow that was drunk jumped out and ran to the police station—his brother was a policeman—and said that his car had been stolen. He was white and in those days you couldn't say nothing. They wouldn't have believed us, as blacks. We didn't have money, but very few people had cars in those days.

I got to the hospital and it was cut around my eyes, cut across the eyelid and it was cut open. [Alberta carried a noticeable scar above her right eye for the rest of her life.] Then I blinked, and when I blinked it dug in and took a chunk out of my face. And they still don't know why it didn't cut my eye out or why at that time I blinked.

I would not let the white doctor sew me up. My mother said I really acted up. I was sitting there bleeding to death and all I wanted was that colored man, that Negro doctor. I wanted a colored doctor to do it, so they went and found a black doctor; he was just an intern, Dr. William Scott, the only black doctor on the staff. He wasn't even a plastic surgeon, just a plain-old doctor that sewed me up. They tried to deaden it and they couldn't ever get it dead, but they let him sew up because that's the only way I would let them sew it up.

Grandmother was there before anybody could notify her. Mother never could understand that. Grandmother had come up; nobody called her but she knew I was in an accident; she expected that I was going to do something like that. That's the way she was, a spiritualist, and she said: "She will be OK. That's going to be her line of work. In her life she's going to be a fighter."

I heard her say all those things. I was always with my grandmother. I didn't know what she meant by that, because as I say, I hadn't even graduated from high school. I had to stay out of school for a whole half term because my face had swollen up, and the kids would come by with cocoa butter and rub it on it at night because it would itch.

Soon after she finished a YWPA course in catering, Alberta decided to travel South and visit Louisiana. The Hill family had stayed in touch with family and friends there, and a friend in Topeka was driving that way with her father. During the trip Alberta experienced the extreme prejudices and practices against blacks that she had not known in Kansas. She suddenly realized the danger of taking her usual strong stand and at least for that trip, she wisely curbed her tongue. On the way back, however, she unexpectedly found herself on the better end of the segregation bargain.

In 1940 I went to Louisiana and I was riding with a friend of mine. Her dad, Mr. Avery, said he was going to Texas and he would take me for a certain amount of money. I said, that's one way I'll get there. Oh, it was so exciting. Guess what? We got in the car and I said goodbye to Mother and we went to Oklahoma. We were hungry and we stopped and went to the restaurant and they told him to go around the back. They didn't serve colored. [Mr. Avery] said, "What do you want?"

I said: "I don't want nothing that comes from the back, because it's probably been messed on. I don't want to eat it. I won't eat." So I didn't eat. Then he took us to Dallas and we ate there because some of his family was there and we ate with them.

Then he took us to Terrell, Texas, Louise and I. He said, "I've got to go back to Dallas." He left us there for five long days, down in the little country town. We went to church. They didn't have a road; they just had wagons. Honest, it was terrible. And I just said, "I have paid him the money." And so we got some boys we found, friends of the people that we met there, and they took us. We could have been kidnaped and murdered and nobody would never know the difference. But they took us to Dallas and I caught up him and I said: "Give me my money back. I'm going to go and get me a ticket and get a bus or a train. Just give me my money. You didn't have any business." He was having a ball.

So he said, "OK," so he had to go back to Terrell, Texas, and got my suitcases and clothes and things, and then he took us on to Shreveport. When we got to Shreveport I had him stop and drop me off and go into a grocery store. I was going to get some lunch meat and some bread. And I stood up there, and people were coming in and this man was waiting on everybody. And I said, "Wait a minute. Hey! I was here first." You know how I am. [I did, indeed, know how she was.] And they just come in. "I want to be waited on."

He looked around at the people and he looked at me, he said, "One of them Northern niggers." And all of a sudden the light went on. Mother says, "Just remember when you're in Rome, you have to do like the Romans do." And I thought about that and I said, better shut my mouth. So he got some meat and slapped it—with his hand on it, slapped it all on the scale and rolled it up. "Here it is gal." And he charged something and I couldn't eat that because he's had his hand all on it.

Then I went to my cousins on my mother's side. These were farmers and several of her nieces and nephews went to a college right across the line over in Texas. They had cars, so I never got to go into a streetcar or to a drinking fountain. I never got the flavor of the state because they were college kids; they had places to go and do that had nothing to do with the whites. Every morning they wake you up and it'd be smelling so good, and you'd say, I'm getting fat. I had gained five pounds and I said, I better get back to Kansas because I'm gaining weight.

When I got ready to go home, they took me to the station. The Southern Belle was a train and we got in but we had to sit in the back of the train, and in the front, all the whites. But, now, it was summer, it had to be in June or July, August, because it was hot. And they had air conditioning. And we were nice and cool because there weren't too many blacks on there. But up in the front, where the white people were, it was packed. And they were hot and they tried to come back where we were and the conductor said "Un-huh, that's for the Negroes." And he wouldn't let them come back until we got to—I think it was St. Louis. They couldn't segregate [there]. They had to stop there and the people from up there were just pouring in. And then they got hot back there where we were. I always look at that and say that was a blessing to be segregated because we enjoyed the cool air conditioning until we got there and the rest of the way home, it was hot. They said, separate but equal; they were separate but definitely unequal. But that was way back then.

That is doubtless one of the few, if not only, cases in history when segregation worked in favor of blacks.

Back home in Topeka, Alberta found a job as a cashier in a theater owned by the Malory family. In talking about the job, she mentioned, simply and almost casually, several of the issues blacks faced in 1940. The first was "passing." The fact that her friend Dorothy Little's family had light-colored skin meant that they were more acceptable to whites than their darker-colored compatriots. Some such light-skinned coloreds could even pass as white, moving into far better-paying jobs where they would be treated with much more respect.

When that YWPA program ended, I went to work at a theater, the Ritz Theater taking tickets. That's how I met Dorothy Little. Beautiful woman. She's the one that was married to the Mills brother.[3] *Dorothy and I became friends then. Her dad was a detective with the state, because they didn't look black really.*

First we were ticket takers, then ushers, then Dorothy taught me how to be a cashier, how to do the money, how to write the reports out, then she left and went to

California [when her husband who was in the armed service was transferred] and I became the cashier and assistant manager. They needed a licensed cashier and they got permission from the owners of the theater, because I was the only black licensed one. I don't know who booked the bands, but they had Jimmy Lundford and all the black bands and I would sell the tickets. And then I'd get to come out once and they would play a medley for the lovely cashier and they cheered.

The war broke out in '39 and this was '40, getting close to '41. I was the president of a professional women's club called Semper Fidelis (always faithful), like the marines. And we used to bake cookies for the soldiers that came out at that air base, Forbes Field.

When Dorothy went to California then I became the ticket seller. And then all the men we could get to run the projection, they would get their Dear John letter, "Uncle Sam wants you," and they left.

The Malorys said, "What are we going to do?"

So I said, "I guess I'm going to have to run it."

And they all thought I could do everything, too, so I went upstairs and Arlen showed me how you run the projector. There would be two projectors and you'd switch from one to the other; and then you push the thing to get the light behind them. It the old-fashioned one, not like you have nowadays. And I can just remember when Gone with the Wind came. Gone with the Wind had about nine or ten reels and I was real thin and skinny anyway. And you had one program in the afternoon and one at night because it ran so long. And I had to lift the reels up and had to light them. So that's what I did until they would get another projectionist, and then I'd go back down to the ticket office. They made me assistant manager and I took the money up.

And then the federal government came—I'm always being involved when the federal government comes. Down the street they had a plant, Morrell's packing plant. And they were putting the egg plant in there where they were doing the frozen eggs to send to the boys overseas. That was the nastiest stuff I've ever seen in my life—frozen, powdered eggs. Nasty.

They had to hire women to crack those eggs. They could take two and three eggs in one hand and crack them and the pan was down at the bottom where most of the bottom girls—when I say "the bottom," they were the streetwalkers and things. During the war they hired them, and they needed a supervisor that those girls would mind. Every time they got somebody in there, they'd run them off [saying] "We don't have to listen to you. You think you're better than us."

And they asked, "Who can we get?"

They said, "Get the ticket seller, Alberta." So I went to work in the daytime down in Morrell's egg company and then I'd rush home and change, because I just had to look good for my theater to sell tickets, wear pretty blouse or sweater or whatever, because they never saw the second half. On Saturdays I'd go to the beauty shop and the Atkinson girls would fix my hair up, so I was in good shape.

So that's what I did at the ticket window. All those soldiers. Uncle Sam had called them up and I could get the pick all of them. Looked good, too—maybe not that good. All I had was a gift of gab.

Someone told those boys I'm not married. And one of my friend Glenda's cousins was in the service and came down to the theater. He told her he wanted to come back and marry me.

I told her, "Un-huh."

She said, "You've seen him come to the window; he's one of us."

Couldn't pick him out of the window.

He kept saying, "I'm going to marry you." And I didn't know nothing about him. So he went back and told his commanding officer he found the woman he wanted to marry, she was a ticket taker in a theater, and he needed a furlough to come home to marry me.

So he wrote back to his cousin, to Glenda, and he told her he was coming home. She said, "Oh, Alberta, you got to marry him!"

I said, "I don't even know him! I don't know nothing about him. Where does he—crazy!"

Mary said: "OK. Come on over to my dad's house, and stay and we'll eat and everything and then we'll go down to the train station and meet him in the morning when he comes in and we'll see about this." All us girls used to hang out at Mary's dad's house—Jeanetta Dixon, Glenda, Mary. So we stayed over at Mary's that night and laughed and partied, and said we'll all wake up and go down to the train station so they could look him over so they could approve or disapprove of him, but we didn't go there. We didn't wake up. We stayed up half the night—and we went to sleep and we didn't wake up. The train had already come in. So they went to see him over to Glenda's house. I went home.

This was 1941 and all of my friends had been married and some of them divorced and I was the only [single] one and they wanted to party and they said, "It's time for you to get married."

And I said, "Well, why me?"

They said: "Alberta, you're going to have to marry him because we need to party. He hasn't had anything exciting to do for a long time. We want to have a party. Not just one day—two or three days. You ought to get married."

I said, "I got nothing better to do."

So they got the guy, brought him around, and took him out to see Mother. She was out doing something in the yard and I said, "Mother." I couldn't even hardly know his name. I said, "Mother, we're going to get married."

She had never heard me talk about Ike Gooch.[4] *She said, "How do you do, young man."*

She said: "OK, Alberta, I'll tell you this; it's the only advice I'm going to give you. One of the things that you don't play with is the Lord. And when you do, if you make your bed hard, you got to lay on it. In other words, you can't come complaining to me about something, because you're playing with God, but I don't tell you what to do. You're supposed to be grown enough to know, and I realize that. I hope you happiness."[5]

So we went to the courthouse with all of my friends, four or five of them, to get all the papers and the license, all of that. I got that. And this white judge or whoever he was that was in the courthouse, he married us. Just as he said, "I now pronounce you man and wife," the tower bells on the courthouse rang, like they did every day at twelve o'clock. And I said: "Oh, Lord, what have I done. I don't know anything about this man. I don't even know whether he's a man or a woman except he was in the army. Oh, Lord, we could have done this a better way." There was no love, no liking, no nothing. I knew what Mother was talking about. Oh, Grandpa's going to be mad, too. Oh, I remembered everything, now that it's too late. Well, make the best out of the situation.

So we went down and we got a room up over the cafe right next door, because I wasn't going to go home. Ike and I went downstairs to the cafe and they partied. And you must remember I didn't drink, I didn't smoke. But I drank milk and I loved to dance, I loved being with the kids, with the gang. That's all I knew—milk. I finally learned how to drink Coke and anything that was red, red pop, strawberry, orange, but I didn't drink beer or anything because it wasn't sweet. "Red pop," that's what they called me. I drank my red pop and we got chili and they got whiskey and they drank it. And Ike was a party man. And I thought, I don't know whether I'm man or woman in here. Oh, Lord, what am I going to do?

Soon after the wedding the army transferred Ike Gooch to San Luis Obispo so Alberta followed him to California. Gooch served as a mess sergeant in a racially segregated unit. Segregation for all black and Japanese American service people in the United States remained in place until after the end of World War II. In 1946 President Harry S. Truman, feeling both national and international pressure, appointed a Civil Rights Commission to investigate and recommend actions with regard to minority citizens. In 1948 their report recommended several changes, including integration of federal services. On July 26, 1948, Truman, acting as commander in chief, issued two executive orders. Executive Order 9980 created a Fair Employment Board to eliminate racial discrimination in federal employment. Order 9981 followed quickly, stating: "It is hereby declared to be the policy of the President that there shall be equality of treatment and opportunity for all persons in the armed services without regard to race, color, religion or national origin. This policy shall be put into effect as rapidly as possible, having due regard to the time required to effectuate any necessary changes without impairing efficiency or morale." Blacks and other minorities would now serve in integrated units.[6]

The Gooches lived in Morro Bay in San Luis Obispo County along with several other black families. Here Alberta gained some insights into life beyond her relatively sheltered existence in Kansas.

At Morro Beach Inn they had the cabins and motor home cabins for the soldiers. The soldiers worked at the camp guarding the coast and there was nothing to do there. I learned to crochet and embroidery and listened to the soaps on the radio.

Then I met some fascinating women. Most of the women were from Mississippi, Texas, Georgia, from down South, and they all had stories to tell. I was born at Shreveport, but I was a baby when Mother moved me to Kansas. They could tell I was a Kansas square, because they would have the parties and I didn't drink, didn't even drink beer, so they would have to get Kool-Aid or pop for me. And I didn't smoke. They knew I didn't know anything so they were just telling me. They would be with their cooking and doing stuff and they would be just telling tales, and they knew they had me. I was a captive audience and I think that they were sincere.

The one from Louisiana would tell me about the seven daughters of the seven sisters and about all the weird things [they would do]. They could take a hair from your head and plant it in a tree and if it grew, you would get weaker and weaker. Ah! [That "Ah!" definitely said she was being polite but not believing a word of it.]

One girl, beautiful, I don't know what her name was. She was a prostitute, but a call girl, not a streetwalker. She worked with a company so that she went to clubs and yachts, and they were pretty well off, but she was good-looking.

In Morro Bay where we lived, when the boys would get their time off or they'd be able to come home for the weekend, we'd go down to Morro Bay Inn that was up in town and they would drink and we would dance. They'd have a band, two or three people playing something, and Ike and I used to do the jitterbug. He would throw me up and clap and stuff. People would wait for us to come so—and I didn't know this at the time—they didn't charge Ike and me anything for drinks if he and I would dance. Oh, he would throw me out and I would come on back and up through his legs and over his head. Jitterbugging. "In the Mood" would be playing; that was one of our favorite songs. They'd put it on and yell, "Come on Gooch."

I remember one time we went down there and they had drinks. I was having my usual stuff, and they said, "You'll like this; it's sweet." Whatever it was, this was a knockout kind of thing. They said: "You ought to try this. You might like it."

I said, "Not if it's got alcohol in it."

"Oh, you won't even know it's got alcohol."

I think I took two sips off of that and, "It may be OK, but I know this has got alcohol." Never did like alcohol. It didn't taste that bad, but they said, "Just taste it." I passed out. They had to carry me out, had to carry me to the car and carry me home.

Much as Alberta enjoyed her adventures in Morro Bay, there were difficulties as well. And some of her experiences made her, and her friends, realize just how protected her life in Kansas had been.

I remember when they had a scare. It was pitch-black, late at night and they thought they had spotted a Japanese sub out on the coast. They were shooting those great big millimeter guns that shook the windows and knocked stuff off the tables. We were just across the highway. It was so powerful that two miles down at Morro Beach Inn, on the other end downtown where the stores were, it knocked plate glass windows out. And all of them were walking around in the dark. One of them had a flashlight and they were counting to see if we were all there. And one of them said, "Where's Mrs. Gooch?"

Rosetta said: "You know where she is. Nobody could sleep through this." So they came and Rosetta had a key because her husband was a master sergeant. She had a key to come in and they woke me up and they talked about it and said: "Nobody, nobody can sleep like that. Didn't you hear that?" The pictures had fallen off [the walls] and dishes up in the cupboard had rolled off. I woke up looking at them. But I didn't know I could sleep like that. I still sleep that soundly.

But living with Ike down the coast, I got bored and moved with Dorothy into Los Angeles and Ike could come up there when he was off. He loved that because there were a whole lot of things to go to. In my house [growing up] you didn't have cussing. Sometimes kids would fight—and when I say fight, that doesn't mean that licks were passed. When I say fight that means you hollered back and forth. They might have been across the street, because you didn't ruffle your clothes or get dirty. You'd say, "You so and so and so and so," whatever language you used. It would be a great verbal kind of contest.

It was only after I had got married to Ike Gooch, out in California, with Dorothy in Los Angeles and she would take me out to the clubs or downtown shopping that I would hear people using "S-Bs" and so forth. I was expecting them to fight and Dorothy would say: "Oh, grow up, Alberta. Grow up." But I did not know about that kind of language. And then she said, "I'm going to take you down Central Street." And then she took me a place and they showed a pornography thing.

I said: "Why is that man dressed in women's clothes? Well, why is he doing his hands?" Dorothy didn't know what to do with me. Growing up I was having too much fun playing tennis with Dorothy's brother. We'd go out and we'd play tennis or anything that had to do with sports. That's where I was at. I wasn't into anything bad.

Then while I was living in Los Angeles, I started working at a nightclub, the Plantation, as a waitress in those short skirts. I started off just working on the weekend and they put me on the table where all these movie stars used to come because I had a gift of gab and they loved me. They would call for me to come, so I started working five days a week. The girls didn't work [full-time] then, just the men worked, but I did. Some of the girls didn't like it because they had been there a long time but the fellows wouldn't let them touch me.

And while I was working at the Plantation, I got this big thing. I've got to do my civic duty. Everybody had to pull their weight. Yes, we had things that were rationed. Yes, we couldn't have this or that, but I should be doing something. I told Dorothy, and she fell out laughing: "You're crazy. You are working."

"Yes but I could do my civic duty." So we looked in the paper and she saw a place that made the screws and bolts for airplanes. So she borrowed a car, a convertible, and we dressed—she always looked nice, her hair all done and

everything—and took me there to interview for the job and came in with me. But I told them I was a serviceman's wife, stationed there but I was living in Los Angeles, but I thought that I needed to be doing my civic duty, something for my country and all that. And Dorothy was sitting there and he was looking at her because she looked like a movie star.

He said: "Let me tell you something, lady. If you've got the nerve to come here dressed like this, in a Cadillac" (it was a Cadillac convertible) "and ask for this dirty job making screws, I'm going to give you a job. But I'm going to guarantee you that you won't last."

I said, "I've got to do my civic duty."

So Dorothy showed me how to get on the busses and transfer downtown. It took me longer to get there than it did the actual work. It's a long ways. You got on the bus and you went downtown and you transferred and got on another bus to get there. I think I might have worked maybe two weeks, but I still kept my job at the nightclub, because that's where I was making my money. I stood up there and pretty soon, I'd go to sleep. And the people around there liked me and one girl especially said, "You go outside and catch some fresh air and I'll keep yours going while you're there."

I'd come back in and say, "Thanks. Do you need to get some rest?" And I would do hers. So everybody got a little rest, but it started taking a toll on me, and you had to be precise, push it in, cut it out. The bolts from the airplane would come out and you had to do so many of them a day. But I just wanted to show that man that I could do my civic duty, and I'd have been OK if I'd quit the night job and got some sleep, but you work at the nightclub you went on at say seven or eight o'clock at night and you work until two in the morning and then you went some place to eat breakfast before you lay down to take a nap and then you're up again at five to catch a bus or a trolley car downtown. I did it for a while, but it wasn't long.

Isaac Gooch had served in the United States Army since May 11, 1941. With the German surrender on May 8, 1945, and the Japanese surrender on September 2, 1945, soldiers were being discharged from active duty as their bases were being diminished in numbers or closed altogether. Since Gooch was nearing time to be discharged, Alberta and Dorothy decided to drive back to Kansas to set up housekeeping before their husbands returned. During that trip they passed through Utah in what was the worst winter on record to that time.

When Ike said he was getting out of the service and we had to go back to Kansas, I told them at the nightclub that I was leaving. The women were happy, but the men weren't. So they had three bars to say goodbye. Then they partied and they took pictures. They said, "Champagne is not like drinking alcohol." I had never tasted champagne, so I took a sip at this bar and I took a sip at the next one to say goodbye. And by the time I got to the third bar, I didn't know nothin'. Alcohol and me—whoosh—but champagne, I had never tasted champagne and it didn't taste like alcohol and it was bubbly—didn't make any difference anyway.

In 1947 Dorothy and I drove back to Kansas and stopped in Utah in the dead of the winter, in '47. If you were here, you know how bad that one was. We were going to stay two or three days; Dorothy's brother and sister-in-law lived here. Dorothy and I said, "Where did we have to go [out for the evening]?" There was no place for blacks for us to go, but one little place, a hole in the wall down somewhere.

Between the weather and the shortage of activities for blacks in Utah, Alberta was glad to return to Topeka, where the minority population was larger and where the number of services available for them—and provided by them—was far higher.

Kansas was home and glad as Alberta was to see her parents again, she immediately ran into one of the continuing problems in her family: her father's belief that he could order his wife around and back up his demands with physical force. While today's reader may be shocked at a husband hitting or even threatening to hit his wife, in the mid-twentieth century, it was not at all an uncommon practice in all parts of the nation, and among all communities, at that time and for several decades more to come. True to her character, Alberta stepped into the fight.

Dad was always jumping on Mother, but Mother was a scrapper, she'd fight him back. He had jumped on her one day and I said, "Mother, I don't believe in any man hitting a woman." But anyway Dad, he hit on Mother. I know I used to hear them at night time and Mother never cried, because Mother was a slugger, and she was little, too, almost five feet weighing eighty-nine or ninety pounds. I said, "The next time, Mother, the very next time." We had a fireplace in the floor and then you had an iron in there that you turned, pushed down and then turned it on and off. I said, "You take that thing and you hit him."

I had told a friend of mine that I lived with in Garden City, Betty, to do the same thing, because they had a fireplace. Bob would get drunk and beat on her.

She was real light [skinned] and always walking around with black eyes. I just said to Betty: "Betty, I don't know why you come with these black eyes. If he ever jumps on you again—because I would never let no man hit me, Gooch would never hit me." And so Betty did. One day he came in drunk. She picked up that [fireplace item] and hit him, and he was so stunned he jumped and run and got in the cab, took it to the next light and had to stop for the light and passed out. And the police came and put him in jail because he was drunk, not because she had hit him in the head. He had a big bruise up on his head, a big knot. He never touched her another day.

And I was telling Mother that, I said: "I told Betty and I'm telling you the same thing. I can't take care of you. I can't help people if they won't take care of themselves."

Daddy came home, all of us had gone, and he jumped on Mother. She grabbed that and hit him in the head, good old gash and he went to the hospital.

I went up there to see him and he said, "See what your mother did to me? She done put me in the hospital." He had a bandage all around his head.

And I said: "Daddy, what gave you the right to hit a woman? The Bible don't tell you that. The Bible says you are supposed to look after women."

"She made me mad and she did this—"

I said, "Mother has worked all of her life taking care of us, even when you couldn't work. Mother has worked and paid the rent."

Then he said, "Well, I'm going to move. I'm leaving your mother and I'm filing for divorce. And I want to move in. Will you let me move in with you?"

I said, "Un-uh. If you leave, if anybody moves in with me, it's going to be my mother."

You know my daddy quit speaking to me for three or four years. I would see him on the street and say, "Hi, Dad." I'm always going to speak. My grandmother said, "A good hello never hurt anybody." She used to walk down the street and speak to white folks, standing by the bus sign. She'd say, "Howdy there," and they'd look at her as though she was crazy. I'd say: "Grandma, you don't know those people. Look at them. They don't want to speak to you." She said: "A good howdy and good hello never hurt nobody. Makes you feel good. You say hello to them so you can feel good." That was her philosophy. So I would speak to my dad, and then, I, when I had come out here to Utah, and I went back home, I went to see my dad, then he would talk with me. So that was a lot of years. He would talk, but we were never close.

Alberta immediately settled in to life in Topeka. She bought a house and was gladly welcomed back to her old job in the theater, but with added responsibilities. She was all ready to welcome Gooch home, but that did not go quite as smoothly as she had expected.

I had kept all of the checks that the army sends to wives, because I didn't need it; I was making money. They had to send me a letter and said cash them otherwise they were going to disqualify them. So when I got back home before Gooch, I put it all into the bank and when he got out of the service, we bought a house, and I had it California-stuccoed, right on the corner. It was in Washburn, not far from the Washburn University. The neighborhoods were integrated. It wasn't a black neighborhood, but they had blacks in the neighborhood. Black people lived all around in that area, not on that street, but behind us and all around. All the rest of them along the street this way and that way were white and if you walked about half a block back behind there, there was a black neighborhood—most of them back there were black. So it was what you call a mix. That's the way Kansas was.

The minute I got back, I looked for a job. Mrs. Malory the owner of the Ritz Theater said any time I left and came back, my job was always waiting. But when I was at home one of the times, I did call Mrs. Malory up and she started crying and said, "Can you get over?" Mr. Mallory had died. So all the business of the theater—I took over and did it all. So I was working there when Gooch came back.

Right away he went down to Garden City, outside of Garden City to work with his father.[7] *So I stayed up in the house. He went down to see his father, his brother and sister-in-law, nieces and nephew and didn't even know any of them. But he went down there and he decided to stay in Garden City because he could make more money. Now I'm up in Topeka in our home. I was working every day at the theater, and he went down there. He said he was going to stay in Garden City and he was working at a hotel. He was a bellhop at the Wheat Farmer and in the wintertime when there was no planting and the snow's on the ground they came to town at the hotel. They got women for the farmers and then they'd go right across the Colorado and get liquor [because Kansas was a dry state]. I could make a lot of money, bring it home, and I'd put it in the bank and we'd pay on the house note.*

Eventually Alberta moved to Garden City to be with her husband, but she frequently made trips back to Topeka to see her mother. She occasionally came with her brother, David, who was then living in Great Bend, not far from Garden City and on the way back to Topeka. By this time David had married his childhood sweetheart Odessa Divers; they had four children, David Junior, Marian, James, and Michael. Those children went on to become an assistant in a mortuary, a supervisor for Bekins Storage line, a nurse, and a college professor, a long jump up from the two-room shack in Louisiana where their father had begun his life. During World War II, David had worked in a defense plant in Oregon where he completed his General Educational Development (GED) test. For a time David worked at the Santa Fe Hospital as an orderly and a part-time janitor, but eventually he attended the police academy and became a police officer. He was for a time the only black police officer in Great Bend, Kansas.[8] He and Alberta were still very close and during one incident, she displayed her affection for him as clearly as he had for her all those years before when he jumped into the bottom of the outhouse to rescue her hat.

I was living in Garden City with my husband and I came home to Topeka and then David and Wanda were giving me a ride back to Garden City before they went back to Great Bend, down near the border, right across from Oklahoma and right across from Colorado.

A whole bunch of brothers came in. They had nothing against me and they said something and David gave them [demonstrates a fight]. And David said, "I'll take you on, come on." And I grabbed my bottle and got up.

When I interviewed David during one of his visits to Alberta, they demonstrated how he had his fists already raised while she stood back-to-back with him, holding her bottle, ready to break it over anyone who came at him from behind. They proudly reported that they had won the match quite handily. I was not about to question a pair who had so amply shown their fighting skills.

That was way before [David] became a policeman. He was a good policeman. After he became a police officer, he went down there, they all became friends—that whole family of them. And they said, "Oh, didn't we have a good time." That's what they called a good time. That reminded me of when we were kids. David, when he was little and [had] all that curly hair, the girls loved him. And they teased him and the boys wanted to fight him, but they couldn't fight him because his big sister was right there. And anytime he had a problem, he never went to Mother, he always came to me if he needed money, all of his life, if something came up, always paid it back, but he always knew that it was here.

I could see from the affection in their conversations that they were still looking after each other. Unfortunately Alberta's relationship with Isaac Gooch was not going nearly so well. They moved back to Topeka, but severe strains were developing in the marriage. She remained independent, feisty and completely her own person. In many ways Gooch was going his own ways, too, but Alberta explicitly said that she did not want to include any details about that; in fact, she didn't talk about them at all. She did say that when a situation did finally reach the point that she feared real trouble, she played her trump card, "I'll tell David." Eventually he did threaten abuse and Alberta filed for a divorce, but the process took a fairly convoluted route before she was finally free.

I think I was married at least seven or seven and a half years to Isaac Gooch, but because I had gotten so independent, he raised a hand. This was Gooch. Of course, Gooch didn't have a mother. His mother died when he was born. His father raised him. He just raised his hand, and you know me, I just stood there and said: "Go right ahead. I ain't moving a bit. I already talked to my brother and he doesn't like you and he'll come over here and I know you don't want him to jump on you. Go right ahead on, but David said just let him know." He did not allow nobody to pick on me. All I had to do was tell him and here he would come. He was a policeman in Garden City and a whole lot of people were scared of him.

I moved out and went to the lawyer and got some divorce papers, and this lawyer carried it through. I think that was in '46 or '47. The first time I went they heard about the emergency divorce, but that didn't last because I had to go out of town and stay. You could get an emergency divorce if you were rich and you had money. What was your reason for getting an emergency divorce? Mine was I wasn't going to be in Topeka any longer. I going to be moving to California—Dorothy was there, too. She's going to be moving to Chicago, and she's going to live in Chicago. And he said, "Divorce granted." But it was granted if you stayed out of town. Dorothy and I went to Chicago and it was too cold. So we went to New York then went to Washington, D.C. And then we came back home to Topeka, and the minute I came back to Topeka then I was in the same house. We hadn't moved any furniture or anything. So the divorce was thrown out.

Further divorce proceedings were interrupted by a severe illness. In the 1940s appendicitis was still frequently fatal. Penicillin had been discovered in 1939, but it was not yet widely used. Even so, Alberta's case was far worse than simply having a bad appendix.

I always kept Mother with me because she and Dad had divorced. Mother was living with me [in the house Alberta and Gooch had bought], and when she came in from work, she found me on the floor. My appendix burst.

Now, you got to know Topeka. This is in September or October of '48. We went to the hospital and they put you [blacks] out in the hall; they don't have room for you. But they didn't let blacks operate on you. They could allow an intern, a black doctor, Dr. Willard, to treat me after the surgery, but whoever operates on you, when they sent you home, they sent your black doctor the papers that said what happened. They said my appendix had burst and the poison had gone all through my body and just gave me pain pills because there was nothing they could do for me. In those days, anytime your appendix burst, you died. That was fifty years ago. How the Lord has let me live—honest to goodness, that's remarkable.

Anyway, as I lay there, Dorothy said, "They are letting her lie there and die." And she got on a plane, little old dinky plane at that time, and came home and said, "Where's the doctor?"

"Well, he sent some pain pills over by Gooch, her husband, and said that's all he could do." So Dorothy went to the Santa Fe Hospital and got a white doctor—and you know that was a no-no. White doctors didn't go into black homes. They had a black doctor and he might come and reach in his pocket, blow the dust off his pills—for what good it did—blow the dust off his sugar pill and give it to you. You just didn't have doctors. Your health just was something Grandmother went out in the field and came back or went to the drugstore and got stuff.

So anyway, Dorothy went and got this white doctor, Dr. Ford and brought him in the house. Now, I don't remember this, but Mother and Dorothy told me later, because he'd go over and look in my eyes. All I remember is I was laying there, never in pain because I guess they had given me the pain pills. And he said, "I can't do nothing." Everybody thought I was clinically dead, even Dr. Ford, including my mother.

Dorothy said, "You will do something."

He said, "Well, can you make her angry?"

Dorothy said, "She doesn't get angry. She's just always full of fun. The only time you can make her mad is if you do anything to her mother."

My mother said he had her go over and touch me in the stomach; Mother always used to rub my stomach, because I'm the baby girl. Then he hollered at her and said: "Quit that! You're spreading the poison."

The only thing I can remember, the whole time I was sick is that my eyes barely opened a crack and I said, "What's that white Paddy doing in my house talking to my mother like that?" And then I thought, "I will never speak to him as long as I live."[9]

But that doctor came to the house three times a day, early in the morning, noon, and night. He had read in a journal where they were experimenting with the new something for peritonitis and he said, "I can try it on her, but I don't think—"

And Dorothy said: "Try it. Try it. Whatever it was." And it was one side with penicillin, and the other side was sulfa, the combination of those two. But somebody had to be by my bed twenty-four hours a day or come in and give me water, liquid, so that the sulfa wouldn't burn me up. It took months and months and months. They would come and pick me up and carry me to the bathroom for a sitz bath three times a day, and after about five or six months, they would let me slowly walk to the bathroom and then they would carry me back. And then about eight months, they would let me stay up for two hours, but I had to sleep six. It was like that. And I was so thin; I weighed 130 pounds when my appendix burst, and when I finally came to Utah I weighed sixty-six.

The people would come by and say, "Oh, I know she can sing." I can't sing; my voice is bad, but they would say, "she can sing, because, look, she's got birds like a canary" and all those funny things. [Alberta acknowledged a degree of hallucination here.] They would bring me milkshakes, because I couldn't have solid food, so I drank milkshakes, five and six a day. And my friends would cook celery or potato soup and strain it through those mesh cloths because nothing was supposed to go down there. I would scratch my stomach and it had to be liquidy. I still love strawberry shakes. But for years I would not eat chicken soup or tomato soup, because all I could have was some kind of soup.

First Dr. Ford had told Mother I would never walk; I would always be in a wheelchair, in a vegetation state because of the poison in my body. And as I kept getting a little stronger and a little stronger and a little stronger, he would say: "I didn't save her. What did?"

I remember all through my sickness I was saying, "Oh, now the Lord's going to let me go." Then one day while I was in bed, just lying there, a white light came and sat on the end of my bed and said: "You will not die. I have work for you to do." And I did.

Years later when I would go back to Kansas and take Mother to the doctor he would look at me and stand there and just shake his head. "I don't believe it." He would always tell people it was a higher power—someone else, not him.

After I got well and I could get up and walk, and after Dr. Ford let me stay up for two hours and then go to bed for two, I could go down to the cafe, across the street from the apartment and they had a cot in the back room. The cafe was going down and my husband could not keep it up because he was too busy running around. And sometimes the cook would not show up or sometimes a waitress wouldn't.

This time Alberta opted for the formal divorce which would take longer, but which would hold. At that point, all she wanted was to be free.

So the second divorce was '48. That was when it really happened. Because I had gotten up with being sick with the peritonitis, and I went to the cafe and it was going down, and so I moved out and said, "Ike, you can have everything in the whole house."

I went to stay with my friend and the lawyer said: "I'm sorry. You're going to have to take some of the things with you. I cannot process this divorce because you worked hard and your money is tied up in this. You can give him the house." Because we got it with the GI bill. So we divided up everything. I said: "Do what you want to do. I don't want any—I don't want to even be remembered."

So he said: "OK. Have your mother come and I'll give her half the dishes, half the linen, half of . . ." You know. So he gave me the car, because we had $5,000 down on a brand-new car.

I said: "Give that to Ike, because he's going to want it, he's going to spend it and throw it away. I'll take the Chevy." And he gave me the cafe, the partnership in the cafe. So I had the car to get where I wanted to go, and I moved out of the house and he had the house. When I saw him after forty some years later we went by, we didn't go in. We looked at the house and he said he had sold it.

I got an apartment right up from, across the street from the cafe, and Mother's furniture and everything could move in there with me, because she lived in the house with me. But she stayed in the house until everything was done with Ike. I got the cafe and the car, and we had put two or three thousand—I don't remember how much that we had put down on a new car. He got that money so he could buy him a car. And he got the washing machine, washer and the dryer. They had just come out. In fact, when they put it in the first day they put it in and tried to wash, the water ran everywhere so they had to come back and they had to do things with it, but we had a washer and dryer.

Although the marriage did not last, the attraction between Isaac and Alberta is easy to understand. Both were civic-minded people who thought beyond themselves and were committed to righting what they saw as wrongs, and both went on to become actively involved in their own communities. Isaac married again and with his wife, Willie Belle, raised three children, two sons and a daughter. He worked as foreman for a hydraulics plant and was active in the American Legion and a member of the Prince Hall Masons.[10] His daughter, Cynthia, recalled that her parents "made sure we were involved in many educational opportunities and in civic organizations in our community." Moreover, "Higher education in our household was not an option, but an expectation."[11] The expectation paid off. By 2000 their oldest son earned a bachelor's degree, joined a fraternity (closed to minorities when Isaac was growing up, but accessible to far more people by the time his children were in college), married, and had four children. Their daughter, Cynthia, was working on a PhD in educational administration at the University of Nebraska-Lincoln and was the assistant director of admissions for multicultural recruitment. She was also involved in her church, the Urban League, the Girl Scouts, and other community organizations. Near the end of his life Isaac Gooch developed Alzheimer's disease and died December 27, 1996, in Kansas.[12] But in 1948 Alberta's divorce would not be final until she had made an even bigger move than the apartment across the street from the cafe.

CHAPTER 4

A SHORT VISIT TO UTAH

Leaving Gooch and moving into a smaller apartment with her mother eased many of the strains in Alberta's life, but problems with the cafe continued and her health was not improving. Finally Dr. Ford took a firm stand.

So Dr. Ford said: "You are getting too involved. People are coming around. I want you to be quiet. You're not well yet. We've got it under control, but it's still in your body. Now, I want you to go away somewhere and rest, maybe six or eight weeks, to get away from here, somewhere quiet."

I said, "Oh, Lord, I don't want to go nowhere."

And then one day in the cafe a Pullman porter came and said, "You ought to go to Salt Lake."

I said, "I ain't lost nothing there. When I was there that was a sad place." In 1947 Dorothy and I drove back by here and stopped in Utah in the dead of the winter, in '47.

But he said: "But Raymond and Blanch are having a lot of problems. You could save that marriage. Raymond respects you because you don't drink."

Dorothy's brother and sister-in-law, Raymond and Blanche Little, lived in Utah. Blanche and I went to the same elementary school in Topeka, Kansas, McKinley, so we knew each other from birth, and during the war while I was in San Luis Obispo with my husband, Blanche moved into my house with my mother until Raymond came [back] from overseas. Then when Raymond got out of the service, he came by my house and picked her up and they started driving and when they got here [Salt Lake City], they just stopped.

I called Blanche and she said, "Come on." And that's how I got there, with the understanding that I have the cafe, I have an apartment, I have all my furniture, I had a car, but my mother was in my apartment, so I didn't have to worry about that. I thought I was just going to be here for six or eight weeks.

Alberta arrived in Salt Lake City and immediately knew she was not in Kansas anymore. Not only was the elevation higher, the air drier, and the land far less flat, the population was very different. Where Topeka had a substantial black community that maintained its own restaurants, theaters, even funeral parlors, Utah like most of the Mountain West had a very small minority population, and the largest group, Native Americans, primarily lived on their own reservations. Reverend France Davis observed that even "when I first came here [in 1972], African Americans were more invisible than visible."[1]

In 1949 Utah reflected much of the rest of the country outside the Deep South: racial segregation was in most cases de facto rather than legislated and enforced by custom and realtors rather than by legal codes, but the neighborhoods certainly did not have the congenial mix Alberta had known in Topeka. Moreover, the dominant local religion, the Church of Jesus Christ of Latter-day Saints, held specific beliefs that impacted both their own members and attitudes within the community at large.

Ronald Coleman observed that "the history of Blacks in Utah is a microcosm of the history of Blacks in the United States."[2] Some blacks arrived in Utah long before the Mormons, like James P. Beckwourth, the legendary trapper for the Rocky Mountain Fur Company, guide, Indian fighter, and hunter.[3] When the Mormons arrived in 1847, several blacks arrived as free people, like the families of Isaac and Jane Manning James, Elijah and Mary Ann Able, and Fredrick and Ellen Sion.[4] Some came with the Mormons as slaves, including some in the first wagon train. When Brigham Young with one hundred and forty other men, three women, and two children entered the Salt Lake valley in July of 1847, there were three black slaves: Hark Lay, Oscar Crosby, and Green Flake, who reputedly drove Brigham Young's carriage into the valley.[5] All were later freed, as were other slaves who were brought into the territory.

Most slavery in the new territory, however, victimized not blacks of African descent but Native American peoples. It was this group that prompted the drafting of a territorial slave law in 1852. This law, like those in several Northern states, including the one that the Mormons had known in Illinois, was patterned after one originally passed in New York. Its goal was to provide a pathway to ending slavery without going to war.[6]

When the Mormons arrived in 1847 the area that had been a part of the Spanish Empire and, more recently, of Mexico, quickly became federal land. The question of slavery, along with any number of other issues, joined the general conflict between Mormons and the federal government. In fact, "The question of sovereignty—or determining who possessed and could exercise governing, legal, social, and even cultural power—is at the crux of Utah Territory's early history."[7]

The arrival of the railroad through Utah brought more black individuals and families into the area. It also opened employment opportunities, both with the railroad itself and with access to jobs in mining, construction, and other fields throughout the area. At the same time, many of the restrictions on blacks and other minorities in other parts of the country came with them. By the time Alberta arrived blacks were allowed into movie theaters, but were often required to sit in the balcony instead of the main floor. While they could provide the music for dancing in venues like Lagoon, Saltair, and Rainbow Gardens, they were restricted from dancing or swimming there. A major change occurred, however, just about the same time Alberta arrived. "The breakthrough in Utah was the result of the determined efforts of Robert E. Freed, a prominent leader in civil rights. When the Freed family and their partner, Ranch Kimball, took over the lease of Lagoon, the terms forbade Blacks in the swimming pool and the ballroom in accordance with a Farmington town ordinance. By the late 1940s, Robert Freed had succeeded in fully opening Lagoon to Blacks; and when his company acquired Rainbow Gardens (Terrace), the same policy was adopted."[8]

In time Alberta would encounter and work to improve all of those issues. Her initial assessment of Salt Lake City, however, was simply:

"The dullest place that I had ever seen. I asked, 'Where do you go and what do you do for fun?' I don't think that we saw hardly any black people at all. We went downtown and stood on the corner there and looked like there was very few black people there. There were very few places that you could go. The only one that I remembered was the Porters and Waiters Club . . . that was where the black

people went. There was another little place that they had somewhere . . . it was right across from the Union Pacific Station down there. They had food, ribs, and the people played cards and stuff. And then they had music and you could dance. That was the only place that you had the chance to socialize. It was like you were invisible or something unless they had to go around you. And they made sure that they didn't touch you. They acted like the black was going to rub off on them or something like that. . . . You couldn't go into the bowling alleys—but I wanted to take my kids, which I never did. At the skating rink, you had to wait 'till eleven or twelve o'clock at night. I mean all of those indignities you had to suffer."[9]

Nonetheless, the six or eight weeks she had planned to stay in Utah became more than fifty years, a stay imposed by Alberta's own enormous faith.

I came in August, August 10, and in September, I thought I could get ready to go home, but I couldn't leave, something came up. And then in October, I said, I've got to go home because I've got a cafe to run; I've got to get home. And every time I had a ticket, but I couldn't go home.

Finally I was washing dishes by the window; it was facing the mountains. I did fall in love with the mountains. I didn't like Utah, but I loved the mountains. I was looking out at the mountains and then I said, "Oh, no." You know how a light bulb goes over your head? I said, "Oh, no, Lord, not Utah. Why not California? Chicago?" I had friends. "Washington, D.C. Not Utah." I really had a time, standing at that window washing dishes, realizing that this is where the Lord was going to let me stay. I thought, I leave my mother—then I felt maybe I'm mistaken. Maybe I can deal with the Lord. I'm always figuring out deals. Maybe if I do the Lord's work, then maybe he'll let me go home. But how do you make deals with the Lord?

Now, my grandfather was a minister, and I taught Sunday school. Even from the age of six or seven I could sing; I knew all the songs. I read the Bible, all the stories from Genesis to Revelation, and I can preach like nobody. I could really throw scriptures around, and my grandfather would always talk about missionaries and going to Africa. We would have occasionally, every three or four years, a missionary come in and tell us about the work that they were doing. That was so inspiring, and I was always assured that the Lord was going to call me, and I could go to Africa and be a missionary. I did not know about home mission, where you go right where you are. Even when I was little and my grandpa was a minister, every Sunday, my grandfather taught me—I always knew that I was going to be special. I never called this home, though. I just was here because the Lord would not let me go home. The Lord sent me here.[10]

Nonetheless, even with word from the Lord, Alberta was still a pragmatist. She immediately started thinking of what she would need to do if she was going to stay in Utah, although at this point, she was still thinking it would be a relatively short calling from the Lord.

Then I said: "If I'm going to stay here, I've got to go to work."

Blanche said, "We'll take you down and see if you can get work in the theater." I was a projectionist at the Ritz Theater during the war, only because they couldn't get a man. I was a cashier, licensed and bonded, and whenever they brought a big band through Topeka, I would have to close up the theater and then go down to the city auditorium and sell tickets.

So I went down to the employment agency and they said: "We don't hire colored. We don't want colored people."

"Well, what do you hire colored to do?"

"Well, you could do day work or housekeeping or linen service."

So I went back to Blanche's, got a newspaper, and Blanche said: "You don't want to do that. That's beneath you."

I said: "My mother said anything that's honest is not beneath you. You do the best job you can as long as it's honest. If you can scrub the floor or wash the windows better than anybody else, if nobody can come in and do it any better, then you are OK."

As Alberta checked the newspapers she found an ad placed by Helen Sandack, wife of Wallace Sandack, an attorney and lynchpin in the Utah Democratic Party. The Sandacks' attitude about race and inclusion is clear from a story Helen shared about her husband. The family lived in Federal Heights, the lovely neighborhood just north of the University of Utah. In the 1960s when neighborhoods were becoming more integrated, Wally was asked how he'd feel if a black family moved in next door. He responded, "I wouldn't care as long as they didn't mind living next door to a Jewish family."[11] Alberta, and for that matter, the state of Utah, greatly benefited from the Sandacks' generosity and compassion.

I looked in the paper and on the first of November, I called the Sandacks and went out to their house.

"Do you have references?"

"Nope."

"Do you do this kind of work?

"Nope. But I sure like to clean house and watch kids."

And I started working for them November, the seventh, 1949; I remember because it was the election [day]. Why they hired me, I will never know, because I said, "Nope."

Helen Sandack later admitted that she was looking for a live-in housekeeper because she had recently experienced some difficulties with the last one and was determined that the woman she hired would have good references. Despite Alberta's continual "nopes," she continued talking with her, finally asking if she liked children. Before Alberta could answer, Helen said, "my eight-month-old baby [Arthur Frank, Artie] came crawling in and the smile on her face told me everything I needed to know."[12]

Alberta went to live in the Sandack home and work as a housekeeper and nanny for their four children, Nancy, then seven, the twins Roger and Richard, and baby Artie. She moved out when she married Harold Lloyd Henry, but returned for a time after her marriage when the Sandacks' fifth child, Susan, was born.[13] Her relationship with the family transcended racial or religious traditions and they moved far beyond being just employers or employee. Alberta herself said, "They let me love the kids just as if they were mine . . . and they still consider me like the family. And I consider them my family."[14]

Obviously the Sandacks agreed. I was deeply touched when Helen Sandack, the white daughter of a wealthy Jewish businessman[15] and wife of a prominent attorney and politician, said of the black Baptist daughter of a Louisiana sharecropper, "Alberta became my very best friend."[16] The respect the Sandack children held for Alberta was demonstrated when Nancy returned from school at Mills College for Passover. Usually she came with a crowd of friends to go skiing or hiking in the mountains, but this time there was only one young man. Her parents immediately realized that his presence carried romantic implications, and neither approved of him. Both remained polite. Wally, in fact, remained so stiffly formal instead of engaging in his usual light-hearted teasing, that Nancy finally became angry with him. Alberta observed all of this as she served the Passover dinner. Then she quietly took Nancy aside, shook her head and said, "Uh, uh, he's not one of us." Nancy burst out laughing for the first time since her arrival. Shortly thereafter she quietly dropped the young man.[17]

Alberta became such an integral part of the family that the children, all grown, still called her "Berta" and included her in their families' activities up until the time of her death. Once when I went to see Alberta, she joyfully told me she had just attended the bar mitzvah for one of Wallace and Helen's grandsons.

Just three months ago Artie's son went to bar mitzvah so [her daughter] Julia had to take me up to Jewish temple for his bar mitzvah because I had been to Artie's bar mitzvah, too.

The Sandack family gave Alberta great support in everything she did, but she gained even more support from Harold Henry, whom she had met shortly before she went to work for them.

Right after I came here in August, Blanch took me down to the Porters and Waiters Club in Salt Lake City; that's where all the railroad guys would go into if they lived here in Salt Lake. She introduced me around, a friend from Topeka, Kansas, and that's when I met Harold. By that time they used to call me the Tonk Queen, because I always played tonk. Tonk is a card game.[18] *And I said, "If you don't like that I can beat anybody playing dominos and checkers, because my daddy taught me how to play games. And I make a lot of noise whether I'm winning or losing, so it doesn't matter." And that's when they introduced me to Harold.*

I said, "He think he's a domino player, too? I'll take any of them on." But he had the prettiest eyes, and green eyes. Most black people have brown eyes. And I just looked at him and I remember saying that to myself, I guess that's who the Lord is going to pick out for me to marry to take care of me, but I'm not having none of it. Then Harold started coming over to Blanche's house where I was living and we would play tonk and then we'd play dominos. I'd say: "Don't let me beat you. If I beat you I'd rub it in the ground." And he'd come back again, so we just started dating.

Harold Henry led Alberta to several other important associations, including her involvement in a local church. Alberta observed several times that when a person moves to a new location he or she should immediately become involved in a local church for both religious and social reasons.

I was still working at Sandacks' and some of Harold's friends would come and bring me down to New Pilgrim Baptist Church.[19] *I joined New Pilgrim, because any time you're at a place, you're supposed to join a church. My grandfather's church was the Church of the Living God, the one that he founded. I was baptized in the Church of the Living God.*

And so I joined the church and they had a convention in Ogden and I went. First time I'd ever walked in there and they knew me. I looked up and they voted me in as a president of the Utah and Idaho Baptist Mission. And I had to go to Pocatello, Idaho; Ogden, Utah; Helper, Utah; all around where there was a black and a Baptist church. I never was gone long from the Sandacks, always over the weekend.

The Sandack family completely supported Alberta in those activities, and she greatly appreciated that support. She enjoyed both attending church and working at the Sandacks. Then a few months later Harold came back into her life. She enjoyed him even more.

He looked me up in November, after I was gone to work at the Sandacks. He would come out there, and we'd play dominos. And Artie, the little baby, would come down and sit on Harold's lap and on mine while we played dominos. But I mean, he'd come out to the house; he didn't stay out to the house, because I didn't live with nobody, but he would come out and we'd play and then he'd go back to down to his place. Then after we were married, when he would come into town, then he would stay. We had to be married, so our whole married life in our room so anybody come down would see that, you don't live in sin, give them ideas. That was the way it was arranged.

So we got married fifteen months later in 1950, November 17. And our marriage night, we went back to the house, put the dominos out, and Artie came and sat down on our laps till he got to sleep, and we'd put him in our bed while we played dominos all night long. He was a lovely person. Married forty-six years, married in 1950 and he passed away June 10, 1996.

"He was born in Denver [Colorado on November 23, 1907]. His mother came to Ogden [Utah]. That was when he was eleven years old or younger. He went to school in Ogden and ... [blacks] weren't allowed to go in swimming pools, but they would go down to the river. His mother took in washing clothes for white folks and he would go down on the railroad tracks and pick up coal and stuff so they could have it.[20] *In the summertime they would follow behind an ice truck to pick up chips of ice and stuff to take home ... then he went to work for the railroad."*[21]

Harold was a hard worker who supported their family both financially and in their many activities. He also had another quality that Alberta greatly admired.

Harold would never hit a woman. "You can walk away," Harold said, "You can put your hat on and walk out the door quicker than you can fight anybody." And if he ever heard of somebody fighting, he said, "That's a shame. Their parents didn't teach them right."

"He was thirteen years older than me. He had been married twice before; I was his third wife. He had two sons, Warren and Jr. Harold Jr. was killed in an airplane during World War II. Warren, his other son, was hurt out there. Harold [her husband] was inducted right here from Utah.

"In World War II Harold was stationed in England. And they put the blacks way out in a little place, I guess they were giving them the honor, because they made sure that the blacks did not come in town to socialize with the white girls. The white girls and everyone didn't mind them except that the white soldiers were calling them 'coons,' 'niggers,' and 'colored,' and everything.

"He was with the communication. They had to go ahead and set up communications. And that day that they were supposed to go [D-day, June 6, 1944] they changed it for the black fellows in the company he was in and said they wouldn't take them, but the white ones, they took them. And Harold said the next day when they got there, all you saw was bodies floating around.

"So their group, they held them back, and didn't let them go. Had they been, they would have been some of them killed in France and Holland and then in Germany."[22]

Segregated units of the United States military had existed since the Civil War. Harold had served as a member of the Fortieth Signal

Construction Battalion in northern France and Europe. The battalion had been organized in direct response to the war on July 31, 1942 and activated on September 21, 1942. The Fortieth Battalion left for England on January 12, 1944, waiting for D-day. They arrived in France thirty days after the initial D-day landings. Harold's unit constructed cable connections across northern France, allowing communications to flow for the Allied forces. The Fortieth Battalion went on to support missions in Luxembourg, Belgium, and Holland, eventually entering Germany on December 8, 1944. It remained in Germany until the end of the war, after Japan surrendered on August 14, 1945. Most of the members of the Fortieth returned home safely.[23]

Alberta was struck by the irony that the prejudice against blacks taking part in the initial D-day assault meant that far more of them lived through the invasion than did the whites who were given the privilege of entering first. It is one of the few times that segregation worked to any kind of advantage to those who were being demeaned. But Alberta was not alone in recognizing the effects of segregation. During World War II people around the world were not necessarily shocked by Japan's and Germany's claims of racial superiority, even if they didn't believe them. A few people may even have accepted their proclamations of racial superiority, but the idea that any race should be eradicated seemed too ridiculous to take seriously. Then the concentration camps were captured and their horrors fully revealed. Thoughtful Americans could not deny that these horrific actions were only enlarged reflections of many of their own attitudes about minorities and ethnic groups, especially blacks. The racial attitudes in America were beginning to shift.

After the war, Harold returned to the railroad where he worked as a porter and waiter for a total of thirty-three years, retiring in 1972. Seven years later he recalled his time on the railroad, starting as a waiter on a dining car in 1937 for twenty-five cents an hour. It "was up at 5:30 a.m., closed down at 9 p.m. He worked up to 240 hours straight time . . . thirty days a month. His pay worked out to about $65 a month." He added, "Of course, you had some fresh money, too—tips." He was serving food on china plates with real silverware since this was before the days of throw-away paper and plastic. He worked for the Union Pacific on the short line from Salt Lake City to Butte, Montana, for the Union Pacific and also the longer runs between Los Angeles and Kansas City and Chicago.[24] Harold and Alberta took a honeymoon trip together on the train to visit her family in Topeka.[25]

Alberta was glad to share that railroad run with Harold. Even more she was delighted to talk about the way that his work led to a happy reunion in Utah with one of her old friends from Topeka. She was absolutely charming as she re-created the dialogue between the two men.

There was a man in Ogden that was the coach of the team [the baseball team that she had played on as a girl]. I didn't even know that he and his wife had moved to Ogden in Utah. He heard that I was here; he heard that I was married to Harold. He told Harold on the railroad he ran on, "Your wife used to play on my ball team."

He and his wife came over and told Harold about me. "She was a lefty, and we had her."

"What position did she play?"

"Well, she could play all the positions. Sometimes she pitched but most of the time she was on first base." He was so glad to see me.

It was evident from the delight with which Alberta told that story that she had been glad to see him, too. She appreciated Harold's concern for her and his great delight in her athletic abilities. Even more, she appreciated his attitude about violence and his concern for her well-being. Mavis Blackburn, a family friend and neighbor observed that Harold was quiet, gentle, and supportive. "He complemented Alberta."[26]

When Harold went looking for a house they could buy, he encountered the de facto segregation that existed in states outside the Old South. While no official law forbade certain areas to blacks or any other groups, they found it impossible to secure housing east of Tenth or Eleventh East in Salt Lake City. The line extended further west in the southern portion of the valley. This in turn led to an increased black population in the city's west side schools, whereas no black pupils were found on the east bench, creating a segregated school system even though no segregation existed in law.[27] Among Henry's papers is the realtor's card for the house they eventually bought. Clearly printed across the bottom is "Must be sold—will sell to colored." Discrimination in housing would persist for years. Even after the passage of the Civil Rights Act in 1964, Salt Lake City blacks still faced racial problems, especially in housing.

"We knew the code books were written for the real estate. If the people signed it, they didn't want colored to buy their house, even if you wanted to sell it, you couldn't sell it to me.

And if you got a real estate person . . . they just took you down to Central City to those dead-end streets and little shacks down there or in some other little place. [Harold] didn't want to get one of those. He said that we're going to buy a home. And he went down on Post Street and Mrs. [Florence] Lawrence had a house across the street that wasn't over a year old and it was up for sale. We bought it and he moved me in there."[28]

Florence Lawrence, like Alberta Henry, was active in improving the lives of blacks in Utah. Among her many good works Lawrence and Bernice Bent helped establish the African section of the Peace Gardens along the Jordan River. Bent also led Project New Hope, a program for "kids who had been 'kicked out' of school." The objective of the program was simply to help them find new courses and give direction to their lives.[29]

All the while Alberta was working with civic groups, she and Harold remained faithful members of the New Pilgrim Baptist Church, but eventually they decided it wasn't filling their needs or expectations. On November 17, 1954, Alberta and Harold became charter members of the New Hope Baptist Church in Salt Lake City.

Alberta also helped to organize the Sunday Anderson Westside Aging and Adult Services Center. She gave the deed to the county and then was somewhat disappointed when they called a press conference but did not invite her.[30]

I just kept working in the church and we decided that Pilgrim people wasn't going to do anything and they weren't going to let us do anything, so we established the New Hope Baptist Church. It was a younger group with friends, younger people; the minister was a young minister and we did everything. We went out and we got money, we put our money in and we paid for the church. It was down on First West. It's still there, the building—a little house—we had it turned into a church. My husband just loved it and everyone that was there, because it was like a family. We'd go to the hospital and nursing home, and if your house was dirty, we would go into your home and we would take buckets and we would clean it up. We'd get money and bring you food—didn't no one have to ask you to do it. Take your clothes to the laundromat and clean them and bring them back. It was so much fun.

I was a church clerk for twenty-two years and I helped people when they died. I fixed up all their obituaries and all those things, whatever their legal needs were, because I worked for the Sandacks and I learned all of these things. When I say I learned about the city, I learned about the people, but then I learned about the legal things.

Harold was pleased with Alberta's church activity and he was also supportive when she developed still more physical problems.

"Mr. Henry and I got married . . . and then I had to have another operation . . . because the adhesions from my appendix bursting was rolling up into my stomach and kept me down. . . . Mrs. Sandack had gotten me with a Dr. Urshler who did diagnostic study, who was watching me, so he had me do that. Then he saw that I had tumors and said that if I keep working that I will never get well. The doctor said, 'You need to really rest.'[31]

"But soon after the year [of recuperation] was up after my operation, I . . . went back and forth up to the Sandacks, because they would go out of town. And even after I got my kids, I would take them up there and I would stay in the house and look after the kids in the house for them while they were gone."[32]

Those kids Alberta and Harold adopted were their son, Wendell, born January 24, 1957, named for an old family friend, a relative of Alberta's first husband, Isaac Gooch, and their daughter, Julia, born October 10, 1958, and named for Alberta's mother.

Alberta and the children adapted well to Harold's erratic schedule, which would reflect the timetables of the trains or "runs" between various cities. He could be in Salt Lake for a few days and gone for a few, but it was never regularly the same sets of days. Alberta recalled one year when Harold would be on the road for Christmas, so she and the children went to Topeka for the holidays and celebrations in Salt Lake would come a little late. They stayed with her mother, but the part of the trip she remembered best was a visit with her father.

One year I decided to take the kids home for Christmas. It would have been in the early sixties. My kids were young, four or five. Now, they had the Christmas tree at home here and they had all the big toys because Harold felt that they ought to have everything, but I wanted them to be home for Christmas with their grandmother. It was one of the worst Christmases. It was cold and the roads were frozen.

One of my friends Mary King was Wendell's godmother. Mary had married a real-old man, Roy Jenkins, real, real, real old. He had bought her a white Cadillac, brand new Cadillac. Mary came over and she said, "We ought not to be going out." She said, "I had to creep because, if you even go fifteen miles an hour, you might slide off the road, and this is a new Cadillac."

Mother always gave money or she bought socks and underwear and a whole bunch of useful things for the kids, all alone, and for Christmas, I knew we were getting the same thing. My daddy, the children's grandfather, James Hill had never ever given me anything or the kids anything, and I told Mary, "Let's go see what Daddy is going to give us." So I called him and I said, "We'll be over."

We crept and we talked and we enjoyed it. When I got there, Daddy, he'd gone out for a little car. No bigger than this [two or three inches] and the wheels could come off and you just sit down and roll it back and forth. Wendell had a great big one at home. And for Julia, [he had] one of them little dolls with no clothes on it. And I said, "Thank you, Daddy."

Mary and I went back to the car. We got to laughing. We couldn't drive fast. We had to stop the car fifteen times. And then I would hold this here little car and that little doll up, and Mary said, "$20,000 Cadillac," and then we would laugh some more. If you could have seen two grown women, forty-two years old—but we laughed. We got home and we couldn't walk; we kept falling down. Not that the ground was slippery, but we were falling because we were laughing so hard. Mother heard us coming because we were laughing so hard. She opened the door and we showed it to her. Mary and I still, every time we'd get together after that, we would say, "What about the little car?" We could have almost have wrecked that Cadillac.

Those kids were home with Mother when Mary and I got in the car. They were asleep by the time we got back so Mary and I went to get one of those little Christmas trees that you can get at the ten-and-fifteen-cent store. Mother didn't have a Christmas tree; Mother was a Jehovah's Witness. But for the kids, she let us bring that one in. So we put that little car and that little [doll], and of course, Mother's socks and underwear and stuff. And Mary had bought them shirts and Julia a dress and we had that under the Christmas tree. Christmas at home had big dolls and big everything. Wendell came and looked and Mary and I stood there and looked at him. Oh, he wouldn't touch nothing. And he said, "Mom, do we have Christmas at home?"

And I said, "Oh, yes. Yes, your dad has everything ready for you at home."

"I want to go home." So Mary and I walked around saying, "Little tree, little Christmas, big tree, big Christmas." It was a few days after Christmas when they got home, but oh, the juicy stuff was under there. He said, "Now, that's Christmas. That's Christmas."

And that's the only thing that my father ever gave my kids. My father never gave me anything, but I never wanted anything, so I never harbored any ill feelings about my father, except maybe once in a while.

I admired the honesty of that "once in a while." Back home in Salt Lake City, they celebrated with a lot of gifts. Alberta's daughter Julia said Christmas was always wonderful. She also observed that life generally in the Henry household

> was great. It really was. Growing up, we just had the best. All I can ever think of is having a wonderful childhood. I was always really involved in school. At home we always played Monopoly, played cards with my dad, played dominos. My dad was on the railroad so my mom was kind of like, the neighborhood kids, all the kids would come over and she'd take us to the park. When my dad was out of town, we'd always go to Taco Bell and Arctic Circle. She was good, too, but it was party time when my dad was gone.
>
> We always had our breakfasts served. All the kids would come over and we'd all walk to school together while she was teaching; we would call it our four-course breakfasts. She'd always do the toast first, and cut them up in little [pieces].[33]

Since those kids at the house reflected the entire neighborhood, Julia observed that "color has never been an issue in our family, ever." Nonetheless, when Alberta felt something was wrong in the school—teachers were being unfair or administrative issues were being handled inappropriately (or not handled at all)—Julia said very firmly:

> She would go to bat for our civil rights whenever. Being people of color, being black in Utah—it was a challenge. It was hard. There was a little subtle racism, I thought at times. I noticed being in high school, I always felt I had to do double to prove myself, in order to be as good as [others]. I just had to try a little bit harder to make that mark. There was this one

> particular incident, I think I was in junior high school, and I got As in all my classes but this one teacher. This particular teacher would not give me an A. Even though I did all the work; I passed all my tests with flying colors. Finally my mother took me out of the class. She said, "I can see here you can't separate the color issues."
>
> There were times when she was gone, but we always supported her in what she did, because I could see where it was benefiting the community, especially here in Utah. And of course my mother wasn't involved with the youth then; it's not until [I was in] junior high school She would always force me into it. "You're going to do this." And I went [*sigh of exasperation*]. But you know, that was some of the best times I had in my life.
>
> I did all the activities that everybody else did. I was in the band; I played the flute. That's something I really enjoyed doing. Being able to play for the high school graduation at the tabernacle was really neat—and I was the only black in the band. You know, you get used to that, like at Franklin Elementary, I can only remember two or three other black kids in the whole school.[34]

Julia learned to deal with issues like being the only black child in a group or being involved in various activities—her own and her mother's.

Wendell was a different story. Alberta didn't want to say much about her son. However, she did talk about some changes at Franklin Elementary School that upset her and may reveal an insight into both his difficulties and her entrance into working for changes in schools and in the larger community.

One outgrowth of the civil rights movement of the 1960s was a push toward group discussions among minorities or others who might face specific social problems. It began at Franklin Elementary School when Salt Lake School District, like most districts in the region, rotated the school's principal. For several years Franklin's principal had been Artie Tucker, with whom Alberta worked closely and harmoniously. Then, as part of the school district's regular rotation of principals:

> *They put a woman in. Don't put her name because she's dead so you don't speak ill of the dead. She put my kids together [with the other black] and Hispanic kids so they could talk. She wanted to talk to them separately. I said, "You can't do that." She didn't know enough about us to do that. Mr. Tucker never did that.*

In elementary school there was no such thing [as segregation] in those days. All the kids just played together like they were one. And she was really trying to separate them away from the white kids.

At Jordan Junior High School, however, Wendell encountered a far more serious situation, one that struck him very personally.

The boys were outdoors one winter throwing snowballs at Wendell. Wendell was sitting on the ground looking at them, because he was kind of chunky, and the janitor went by and one of the kids hit him with a snowball and Wendell just cracked up. He was laughing so hard, and the janitor went over, grabbed him, "You think it's funny?" and shoved his face down in the snow, made his nose bleed. I went over and talked to [the principal] and she said, "I'll just talk to him." I think that's one of the reasons my son didn't like school anymore. He was going to junior high and didn't want to go anymore, from just that one incident. I really wanted to do something about that janitor. I could have got him to lose his job. But Harold said, "You don't want to do that because it will send the wrong message out."

Whether getting the janitor fired would have helped Wendell remains a moot question. Alberta observed only that Wendell didn't like school and his family

Couldn't keep him away from the drugs.

The drugs led Wendell into a range of difficulties. Among Alberta's papers are newspaper clippings reporting he was shot in the leg at twelve years old by a neighbor who thought he was a prowler.[35] Another article indicates that in 1986 he was caught trying to escape from the Utah State Prison. That attempt added nine years to his sentence, but he would be granted a hearing on a new parole date in a few years.[36] Wendell wouldn't make it to that hearing; he died in prison in 1988.

If talking about her son was painful for Alberta, for her daughter, Julia, it was a happy chance to remember a brother she dearly loved. "He had a big heart—very good-hearted—very personable. He was a people person. He would give you the shirt off his back even if it was his last shirt. He would help anybody, even though he didn't really have [much]. I can't remember him working a job. To be honest with you, I can't. And so my dad would help him and I would help him. He'd always share whatever my mom and dad did for him, whoever didn't have a place to stay they could stay at his place. He would feed them. He only did detriment to himself; he never hurt anyone else."[37]

And given Wendell's problems, Julia "felt really obligated, once he started going down the different path that he took, I decided I'm going to make up for it and make my parents proud. Of course I always reaped the benefits. If I got As I got paid for them, got new outfits. I thought, I can do this. And then my mother always had that drive to motivate. She was always totally involved in the school district, in schools, it made it easier. I never felt compelled to sluff school like the other kids did stuff. I just felt that I should be the achiever because my brother was always the wayward child."

And she did, indeed, succeed. Alberta's papers include clippings showing Julia as president of the eighth grade at Jordan Junior High School.[38] She graduated from West High at seventeen and, Julia recalled, "received a four-year academic scholarship to Westminster right out of high school and I went for two years. Then I decided I wanted to get married at the ripe age of nineteen."

Part of Julia's motivation to succeed came from her mother's involvement with her schools. When her children started kindergarten at Franklin Elementary School, Alberta volunteered with the PTA. She greatly enjoyed working with the children and met a great many people she liked. One of the things she did not enjoy, however, was the pervasive social impact of the LDS Church in Utah, and she let it be known that while she was a tolerant person, she would not be pushed around, even gently, by things like the use of LDS terminology, talking about the local ward or referring to people as "brother" or "sister."

My kids started kindergarten and first grade and I had to go over and stand on the corner and watch them go in and when they came out I'd go and watch them. Then I got brave enough to go into school with them, got involved with the PTA. "I'm not your sister, I'm Alberta Henry." Everybody—sister and brother and they would talk about the ward and the one minority is coming on: "All of us don't belong, I'm a Baptist." Most of them didn't like it because they couldn't talk the missionary stuff because I wouldn't allow it.

Nonetheless, Alberta continued to volunteer at the school, and Franklin Elementary School's principal, LeRoy Nelsen, quickly recognized her abilities. "She was vitally interested in the welfare of all the kids—not just her own or just the black kids. She was intelligent, bright, energetic, but she was working as a domestic, and I felt she was capable of more complicated work. I suggested she go to the university and get a degree."[39] In time Henry followed Nelsen's suggestion and earned a college degree, but not until after she had already provided a great many benefits for other students, including serving as an officer in Franklin's PTA.

I [was] made vice president [at] Franklin Elementary School. The president went to Mexico for three whole months over Christmas, and I had to take over. I did not know that she wrote back to one of the members of the PTA and told her to get a Santa Claus. That was my job. I'm the acting president of the PTA, so I got a Santa Claus. In all the history of that school [only once did] they ever had two Santa Clauses, one tall and thin and other short and fat. We had to put one down in one corner and the other down in another and hope they never met.

Apparently the Santa situation worked out satisfactorily. While Alberta was working in the PTA, another school principal with whom she worked recognized her natural leadership abilities. He also realized that with both of her children in school, she could become involved in a number of other areas.

Every time I came into the school, there he was. Artie Tucker. The principal says, "Alberta, you've got so much time on your hands, why don't you get on some boards." He's on the board of the Salt Lake School District Credit Union. Whenever I see him [now], he says, "I'm the one who started you off."

Tucker may have been right, but he likely had no idea just how much he was starting. Alberta's entrance to public life in Utah would alter her own and her family's lives, but it would alter the state of Utah even more.

CHAPTER 5

BUILDING A FIRM FOUNDATION

Mr. Sandack would say, "Well, what does the Lord want you to do?"

And I would say, "I don't know." I still don't know what the Lord wants me to do, but if you see my Bible in there, lying open, it's because I'm looking for scriptures. And my Bible just kept flipping over to where Christ repeats himself three times: "If thou lovest me, feed my sheep."[1] Now, what does it mean, "feed my sheep"? And I kept saying, "I don't know," but my Bible kept opening up. That's everything.

Following both her Bible's inspiration and Artie Tucker's advice to become more involved in the community, Alberta joined several local organizations in the early 1960s, largely just to let people see her black face in the crowd but also to motivate the local black community to solidify and to become more involved in civic needs and organizations. The apathy she felt in that black community troubled her greatly. When an interviewer asked, "In characterizing the African American community [in Utah] over the years, can you tell us about some of the changes?" her reply was:

"What community?

"Every place I've been they've had a community. The people who lived in North Topeka[2] *and all were black and when some of us got sick, we would go to a neighbor's house and stay if we had the chicken pox. We don't have that kind of community here. It's not that closeness thing that everybody knew everybody and if I got in trouble a neighbor could whip me.*

"You could look around where I'm living at. Do you see any blacks? Do you see anywhere around here? When I lived on Post Street [in Salt Lake City] there were about five or six families—that was about as much of a community as you were going to get. Our community for us blacks was in the churches that we go to, and we all don't go to the same church. My daughter belongs to the Faith Temple . . . but I'm a Baptist, a fighting one. And there's where we were born, and the children are blessed. When you die, you know my husband died, and they had his funeral right there at the church. To me, that's where a community is in Utah."[3]

The situation for blacks in Utah had already changed greatly from 1948 when Alberta arrived in Utah to the 1960s when she started becoming involved in community affairs. The minority population of Salt Lake City had grown in both numbers and activity. "Blacks formed local lodges of the Odd Fellows and Elks. The Ladies Civic and Study Club of Salt Lake City, the Camelia Arts and Crafts Club, and the Nimble Thimble Club were three Black women's groups. The Nimble Thimble Club was responsible for initiating the idea of building a community center for Blacks. . . . Besides joining the various fraternal and social groups, Blacks often went to dance and to listen to the music at some of the local nightclubs. Dixie Land, the Jazz Bo, the Porters and Waiters Club, and the Hi Marine were places where Blacks and some whites went for entertainment."[4] All that notwithstanding, Alberta knew the Lord had a reason for keeping her in Utah. So she followed her grandfather's advice and kept going to church. She was not surprised when the core of her involvement with the larger Salt Lake community started with helping a friend from church, Mignon Richmond.

Mignon Barker Richmond had graduated from Utah State University in 1921, the first black to graduate from a college in Utah. She went on to become a prominent leader in the black community, serving on several boards and committees. Eventually Salt Lake City honored her by naming Richmond Park at 450 East Martin Luther King Boulevard for her.[5]

We were at church; it came about at one of the meetings. That was how I got acquainted with Mignon. She had stories to tell about Utah and I wanted to know them. I would take the cue from her. Mignon didn't drive. I said, "I have the time, so I'll come too."

So I went to church and I picked up Mignon Richmond. She's the only black, she and Albert Fritz, who was president of the NAACP then they were the only blacks in the fifties that white people knew about in Utah. If you ask if they know any blacks, they'd say, "Do you know Albert Fritz? Or do you know Mignon Richmond?" So I started picking Mignon up and we'd go to this board meeting and we'd go to another one. And that's how I really got involved because she had to come off from those boards. She had Alzheimer's, but at first she was serving and she would be there as a reminder of blacks. So she got me really involved in all of the others.

Alberta was already aware of one of the most important gathering places not only for the black community, but for many others on the west side of Salt Lake City as well: the Nettie Gregory Community Center at 742 West South Temple. Nettie Gregory and her husband, William, both natives of Tennessee, had settled in Salt Lake City where he worked for the railroad. Her daughters observed that every Twenty-Fourth of July, they would join the crowds to watch the Pioneer Day parade, "clapping and cheering as loudly as anyone"[6] regardless of the fact that everyone in the parade was white. William and Nettie recognized the need for wholesome activities for young people on the west side of Salt Lake City, so they organized some programs at the Calvary Baptist Church. They quickly found that the church could not accommodate the many young people who came. William then donated a small parcel of land, and Nettie networked with black women's clubs to raise money to build what would become the first civic building in the area. She died just months before construction was completed in 1964, and the building located at 742 West South Temple was named in her honor.[7]

It's incorporated under the Gregory family, Mr. Gregory, it was his wife that went out both times in the early 1960s and got donations to build something. The black people were so mad because she built the building [by] the railroad tracks—and that's where all these blacks are—that they wouldn't help her. But the Four-Five Club[8] and the different other clubs—they had helped her out and the men went over and built that Nettie Gregory Center. They named it after her. It's a community center when it was first built and the county had a recreation director that they put in there, but then they built the Northwest Multipurpose Center and they pulled out all the help, so then it became a community thing.

Enlarging that "community thing" was Alberta's goal, but early in her civic involvement, she recognized that it was not just the white community that needed education. As she was serving with the Baptist Women's Missionary Society she observed:

The black community themselves, I could hear disparaging remarks about what I was trying to do, but I never would tell them, so I never did feel bad about it if they did believe them. "Oh, she's so much better than anyone else." "I wish she'd get off that kick." Everywhere I went I took a Bible. I tried not to let nobody know what I was doing, because this is one of Grandma's sayings and Grandpa's, "Never let your left hand know what your right hand is doing."[9]

But they knew anyway. It was hard to miss Alberta's work in so many areas. Her name appeared in newspapers and was mentioned by leaders from both the black and the white communities. But within her church, she was still running into criticism, disagreements, and even power struggles no matter how good her good works were.

I was with the Utah-Idaho Baptist Association from 1960 to 1966 going around doing all that. Then I decided that's kind of nice, but kids were not going to school. I'd see wherever black kids were going to school, and they weren't in the schools. I went up to the University of Utah and it looked just so foreign because very few blacks were going to school up there.

"[But] without education, you are not really going anywhere.... You've got to have an education. Now, I don't mean you got to get a PhD. I am not talking about that. I've seen some people, Lord, forgive me if I say this, but they have PhDs and they're fools. That's all they've got. You got to have a whole lot of other things to go along with. But to be able to stay in and get whatever you want, and do whatever you want to do, you've got to get an education and it's got to be well rounded. That's what I always told students. If I can and go and I don't know too much and I can go and I can learn about it and can do anything, I can go anywhere."[10]

So we picked out four different students from four different churches and we put three of them into the university, one of them left town, so we only got to put three of them in. But the money came from the Jewish community so that I could do it—give it to me working with the Utah-Idaho Baptists Association. The next year, '66, the ministers wanted me to go out and raise some money, but they would select the students. And I said, "Hell, no." Excuse my language, but that's exactly what I said.

What do they mean? I developed this program, went out and done the work and now they want to give [an oratory] contest or something and then name whatever one of their friends' friends and I didn't take it like that. I went to the missionaries to see what the kids in the school had. They didn't have to have great grades. They didn't have to write no poem, but they had the desire and wanted to go and I found out that if you wanted something, they're the best students to get. And I got home and one of the ministers knew that I had gotten sick and he came over and he raised hell and I was going to be sick because I was at the church and—I wouldn't say anything but you could tell from my face that I was really mad about it. I went home and Harold called Dr. Ershler and Dr. Ershler came out to the house and then he said, "I'm going to put you in the hospital for three days because I want do some tests on you."

Now he didn't let me know that he knew what was going on. So I said, "Not until I write a letter of resignation." A real nice letter of resignation, but I wanted to send it bad. And then I went on to hospital for the three days. But I resigned from the association—to think that those ministers wanted to take over a program that the women built and ran—it's a man's world. You couldn't tell me that then, but it's a man's world.

So when I came out of the hospital Dr. Ershler said, "You will stay in for about eight months." Dr. Ershler had me doing all the tests. They did not know where the peritonitis had went to. They knew it was all through my body. They knew it would always be there. But it always goes into some kind of form and then they found fibrosis or a tumor, but it was too small; he couldn't do anything with it. Just doing nothing but resting, then when I did have the operation, he took out the tube and found dead tuberculosis cells in it. So then he had me go through a program and take a lot of pills.

Then the students came and said they had went to the association and they said they didn't have a program. That was Mrs. Henry. Nobody was there to raise the money. See, the men hadn't raised any money. I went and got the money from the Sweets and the Franks and the Sandacks and the Roses, but they didn't have those connections. So that's when I told the students if I could plan—I couldn't go out, but I could plan for them.

"The students came in—it was Grover Thompson and Tony Harp. And, by the way, Tony Nathaniel Harp was one of those students that came that I had put [into the university] early. Do you know what she is doing today? She is a state senator in Connecticut, is that not exciting to know that one of those students has gone all the way up?"[11]

That's how it got started.

What got started was the Alberta Henry Education Foundation (AHEF), incorporated in 1967, soon after Alberta had refused to allow the men in her church to take over the work she had begun there. Alberta was always quick to note that while it bore her name, she was not the only one involved. The initial governing board consisted of Virginia Hiatt, Thomas Godfrey, Charles Nabors, Sandra Day, Ben Roe, and Henry Adams. A great many others also provided good services and donations. Ben Roe who worked with fundraising for several organizations observed that "no matter how much money I raised, Alberta Henry always found students who could use it."[12] Alberta's papers include dozens of letters from young students she helped, and even more from those same students after they had achieved more than they (or even she) could have imagined as the youngsters they were when they first met her.

By 1969 the foundation was helping twenty-seven students, some with money from the foundation itself, some with receiving help from groups like Equal Opportunity Grants, some with only tuition, others with only books. By 1971 it was helping thirty-one students and a dozen others had graduated, but they still had thirteen prospective new students. Among those AHEF students were several who would achieve both local and national prominence.

One was Shauna Graves, who earned her law degree in 1990. She said at the time, "Although they called my name to receive the diploma, I know that without the help of some very special people I would never have been there."[13] She and Alberta formed a great friendship that lasted the rest of Alberta's life. She later wrote to Alberta: "Without you my life and the accomplishments I've made would not have been possible. . . . You always made sure that young people were involved in something. . . . During junior high and high school you intervened whenever it seemed like we might be in trouble, and you rewarded our academic efforts. . . . You have been there for me professionally and personally."[14] Shauna Graves Robertson worked for the Salt Lake Legal Defenders Association and eventually became the presiding judge in Salt Lake County, breaking trails both for blacks and for other women of all colors.

Solomon Cachon observed that nowhere in the elementary, junior high, or high schools he attended was he encouraged to go on to college. He entered Westminster College in the fall of 1969, eventually becoming a lawyer and a member of the Utah Bar.

Tallie Lee Cavaness had entered the University of Utah in the fall of 1969 on the GI Bill. The AHEF began sponsoring him the next year. He graduated with bachelor's degrees in both computer science and electrical engineering, and then added a law degree. He became a member of the Utah Bar Association and worked as a technical writer and contract administrator for Hercules Aerospace.

Marsha Boyd Hodges received help from the AHEF for both her bachelor's degree and the training required to qualify for police work. She became a probation officer in the Salt Lake area.

All of them, and many more, gave credit to Alberta Henry for helping them financially and even more for giving them their ability to trust themselves.

Alberta, of course, gave the credit to the Lord.

"The Alberta Henry Education Foundation is the love of my life. I was with the Utah and Idaho Association going up and down finding out this was how Utah was. They were really bright kids. Their parents did not hardly stay in Utah. The girls were bright, and they would get good grades. But none of the boys would because the teachers didn't understand the boys.

"I was never any more happier than to come and have the Lord give us a foundation that we never had to have federal dollars, state dollars, none of that money. In the earlier days, we had the Bamberger Foundation and the Travis Foundation. But that was just only for a short time. The rest of the money now came from people. What people? The people of Utah. The black people? No. So that gives me great joy to say they supported a thing that they saw that was really good. . . . To me, that gives me great pleasure, and I'm just as happy sitting here. And if they don't remember me and put me in anything, that's why I'm calling to tell you that they did, you know. I'm not going to go out and broadcast, or say I've done all those things. I didn't really do them. How I done them, I never know. But the Lord knows.

"And we had forty and fifty and we were putting them in, because we didn't have students at the university until the Alberta Henry Foundation came along and started putting them in. As you heard me say, that Grover Land said to me that we need to go and I said that I would plan and you all do the work. And then they kept coming until I couldn't do it, so Mr. Sandack and Virginia [Hiatt, a Presbyterian member of Church Women United] decided that we would go into a foundation.

"So, I went to Mr. and Mrs. Sandack, and four of their friends gave me money, so I could put them in while I was president of the association. During that time, in six years, in 1966, I sent in my resignation to the association because they didn't want me to do the things the way I wanted to do them—to just pick any student, not the high grade student. But I picked the ones who really wanted it, but their grades were low, because they didn't go along with the idea that some teacher had in mind. Their grades might have been just 0.1, but they had something about them and they said, 'No, we will do something else.' So, I went home and the doctor put me in twenty-one pills-a-day because the peritonitis was acting up and kept me in for eight months.

"They kept coming and I kept planning things for them—like giving them little things, having a banquet, selling iron board covers, cupcakes—and they still kept coming. It got up to be six and then eight students. Then Mr. Sandack and Mr. Hiatt decided that it ought to go into the foundation. So, it went into the foundation and the students named it the Alberta Henry Education Foundation. I told them they couldn't do that ... 'I'm not dead yet. You can't name it that.' But they insisted and that's how it became, and now we got over three hundred students that we are looking for, and I think we might have found maybe ninety some of them. They are of all races and all colors, yes every race, Native Americans, Asians."[15]

The Jewish community was involved because A. Wally Sandack was the one that got its chartered papers and it was the Jewish people when I first started putting these kids in school. It wasn't the foundation then it was just the Jewish ones that gave me the money, nobody else. I got a list of those seven families—the Franks, the Sweets, Sandacks that gave me the money to put students in and then when the students kept coming.

And I had gotten the peritonitis and I was sick, the doctor had put me in for eight months, I couldn't do it so I just had to borrow money from Colleen Sweets and then we'd raise the money, I'd pay them off, then we'd look up, there's be some more money and we never could catch up, so that's why we had to turn it into a foundation.

But the heart of the foundation when it started was Ben Roe. He was the foundation. He was the one who went out and talked to the chamber of commerce and people with money, and he got the Bamberger Foundation, he had them come in and selected ten students and they would fund them and they did over ten years of the foundation. They helped provide some of the seed money to get it going.

Jim Rock did more—he took over the treasurer, no, financial secretary. He's the one that when they selected the students, they went to him, and he was the financial aid officer. What he did was take the money the foundation had and [use] it with basic scholarships and other kinds of things so that we were able to give more students money. You could get more money when you did that. All of the different universities—Westminster, Utah, Technical College [now Salt Lake Community College].

I had all the backing with Dr. Boyer Jarvis for the foundation. Dr. Boyer Jarvis served as vice chairman under me the whole time, fifteen years I think it was that we served together, and at all the annual meetings, he got the university or some other place that didn't charge us much to have our annual meeting. He was the vice president of the University of Utah. When I talk about the foundation, it was a catalyst with the university, so all of those things that I really needed, that's how I could get them. And Norm Gibbons who was professor over the student affairs when I needed him or some students that were not on the foundation and they needed help—their parents maybe made a little bit too much money and the foundation could not pick them up, then I got Boyer and I would send them up to Norm Gibbons and he would get them the kind of assistance that they needed so no one could fall between the lumps—he took one, he took two, but he took them all.

Christ United Methodist Church, they started giving us money and they had different groups up there that raised funds. And every year, that's thirty-two years, Christ United Methodist Church has given money to the foundation to assist students. The Christ United Church is the one that came with us and is with us today. The Presbyterian Church, the first lady that helped me to set up the foundation, Virginia Hyatt, came from Church Women United and she was from the Presbyterian Church.

The foundation [helped] over three hundred and some students with no federal dollars. The students and the board named it the Alberta Henry Foundation over my objections, because I wasn't dead. I thought you had to be dead and then you got—well, anyway, over three hundred and some students that we were mentors to, and they came from LDS Church, Catholic, from every denomination. You want to see the tie-in? My tie-in came through the foundation, which is thirty-two years old now and working with parents of these kids. That's a marvelous record.

That marvelous record began small but grew as more and more people learned of the possibilities it offered students who needed help. Wallace Sandack used both his skill as an attorney and his contacts with other competent people to make certain the program could remain in effect for a very long time. He established the organization as nonprofit and tax-exempt and clearly stated the purpose for the organization:

> The foregoing purposes of the corporation will be accomplished primarily by fostering the development, operation, and awarding of scholarship for tuition, books, board and housing for needy students at college, junior college, university and/or vocational training school level in the State of Utah, whose financial means would otherwise deny them this benefit, and without regard to the sex, color, creed, religion or national origin of such persons.[16]

Many of those students received full or partial tuition; some just got money for books or lab fees. Each case was decided independently, based on student needs. They moved forward with their education and then more students came asking for help. Alberta became known for going after students who didn't see college as an option. Solomon Chacon wasn't planning to go to college when he graduated from high school in rural Colorado, but Alberta told him that if he could be admitted to the University of Utah, she'd find a scholarship for him. "She started talking about college, and it was scary. . . . I didn't even know anyone who'd been to school."[17] He worked to be admitted and she worked to find money for him, a small amount, but enough to make up the difference between what he had and what he needed to attend school. Chacon became an attorney in Salt Lake City, the first professional from a very large family.[18]

Alberta's assistance often went beyond money. When Harvey Boyd encountered difficulties as he started an architecture program at the University of Utah in 1969, Alberta helped him contact the dean of the department and found a local architect who mentored him through the program. Boyd became an architect in Salt Lake City and an officer in the Alberta Henry Education Foundation. He is still the contact person listed on the Alberta Henry Education Foundation website.[19]

She even impacted those for whom no financial aid could be found. Andrew Valdez, who would become a judge in the Third District Court, wanted to go to college after he graduated from West High in 1970, so he approached Alberta for funds. She told him there was no money left for the next year, but she found a job for him at a post office. Valdez said: "Instead of just saying, 'No, I'm sorry,' she made the extra effort to find me a place to work as opposed to giving me free money. [She was] a community mom. If she didn't have an answer, she'd find one for you."[20]

Michael Styles remembers her as a direct mentor. "She turned a rebel without a clue into a soldier with a cause." He was a shy young man, and he was impressed with Alberta's forthright approach to problems and her aggressive style. He became active in public affairs, fighting for causes as he had seen her do. Styles later became the director of the Utah Office of Black Affairs.[21]

Alberta directly influenced the expansion of prospects for many young people in the Salt Lake City area through the foundation. While it was initially started to support black students, it quickly expanded to include disadvantaged people from every race and many ethnic groups. By 2005 the AHEF had directly supported over two hundred students.[22] She saw them become doctors, lawyers, judges, teachers, and public servants in a vast range of areas and she was always interested in their welfare. Occasionally she ran into them in ways she was not expecting. When Nanette Roundy, niece of Alberta's good friends and neighbors Vaughn and Melva Blackburn, wrote a paper praising her and the foundation for an Ethnics 2550 class at the University of Utah, the teacher added an unusual note. Roundy brought her teacher's note over for Alberta to see: "I agree, especially since I am an Alberta Henry Education fund scholarship recipient. She is special."[23]

As the chair of the foundation from 1967 to 1980 Alberta devoted much of her time to middle and high school students, yet as she gained visibility in the community, others saw her as a valuable candidate to increase educational opportunities for many more students. And by then it was not just the black community that knew Alberta and gathered at her home. She was as gracious and welcoming as ever, but she was genuinely surprised that the reaction from the white community was different from what she had expected.

So then when the university and I had a luncheon at my house, for the foundation, a lot of them brought their kids. It was on the west side of the street, the biggest house on the block. They'd look around—they had never been in a black house. I always laugh about that, because I could never understand. I had worked for the Sandacks, I had catered parties. So it was no big deal. So why was it a big deal for them to come to a black house? I never understood that. I still don't. Except that I know that everybody's a product of their environment.

However amusing those visitors' reactions may have been, they were learning, like many others, that Alberta was a person with a family and a home, just like everybody else, even if her activities were a good bit more active than lots of others. Alberta encountered influential people in her varied endeavors and organizations, and those contacts encouraged more cooperation among all of them.

"All I ever did was go to meetings. All I ever did was go wherever I thought they had a board meeting, or anything that had money, or something that would be advantageous and good for the black community. You heard me say just in even one year, I would have maybe thirty or forty boards and agencies that I would go to, because I knew it would reckle them.[24] *Most of the time, they'd never seen a black. Then, on top of that, Governor Rampton came in and appointed me to Brooklyn Institute. I would be up in Snowbird with the whole bunch, and I'd be the only black. I even got to go with the bid committee to select the Third Judge. That's when we got Judge [David K Winder], and there I was the only black. Then here come again an energy commission and Governor [Calvin] Rampton said, 'Alberta will be on that.'*

"So I was supposed to break the ice for all the places and for people. I would read all the stuff at home, and I would battle in it like I had been in it for years. I took a physics class and I [audited classes] when you don't want credit, you don't degree, because I didn't know anything about physics. Did you know that the teacher read my paper for the whole class and there were almost a hundred of us? I was embarrassed.... He read and he said, 'She's not getting a grade, but if I would give it a grade she would get an A.' All because I got into it and I loved it. You know, if I hadn't been on the energy committee, I probably wouldn't [have] been able to pass that class."[25]

Alberta's alliances with so many people led her to still other avenues. She approached Governor Calvin Rampton about securing funds for minority needs in the legislature.[26] He agreed and asked her to join on the Governor's Black Policy Advisory Council. She worked on the council from 1971 to 1979, serving as chair from 1975 to 1976. In 1973 Rampton named the week of August 13 as Alberta Henry Education Foundation Week.[27] All the while, she continued her involvement with the NAACP.

When Jim [James Dooley] became president [of the Salt Lake City NAACP] he did stuff there with youth, he tried really, but he couldn't [do everything] so that's why they called me in to be the youth director and so that's where I had youth meetings for the NAACP.

James Dooley was elected president of the Salt Lake City NAACP in 1969 and by 1974 he knew he had found a good ally in Alberta Henry. They looked for ways to highlight and reward positive behavior from the young people. In 1978 Dooley suggested that the group start naming the Distinguished Youth of the Month. Winners were given a twenty-five-dollar savings bond and the opportunity to spend a day with the black professional of their choice. The first winner, Tonya McFarland, chose Alberta Henry because "I like the things that Mrs. Henry does. I wanted to get to know her better." McFarland shadowed Alberta for a full day, going in and out of schools, answering calls in her office, and having lunch in the Panorama Room at the University of Utah.[28]

As a youth director, Alberta supervised games and crafts, but she quickly displayed what would become her trademark in dealing with civic activities: look for lots of options and don't settle for the obvious ones. She took a particularly proactive stance with the young people. She became concerned that school counselors exhibited prejudices toward several groups of students—and she wasn't the only one who recognized that frequent, almost casual kind of prejudice. A high school counselor told young Phillip Notarianni, son of Italian immigrants, that he could find a job in the mines like the rest of the Italians. Phil didn't like either the attitude or the advice. He went on to earn a PhD in history, teach at the University of Utah, and serve as director of the Utah State Historical Society.[29] Alberta observed exactly that kind of dismissive attitude toward black students among too many school personnel.

They would send students to the counselors and the counselors would say, "Oh you can go and work places you choose." They would not tell them about scholarships that were available. If the kids were not in school, the counselors would alert me and I'd go out and find them to stop the dropout rates. Marsha Boyd was working with me over at the Nettie Gregory Center with the youth and she was a student on the Alberta Henry Education Foundation going to school at the University of Utah.[30] *[She was one of] four blacks hired, one in each school as counselor-aides, they were all going to the University of Utah, and they had a program where they would pay students and I got to select the blacks, and Marsha was one of them. [She] knew where all the kids were hanging out. She'd get in my car and we'd go out and pick them up and bring them back to school. We were worse than truant officers.*

Marsha Boyd and the other three young black university students that Salt Lake School District hired to counsel high school students had an enormous impact. They worked with young people who were performing poorly and appeared to be in danger of dropping out of school, helping them see options and possibilities they had never known. She and Alberta became a formidable team, both of them constantly on the lookout for ways to help children and young adults, especially minority students, to find ways to explore, grow, and succeed. They recognized the value of music, but knew few of those students' families could afford musical instruments; in 1971 they opted for something very simple: a drill team.

The year before I had taken the NAACP youth students on a bus; we got the bus and raised money and we let adults come in with us to go to Asilomar. Every other year NAACP held a regional meeting at Asilomar, California. That's right outside Monterey; it's right on the beach. I had taken sixty some students and the rest were adults and the NAACP's Jim Dooley. He took credit, but really, the students did it because I helped them arrange to go out to get us donations and everything to have a bus to take us there and back. And the parents would let the students go. While we were there, they had some drill teams and they gave prizes to the drill teams.

Marsha saw them and said, "We can do that. We can do better than that."

I said, "We can?"

"Oh, yes."

And the girls looked at them. "We don't have us one."

So between the girls and Marsha, that's how that drill team came about. Two years later, when I took them back to Asilomar, they won the trophy for the best drill team. But I had ripped them up[31] *and I had them crying the day before they were to perform. "You got out here and you've seen some boys" [imitates crying]. I said, "Cry all you want to but you're not shaking your hips."*

They were scared. They had never been out of Utah. A lot of them had never been around a lot of blacks. Coming from Utah, you don't see that many blacks. They were out there with blacks from all over the region. And when they got up there they snapped to it, I mean they were precise. They won a prize and I got an award, but it was Marsha that did the drill team.

Marsha became the director of that group of girls at the Nettie Gregory Center, but they needed a title. They wanted a name that would distinctly identify the members as both black and very hip, so they adopted a term from a style of popular music then being applied by blacks to themselves: the Soul Sisters Drill Team. The name reflects yet another shift in the language designating black Americans: "Soul" meant black, but it carried connotations of inclusion as well as identification, frequently coupled with "brother" or "sister." The drill team performed in various places, but especially in schools helping children and young adults broaden their horizons. In 1973 they were named Outstanding Youth Group at the NAACP West Regional Conference in Pacific Grove, California. Team members included Susie Bell, Marla Boyd, Cathy Christie, Cheryl Christie, Shauna Graves, Julia Henry, Vanessa Jackson, Ramona Rae Lytle, Cathy Mason, Phyllis Spight, Mary Ann Wallace, Angela Woolfork, and Shauna Benns. Benns later remarked that traveling to cities in California gave her both a taste for travel and the knowledge that it really was possible for her, a young black girl, to travel and see more of the world.[32]

Alberta's and Boyd's work with the youth was paying off. All those Soul Sisters on the drill team not only stayed in school, they became leaders. Jackson was corresponding secretary of the youth branch of the NAACP and a member of the Black Student Union (BSU) at West High School. Graves was the vice president of the BSU, a member of the NAACP Youth Board and Youth Choir. Lytle was membership chairman of the Youth Branch of the NAACP, a Girl Scout for eight years, a member of Sears Fashion Board Pace Setters, and a member of the BSU, pep club and junior choir at West High. Mason was a member of the Distributive Education Clubs of America (DECA) and treasurer of the BSU at West High. All of the team members, in fact, were involved in positive and educational school and community activities.[33] Being on the team gave the girls themselves opportunities to perform, travel, and grow, but those girls also became role models for younger children of all races and backgrounds. All of them were becoming exactly the kind of positive role models Alberta had realized black youth needed.

Whenever I went out to speak to some of the students—the teachers would invite me—I took the drill team or an acrobatic bunch or a [high school] senior or something. And that was my visit to that school. And the students would be clapping and some would ask, "Can we have your autograph?" I always think about those little kids and their faces. They were so impressed.

While Alberta worked with organized groups like the drill team, she was also involved with a range of other activities. Often when projects were under way, making centerpieces for tables at a dinner or arranging items for an NAACP meeting, the young people from the neighborhood or the organizations gathered at the Henry home. By that time both of Alberta's children were teenagers and became greatly involved in whatever was going on. Her daughter, Julia, said:

> I remember times she'd have all the youth over and we'd be making table decorations for the banquets. She's got an imagination. [*Said with great emphasis*] We'd tell her, "Will you quit thinking!" She would think up these decorations and then we would make them. We'd have them there at our house on Tenth West, big dining room table full of stuff. I remember going with her to Zims arts and crafts store so many times.
>
> And then she started a drill team at the NAACP. I had to be involved in that. "If I'm going to be a part of something, then my daughter is darn well going to be a part of it, too." They were mainly black kids from the community. We would go to the Nettie Gregory Center. That's where we would migrate and have our little dances. We made our fun. Even if we just went over there and hung out, there were always programs over there that were easily implemented by Mrs. Henry and the NAACP.[34]

Shauna Graves Robertson, an AHEF student during her law school training at the University of Utah, agreed that the whole black community of Salt Lake City seemed to congregate at the Henry house on a regular basis.[35] Alberta joined groups where she was obviously needed, like the

NAACP youth program, but she also joined some other groups, primarily to provide the presence of someone who was not white. In time she would serve on the board or as an officer in more than forty local organizations.

Often I was the only black and I was there to sensitize people, because none of them had ever even been close [to blacks—and probably not a lot of other minorities, either]. And then if they had money, I wanted to see if they had programs like State House Fellows. I would get them so they would let a black be a State House Fellow, work for the commission; there wasn't a black that was in politics. So my involvement in all of those boards was for a reason to get people to know, and most of them did get to know me.

Alberta certainly did help Salt Lake residents of all colors get to know her. She also made them more aware of their own communities, as well as the larger community that includes all of us. At the same time, blacks in other parts of the country were also raising awareness of issues in their own areas. Alberta's entrance into civic involvement coincided with the rise of the civil rights movement throughout the United States, especially in the Deep South. Beginning in the 1950s, and throughout the 1960s, a rapid and dramatic upheaval in civil rights protests swept through the courts and across the nation. *Brown v. Topeka* had alerted people in the North and West to the existence of legal segregation in the South, but also to the broader problems in employment, education, and civil intercourse across the country.

When John F. Kennedy was elected president in 1960, he proposed a range of programs, but they were largely rejected, both by Congress and by the general populace. When Lyndon B. Johnson became president following Kennedy's assassination in November 1963, he found both Congress and the nation far more amendable to dealing with social issues. By that time the civil rights movement had forced citizen's attention to the grievous conditions spawned by segregation and the need for change. In a relatively short time, a series of laws were passed that created the most far-reaching civil rights legislation enacted since Reconstruction. The next year Johnson urged passage of several bills creating what became collectively known as the Great Society.[36]

Johnson's Great Society program recognized the inequities in American society and attempted to find ways to remedy them. These federal domestic programs addressed the very real problems of health care, housing, nutrition, and education among America's poor by attacking concerns in specific areas including city planning and urban design, day care and education, housing and medical care, crime and juvenile delinquency, vocational rehabilitation, and programs for the elderly. Johnson's Economic Opportunity Bill of 1964 created the Office of Economic Opportunity (OEO), operating directly under the Office of the President, which oversaw virtually all of the new programs designed to provide pathways for the poor to join in finding solutions to their own problems. The Community Action Program (CAP) included adult basic education and assistance programs for children in need. Work experience programs helped unemployed fathers and mothers both gain experience and find real jobs. Volunteers were recruited to aid in many of these causes through Volunteers in Service to America (VISTA), a domestic service patterned after Kennedy's Peace Corps. The laws created employment and investment incentives for small businesses and specific programs aimed at helping the rural poor and migrant workers.[37] Community involvement on the local level was both integral and essential in these programs.

Urban slums, with their inadequate housing and high crime rates, threatened the decay of many cities. Johnson's response was the Model Cities program under the Department of Housing and Urban Development (HUD). It emphasized the coordination of various local and national agencies and utilized information on population trends, unemployment figures, crime statistics, and urban planning. Model Cities projects under the direction of local leaders were established in over two hundred urban areas around the country, including Salt Lake City. The program was designed to aid disadvantaged citizens in a specific area in upgrading their own habitats. More specifically it helped to raise the standard of living for disadvantaged citizens in urban areas.[38] It worked congruently with the Community Action, Neighborhood Youth Corps, and VISTA volunteers.[39]

Education reforms extended from preschoolers to adults. Job Corps opened in 1964 under the Department of Labor to provide opportunities for learning a trade, and, if necessary, also earning a high school diploma or General Educational Development (GED) certificate to young people ages sixteen through twenty-four.

One of the most innovative of those programs was Head Start for preschool children initiated in 1964. Studies showed that children from poor families or families in which English was not spoken at home failed to succeed in schools at alarming rates. Head Start was designed to provide underprivileged children with many of the same advantages as their wealthier neighbors who were sent to preschools where they learned the rudiments of reading, math, and behavior in classes as well as at home.[40] As students began to enroll, teachers discovered children "who in many cases had never opened a book or touched a pencil, had never eaten an apple or used a knife and fork, and, in some cases, had never talked because no one talked to them."[41] Many of the children had physical as well as societal problems that impinged on their learning. Medical examinations of the children enrolled in the Jacksonville, Florida, Head Start program, for example, showed 52 percent were anemic, 45 percent needed dental care, 31 percent had problems with hearing, and 25 percent had problems with their eyes, 5 percent being partially blind.[42] Growing out of those studies that showed how desperately children of poverty needed help to succeed in school, and eventually in life, came the Children's Television Workshop and its landmark program, *Sesame Street*, a radically innovative program for educational and entertaining children's television.

Promoters of the Head Start program in Salt Lake City included Governor Calvin Rampton and Esther Landa, long a valiant advocate for social and political causes. The school would function as both a day care center and a nursery school for underprivileged children in the area. After intense lobbying with various governmental bodies, Rampton and Landa finally launched Salt Lake City's Head Start Center in 1967.[43] They began to look for people they knew would work well with children.

They knew me by now, [so] I went to work in 1967 to '72 at the day care center. At that time it was great. They wanted a Head Start day care and Esther Landa and I think Mrs. Calvin Rampton, they recommended that they hire Alberta Henry. So I get a letter in the mail saying that they want to hire me. I went to Dr. Ershler, the doctor that Mrs. Sandack had got for me that was keeping me alive, and he said, "Yes, you can do that from eight to five—if you just work from eight to five, come home and rest, be with your kids."

He thought she could handle eight hours a day, but no more than that. So she took the job, but she still maintained her membership in nearly four dozen organizations and frequently held meetings in the evenings at her house. She showed up for Head Start every day, so technically she was following Dr. Eschler's orders and working (for pay) only eight hours a day.

It was no surprise that the people behind the Salt Lake City Head Start program wanted Alberta Henry. Her affection for the children was evident to everyone who saw her with them. Nearly thirty years later one parent expressed gratitude for Alberta's efforts to help her child when he attended the Head Start program. At that time the woman had been "a single mother of four and had to work a job and a half to support them." Her three-year-old son was enrolled in Head Start, and she wanted him to experience the same loving environment he had at home, but wondered if he would find that at the center. When she put him into the program, she met Alberta, who would be one of his teachers. "It was easy to see she loved kids, and I knew Jon was in good hands. Then one day I was a little late in picking him up and . . . found him wrapped up tight in Henry's arms while she twirled round and round, laughing almost as hard as he. She was treating him the way we did at home and he loved it. Alberta's were the best possible hands he could be in!"[44]

So I went to work at the Head Start. It was down there where the general hospital used to be on Twenty-First South.[45] *And they had all those buildings just behind there, not on State Street but on Twenty-First. We had to go in there and we fixed it up and put shelves and small toilets and everything, playground. And that's how Head Start day care got started.*

And then we moved it into Central City, once they had that built. Liz Crookston was the director of day care and did the evaluation for the University of Utah. Now you heard me say that I had never been to college; I had graduated from high school, but I was an aide in the [class] room and a lady from the university came down to evaluate all the teachers and aides. She evaluated me and I evaluated as high as the teachers who had the degrees and she recommended that they move me up to be a teacher with a room.[46] *So I went back to Dr. Ershler; he said it's still the same.*

So I became a teacher at Head Start day care down in Central City. They were to hire a teacher with the degrees to work with me to teach me how to do lesson plans and all the things that they do in college. They got a beautiful lady named Elizabeth, and for a few days she worked with me, and then she went to Liz and said: "I can't work with her. She already knows all these things." Then she said, "But I'd like to have the other three-year-old room so we can work together."

But if you go downstairs, you see my library, that's all I ever did when I was little was read. And I've got all kinds of books, and then I have a World Book and the other book with all the kid's stuff in it. All you got to do is read and set up and make the day care plan. If you're going to the zoo, animals and things—that's simple. I did that with my kids and so that's what I was doing. And then I was happy. I was happy—until the federal government got involved.

They sent a man down and said that Head Start was a good program, but unless we got the parents involved, we did no good. If we got the kids brought up to a certain level and they had to go back into that same environment. Now, I had the foundation, so I was already going into the schools, because there were parents with kids in the day care but they were in elementary school, too. And they had parents that had kids in the junior high school that I was picking up and putting in college with my foundation. And with the New Hope Baptist Church I had another [connection] and with the Utah and Idaho Baptist Association, I had a whole lot of things that I could pull from.

But the federal government recommended that I become parent coordinator and I cried and said, "I quit." I just wanted to be in the classroom, because the cute little kids, the little sugar pudding pie babies. So they had to make a deal with me for me not to quit. I could be a parent coordinator until four o'clock, from eight to four, and then four o'clock I could go into the classroom and when the teachers left at four thirty and five, then I would have all the kids until their parents picked them up. Now, you can't hardly beat that. I mean, that's the best of two worlds. So I said yes, and going along merrily, and at Christmas and I would go out and get the different [groups]. The Church Women United, they would buy all the presents for Christmas and things for the kids. There was another group, they would come in and be [like] grandparents to the kids. I loved that, and I said I would never leave, because I could bring my kids. My kids, by that time, were ten or eleven and twelve. I didn't go to work until they were eleven. Wendell was eleven and Julia was ten, going on eleven. So that's when I went to work at the Head Start day care and that's where I stayed.

In 1971 I was sitting there in my office as the parent coordinator, saying I'll go out and visit these parents, I got to get them a job, make sure they are getting the kids to the doctor. The phone rang and said, "Alberta Henry?"

"Yes."

"This is the regents president of the regents in the something or other—at the University of Utah."

"Yeah, What do you want?" Oh, I was mad because I had just got a call before then that said a principal at Jordan had kicked some kids out of school. I said, "Let me go over to that bird-head school. That's where my kids go to school."

I thought maybe when that call came, it was another one of the calls or one of the parents, and I was going to say, I'm on my way. Now, I'm still at the day care, at Central City day care, but I have kids in school, elementary and junior high.

And this phone [caller] said, "Well, what we're doing, we've done our study and everything, and the university has granted you an honorary doctorate degree." I didn't know what an honorary doctorate was. What was that? I didn't have the slightest idea what that is. "And we're calling for you to confirm—"

I said: "I don't know. I'm awfully busy. I'm going out here. I'm getting ready to burn one of those junior high schools down."

And the man just got tickled, and he laughed and he said: "I'll tell you what, Mrs. Henry. Tell us if it's all right with you, just give us your approval, and then you can go and burn the school down."

I said, "OK, whatever that is." Now, I didn't know what an honorary doctorate was. In fact, I didn't know when they were putting the cap on me and Governor Rampton and Senator Bennett and this other man and all of them were there. Mr. Sandack got the biggest kick out of me, because I've got a mouth, you know.

Everyone who met Alberta quickly learned she had a mouth. More than that, she knew how to use it. She became the first black person to receive an honorary doctorate from the University of Utah. The second was Reverend France Davis in 1973.

Ten or twelve years later they gave one to Reverend Davis. And they should. He's a powerhouse.

But even with that honorary doctorate Alberta often said she'd have been content to stay with Head Start forever, but she soon recognized she was needed in a wider field.

Then in 1972 I came home from work at Head Start and there was a letter in the mail. The Board of Education for Salt Lake City had met a week or two weeks ago and agreed to hire me as the minority consultant for the black population.

The only reason they could not reach me by telephone because I was never home. After I got away from the day care center, I was the chairman of the Model Cities education, and I loved that. Oh, we had a whole bunch of good programs. Darlene Ball, who was on the education committee, I'm quite sure she recommended me to be hired, because she loved the way I chaired the meetings with Model Cities, but I had learned that from Esther Landa. I had watched her several times and I thought, she could do it like a man. She could really handle those meetings and was being fair, too.

So I went back to Dr. Erschler again, because I had him for a doctor until he retired; that was thirty-one years. He said: "As long as you don't overdo it more than the eight hours, I think you're kind of getting carried away, Alberta. But I think you could." So Harold said, OK with him. So I had to tell the day care and give my notice that I had to leave because I was being hired as the minority consultant at the Salt Lake City School District. It was a sad day.

But do you notice the pattern in here? I had nothing to do with any of this. I prayed and I went to church—it was like the Lord says, there are others out there, there are kids in the elementary, junior high school, and high school that need you. It was just like He was moving me along to do all these.

Apparently this time the Lord was moving her to a position where she would have even more influence, officially as well as unofficially, than she had known in any of her previous work.

CHAPTER 6

THE SALT LAKE SCHOOL DISTRICT

When Alberta signed on with Salt Lake School District, she was probably aware that she was walking into a firestorm, or more accurately a range of firestorms. The district was experiencing problems on several different fronts, from aging school buildings to minority students' needs to diminishing student numbers. District officials had tried for several years to analyze those needs and find the unintended consequences of earlier decisions.

In the decades following World War II, Salt Lake City, like other large cities across the country, found that residents were moving from the central city to the suburbs, leaving behind those who could not afford the newer, larger houses in outlying areas. Consequently school enrollments shifted in the same direction as those moves. By 1959 the district's school population had risen to forty-two thousand, and twenty new schools were built or under construction. The new schools, however, were on the outskirts of Salt Lake City where the population had increased, while the inner city population continued to drop rapidly as the area became more and more commercial. Moreover the schools in the central city were not only losing students but the buildings themselves were old and physically deteriorating, most no longer meeting building code requirements. They would have to be closed, never a popular option with parents or students. To deal with these and related issues, the Salt Lake School District hired Arthur C. Wiscombe in 1969.[1]

Wiscombe came from a solidly Mormon background. He also carried an impressive vita. He held a master's degree from Harvard with additional classes at Columbia, where he and his family lived on the edge of Harlem and had contact with the black population there. He completed his PhD at the University of Colorado. He had taught at both Brigham Young University and the University of Utah and served as a principal and an assistant superintendent in Uintah County.[2]

When he arrived in Salt Lake City District, Wiscombe tackled the problem of closing schools and realigning enrollments. Obviously the first targets had to be those central city schools that held the greatest structural dangers. Wiscombe proposed closing six elementary schools, moving ninth grades to high schools and sixth grades to middle schools. Those middle schools would be located in the new suburban neighborhoods, essentially a ring around the inner city where most minority students lived. He suggested that busing those students from the central city to the middle schools would give them more opportunities. That was probably true, but not all of the parents in the central city wanted their children bused every day.

Difficult as closures were, all educational issues were greatly complicated by the needs of minority students. In 1954 when the Supreme Court had declared segregation illegal in the case of *Brown v. Board of Education*, Dr. Allen Bateman, Utah state superintendent of public instruction, had responded positively to the ruling. "The decision is fundamentally right. If we [the United States] hope to maintain our position of leadership in the world today with the people of other races and nationalities, we must do everything possible to show that we are actually practicing equal treatment of all peoples within our country."[3] That same year the Utah State Department of Education Committee launched a study to determine whether segregation, de facto or otherwise, could be impacting its own schools. The analysis concluded that although Utah did not mandate segregated schools, minority students faced racism when they tried to obtain scholastic honors. Young minority people became frustrated with the discrimination they faced in jobs and in the professional services in Utah. For black teenagers, school was not seen as a viable option. A study indicated that they knew that "they [would] not be given an equal chance to use their knowledge and training in the open market."[4] The study concluded that although Utah's schools were integrated, on many levels minority students faced racism sufficiently severe as to greatly reduce if not eliminate altogether their chances for higher education.[5]

From 1956 forward, public opinion surveys showed a steady rise in positive attitudes among white Americans in all parts of the country to the concept of integration in both schools and public facilities. By the early 1970s, however, such support for integration had leveled off and even occasionally dropped.[6] Minorities still needed better avenues for integration into the American mainstream and access to the American dream, and most people acknowledged that those avenues ran through the public schools—they just could not agree on how to pave the road.

The Salt Lake City School Board attempted to find some solutions to problems within the district using both federal and local resources and developing alliances with other community organizations. By the beginning of the 1970s, they had made some progress. In 1971 Governor Calvin Rampton implemented Negro History Week in Utah schools and Wiscombe helped to establish school improvement councils in three intercity junior high schools to "involve a large segment of the parents . . . through School Community Councils and the PTA"[7] but it was still clear that minority students and their parents wanted much more than a token week or committee. Early in 1971, the board had approved an early childhood education program "to be funded by Model Cities for $115,000."[8] A Black Opinion Survey of the Salt Lake City Schools was undertaken to determine needs. James Dooley, president of the Salt Lake City Chapter of the NAACP and J. B. Stewart, chair of the organization's educational committee, spoke to the board about the survey. The board acknowledged a number of problems in the schools, especially in "certain schools as they relate to our minority groups" and noted that they would deal with any questions brought before the board.[9]

As Wiscombe continued to push for better accommodations for all students, a crisis at West High pushed the issue of minority students to the front of the agenda. West High music teacher James D. Maher had a disagreement with four black students that ended with him calling them "niggers." At the next school board meeting James Dooley, president of the Salt Lake NAACP, insisted that the teacher be fired and suggested such attitudes were among the reasons so many black and Hispanic students dropped out of school. The discussion became more intense as it went on. The teacher was put on paid suspension and the four students were also suspended, but would be tutored at the district office while the situation could be examined more closely. The problem grew a few days later when

FIGURE 1. (ABOVE)
The Hill family on the front porch of their home in Louisiana, taken shortly before they moved to Kansas. Left to right: Alberta, Julia, Nevada, David, James, Rosetta Mazie. Courtesy of Gilbert Lebya.

FIGURE 2. (LEFT)
Alberta Hill age seventeen. This photo was taken just before the auto accident that scarred her face. Courtesy of Gilbert Lebya.

FIGURE 3. (TOP LEFT) Alberta and Isaac Gooch with her parents, Julia and James Hill. Courtesy of Gilbert Lebya.

FIGURE 4. (TOP RIGHT) Isaac Gooch at the time Alberta Hill met him. Courtesy of Gilbert Lebya.

FIGURE 5. (ABOVE) Dorothy Little, her friend Olga, and Alberta Hill. Courtesy of Gilbert Lebya.

FIGURE 6. Unidentified friend with Alberta and Dorothy Little. Courtesy of Gilbert Lebya.

FIGURE 7. Alberta Gooch, front row, third from the right, with the staff of the club in California where she worked while her husband was stationed during World War II. Courtesy of Gilbert Lebya.

FIGURE 8. Harold Henry soon after he met Alberta. Courtesy of Gilbert Lebya.

FIGURE 9. Alberta Henry at the time of her marriage to Harold Henry. Courtesy of Gilbert Lebya.

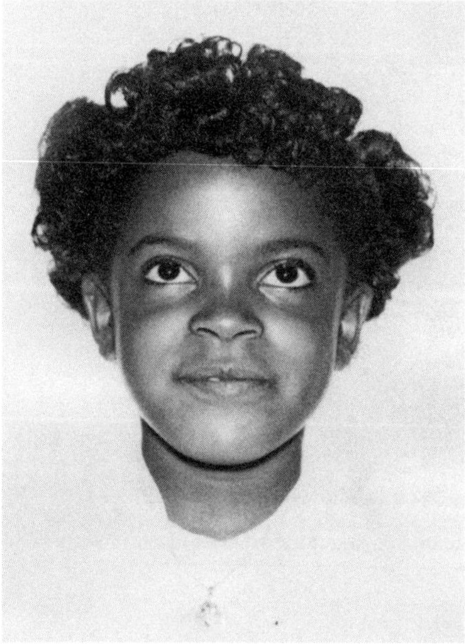

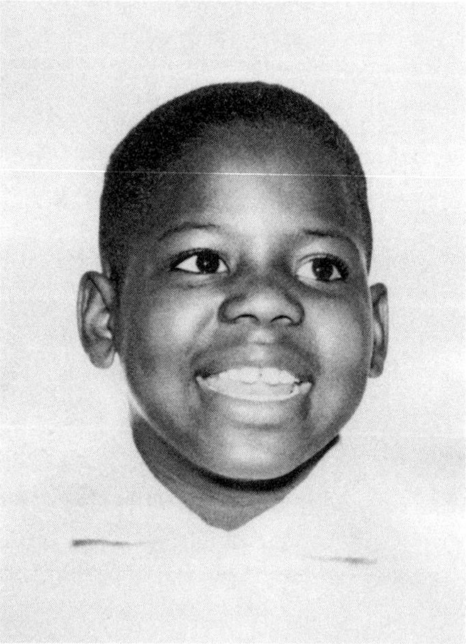

FIGURE 10. (TOP) Woodrow and Emma Brown, Julia's godparents, bracket Wendell, Alberta, and Julia at Christmas. Courtesy of Gilbert Lebya.

FIGURE 11. (ABOVE LEFT) Julia Henry at about age 10. Courtesy of Gilbert Lebya.

FIGURE 12T. (ABOVE RIGHT) Wendell Henry at about age 10. Courtesy of Gilbert Lebya.

FIGURE 13. Harold Henry near the end of his life. Courtesy of Gilbert Lebya.

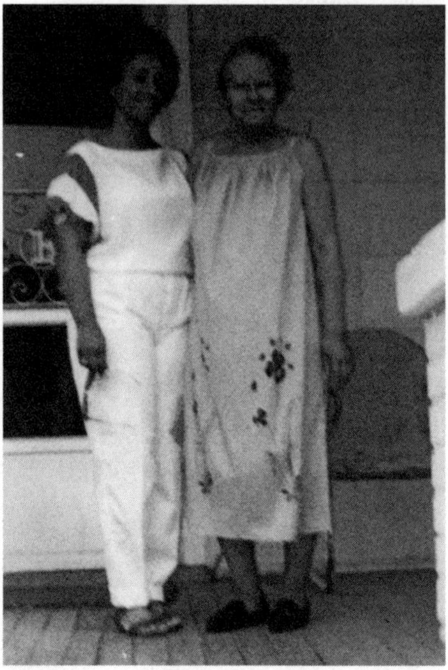

FIGURE 14. (TOP LEFT) Alberta Henry with her daughter Julia at Ian Cumming's party to celebrate his acquisition of a portrait of Helen's father, Arthur Frank.

FIGURE 15. (TOP RIGHT) Julia Henry with her grandmother and namesake, Julia Palmer Hill. Courtesy of Gilbert Lebya.

FIGURE 16. (RIGHT) Harold and Alberta Henry in their living room. Courtesy of Gilbert Lebya.

FIGURE 17. Alberta Henry studied the Bible all her life, a habit developed under the tutelage of her grandfather, J. J. Palmer, a minister in the Church of the Living God. Courtesy of Gilbert Lebya.

FIGURE 18. Alberta Henry sits comfortably in church. She felt strongly that wherever she might live, she should be affiliated with a church. Courtesy of Gilbert Lebya.

FIGURE 19. Alberta Henry delighted to have received an honorary doctoral degree from the University of Utah. Courtesy of Gilbert Lebya.

FIGURE 20. Alberta Henry receiving her Bachelor of Education degree from the University of Utah. Teachers in the Salt Lake City school district could no longer complain that she was not their equal in education. Courtesy of Gilbert Lebya.

FIGURE 21. Alberta with the Sandack family at Ian Cumming's party to celebrate his acquisition of a portrait of Helen's father, Arthur Frank. Front row, left to right: Joey Borgenicht, standing next to his mother, Nancy Sandack Borgenicht, Alberta Henry, Susan, the Sandack's younger daughter, Helen, and Roger Sandack. Back Row: Arthur Sandack and his wife, Debbie; Jonathan (affectionately known as Casey), Rick's son; David Payne, Susan's companion, Rick and Wallace Sandack.

FIGURE 22. Alberta Henry in her living room beside a few of the many recognitions and honors she received. Courtesy of Gilbert Lebya.

FIGURE 23. Governor Calvin Rampton with Liz Benns, her mother, and Alberta Henry. Courtesy of Gilbert Lebya.

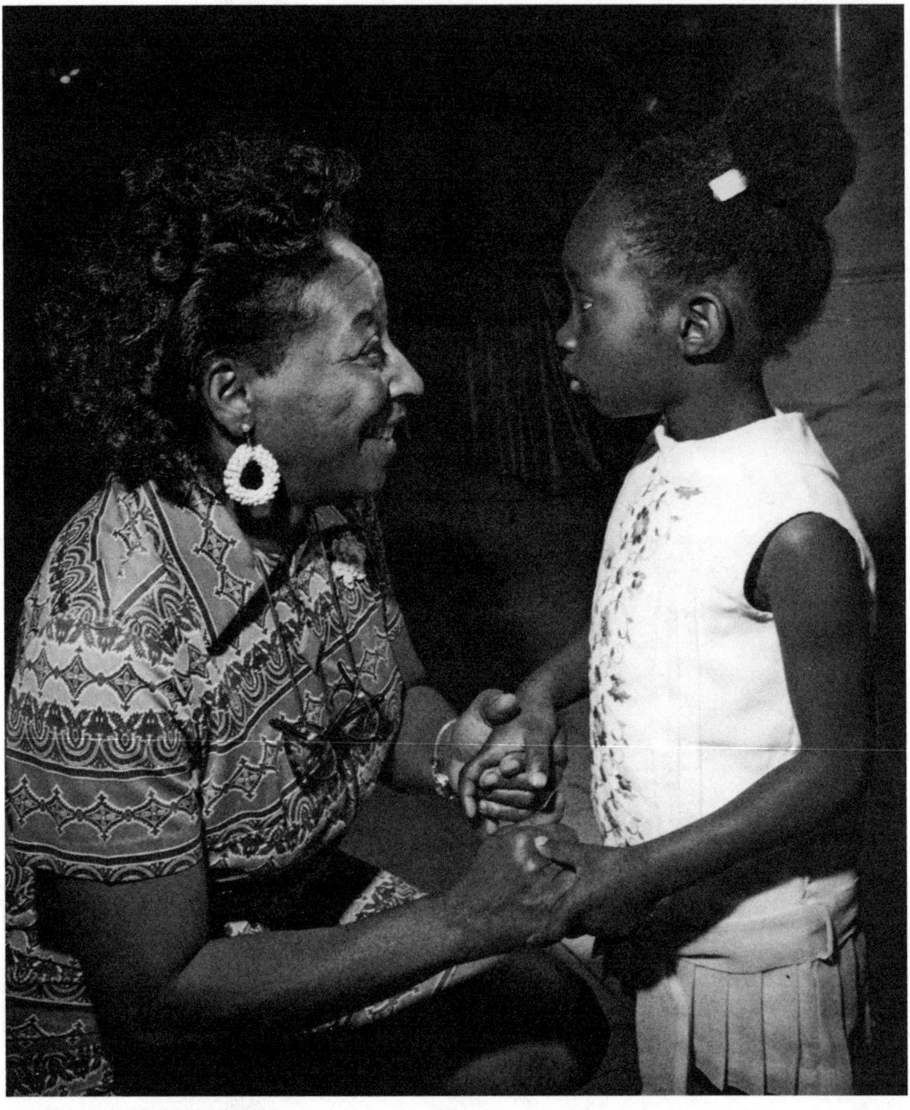

FIGURE 24. Head Start teacher Alberta Henry with one of her charges, Elizabeth Benns. Courtesy of Gilbert Lebya.

FIGURE 25. Alberta Henry voting at the State Democratic Convention. Courtesy of Gilbert Lebya.

FIGURE 26. Alberta Henry visiting with another delegate to the State Democratic Convention. Courtesy of Gilbert Lebya.

FIGURE 27. Alberta Henry's granddaughter Denitra being honored with an award for scholarship by Governor Olene Walker. Courtesy of Gilbert Lebya.

FIGURE 28. Mrs. Richard McFarlane holds her son Richard while Alberta Henry talks with Tonya McFarlane. As part of an NAACP program to encourage young people to examine job possibilities, Tonya asked to shadow Alberta Henry for a day. Courtesy of Gilbert Lebya.

one hundred white parents arrived at the district offices demanding that Maher be reinstated. Wiscombe proposed a task force to look into the issue. To head such a group, he recommended Robert Freed, Utah chair of the U.S. Commission on Civil Rights. Meanwhile to maintain order and safety, policemen would be stationed in every school.[10]

But the problems continued to grow. One example can be seen in the minutes of the district board meetings for the early weeks of 1972. They revolve around a crisis at Horace Mann Junior High School. Alberta already knew Horace Mann well; her young friend and sister truant officer Marsha Boyd was the black student from the University of Utah assigned to work with the students at that school. Alberta called Horace Mann "a bad, bad, bad place."[11] She was not alone in that assessment.[12]

Dooley and Stewart attended the February board meetings and brought with them several parents of Horace Mann students. Four of those parents, Solomon Chacon, Simona Chavez, Alfredo Chacon, and Tina Garcia, spoke to the board asking that four actions be taken: first that "corporal punishment and brutality be abolished in the schools"; second, "Mr. H. William Gradt, teacher at Horace Mann be 'fired'"; third, "racism be eliminated in schools," and fourth, "all policemen be taken out of schools." The parents made several other specific suggestions for positive actions, such as providing a multilingual cultural program to give students pride in their heritage. At the same time, another Horace Mann parent present disagreed with both the requests and the suggestions. The board asked that all those parents meet with the appropriate district personnel, including Joseph Sandoval, the district's minority counselor, before their next meeting. Stewart observed that while the Black Opinion Survey was useful, it was only a beginning in the study of a highly complex problem.[13]

A few weeks later some of those same Horace Mann parents returned with several others, this time accompanied by a man who claimed to be an attorney but was identified in the minutes of the meeting only as "Bill." Whereas the group had previously been part of Dooley and Stewart's prearranged agenda item, this time the parents asked to speak during the board's scheduled thirty-minute open forum at the beginning of each 7:30 p.m. meeting.[14] Each of six parents took over five minutes, exceeding the allotted thirty-minute limit. When the group was informed that their time was up, Bill protested that he had several more speakers lined up. Board member Dan Bushnell asked if the group was aware of the community relations council within each school and suggested they become involved with the one for their school; group members replied that the council "doesn't mean anything." Then H. Wayne Wadsworth, attorney for the board, advised the group that they were in violation of state and city ordinances and would have to desist, but Bill simply replied they still had more speakers. At that point board chair William W. Cannon recessed the meeting and the board left the room, whereupon some of the angry parents moved into the vacated board members' chairs and passed motions approving all of their demands. When the parents were finally persuaded to leave at 9:00 p.m., the board returned and worked part of the way through a lengthy agenda of highly varied items: requests from the University of Utah Department of Education; a letter of appreciation from Esther Landa for the board's kindness following her husband's death; the legal relationship between the district and the state relative to gasoline purchases; and discussions of budget issues, including several properties such as the lease or sale of the recently closed Longfellow School. Finally at 10:30 p.m. the board postponed the remaining items and asked that those who had prepared reports please return with them to the next board meeting.[15]

The evening was both tragedy and farce. Obviously, the parents did not trust the all-white school board, while the board, and doubtless all those people whose carefully prepared presentations had been postponed, were understandably unhappy with the group's behavior. Board meeting minutes indicate no further presentations from the Horace Mann representatives, but both the board members and the representatives of the NAACP and other minority groups continued to work together on school issues including the Black Opinion Survey. In addition, both board members and the representatives of the black community apparently attempted to make connections with each other. In February 1972 Mrs. Ernest Otera, PTA president of Jackson School, invited board members to attend Black History Day and that same month the board adopted a program of minorities studies to include a survey of every black and Hispanic household in the district.[16]

Results from the Black Opinion Survey, the first investigation to determine black education-related sentiments in the district, showed that parents felt their children were not receiving an appropriate education. Alberta Henry, who was still working with the Head Start program at the time, later summed up the situation: "the schools were discriminatory . . . the teachers were Mormon and racist and biased."[17] After learning about the perceived discrimination, the board agreed to establish an advisory program and requested input from prominent blacks in the community. Although the board apparently, and probably sincerely, had the black population's interest in mind, the black leaders wanted to make transformations in education their own way. Consequently the school board dissolved the advisory board and tried a different tactic.[18]

The board then hired a white man to be their liaison with the black community.[19] Alberta had encountered him at the Central City Day Care Center where he had come to hear complaints from blacks which he would then relay to the school board. Alberta felt that he would misinterpret anything she told him. Thus, she and the NAACP informed him that they did not require an interpreter. She stated: "You can't tell them what we want to tell them. You would tell them what you [want] to tell them."[20] Although the man was evidently sincere as he tried to convey the black community's needs, Alberta understandably felt it was important to present black input that was not filtered through the voice of the white community. Apparently, she was not alone. On April 13, 1972, James Dooley sent a letter that "questioned the district's ability" to deal with the problems of minority and economically disadvantaged children; he further criticized the district's use of Title One funds."[21]

Finally, the Salt Lake City School Board decided to hire a minority consultant specifically for the black student population. They had earlier hired Joe Sandavol to aid Hispanic students,[22] probably because it is much easier to recognize the problems of students for whom English is not their primary language than it is to see the societal issues plaguing minority students who are native English speakers. Given the responses to the survey, the district realized that black students were not receiving an appropriate education and thus feared "something bad" would happen if procedures did not change.[23]

Darlene Bowe, advisor to the committee representing the Salt Lake City School Board, was at the time also serving on the Educational Task Force for the Model City in Salt Lake City. Chairman of that committee was Alberta Henry. Bowe and several other people had noted that Henry's administrative abilities showed clearly in the way she handled discussions, sometimes heated, about everything from the expenditure of funds to establishing a Peace Garden.[24] Bowe and Alberta had worked well together as they tried to solve the district's challenges for black students.[25] She suggested that the board hire Alberta Henry as a minority consultant, and the board voted to employ her as a link with the black students. She joined Joseph Sandoval as a Salt Lake School District minority counselor.

Although Alberta was reluctant to leave the day care center, she realized that the consultant position would give her daily, official access to classrooms and she could return to the school board with explicit, first-hand information—and her recommendations would be taken seriously. So in August 1972 she signed the papers to become Salt Lake District's minority consultant for the black student population, primarily because she saw it as a calling from the Lord.[26]

Do you notice the pattern in here? I had nothing to do with any of this. I prayed and I went to church—it was like the Lord says, there are others out there, there are kids in the elementary, junior high school, and high school that need you. It was just like he was moving me along to do all these things. The black community knew me by now, because after I had my kids I went to work in 1967 to '72 at the day care center, but then after I left work I went to different meetings but I just kept going. And then by working at the day care, the parents had kids in elementary and junior high school, so they had problems with their kids. So naturally, I went out to those schools to help the parents of the kids that were in my day care. But don't ask me how I know how to do all those things. I have no idea, but the Lord told me to just go and not worry about what I was to say or do, that he would put the words in my mouth. And whatever I was asked to do, somehow the Lord helped me to do it. Whenever I was—You can do anything with the Lord.

As minority consultant I was an administrator and they [district personnel] didn't like it. They just didn't want a black in there, the people close to me. They'd never had one at the office, and I had to go out and pull black people to come in because they had to know that this was their administration building and they should be there. "Yeah, but they don't treat you right." They wouldn't even speak to me, a lot of them.

Gerald Allen, an elementary school principal in the Salt Lake School District when Alberta Henry worked there, supported her contention that administrators initially neither wanted nor respected her. He suggested that one of reasons for their animosity can be traced to the way she was initially introduced to its principals. Superintendent Wiscombe simply brought her into a meeting of all school principals and announced that she would be overseeing black minority issues and principals would be required to cooperate with her. It was not an auspicious beginning. Some principals openly said she was nothing but a token to placate the NAACP; others doubted the need for such an office no matter who filled it. Nearly all were offended by the fact that while they held master's degrees and doctorates, they were required to take orders from Alberta, who at that point had an honorary doctorate from the University of Utah but no "real" college degree. She was perceived as an enemy, but an enemy with the power to get them fired.[27] That prevailing attitude unquestionably made her job more difficult, but her own assertive nature was doubtless also a factor. As her brother David observed: "She's aggressive. She used to be aggressive as a child—very alert and aggressive. If she figured you were wrong, there would be a big debate coming on."[28] Another factor was simply that few of the people in the district had any experience in dealing with minorities of any kind.

"I was the first black in the Salt Lake School District. People wouldn't speak to me and they would walk way around me. I know they hired me to boot them down. By the time I left, they didn't want to let me go because I was fighting all of their battles for them. I had to devise an instrument, walk down the hall every day and say, 'Hello, how are you?'

"Then they would have to say, 'How are you?' Right?

"I would say, 'Wonderful, oh, beautiful,' and then keep walking. I did that every day and in every office I would stop and say, 'It looks pretty' and would say, 'How are you?' And so they got to wondering why is she wonderful all of the time? They were sick sometimes but I was never sick. Why was I not sick?

"But then the teachers in the school didn't like it because I would tell them that they were prejudice[d] and they had to teach all of the kids the same."[29]

Now, I cannot tell you how I knew how to do all these things. But the Lord had said if I'd go, I did not have to take any thought of what I'm going to say or what I'm going to do, that he would be with me. So I took that as literally. But in an important meeting, he would keep my mouth closed, and sometimes I'd listen, trying to find out where, what, and how, and then I would speak. It was like everybody had already exhausted all their avenues, and whatever I was saying was just what they needed to hear to bring them back and get them to where they needed to go. Maybe it wasn't everything they wanted, but [there was] something for everybody.

Nonetheless, Alberta freely admitted that her own forthright attitude became an issue. As she had said earlier:

I don't sugarcoat anything. In fact, I don't know how to do that. I didn't like myself very much in those days, but I had a job to do. I usually wasn't very nice.

Gerald Allen, who had sympathized with Alberta during her introduction to the district's principals, recalls his first personal meeting with her as volatile. Several of the older boys in his elementary school got into a fight and, in accordance with district policy he suspended the lot of them. District policy also required that before they could be sent home someone at the home had to be notified. Allen succeeded in reaching parents for all but one boy who happened to be black. As the child watched all his friends and former combatants leave, he became more and more upset at being kept in the principal's office. When he tried to leave and Allen restrained him, the boy bit him on the arm. Startled, Allen jerked his arm away, cutting the boy's lip in the process. The boy raced out of the office and Allen continued trying to reach someone at his home.

A few hours later the boy's mother showed up in his office with Alberta, both of them furious. As Allen put it, "I'd never been yelled at so thoroughly by two black women before. When they stopped for breath, I asked them if he had told them he bit me." Apparently the boy had neglected to mention that detail. When Allen explained exactly what happened and how the boy's lip came to be cut, both Alberta and the boy's mother agreed that he had acted entirely appropriately and stayed within district guidelines. Allen went on to achieve a good working relationship with both the mother and Alberta, something not all principals or administrators in the district managed to do.[30]

One who did was Corrine Hill, a white administrator in the Salt Lake School District. She described the racial situation in Salt Lake City in the 1970s as one of simple neglect rather than outright bigotry. As an example she recalled one of her earliest experiences with Alberta. Hill had prepared a pamphlet showing children in various situations—playing with other children, visiting with older adults, sitting in class and so forth. Alberta stormed into Hill's office with the pamphlet and said (with a good deal of emphasis), "You've done it again." When Hill asked the problem, Alberta showed her the various photographs used in the pamphlet and said, "Look at that. There is not a single black child—not a single child of any color except white." Hill immediately recognized the problem and apologized, adding, "I know how you must feel." Alberta exploded. No white person, she maintained, could possibly know how it feels to be constantly pushed aside, held back and dominated unless they had actually experienced the bigotry behind those actions. Hill's next project was far more inclusive, and she and Alberta became close allies.[31]

Alberta Henry's explosive reactions to the situation with Allen's student and to Hill's pamphlet demonstrate another of the difficulties some people had in dealing with her then and may account for their refusals to talk about her now. No one, whether they admire or despise Alberta Henry, denies that her approach was usually personal, forceful, and hands-on—which often meant that someone else's hands were moved off.

Alberta's tactics didn't change, but the situation in the district did. "By 1973 it was clear that Wiscombe did not enjoy the necessary support of the board. An executive session lasted until midnight apparently unable to reach a consensus as to whether Wiscombe should be retained as superintendent."[32] School board elections followed and several new members joined the board, but the makeup of the board had already been shifting significantly. In a 1971 meeting of members of the "Mexican-American community, including veteran teacher Robert Archuletta, a decision was made to organize a campaign to give the minority community a voice on the board." Their choice was Dr. Eugene Garcia, a PhD teacher at the University of Utah.[33]

Wiscombe submitted his resignation to the board on February 6, 1973. "In a sense, Wiscombe was a victim of the very revolution he had championed and which was engulfing America's urban school systems in the 1970s."[34] Wiscombe himself later said he was "caught up in a whirlwind of so many deep negatives that are so volatile, so political that virtually all [my] energies are burned up just dealing with fires and emergencies and the politics involved in these kind of situations."[35]

Ironic as was Wiscombe's falling prey to his own revolution, another irony came with the choice of his successor. On September 1, 1973, a much younger and all-Mormon Salt Lake City School Board hired as its new superintendent an Italian-born Catholic turned Methodist who had worked in areas from New York to California but had never been in Utah. Donald Thomas would serve until 1984 and proved to be one of Alberta's strongest allies.[36] Thomas, like Henry, was an outsider. One of the first things he recognized when he arrived in Salt Lake City was that Utahans of all races had very different experiences with other races than those he had known, which is to say, almost none. "I grew up in Chicago Heights, Illinois, where we had forty percent African Americans. I went to school with them. My debate partner was black, Willie Washington."[37]

Thomas's recognition of other people's unease with minorities helped in his support of Alberta Henry. It also altered the Salt Lake School District. His own ease with minorities was apparent in his first meeting with James Dooley, president of the Salt Lake Chapter of the NAACP.

> The first time that Jim Dooley came to me, he said, "Dr. Thomas, we've got eighteen demands."
>
> I said, "Let's write them all down."
>
> He wrote them all down. [They were] like, "We want three central officers and we want four principals and we want this . . ."
>
> And I said [*indicating he was pointing to the list*]: "Now Jim, this stuff right here is a bunch of nonsense and you know it and I know it. This stuff I think I can do." What another individual would have said was "Well, Mr. Dooley, I think these are good ideas, and I must give them due consideration." Or "I appreciate . . ." But if it's a bunch of nonsense, it's a bunch of nonsense.
>
> He put [out] his hand, and said, "Don, thanks. You're the first person that has treated me as a human being. You're the first person in Utah that has treated me as a man, rather than a black man." And I thought that was a very telling statement: that people either were intimidated by him or would try to be overly solicitous. He's just another human being. I would have done the same with anyone else that would have come in. But he was really a great asset to the district. He provided some of the training, did some of the workshops. He was a good man.
>
> The people here are good people; they are all very fine school people. They just did not know how to work with a black person. What they lack is any background and any experience in growing up with minorities, particularly blacks, and having any kind of social relationship. If you have grown up with blacks, played football with them, had them in your home,

it's a natural thing. But if you've never been with them and particularly if you've never worked with them, it was hard to adjust to being supervised by a black, particularly by a black woman. They were a little bit fearful that somehow she would do something to hurt the system but Alberta was a great asset to the district.

We had a system called optional instruction programs, where we put different programs within the various schools in order to attract more students to that school where the enrollment was declining.[38] We had an open education program. We had eight optional instructional programs at eight different schools, and they all attracted students. They all had a waiting list and that helped with the enrollment in those schools where they had declining enrollment. We had closed a lot of schools. Then also we opened up our school district to the other districts, Jordan and Granite, if any of them wanted to come. We had about three or four hundred students from those other districts coming to Salt Lake City.

But with minorities, you have to have outreach if you want them to get involved in education. They feel like they don't have the clothes; they don't know how to talk to teachers. But if you get a minority person who talks to them and tells them it's good to come to school, parent conferences, and so on, they feel more comfortable. The young lady that was at West did a good job in getting more of the minorities to come to the parent teacher conferences, open houses and that.

I enlarged [the minority consultant's] responsibilities, including staff development and also did some public relations and some training for principals. And that was not a very easy thing for the system to accept. The whites feared that the blacks were going to be too militant; people here have no idea of what militancy is. And the blacks always feel like they are not going to be told the truth or they are not going to be listened to, but with Alberta, I got instant credibility because she and I and Jim Dooley worked together and we devised staff development and Jim and I did consulting together, so it really worked out well.

We had the principals and administrators go out and eat soul food and we had them take Alberta out to lunch. I had one principal say, "I had lunch with Alberta. You know, she eats the same way we do," which is really a great revelation.

There was an occasion where we were at a conference, all the administrators, and Alberta said, "I hope that next year we have our conference at

> another place where I could get a cup of coffee and where I feel more free to do things that would be what I like to do."
>
> And one of the administrators, and he is one that I highly valued, I think he's one of the best people I've ever worked with, said, "Well, Dr. Thomas, I don't believe that any of the people here have prejudice toward the colored folk." And Alberta started to cry and she walked out. And he said, "Don, what did I do?"
>
> I said, "You didn't do anything, except we don't refer to them as 'the colored folk.'"
>
> He really did not mean anything. He just did not know. But she was hurt. I explained it to her and she was all right.
>
> One time Alberta visited a school and the principal called me and said, "Dr. Thomas, Alberta's here."
>
> I said, "Yes."
>
> And he said, "What should I do with her?"
>
> I said, "What would you do with any other visitor? She's a part of the district. Show her around. If I were to visit, what would you do?"
>
> Well he would introduce me to some classes, say hello to them—
>
> "Do the same thing with Alberta." Do you have to instruct a principal as to what to do with a central office visitor?
>
> But otherwise, after they had the staff development, and we ate together; we would go to conferences together, I think it worked out that they became very accepting of Alberta. Being able to work and see that Alberta is a human, just like I am, has feelings, gets hurt, has other children, the same way, I think they did become more sensitive to [other] minorities.[39]

There were a lot of people who didn't know what to do with Alberta at first, and a great many of them were very negative. Since Alberta's initial introduction to all the principals in the district had gone so badly, Thomas suggested the one-at-a-time approach.

So Dr. Thomas had to have all the principals meet me, first the elementary, two times and then he had Robert Archuletta to go along with me, because he was the only other minority there at the time, and ask them what was wrong and how they viewed me. And all the principals except three of them, even one in junior high school and one in high school and one in elementary said they were intimidated by me.

That hurt me, and I sat up and said: "Dr. Thomas, how can they be intimidated by a little black woman. I don't have any money. I don't have any prestige. I don't—"

And he said, "You've got to realize that you are important."

I said: "I don't. I give all my money away to all these projects."

He said: "It's not the money. You have integrity. People believe in you. You might be hard, but you are fair. Any time anybody has integrity and will speak out for justice and things, they are important."

But I can't see it. I still don't see it.

I didn't know what I was doing, but I went to all the supervisors with Dr. Thomas. You always go down and talk to them about it, mostly to develop things. I developed the parent-coordinating thing. I developed workshops that included black history, minority history and he came to one and he loved it so much that every workshop I did, I had to plan it around whenever he was in town because Dr. Thomas insisted on being with it. He became a part of the workshop; that always gave my workshops credibility with the white teachers.

Despite all that, Alberta recognized teachers could raise one substantive objection to her supervision: She had been given an honorary doctorate, but she had never earned a college degree in the usual fashion. Initially she questioned the need for one, but Donald Thomas knew better.

"They have a degree so a letter [diploma] was hanging up there [and she did not].

"Dr. Thomas said, 'Let's rectify that. You go and get the degree.'

"I said that I really didn't need it because the Lord gives me what I need.

"He said, 'I've proofed your record.'

"I didn't think that nobody knew that I had already applied for the university. I wanted to go and show my students, all of the students of the foundation: 'If I go and get an A or B, I expect you to get the same.'"[40]

Thomas knew that Alberta's lack of a college degree presented genuine obstacles to her credibility among the district personnel. He observed,

> Not all teachers and administrators appreciated her. The teachers knew she didn't have a degree. She got an honorary doctorate degree. Now after she got the honorary doctorate degree, people would say, "Well, that's not

> a real degree." And people thought maybe she was illiterate or something because she didn't have a degree, but she knew what she was doing.
>
> So I worked with Boyer Jarvis, the vice president [of the University of Utah]. I said to Boyer, they've criticized her because she doesn't have a degree. Let's get a degree. Let's use independent study, and they would give her the course and I would supervise the independent study. She got a legitimate degree through independent study and she also had the honorary doctorate degree. Now nobody could criticize her.[41]

In 1972, while in the process of earning her degree, Alberta met France Davis, then a graduate student and a teaching fellow at the University of Utah. Davis is black, born and raised in Burke County, Georgia. After graduation from Waynesboro High School he attended college at Tuskegee University in Macon County, Alabama. After his time there he joined the civil rights movement, marching with Dr. Martin Luther King. He "then dropped out of school, went into the military, during the Viet Nam days, spent four years there then got out, and returned to college in Oakland, California, at Berkeley and then graduated from University of California, Berkeley, Westminster, University of Utah, and Northwest Nazarene College."[42] In 1973 Calvary Missionary Baptist Church in Salt Lake City lost its minister and asked him "to fill in as pastor until they could find one."[43] He's still there, recognized by members of the congregation, the general public and the media as an outstanding force for any good cause in the area.[44] In 1983 when New Hope Baptist Church closed, Harold and Alberta Henry transferred their membership to Calvary Baptist Church, where they remained for the rest of their lives, serving in a range of positions.

Calvary Baptist Church "began in 1892 as a prayer group in the homes of the city's growing African-American community." For over a century it has "been a center of exuberant faith in Salt Lake City.[45] It was that exuberant faith, and the accompanying good works, that brought the Henry family to Calvary. As soon as Alberta had met France Davis, she recognized that he would be ideal to help in her good works, beginning with the youth at the Nettie Gregory Center.

I had Reverend Davis come over and talk about parliamentary procedure and holding meetings and how to be a good chairperson.

It was a new topic for most of the youth, but they found it fascinating and many of them eventually found it useful.[46] Henry continued to call on Reverend Davis for help. She called on him so frequently, in fact, years later he joked, "Every time I looked around, she continued to call—as though I had nothing else to do."[47] Davis apparently said "yes" to her frequent requests.

Alberta also reached out to black parents to listen to their ideas, but also to train them in the ways they could help their children in school. She conducted black parents workshops which included other races and often Salt Lake School District administrators as well. Recognizing the need to have administrators aware of what she was doing and to get both their input and support, her first meeting in September of 1974 was for the State Board of Education. The next in 1975 was at Magna Elementary, a school in Granite District; apparently Alberta's usefulness was becoming more widely known. In following years the meetings were held at Edison and Jackson Elementary Schools (1975), Northwest Intermediate (1976–1977), South High (1978), and both East and West High Schools (1979).

At the same time, she was creating help for students, she also provided tools for both parents and teachers: a black curriculum in 1978, a pamphlet titled *Parents' Rights and Responsibilities* in 1978 (revised and reprinted in 1982), a resource unit on Dr. Martin Luther King Jr. in 1979, a *Blacks in Utah* calendar in 1985, and *Contemporary Blacks in Utah* resource book in 1986. The book included information on black history in Utah, the Alberta Henry Education Foundation, and brief biographical outlines of outstanding Utah blacks, ranging from Dr. Afesa Marie Adams, associate vice president for academic affairs at the University of Utah, to Senator Terry Lee Williams, the first black elected to the Utah state senate. At the same time her value as a public speaker was becoming more widely known. By the mid-nineties she had filled more than five hundred speaking engagements. Her work with other groups, like the youth groups she had started, also contributed to local schools.

We helped parents to organize awareness trips for young people, so that they traveled to places both in the United States, to places like St. Augustine, Florida, and to places outside of the United States like New Zealand. We also worked together to organize a manpower training program called OIC, Opportunities

Industrialization Centers, which was a program designed to help people either in dead-end jobs or without basic education, minimal education and without job skills so that they could become self-supporting and self-sustaining. And so we worked together in terms of those. We then spent time with the state board of education making resources available to them, helping them to understand the importance and the need for broader education that included not only the majority but people of African American descent and others as well.

I brought the OIC in 1974 and I was chairman for twenty-four years here in Utah, and when the other chairman coming after Reverend Davis messed up, they called me from Phoenix, Arizona, and Reverend Sullivan made me the acting chairman to get it started [again], but I never could. For four years I did that.

Failure to restart OIC, holding a degree or not, Alberta was still having an impact in Salt Lake City schools. No one was more keenly aware of that than Donald Thomas.

> What Alberta was able to do that none of the other people could do was that if you had a problem with a black parent, even when the parent was totally irrational, Alberta could get that parent to understand. Where if we [white administrators] had dealt with that parent, they would just think we were racist, but Alberta would say, "Now let me explain to you the policies of the district, and let me explain to you why they made this decision." And she would bring the parent in and I'd talk to the parent and she'd be there. And there's a different dynamic when she's there than "You whitey, you don't understand." Alberta would say, "Now just a minute. This guy's OK." And she would be able to resolve a situation that we just would not have been able to resolve.[48]

Alberta's daily efforts on the front lines in the schools were clear to parents. Brenda Diaz talked about a time when her daughter was involved in fights at school. "[She] was always in trouble when she went to Roosevelt . . . and we lived right around the corner from it. I think [she] was about twelve and she stayed in trouble for a whole week, and Miss Alberta was up there every day that whole week, to see about her, never lost her temper, never lost her patience. It was like, 'Tanya, what am I going to do with you?' Trying to straighten things out with whoever she was having a problem with."[49]

Diaz went on to work with Alberta Henry in several community groups, including the NAACP, in several cases dealing with problems in the schools herself. But she knew "if anything was going on in the schools, what the problems were, connecting with the teachers, that we could adjust to make it better for them, and Alberta working with the school district, they always heard her because she was there to see what was going on with those children, if they were having problems, or whatever—she was there. That's a lot for one person to do, but she was dedicated to it, she was good at it, she was fair, she was an outspoken person and she was just not going to let some things happen."[50]

Brenda Diaz appreciated Alberta's concern for her daughter and her intervention on the part of other students. Many principals, however, viewed that kind of direct action as interference with their responsibilities, but Alberta often saw such a confrontational approach as necessary. Thomas observed that occasionally he still had to step in to back up her decisions as she began working directly in the schools.

> I have an Alberta story that very few people will believe. Alberta had a friend in the Granite School District. The friend had a child in kindergarten. The child had a fight with a white child in at the kindergarten level. The principal of the school called the police, had the black child handcuffed and taken to the police station. The mother called Alberta very upset. Alberta called me and said, "You need to do something, because the mother is very upset and they handcuffed the child and took him to the police station."
>
> I called and said to the principal, I understand that it occurred and that the child, the black child was taken to the police station, but not the white child.
>
> He said, "That's true, because the black child started the fight."
>
> I said, "You are dismissed. I'm firing you as a principal in the Granite School District."
>
> He said, "You can't do that."
>
> I said, "You're fired, and I want you to go to the district office and tell your superintendent that I have dismissed you as a principal of the Granite School District."
>
> Well, he went to Reed Call, and Reed Call called me. Reed was the superintendent [in Granite District] then. Reed said: "Don, what are you doing? You can't fire my principal."

> I said: "Reed, I have fired your principal for what he did, which was unjust and I want you and Alberta and the mother and the principal to get together and solve the problem. And after the problem is solved, I will reinstate the principal." And he did. He got them all together; they resolved the problem.
>
> Alberta [called on the phone from the meeting and] said, "Don, We've settled it and they've apologized to the family."
>
> So I said, "Put the principal on the line."
>
> And the principal said: "Hi, Dr. Thomas. I think we've got it settled."
>
> And I said: "I appreciate that. I am hereby reinstating you as principal in the Granite School District." And that was it.
>
> Reed knew that if they didn't settle it, they were going to have a big PR problem. Reed was a good superintendent and knew they were wrong. Had he known what was happening, he would not have permitted it. Reed is a wonderful human being. You can talk to Reed and we still are good friends. But I think that as a result of what we did in Salt Lake City, other individuals began to be more sensitive to minorities. It also was a time when we were getting an influx of other minorities, like the Tongans, we had other Polynesians and we had Russians. We had more Hispanics coming in. So I think what we did kind of set a tone for dealing more effectively with minority groups.[51]

Alberta knew she was easily recognized by parents, students, and teachers. She also knew that many of them appreciated what she was doing, but not all.

There was a teacher over there [Horace Mann Junior High], he won't forgive me to this day. He swore that I went after him and got him fired. I had no power at that school. He was going to take me to the board, but he never did.

The teachers would see me coming and they'd say, "Oh-oh, look who's here." Elementary, junior high, and high school, they'd go in a panic. And I'd come in smiling and just happy, because I made it a habit. Sometimes not even go in to do any work [at the office], just visit the schools. That's the only way that you can get the kids to know and stay in class, because they've got to see you. So sometimes five schools a day, that's what I'd do. Sometimes spur of the moment. Sometimes I'd get to work and they'd say, we've got a problem over at this school and I'd go over to that school. I had the reputation, she's tough, but she's fair, and word got around that I would go out of my way.

And the one that sticks out the most was at Riley Elementary. Two black students had been fighting and calling each other "nigger." And they didn't do anything about it. About a week later, two white students were against two black students and they were calling the black students "nigger." They wanted to expel the white students, and the [white] mother did not think it was right. "You call Alberta."

I didn't know about the black kids but she did. Her son had said: "They called each other that. I didn't see anything wrong with it."

And so I asked [the principal], "Now what did you do with the black students?"

"Well nothing. They said that they understood—"

I hit the table. "If it's not wrong for them to say it, then it's not wrong for him. It's wrong, but you have to help them understand it." I was jumping on them because they had to see that fairness went every kind of way. Where did the white kid get it from? By the time I left the board I had more white parents calling me to the schools than I did blacks.

There was another one but at Jordan Junior High School. I got an SOS at the superintendent's office. You've got to go to Jordan Junior High immediately. We've got fights going on and everything. So I rushed over there. The principal had all the kids that were in a fight—Hispanics, blacks and whites. They were all talking at once.

I said to the principal: "Can I get it quiet in here a minute? I want to know who was fighting. I mean the two that were actually fighting. That's what I want to know. I don't want all the little stories." I looked around. They wanted to tell their little stories. I didn't want to hear it.

It was a Hispanic and a white girl. The Hispanic said, "She told all the kids to come over by my house; she's going to beat me up later."

The white girl didn't say anything. "OK," I said to the white girl, "Why are you fighting?"

"So and so said she said so and so about me and so and so."

The other girl hit back, "But her friend said so and so."

I said, "Wait just a minute." I got my purse out and got two dollar bills out and I hand one to the white girl's friend and one to the Hispanic's. "Thank you. Was there anybody else?"

"Why do they—they didn't get hit." The whole group was really upset.

I said, "Any time anybody can just make a suggestion or tell a lie and get others to do the fighting and get others to get hurt, I'm going to pay them." The principal hasn't got over that yet.

But it made a lasting friendship. They had never heard anybody solve a problem like that. Years later the Hispanic girl started going with my son and used to come over to visit.

And when I left those school board offices, the people who wouldn't even speak to me, wouldn't shake my hand [when she first arrived] always said, "Oh, Mrs. Henry, you can't leave us because you help us solve all the problems." Any time anybody in that whole building had a problem, they came to me.

You'd be surprised how many times the board had problems and they had given it to an administrator, to a principal and months would pass and it would never get done. It wasn't my problem. I'm going around doing what I'm supposed to be doing and the board would have me called in.

The best one was right off of Fourth South and Eighth East. They had some land and they had a house there that they wanted torn down, a little house sandwiched in between, they needed it for the parking lot of a playground over there at that school. A woman lived there and she had lived there for years. She had a dog. They wanted that land but were supposed to relocate her and all the places they had would not take her dog—and she was not going to leave without her dog. Every time one of them went over there, she would open the door halfway with the screen locked and she would not let them in. This went on for a year and a half and the time was coming up that they had to start work because they were going to remodel that school and they needed that land. They said, "Get Alberta."

I said: "Oh, Lord. What is this?"

They said, "If you can go and talk to her and see what you can do."

So I went over and knocked on the door and said, "I'm Alberta Henry."

She said: "Oh, I read about you. Come on in." But they had told me she wouldn't let nobody in the house.

I sat down and said, "What is it?"

"I told them I'd be glad to move but they won't find a place that I can move with my dog. And I don't have a lot of money. They just want to get me there and I have to have some place that I can really afford."

So I knew it had to be someplace that was cheap. I said, "OK, I'll go to work on it."

"How much time are you going to give me?"

I said, "They said they need it right away."

She said, "You can take all the time you want."

I said, "Right on!"

I found the house. I went to several places. I looked at some things and talked to people. And I finally went down one of those dead-end streets. They had a dog run beside one of the places. I knocked on the door. Cupboards were falling apart; it needed painting in the kitchen. The man said he would rent it to her and she could bring her dog. I said: "OK, give us a month. I don't want her to move in."

I went back to the board and told them, "You have to have a man go in with the keys and you have to fix things and paint it and I have to come inspect it."

So I took her over and I said: "You see all the work that has to be done. I don't want you moving in until I get all that done."

She went out and saw that dog run around the side of the house. She was so happy. She said, "Will you call me?"

I said: "When they get that work done. They're not going to get off of that."

Oh, they were mad. "Why do we have to do that?"

I said: "You don't want to do it? OK, forget it. You don't want her to move, she'll stay there."

The superintendent came in and said, "You will send a crew over there." They did a very good job, but they didn't go over and beyond what they were supposed to do. I took her over. We both went over it. The cupboards weren't falling off. They had painted it. I thought they could do a better job, but she was happy and so they had to move her.

I'm glad I got that done. That was one of the toughest and the longest ones.

But I got tickled at them when West High School wanted to tear down the buildings and houses across from West High School and I think they put a parking lot across the street. Marshalls sold their house and another man sold his house. They boarded the building up but squatters got in there. They tore the boards off the windows and got in. There were two or three families; they had several kids. And the district officials went over there and they sent their lawyer over there. The squatters ignored them. And the police went over there, but you can't just put them out on the street; there's a law against that.

So you know what their answer was: "Get Alberta."

I said: "OK, when I go, who do I call? Can I call the lawyer?" He was a pompous ass kind of a man. I wanted him because he had alienated them so bad that when I came, they were so glad to see me.

"Oh, Mrs. Henry. Yes." My reputation by this time had exceeded me.

I think she actually knew that was a malapropism; she grinned broadly, but she didn't slow down.

I said: "I don't want you to move anywhere. Tell me what you want. I want you to tell me what you need." And of course they had to tell me what everybody had done to them.

And I said: "OK. Tell me what would it take you to leave here? You know you are going to have to leave sooner or later. What will it take? What do you want—not what they said."

"Well, if we had a place where we could stay until we got a permanent place and if we had maybe a week somewhere."

I said: "Right behind there, right down the street from West High is a little motel that rents rooms. OK if we can get that for you? And you all can have enough room, be nice and warm? Ok if we move there?"

"Yes. Enough for one week."

I said, "No, no, no, no." They looked at me, surprised. "Two weeks. They have a swimming pool there, too. Two weeks. I'll take your proposition back and I'll bring it back to you." I said: "No, I'm going to call. Let me go across the street over to West High and I'll call and have the lawyer come. He's the one that has to write up the thing."

He came. Now my thinking was he did not really care for blacks. Period. And he didn't want a black to do something he couldn't do. And his face was red. And I'm going to make him talk to me. I said, "For two weeks, and the board will pay and they will move out—tonight if you go down there and make arrangements for four rooms for two weeks."

It's funny he didn't have a heart attack. He didn't say more than he had to say. "Well, why can't we just do it for a week?"

I said, "Don't do it at all. I'm through."

"Wait! Wait! Wait! Come back."

"I have told you what I have negotiated. Now you want to re-negotiate something? You go ahead and do it." They weren't going to let him in. He did it and they came out and they shook my hand, hugged me. I picked them up from there and took them over to the motel.

But that was so much fun, watching the discomfort of that lawyer. And the board thought it was great.

That approval by the school board gave Alberta Henry so much credibility that she was frequently interviewed by various media about education and black issues. She was a regular guest on Jackie Nokes's daily local talk show on KSL TV. During one appearance she greatly enjoyed lobbing a bombshell into the conversation.

Alberta had lived in Utah for twenty-two years before she learned that Utah Territory had passed a law governing slavery. She felt angered that Utah was the only Western state to pass such a law and frustrated that the fact was not included in history books or encyclopedias. (It wasn't then; it is now.) She felt so strongly about this issue that she insisted that the entire text of the act be included in this book; it appears as Appendix C.

Nonetheless, she told the following story with great pride and delight—and a lot of outright giggles from both of us.

When I found out, I went on Jackie Nokes's program on channel five and they were asking me about coming to Utah and they wanted to know about the Alberta Henry Education Foundation, and I waited. When she said, "It's been so nice, Alberta, having you here and telling us about black history and everything."

I said: "I didn't tell you everything, because Utah was a slave territory. They had slaves." The fellow that was carrying things—they were closing up—he dropped the mike, and she said, "OK, goodbye—have to go."

And she ran over to me, and I'm sitting there, little devil, and laughing. Oh my stomach hurt, because I knew what I had done. I just wanted to get it in, but I didn't want to discuss it. "A slave territory." And I didn't say state: "Slave territory. They had slaves here." I shut up real quick. And that was the end of the program. They had to cut it off. I said, "I've got to go."

She said, "You've got to come back."

And I said, "OK. Call me at the office."

When I got back to the board I ran to my room and started laughing and shut my door. The switchboard lit up at channel five. Nobody could get in. Nobody could get out. People were calling and one or two of them—they were historians—and they wanted that woman—me—that woman, Alberta, not Mrs. Henry, that woman, they wanted her fired for getting on the air spreading lies. The switchboards at the board of education had lit up and nobody could get in. So channel two called Dr. Thomas, and they wanted me on. I'm sitting there laughing and Dr. Thomas walked in and said, "Now what have you got yourself into this time?"

I said, I said: "Nothing, Dr. Thomas. Can't you see my halo on my head?" I said: "All I did was wait till the very end of the show, Dr. Thomas, and I dropped a bomb and said Utah was a slave territory, and I can prove it by an act, a legislative act, a territorial legislative act."

Now, Dr. Thomas knew I never lied. I had the stuff. And he said: "This is really tickling you, but they want you to come before the board of education, but I'll tell the board what it is, so you don't have to worry about coming before the board. They are calling for your resignation, but I knew, knowing you, I knew that you were really enjoying this. Don't worry about it. But Alberta, you do have to go back."

I said: "I'm not worried. They're the ones worried." And I said: "I will come with the stipulation as long as you let me bring a historian, Dr. Ronald Coleman, because I got it out of The Peoples of Utah, *and I talked to him about it."*[52]

He said: "Fair enough. I'll set it up for you."

He called Dr. Coleman. He said, "Yes I would meet them."

So a few days later we went back. And Jackie Noakes said, "Well, she caused quite a stir and she's back here."

I said: "I'm back here, but I'm not back here to discuss it. I really think people ought to hear it from a historian, Dr. Ronald Coleman, assistant professor at the University of Utah" (I think he was at that time). And I said, "He is here and he will explain." Now, why? He is a man. They didn't say he is lying. The telephones didn't light up when he told them. And I'm sitting there [rolling her eyes, looking very smug] like a cat that ate his canary. I've had a ball doing that.

But the idea that historians did not know that and for a long time—I didn't know they had lynchings here. Helen Papanikolas told me that and showed me the pictures, and I said, "I want to put it in my lecture."

She said, "Oh, but they don't like you to talk about it."

I said, "Why, it did happen?"

And she said, "Yeah, but some of the people are still alive that were there at that time, and they'd be embarrassed."

And I said, "But how embarrassed was that man when they cut his fingers and cut different parts off him and kids watching—that was embarrassing."

She said, "I'm just telling you." So I just slip it in whenever the time was right.

She told that story in a way that would have made Jay Leno proud. By the end she was sitting there, with her arms folded on the table, gazing at the ceiling with a look of absolute innocence on her face, the archetypal picture of a kid who has just piled up old papers and given another kid the book of matches. By the end we were both laughing uproariously. Finally I asked if she had any qualms, as a good Christian, about enjoying other people's discomfort so much. Her reply was:

No. Really, I think the Lord wants us to enjoy ourselves. And I didn't say anything negative. Do you think the Lord would be displeased with me getting some enjoyment?

I observed that anyone who created the duck-billed platypus had to have a sense of humor.

I'm glad you said that, because the other day I said: "It gave me so much joy. I'm praying, Lord, please have mercy on me, but it gave me so much joy." And you do the same, come on.

She's right; I do. And both of us suspected that we were not alone in that.

While Alberta was putting out individual fires, she also looked for ways to change attitudes among both whites and minorities. She organized a women administrators' group in the district. Women had only begun moving into administrative positions at the time and she felt the mutual support was necessary. She also arranged for a trip on the Heber Creeper railway into the Heber valley for administrators before school began in the fall. It gave them all a chance to visit and become better acquainted in a completely neutral atmosphere.

Concerned though Alberta was with cooperation among district personnel, she was particularly concerned about the black students' negative views of themselves. In 1973, soon after joining the district, she established a black honor society to give young black students a source of pride and a goal to reach. She was shocked when people criticized the group as racist for being limited to black students. Jim Rock, who calls himself her "honorary son" and served as secretary-treasurer of the Alberta Henry Education Foundation, teased her, saying, "It was a great learning experience to see yourself as a racist."[53]

The group was quickly renamed the Rainbow Honorary Society and opened to all students. The organization was designed to improve students' self-esteem and to help each appreciate his or her own ethnicity. In the process it raised their educational prospects. In 1974 twenty-six students with a 3.5 grade point average qualified for the honor society and after that the number rose every year.[54]

Alberta recognized that students needed incentives to achieve good grades—college still seemed impossible to many of them—so she organized trips funded by donations and student projects. In order to go on one of the summer excursions students had to earn good grades (the honor roll was a real aim but not mandatory), always show up on time for classes and never get into any fights. The trips started modestly but eventually included some exotic places: Denver, 1973; Seattle, 1974; New Zealand, 1975. None was held in 1976 because Alberta was still repaying a loan she had taken out to cover the New Zealand venture. The trips resumed the next year with groups going to San Diego in 1977; Jamaica, 1978; Victoria, Canada, 1979; St. Augustine, Florida, 1980; Mexico City, 1981; Hawaii, 1982; Cancun, Mexico, 1983; Mazatlan, Mexico, 1984; Jamaica, 1985; Disneyland, 1986.[55]

While some people criticized the trips as too expensive and serving only a few students, Alberta countered that the costs were borne by the students, their families, and interested donors. Moreover, those few were setting the examples for others to follow and she saw good role models as one of the most critical elements in changing the attitudes of blacks about themselves. Occasionally she also discovered opportunities to educate the people they visited. In 1975 she served as a chaperone for twenty minority students during a tour of New Zealand.

I was working with kids from all kinds of backgrounds, all kinds of religious affiliations, taking them out of the United States. We'd be in Rotorua, New Zealand, and we'd be going to Hamilton or somewhere and we'd be waving goodbye and the friends we'd met, they would get on the bus with us and we'd say, "You know you said last night when we left you had to go to work."

"Oh, yes, we're going with you." They would ride with us there. They wouldn't bother to call. You'd get there in the meeting and you'd sit among the Maori there an hour or two—it didn't matter what the schedule said. Colored People Time means you're always going to be late. And I didn't want to be like that so I would always stay on time. Reverend [France] Davis is the same way. When he's there at our church, you'd better be on time or he'll get up and start it himself, because he believes in starting when he says he's going to be there. And that's the way I am.

The talk [to a local audience] was to be twenty minutes and ten minutes for questioning. Now, a room full of men, and I'm the only woman and the only black, so I was an oddity. And so I picked over the food as I usually do and tell them I can cut this down to fifteen minutes I don't need to talk for more. So I got up to start talking and a hush came over the room and I see some of them leaning. You know I talk loud anyway. So I said, "You have to realize this that in America blah, blah, blah." And they [in the United States] were still down where Stokely Carmichael said, "Burn, baby, burn," and the civil rights movement. And they [in New Zealand] were way back there [in the 1960s].

I took eighteen minutes by the clock and I said I am ready for questions. They kept me up there one solid hour with question after question. And I finally said: "I was given instruction that I was to speak twenty minutes and allow ten minutes for questions. Do you realize it's been forty-eight or forty-nine minutes by my watch?" Because I was wanting to get back to the food there.

They said, "Oh, we're sorry, we're sorry, but it was so interesting and we really want to know more." They still kind of asked me questions as I was going out the door, but I was really perturbed because I wanted to be with the students.

And when we were in Auckland and we were the guests of the Maori queen, and all the places we went, we would stop and stay with the Maoris. They have all the carvings all the way down and they have blankets on the floor—the same place Nixon went—so fascinating. I thought I'd never get used to it.

The first night there, I knew they were going to be tired because we'd only been in the air seventeen hours and we'd only stopped in Tahiti. And we were sleeping on the floor [a shake of her head]. We just had to take away the pillows and the blankets—you'd run and get yours and put your suitcase behind it. This was brand-new.

Alberta's daughter, Julia, was among the students who visited New Zealand. She recalled: "I'll never forget when she made me go to New Zealand. I didn't want to go to New Zealand because I looked at the map and I saw where the United States was here and New Zealand was clear on the other side of the world." But her mother said, "If I'm going to take kids to New Zealand, you're going to go with me, too." Julia went and "had the best time of my life. I didn't want to come back." She also learned: "We take a lot for granted here in America. Our amenities are so different. We stayed among the Maori people and we slept in a community center, on cots and on the floor. Over there you took cold showers. They had community bathing and it wasn't considered immoral if you had a male friend to shower with." She also noted that the Maori culture was so different. "It was a loving culture. They bonded together as families, very accepting. But the food, now that was another thing. There were some things I was exposed to that I couldn't eat. Abalone. Mussels. They'd just take right out of the ocean. You could find meats that you didn't quite know what they were. That's where we really learned how to eat tomato sandwiches, tomato cucumber sandwiches."[56]

Alberta enjoyed the trip as well, and she also learned things along the way.

We would sit up under the Maori sun two hours while they welcomed you. The women didn't speak; it was the men—they came to you, all the men. It wasn't hot; you didn't sweat, but one day sitting up there two hours I turned red. Kids came in sort of peeling after and they said, "We didn't know blacks could peel." And I started peeling. When I came home, I told my son, "See, I'm black and beautiful." That lasted about three months and then it wore off.

Then we went from Auckland to Wellington. And when we got to Wellington, the Altrusa Club, which I was a member of, had already wired the Altrusa ladies there. We were in a line to meet with the British somebody or dignitary and we had to wear formal gowns and stuff. I took a long skirt and blouse because you just don't have room for all that other stuff. But we all put it on and went through this line and had the meal and the general, whoever was the head of it, his wife was in charge of Altrusa. They came and got me and the next day they came to the Maori, and I went to one of their meetings and I went and stayed in the assembly hall. It was quite an experience. And then they wrote back here to this [Salt Lake City] Altrusa and said the Altrusa Club of Wellington, "We feel was honored to have as a guest Alberta Henry from Salt Lake City, Utah, and she graced the club and explained what the club was doing." So when I got back home and went to Altrusa meeting they had it there. And I was shocked. I always got shocked.

Since such opportunities were open to all students even though the sponsor was the Rainbow Honorary Society, backlash from the white community became minimal, but some people still felt minorities were being given too much attention and funding. Donald Thomas said that he was never criticized by the school board but he heard

> only occasionally from individual board members. They would say, "Don, you're doing too much for those minorities?" Occasionally, not too often, like when we had special programs for Hispanics, they'd say, "Do you think you should do all that? Shouldn't they have more initiative themselves?"
>
> Yes, they should have, but this is a special program to help. They never voted against any of my proposals. I never had a proposal for minority training or for workshops or for scholarships for black students refused.
>
> I think the general attitude was that the district is attempting to be fair and receptive to minority needs. And that became sort of a general attitude that was projected by Reverend France Davis, by Jim Dooley, by Ronald Coleman, by Alberta Henry.
>
> I became a life member of the NAACP. They gave me the Civil Rights Worker of the Year Award, so they knew that the leadership of the district and the people like Rafael Levy and Robert Archuletta, they could see we had a Jew, and we had minorities, we had Darlene Ball and Corinne Hill. They could see that we were trying to be more representative of the community. So it wasn't just one individual. The whole central office was perceived as being more favorable, or at least, honest and fair with minority people.[57]

Support for both Alberta Henry and Donald Thomas increased when the *American School Board Journal* included them in their annual list of the top one hundred educators in the nation. Thomas observed,

> Salt Lake City had more people in that category than any other district in the nation. We had three people identified two years being in the top one hundred, Alberta Henry, myself, and Gary Harwood. I was in the first year, when they identified the first one hundred and then Gary and Alberta were in the second or third year. So Alberta was in good company. We got a lot of publicity out of that. We did it because we wanted to be recognized as one of the best. In fact, the Ford Foundation recognized Salt Lake City as an urban district that works. I think the people were motivated to set up Salt Lake City as kind of a landmark district that was working well. We had good relations with the teachers. We had a good board of education. We had high achievement. We had a high attendance level. We really were doing some exemplary work as an urban district.[58]

All this while Alberta quietly continued taking classes at the University of Utah and in 1980, after eight years as one of the district's minority counselors, she received her bachelor's degree. Teachers and administrators could no longer complain that she was in any way unqualified for her job. She had also gained respect and credibility from her activity in the vast range of clubs and organizations in which she served. She felt that the situation for blacks in Utah was improving, but her chief frustration was the apathy of far-too-many people she knew, especially those from the black community.

"I decided that I should run for office so that I could teach people that you don't wait for the day of the election, that you have to go to the mass meetings. So I would have mass meetings at my house and they still didn't come. So I said that I would run for office.

"So in 1972 or 1974, I decided to run [for the Utah legislature in District Six]. After I got off of work from the board of education I would go out and visit the houses and say that the mass meetings are important. Now if I run and when it comes to your mass meeting, you run for delegate. Because if you can get 60 percent of them, they can't bring the thing of race in.

"I was running against another [woman] who had been the legislative chairman for years—an elderly lady. I knew that they were going to discriminate against me. When I put my material out in the stores, they would tear them and throw them away in the wastebasket. I am telling you this so that you know what it was like back then in Utah.

"Still, I got one lady and she was going to be a delegate for me. She paid her tithes in the [LDS Church] and they called her in because she voted for me and was a delegate for me. I cried for days. I loved that lady. She just said that I would make the best candidate, and the church they didn't, they didn't find anything wrong with Mrs. Henry. 'She has done a lot of good things but she doesn't belong to the church.' So that let me know where I was at and that I wasn't going to do it, so I almost 60 percented her. And I would have, but if one delegate didn't come, if they let her go in there while they were voting, change a vote, so I had all but one vote short of 60 percent, they could run a primary and then they could get a task force out. But that didn't bother me any.

"I didn't think the Lord wanted me in politics because my grandfather always said as long as you live don't ever be a politician. I never knew the reason why. It always worried me why my grandfather didn't want me to be a politician.

A missionary, go to Africa or somewhere, but a politician, no. He said that a politician had to lie and no liars are going to get into heaven."[59]

Her grandfather notwithstanding, Alberta had joined the Democratic Party in 1941 and worked with and for it from that time forward. She regularly held the mass meetings for her precinct in her house and attended the state conventions frequently. She again ran unsuccessfully for the Utah House of Representatives from legislative District Six in 1976. In 2000 the Utah Central Committee chose her to replace a delegate to the Democratic National Convention in New York where Jimmy Carter became the nominee. She said she was "greatly impressed with Barbara Jordan," a black representative from Texas who delivered the keynote address at that convention. Alberta was interviewed by television stations and showed up on the evening news. She said that publicity put the Utah Democratic Party in her debt and she "held those markers for years." But through it all she was frustrated by the strong white/Mormon majority, but even more by the apparent lack of interest and involvement from black and other minority communities.[60]

"I've been here twenty-one years, and I have the mass meeting [for her local Democratic Precinct] right here in my house every year. This year [1998], I said, 'This is my last time,' because I had it all the time. I was on the west side in Salt Lake because there's never any blacks. There's only whites. There's never any Native Americans, Asians, or anything. They're all white. Only one time, during election time, I think it was the election with the last president, Clinton. No, it was before that, we had a whole house full of people in here, but no blacks. So to me, my grandkids are not growing up in a black community. All their friends are white."[61]

Frustrated though she was, Alberta kept up her busy schedule with a range of groups. She continued to work with Model Cities representing both the schools and the black and other minority communities. She still served on the boards or as an officer in dozens of other organizations, including the NAACP. She had long been involved in the NAACP, but during the last few years that involvement had become intense and she was getting old. In 1986 she retired from the Salt Lake School District. She recalled that when she was hired there she had been greeted with feelings ranging from skepticism to hostility, but that attitude had changed.

When I left those offices, the people who wouldn't even speak to me, wouldn't shake my hand always, said, "Oh, Mrs. Henry, you can't leave us because you help us solve all the problems." Any time anybody in that whole building had a problem, they came to me.

Harold J. Trussel, who had met Alberta when he was principal of Horace Mann Junior High, reflects her opinion in a letter he wrote to her years later: "I would also like to express my appreciation to you for the things that I learned from you which I believe have made a difference in my administration. You have always been a wonderful example. You, as you are aware, have done much to promote equal opportunities for all students. It was always a pleasure for me to work with you at Horace Mann and now at the Salt Lake City Community School. We had many enjoyable times together. Through all of the laughter and fun, there was much knowledge I was able to gain from you. As I pass your picture in the hallway, I oft times whisper an audible 'thank you.'"[62]

Alberta continued to be concerned about schools long after she left them. Years later as we were talking about her experience in Salt Lake City School District, she observed several problems schools were still having. She felt that the results of those shortcomings were having a negative effect, especially the jobs students were capable of taking and the kind of work they would produce. She was not happy with what she was seeing.

My granddaughter is going to school. She never brought her book in; she used a book with somebody else. The kids don't have all their materials. Did you know that? In our schools in Utah they don't have books. They have to use them over and over again, and they don't have enough because they have so many kids. So, I think they need to take that money and put it into supplies and things. I feel sorry for some of the teachers, because they use their own money to buy supplies. So I say pay the teachers enough and go back to the basics so that the kids can write.

I go to the stores and I would be appalled. They're working but they can't do anything unless they got running things [computers or cash registers]. And I'd already figured it out in my head one day, so I gave the lady, I said, "This is too much money." "Oh, no it's not." She got on her little calculator. I said: "I'm just being honest. I really shouldn't argue with you. Take a paper, a pencil and figure it out. You've given me too much money and you're going to come up short. If it was anyone else I'd just say, 'Heck to it, it's mine.' But I can't take your money." I said, "Call somebody else over." So they called this other man.

"Are you having a problem, Ms. Henry?" because they all know me.

"I'm just trying to give her money back. She gave me too much money."

And he said: "That's right, she did. A dollar and something too much." They can't figure unless they got a computer. They don't ask them to use their heads.

Retired though she might be, Alberta did not slow down. From before the time she went to work in Head Start, she had served in the Salt Lake Chapter of the NAACP. Now it would become her full-time job.

CHAPTER 7

THE NAACP

Fighting the Good Fight

The National Association for the Advancement of Colored People (NAACP) has been fighting for equality among citizens of the United States, or at least, greater degrees of equality, ever since its inception in 1909, but *Plessy v. Ferguson* had legitimized segregation in the United States in 1896. Segregation was used extensively throughout the South, overtly denying black Americans their basic rights of citizenship. At the same time throughout the North and West, equality was fostered, both genuine and pretended, however much actual bigotry might remain. Nonetheless exhibitions of racial hatred simmered across the country and occasionally boiled into public view in the North as well as the South. One of the most startling incidents occurred in Springfield, Illinois, during the summer of 1908. Two days of rioting involved many of the city's "best citizens." Scores of blacks were killed or wounded and thousands driven from the area. While minorities throughout the country had long chaffed under various forms of imposed inequality, the frequently murderous attacks that were common in the Deep South were seldom known beyond their borders. Consequently the ferocity of this public display of racial hatred in the home of Abraham Lincoln sent shock waves through the country.[1]

Soon after these riots William English Walling wrote in the New York City *Independent*: "Yet who realizes the seriousness of the situation, and what large and powerful body of citizens is ready to come to their aid?"[2] That large and powerful body came into being a few months later. During the first week in January 1909 a multiracial group of activists met in New York City to discuss possible options and to create an organization that could implement actions to deal with both legal and de facto segregation. The result was the National Association for the Advancement of Colored People. While "colored" was the polite term for blacks at the time, the organizers also hoped to extend help to other groups including recent immigrants. The mission statement of the NAACP clearly shows its concern for equality among all peoples. The organization would work "to secure the political, educational, social, and economic equality of rights of all persons and to eliminate race-based discrimination."

> **Vision Statement**
>
> The vision of the National Association for the Advancement of Colored People is to ensure a society in which all individuals have equal rights without discrimination based on race.
>
> **Objectives**
>
> The following statement of objectives is found on the first page of the NAACP Constitution—the principal objectives of the Association shall be:
>
> - To ensure the political, educational, social, and economic equality of all citizens
> - To achieve equality of rights and eliminate race prejudice among the citizens of the United States
> - To remove all barriers of racial discrimination through democratic processes
> - To seek enactment and enforcement of federal, state, and local laws securing civil rights
> - To inform the public of the adverse effects of racial discrimination and to seek its elimination
> - To educate persons as to their constitutional rights and to take all lawful action to secure the exercise thereof, and to take any other lawful action in furtherance of these objectives, consistent with the NAACP's Articles of Incorporation and this Constitution.[3]

The organization was officially inaugurated on Abraham Lincoln's centennial birthday, February 12, 1909. Oswald Garrison Villard, grandson of abolitionist William Lloyd Garrison, announced the organization in his New York *Evening Post*.[4] Among the signers of the statement were professors, ministers, rabbis, and prominent writers and social activists including Jane Adams, William Lloyd Garrison, William Dean Howells, Lincoln Steffens, and W. E. B. DuBois, who became the group's first president. The organization's tactics included making speeches, lobbying, and publicizing the issues raised by inequalities. Deciding they needed their own publication to present their case, the NAACP launched a magazine, *Crisis,* named for Walling's favorite poem, "The Present Crisis" by James Russell Lowell.

The NAACP leaders soon became involved in case law to help fight institutionalized segregation and discrimination, much clearer targets to attack than individual or social prejudice. They looked for practices enforced by what were known as Jim Crow laws. Then they aimed at laws with inherent inconsistencies or other flaws that could demonstrate the sheer foolishness of Jim Crow laws. In 1914 their first case came before the court in the *McCabe v. Atchinson, Topeka & Santa Fe Railway*. The case involved an Oklahoma law that required separate but equal railroad coaches, one for whites and another for blacks. That concept had been upheld in *Plessy v. Fergusson*; however, the Oklahoma law excepted luxury units such as parlor, dining, and sleeping cars. They could be used by either race, but not jointly. Since few blacks had the funds for these services, railroads used the law to avoid providing separate black facilities for eating or sleeping. The court ruled in favor of *McCabe* and noted that separate facilities must be available and equal whether use was probable or not. Adding those extra cars would cost the railroad dearly. Years later, Garrett Epps argued that, "Without *McCabe*, the road to *Brown v. Board of Education* would have been much harder."[5]

Brown v. Board of Education came in 1954 from Alberta's hometown of Topeka. Following a long series of cases filed by the NAACP, it demonstrated both the stupidity of and the damage caused by racial segregation, and it would force the entire nation to examine itself in ways it never had before. Since Topeka had institutionalized segregation, de facto segregation, and complete integration all living side by side, both black and white citizens could see models for all three alternatives. Oliver Brown not only recognized the possibilities, he used them. Brown was a welder for a railroad and after hours an assistant pastor in his church. In the early 1950s he had no history of civic or racial activism; he simply recognized a problem in his daughter's education.

The family home was close to the railroad where he worked, the neighborhood bordering on a major switchyard. So his children could reach their segregated school only by threading the dangerous path through the trains on those tracks. When his daughter Linda was about to enter third grade, Brown took her to a school only seven blocks away and accessible through a much safer passage. The principal there refused to accept a colored child in a whites-only school no matter how much safer or more sensible it might be for that child. So Brown turned to McKinley Burnett, head of the local branch of the NAACP.[6]

Burnett recognized that a case like Linda Brown's could test the validity of the separate but equal laws upheld by *Plessy v. Fergusson*, and he had a particularly appealing eight-year-old client to do it. On March 22, 1951, the NAACP filed a case against the Topeka Board of Education on behalf of Linda Brown. Their argument illuminated the inherent inequality of separation asking, "Does segregation of children in public schools solely on the basis of race . . . deprive the children of the minority group of equal educational opportunities?" In addition the legal argument also cited the demeaning effect on children's psyches: "if colored children are denied the experience in school of associating with white children, who represent ninety percent of our national society in which these colored children must live, the colored child's curriculum is being greatly curtailed."[7]

The case worked its way through the judicial system to the United States Supreme Court. On May 17, 1954, Chief Justice Earl Warren announced the court's unanimous decision that segregation of schools violated the equal protection clause of the Fourteenth Amendment declaring "that to segregate black schoolchildren from others of similar age and qualifications solely because of their race generates a feeling of inferiority as to their status in the community that may affect their hearts and minds in a way unlikely ever to be undone. Segregation with the sanction of law, therefore, has a tendency to retard the educational and mental development of Negro children."[8] Kansas school districts dropped their restrictions fairly quietly. Since most Northern and Western schools had no laws on the books requiring segregation, many simply took note and moved on. Some, however, like the Salt Lake City School District, began a systematic examination of their policies. Alberta Henry was very glad to see that done.

Government agencies in both individual states and the nation began trying to find ways to allow all citizens equal access to services. In 1957

President Dwight Eisenhower "sent Congress a proposal for civil rights legislation. The result was the Civil Rights Act of 1957, the first civil rights legislation since Reconstruction. The new act established the Civil Rights Section of the Justice Department and empowered federal prosecutors to obtain court injunctions against interference with the right to vote. It also established a federal Civil Rights Commission with authority to investigate discriminatory conditions and recommend corrective measures."[9]

While most states at least attempted to create better learning circumstances for all students, in the Deep South, federal intervention and armed troops were required to end segregation in schools and other public facilities. Little Rock (Arkansas) High School was integrated in 1957 only after Eisenhower activated the National Guard and ordered them to protect all students.[10] The violence directed at black students and their supporters and the hatred evident among crowds of segregationists around the school appeared in television news broadcasts that shocked the world and demonstrated the moral core of the civil rights cause.

The impact of the *Brown* decision spread to other areas. Segregated bus service, similar to that on trains upheld by *Plessy v. Ferguson*, existed throughout the South: whites could sit in the front section of a bus while blacks were required to sit in the back. If the bus was full, blacks on the rows closest to the front were required to give up their seats to whites, regardless of age or disabilities of either party. That practice was sometimes challenged by black individuals, including Rosa Parks, longtime activist in the civil rights movement. She had joined the NAACP in 1943 and served as secretary, a voter-registration worker, advisor to the youth council, and several other positions. Beginning in the 1940s "she had refused on several occasions to comply with bus-segregation laws, frequently enough that some bus drivers recognized her on sight and simply refused to stop for her."[11] In 1955 she boarded a bus in Montgomery, Alabama, and took a seat in the "colored section." As the bus moved along picking up more passengers, both the colored and the white sections filled. When a white woman boarded the now fully packed bus, Parks was asked to give up her seat so that the white woman could sit down. She refused. She was arrested and put in jail. In protest, local blacks organized a boycott that firmly established the bus system's dependence on their black ridership. The man chosen to lead the boycott was a relatively new minister in the area, Dr. Martin Luther King Jr.[12] As the tactical and spiritual leader of the movement, King and his followers advocated nonviolence, the kind of passive resistance that Mahatma Gandhi had used to free India from British colonial rule. At the same time he noted the need to actively protest unjust laws however pacifist the tactics might be. In time they were joined by other groups, notably the Congress of Racial Equality (CORE).[13]

The idea of nonviolent action spread. In 1958 Barbara Ann Posey, a member of the Oklahoma City NAACP Youth Council, led a sit-in that desegregated five stores. In 1959 CORE members held a sit-in at the lunch counter at W. T. Grant's department store in Miami, Florida. Support for the cause grew. Despite the success of such ventures, and despite the courage of the people who participated, these quiet individual events drew only modest press coverage and most of America was still unaware of just how widespread and demeaning segregation really was. That changed the next year in Greensboro, North Carolina, when Joseph McNeill, Ezell Blair Jr., Franklin McCain, and David Richmond, four freshmen at the North Carolina Agricultural and Technical College, entered a variety store and sat down at the whites-only lunch counter. Despite being refused service, they remained until the store closed and announced they would be back the next day. A local radio station picked up the story. Others joined the students, and within a week Greensboro's downtown lunch counters were packed daily with young blacks, most of them students. They agreed to stop demonstrating when city officials finally agreed to negotiate. Those negotiations proved to be useless since the white city council refused any degree of compromise, so the students returned to sit at lunch counters. Forty-five were arrested on charges of trespassing, resulting in a massive boycott of the targeted stores, even though, in many cases, the stores were simply abiding by the local laws. Similar sit-ins flourished across the South, generating extensive media coverage that affected attitudes across the nation.[14]

In 1961 CORE leader James Farmer chose a target and a tactic that he was certain would draw in the media. While buses and all ancillary services—terminals, restrooms, dining areas, and drinking fountains—were integrated throughout most of the country, in the South they remained segregated. Farmer asked for volunteers, both black and white, to board buses in the North and ride into the South. Blacks would then attempt to use white facilities, and whites would use those designated for "blacks only." They would doubtless be arrested, but if enough came, they could quickly overcrowd the jails and in the process bring the nation's attention to the injustices of segregation. The freedom riders began in April with training in Ghandi's passive resistance. As they traveled into the south, they discovered that the signs designating "colored" and "white" had been removed in some terminals. When they reached Rock Hill, South Carolina, on May 9, however, they were attacked by a large group of whites while the local police simply stood by and watched. Similar and far worse incidents occurred in other Southern bastions of racism, and the national media began showing the entire country the brutality by which segregation was enforced. By the time the group reached Birmingham, Alabama, crowds of attackers were standing by to beat, kick, club, even burn the riders. Police were nowhere in sight, and when Police Commissioner Eugene "Bull" Connor was asked why they had not come to the scene of so obvious an assault, he replied that they had all been visiting their mothers since that Sunday was Mother's Day. The horrifying pictures of the assaults appeared around the world, finally forcing the White House to intervene. President John F. Kennedy proposed a civil rights bill, but when he was killed in Dallas on November 22, 1963, its passage became the purview of his successor Lyndon Banes Johnson.[15]

The succeeding years of the 1960s became rife with violent clashes and civil unrest, in which anger over the Vietnam War became merged with demands for civil rights. Riots broke out in several major cities. From April 11 to 17, 1965, the Watts area of Los Angeles became a war zone resulting in thirty-four deaths and $40 million in damage.[16] During the summer of 1967, race riots erupted in more than one hundred American cities, especially in the inner city ghettos. A riot in Newark lasted six days, left twenty-six people dead and fifteen hundred injured. In Detroit a week-long riot left forty-three killed, two thousand injured, and five thousand homeless. The violence did not end until President Lyndon Johnson sent in nearly five thousand army paratroopers.[17]

Utah avoided any real riots but stories abounded of possible attacks. Polly Stewart, a University of Utah student at the time, had spent the summer of 1964 working in New York City. When she returned home to Salt Lake City, her mother, who worked at the Salt Lake City Library, told her stories were circulating that local blacks had been buying cake picks and that they planned to use them as weapons. Polly said, "There were also some stories about the west desert—but I don't remember the details."[18]

Nonetheless, most Americans, regardless of race, saw patient negotiation and, if necessary, legal actions, as espoused by Martin Luther King and other national leaders, as more effective ways to guarantee genuine civil rights. Both blacks and whites from across the nation traveled to the South to work with voter registration drives and integration of public facilities. Equally important but never so widely publicized were the efforts by many others who recognized the far-more subtle forms of discrimination and even segregation in their own areas. Alberta Henry was among those who worked for change in the small corner of the world where she knew the Lord had brought her.

And the world did change. In 1952, just two years before the *Brown* case, "only 15 percent of blacks over age 25 were high school graduates. . . . By 2002, that number had grown to 79 percent. The number of black college graduates has risen from about 252,000 in 1957 to 3.5 million in 2002." The *Brown* decision "forever changed our view of what it meant to aspire to an equal and just society."[19]

Much of that change in Utah was encouraged by the local chapters of the NAACP. The Salt Lake Branch had been organized on February 10, 1919, just ten years after the national NAACP. Reverend George W. Harts served as its president.[20] Alberta Henry first became involved with NAACP Salt Lake City Branch early in the 1960s, especially while she was working with the Head Start program. She had not joined it earlier because so many local blacks felt the organization did not help them in the rudimentary kinds of things they needed most—like getting jobs. Volunteering in such an organization often involves many hours of work and frequently draws the ire of both insiders and outsiders. Betty Sawyer, who served as president of the Ogden Branch of the NAACP for four years observed, "If you're not a die-hard, you'll do it for a year and then stop." During her tenure Sawyer "endured criticism from inside the black community and discrimination from outside of it. And people always wanted her to do more."[21]

Alberta Henry was always ready to do more, Dr. Ershler's warnings notwithstanding. In 1980 while she was still working full-time for the Salt Lake School District and active in forty other organizations, Alberta was elected president of the Salt Lake Chapter of the NAACP with Wilfred Bocage as vice president. She was the first woman to serve in that position. She had worked with the NAACP for years in a range of activities and responsibilities and one of her chief concerns with Salt Lake City was that there was not an identifiable black community as there had been in Topeka.

I had forty or so agencies that I was on boards with all at one time. It wouldn't have been bad, but I was chairman of several of them. I was chairperson of the Utah and Idaho Baptist Association. Then I had the Alberta Henry Education Foundation. And then I was also the chairman of the Governor's Black Policy Council when Governor Rampton brought that in. And then that's where we heard of OIC [Opportunities Industrialization Centers] and I thought it ought to go in Ogden because there were more black people in Ogden because of the railroad.

"At that time I was the youth advisor in the NAACP, and we had over one hundred students and I would take them to Asilomar, California [a conference center near the beach on the Monterey Peninsula]. See, the black folks were somewhere else and everybody kept saying, 'You ought to run for president.' And I said, 'I'm backing Jim Dooley.' Finally, when Jim Dooley said he wasn't going to run again, then he said, 'You should run.' So I did run, and we won, and there were no people hardly there. I don't think over eight or nine people were still coming to the meetings. There was no money. So Mr. Lanorst Bush took the foundation and we started building on the NAACP.

"I've done a lot of the committees and all the different groups under Jim [Dooley], but Jim took credit for them, and that's rightly so because he was the president."[22]

Brenda Diaz, who also worked with Alberta helping children through the NAACP, greatly appreciated what she was doing to help minority youth. "I was the outreach worker and I was the youth advisor. We had a youth group and got them involved in activities like getting to know people for your arts, crafts, information, being able to mingle, being able to talk about your ethnic background, that sort of thing ... to be able to connect with their black ethnic background.... My thing was getting information to the children in schools, giving their moms information about what college was available and getting scholarships all over the United States and getting jobs."[23]

Given all her experience and her long list of allies, Alberta entered the position of president of the Salt Lake Branch with several priorities. She was deeply concerned that the organization observed all proprieties, to ensure its credibility with members, media, legislators, and the general populace. Remembering what she had observed in Esther Landa's chairing of meetings and what she had learned from Daily Oliver, a lawyer for the Utah-Idaho Baptist Association, and Reverend France Davis about parliamentary procedure, she was particularly careful in handling discussions and making decisions. She was scrupulous about clearing all proposals and financial questions with the board of directors and established protocols to give the organization stability and maintain that crucial credibility.[24]

"One of the things I wanted to build on was accountability and accessibility—accountability mostly: that we were accountable to the people to see the things and help the people here in Utah. We were having a lot of problems.... There was nobody that was working with them. So, that was what mostly what my thing was. It wasn't national NAACP, because I didn't see what national was doing for us. They didn't come in here and fight our battles for us."[25]

Other blacks, individually and as groups, were also keenly aware that they needed to take part in public discussions. Reverend France Davis observed that he and members of his congregation

> are actively involved in the political system but never involved in the partisan politics. We believe that the laws that are passed, that the ordinances that govern our community impact upon this church and its members and that we ought to be actively participating in that process. Where partisan politics are concerned, we encourage people to run for office; we never tell them what party to run for nor do we provide them with any kind of endorsement for whatever it is they are doing.
>
> Our involvement is in those things that impact upon the lives of the members and on this congregation. When Congress passed the Martin Luther King holiday bill, Alberta and I and others got Utah to agree that they would keep the Martin Luther King holiday bill too. There was a time when taxation was being imposed on some nonprofit facilities like churches and some others it was not, so we got actively involved, took a stance, and got that reversed. So whatever affects people and causes them to hurt economically, politically, socially, or otherwise, we get involved and take a stance.[26]

So Alberta Henry took a stance, actually, she took lots of stances. Hard as she worked to establish credibility, she worked harder still to overcome the remaining vestiges of racism in the community. "We cannot afford to view the civil rights movement as a phenomenon of the sixties and seventies," she said in 1991. "Instead, we must view civil rights as what they are—a fundamental guarantee of equal citizenship for all Americans."[27] She recognized that equal citizenship required equal recognition, something she did not always find forthcoming. For example in 1983 when the United States Congress declared the third Monday in January to be Martin Luther King Jr. Day, the Utah state legislature, like several others across the country, opted for a more generic name, Human Rights Day, and even that was not particularly observed. Public offices, for example, remained open. Alberta and other black leaders in Utah recognized the need for a holiday specific to black Americans, so they threatened a lawsuit to make Martin Luther King Jr. Day a true celebration for all citizens.[28] To both protest and publicize the issue, Alberta refused to speak at Salt Lake Community College on Martin Luther King Jr. Day on Monday, January 16, 1989, when all classes were held on their regular schedules. Instead, she spoke a few days later, noting her objections to business as usual on the declared holiday. Her actions raised a ruckus. She said the flap made her feel as though she were part of a soap opera.[29]

Many local blacks agreed with her. They felt that a generic name and business as usual meant inadequate observance of something very important to them. Many, probably most white Utahns, however, could not understand why anyone was so insistent on calling the holiday after the slain black leader. After all, Human Rights Day certainly covered the principles for which King had fought. Those good citizens simply did not realize that while the entire community happily joined in celebrations that Asian and European immigrants had brought with them—Columbus Day or Kite Day or Saint Patrick's Day—even if government and business offices remained open, blacks had no holiday that they could claim as their own.[30] Their ancestors had, after all, been kidnaped and shipped to America, cut off from the customs and celebrations of their homelands, unlike voluntary migrants who brought the customs, traditions, and even recipes of their ancestors with them.

Like many Utah blacks Wynetha Bridgewater, who had grown up in Salt Lake City during the 1940s and 1950s, felt very much at home in her own neighborhood in southwestern Salt Lake City, but she joined in the wider city activities as well. Her family attended Twenty-Fourth of July parades and recognized the shared heritage of all Utahns with those early Mormon pioneers. Nonetheless during her childhood there were no minorities represented in the parade, so she felt only a limited connection. Although she enjoyed celebrations based on other cultures, she wanted one of her own. When Congress declared Martin Luther King Jr. Day, she was glad and grateful that her heritage finally had its own holiday.[31]

While Utah was not alone in its lack of observation of the King holiday, many black Utahns still felt an extra level of discrimination. Not only was the state predominantly white, it was also predominantly Mormon and for many years the LDS Church had maintained a policy blacks, and many others, felt was fundamentally racist. The church as an organization had denied its priesthood to any male of black African descent while granting it to men of all other racial and ethnic backgrounds. That had not always been the case, earlier in LDS Church history, and the policy bothered a lot of people, both within and without the church itself.

During the beginnings of the LDS Church in the 1830s and 1840s, when slavery was still legal but the abolition movement was growing, several free blacks had joined the LDS Church. While some white LDS members agreed with the extreme Northern abolitionists like William Lloyd Garrison in demanding slave owners instantly free their slaves with no compensation, Joseph Smith, first prophet and president of the church, was probably more a gradualist but was decidedly in favor of slavery's demise.[32] Black LDS members apparently recognized Smith's intent. Jane Elizabeth Manning James, a free black woman from Wilton, Connecticut, converted to Mormonism along with her family in the early 1840s and traveled to the LDS headquarters in Nauvoo, Illinois, by foot since blacks were restricted from many forms of public transit in the Northern states. When Jane and her family arrived in Nauvoo, they stayed for a time with Joseph and Emma Smith. James described Smith as "the finest man I ever saw on earth."[33]

Whatever their personal feelings on slavery or abolition, the Mormons welcomed blacks into their religion and initially the priesthood was granted to all worthy males regardless of race. "During the first two decades of the Church's existence, a few black men were ordained to the priesthood. One of these men, Elijah Abel, also participated in temple ceremonies in Kirtland, Ohio, and was later baptized as proxy for deceased relatives in Nauvoo, Illinois. There is no reliable evidence that any black men were denied the priesthood during Joseph Smith's lifetime. In a private Church council three years after Joseph Smith's death, Brigham Young praised Q. Walker Lewis, a black man who had been ordained to the priesthood, saying, 'We have one of the best Elders, an African.'"[34]

Because there was no official statement of the reasons behind the priesthood exclusion other than that it was pronounced by prophets as ordained by God, many people both inside and outside the LDS community speculated as to why a specific race was denied the right to hold the priesthood. Despite this discriminatory policy, many blacks remained strong members for several reasons. Their roots in Christian fundamentalism made them acquiescent in accepting the doctrines and the self-reliance, unity, and independence from outside institutions which were mirrored in the Mormon Church.[35]

Nonetheless, given the unspecified reasons for the priesthood restrictions, Mormons who were prejudiced against blacks, whatever their own individual reasons, could easily believe they had a valid religious reason to maintain such judgments and did not feel it necessary to view or treat blacks as equals.[36] Although such a policy probably suggests extremely poor treatment for blacks, it apparently had far less impact than might be assumed. After extensive study Ronald Coleman concluded that "The bigotry and discrimination encountered by blacks in Utah was no more severe than in other Western states between 1847 and 1910. Belief in white superiority and black inferiority was generally shared by Mormons and non-Mormons alike."[37]

Over the years several Mormon leaders had opined that such restrictions would be lifted. In 1852 Brigham Young had said, "time will come when they will have the privilege of all we have the privilege of and more."[38] That time came on June 9, 1978, when LDS President Spencer W. Kimball announced that henceforth the priesthood would be given to all worthy male members, regardless of race.[39] The local media immediately approached Alberta for a comment.

"I was sitting at the board of education, and the newspaper—I don't know why all of them [reporters] always like me—it just hit me. And the switchboard would always put them through really quick. They always wanted to get what I felt as

a president of the Alberta Henry Education Foundation: 'Kimball is having a revelation, and we wondered what you've got to say.' I would say, 'You don't know what I'm saying. He's saying it's for men. I'm a woman.' And by that time you heard it over the radio, and everybody was all, 'What did Alberta Henry think about it?' I said, 'I'm not going to make any statements; I'm not a man. He didn't say a revelation said let the women in. Now you can call me back when he do that, will you?'"[40]

I told Alberta she knew perfectly well why they called her, and she grinned, but she stuck by her answer. She had long recognized the need for black Utahns to be an integral part of the larger society around them. She repeatedly said she had joined so many civic and service organizations, serving as an officer in several of them, in part,

Just to let them see a black face.

And now that the restrictions on the LDS priesthood had been lifted and Alberta could see far more black faces in both that church's membership and leadership, she recognized it had removed any implication that Mormons officially denigrated blacks.

So, in the late 1980s, she decided it was time to tackle the elephant, if not in the living room, at least in the city. She went to the LDS Church offices, walked in the front door and asked to speak with someone about the possibility of a closer working relationship between the church and the local black community. She was directed to Stuart Reid, at that time a member of the church public relations staff. She explained what she wanted and Reid noted that church officials, especially Gordon B. Hinckley, then a counselor in the church's First Presidency, felt the need to reach out to create more harmonious community relations. Reid introduced Alberta to Hinckley and the two became fast friends.[41] Alberta confirmed that statement. She observed in several of our visits that any time she called, if he was in the office, he took her call immediately. She spoke very fondly of her respect and affection for him.

Alberta also became friends with Reid. She invited him to attend a meeting of the Board of Directors of the Salt Lake City Branch of the NAACP, even to consider serving on that board, and he agreed. He went to the next meeting and sat there listening as board members discussed him in the third person. They debated the value of adding him to their group, some arguing against his inclusion by saying, in effect, that he had not paid his dues to local blacks. Reid recalls it as a "very uncomfortable experience," but acknowledged to the board that he had not to that point spent much time in the black community. Some board members asked why an alliance with the LDS Church was needed, so Henry argued strongly that it would be advantageous to the NAACP to have such a link. As was so often the case, Alberta Henry's arguments carried. The board voted to add Reid to their number, and he worked for six years under Henry's leadership. "We had a warm and friendly relationship," Reid says. "She was a very caring person and concerned for the African American community, but also for the whole community as well." When Alberta retired in 1992, Reid continued to serve on the board under her successor, Jeanetta Williams.[42]

CHAPTER 8

ONE LAST GREAT BATTLE

Whatever else Alberta Henry accomplished during her time with the NAACP seemed to be subsumed into the one great cause she lost: the William Andrews case. But that case had started long before she became president of the Salt Lake Branch of the NAACP.

On the night of April 22, 1974, two men broke into the Hi-Fi Shop, a music store in Ogden, Utah. The intruders forced five employees and customers into the basement of the store and during the violent rampage that followed the imprisoned victims were tied up, one woman was raped, and all were forced to drink caustic drain cleaner in an attempt to kill them. When death by Drano proved too slow, all five were shot, three fatally, one left severely disabled. These actions forever changed the lives of those involved and aroused feelings among all races throughout the region. Citizens and officials alike called for the death penalty even before the culprits were known. The case evoked local and national outrage because the agonizing torture the victims had endured had all been carefully planned in advance.[1]

Shortly after the crime, incriminating information surfaced that pointed to Dale Pierre Selby and William Andrews, both black servicemen stationed at Hill Air Force Base a few miles south of Ogden. They were charged with homicide, a crime carrying the possibility of the death penalty. A third man, Keith Roberts, assisted in the theft, but since he had stayed in the vehicle, he was tried separately and convicted of aggravated robbery. Both Selby and Andrews were identified by one of the surviving victims and a fellow serviceman testified that they had told him they committed the crime. They were arrested, tried, convicted, and sentenced to death. After his conviction Selby admitted that he had committed the rape but that they had both brought drain cleaner with them, intending to use it to kill any witnesses. He also confessed that he had shot all five victims when the drain cleaner failed to act quickly enough. That shooting occurred, however, after Andrews had left the shop.[2]

Although the two men were tried together and both sentenced to death, the fact remained that only Selby had committed murder. Andrews—however culpable he was as an accomplice, however horrible his participation in the tortures, however guilty he may have been in premeditating murder by drain cleaner—had not actually killed anyone. The case became the center of a long and crucial legal battle over the death penalty in general and over his execution in particular.

In Utah, as in the rest of the nation, controversy over capital punishment was rampant. Racial inequities clearly existed between punishment for crimes and particularly for the use of capital punishment. A study of executions in the United States between 1930 and 1967 showed that while blacks constituted only 10 to 12 percent of the population, 50 percent of prisoners executed were black. However, 97 percent of those executions took place in the Southern states, the home of the old Confederacy where legalized segregation had existed for the entire duration of that study. The balance in the rest of the country was far more racially proportional, yet arguments could still be made that race affected jurors' decisions and the court's punishments.[3]

Beginning in 1967 states had ceased executions pending decisions in several death penalty challenges working their way to the Supreme Court. Then in 1972, in the case of *Furman v. Georgia*,[4] the court "nullified all death sentences imposed without statutory guidelines." Across the nation death sentences were placed on hold until legislatures could clarify their laws, leaving more than six hundred prisoners in limbo on death row. The ban was lifted in 1976 with decisions made in two cases on the same day: *Woodson v. North Carolina* and *Gregg v. Georgia*.[5] Those cases mandated that the death penalty could be constitutional if "it is imposed in a two-stage procedure accompanied by specific guidelines that take into account differences in individual defendants and their crimes."[6] That same year just such a case appeared in Utah.

On July 19, 1976, Gary Mark Gilmore, paroled from the federal penitentiary in Marion, Illinois, only three months earlier, killed a gas station attendant in the course of a robbery in Orem, Utah. The next day he moved on to nearby Provo where he robbed a motel and killed the manager, Ben Bushnell, who was lying on the floor as Gilmore had ordered him to do. A guest at the motel, Peter Arroyo, found the body. He later testified that he had seen Gilmore in the office only a few minutes earlier, holding a gun and a cash box. Moreover, in the course of shooting Bushnell, Gilmore had shot himself in the hand and left a trail of blood to the bushes where he dumped the gun. Blood and ballistics tests verified that the gun was the murder weapon and Gilmore was the shooter. The evidence was so overwhelming that Gilmore's counsel could offer no defense at all: Gilmore had unequivocally committed the crime. He demanded the death penalty and attempted suicide twice while he was in prison even though his lawyers were attempting to free him. On January 17, 1977, Gary Gilmore became the first person executed in the United States after the ten-year moratorium ended by the *Woodson* and *Gregg* decisions. He chose execution by a firing squad rather than by hanging, the only other option available at the time at the Utah State Prison. Shortly thereafter several other states reinstituted capital punishment.[7]

An overwhelming majority of Utahns favored capital punishment. In 1973, a year before the Hi-Fi Shop murders occurred, a Salt Lake City newspaper poll indicated that "87 percent of the Mormons and 76 percent of the non-Mormons favored the death penalty."[8] Moreover, the horrific details of the Hi-Fi case bent jurors' decisions and public opinion against both Selby and Andrews. The evidence in the original trial made proof of Andrews's innocence difficult because the jury only saw premeditated rape followed by equally premeditated and carefully planned murders. Andrews's role in the crime did not seem distinct or different. The sheer heinousness and the premeditation involved in the tortures preceding the murders doubtless also impacted the attitudes in favor of the death penalty.

In 1986, after the Tenth Circuit Court of Appeals in Denver denied Selby and Andrews's joint appeal, Andrews's attorney managed to have the cases separated. Exhausting all options with the judiciary, Selby made a final, futile appeal to the Utah Board of Pardons,[9] the only body authorized by Utah law to grant such pardons. Both men had served thirteen years on death row when Selby was executed on August 28, 1987. He was offered a choice in the method of execution: firing squad or lethal injection, but he refused to choose. His execution was the first in Utah by lethal injection and the first since Gary Gilmore's death by firing squad in January 1977.[10]

Alberta Henry distinguished sharply between the two men. While she disagreed strongly with the concept of capital punishment, she acknowledged Selby's absolute guilt. When I asked Alberta what she thought of Selby, she replied with a visible shudder:

Oh, he was a bad one.

She felt quite differently about Andrews and so did his lawyers. They wanted the state and parole board to examine his involvement in the case independent of Selby's actions. They acknowledged that Selby and Andrews had both brought Drano to kill witnesses, but stressed that since Selby had confessed that he alone shot all five victims and he alone committed the rape, Andrews was only an accomplice. Andrews's legal team maintained that an accomplice could not be held responsible for the actions of his partner, only for those crimes in which he had actually participated. They had a hard fight to prove this to a community so outraged by the horrors of premeditated torture and murder.

Alberta was also well acquainted with the obstacles blacks faced in the white justice system as she tried to save the life of William Andrews. She sincerely believed he was a gullible young man caught up by a sociopath. In addition to her attempt to save Andrews's life, Alberta used his conviction to voice her opinion concerning capital punishment in Utah. Through her position as the NAACP president, she united the black community—and much of the community at large—in support of Andrews, and she publicly addressed the racial implications of Andrews's sentence. Through all of this she knew she was putting her own professional and civic reputation at stake.

To win life for Andrews his lawyers and proponents had to prove that his role in the murders was more complex than Selby's and should not, therefore, warrant the death penalty. In presentations to the courts they admitted that Andrews had participated in the Hi-Fi Shop crime but not as a murderer. Indeed, he and Selby brought poisonous Drano to kill victims and forced them to drink the substance, fully intending to kill them, but while Andrews loaded the car with stolen merchandise, Selby shot all five victims when he realized the Drano was not working quickly enough. However horrifying his part in the crime, Andrews was not the trigger man. Prosecutors maintained that Andrews helped administer the caustic drain cleaner, which alone could have killed the victims given time, and he also knew Selby intended to kill them. The court concurred that Andrews was just as responsible for the murders as Selby because the poisonous liquid would have eventually killed the victims and felt that Andrews understood and expected what Selby would do and did not stop him.[11]

Andrews's death sentence, however, led many, especially in the black community, to see the penalty as an example of racism rather than justice. Some ventured that he was more likely to receive the death penalty rather than a lesser sentence because of his race. Others suggested that capital punishment was too severe for the extent of his involvement. Some national black activists, such as Jesse Jackson, wanted to organize a protest march on LDS Church Headquarters to bring pressure for a reduction in the sentence. Alberta, along with the rest of the local black leaders, knew that the only agency that could alter the sentence was the board of pardons. Nonetheless, she contacted LDS President Gordon B. Hinkley who verified the fact that the church had neither authority nor opinion in the matter at all. This was purely a civil issue. After many communications local leaders convinced the national activists that any of the marches or other actions they were proposing would only create ill will where local black leaders had established a congenial and mutually supportive relationship.[12]

The argument that the jury had sentenced Andrews to death because of his race and/or background was not the first time this topic had been approached in the courts. In 1987, when Warren McClesky's attorneys appealed before the U.S. Supreme Court, they argued there were racial disparities in capital sentencing. They noted if the victims were white and the offender black, the perpetrator was more likely to receive the death penalty than if the victims were black.[13] To justify its ruling in the case, the court stated: "Apparent disparities in sentencing are an inevitable part of our criminal justice system. . . . Where the discretion that is fundamental to our criminal process is involved, we decline to assume that what is unexplained is invidious."[14] The McClesky case confronted the factor of race in relation to the conviction throughout the nation, but viewing all the men executed in Utah, their ethnicity did not appear to be disproportional to the general racial distribution of the state. In fact religion might be the determining factor in cases in Utah. Gillespie points out that of the forty-seven men executed in Utah, twenty-five were not Mormon, eight were Mormon, and fourteen were unknown. Most of the men who were not Mormon had recently come to Utah from outside of the state or were passing through at the time of their crimes.[15] Capital punishment, however, had a long history as an issue specific to black citizens in the United States.[16] Accordingly it was natural for the NAACP to act on a political and social interest in the Andrews case. Moreover, Alberta wanted to bring the black community together to prove to Utah that the black population would not sit idly by and let it execute a man that many of them considered innocent of the specific crime for which he was charged.

By the time Andrews challenged his sentence in the late 1980s, Alberta had served for nearly ten years as the president of the Salt Lake City Chapter of the NAACP. With opposition to this case came increased visibility and she saw that as an opportunity to strengthen equality in Utah. Many thought the Andrews's case presented the ideal opportunity to show both the state and nation the premise that even in twentieth-century Utah blacks faced a prejudiced atmosphere. Since Andrews had not actually killed anyone, Henry and others believed his execution was based on his color of skin. The overall historical experience of black Americans, with a system that permitted questionable executions, reinforced the NAACP's sentiment.

In June of 1992 Andrews's lawyers requested a second hearing with the board of pardons. After two days of hearings, the board rejected the request with a two to one vote. The lone dissenter, Victoria Palacios, said she felt that "life with parole was the appropriate punishment for Andrews."[17]

Andrews was scheduled to die on Tuesday, August 22, 1989, but four days earlier on August 19, the Tenth U.S. Circuit Court of Appeals stayed the execution for 160 days, or "until further order of the court."[18] The day after the state announced the delay, Alberta gathered the black community in a meeting to assert that the state of Utah made Andrews a "victim of racism." At a press conference earlier that day Henry uttered: "Utah, a pretty great state? Yes, it might be *if* you are white." She wanted to retain a positive air but felt that the justice system in Utah was "corrupted by prejudice."[19]

Alberta again employed the Utah black community to fight for Andrews's life. At a NAACP-sponsored meeting on September 11, 1989, she urged the people not to forget Andrews and maintained: "If Andrews can't get justice here in Utah, then we *all* are at the mercy of unjust laws and blood atonement people. . . . We must continue our prayers for William Andrews for if he is murdered by the State, Utah will never-ever live it down. (This we pledge.)"[20] She also issued a press release for a rally to support William Andrews. It went to media outlets, but also to members of the NAACP, larger black community, and Christian churches of Utah to illustrate the implications involved in Andrews's case. Alberta postulated that, if Andrews did not receive justice, then all blacks suffered the consequences. Therefore she urged citizens to unite and show the nation how "blacks and Christians" felt about equality in Utah.[21]

To highlight her main point, that racism was the dominant cause of Andrews's execution, Alberta pointed to white convicts in Utah who had committed murder but had not received the death penalty. She referred to Joseph Paul Franklin, an avowed racist who shot two black joggers in August 1980. She also brought attention to an infamous Utah murderer, Mark W. Hoffman, a white Mormon, who produced forged copies of what he convinced buyers were Mormon historical documents, then killed two people in October 1985 with homemade pipe bombs to keep them from exposing his schemes. Both of those killers received life in prison instead of the death penalty. To this, she asked:

> *"Did they deserve to die? Did the people cry for the death penalty? Do the press and television fill their papers and screens each anniversary to make sure no one forgets. No, only the Hi-Fi story. . . . Did the punishment fit the crime? No."*[22]

She pointed to these cases as evidence that because of his race, Andrews was more certain to receive the death penalty than a white person.[23] Others disagreed. Robert Stott, the attorney who had prosecuted both Franklin and Hoffman, insisted that a jury decides whether to impose a death sentence based on convincing, "smoking gun" evidence. He agreed that Franklin's crime was blatant admitted racism with obvious premeditation—hiding in a field waiting to shoot the two black men. The jury found him guilty in only five hours, but could not get unanimous agreement on the death penalty, so Stott continued to press the case. "In the past 15 years, we've never had a death penalty case that we spent so much effort in trying to obtain the death penalty as in the Franklin case." The problem, however, was that it did not have the clear-cut evidence presented by the Hi-Fi murders. "There were no eyewitnesses, no fingerprints, no smoking gun. It was a circumstantial case. . . . What we learned from the Franklin case—and other capital homicide cases since—is that the single most important factor in a death case is not race or politics, but the strength of the evidence."[24] The *Deseret News*, an LDS-owned newspaper, responded to Henry's comments by stating, "It is a serious mistake to make the issue one of racism in Utah." The article suggested that if Selby and Andrews had been white, the outcome would have been the same.[25] Various letters to the editor in both local newspapers suggested the same thing. "I frankly wouldn't care if he is white, green or purple. I feel the death penalty is justified."[26]

Alberta remained steadfast. She requested all the good and decent people in Utah

"to come forward now and stand as Ms. [Victoria] Palacios and let the world know we are not all like those who are spiteful, vindictive and seeking revenge. Their hatred for all black people runs deep and there is no place in their hearts for equal treatment under the law. I hope and pray that we as Christians can forgive them and pray for those who think it is alright to kill blacks for any reason even if there is no one killed."[27]

Alberta's willingness to take a stance against such a controversial case raised both applause and outrage in the community. Shortly after the NAACP held the 1989 meeting for Andrews, she received a supportive letter that stated: "Thank goodness there are people such as yourself who are in the position to stand up for the rights of people such as William Andrews. . . . I am white and I am Catholic and what they are doing to Mr. Andrews is a disgrace to our so-called civilized society." The letter writer also noted that Andrews did do an "ugly thing" but others (whites) have done worse and did not receive the death penalty.[28]

Evidently a number of Utahns of various races and ethnicities agreed with Henry, but not all. She received letters that criticized her active support for Andrews; some even offered threats. One anonymous critic sent a letter saying: "I cannot believe you are so ill-educated and irresponsible to say that a black person (in Utah) can be picked up and put on death row and executed *'only because they are black'* . . . Mr. Andrews is on death row because he assisted in the torture and murder of innocent people, not because he is black. . . . If this is a barbaric, racist state, then get the hell out! However, it is not!"[29] In a letter still more condemning, and far more vitriolic than any others, Reverend Ema White, who praised herself as a "proud white racist," criticized Alberta Henry and her associate James Gillespie for their membership in the NAACP. According to the minister, because of black organizations, Henry and Gillespie had become racist themselves. White also suggested that her view appeared to be that "niggers have the right to kill whites. Its [sic] only racial when whites kill niggers." Reverend White went on to suggest that "all you nigger bastards go back to Africa and starve to death."[30] The range of responses to Henry's actions conveyed the complexities of the Andrews case concerning both racial attitudes and the horrors of the crimes.

In 1989, hearing of Alberta's determination to preserve his life, Andrews wrote a poignant letter in which he imparted his feelings pertaining to the actions taken by the NAACP, the Hi-Fi Shop murders, the effect the crime had on the black community, and the death penalty. Andrews's letter provided a glimpse into the life and emotions of a black man who had lived for nearly seventeen years on death row. It also illustrated that Alberta and the NAACP had helped him realize that his actions reflected on his race, whether fairly or not.

> Dear Mrs. Henry,
>
> I am writeing to express my gratitude for the concern yourself and the N.A.A.C.P. has showen concerning my case. Please accept my apology for the shame and embarrassment I brought upon the Black Community here in Utah. At the time when I participated in the crime at the Ogden Hi Fi Shop back in 1974 I was very young and very stupid. I did not have no idea

> of the harm I was doing to the crime victims, or its social impact on the Black Community, or its impact on the community as a hole. I know to you it may seem un-reasonable that a 19 year old Black man in America could be so un-aware but I can assure you that not only was I stupid but sence I have been here in this prison I have met young Black men that are just as socially un-aware as I was. I have met many young Black men in this place that either don't care or are un-aware of how crime commited by Black people is reflected on the Black Race as a hole. Now that I am much older and much more concerned about my people, I have the benefit of hind sight and can trace my lack of social awareness to my up bringing. All of my life no one ever impressed upon me how the actions of one Black person will be seen by the other races of the world as representative of the Black race as a hole. I realize that judgeing the entire race by the actions of one is wrong but it is a fact that we live in an imperfict world. It is a fact that in this imperfect world, that Black People are very often judged by the actions of Blacks who are the example of criminal behavior. I realize now that my actions back in 1974 at the Ogden Hi Fi Shop has contributed to the negative image Black People are unjustly suffering from to this day. I am very ashamed of myself for contributing to that negative image. I pray some day I will find a way to be a more positive image to my people and for my people. I also realize the harm I coused the victims of that crime and I do feel grate remorse becouse of that. But I do not believe my participation in that crime should warrant the death penality. Some members of the Board of Pardon seem to think I have not showen enough remores for that crime. I can only express to them or anyone else how I feel with my words and my actions. I would like to do more to recompense for my crime but my circumstances wont allow for it. All I can do is hope and pray. It is my hope that some day I can be of service to the community as a hole and try to make the world a better place for all. But I realize it is all in the hands of God. What ever Gods will, let it be so.
>
> Once again, thank you for your concern and will you please convey my gratitude to the others that you are awear of who are concerned for my well being also. God bless you and all you stand for.[31]

By the middle of 1992, the death penalty seemed inevitable for Andrews, but Alberta fought until the bitter end and for her it was very bitter. She planned another rally in honor of William Andrews on June 1,

1992, to reiterate the racial implications of the case. As Henry spoke to the gathered citizens, her voice resonated with her fiery views:

Why are we here today? Why have we gathered at this time and place? Are we here because we are happy? Sad—Mad? [Or are] we just fed up with the criminal justice system? I'm here because I can't take it any more—I'm pushed to the edge with the two kinds of justice given out here in Utah. For almost eighteen years—I had hoped and prayed—and I knew in my heart that there were good, honest, and fair thinking people who would come forward and raise their voices and say, "It's not right and we will not let you execute William Andrew—he did not kill any one and he did not get a fair trial." I did not give up hope for I had come to know and love over the past forty some years thousands of wonderful people. But I waited—and waited for some judge—the governor or just one prosecuting attorney who would say "William Andrews did not get a fair trial." Of all the people here in Utah who have killed we did not give them the Death Penalty . . . I'm now ready—Are you? I'm ready to let them know they can't kill Andrews, who has killed no one. We—will not—We cannot—We—must not be silent. The time is now—now—now for justice.[32]

The argument relied upon six main points for preserving William Andrew's life: 1) He did not kill anyone. 2) He did not shoot anyone. 3) He was not present when anyone was killed. 4) An all-white jury was selected for the trial. 5) The prosecutor made a racist comment that could bias the jury. 6) A note saying "hang the niggers" was found by jurors. Although Alberta and a great many others tried unceasingly to halt the execution of William Andrews, in the summer of 1992 when the Utah Supreme Court denied his fourth appeal, it guaranteed his life would end. Andrews's lawyers tried for a petition to the court, maintaining that the defense had ineffective counsel and that racial attitudes prejudiced the whole case. To halt Andrews's July 30, 1992, execution day, the attorneys tried to use a new statute, available only after April 27, 1992, of life without parole. Prosecutors argued that the rule was not meant to be retroactive and could not be applied to Andrews's case. Consequently, the Utah Supreme Court voted in a four to one ruling to support Andrews's death sentence.[33]

Following the court's decision, Alberta called an emergency meeting for members of the NAACP. They voted to hold nightly vigils in front of the governor's mansion, asking Governor Norman Bangerter to persuade the board of pardons to stay Andrews's execution, until its next meeting. Opponents of the death penalty in general, and people who were concerned with the Andrews case specifically, met at her home. Alberta herself went daily taking Julia, then fifteen years old, with her.[34] Forty clergy and religious leaders from Utah signed a letter to Governor Norman Bangerter asking him to prevent Andrews's execution. However vehemently the participants pleaded, Bangerter explained that the governor of the state of Utah has no statutory power to alter or commute sentences. Only the board of pardons could commute Andrews's sentence. Bangerter did have the authority to postpone the execution, giving the board time to review the case; however, that seemed pointless since the board had already refused to hear Andrews's case again. Thus the governor declined to intervene and Andrews moved closer to death. Alberta and Jenetta Williams led a petition drive and collected 1,500 signatures. They presented those petitions to the board of pardons, to no avail.[35]

Many people felt the decisions were entirely racial and some charged the LDS Church with being complicit in the culture of racism thought to have brought them about. Boyer Jarvis, a Mormon and a retired University of Utah professor was quoted in the *Salt Lake Tribune* that Utah had "an abundance of two kinds of justice—one for members of the white majority, another for blacks." His statement was repeated in national papers as well.[36] The day before Andrews's scheduled execution, Salt Lake City's black organizations came together in a last-minute attempt to halt the action via a restraining order. Their reactions during this time reflected the brutal impact the case had on the black community. The groups maintained that the execution "will be a symbolic means of executing the black community and will destroy [our] hopes of achieving equality."[37] Many blacks believed that Andrews's death would heighten racism and discrimination. Alberta Henry contributed to this rhetoric, stating: "[The execution] is blatantly racist. If they murder William Andrews, Utah will never be the same for us again."[38] Attorney General Paul Van Dam voluntarily agreed to delay the execution, while the U.S. Supreme Court reviewed the case, but the court voted seven to two for execution, just minutes before Andrews would be executed.[39]

After seventeen years on death row, longer than any condemned inmate in the United States until that time, William Andrews was executed on

July 30, 1992, by lethal injection. Before the deputy read Andrews the death warrant, Andrews "mouthed the words 'I love you,' and blew a kiss" to his sister Audrey Minter Boson, and his niece Minnie Minter, the only family members in attendance. The prison officials beside the gurney asked Andrews for his last words. They reported that he said: "Thank those who tried to keep me alive. I hope they continue to fight for equal justice after I'm gone. Tell my family goodbye and that I love them."[40] The Andrews family sent personal cards to Henry and the NAACP, thanking them for their efforts in the case.[41]

Alberta knew that despite the failure to keep Andrews alive, she had done everything possible to save him. She also knew she possessed the position that gave her credibility as one opposed to all forms of discrimination. Members of the Salt Lake NAACP had fought long and hard to save his life and many of them wanted to maintain their focus on guaranteeing rights for everyone. Within days of Andrews's execution Alberta helped to organize a committee on equal justice made up of three groups: clergy, lawyers, and citizens. Most of the two hundred in the group had signed up to join following a memorial service for Andrews. Reverend Janet Swift, co-chairwoman of the committee, said, "I'm very, very concerned that we don't lose our edge."[42] Although her experiences with William Andrews had strengthened Alberta's resolve to forward the fight against discrimination in Utah, the intensity of the public clamor over the issue and the refusal by both the courts and the public to reconsider the questionable elements in the crime seemed to shock her. William Andrews's execution left Henry dejected and, to a degree, embittered.

"The only one we lost that hurt me real bad was William Andrews. I didn't like the lies that they told that said he had killed somebody, when he hadn't. Said he had raped somebody and totaled for sixteen or seventeen years, which was a lie. He hadn't done any of those things. So I thought he should, if anything, get life in prison, because the state has to live with that. It just doesn't go away."[43]

Although the Andrews case occupied much of her time, Alberta was keenly aware of other issues, too. She had moved into major fighting form over the Rodney King incident. On March 3, 1991, Rodney King, a black man, was stopped for drunk driving by four Los Angeles police officers. He was arrested only after several minutes of severe, violent attacks with clubs and nightsticks. The incident was caught on home video and shown repeatedly on television stations across the country, clearly presenting King as a victim of police brutality. Alberta immediately recognized the need to involve the entire community on the issue.

> *If I don't agree with something that someone else says out in the community, it really doesn't matter because we're not going to come together. When Rodney King got beat, and I was president of NAACP, I said, "They're going to have a community thing out at Nettie Gregory." And we'd call the community and that's the only time the community gets to come in on the decision is if the leaders would ask them to come together.*

The four police officers who had been taped beating King were acquitted and riots broke out in Los Angeles. Utahns, both black and white, reacted with both anger and sorrow. Cedar City Police Chief Pete Hansen said, "I am just sick. I absolutely couldn't believe it. I don't mean to take a shot at the jury, but the tape was condemning." Other officers noted that the system, not just those officers, had been on trial, and that the case had made crime prevention and law enforcement much more difficult because the public had lost so much respect for the police. Ronald Coleman, a black professor at the University of Utah, said, "It raises the specter of fear for the welfare of a large number of men of color who are unfortunately potential victims." Alberta echoed his fears: "It has already sent the message that police can use force on anyone, but [afterward] dismiss it and say it was justified [but the riot] did not have to happen." The Salt Lake City Branch of the NAACP organized an open forum on the King trial for May 4, 1992, to air local issues and allow discussion by people from a broad spectrum of the community.[44] Once again Alberta was working locally to get ahead of the problems.

While Alberta usually worked in concert with other black leaders, occasionally they disagreed and when they did, she did not hesitate to state her views. In 1991 when President George H. W. Bush nominated a black man, Clarence Thomas, to become a justice of the Supreme Court, Alberta was "totally surprised." She had not been expecting the Republican president to choose a black and observed that "nothing was said (or known) that he was not a qualified person," declaring he was certainly "as good as anyone else."[45] Other national and local NAACP leaders, however, took a different stand. James Gillespie, president of the Ogden Chapter of the

NAACP, complained that Thomas had criticized the NAACP and was not sufficiently concerned with the needs for job opportunities for blacks.[46] Bill Watkins, a teacher from the University of Utah, criticized Thomas's work as an Equal Employment Opportunity official and voted with the majority of the Salt Lake Chapter's NAACP membership to uphold the national association's opposition. As the chapter president, Alberta granted the chapter's right to take that stand but she did not alter hers, observing a newly emerging attitude about black men. "I think there is a [tendency] to bash black male men, and I'm just about fed up with it."[47] "He is still black, and he still came up the hard way—like a lot of us—to get where he was."[48] The split in the Utah NAACP was not so unusual as it may seem. Thomas's nomination created strong feelings on many sides, creating some of the oddest political alliances in U.S. history.

Through all these high-profile cases, Alberta kept working on the more mundane issues of prejudice, both by protesting what she saw as wrongs, great or small, and by building bridges just as she always had. In 1991 she sent various groups and agencies thirty-eight forms in two months, all responding to complaints from minority citizens about discrimination in housing, harassment from police, unfair treatment on a job, and verbal assaults using defamatory epithets.[49] She complained when Utah's senators, Orrin Hatch and Jake Garn, fought against the Civil Rights Act of 1990 despite Hatch's protests that it was "a pathetic bill" that would be a "litigation bonanza for lawyers."[50] She issued an official letter of complaint on NAACP letterhead protesting Utah Code Ann. #13-7-3 which, she said, "severely restricts the availability of effective legal redress for civil rights abuses and violations by private businesses."[51]

Always on the lookout for positive racial interactions, in 1992 Alberta and the board of the Salt Lake City Branch of the NAACP arranged a visit and speaking engagements for Rosa Parks, the black woman from Montgomery, Alabama, whose refusal to give up her seat in the bus to a white woman had sparked the bus boycott and demonstrations that brought Martin Luther King Jr. into national prominence. Since Alberta was tied up with the Andrews case at the time, she asked her vice president, Jeanetta Williams, to take charge of the Parks visit.

We were working with Willie Andrews so I didn't go when we brought in Rosa Parks. Jeanetta went with her and I stayed home. We were working on the third appeal and I was sharing. If you give a vice president a job to do, if you sit there and are helping you watch and tell him or her, you need to do this. Do you need any help? Are you getting it done? I called her and I started letting her do all the things.

When they discovered that the cost of Parks's speaking fee and the amount necessary to bring her to Utah was $10,000, far more than the local chapter could possibly manage, Alberta turned to Stuart Reid, the man she had met when she walked into the LDS Church office building looking to establish ties. The LDS Church paid $7,000 and arranged for Parks to speak at BYU as well as those appearances that were already scheduled. Parks's visit to BYU was far bigger than anyone had expected. She had originally been booked just to talk with political science majors, but so many people showed up that her presentation was moved to a large auditorium with her message broadcast into other areas on campus. Those other areas also quickly became crowded. Many students simply skipped their classes and a great many teachers gave quick handouts and then excused their entire class to attend. Attendance at her speeches in Salt Lake City was also extremely high and her remarks were well received. The visit was a huge success. Alberta felt confident that she could finally retire and leave the Salt Lake Branch of the NAACP in the good hands of her vice president.

CHAPTER 9

RETIREMENT—SORT OF

By the end of 1992, soon after William Andrews was executed and the Salt Lake City NAACP brought Rosa Parks to Utah, Alberta decided it was time to slow down. She had retired from the Salt Lake School District in 1986 and was now seventy-two. She officially retired from the presidency of the Salt Lake City Chapter of the NAACP on December 31, 1992. Both of those retirements occasioned a spate of news stories reviewing her career and praising her efforts. She appreciated them, and recognizing their value to the black community as a whole, acknowledged one of them in a letter to the editor.

"How does one say thanks for such a beautiful picture and story about black history in Utah?" she asked in a letter to the editor of the Deseret News, noting that "if it was in my power, I would certainly give [the authors] an award for they earned it with the complete picture of black history in Utah."[1]

By then Alberta had worked in the Salt Lake Chapter of the NAACP for more than thirty years, serving over a decade as its president, assisted during the last several years by her friend and protegee Jeanetta Williams. Among other duties, Williams had handled the Rosa Parks visit and helped organize protests in the Andrews case.[2] Many observers felt that when Alberta retired, "she was fortunate to have a committed successor in Williams."[3] Alberta felt the same way. She was weary of fighting what seemed to be the same old battles and wanted to do more with her family. A lot of people thought she deserved a rest. Reverend France Davis summed up the position of blacks in Utah at the time he arrived in Utah in the early 1970s and compared them with the differences thirty years later.

> They were minimally formally educated. The goal of many of them was simply to get a good job at Kennecott, working in the mines, and that would have been the top of many people's world during that time. Many of them had come to this area getting away from wherever they came from and were themselves struggling with their identity, trying to find themselves and their place in the world.
>
> Since that time the number of college graduates has continued to swell. We have more African Americans who are now teaching in the public schools than we had college graduates in 1972; now we have more that are teachers. And that does not count people who work in engineering and business and pastoring churches and other kinds of roles. So the community continues to improve. Calvary and people like Alberta have been at the center of much of that improvement. And it's been our goal to say where we are as examples. Alberta earned her own degree since I've been here, for example. But many of us have been examples to say here we are; we could do it, so can you. And those have been good role models for our young people as well as for some of our older people.[4]

Having served the community so well for so long, Alberta could now focus more on her family, where she had a lot to do. She had always maintained close ties with her parents and siblings, and during retirement her involvement with them increased sharply. In 1988 she had recognized that her mother Julia, who was still living in Topeka, had reached the point of needing care and wanted her to be closer. She arranged to move her mother into the Jackson Towers in Salt Lake City and later to her own home where she could be close enough to help her.[5] Alberta was happy to take care of her mother but was even happier to spoil her a little. She delighted in talking about specific incidents in their time together.

I brought her out here to take care of her. She had a stroke so she was in a nursing home. I had her almost five years. When she wanted something sweet. I said, "Ice cream?"

"No."

"Graham cracker?"

"No."

"What about an apple pie?"

"Yeah."

I said, "I'll fix it for you." And it took an hour for it to [bake] because we used those Mary Somebody frozen apple pies. So I put one in at nine o'clock and it came out at five minutes after ten and she came down and had a little bit of it, just enough for her.

And she said, "Is everything OK at the house here?"

And I said: "Everything is fine. The dishes been done and I had two pieces of your apple pie."

It wasn't just pie. Alberta fixed anything she could for her mother.

Mother said, "Oh, I love this sauerkraut." She asked me to fix her spare ribs, the thick ribs. I think she called it the back ribs, and I cut off the rest of the fat—and I cooked it and put the spare ribs in it. I just tasted it once to see if the sauerkraut were OK.

Much as Alberta enjoyed this chance to help her mother, having her close also proved to be an opportunity for her daughter. Julia Henry had been named for her grandmother and had met her a few times in Topeka, but when her mother "brought my grandmother out here, when her health failed, I got a chance to spend quality time with my grandmother. I would come over and give my mother a reprieve so she would go to Wendover on the weekends, so then it was party time for me and Grandma and the kids." They would go to Taco Bell or Arctic Circle. Or "we'd get Kentucky Fried Chicken, and we'd let Grandma do her own thing, get off of her routine, her regimen and diet . . . the first day when mom would leave, I'd fix her regular routine, but the next day when she'd gone—like she'd leave on a Friday and stay all day Saturday and leave late Saturday night or early Sunday morning—Saturday was party day. We'd drop the regimen and kind of put her blood sugar out of whack, but we let her move when she wanted and do what she wanted."

Julia observed that although she herself is adopted, during the time her grandmother lived in Salt Lake City, she realized that they share many similarities. Although it was "only four years, what's funny, what's ironic is that I was never raised around her, but I have a lot of her personality—very stoic. I'm not really an affectionate type person. I'm getting better now in my older age, but my mother tells me all the time: 'You're like your grandmother. I don't understand that because you weren't raised around her.'"[6]

By 1990 Alberta's mother was needing a lot of care. Both Harold and Alberta had some health issues and Alberta was still in the midst of the fight to save William Andrews's life, leading the Salt Lake City Branch of the NAACP, working in dozens of other organizations when she suddenly became ill. She summed up the year in a letter, apparently a belated Christmas message, to friends and family, early in 1991. At the top was her name, address, and the title "The Henry's Home in 1990."

"1990 has passed and gone, 1991 is almost a month old and God has blessed us all to be alive and in fair health. 1990 was a rough year and found us all sick and in and out of hospitals.

"Mother was in the hospital in April with blood clots that moved up to her lungs. It was touch-and-go for several days. She was again in the hospital in October for fourteen days, her lungs and chest cavities were filled with fluid from the blood clots. They operated on her and put a tube in her chest and sent her home with around-the-clock nurses. (Every eight hours.) They would drain the tube and then put antibiotics in. This process went on for almost a month until December 1, 1990. So if I did not write you can see the reason why.

"We thank God that she is making good progress now but is still on oxygen and a man comes in three times a week for her therapy. Also a nurse comes twice a month to check her out, and twice a week an aide comes to bath, wash her hair, and clean her room. She also has a senior companion who comes once a week to read to her (the Bible). Eat lunch and talk for three hours.

"Harold was rushed to the hospital on October 29th (just three days after our NAACP Annual Banquet). They worked on him for half an hour before taking him to the hospital. He had a kidney infection that triggered his diabetes and caused his weakened heart condition to react. So then I had two people in the hospital, my mother on one floor and my husband on another floor. I drove twice a day, twenty miles, and hobbling up and down the halls with the help of a cane for my bad leg and side.

"A quick call to my brother, David, in California and he was here within eleven hours, staying until they were both home and doing better.

"I have been sick with a bad eye and unable to walk without pain, or without a cane. Most all of 1990 I have had muscle spasm in my right side. I was put in the hospital on April 24th, and scheduled for an eye operation the next day. They thought I had a detached retina but on further examination they concluded that there was hole in the back of the eye. So for eight months they treated it without having to use laser.

"The muscle spasm I was having turned out to be a broken vessel in my knee that spreaded infection in my body. It is called, (iliotibial band syndrome.) A very fancy name yes? So, for nine months of pain, limping, and dragging myself around, I was sent to specialist who gave me some very powerful medicine which removed the infection out of my body. The Lord has really blessed our family.

"Well, 1991 came in and I can now walk without a cane or any pain. My daughter, her husband, and three grandchildren are all well. They came every day, back and forth to the hospital giving assistance and moral support. The Lord truly blessed us to have such a wonderful family and friends.

"The doctor finally released Harold after two months to go back to work. (January 3rd.) I was reelected as President of the Salt Lake Branch NAACP for two more years. I have already served ten years, and if God willing and I finish these two years which will be twelve years total. I will not run again. That's a promise.

"Give our regards to everyone and may God bless and keep you all.

With love and best wishes,"[7]

Julia Palmer Hill Brantly died on April 22, 1992, in Holy Cross Hospital. She was buried in the Mount Hope Cemetery, Topeka, Kansas.[8] Then in 1993, Alberta's sister Rosetta Martin, by far the most rebellious of the Hill children, was released from prison and had no place to go.

Rosetta had left [Kansas] and was living in Oregon or somewhere. I don't know all the places she was living. She got married five different times. I don't even know if she got divorced from any of them except the next to last one. The last one died.

Rosetta's checkered past notwithstanding, Alberta invited her sister to live in her home. A few years later, Rosetta suffered a stroke and required care, but not for long. She died on May 22, 1998.[9]

During the time that Alberta had been caring for her mother and sister, her husband, Harold, became ill. In 1994, when his illness became extreme, their daughter, Julia, and her husband, Daniel Cosby, moved into the Henrys' home in West Valley City to help Alberta care for him. Julia said, "I just came home one day from work on a Wednesday and Daniel tells me, 'Call your mom and dad and tell them we're moving in Friday.' Because my dad was starting to go downhill and I could see the stress toll on my mom." With them came Julia's daughter, Patrice, by her first husband, Robert Sawyer, and the Cosbys' two children, Daniel Julian and Denitra Lashae, by then seven and six, respectively.[10]

Alberta always spoke of Harold with great affection and respect, an attitude reflected in her response to an interviewer who asked: "In almost fifty years here in Utah, what stands out as being your happiest experience, your happiest moment? What has been delightful about living here?"

"Marrying the husband that I married, because everybody don't have a good marriage. I used to tell the women that came here, and they said "Oh, your husband is so good looking." And I'm watching him. I'm not letting him go anywhere. I knew he wouldn't go anywhere in the first place, because my husband dearly loves me.

"And the kids, which I thought I would never have. And for people to call me and say, 'We've got this kid,' or, 'We've got that one,' from the agency—the children's agency in Ogden. I didn't know anything about it, but they said this fits your household. And then, when I got my one son, which was a delight.... [someone said] You'd need to have another child and you got another one. And we'd thought in the range of two or so . . . those were the happy days."[11]

Harold and Alberta had been married for forty-six years when he died on June 10, 1996. One of my visits to Alberta fell on June 10 three years later. That was when I learned it was still a difficult date for her.

I was glad that you are coming. Harold died three years ago on the 10th of June. I get remorseful and my mind gets back. I always have gone somewhere and had people around so I don't get sticky and think about June the 10th. I think it was the last year they had me on the 10th of June go to American Express. I said, Oh, I'd welcome that. And he said, "Oh, it's so good of you to come." Then in '98 I was at Pilgrim [New Pilgrim Baptist Church], I think it was speaking for a group that had adopted a whole lot of multi-colored kids. They came and got me on June the 10th of '98.

It just don't seem like three years ago. I've been telling everybody two years ago and Julia said, "Mother, it's been three years ago."

I said, "But it only seems—"

She said, "Mother. It's been three years ago. 1996. This is '99 now, Mother, OK?" So be quiet.

With Harold no longer needing care, Julia and Daniel considered moving. As Julia said, "We had no idea we were staying after he died."

But Alberta simply asked her, "Why do you need to move out?"

Julia replied, "Well, you know, we really don't have to."

So they stayed. Among their many good services to Alberta, Daniel hung her many awards on the living room wall. It was both a beautiful and an impressive display. Alberta appreciated it, but she did not put a lot of emphasis on her awards.

I can show you all those awards, fifty of them, that one in the corner with the clock on it, that came from the State Board of Education for the Black Curriculum. I was chairman of the advisory board for the state board. I had so many titles I didn't know which hat I was wearing all the time.

"Every night, I said, 'I don't want them. Why are they doing this? I don't actually ever do anything.' Now you heard me say as of today right now there is peritonitis in my body. I was a hired teacher and I climbed on the tricky bars and hung upside down with the kids. Now how could anybody with poison [in her] body do that? Nobody can. It has to be the Lord. The Lord sent me here. And how would anybody hire me as a head teacher if I didn't have a university degree? I had never been in a university. It can't be me."[12]

The Lord said, don't let your left know what your right hand is going to do. Going out and trying to get awards and praises for what you do, it won't add none in heaven. Every time I got an award, I said, Lord, you're making it hard. I'm trying to build my timber up in heaven to get my reward so that when I'm gone the Lord will say, "Well done, thou good and faithful servant, you've done so much, come on up high" and all that.[13] *How am I going to get that if you keep on awarding me down here?*

When I observed that the Lord also said, "Don't hide your light beneath a bushel,"[14] she replied,

Right. I will, but you don't have to award me.

The Cosbys remained with her until 2001 when Julia and Daniel divorced. Daniel Julian moved in with his father. Julia's daughter Patrice married Jason Dechameau and moved on with her own life, leaving only Julia and Denitra with Alberta.

In 1999, just after her parents had separated, Denitra had emergency brain surgery to correct an epidural abscess. A rare infection had dislodged from the sinus cavity and entered the lining between her brain and the bone. Denitra missed the first semester of her first year in junior high school, staying home with her grandmother during the day. Both Julia and Alberta credited her recovery to faith and prayers. Denitra recovered completely and grew into a lovely young woman. Alberta very much enjoyed having her close.[15]

Despite the joy Alberta found in her family, she was still involved in the community, albeit not so intensely as she once had been. When she stepped down from the presidency of the Salt Lake City Chapter of the NAACP in 1992, she remained on the board of directors. Initially she had been very happy that Janetta Williams could take over for her. As time passed, however, Alberta became increasingly concerned about the way the organization was being run. Even when she was criticizing Williams, however, I heard a note of sadness in her voice, very different from the tone she used when she talked about the time when they had once shared great friendship and commitment to a common cause.

Part of the problem was the difference in style. Alberta's style was hands-on, face-to-face, and frequently in-your-face. When issues arose in any of the organizations of which she was a part, she immediately called or went herself. Williams has opted for more modern, technological methods, like email and a webpage, but some members found things like the answering machine which Alberta felt was too impersonal and too easy to ignore.[16] Williams expanded the influence of the local organization, even holding a seat on the national board of directors for a time. She also recruited local corporate sponsors, a practice Alberta believed risks a conflict of interest.[17]

Another difference is emphasis. While Alberta recognized the needs of all minority groups, she saw the NAACP as the organization to focus on the needs of blacks. Williams conversely says, "The NAACP is a civil-rights organization with memberships that are reflective of all ethnic groups."[18] That was, in fact, part of the logic the national NAACP used when it chose to maintain the organization's name in the 1960s and 1970s when "colored" and "Negro," the previously polite terms for racial identifications, were replaced with "Black" and "African American" or "Afro-American."[19] Nonetheless, Alberta Henry had tutored Williams to take her place and was both surprised and disappointed that her protegee was taking such a different approach. Worse, she—and others—saw some real problems in procedures and decisions.

The president do not make all the decisions and do not involve the board. That's what they did. They just took over and they don't let the board do anything. Then they moved all the board stuff [equipment—computers, fax, etc.] out to their house—so I called a meeting of the board [since] I was on the board, and I said: "Let's try to straighten this out. You have to get permission from the board. When the board moves and seconds anything you put it in the minutes, when the board moves and seconds you can spend $2,000 to get a computer or something else."

[But] you go to the store and you get something that's $3,000 and you get a fax machine and other things, the board did not approve of that. And we get in trouble doing that. Did you ask the board? You want to take all the people to national and you want the board to pay for that but on the minutes it's moved and seconded that only the president gets all the money. Anybody else who wanted to go, they were paid and prorated for some of their workshops. You can't do that. They going to do that anyway. If you don't do something right—and I tried to help them straighten it out—and I fear that it's illegal.

I said, "You don't want me on the board." And that's when [the name of another board member escaped her] resigned first and another lady resigned, and when I went to that meeting, I said: "Look, I am resigning, but I will send you a letter. I will send you a letter of resignation. Don't you try to do me like you did those other people." I said, "I will sue you. I will send you one, but I will have nothing more to do with you because it's not right. And even if you was my mother, I would tell you it's not right."

It's been going down and down. Most all of the old board members have resigned. Once she go out and speak to [someone]—It didn't go before the board and the members called me and Julia said, "Just whatever she wants." It looks like they are in the pockets of the police and the chamber of commerce because [those organizations] have been giving them money to do things with. And you can't take money like that. You cannot take money from the police or the people that have oppressed your people.

That was 1997. By then Williams had been president of the local NAACP for five years and other members and board members had also expressed concerns. Alberta, along with Larry Houston, Leslie Reynolds, and Bonnie Dew, resigned from the Board of Directors of the Salt Lake City Chapter and made at least some of their concerns public. The local media reported that they questioned the way Williams was using the organization's fax machine for a private business. They were concerned that several NAACP members were given full compensation for travel expenses to an out-of-state conference. "We've generally only paid 50 percent for the delegates in the past," said Houston, observing the NAACP's nonprofit status and limited funds. Williams declined to respond to their comments, although she had said earlier that some board members were ineffective, sometimes wanting to deviate from policies of the national organization. Alberta said that resigning from the board of the organization was one of the hardest things she ever had to do, but she felt she had no choice, in part because she did not want any sort of stain to become attached to the Alberta Henry Education Foundation, which is dependent on private contributors.[20]

Such a public break in the black community shattered decades of tradition. That community, both locally and nationally, had usually maintained a united and frequently silent front in order to protect their own safety and to allow them to affect changes they saw as essential. Comedian Bill Cosby shattered that facade in May 2004 at a gathering in Washington D.C. commemorating the fiftieth anniversary of the Supreme Court's decision in *Brown v. Board of Education.* Cosby suggested, rather forcefully, that many blacks were squandering the prizes won in the 1960s and 1970s civil rights movement; they were dropping out of school, becoming pregnant too early and out of wedlock, and supporting musical groups that use vulgar and racist language. He was immediately criticized by black leaders who agreed while there were problems within the black community, he should not air their dirty laundry in public. Cosby's response was "Your dirty laundry gets out of school at 2:30 every day, it's cursing and calling each other n—."[21] Those black leaders criticized Cosby, not so much for what he said as for breaking the united image they felt their community needed to maintain.

The situation in Salt Lake City NAACP continued to deteriorate so much that in 2002 one observer noted there "has definitely been a rift in the community."[22] That fall several disenchanted NAACP members, led by Michael Styles and Charles Henderson, asked Alberta to challenge Jeanetta Williams for leadership of the Salt Lake City NAACP. In a demonstration of her long-held religious beliefs she said, "If I can get up one more time, that tells me the Lord wants me to finish the work I started."[23] Several people were concerned that the strain of running and, if she won, of managing the organization, would be too great for Alberta, then seventy-eight years old. Styles said that he quit worrying when he started receiving phone calls from Alberta every morning about 7:00 a.m. asking if he had checked the lists, contacted people, or in other ways appropriately managed her campaign. Obviously Alberta Henry was still in fighting form and ready to run her own show. Styles felt even less concerned when she started complaining about all the trouble he was getting her into, even referring to him as "Trouble" when she spoke of him to others. He felt he had truly arrived if he had become number one on Alberta Henry's troublesome list.[24]

Alberta and her supporters campaigned hard, but on November 4, 2002, "in an election that remained contentious to the end, Jeanetta Williams . . . retained her presidency of the Salt Lake City Branch of the National Association for the Advancement of Colored People." The election was decided, at least in part, by Williams's appeal outside the black community. The members who voted "included large numbers of white and Pacific Islanders"—so many, in fact, that "Henry and other members of the branch said they suspected election protocol violations and planned to file a complaint with the national organization."[25] Although she was discouraged by the loss, Alberta returned home to enjoy the same quiet life she had before the election. "I go to church. I volunteer. I tell you my life is perfect."[26] She continued to visit friends, volunteer, and opine on life in Utah.

Then in the winter of 2003 Alberta was diagnosed with cancer and began treatments at the University of Utah Hospital and the Huntsman Cancer Center. Treatment bought her some time, but by July of 2004, she needed care all day. By then Patrice was divorced and back with the family in their West Valley City home. She gave up some promising job opportunities to stay home during the day to care for her grandmother. Julia describes her oldest daughter as loving and caring, attributes that Julia herself had long shown in working with her mother and caring for her father. Both women would need those qualities during the next year. Julia had married Gilbert Leyba and had baby daughter, Adrian, in 2004. The entire family adored the baby, but it meant that Julia and Patrice were sandwiched between two generations, both requiring a lot of care. To simplify the situation, they arranged a room just off the kitchen for Alberta to facilitate her care, and someone always stayed nearby.[27]

Despite Alberta's illness, or maybe because of it, a great many people dropped by to pay their respects and say goodbye. So many came, in fact, that at one point Alberta told Reverend France Davis: "Reverend, make these people leave me alone. I'm trying to die."[28] Nonetheless, she kept receiving visitors—family, old friends, students she had helped to become competent, contributing adults. Shauna Graves Robertson, a member of the Soul Sisters Drill Team and an AHEF scholar, by then a judge with the Salt Lake County Justice Court, helped put Alberta's legal affairs in order. Alberta's good friend Mary Schultz came weekly and helped her sort through her voluminous files and papers, preparing them for donation to the University of Utah Marriott Library, Special Collections. Alberta, as she always had, spent a lot of her time studying her Bible. When the visitation team from Calvary Baptist Church came to see her, she asked them Bible questions and sent them away with assignments to locate scriptures for her.[29]

Medicine, determination and, in Alberta's view, prayer helped prolong her life, but the cancer was winning. In May 2005 Alberta Henry was moved into the Care Source Hospice where she died just a few days later on May 11, 2005.[30] Once again, tributes poured in. Harvey Boyd, one of the earliest recipients of help from the Alberta Henry Education Foundation and now its director, said: "She gave hope to a lot of people.... She helped people visualize their dreams.... She thought everyone had potential." France Davis, pastor of Calvary Baptist Church, Alberta Henry's minister and friend, compared her to Rosa Parks. "She was a voice for the voiceless. She had a way of breaking down barriers." Helen Sandack, Henry's first employer in Utah and her good friend, observed, "She's made the most of her life by giving and caring."[31] Stuart Reid, that young man from LDS Church Public Relations who had accompanied her to a meeting of the NAACP and eventually found himself a member of the board, said: "More than any person I know in the community, she sacrificed her time and energy to build the community. I have a lot of respect for her, and I know [LDS] President Hinkley does as well."[32] Her daughter Julia spoke of her own great love for her mother and acknowledged Alberta as her own personal role model, calling her, "just a very strong person, a pillar of the community, an advocate for civil rights [who] loved to help people . . . She made a lot of impact on a lot of people's lives." Jeanetta Williams, Henry's protegee, who remained as president of the Salt Lake City Chapter of the NAACP despite Alberta's challenge for that office in 2002, issued a formal statement: "We are saddened to hear about her death. Our condolences go to her family. She was very dedicated to the NAACP and the civil rights movement." The message was read at the homegoing service, but Williams did not attend.[33]

Alberta had done all those things, but she gave credit to the source she always cited.

"All of these things just evolved; I never planned any of them. The Lord had a job for me to do. He sent me here and gave me a husband to do that. And then when he thought I was rested in 1967, I went to the day care. I never went out and applied for a job. How do you account for me doing that if it wasn't for the Lord?"[34]

EPILOGUE

Alberta had said that her homegoing service (not a funeral) was not to be a gloomy affair, because she so completely believed that she was, in fact, going home. Reverend France Davis, her pastor and also her old friend and compatriot in so many good causes, conducted the service. He reported that she had told him, firmly, several times, that she did not want it to be a gloomy affair. The whole congregation chuckled at that "firmly." Everyone present recognized and appreciated Alberta's strong stand on her final issue on this earth.

She had requested three songs: "Peace Be Still," "Your Grace and Mercy," and "Midnight Train to Georgia" by Gladys Knight and the Pips. The choir sang the first two during the services, and the organist played the last while the coffin was being closed. The services began at noon on May 17, 2005, at Calvary Baptist Church and ended only a little past 1:00 p.m., allowing attendance by many people who could only come during their lunch hours because they simply could not afford to miss an hour of work. They were part of the broad range of people from Alberta's public and private life, a range which demonstrated the breadth of her influence. The entire Sandack family, her first employers and lifetime friends, were there. So was Esther Landa's sister Ruth, since Alberta's friend and mentor was too ill to come. Former governor Calvin Rampton attended, and Salt Lake City Mayor Rocky Anderson spoke, noting that he had first met Alberta in her home when she was organizing protests against the execution of William Andrews.[1] Philanthropist Jon Huntsman had been scheduled to speak, but at the last minute he could not make it, so his son, Governor

Jon Huntsman Jr., along with his wife and daughter, came to offer their family's condolences to Alberta's family.

Reverend Davis took the theme for his eulogy from 2 Timothy 4:6–8: "For now I am ready to be offered, and the time of my departure is at hand. I have fought a good fight, I have finished my course, I have kept the faith: Henceforth there is laid up for me a crown of righteousness, which the Lord, the righteous judge, shall give me at that day: and not to me only, but unto all them also that love his appearing." Alberta, he said, had fought a good fight, against racism and intolerance and for better education and jobs. He noted that she stayed in Utah only because she felt the Lord wanted her here; she lived with a sense of mission, and he challenged the people in attendance to truly pay their respects to Alberta by finding their own missions.

Among the speakers were government officials, old friends, and scholars who had been aided by Alberta. Shauna Graves Robertson, an Alberta Henry Education Foundation student and currently the presiding judge in Salt Lake County, read the obituary; she also recognized several people present who, like herself, were members of one of the first groups Alberta had formed: the Soul Sisters Drill Team. Its aim had been to help teenage black girls raise their own evaluations of themselves; given the heights Robertson and the other members have attained, the drill team achieved that goal.

Robertson also thanked Alberta's daughter, Julia, for sharing her mother, observing that the Henry house was always full, the whole black community of Salt Lake City seeming to congregate there regularly. Ronald Coleman, professor of history from the University of Utah, noted that the Board of Directors of the AHEF were working to help the program continue. "We can think of no better way to honor Mrs. Henry's life work than to make sure opportunities are available."[2] Patricia Palmer read a resolution from the Salt Lake City Chapter of the NAACP honoring Alberta for her life's work since Jeanetta Williams could not attend the homegoing service.

There were "Amens" from the congregation when anyone talked about Alberta as a worker or a fighter; there were chuckles when she was described as "feisty" or "firm." There was, as Alberta had asked, more laughter than tears. Immediately following the services, she was buried beside Harold in Mount Olivet Cemetery in Salt Lake City. She will remain forever in the state she only intended to visit, and she will rest in a city where she rarely ceased to work.

Alberta Henry applied for only one job in Utah: working as a domestic for the Sandack family. All the other positions, paid and unpaid, that she held—in Head Start and Salt Lake School District and the many organizations she joined and led—came only because someone asked her to accept them. Alberta herself felt strongly that it was the Lord who brought those positions to her, saying in nearly every conversation we had, "All I know is, the Lord has work for me to do." She may have been unhappy that the Lord wanted her to stay in Utah, but she stayed because she genuinely believed that the Lord knew what He was doing. A lot of people from a great many faiths would agree with her that the Lord did indeed know what He was doing and Utah is better for it.

There are still those who maintained that in the late twentieth century much was still the same. "Relations between blacks and whites in this country have been based since the beginning on a conception of two socially distinct groups, defined largely in terms of physical characteristics, though with social categorization enforced. . . . There is no evidence that this virtually absolute differentiation of the American population has been reduced by any of the changes of the last four decades. . . . What has changed [by 1985] is the normative definition of appropriate relations between blacks and whites."[3] By the twenty-first century, American society has reached the point that blatant racism is "no longer socially acceptable."[4] Nonetheless, racism has certainly not been eliminated. On their website the Ku Klux Klan offers "A Message of Hope and Deliverance to White Christian America" along with tee-shirts,[5] and the Aryan Nations, Skinhead Division, proffers "A Sword of Truth" on theirs.[6]

In Utah the situation has improved over the years. In 1984, Ozwald Balfour, community affairs director of the University Of Utah's black student union observed that, although "there are more opportunities for blacks in this state than others, we still have a long way to go before all discrimination—here and elsewhere—is eradicated."[7] Since then minorities have increased in both number and influence in the state, yet inequities still exist. The 2010 census reported that Utah is still predominantly white, 86.1 percent. The minority population (black, American Indian, Asian, and Pacific Islanders) of 13.9 percent is certainly higher than the 1.7 percent it was in 1950 soon after Alberta arrived, yet blacks still comprise only

1.1 percent of the state's population.[8] Perhaps even more significant, the power structure in Utah remains white. In 2005 no minority candidates filed to run for office in Salt Lake City, despite "the fact that over fifty percent of all children in the Salt Lake City School District are ethnic minorities."[9] By 2014, however, former Saratoga Springs's black woman mayor Mia Love raised more than $500,000 in three months to run against incumbent Jim Matheson, whom she had come close to defeating in 2012.[10] By the 2016 election she garnered nearly 54 percent of the vote and served in the United States Congress, continuing to serve until she lost a tightly contested race in 2018 and became a CNN commentator, promising 'unleashed' talk.[11]

Alberta Henry herself reflected that changing attitude. In 1974 she said, "I'm not going to come out (among whites) until I feel comfortable there . . . I'm going to stay where I'm at and learn to handle myself."[12] By the next decade, she apparently did feel comfortable being among whites and other groups as well. In the mid-1980s the Henry family moved to West Valley City, a predominantly white suburb of Salt Lake City, occasioning very little fuss. Their next-door neighbors, Von and Mavis Blackburn, both white, recall no real difficulty about a black family moving into the area. The Blackburns themselves became such good friends with the Henrys that when their son was born, they took him over to meet Alberta even before they took him into their own home.[13]

Alberta Henry helped bring about such a congenial atmosphere, even though her tactics were sometimes highly abrasive. She helped, occasionally shoved, both the majority and minority populations to become more aware and appreciative of each other. In the process she stepped on a lot of toes—a black woman telling white men about her civil rights was a more than slightly frightening idea in the decades following World War II for both blacks and whites. Nonetheless, over those years she helped to alter white people's perceptions of blacks and blacks' perceptions of themselves. I never did figure out which one of those changes pleased her most.

Alberta built upon the efforts of great national leaders like A. Philip Randolph and Martin Luther King Jr. Like many others all over the country she applied her own talents to solve the specific problems in her own area and to make that area better for everyone who lived there. Many people recognized that Alberta Henry helped make the civil rights movement a success by "working in the vineyard" where the Lord had planted her.[14] Judge Tyrone E. Medley, judge of the District Court for the Third Judicial District, State of Utah, and the first black appointed to the bench in Utah observed:

> I'm a strong believer in history. Without question I am the beneficiary here in this state of those civil rights workers who went before me and plowed the way. The Alberta Henrys of the world, the Albert Fritzes of the world, I hope they understand that I do appreciate and understand what they did by paving the way for me. I am the beneficiary of their works and efforts. I'm certainly hoping at the end of my tenure as a judge, I hope my performance record, I hope that track record as a judge will be such that when African Americans are screened and interviewed for judicial positions that it won't be such a nuance. I can tell you that it is not easy being the first and only African American judge in the state of Utah. I certainly hope that my career will have inspired some to pursue this type of career. I also hope that my career will have sensitized the powers that be that there is really nothing that African Americans cannot do, that we are not limited to the traditional stereotypes. So, in that way I would hope that I made some contribution.[15]

To that, Alberta Henry would say "Amen."

APPENDIX A

TIMELINE OF ALBERTA HENRY'S LIFE AND AFFILIATIONS AND HONORS

TIMELINE OF ALBERTA HENRY'S LIFE

1907 **Harold Henry born in Denver, Colorado.**

1909 National Association for the Advancement of Colored People (NAACP) organized.

1914 World War I began in Europe.
Salt Lake City Chapter of the NAACP organized.

1917 **Rosetta Hill born.**
United States entered World War I.

1918 World War I ended.
President Woodrow Wilson issued a statement condemning lynching.

1919 **Nevada Hill born.**

1920 **Alberta Hill born.**

1921 **David Hill born.**

1923 **The Hill family moved from Louisiana to Topeka, Kansas.**

1932 **Alberta Hill graduated from McKinley Elementary School, Topeka, Kansas.**

1935 **Alberta Hill graduated from Curtis Junior High, Topeka Kansas.**

1938 **Alberta Hill injured in an auto accident that left a scar on her face for life.**
NAACP lawyers Charles Houston and Thurgood Marshall won a legal challenge that allowed a black student admission to the University of Maryland.

1939 **Alberta Hill graduated from Topeka High School.**
Daughters of the American Revolution refused to allow Marion Anderson to sing in their Constitution Hall in Washington, D.C.; the concert was moved to the Lincoln Memorial where an estimated seventy-five thousand people attended.
World War II began in Europe.

1940 **Alberta Hill worked for the Ritz Theater, Topeka, Kansas, as projectionist, cashier, and usher.**

1941 Japanese attack on Pearl Harbor brought the United States into World War II.

1942 **James and Julia Hill divorced.**
Alberta Hill married Isaac Gooch.
Congress of Racial Equality (CORE) was organized and used direct, nonviolent challenges to Jim Crow practices.

1945 World War II ended.

1946 **Alberta Gooch became a licensed two-way radio dispatcher for the City Cab Company, Garden City, Kansas.**

1947 **Alberta Gooch was the co-owner and manager of the Jenkins Cafe, Topeka, Kansas.**
The Brooklyn Dodgers hired Jackie Robinson, breaking the color line in professional baseball.

1948 **Alberta Hill Gooch suffered an appendicitis attack and moved to Utah to recover.**
Alberta filed for a divorce from Isaac Gooch.
President Harry S. Truman integrated the United States military forces.

1949 **Alberta Hill began working for Wallace and Helen Sandack.**
Alberta Hill joined the Salt Lake City Chapter of the NAACP.

1950 **Alberta Hill married Harold Lloyd Henry.**

1951 **Harold and Alberta Henry joined Pilgrim Baptist Church.**

1954 **Harold and Alberta Henry became charter members of New Hope Baptist Church.**
The United States Supreme Court ruled racial segregation of schools unconstitutional in the case of *Brown v. Board of Education of Topeka.*
Rosa Parks was arrested in Montgomery, Alabama, when she refused to give her seat on a bus to a white woman.

A study by the Utah State Department of Education concluded that although Utah had no legally segregated schools, minority students faced discrimination when they sought scholastic honors.

1957 **Wendell Henry born.**
Arkansas Governor Orval Faubus ordered the National Guard to prevent integration of black students into Little Rock's Central High School; President Dwight Eisenhower sent federal troops to enforce integration.
President Eisenhower sent Congress the Civil Rights Act of 1957, the first civil rights legislation since Reconstruction.

1958 **Julia Henry born.**
Oklahoma City NAACP Youth Council organized sit-ins to integrate five stores; the practice spread through the Midwest and South, generating television coverage that spread the story across the nation.

1959 Black Muslims' rejection of Christianity and hatred of whites was reported in a two-hour television documentary.

1960 **Alberta Henry was elected president of the Utah-Idaho Baptist Association and began traveling throughout the region, encouraging people to register to vote and stressing assistance from within the black community.**
A sit-in at a lunch counter in Greensboro, North Carolina, set off a chain of demonstrations against segregation in public facilities.

1961 The Student Non-violent Coordinating Council (SNCC) formed.
Freedom rides on public transport began in Southern states to force integration.

1962 Students for a Democratic Society (SDS) formed and began demonstrations for equal treatment of all races.

1963 Civil rights marchers in Birmingham were jailed, beaten, shocked, and otherwise abused; much of the abuse was broadcast on national television, informing the country outside the South of the problems blacks faced.
While incarcerated for leading freedom marches in Alabama, Martin Luther King Jr. wrote the "Letter from Birmingham Jail."
Medgar Evers, NAACP field director, was shot and killed in the driveway of his home in Jackson, Mississippi.

President John F. Kennedy was assassinated in Dallas, Texas.

1964 Civil rights workers Michael Schwerner, Andrew Goodman, and James Chaney were killed and their bodies hidden in Meridian, Mississippi.

Congress passed the Civil Rights Act guaranteeing federal protection of fundamental rights for all citizens.

Civil rights advocates marched from Selma to Montgomery, Alabama, meeting violence and abuse along the way.

1965 Voting Rights Act passed by Congress, giving all American citizens equal rights to vote.

Thirty thousand voters, early, all black, were registered in the Southern states.

Race riots erupted in American cities, notably in Chicago and the Watts section of Los Angeles.

Governor Calvin Rampton signed Utah's first Civil Rights Bill.

1966 **Alberta Henry resigned from the Baptist Women's Missionary Society.**

Race riots occurred in more than twenty American cities.

1967 **The Alberta Henry Education Foundation incorporated.**

Alberta Henry hired as an aide and then a teacher in the Salt Lake City Head Start Center.

Head Start programs for early childhood education began in Salt Lake City.

1968 Martin Luther King Jr. and Robert F. Kennedy assassinated.

Anti–Vietnam War protestors demonstrated in the streets outside the Democratic National Convention in Chicago.

1970 **Alberta Henry organized the Soul Sisters Drill Team at the Nettie Gregory Center with Marsha Boyd as director.**

Alberta took the drill team to perform at the national NAACP semiannual conference in Asilomar, California.

Alberta Henry attended the national NAACP conference in Chicago.

1971 **University of Utah awarded Alberta Henry an honorary doctorate degree.**

Alberta Henry became the youth advisor for the Salt Lake City Branch of the NAACP.

Governor Calvin Rampton implemented Negro History Week in Utah schools.

1972 Alberta Henry was hired as a minority consultant for Salt Lake City School District; she worked with Joe Sandoval, who had been hired earlier.

Alberta Henry helped organize the black student honor society in Salt Lake School District. The name was later changed to the Rainbow Honorary Society to include all interested students.

Alberta Henry became chair of the Educational Task Force for Salt Lake City's Model City Program.

1973 Alberta Henry entered the race for Utah House of Representative District Six.

Alberta Henry took members of the black student honors society with GPAs of 3.0 or better to Denver, Colorado, for an educational experience.

Alberta Henry became the first vice president of the Salt Lake City Branch of the NAACP.

The Soul Sisters Drill Team was named Outstanding Youth Group at the West Regional Conference in Pacific Grove, California.

Donald Thomas was hired as superintendent of Salt Lake City School District.

Governor Calvin Rampton declared the week of August 13 to be Alberta Henry Education Foundation Week.

1974 Alberta Henry took members of the black student honors society with GPAs of 3.0 or better to Seattle, Washington, for an educational experience.

Dale Pierre Selby and William Andrews robbed the Hi-Fi Shop in Ogden, where they tortured five people, killing three in the process.

1975 Alberta Henry spearheaded a visit to New Zealand by twenty minority honor students and five adults.

1976 *Reverend Robert L. Harris of Ogden was elected to the Utah State House of Representatives, the first African American elected to public office in Utah.*

1977 Alberta Henry took members of the Rainbow Honorary Society with GPAs of 3.0 or better to San Diego for an educational experience.

1978 Alberta Henry took members of the Rainbow Honorary Society with GPAs of 3.0 or better to Jamaica for an educational experience.

President Spencer W. Kimball of the Church of Jesus Christ of Latter-day Saints announced that the church's longheld policy of restricting its priesthood from black men had been lifted.

1979 Alberta Henry took members of the Rainbow Honorary Society with GPAs of 3.0 or better to Victoria, Canada, for an educational experience.

Alberta Henry became the third vice president of the Salt Lake City Branch of the NAACP.

1980 Alberta Henry took members of the Rainbow Honorary Society with GPAs of 3.0 or better to St. Augustine, Florida, for an educational experience.

Alberta Henry graduated from the University of Utah with a bachelor's degree.

1981 Alberta Henry took members of the Rainbow Honorary Society with GPAs of 3.0 or better to Mexico City for an educational experience.

1982 Alberta Henry took members of the Rainbow Honorary Society with GPAs of 3.0 or better to Hawaii for an educational experience.

1983 New Hope Baptist Church closed and Harold and Alberta Henry transferred their membership to Calvary Baptist Church.

Alberta Henry took members of the Rainbow Honorary Society with GPAs of 3.0 or better to Cancun, Mexico, for an educational experience.

1984 Alberta Henry took members of the Rainbow Honorary Society with GPAs of 3.0 or better to Mazatlan, Mexico, for an educational experience.

1985 Alberta Henry took members of the Rainbow Honorary Society with GPAs of 3.0 or better to Jamaica for an educational experience.

1986 Alberta Henry took members of the Rainbow Honorary Society with GPAs of 3.0 or better to Disneyland for an educational experience.
Alberta Henry retired from the Salt Lake City School District.
Alberta Henry became president of the Salt Lake City Branch of the NAACP.

1987 *Dale Pierre Selby was executed for his part in the Hi-Fi Shop murders.*

1988 Wendell Henry died.
Alberta Henry brought her mother to live in Salt Lake City.

1991 Rodney King, who was black, was beaten by police officers in Los Angeles attempting to arrest him; the case became a focal point for charges of police brutality against minorities.
Clarence Thomas, a black federal judge of the United States Court of Appeals for the District of Columbia Circuit, was nominated and confirmed a justice of the United States Supreme Court.
Salt Lake City NAACP opposed Thomas's nomination.
Alberta Henry observed of Thomas that "He's as good as any other."

1992 Alberta Henry's mother, Julia Palmer Hill Brantly, died in Salt Lake City.
Alberta Henry retired as president of the Salt Lake City Chapter of the NAACP, succeeded by her protege, Jeanetta Williams.
Salt Lake Branch of the NAACP brought Rosa Parks to Utah.
William Andrews was executed for the Hi-Fi Shop murders, despite efforts by Alberta Henry and others to prevent it.

1996 Harold Henry died in Salt Lake City.
Isaac Gooch died in Kansas.

1997 Alberta Henry, along with Larry Houston, Leslie Reynolds, and Bonnie Dew, resigned from the board of directors of the Salt Lake City Chapter of the NAACP over concerns about the way the program was being run.

1998 Rosetta Hill died at her sister Alberta's home in Salt Lake City.

2002 A group of concerned NAACP members asked Alberta Henry to challenge Jeanetta Williams for the presidency of the Salt Lake City Chapter; Alberta ran but was defeated.
2003 Alberta Henry was diagnosed with cancer.
2005 Alberta Hill Henry died and was buried in Salt Lake City.
2009 Julia Henry Lebya died and was buried in Salt Lake City.

AFFILIATIONS AND HONORS

Democratic Party, Member: 1941–2005
  Chair of local mass meetings: 1955–2000
Delegate, Salt Lake County and Utah State Democratic Conventions: 1971–2000
Alternate Delegate, Midterm Democratic Convention, Kansas City, Missouri: 1974
Candidate for State Legislative District Six: 1974, 1976
Delegate, National Democratic Convention, New York City: 1976
Delegate, National Democratic Conference, Memphis, Tennessee: 1978
Semper Fidelis, President (professional women's club in Topeka, Kansas): 1941
Black Championship in Tennis, Topeka, Kansas, First Place: 1942
Negro Tennis Tournament, Women's Singles, First Place: 1942
Salt Lake Branch, National Association for the Advancement of Colored People (NAACP)
  Alberta joined the Salt Lake Branch, NAACP: 1949
  Albert Fritz Civil Rights Worker of the Year Award for Untiring Services to Humanity, NAACP: 1971
  Youth Group Award for Faithful Service to the NAACP Youth: 1974, 1979
  Youth Advisor: 1971–1977
  First Vice President: 1973–1978
  President's Award for Outstanding Service to NAACP: 1976
  Third Vice President: 1979–1980
  President: 1981–1992
  Appreciation Award as outgoing president: 1981–1992, 1993
  Martin Luther King Award: 1988
  Rosa Parks Award, Salt Lake Branch NAACP: 1995

New Hope Baptist Church, Charter Member: 1954
  Clerk: 1954
  Missionary President
  Sunday School Superintendent
  Sunday School Teacher
  President of the Usher Board
Utah-Idaho Baptist Women's Association, President: 1960–1966
  Missionary Department
"Gospel Hour," announcements and gospel music Sunday mornings, KSXX Radio Station: 1966–1967
Franklin Elementary School PTA Board: 1967–68
Alberta Henry Education Foundation: 1967
  Founder: 1967
  Chair: 1967–1980
  Emeritus Chair: 1980–2005
Western States Women's Convention, Financial Clerk: 1968
Black Advisory Board, University of Utah, Chair: 1969–1971
Governor's Commission on State House Fellows for the State of Utah: 1969–1979
Commendation from President Richard M. Nixon, in Recognition of Exceptional Service to Others: 1970
Beehive Lodge of Elks Citizen's Award: 1970
Honorary Degree, Doctor of Humane Letters, University of Utah: 1971
Brookings Institute Wasatch Front: 1971–1972
Governor's Black Policy Advisory Council: 1971–1979
  Chair: 1975–1976
Model Cities, Education Task Force Chair: 1971–1973
Community Service Council, Minority Committee Chair: 1971–1977
Utah State House Fellows Commission: 1971–1977
FCC Radio and Telephone Operator, third class permit: 1972
Students' Award, Utah Technical College: 1972
Black Honor Society/Rainbow Honor Society: 1972–1986
Altrusa Club of Salt Lake, Presentation of Honors: 1972
  Honors Award for Outstanding Community Service: 1973
  Member: 1973–1985
  President: 1979–1980

Blacks Unlimited, Founder and Chair: 1972–1989
Utah Endowment for the Humanities: 1972–1978
Biography entered as a permanent record in the Community Memorial Chapel Honors Library of Living History: 1973
Westside Community Council Board, Social Service
  Committee Chair: 1973–1976
YWCA Board of Directors: 1972–1978
Utah Advisory Committee, Commission on Civil Rights: 1973–1979
  Chair: 1975–1976
Salt Lake Association of School Administrators: 1973–1986
  Social Committee Chair: 1983
  Secretary: 1981–1982
Traveler's Aid Society: 1973–1979
  President: 1977–1979
Manpower, Employment Training Administration Council Board: 1973–1982
Blacks in Utah, Moderator, KCPX Television: 1974–1978
Utah Opportunities Industrialization Center (U/OIC): 1974–1995
  Instrumental in bringing OIC to Salt Lake City: May 1974
  Vice Chair: 1977–1990
  Award of Merit, Director of the Year Award: 1985
  Vision Award for Outstanding Service to the Community and State: 1993
  Chair: 1994
  Distinguished Service Award, Utah: 1995
  Award of Merit, Director of the Year: 1995
Black Parents Workshops, Director, with programs developed in several areas
  State Board: September 1974
  Magna Elementary, Granite School District: November 1975
  Edison Elementary, Salt Lake School District: November 1975
  Jackson Elementary, Salt Lake School District: April 1976
  Northwest Intermediate School, Salt Lake School District: December 1976
  South High School, Salt Lake School District: May 1978
  East High School, Salt Lake School District: March 1979
  West High School, Salt Lake School District: May 1979

Published curriculums
Contribution of Eighteen Blacks: 1978
Resource Unit on Dr. Martin Luther King Jr.: 1979
United Way of Salt Lake City, Member, Board of Directors: 1974–1977
Campfire Girls Woman in the Community: 1975
Diana Award from Epsilon Sigma Alpha International Granting Membership in the Distinguished International Academy of Noble Achievement for Exceptional Service to Humanity: 1975
Golden Deeds Award, "For Compassion, Dynamic Leadership, Resourcefulness and Example in Building Bridges for Understanding," Exchange Club: 1975
Utah Student Cultural Exchange Committee, chaperoned twenty students to New Zealand and was guest speaker for the Rotary Club while there: 1975
Exchange Club Golden Deeds Award: 1975
Utah Technical College (now Salt Lake Community College) Service Award: 1975
Governor's Blue Ribbon Commission on Energy: 1976–1977
Governor's Black Policy Advisory Council, Chair: 1975, 1986
Utah Black Community Honors, "A Tribute to a Great Humanitarian": 1976
Distinguished Woman of the Year Award, Women's Resource Center, University of Utah: 1976
Utah State Board of Education Advisory Committee: 1976–1986
Committee on Education for Black Students, Chair: 1976–1983
Community Service Award, Westminster College Alumni Association: 1977
Listed in *Who's Who in Black America*: 1977–1978
Listed in *Who's Who in Politics*: 1977–1978
Listed in *Personalities of the West and Midwest*: 1977–1978
Salt Lake City Accountability Plan: 1977
Utah Mother's Association, Nominee for Mother of the Year: 1977
Westminster College Alumni Association Community Service Award: 1977
Manpower Planning Council/CETA: 1977–1982
Youth Task Force Chair: 1977–1980
Executive Board Chair: 1981–1982

Significant Segment Chair: 1981–1982
Published pamphlet, *Parents' Rights and Responsibilities*: 1978, revised 1982
State Board of Education Committee on Course Content for Cultural Awareness: 1978–1979
Salt Lake City Community Intermediate School (SLIP): 1978–1987
Chair: 1980–1987
Utah Federal Judicial Selection Commission, committee to select Utah's Third District Federal Judge: 1979
Salt Lake School District Women's Administrators: 1979–1986
Coordinator: 1979–1984
Community Service Award: 1979
Alberta Henry Education Foundation for Remarkable Achievements: 1980
Bachelor of Science Degree in Education, Cum Laude, University of Utah: 1980
Honorary Member, Phi Delta Kappa: 1980
Advisory Council, Graduate School of Education, University of Utah: 1981
Honorary Life Membership, Utah State Human Services Conference: 1981
Children's Museum of Utah Board of Directors: 1981–1982
Health Advisory Council, Utah State Department of Health: 1981–1986
Ethics and Disciplinary Committee of the Utah State Board: 1982–1986
Inducted into Salt Lake Council of Women's Hall of Fame: 1983
Orrin G. Hatch Advisory Committee to Review the Legislative Agenda of the 98th Congress: 1983
Calvary Baptist Church, Member: 1983–2005
Missionary Society President: 1986–1991
Published *Blacks in Utah* calendars: 1984–1985
Outstanding Guest Speaker, Dugway Proving Ground: 1985
Published *Blacks in Utah* resource book: 1986
Family Counseling Center Board of Directors: 1986–1989
Utah Mathematics, Engineering, Science, Achievement/Minority Engineering Program (MESA/MEP) Board of Directors: 1986 –1988
Governor's Black Beehive Award, in honor of Martin Luther King Day: 1987

Utah State Office of Education Black Advisory Board Award: 1987
Outstanding Achievement Award, YWCA Community Leadership: 1989
Distinguished Service in Alternative Education, Salt Lake Community Intermediate School: 1990–1991
Outstanding Service to the Community, Community Service Award, *Mountain West Minority Reporter Sentinel*: 1991
Honorary Member, Delta Kappa Gamma Society: 1992
Renie Cohen Memorial Civil Liberties Award for Years of Dedicated Service, American Civil Liberties Union: 1992
Appreciation of Lifetime of Dedicated Service to the Furtherance of Equality for All Americans, Federal Bureau of Investigation: 1993
Appreciation Award, Community Relations Service for "Leadership in Addressing Minority Issues," United States Department of Justice: 1994
Appreciation Award, Utah Defense Depot, Ogden, Utah: 1994
Community Leadership and Service Award, Catholic Community Service of Utah: 1996
Honored by National Conference for Community and Justice: 2000
Utah Humanities Council Mayor's Award: 2003
Honorary Degree, Doctor of Humane Letters, Salt Lake Community College: 2003

APPENDIX B

A SAMPLING OF STUDENTS ASSISTED BY THE ALBERTA HENRY EDUCATION FOUNDATION

The Alberta Henry Education Foundation has aided over two hundred students to achieve their educational goals, sometimes with tuition, sometimes with books, and often with just enough bridge money to allow them to finish or to meet specific needs. Nearly all of them also worked full- or part-time while they were in school. Perhaps as important as the money the foundation granted were the people involved who offered mentoring, advice, and the assurance that the individual's goals were worth the time and effort they required. Unfortunately a complete list of those students and their current whereabouts is not available, but the following few samples indicate the kinds of achievements made possible by AHEF assistance.

TIMOTHY ALLEN

With help from the AHEF, Timothy Allen became a lawyer.

WILLIE ALLEN

Willie Allen graduated from the University of Utah with help from the foundation and went to work in the film industry in Los Angeles.

HARVEY BOYD

Harvey Boyd entered the University of Utah in 1968, majoring in architecture. He had worked that summer and saved enough to meet most of his basic needs, but the foundation provided bridge money to help him with school expenses. He became an architect in Salt Lake City and a volunteer with the AHEF to ensure scholarships for deserving students.

SOLOMON CACHON

Solomon Cachon entered Westminster College in September 1969. He observed that in no ways did the elementary, junior high, and high schools he attended encourage him to go on to college. In college he became more confident, involved, and outspoken about the problems of minorities, becoming a lawyer in Utah.

TALLIE LEE CAVANESS

Tallie Lee Cavaness began school at the University of Utah in the fall of 1968 on the GI bill. The next year the AHEF began sponsoring him as a major in mathematics. He graduated with both a bachelor of science in computer science and a bachelor of science in electrical engineering. He went on to receive a law degree from the University of Utah Law School and become a member of the Utah Bar Association. He worked for Hercules Aerospace as a technical writer and contracts administrator until his death in 2001.

SHAUNA BENNS EDMONDS

Shauna Benns attended Utah State University, along with her friend Sheila Peak, at least in part because they thought that if they put some miles between themselves and Alberta Henry, she wouldn't check up on them so much. It's true she didn't just drop in as she did with students at the University of Utah, but she still kept track. Benns recognized and appreciated the value of Alberta Henry's concern and watchfulness when she became an adult. She graduated in early childhood education and business. She taught for several years then went into insurance because she needed more than teacher's pay, but with plans to return to teaching after retirement.

DARIUS GRAY

Darius Gray attended Brigham Young University on an AHEF scholarship. He helped found the black LDS group, Genesis, and became an author, helped to produce documentaries, and mentored many others in several fields.

JOE GRAY

Joe Gray was a senior by the time the AHEF began helping him. He had put himself through three years of school and taken time off to serve in the army before he applied for aid. By his final year he had used all of his eligibility from an athletic scholarship, so the foundation provided a small amount to help him graduate. He worked for State Farm Insurance in Colorado.

TONI HARP

Toni Harp received help from Alpha and Omega, one of the precursor organizations to the AHEF. She went to University of Chicago in October of 1967 and the foundation came into being that December. Harp was instrumental in the preliminary work to help establish the AHEF. She went on to become state senator for the Tenth District, New Haven, Connecticut, from 1993 to 2013. In that year she was elected mayor of New Haven, taking office on January 1, 2014.

MARSHA BOYD HODGES

Henry worked with Marsha Boyd while Boyd was a student from the University of Utah, hired by Salt Lake School District to counsel high school students who were performing poorly and were in danger of dropping out of school. With a little help from the foundation, Boyd became a probation officer and continued working with the same sorts of young people she and Henry used to track down and put back in class.

KIM HOPKINS

Kim Hopkins was an eighth grade student at Westlake Junior High School when he first encountered Alberta Henry. He was one of the students with grade points above 3.5 included on a trip to Pacific Grove, California. The AHEF helped him to attend Utah State University. He became a teacher at Hunter High School in Granite School District.

INGRID LAKE

Elizabeth (Ingrid) Lake was working and had some tuition aid and received only a small AHEF grant to help meet her basic needs. She attended the University of Utah with an interest in nursing but shifted to education and became a teacher in California.

SHAUNA GRAVES ROBERTSON

Shauna Robertson received her bachelor's degree from the University of Arizona and then the AHEF funded her graduate work at the University of Utah. She served as a lawyer with legal aid and is currently the presiding judge in Salt Lake County.

MICHAEL STYLES

Michael Styles became the director of the Utah Office of Black Affairs, and remained good friends with Alberta for the rest of her life.

GROVER THOMPSON

Grover Thompson worked for the state board of education while he attended college, paying most of his own bills. The AHEF provided enough support money to make up the difference. He graduated from the University of Utah with a degree in English. In 1972 he was elected student body president on a write-in campaign and served during the 1972–1973 school year, the first black student to hold that position. The following year he was accepted to the University of Utah Law School.

CLIFFORD WILLIAMS

While his work provided enough for basic living needs, Clifford Williams received AHEF aid with tuition for school at the University of Utah and later worked for the California university system.

KAREN WALLENBERG

Karen Wallenberg studied architecture and worked with Harvey Boyd, another AHEF student.

JUDEE LAWRENCE WILLIAMS

Judee Williams received AHEF help to attend the University of Utah and worked in affirmative action at the University of Utah and as a manager for internal communications, community, and government relations for the Phillips Corporation in California.

APPENDIX C

AN ACT IN RELATION TO SERVICE

Alberta was most insistent that this act[1] be included as an appendix to her life story. While she acknowledged that slavery actually existed in nearly all Western states, especially the Spanish enslavement of Native Americans in New Mexico and Arizona, she felt strongly about the fact that Utah was the only Western state or territory to legalize slavery. In fact, this law is patterned after the ones adopted in Northern states to end slavery.

SEC. 1 [Service due in other states or territories shall be binding in this territory]

Be it enacted by the Governor and Legislative Assembly of the Territory of Utah, that any person or persons coming to this Territory and bringing with them servants justly bound to them, arising from special contract or otherwise, said person or persons shall be entitled to such service or labor by the laws of this Territory: *Provided*, That he shall file in the office of the Probate Court, written and satisfactory evidence that such service or labor is due.

SEC. 2 [How contracts for servitude may be proved]

That the Probate Court shall receive as evidence any contract properly attested in writing or any well proved agreement wherein the party or parties serving have received or are to receive a reasonable compensation for his, her or their services: *Provided,* That no contract shall bind the heirs of the servant or servants to service for a longer period than will satisfy the debt due his, her or their master or masters.

SEC. 3 [Servants brot from U.S. May be retained in servitude for life]

That any person bringing a servant or servants, and his, her, or their children from any part of the United States, or other country, and shall place in the office of the Probate Court the certificate of any Court of record under seal, properly attested that he, she, or they are entitled lawfully to the service of such servant or servants, and his, her, or their heirs shall be entitled to the services of the said servant or servants unless forfeited as hereinafter provided, if it shall appear that such servant or servants came into the Territory of their own free will and choice.

SEC. 4 [Servants may be forfeited Fines and imprisonment for sexual intercourse with African race]

That if a master or mistress shall have sexual or carnal intercourse with his or her servant or servants of the African race, he or she shall forfeit all claim to said servant or servants to the commonwealth; and if any white person shall be guilty of sexual intercourse with any of the African race, they shall be subject, on conviction thereof, to a fine of not exceeding one thousand dollars, nor less than five hundred, to the use of the Territory, and imprisonment, not exceeding three years.

SEC. 5 [Duties toward servants]

It shall be the duty of masters or mistresses, to provide for his, her or their servants comfortable habitations, clothing, bedding, sufficient food, and recreation. And it shall be the duty of the servant in return therefor, to labor faithfully all reasonable hours, and do such service with fidelity as may be required by his, or her master or mistress.

SEC. 6 [Master may punish servants Forfeit of servants by cruelty]

It shall be the duty of the master to correct and punish his servant in a reasonable manner when it may be necessary, being guided by prudence and humanity; and if he shall be guilty of cruelty or abuse, or neglect to feed, clothe, or shelter his servants in a proper manner, the Probate Court may declare the contract between master and servant or servants void, according to the provisions of the fourth section of this act.

SEC. 7 [Transference of servants]

That servants may be transferred from one master or mistress to another by the consent and approbation of the Probate Court, who shall keep a record of the same in his office; but no transfer shall be made without the consent of the servant given to the Probate Judge in the absence of his master or mistress.

SEC. 8 [Fine and imprisonment for transferring servants contrary to law]

Any person transferring a servant or servants contrary to the provisions of this act, or taking one out of the Territory contrary to his, or her will, except by decree of the Court in case of a fugitive from labor, shall be on conviction thereof, subject to a fine, not exceeding five thousand dollars, and imprisonment, not exceeding five years, or both, at the discretion of the Court, and shall forfeit all claims to the services of such servant or servants, as provided in the fourth section of this act.

SEC. 9 [Servants to be sent to school]

It shall further be the duty of all masters or mistresses, to send their servant or servants to school, not less than eighteen months between the ages of six years and twenty years.

NOTES

INTRODUCTION

1. Henry, interviews with the author. Henry gave her original papers to the University of Utah, now available through the J. Willard Marriott Library Manuscripts Collection. While I was copying her papers for myself, I also made a set, which I donated to the Utah State Historical Society.
2. Kemp, telephone interview. Kemp served on the Salt Lake City School Board for twelve years.
3. Whitley, ed., *Worth Their Salt* and *Worth Their Salt, Too.*
4. All Bible verses used in this book come from the King James Version.
5. Sandack, interview.
6. O'Neal, "Raising Her Voice"; Freimann, "Can Change Occur to a Set Society?"

CHAPTER 1

1. Cronon, *Black Moses*, 33.
2. "D. C. Stephenson Trial: 1925," in Knappman, ed., *American Trials of the 20th Century*, 100.
3. *Plessy v. Ferguson*, 163 U.S. 537 (1896). See also Cornell Legal Information Institute, law.cornell.edu.
4. Fireside, *Plessy v. Ferguson*, 5–12.
5. Ibid.
6. Urofsky and Finkelman, *Constitutional History of the United States* 1:483.
7. Daynes, ed., *Fulfilling the Founding*, 282–83.
8. Fireside, *Plessy v. Ferguson*, 5–12; and Urofsky and Finkelman, *Constitutional History of the United States* 1:483.
9. Jim Crow Museum of Racist Memorabilia, ferris.edu/jimcrow. "Jim Crow" was a derogatory term for blacks.
10. The family had always known that James was born in Oklahoma, but only in the late 1990s (when Alberta's brother David's son, Michael Hill, began to trace the family genealogy) did they learn that it was a reservation. Information on the Hill family is available on the Ancestry website in both the Hill and the Wilson family trees.
11. The town is spelled "Hoossten" on Alberta's birth certificate and she pronounced it with the double "oo" of "boot."
12. Litwack, *Trouble in Mind*, 114–67.
13. W. E. B. DuBois quoted in Litwack, *Trouble in Mind,* 116.
14. Information for the family in Alberta Henry's notes for her personal intended autobiography, in Henry papers.

15. The Hill family tree on Ancestry says Julia was born September 16, 1901, in Benton, Bossier, Louisiana. Her marriage to James Hill is dated as December 9, 1917, and Rosetta Maria Hill's birth as April 29, 1917, in Shreveport, Louisiana.
16. David was named for his father's brother who had died young.
17. "Step on" could include teasing, bullying, even abusing.
18. Weiler, *Utah's African-American Voices*.
19. David Hill, interview.
20. Alexander, review of Bagley, *Blood of the Prophets*, 170. For more information and photos on lynchings, see Williams, *Eyes on the Prize* and the PBS television series with the same title based on his book.
21. Jackson, *Racism, Injustice, and the Death Penalty*, 99.

CHAPTER 2

1. Horace B. English quoted in "Brown v. Board of Education: 1954," in Knappman, ed., *American Trials of the 20th Century*, 244.
2. Packard, *American Nightmare*, 65–66; and Daynes, ed. *Fulfilling the Founding*, 212–13. See also, "Exodusters," National Park Service, nps.gov/home/learn/historyculture/exodusters.htm; "Exodusters," Kansas Historical Society, kshs.org/kansapedia/exodusters/17162; and "Singleton Benjamin, 'Pap'" entry, civilwaronthewesternborder.org/encyclopedia.
3. Weiler, *Utah's African-American Voices*.
4. David Hill, interview.
5. Louis was a professional boxer from 1934 to 1959. Known as the "Brown Bomber," he became the first black boxer to achieve nationwide respect.
6. Schmeling's knockout of Joe Louis became the stuff of legend, topped only by the rematch when Louis took his title back in only two minutes and four seconds in the first round. More important in many eyes was a black American winning over an avowed Nazi who proclaimed racial superiority. See International Boxing Hall of Fame, ibhof.com; video of the fight is available on YouTube, "Joe Louis vs. Max Schmeling—1st Round Knockout."
7. "Colored People Time" was a derogatory reference suggesting that blacks couldn't read a clock so they were slow and unreliable.
8. David Hill, interview.
9. Restrictions on women having money or accounts in their own names or even inheriting money or property were common at the time, and for a number of years later as well, even though the Albion B. Emery probate case in Utah had broken that rule in 1895. The court ruled that Susanna Bransford Emery, widow of Albion Emery, was entitled to receive his holdings in the Silver King Mine in Park City, establishing the precedent that a woman could inherit in her own name. Nonetheless, it would be years before women managing their own money became common. See Dykman and Whitley, *The Silver Queen*, 37–47.
10. Weiler, *Utah's African-American Voices*.
11. One of Alberta's and Martha Patterson's appearances is commemorated in the "Annual Program for the Prince Hall Chapter of the Order of the Eastern Star, August 22, 1934," in Henry papers.
12. "Playground Notes," clipping from unidentified newspaper in Henry papers.

13. "Negro Net Tournament to Be at 20th-Kansas," clipping from unidentified newspaper in Henry papers.
14. See Cronon, *Black Moses*.
15. Such places were known as "Sundown towns" or "Sundowners" because they had explicit laws stating than any colored people caught out after dark could be subject to arrest, and in reality, much worse. See Loewen, *Sundown Towns*.
16. Typed talk in Henry papers.
17. Graduation program, Topeka High School, June 2, 1939, in Henry papers.

CHAPTER 3

1. Kennedy, *Freedom from Fear*, 252–54.
2. "Chica" is a Hispanic word for a girl, but it often refers to a particularly hot, energetic, or aggressive young woman, a leader. Alberta enjoyed the use of current slang, no matter what source it came from or the period she encountered it.
3. The four Mills Brothers made up a black quartet, popular from the 1920s through the 1970s. They were popular for so long and known so widely that the last brother's death was reported in the *New York Times*, undated clipping in Henry papers, also online, "Donald Mills, Last of the Singing Mills Brothers, Dies at 84," *New York Times*, November 15, 1999. Several of their numbers are available on YouTube.
4. Isaac Gooch was a year older than Alberta, born July 15, 1919.
5. The irony in Julia's concern is that she and James were divorced a few years later.
6. Truman Presidential Museum and Library, trumanlibrary.org; McCullough, *Truman*, 915; and Dees, Jr., and Hadley, *Jim Crow*, 106.
7. Garden City is in the southwest corner of Kansas, near the Colorado border.
8. David Hill, interview.
9. "Paddy" was historically a derogatory term used to describe Irish immigrants, but in some areas it became a generalized term used by blacks against whites. Alberta said she used it in school and "could always make the white kids mad when they called me 'nigger.'"
10. Masonry among black men in the United States began during the Revolutionary War when Prince Hall and fourteen other free black men were initiated into Lodge No. 441, Irish Constitution, attached to the 38th Regiment of Foot, British Army, garrisoned at Castle Williams (now Fort Independence), Boston Harbor on March 6, 1775. When the British army left Boston, Lodge No. 441 granted Prince Hall and his brothers authority to meet as a lodge, African Lodge No. 459. The Prince Hall Masons became an important element in the fight against slavery before the Civil War and in the fight for civil rights during the twentieth century.

    Other well-known Prince Hall Masons include but are not limited to Thurgood Marshall, associate justice, U.S. Supreme Court; Alex Haley, author; Booker T. Washington, educator and founder of Tuskegee Institute; Charles B. Rangel, U.S. congressman from New York; Louis Stokes, U.S. congressman from Ohio; William "Count" Basie, orchestra leader and composer; Nathaniel "Nat King" Cole, pianist and singer; W. E. B. DuBois, educator, author, and historian; Medger Evers, civil rights leader; Andrew Young, civil rights leader and former mayor of Atlanta; Thomas Bradley, former mayor of Los Angeles; Sugar Ray Robinson, mid/light heavy boxing champion; John H. Johnson, publisher of *Ebony* and *Jet* magazines; and Carl B. Stokes, the first black person elected mayor of a major American city, Cleveland, Ohio. "Who Is Prince Hall?" www.mindspring.com/~johnsonx/whoisph.htm.

11. Cynthia Gooch, daughter of Isaac Gooch by his second marriage, telephone interview with and email to the author.
12. Gooch, email.

CHAPTER 4

1. Davis, interview.
2. Coleman, "Blacks in Utah History," 115.
3. Ibid.
4. Wolfinger, "Jane Manning James," 14–31; and Coleman, "Blacks in Utah History," 116.
5. Green Flake's owner, James M. Flake, was a Southerner who had joined the LDS Church in 1843. Soon after his conversion James Flake either freed or sold nearly all of his slaves, but retained his wife Agnes's personal maid, Liz, and Green. Green Flake was freed "apparently—when his owner, a Mrs. James M. Flake, gave him to the LDS Church as tithing." Brigham Young simply accepted Green and then declared him free. Lee Benson, "No Slaves in Utah Territory? Think Again," *Deseret Morning News,* August 9, 2000. A story exists that when someone gave Brigham a slave as tithing then later asked to have him back, Brigham refused, saying, "You gave him to the Lord and the Lord doesn't keep slaves." True or not, that certainly reflected the attitude of most Mormon pioneers.
6. Utah Territory's slave law appears in this book as Appendix C. The law was passed after Batiste, a Ute trader, came into the area with two children, a boy and a girl, and offered them for sale. "When the Mormons recoiled at the idea, Batiste said if they did not buy them he would kill them." When they still refused, he killed the boy. Charles Decker then "agreed to give Batiste a gun for the girl. Decker took the girl to his sister Lucy, Brigham [Young]'s first plural wife, to raise. Lucy named her Sally and reared her as her own." Arrington and Bitton, *Brigham Young*, 210.
7. Rogers, *Unpopular Sovereignty*, 5.
8. Coleman, "Blacks in Utah History," 136–37. Rainbow Gardens featured a swimming pool fed by natural warm springs with a restaurant, shops, and other amenities. Lagoon is an amusement park in Farmington, halfway between Salt Lake City and Ogden.
9. Weiler, *Utah's African-American Voices*.
10. As I had with the Alberta's spiritual experience during her illness, I included her story of standing by the window and knowing she would stay in Utah in the short biography I did for *Worth Their Salt, Too*. Once again, when she read the manuscript, she was surprised to see this story included. She said she had told this same thing to every reporter or interviewer she had ever met and none had ever included it in their finished work. I was amazed. I began to wonder if my attitude stemmed simply from my own faith, but simply concluded that this had to be included in Alberta's biography because her faith in God was the center of her life and everything she did stemmed from that faith. Her faith was the reason she had stayed in Utah and the reason she had such a great impact on the state. She noted frequently how her grandfather J. J. Palmer's preaching and knowledge of the Bible led to her deep spiritual beliefs and her faith in the Bible and in herself. *Worth Their Salt, Too,* 251–52.
11. Helen Sandack, interview. See also, A. Wally Sandack papers.

12. Wallace and Helen Sandack, "Tribute to Alberta Henry," n.d., in Henry papers.
13. Helen and Wally Sandack to Alberta Henry, n.d., in Henry papers. Sandack, interview. Nancy Sandack Borgenicht became the founder and director of the Salt Lake Acting Company, serving as director of development until her retirement in 2013; Roger and Arthur are both attorneys in Salt Lake City; Richard became a writer and journalist in Los Angeles; Susan formed the Repertory Dance Theater, handling their finances and grant proposals.
14. Weiler, *Utah's African-American Voices*.
15. Helen Sandack's father was Arthur Frank, founder of the Arthur Frank chain of clothing stores.
16. Sandack, interview.
17. Wallace and Helen Sandack, "Tribute to Alberta Henry," in Henry papers. Sandack, interview. Alberta herself recalled saying exactly those words to Nancy.
18. Also known as tunk, it is a matching game similar to rummy.
19. In 1948 the church was called Pilgrim Baptist Church. When a new freeway forced relocation of the building in 1955, it was renamed New Pilgrim Baptist Church. When Alberta joined Pilgrim in 1948, she met Reverend Jesse Killings, who had become pastor just the year before. On November 17, 1954, Reverend Killings was elected pastor of New Hope Missionary Baptist Church, with twenty names on the membership roll. Alberta Henry was one of them. Reverend Killings remained an influential person in Alberta's life for several more years. Davis, *Light in the Midst of Zion*, 43–51.
20. Coal-burning furnaces were the usual method of heating homes in that period.
21. Weiler, *Utah's African-American Voices*.
22. Ibid.
23. "40th Signal Battalion" entry, history.army.mil.
24. Douglas L. Parker, "Railroader Recalls Old Days," *Salt Lake Tribune*, n.d., in Henry papers. The year used here is calculated from his age given in the article. The railroad companies employed nearly 240 blacks. See U.S. Census Bureau, *Census of Population: 1960*, part 46, 260. People working on the railroad would travel specific routes, staying in one town, sometimes overnight, and work on the return train to its original starting point. Depending on the length of the trip, they could be gone for two, three, or even four days, and then they would have several days off.
25. Weiler, *Utah's African-American Voices*.
26. Blackburn, telephone interview.
27. See *The Daily Utah Chronicle*, November 23, 1964, 2.
28. Weiler, *Utah's African-American Voices*.
29. Lawrence was also interviewed by Weiler, *Utah's African American Voices*. The Peace Gardens are located at 1060 South 900 West. Telephone interview with Salt Lake City Parks with the author, September 18, 2000.
30. Sunday Anderson, 868 West 900 South, was established June 17, 1978, and still provides aging and adult services, sponsors events, offers transportation, and serves lunch daily, Monday through Friday. See slco.org/aging-adult-services/sunday-anderson-westside.
31. Weiler, *Utah's African-American Voices*. Dr. Ewin Urshler remained her doctor until he retired, thirty-seven years later. During that time Alberta had two more major operations.
32. Ibid.

33. Julia Henry Lebya, interviews.
34. Ibid.
35. "Bullet Strikes Boy, 12, in Leg: S. L. Man Jailed," *Deseret News*, and "S. L. Youth Shot, Suspect Held," *Salt Lake Tribune,* both on the same date, April 4, 1969, and both in Henry papers.
36. "Escape Attempt Adds 9 Years to Burglar's Sentence," *Salt Lake Tribune,* August 24, 1986, in Henry papers.
37. Julia Henry Lebya, interviews.
38. "Eighth Grade Officers at JJHS," *Sunset News*, October 28, 1971, copy in Henry papers. Jordan Junior was in Salt Lake City District, but was later closed.
39. LeRoy Nelsen, telephone interviews.

CHAPTER 5

1. Christ's injunction to Peter shortly before the crucifixion, John 21:15–17.
2. The transcription of this interview says, "north of the peak," but Alberta was obviously using her usual reference to North Topeka.
3. Weiler, *Utah's African-American Voices.*
4. Coleman, "Blacks in Utah History," 135.
5. "Utah's People of Color," *Salt Lake Tribune*, December 27, 1998; and "Richmond Park," www.slc.gov/parks.
6. Laurie Sullivan Maddox, "Social Club Nourishes Utah Roots of L.A. Blacks," *Salt Lake Tribune,* July 27, 1997.
7. "Nettie Grimes Gregory" entry, Utahns of Achievement, historytogo.utah.gov/people/utahns_of_achievement.
8. A local service and social club, not to be confused with the large retailer of a similar name.
9. Christ's warning that his followers should not flaunt their good works, Matthew 6:3.
10. Weiler, *Utah's African-American Voices.*
11. Ibid. Toni Nathaniel Harp served in the Connecticut legislature from 1993 to 2013 then was elected mayor of New Haven, assuming office on January 1, 2014.
12. Rock, ed., *Blend of the Two*, 118.
13. Shauna Graves to Alberta Henry, June 18, 1990, in Henry papers.
14. Shauna Graves Robertson to Alberta Henry, January 11, 1993, in Henry papers. See also her position as judge in Salt Lake County, slco.org/justice-court/honorable-graves-robertson.
15. Weiler, *Utah's African-American Voices.*
16. A. Wally Sandack, articles of incorporation of the Alberta Henry Education Foundation, December 6, 1967, in Sandack papers.
17. Solomon Cachon quoted in Lois M. Collins, "Fund Gives Able Youths a Shot at College," *Deseret News*, April 25, 1991.
18. Deborah Bulkeley, "Henry Remembered as a Life-Changer," *Deseret News*, May 16, 2005.
19. Ibid.; Boyd, telephone interviews. For further information on the Alberta Henry Education Foundation, search for "Alberta Henry" in the University of Utah Web Archive, archive-it.org/collections/2278.
20. Andrew Valdez quoted in Deborah Bulkeley, "Henry Remembered as a Life-Changer," *Deseret News*, May 16, 2005.

21. Michael Styles, remarks at the homegoing service for Alberta Henry, May 17, 2005.
22. Harvey Boyd quoted in Deborah Bulkeley, "Henry Remembered as a Life-Changer," *Deseret News*, May 16, 2005. Boyd kindly provided information on the foundation and helped me contact several recipients. Boyd, telephone interviews. Appendix B lists just a few of those scholarship winners and some of their achievements as adults.
23. Note on a paper for Nanette Roundy, copy in Henry papers.
24. "Reck" is an archaic verb meaning to have a care, concern, or interest in someone or something. Alberta's concern was making other people have a care, concern, or interest. "Reckle" achieved a very different meaning in modern street slang, but I'm certain Alberta did not intend that usage in her statement.
25. Weiler, *Utah's African-American Voices.*
26. Notes for a speech in Henry papers.
27. Calvin L. Rampton, Proclamation, August 13, 1973, in Henry papers.
28. "NAACP Pat on Back," *Salt Lake Tribune*, February 24, 1978.
29. Notarianni, interview.
30. The scholarship remains one of the opportunities available through the Alberta Henry Education Foundation.
31. "Ripped" in this context meant encouraged, dared, worked them hard. It has no relation to the definition in current slang relating to drugs or alcohol.
32. Edmond, telephone interview.
33. "NAACP Drill Team," *Sunset News*, October 4, 1973.
34. Julia Henry Lebya, interviews.
35. Shauna Graves Robertson, telephone interview, and her eulogy for Alberta Henry at her homegoing service, May 17, 2005.
36. Johnson's Great Society speech (1964), in *Papers of the Presidents, Lyndon Johnson* I:704–707; and Andrew, *Lyndon Johnson*, 5.
37. Andrew, *Lyndon Johnson*, 64–67.
38. Model Cities reports are available on microfilm from the Archives of the Library of the Department of Housing and Urban Development in Washington, D.C. Many of the records on Model Cities can be accessed at modelcities.org.
39. Kotz, *Judgment Days*, 182.
40. Both historical and current information on Head Start is available at Administration for Children and Families, acf.hhs.gov.
41. Kotz, *Judgment Days*, 76.
42. Ibid.
43. *Sunset News*, May 23, 1968; Henry, interviews with Kelen, 123, 161, and 176; Goldberg, "Esther Rosenblatt Landa," 234; and Henry, interviews with the author.
44. Shonni Schwin, "Grateful Parent," letter to the editor, *Salt Lake Tribune*, May 20, 2000.
45. It was on the northeast corner of 2100 South and State Streets, current site of the Salt Lake County offices.
46. Alberta said some others from the University of Utah came through to evaluate as well; she could not remember any names, but none of them overturned the decision.

CHAPTER 6

1. Buchanan, *Culture Clash and Accommodation*, 192.
2. Ibid., 194.

3. Allen Bateman, *Salt Lake Tribune*, May 18, 1954, quoted in Peterson, "Utah's Politics since 1945," 20.
4. Smith, "Social Status of the Negro in Utah."
5. Coleman, "Preface: African Americans in Utah," 68.
6. Schuman, Steeh, and Bobo, *Racial Attitudes in America*, 78.
7. Minutes of Salt Lake School Board, March 30, 1971.
8. Minutes of Salt Lake School Board, March 16, 1971.
9. Minutes of Salt Lake School Board, May 18, 1971.
10. Buchanan, *Culture Clash and Accommodation*, 201.
11. Henry, interviews with the author.
12. Horace Mann was located in an area of downtown Salt Lake City rapidly becoming more commercial than residential and was plagued by gang violence. I had observed classes taught by a friend there in the early 1960s as part of my teacher education program at the University of Utah. I sat at the back of the room and watched her present material and lead discussions among the students, some participating, some obviously bored, others looking extremely anxious. After the students had gone home she spoke candidly, referring to the school as the "switchblade center of the West." She told me that a few days earlier she had come into her classroom on the third story of the building and found a group of students dangling another student by his legs out of the window above the concrete below. Not daring to shout for fear she would startle the boys and they would drop their victim, she simply said: "Haul him in. It's time for class." Then she sat down at her desk so her class could not see her shaking hands and knees. She made no mention of the races or ethnicity of any of the boys involved, but it was clear that she dealt with both pranks and hostilities on a regular basis.
13. Minutes of Salt Lake School Board, February 1 and 15, 1972.
14. This period was reserved for individuals or groups with specific or even emergency issues. Usually the speakers took only a few minutes and the board referred them to appropriate district personnel; reports and discussions generally followed within one or two subsequent board meetings.
15. Minutes of Salt Lake School Board, June 1, 1971.
16. Ibid.
17. Henry, interviews with Kelen, 205.
18. Ibid.
19. The man's name is not included in public records and personnel records are sealed. The information about him here comes solely from Henry's interviews.
20. Henry, interviews with Kelen, 206.
21. Minutes of Salt Lake School Board, May 2, 1972.
22. Minutes of Salt Lake School Board, May 4, 1971.
23. Henry, interviews with Kelen, 206.
24. "Coordinating Council—People Working Together," *Salt Lake Model Neighborhood News*, December 30, 1971; and *Northwest News*, June 1976, both in Henry papers.
25. Henry, interviews with Kelen, 201–4.
26. Henry, interviews with the author; Henry, interviews with Kelen, 206–7.
27. Allen, interviews. Allen was one of the few principals I approached who would talk with me about Alberta's time in the Salt Lake School District. Most retained their distrust of her and anyone they perceived as backing her. When I approached a man

I knew had been a principal in that district and asked him about Alberta, he simply replied, somewhat vehemently, "Oh, that nigger!" And walked away.

28. David Hill, interview.
29. Weiler, *Utah's African-American Voices.*
30. Allen, interviews. Both Henry and Allen said that they came to like and respect each other. In fact, when I told her what he had said, she grinned broadly and said, "He is a lovely man."
31. Corrine Hill, interview. Hill worked in local, state, and national education positions, eventually becoming Governor Michael Leavitt's education deputy. "Education Leader Corinne P. Hill Dies," *Deseret News*, August 10, 2003.
32. Buchanan, *Culture Clash and Accommodation,* 209.
33. Ibid., 210.
34. Ibid., 212.
35. Arthur Wiscombe, oral history, June 28, 1973, quoted in Buchanan, *Culture Clash and Accommodation,* 213.
36. Alberta told me firmly that the one person I absolutely had to interview was Donald Thomas. When I called to make an appointment, he was extremely gracious, as he was through our entire meeting and subsequent telephone calls.
37. Thomas, interview.
38. At that time optional instruction programs usually involved an emphasis on a specific field—science, humanities, history, automobile repair, or any other area. They would draw students with interests in those specific areas. Today optional instruction programs range from specific fields to home schooling.
39. Thomas, interview.
40. Weiler, *Utah's African-American Voices.*
41. Thomas, interview.
42. Davis, interview.
43. Davis, *Light in the Midst of Zion*, 63; and "Utah Civil Rights Legend France Davis Marks 43 Years as Calvary's Pastor," *Salt Lake Tribune,* April 24, 2017.
44. Doug Robinson, "Rev. France Davis: A Force for Good," *Deseret News*, December 3, 2002.
45. McKenzie Romero, "Calvary Baptist Church Celebrates 125 Years in SLC," *Deseret News*, November 13, 2017.
46. Davis, interview.
47. France Davis, eulogy at homegoing service for Alberta Henry, May 17, 2005, quoted in Deborah Bulkeley, "Speakers Remember Henry's Good Works," *Deseret Morning News*, May 18, 2005.
48. Thomas, interview.
49. Diaz, interview. By coincidence, Diaz had been one of my students at the Skill Center twenty years earlier, learning what she needed to do to increase her job potential; she succeeded very well.
50. Diaz, interview.
51. Thomas, interview.
52. Papanikolas, ed., *Peoples of Utah.*
53. Jim Rock, "Alberta Hill Henry," n.d., in Henry papers.
54. "A Minorities Education Report," newspaper clipping in Henry papers.
55. Henry, interviews with the author, and notes in Henry papers.
56. Julia Henry Lebya, interviews.

57. Thomas, interview. Thomas said he had a very different experience in his next job:

> After I left here, I went to work for Governor Riley of South Carolina. They're colored by the Civil War still, and in private discussions they refer to the Afro-Americans as the "undeserving ones." I heard that, and I said, "Say that again?"
>
> One legislator said, "Well, we shouldn't spend so much money for those undeserving ones."
>
> "Who are the undeserving ones."
>
> He said, "Well, you know."
>
> I said, "No, I don't know. I'm from Utah."
>
> They think they are not deserving of a good education, but Governor Riley was great. He said, "They are deserving."

58. Thomas, interview.
59. Weiler, *Utah's African-American Voices.*
60. Henry, interviews with the author, and Henry's resume in her papers; those papers also include her campaign materials and mementoes of the Democratic National Convention.
61. Weiler, *Utah's African-American Voices.*
62. Harold J. Trussel, principal, to Alberta Henry (on West High School letterhead), June 30, 1989, in Henry papers.

CHAPTER 7

1. Mary White Ovington, *How the National Association for the Advancement of Colored People Began,* 1914, reprinted in 1949, unpaginated pamphlet in Henry papers; digital copy available at Civil Rights Digital Library, crdl.usg.edu.
2. William English Walling, "Race War in the North," *Independent* (New York City), September 3, 1908, quoted in Ovington, *How the National Association for the Advancement of Colored People Began.*
3. "What is the Mission of the NAACP?," naacp.org/about-us.
4. *Evening Post* was a supplement to the *Nation,* a magazine still in operation. See thenation.com.
5. Urofsky and Finkelman, *Constitutional History of the United States,* 1:494. See also, "What's the Most Important Supreme Court Case No One's Ever Heard Of?" *Atlantic Monthly,* May 2013. The article features views from a range of authors, each choosing a different case.
6. "Brown v. Board of Education: 1954," in Knappman, ed., *American Trials of the 20th Century,* 243.
7. Ibid.
8. Supreme Court decision quoted in Urofsky and Finkelman, *Constitutional History of the United States,* 782, and in "Brown v. Board of Education: 1954," in Knappman, ed., *American Trials of the 20th Century,* 242–46.
9. Eisenhower Presidential Library, Museum, and Boyhood Home, eisenhower.archives.gov.
10. Schuman, Steeh, and Bobo, *Racial Attitudes in America,* 22.
11. Payne, *I've Got the Light of Freedom,* 416.

12. Packard, *American Nightmare*, 246–49.
13. The Congress of Racial Equality (CORE) was founded by a group of students in Chicago in 1942. Originally named the Committee of Racial Equality, its makeup was interracial students, some of whom were also members of the Chicago Branch of the Fellowship of Reconciliation (FOR). All were followers of Mahatma Gandhi's tactics of nonviolent resistance. In that same year they organized sit-ins at segregated facilities. Sit-ins remained one of their foremost tactics until formal segregation was ended. See congressofracialequality.org.
14. Sitkoff, *Struggle for Black Equality*, 67–73.
15. Ibid., 97–108; Packard, *American Nightmare*, 260–61. Details of Kennedy's assassination are available from several websites, including the Kennedy Library, jfklibrary.org.
16. Civil Rights Digital Library, crdl.usg.edu.
17. Kotz, *Judgment Days*, 380–381; and Colburt, ed., *Eyewitness to America*, 494.
18. Stewart, interviews. Cake picks certainly could become weapons. They are designed to cut layer cakes smoothly, using a metal rod about eight to twelve inches long with tines several inches long extending out in a line from one side like teeth from a comb—and it was for that comb-like quality that blacks were buying them. Large and bushy Afro hairstyles had come into vogue and regular plastic combs broke in them. Cake picks worked perfectly, as I observed while I was teaching at the Clearfield Job Corps Center during the late sixties. I was impressed by the ease with which my black male students could comb their hair with them.
19. Robert Grey Jr. quoted in Deborah Bulkeley, "Brown Set the Tone for Change in Utah," *Deseret News*, May 17, 2004. Bulkeley noted that Grey would "become the second president of color of the American Bar Association." Her statistics come from the 2002 census.
20. "The Origin of the Salt Lake Branch NAACP," in the program for the 77th Annual Life Membership and Freedom Fund Banquet, October 25, 1996, in Henry papers.
21. Betty Sawyer quoted in Tim Sullivan, "S.L. NAACP Hits a Crossroads," *Salt Lake Tribune*, November 2, 2002.
22. Weiler, *Utah's African-American Voices*.
23. Diaz, interview.
24. Davis, interview. Alberta commented several times on her respect for Esther Landa and several others have noted the care both women took in following procedures.
25. Weiler, *Utah's African-American Voices*.
26. Davis, interview.
27. "Civil Rights Zeal in Utah Endures, NAACP Says," *Deseret News*, January 21, 1991.
28. Dave Jonsson, "NAACP Leader May File Suit to Ensure King Observance," *Salt Lake Tribune*, January 19, 1990.
29. "NAACP Leader Says Racial Bias Still Lingers among Many Utahns," *Deseret News*, February 19, 1989.
30. Alta Miller describes the way the entire community would celebrate the holidays of many immigrants to Bingham Canyon in "Short Sketch of My Life," 145–47.
31. Bridgewater, interviews.
32. "Within the context of American politics in 1844, however, even gradual emancipation was a radical proposal. . . . For instance, Elijah P. Lovejoy [a white Presbyterian

minister] had been murdered in Alton, Illinois, for his advocacy of abolition." Wolfinger, "Jane Manning James," 267n53.

33. "Life Sketch of Jane Elizabeth Manning James," Wilford Woodruff MSS. See also Bushman, *Joseph Smith;* and Lythgoe, "Negro Slavery and Mormon Doctrine."
34. "Race and the Priesthood," lds.org/topics/race-and-the-priesthood; the statement by Brigham Young is quoted from Historian's Office General Church Minutes, March 26, 1847, LDS Church History Library, Salt Lake City, spelling and punctuation modernized. See also Embry, *Black Saints in a White Church*, 38–39. Embry also joined Alan Cherry for an entry on "Blacks," in Ludlow, ed., *Encyclopedia of Mormonism*, 1:125.
35. Coleman, "Blacks in Utah History," 140.
36. Allen discusses this issue in his senior thesis, "Fighting the Good Fight in Zion."
37. Coleman, "A History of Blacks in Utah," vi.
38. Brigham Young papers, February 5, 1852.
39. "Carter Praises LDS Church Action," *Deseret News,* June 10, 1978. The full text of official statements on that revelation can be found at lds.org/topics/race-and-the-priesthood.
40. Weiler, *Utah's African-American Voices.*
41. Reid, telephone interview.
42. Ibid. Alberta agreed that they developed a very congenial friendship.

CHAPTER 8

1. Corey Peterson, "Three Murdered as Burglars Invade Ogden Hi-Fi Shop," *Ogden Standard-Examiner,* April 23, 1974. Kinder, *Victim*, 29–45. Kinder's book recounts the murder, arrest, and aftermath relating to the Hi-Fi murders. It focuses particularly on one of the victims, Cortney Naisbett, who remained disabled for the rest of his life from the torture he endured. See also Glen Warchol, "Hi-Fi Torture Victim Dies 28 Years Later," *Salt Lake Tribune*, July 15, 2002.
2. "Two Airmen from Hill AFB Held in Brutal Ogden Murders," *Ogden Standard-Examiner*, April 24, 1974; and Kinder, *Victim*, 104–41.
3. For a discussion of racial impacts on sentencing, see Paternoster, *Capital Punishment in America*, 15.
4. *Furman v. Georgia*, Cornell Legal Information Institute, law.cornell.edu.
5. *Woodson v. North Carolina* and *Gregg v. Georgia*, Cornell Legal Information Institute, law.cornell.edu.
6. Crew, "Death and Resurrection of Capital Punishment," 44–49. For more information on the death penalty and the Gilmore case see *Furman v. Georgia* entry in Hall, *Oxford Companion to the Supreme Court;* and Haines, *Against Capital Punishment*, 57–58.
7. For a brief discussion of the trial with accompanying references, see "Gary Mark Gilmore Trial: 1976," in Knappman, ed., *American Trials of the 20th Century.* See also Samuel G. McFarland in *Journal of Criminal Law and Criminology*, Fall 1983, 1014–32; and Welsh W. White, *University of Pittsburgh Law Review*, Spring 1987, 853–57. Norman Mailer fictionalized the Gilmore case in *The Executioner's Song,* which won a Pulitzer Prize and was later adapted to a television film of the same name by NBC.
8. Poll published in the *Salt Lake Tribune*, December 16, 1973.
9. Kinder, *Victim,* 309.

10. L. Jerry Spangler, "Selby to Pay for 1974 Hi-Fi Murders," *Deseret News*, August 28, 1987; Gillespie, *The Unforgiven*, 23, 151–54; and Kinder, *Victim*, 314.
11. Local papers carried news of that decision and discussion of it for days, as did several national outlets. The *New York Times* quoted Alberta Henry saying: "We said nothing when they executed Selby, but we're saying that no one who didn't actually kill should receive the death sentence.... We feel there is no justice until everybody gets the same treatment.... If you give us the same treatment that you give everyone else, then you won't hear from us." Robert Reinhold, "Salt Lake City Journal; 1974 Case Still Strains Race Relations in Utah," *New York Times*, August 31, 1989.
12. Henry, interviews; and Reid, interview.
13. Haines, *Against Capital Punishment*, 76–79.
14. Justice Powell quoted in *Chicago Tribune*, April 23, 1987. For a discussion of the decision, see *McClesky v. Klemp* at Cornell Law School, lawschool.cornell.edu. See also Kirchmeier, *Imprisoned by the Past*.
15. Gillespie, *The Unforgiven*, 25–26.
16. For more information concerning capital punishment specific to blacks, Utah, and the nation, see Haines, *Against Capital Punishment*; Hood, *Death in the Balance*; Jackson, *Legal Lynching*; and Sillitoe, *Friendly Fire*, available at signaturebookslibrary.org.
17. "Pardons Board Denies Andrews a 2nd Hearing," *Salt Lake Tribune*, undated clipping in Henry papers, but probably close to June 18, 1992, the date that the *Deseret News* ran the same story with an almost identical headline, "Pardons Board Refuses Andrews a 2nd Hearing."
18. Tenth Circuit Court decision quoted in *Deseret News*, August 20, 1989, and *Salt Lake Tribune*, June 13, 1992.
19. Jan Thompson, "Utah Justice System Is Corrupted by Prejudice, NAACP Leader Says," *Deseret News*, August 20, 1989.
20. Alberta Henry, "News from the President's Desk," *Salt Lake City Branch NAACP*, September 1, 1989, in Henry papers.
21. Alberta Henry, press release, *Salt Lake Branch NAACP*, and William Andrews's rally speech, June 1, 1992, in Henry papers.
22. Alberta Henry, press release, *Salt Lake Branch NAACP*, June 1, 1992. Henry also questioned the case of George Wesley Hamilton, a white man who had sexually abused and murdered a nineteen-year-old woman who attended Southern Utah State College. He was charged with second-degree murder. Later she challenged the case of Steven Ray Stout, who on January 22, 1988, bludgeoned, stabbed, and strangled two women in West Valley City. He received two consecutive life terms instead of the death penalty.
23. Marjorie Cortez, Joseph Bauman, and Valerie Schulthies, "Board Denies Andrews' Request for Clemency," *Deseret News*, August 18, 1989, August 24, 1989.
24. Jan Thompson, "Evidence, Not Race, Prompted Death Penalty, Prosecutor Says," *Deseret News*, August 27, 1989.
25. "'Racism' Cries Not Justified in Debate about Andrews," *Deseret News*, August 23, 1989.
26. V. Hadley, "No Joy," *Salt Lake Tribune*, August 28, 1989.
27. Alberta Henry, press release, *Salt Lake Branch NAACP*, June 1, 1992. See also Marjories Cortez, Joseph Bauman, and Valerie Schultes, "Board Denies Andres's Request for Clemency," *Deseret News*, August 18, 1989.
28. Coletta Sume to Alberta Henry, August 21, 1989, in Henry papers.

29. Anonymous to Alberta Henry, August 24, 1989, in Henry papers; emphasis in the original.
30. Reverend Ema White to James Gillespie and Alberta Henry, n.d. [ca. 1989], in Henry papers.
31. William Andrews to Alberta Henry, August 31, 1989, in Henry papers. Spelling and punctuation appear as in the original; in any cases where there is a question caused by my inability to read his penmanship, the traditional forms have been used.
32. Alberta Henry, William Andrews's rally speech, June 1, 1992, copy in Henry papers; NAACP, "We Need Your Attendance to Stand Up for Justice and Decency," June 1, 1992, copy in Henry papers.
33. Marianne Funk, "Hi-Fi Killer Gets July 30 Death Date," *Deseret News*, July 2, 1992.
34. Rocky Anderson, remarks at the homegoing service for Alberta Henry, May 17, 2005.
35. "Petition for Commutation," *Deseret News*, June 27, 1992. Within two weeks the board of pardons was flooded with letters from around the world asking for clemency for Andrews. Laurie M. Wirth, "Letters Urge Utah Not to Execute Andrews," *Deseret News*, July 8, 1992.
36. Dirk Johnson, "Utah Execution Hinges on Issue of Racial Bias," *New York Times*, July 19, 1992.
37. All of the Utah newspapers carried the story, but so did a remarkable number of national papers, including James Coates, "In Utah, a Bitter Execution Debate," *Chicago Tribune*, July 29, 1992.
38. James Coates, "In Utah, a Bitter Execution Debate," *Chicago Tribune*, July 29, 1992.
39. University of Minnesota Human Rights Library, hrlibrary.umn.edu.
40. Gillespie, *The Unforgiven*, 29. "Andrews Executed by Lethal Injection," both *Deseret News* and *Salt Lake Tribune* used the same title on the same day, July 31 1992.
41. Notes and letters in Henry papers.
42. Amy Donaldson, "S.L. Panel to Document Racism," *Deseret News*, August 4, 1992.
43. Weiler, *Utah's African-American Voices*.
44. David Clifton and Chris Jorgensen, with contributions from Jon Ure, "Utahns React Angrily to Cops' Acquittals," *Salt Lake Tribune*, May 1, 1992.
45. "NAACP Leader in S.L. Calls Thomas as Good a Candidate as Any," *Deseret News*, July 2, 1991.
46. Vince Horiuchi, "Black Utahns Differ on Court Nominee," *Salt Lake Tribune*, August 2, 1991.
47. "S.L. Branch of NAACP Opposes Thomas," *Deseret News*, August 6, 1991.
48. Associated Press, "Utah NAACP Leaders Differ," *Deseret News*, August 2, 1991.
49. Carol Sisco, "Bigots Still Bane of NAACP," *Salt Lake Tribune*, September 9, 1991.
50. Tim Fitzpatrick, "NAACP Slams Hatch, Garn for Battling Civil Rights Act," *Salt Lake Tribune*, July 22, 1990, clipping in Henry papers.
51. Alberta Henry, NAACP press release, May 13, 1991, in Henry papers.

CHAPTER 9

1. Alberta Henry, "Desnews Did Justice to Blacks," readers' forum, *Deseret News*, February 28, 1994, responding to an article by Kristan Jacobsen and Amy Donaldson, "After 45 Years, Henry Says She Still Has Work to Do," *Deseret News*, February 3, 1994.
2. "Williams Will Lead NAACP Chapter in S.L.," *Deseret News*, December 8, 1992.

3. Tim Sullivan, "S.L. NAACP Hits a Crossroads," *Salt Lake Tribune*, November 2, 2002.
4. Davis, interview.
5. Alberta Henry, letter to the Department of Public Housing, Topeka, Kansas, January 13, 1989, in Henry papers.
6. Julia Henry Lebya, interviews.
7. Photocopy of a two-page letter in Henry papers; the letter was typed in all capitals and ends with her signature.
8. Obituary for Julia Ida Palmer Hill Brantly, *Deseret News,* June 9, 1992. Soon after Alberta had married Isaac Gooch, Julia and Harold had been divorced; Julia later married Art Brantly.
9. David Hill, interview; and Henry, interviews with the author.
10. Julia Henry Lebya, interviews.
11. Weiler, *Utah's African-American Voices.*
12. Ibid.
13. Matthew 6:6.
14. Matthew 5:15.
15. Henry, interviews with the author; and Julia Henry Lebya, interviews.
16. Tim Sullivan, "NAACP's Ex-boss to Run Again," *Salt Lake Tribune,* October 25, 2002. I tried repeatedly to contact Williams for her input in Alberta's story, using telephone, email, and letters, even letters containing self-addressed, stamped envelopes. I have never received a response of any kind.
17. Tim Sullivan, "S.L. NAACP Hits a Crossroads," *Salt Lake Tribune*, November 2, 2002; Henry, interviews with the author.
18. Jeanetta Williams quoted in Diane Urbani, "NAACP of Utah Re-elects Leader," *Deseret News*, November 9, 2002.
19. "Title Will Keep 'Colored People,'" *Salt Lake Tribune*, September 9, 1991.
20. Jason Swenson, "Concerns Prompt Longtime Leader to Leave NAACP Board," *Deseret News*, August 8, 1997.
21. Don Babwin, Associated Press, "Cosby Upbraids Blacks," *Deseret News*, July 2, 2004.
22. Bonnie Dew quoted in Tim Sullivan, "S.L. NAACP Hits a Crossroads," *Salt Lake Tribune*, November 2, 2002.
23. Tim Sullivan, "NAACP's Ex-Boss to Run Again," *Salt Lake Tribune,* October 25, 2002.
24. Michael Styles, remarks at the homegoing service for Alberta Henry, May 17, 2005.
25. Tim Sullivan, "NAACP Retains Williams," *Salt Lake Tribune*, November 6, 2002. See also Diane Ulibani, "NAACP of Utah Re-elects Leader," *Deseret News* November 9, 2002.
26. Tim Sullivan, "NAACP's Ex-boss to Run Again," *Salt Lake Tribune,* October 25, 2002.
27. Sawyer, interviews; and Gilbert Lebya, telephone and personal interviews.
28. Davis, eulogy at homegoing service for Alberta Henry, May 17, 2005.
29. Ibid.
30. Julia Henry Lebya, telephone call to the author, May 11, 2005: and Deborah Bulkeley, *Deseret Morning News*, May 12, 2005.
31. Jennifer W. Sanchez, "A Life of Service," *Salt Lake Tribune*, May 12, 2005.
32. Reid, interview.
33. Deborah Bulkeley, "Alberta Henry, 84, Treated at Hospice," *Deseret News*, May 10, 2005; and "Activist Alberta Henry Dies at 84," *Deseret News*, May 12, 2005.
34. Weiler, *Utah's African-American Voices.*

EPILOGUE

1. Rocky Anderson, remarks at homegoing service for Alberta Henry, May 17, 2005, from notes taken by the author during the service. Unless otherwise indicated, all information on the funeral comes from those notes.
2. Deborah Bulkeley, "Speakers Remember Henry's Good Works," *Deseret News*, May 18, 2005.
3. Schuman, Steeh, and Bobo, *Racial Attitudes in America*, 201–2.
4. "Voting Rights, 40 Years Later," *Deseret Morning News*, August 10, 2005.
5. "Welcome to the Ku Klux Klan: Knights Party," www.kkk.com.
6. Aryan Nations, Skinhead Division, aryan-nation-skinheads.org.
7. "Utahs' [sic] History Ignores Blacks," *Daily Utah Chronicle*, April 4, 1984.
8. U. S. Census Bureau, 2010 census, factfinder.census.gov.
9. Bradley Snyder, "Races for S.L. Council All White," *Deseret Morning News*, August 17, 2005.
10. Brady McCombs, "Republican Mia Love Raises Another $500K," *Deseret News*, February 4, 2014.
11. "U.S. House 4th District Results: Mia Love Wins," Election 2016, *New York Times*, nytimes.com/elections/results/utah-house-district-4-love-owens. Dennis Romboy, "Former Utah GOP Rep. Mia Love Promises 'Unleashed' Talk," *Deseret News*, January 7, 2019.
12. "Speaker Airs 'Black Pride,'" *Salt Lake Tribune*, February 4, 1974, clipping in Henry papers.
13. Blackburn, telephone interview. A short while after that interview I arrived at Alberta's home to work with her on this book and found an ambulance in front of the house. The door was standing open so I went in and there was Mavis holding an oxygen mask to Alberta's face. She had come over, found her friend very ill, and called the paramedics. She needed to leave so she asked me to take over until Julia could get there. It was obvious both that Mavis was a very comfortable friend to the whole Henry family and that Alberta felt safe in her hands.
14. Shauna Graves Robertson, telephone interview with the author, September 3, 2003.
15. Tyrone E. Medley quoted in Weiler, *Utah's African-American Voices*.

APPENDIX C

1. An Act in Relation to Service, Approved Feb. 4th, 1852, *Acts, Resolutions and Memorials, Passed by the First Annual, and Special Sessions, of the Legislative Assembly of the Territory of Utah, Begun and Held at Great Salt Lake City, on the 22nd Day of September, A.D. 1851, Published by Authority of the Legislative Assembly* (Great Salt Lake City: Brigham H. Young, Printer, 1852), 80–82. Territorial Legislature Records, series 3150, box 1, folder 55, Utah State Archives and Records Administration. Spelling, punctuation, and capitalization appear as in the original. See also, Coleman, "Blacks in Utah History," 120–22. For a full discussion of this law, see Rich, "True Policy for Utah," 54.

BIBLIOGRAPHY

Alexander, Thomas G. Review of *Blood of the Prophets: Brigham Young and the Massacre at Mountain Meadows,* by Will Bagley. *BYU Studies* 42, no. 1 (2003): 170.

Allen, Alex. "Fighting the Good Fight in Zion: The Impact of the NAACP on Social Reforms in Utah and the LDS Church." Senior thesis, Brigham Young University, 1998.

Allen, Gerald. Interviews with the author. 2002–2004.

Allen, James B., and Glen M. Leonard. *The Story of the Latter-day Saints*. Salt Lake City: Deseret Book, 1976.

Andrew, John A., III. *Lyndon Johnson and the Great Society*. Chicago: Ivan R. Dee, 1998.

Arrington, Leonard, and Davis Bitton. *Brigham Young: American Moses*. New York: Knopf, 1992.

———. *The Mormon Experience: A History of the Latter-day Saints*. New York: Knopf, 1979.

Beauvoir, Simone de. *The Second Sex*. Translated by Howard Parshley. New York: Knopf, 1954.

Blackburn, Mavis. Telephone interview with the author. August 3, 2005.

Boesel, David. *Cities under Siege: An Anatomy of the Ghetto Riots, 1964–1968*. New York: Basic Books, 1971.

Boyd, Harvey. Telephone interviews with the author. 2000–2001.

Branch, Taylor. *Parting the Waters: America in the King Years, 1954–63*. New York: Simon and Schuster, 1988.

Bridgewater, Wynetha (Nita). Telephone and personal interviews with the author. May 17–18, 2005.

Bringhurst, Newell G. *Saints, Slaves, and Blacks: The Changing Place of Black People within Mormonism*. Westport, CT: Greenwood Press, 1981.

Buchanan, Fredrick S. *Culture Clash and Accommodation: Public Schooling in Salt Lake City, 1890–1994*. Salt Lake City: Smith Research Associates, in association with Signature Books, 1996.

Bullock, Paul. *Watts: The Aftermath; An Inside View of the Ghetto*. New York: Grove, 1969.

Bush, Lester E. "Mormonism's Negro Doctrine: An HistoricalOverview." *Dialogue: A Journal of Mormon Thought* 8, no. 1 (1973): 11–68.

Bush, Lester E., and Armand Mauss, eds. *Neither White nor Black: Mormon Scholars Confront the Race Issue in a Universal Church*. Midvale, Utah: Signature Books, 1954.

Bushman, Richard L. *Joseph Smith and the Beginnings of Mormonism*. Urbana: University of Illinois Press, 1984.

California Governor's Commission on the Los Angeles Riots. *Violence in the City—an End or a Beginning?* Los Angeles, 1965.

Children's Television Workshop. *CTW Research Bibliography, Research Papers relating to the Children's Television Workshop and Its Experimental Educational Series: "Sesame Street" and "The Electric Company," 1966–1976*. New York: Children's Television Workshop, 1976.
Colburt, David, ed. *Eyewitness to America*. New York: Pantheon Books, 1997.
Coleman, Ronald Gerald. "Blacks in Utah History: An Unknown Legacy." In *The Peoples of Utah*, edited by Helen Papanikolas. Salt Lake City: Utah State Historical Society, 1976.
———. "A History of Blacks in Utah, 1825–1910." PhD diss., University of Utah, 1980.
———. "Preface: African Americans in Utah." In *Missing Stories: An Oral History of Ethnic and Minority Groups in Utah*, edited by Leslie G. Kelen and Eileen Hallet Stone. Logan: Utah State University Press, 2000.
———. Telephone interview with the author. May 30, 2005.
Conot, Robert. *Rivers of Blood, Years of Darkness: The Unforgettable Classic Account of the Watts Riot*. New York: Morrow, 1968.
Crew, Keith. "The Death and Resurrection of Capital Punishment." In *Historic U.S. Court Cases, 1690–1990*, edited by John W. Johnson. New York: Garland, 1992.
Cronon, Edmund David. *Black Moses: The Story of Marcus Garvey and the Universal Negro Improvement Association*. Madison: University of Wisconsin Press, 1964.
Crump, Spencer. *Black Riot in Los Angeles: The Story of the Watts Tragedy*. Los Angeles: Trans-Anglo, 1966.
Cunningham, David. *Klansville, U.S.A.* New York: Oxford University Press, 2014.
David, Jay, ed. *Growing Up Black*. New York: Avon Books, 1992.
Davis, France A. Interview with the author. May 14, 2002.
———. *Light in the Midst of Zion: A History of Black Baptists in Utah*. Salt Lake City: Empire, 1997.
Daynes, Gary, ed. *Fulfilling the Founding*. Boston: Pearson Custom Printing, 2001.
Dees, Jesse Walter, Jr., and James S. Hadley. *Jim Crow*. Westport, CT: Negro Universities Press, 1951.
Diaz, Brenda Moore. Interview with the author. May 14, 2002.
Doctrine and Covenants of the Church of Jesus Christ of Latter-day Saints. Salt Lake City: Church of Jesus Christ of Latter-day Saints, 1981.
Dykman, Judy, and Colleen Whitley. *The Silver Queen*. Logan: Utah State University Press, 1998.
Edmond, Shauna Benns. Telephone interview with the author. July 30, 2005.
Embry, Jesse. *Black Saints in a White Church*. Salt Lake City: Signature Books, 1994.
Fireside, Harvey. *Plessy v. Ferguson: Separate but Equal?* Springfield, NJ: Enslow, 1997.
Fisch, Shalom M. *Children's Learning from Educational Television: "Sesame Street" and Beyond*. Mahwah, NJ: Lawrence Erlbaum Associates, 2004.
Fogelson, Robert M. *The Los Angeles Riots*. New York: Arno Press, 1969.
Foner, Jack D. *Blacks and the Military in American History*. New York: Praeger, 1974.
Franklin, John Hope. *From Slavery to Freedom: A History of Negro Americans*. 3rd ed. New York: Knopf, 1967.
Freimann, Tiana. "Can Change Occur to a Set Society? How African-Americans, the Church of Jesus Christ of Latter-day Saints, and the National Association of the Advancement of Colored People Changed Utah." Senior thesis, University of Utah, 2003.

Friedan, Betty. *The Feminine Mystique*. New York: Norton, 1963.
Furnas, Joseph Chamberlain. *The Road to Harper's Ferry*. New York: W. Sloan Associates, 1959.
Garrow, David J., ed. *Martin Luther King, Jr.: Civil Rights Leader, Theologian, Orator*. Vols. 1–3 of *Martin LutherKing, Jr., and the Civil Rights Movement*. New York: Carlson, 1989.
Gazit, Chana, writer and producer. *Surviving the Dustbowl*. Aired January 29, 2019, on PBS, pbs.org/wgbh/americanexperience/films/dustbowl.
Gillespie, L. Kay. *The Unforgiven: Utah's Executed Men*. Salt Lake City: Signature Books, 1991.
Goldberg, Robert A. "Esther Rosenblatt Landa: Her Price Is Far above Rubies." In *Worth Their Salt: Notable but Unnoted Women of Utah*, edited by Colleen Whitley. Logan: Utah State University Press, 1996.
Goldenberg, David M. *The Curse of Ham: Race and Slavery in Early Judaism, Christianity, and Islam*. Princeton, NJ: Princeton University Press, 2003.
Gooch, Cynthia. Telephone interview and email with the author. November 27, 2000.
Gordon, Ann Dexter, ed. *African American Women and the Vote, 1837–1965*. Amherst: University of Massachusetts Press, 1997.
Haines, Herbert H. *Against Capital Punishment: The Anti-Death Penalty Movement in America, 1972–1994*. New York: Oxford University Press, 1996.
Halberstam, David. *The Children*. New York: Random House, 1998.
Hall, Kermit L. *Major Problems in American Constitutional History*. Vols. 1 and 2. Lexington, MA: Heath, 1992.
———. *Oxford Companion to the Supreme Court of the United States*. New York: Oxford University Press, 1992.
Harding, Vincent. *Martin Luther King: The Inconvenient Hero*. New York: Orbis Books, 1996.
Hayes, Stephen R. *Noah's Curse: The Biblical Justification of American Slavery*. New York: Oxford University Press, 2002.
Henry, Alberta Hill. *Contemporary Blacks in Utah: Resource Book*. Salt Lake City: Salt Lake City School District, 1986.
———. Interviews with the author. 1998–2005.
———. Interview with Jennifer O'Neal. December 14, 2000.
———. Interviews with Leslie Kelen. 1983. Interviews with Blacks in Utah. Special Collections, Marriott Library, University of Utah.
———. Papers. Special Collections, Marriott Library, University of Utah. Copies at the Utah State Historical Society, Salt Lake City.
Hill, Corrine. Interview with the author. May 14, 2003.
Hill, David. Interview with the author. November 18, 1998.
Hood, Donald D. *Death in the Balance: The Debate over Capital Punishment*. Lexington, MA: Lexington Books, 1989.
Jackson, Jesse, *Legal Lynching: Racism, Injustice, and the Death Penalty*. New York: Marlowe, 1966.
Johnson, Lyndon B. *Public Papers of the Presidents of the United States: Lyndon Johnson*. 2 vols. Washignton, D.C.: Government Printing Office, 1965.
Kemp, Carolyn. Telephone interview with the author. November 22, 2004.
Kennedy, David M. *Freedom from Fear: The American People in Depression and War, 1929–1945*. New York: Oxford University Press, 1999.

Kinder, Gary. *Victim: The Other Side of Murder.* 2nd ed. New York: Atlantic Monthly Press, 1982.
King, Martin Luther, Jr. *The Autobiography of Martin Luther King, Jr.* Edited by Clayborne Carson. New York: Warner Books, 1998.
Kirchmeier, Jeffrey L. *Imprisoned by the Past: Warren McClensky, Race, and the American Death Penalty*. New York: Oxford University Press, 2015.
Klarman, Michael J. *From Jim Crow to Civil Rights: The Supreme Court and the Struggle for Racial Equality.* New York: Oxford University Press, 2004.
Knappman, Edward W., ed. *American Trials of the 20th Century: From the Scopes Monkey Trial to O. J. Simpson*. Detroit: Visible Ink Press, New England Publishing, 1995.
Kotz, Nick. *Judgment Days: Lyndon Baines Johnson, Martin Luther King Jr., and the Laws That Changed America.* New York: Houghton Mifflin, 2005.
Lebya, Gilbert. Telephone and personal interviews with the author. July 2013.
Lebya, Julia Henry. Interviews with the author. August 2002.
Leighniger, Robert D. *Long-Range Public Investment: The Forgotten Legacy of the New Deal.* Columbia: University of South Carolina Press, 2007.
Lewis, David. *King: A Biography*. 2nd ed. Chicago: University of Illinois Press, 1978.
Life, Trial, and Execution of Captain John Brown: Known as "Old Brown of Ossawatomie." New York: R. M. DeWitt, 1859. Microfilm.
Litwack, Leon F. *Trouble in Mind: Black Southerners in the Age of Jim Crow*. New York: Knopf, 1998.
Loewen, James W. *Sundown Towns: A Hidden Dimension of American Racism*. New York: New Press, 2005.
Ludlow, Daniel H., ed. *Encyclopedia of Mormonism*. New York: Macmillan, 1992.
Lundgren, Ruth H. Interview with the author. November 16, 2004.
Lythgoe, Dennis L. "Negro Slavery and Mormon Doctrine." *Western Humanities Review* 21 (Autumn 1967): 329–30.
———. "Negro Slavery in Utah." *Utah Historical Quarterly* 39, no 1 (Winter 1971): 40.
Mailer, Norman. *The Executioner's Song*. Boston: Little, Brown, 1979.
McConkie, Bruce R. *Mormon Doctrine*. 2nd ed. Salt Lake City: Bookcraft, 1966.
McCullough, David. *Truman*. New York: Simon and Schuster, 1992.
McMurrin, Sterling M. "The Negroes among the Mormons." Address given before the annual banquet of the Salt Lake City Chapter of the National Association for the Advancement of Colored People, June 21, 1968.
Miller, Alta. "A Short Sketch of My Life." In *Worth Their Salt: Notable but Unnoted Women of Utah*, edited by Colleen Whitley. Logan: Utah State University Press, 1996.
Moore, Christopher Paul. *Fighting for America: Black Soldiers—the Unsung Heroes of World War II.* New York: Ballentine Books, 2005.
Nelsen, LeRoy. Telephone interviews with the author. December 1998.
New Hope Missionary Baptist Church. *History and Aim*. Salt Lake City: New Hope Missionary Baptist Church, 1968.
Notarianni, Phillip F. Interview with the author. 2005.
Oates, Stephen B. *Let the Trumpet Sound: The Life of Martin Luther King, Jr.* New York: Harper and Row, 1982.
O'Dea, Thomas. *The Mormons*. Chicago: University of Chicago Press, 1957.
O'Neal, Jennifer. "Raising Her Voice: Alberta Henry's Efforts to Strengthen Equality in Utah." MA thesis, Utah State University, 2002.

Ozment, Steven. *Protestants: The Birth of a Revolution.* New York: Doubleday, 1992.

Packard, Jerrold M. *American Nightmare: The History of Jim Crow*. New York: St. Martin's Press, 2002.

Papanikolas, Helen, ed. *The Peoples of Utah*. Salt Lake City: Utah State Historical Society, 1976.

Parson, Robert. *Mignon Barker Richmond: Utah's First Black, Woman College Graduate and Distinguished USU Alumnus*. Logan: Utah State University Archives, 1986.

Paternoster, Raymond. *Capital Punishment in America*. New York: Lexington Books, 1991.

Patterson, James T. *Brown v. Board of Education: A Civil Rights Milestone and Its Troubled Legacy.* New York: Oxford University Press, 2001.

Payne, Charles M. *I've Got the Light of Freedom*. Berkeley: University of California Press, 2007.

Peterson, F. Ross. "Utah's Politics since 1945." In *Utah's History,* edited by Richard E. Poll, Thomas G. Alexander, Eugene E. Campbell, and David E. Miller. Logan: Utah State University Press, 1987.

Reid, Stuart. Telephone interview with the author. September 17, 2005.

Rich, Christopher, "The True Policy for Utah: An Ace in Relation to Slavery." *Utah Historical Quarterly* 80, no. 1 (Winter 2012): 54.

Robertson, Shauna Graves. Telephone interviews with the author. September 3, 2003, and June 6, 2005.

Rock, James M., ed., *A Blend of the Two*. Salt Lake City: Friends of the University of Utah Library, 1978.

Rogers, Brent M. *Unpopular Sovereignty: Mormons and the Federal Management of Early Utah Territory.* Lincoln: University of Nebraska Press, 2017.

Rossi, Peter Henry. *Ghetto Revolts.* New Brunswick, NJ: Transactions Books, 1973.

Sandack, A. Wally. Papers. Special Collections, Marriott Library, University of Utah.

Sandack, Helen. Interview with the author. September 3, 2003.

Sawyer, Patrice. Interviews with the author. 2005.

Schuman, Howard, Charlotte Steeh, and Lawrence Bobo. *Racial Attitudes in America: Trends and Interpretations*. Cambridge, MA: Harvard University Press, 1985.

Sears, David. *The Politics of Violence: The New Urban Blacks and the Watts Riot.* Boston: Houghton, Mifflin, 1973.

Sillitoe, Linda. *Friendly Fire: The ACLU in Utah.* Salt Lake City: Signature Books, 1996.

Sitkoff, Harvard. *The Struggle for Black Equality, 1954–1980*. New York: Farrar, Straus, and Giroux, 1981.

Smith, Elmer R. "The Social Status of the Negro in Utah." Paper presented at Utah Academy of Sciences, Arts, and Letters, Ogden, Utah, November 20, 1954. Utah State Historical Society, Salt Lake City.

Smith, Jason Scott. *Building New Deal Liberalism: The Political Economy of Public Works.* New York: Cambridge University Press, 2007.

Stewart, Polly. Interviews and emails with the author. May 2005. *Sunstone*, "An Unintended and Difficult Odyssey (Twenty-Five Years after the Revelation—Where Are We Now?)," March 2003.

Taggart, Stephen G. *Mormonism's Negro Policy: Social and Historical Origins*. Salt Lake City: University of Utah Press, 1970.

Taylor, Quintard. *In Search of the Racial Frontier: AfricanAmericans in the American West, 1528–1990*. New York: Norton, 1998.

Thomas, Donald. Interview with the author. May 12, 1999.

Tobler, Douglas F., and Nelson B. Wadsworth. *The History of the Mormons in Photographs and Text*. New York: St. Martin's Press, 1987.

United States Bureau of the Census. *18th Decennial Census of Population: 1960*. Washington, D.C., 1960.

United States Congress. *Reports of the Select Committee of the Senate Appointed to Inquire into the Late Invasion and Seizure of the Public Property at Harper's Ferry*. Washington, D.C., 1860. Microfilm.

United States Park Service. *Harper's Ferry and the Story of John Brown*. Washington, D.C.: Department of Interior, 1991.

Urofsky, Melvin L., and Paul Finkelman. *A March of Liberty: A Constitutional History of the United States*. New York: Oxford University Press, 2002.

Utah Humanities Council. "UHC Celebrates 30 Years Expanding Minds through the Humanities." *Newsletter of the Utah Humanities Council*, Spring 2005.

Weiler, Kathleen, writer and producer. *Utah's African-American Voices: The Story of African-Americans in Utah*. Salt Lake City: KUED, 1998. Video.

Whalen, Joseph William. *The Latter-day Saints in the Modern World: An Account of Modern Mormonism*. Rev. ed. West Bend: University of Notre Dame Press, 1964.

Whitley, Colleen, ed. *Worth Their Salt: Notable but Unnoted Women of Utah*. Logan: Utah State University Press, 1996.

———, ed. *Worth Their Salt, Too: More Notable but Often Unnoted Women of Utah*. Logan: Utah State University Press, 2000.

Williams, Juan. *Eyes on the Prize. America's Civil Rights Years, 1954–1965*. New York: Viking, 1987.

Williamson, Joel. *The Crucible of Race: Black/White Relations in the American South since Emancipation*. New York: Oxford University Press, 1984.

Wiser, Callie, director and producer. *Klansville, U.S.A.* Aired January 13, 2015, on PBS. pbs.org/wgbh/americanexperience/films/klansville.

Wolfinger, Henry J. "Jane Manning James: A Test of Faith." In *Worth Their Salt: Notable but Unnoted Women of Utah*, edited by Colleen Whitley. Logan: Utah State University Press, 1996.

Woodruff, Wilford. Manuscripts. LDS Church Archives, Salt Lake City.

Young, Andrew. *An Easy Burden: The Civil Rights Movement and the Transformation of America*. New York: Harper Collins, 1996.

Young, Brigham. Papers. LDS Church Archives, Salt Lake City.